T0399324

Language Production

Bringing together the latest research from world-leading academics, this edited volume is an authoritative resource on the psycholinguistic study of language production, exploring longstanding concepts as well as contemporary and emerging theories.

Hartsuiker and Strijkers affirm that although language production may seem like a mundane everyday activity, it is in fact a remarkable human accomplishment. This comprehensive text presents an up-to-date overview of the key topics in the field, providing important theoretical and empirical challenges to the traditional and accepted modal view of language production. Each chapter explores in detail a different aspect of language production, covering traditional methods including written and signed production alongside emerging research on joint action production. Emphasizing the neurobiological underpinnings of language, chapter authors showcase research that moves from a monologue-only approach to one that considers production in more ecologically valid circumstances.

Written in an accessible and compelling style, *Language Production* is essential reading for students and researchers of language production and psycholinguistics, as well as anyone who wishes to learn more about the fascinating topic of how humans produce language.

Robert J. Hartsuiker is Professor of Psychology at Ghent University, Belgium. His research interests include language processing, language production, bilingualism, and self-monitoring of speech.

Kristof Strijkers is a Researcher at the Centre National de la Recherche (CNRS) and Aix-Marseille University, France. His research examines the spatiotemporal dynamics of language production and comprehension, and the neural representations of words in the brain.

Current Issues in the Psychology of Language
Series Editor: Trevor A. Harley

Current Issues in the Psychology of Language is a series of edited books that will reflect the state-of-the-art in areas of current and emerging interest in the psychological study of language.

Each volume is tightly focused on a particular topic and consists of seven to ten chapters contributed by international experts. The editors of individual volumes are leading figures in their areas and provide an introductory overview.

Example topics include: language development, bilingualism and second language acquisition, word recognition, word meaning, text processing, the neuroscience of language, and language production, as well as the inter-relations between these topics.

Sentence Processing
Edited by Roger van Gompel

Speech Perception and Spoken Word Recognition
Edited by M. Gareth Gaskell and Jelena Mirković

Visual Word Recognition Volume 1
Edited by James S. Adelman

Visual Word Recognition Volume 2
Edited by James S. Adelman

Linguistic Morphology
Edited by Davide Crepaldi

Language Production
Edited by Robert J. Hartsuiker and Kristof Strijkers

Language Production

Edited by Robert J. Hartsuiker
and Kristof Strijkers

Routledge
Taylor & Francis Group

LONDON AND NEW YORK

Designed cover image: © Getty images

First published 2023
by Routledge
4 Park Square, Milton Park, Abingdon, Oxon OX14 4RN

and by Routledge
605 Third Avenue, New York, NY 10158

Routledge is an imprint of the Taylor & Francis Group, an informa business

British Library Cataloguing-in-Publication Data
A catalogue record for this book is available from the British Library

Library of Congress Cataloguing-in-Publication Data
Names: Hartsuiker, Robert J., 1968- editor. | Strijkers, Kristof, editor.
Title: Language production / edited by Robert J. Hartsuiker, Kristof Strijkers.
Description: Milton Park, Abingdon, Oxon; New York, NY: Routledge, 2023. | Includes bibliographical references and index. | Identifiers: LCCN 2022042662 (print) | LCCN 2022042663 (ebook) | ISBN 9780367703424 (hardback) | ISBN 9780367703417 (paperback) | ISBN 9781003145790 (ebook)
Subjects: LCSH: Psycholinguistics.
Classification: LCC BF455.L28 2023 (print) | LCC BF455 (ebook) | DDC 401/.9--dc23/eng/20220915
LC record available at https://lccn.loc.gov/2022042662
LC ebook record available at https://lccn.loc.gov/2022042663

ISBN: 978-0-367-70342-4 (hbk)
ISBN: 978-0-367-70341-7 (pbk)
ISBN: 978-1-003-14579-0 (ebk)

DOI: 10.4324/9781003145790

Typeset in Bembo
by MPS Limited, Dehradun

Contents

Contributors

Priscila Borges is a university assistant (prae-doc) at the Department of Linguistics, University of Vienna, Austria. She is interested in the behavioral and neural correlates of implicit naming across development.

Sarah Brown-Schmidt is Professor of Psychology & Human Development at Vanderbilt University, USA. Her research is at the intersection of language processing and memory, with a focus on mechanisms of interactive conversation. Much of her recent research examines memory for conversation, and the impact of traumatic brain injury and Alzheimer's disease on language processing.

Audrey Bürki is a Professor of Neuro- and Psycholinguistics at the University of Potsdam, Germany. She completed her PhD at the University of Geneva. She then worked as a post-doc at the Universities of York (UK) and Aix-Marseille (France), and as a lecturer in Methodology and Applied statistics at the University of Geneva. Her research focuses on the cognitive architecture of the language production system that she investigates with a variety of measures: phonetic analyses, response times, eye-tracking, and event-related potential data.

J.P. de Ruiter is a Professor in Cognitive Science, appointed in the departments of computer science and psychology at Tufts University, USA. His research interest is the cognitive foundations of human communication. He has published on gesture, turn-taking, pragmatics, and the methodology of interaction research.

Mathieu Declerck is a Professor at the Department of Linguistics and Literary Studies, Vrije Universiteit Brussels, Belgium. He mainly investigates multilingual language production and comprehension, processing of dialects, and executive functions.

Karen Emmorey is a Distinguished Professor in the School of Speech, Language, and Hearing Sciences at San Diego State University, USA, and the Director of the Laboratory for Language and Cognitive Neuroscience. Dr. Emmorey's research focuses on what sign languages can reveal about the nature of human language, cognition, and the brain. She studies the processes involved in how deaf and hearing people produce and comprehend sign language and how these processes are represented in the brain. Her research interests also include bimodal bilingualism and the neurocognitive underpinnings of reading skills in profoundly deaf adults.

Chiara Gambi is an Assistant Professor in Psychology at the University of Warwick, UK, and an honorary research fellow at the School of Psychology, Cardiff University, UK. She is interested in the role that prediction plays in language learning and language use in conversation and has studied how speakers represent each other's utterances in joint language production tasks.

Robert J. Hartsuiker is Professor of Psychology at Ghent University, Belgium. His research interests include language processing, language production, bilingualism, and self-monitoring of speech.

Bissera Ivanova is a PhD student in the cognitive neuroscience of language at the Laboratoire Parole et Langage (LPL) of Aix-Marseille University (AMU), France, and is specialized in the spatiotemporal dynamics of syntax in language production and perception.

Sonia Kandel is Professor in Cognitive Science at the Université Grenoble Alpes, France. She works on language processing and conducts her research at GIPSA-lab (CNRS UMR 5126).

Emilia Kerr is a PhD student in the cognitive neuroscience of language at the Laboratoire Parole et Langage (LPL) of Aix-Marseille University (AMU), France, and is specialized in word dynamics and conversation.

Andrea M. Philipp is a Senior Research Scientist at the Institute of Psychology, RWTH Aachen University, Germany. Her research focuses on bilingualism, language switching, and cognitive control.

Vitória Piai is an Associate Professor at the Donders Institute for Brain, Behaviour and Cognition at Radboud University in the Netherlands. She studies language production in adults with and without neurological damage, with a particular focus on electrophysiological methods.

Martin Pickering is a Professor of the Psychology of Language and Communication at the University of Edinburgh, UK. He is interested in language production, comprehension, and their relationship, particularly with respect to dialogue.

Elin Runnqvist is a tenured researcher at the Centre National de la Recherche Scientifique (CNRS), France, working at the Laboratoire de Parole & Langage (LPL) as well as at the Institute of Language, Communication and the Brain (ILCB) in Aix-en-Provence and Marseille, France. Her research interests concern error monitoring as well as speech and language production learning. In particular, she focuses on their neural bases and the extent to which they might rely on or interact with processes of interfacing cognitive skills and actions.

L. María Sánchez is a PhD student at the department of Linguistics and Literary Studies, Vrije Universiteit Brussel, Belgium. Her main research interests include multilingualism, language switching, and cognitive control.

L. Robert (Bob) Slevc is an Associate Professor at the University of Maryland, College Park, USA, where he is affiliated with the Department of Psychology, the Program in Neuroscience and Cognitive Science, the Maryland Language Science Center, and the Center for Comparative and Evolutionary Biology of Hearing. His research focuses on the cognitive/neural mechanisms involved in language production, language comprehension, and the perception/cognition of music.

Kristof Strijkers is a CNRS Research Scientist (PhD in Cognitive Neuroscience and Language) at the Laboratoire Parole et Langage (LPL) of Aix-Marseille University (AMU). His research examines the spatiotemporal dynamics of language production and comprehension, and the neural representations of words in the brain.

Esli Struys is a Professor of Linguistics at the department of Linguistics and Literary Studies, Vrije Universiteit Brussels, Belgium. He conducts research on multilingualism, language control, and the implementation of bilingual education.

Si On Yoon is an Assistant Professor in the Department of Communication Sciences and Disorders at the University of Iowa, USA. Her research interests include how interlocutors produce and comprehend language in complex conversational settings such as multiparty conversation, and how memory affects language use while communicating. She is also interested in the development and use of social pragmatic language (e.g., children and younger/older adults), and in various populations (e.g., individuals with amnesia or Alzheimer's disease).

Greig de Zubicaray is a Professor in the School of Psychology and Counselling at Queensland University of Technology, Brisbane, Australia. His research focuses on cognitive and brain mechanisms involved in language production and comprehension and their disorders.

Introduction

Current Issues in the Psychology of Language: Language Production

Robert Hartsuiker and Kristof Strijkers

People produce language all of the time, but how do we do it? Although language production seems a mundane, every-day activity, it is in fact a remarkable human accomplishment. People can produce language at a rate of about two words (or four to five syllables) per second. Doing so requires coordinating a range of different types of information. This involves constructing a message we wish to express. This message should fit with the social and physical context we are in as well as the preceding discourse. It also involves finding words from a huge mental lexicon, ordering those words given the rules of grammar, determining the speech sounds of those words, and performing a hugely complicated act of motor control, involving dozens of muscles and several effectors, when pronouncing those sounds. Language production in other modalities, like written or sign production, is no less complex and equally requires the retrieval of a multitude of mental representations, which need to be translated in precise and complex motor movements. Yet despite this complexity, language production usually proceeds extremely fluently and accurately (with only one error per 1,000 words according to some estimates). This book is about this fascinating ability to produce language.

The goal of this book is to provide an up-to-date overview of the psycholinguistic study of language production. As detailed in Slevc (this volume) and Kerr et al. (this volume), work in the last quarter of the 20th century has led to a "modal" view of spoken language production that remains very influential to this day. Yet novel ideas and novel findings in the field reviewed in this book provide some important theoretical and empirical challenges for these traditional views, for instance with respect to the division of language production in a number of separate "stages" and with respect to the mechanisms that decide which word to choose.

All chapters are written in an accessible way, so that they are not only useful to professional language production researchers but also to students learning about psycholinguistics, and a more general audience that wishes to learn more about the fascinating issue of how humans produce language. Each chapter consists of a thorough review of one aspect of language production, discussing long-standing questions and classical theories, but also providing an overview

DOI: 10.4324/9781003145790-1

of the current state of the art and how those traditional empirical questions and theories have evolved in recent years, as well as which novel, more recent questions emerged in the field; numerous key references to both earlier and very recent literature are provided to the reader. Five broad topics can be distilled from the various chapters: basic processes of language production, the brain basis of language production, speech monitoring and control, language production beyond the spoken modality, and language production in a social context.

The first three chapters of the book discuss basic mechanisms of speech production: Slevc (this volume) focuses on grammatical processing, Kerr et al. (this volume) on lexical access, and Bürki (this volume) on phonological processing. We consider cognitive theories and evidence from behavioral evidence, but ultimately, of course, language comes from the brain. Chapters 5 and 6 of this book are dedicated to this brain basis of language production and present detailed overviews of neurocognitive accounts and neurophysiological data, where De Zubicarey (this volume) particularly focuses on neuroimaging data and Piai and Borges (this volume) discuss the electrophysiology of language production. After these in-depth overviews of the cognitive and neural basis of basic language production processes, the following two chapters portray how these processes are controlled and monitored in the course of speech planning: Runnqvist (this volume) discusses both classical and recent neurocognitive accounts about the self-monitoring of speech (that is checking one's own speech for errors and other problems). Another control process is discussed by Sánchez et al. (this volume), namely the control for selecting to-be-uttered words in the desired language in bilingual speakers. Speaking is of course only one of several modalities of language production, and, importantly, this book includes several chapters on other language production modalities: In Chapter 8, Kandel (this volume) reviews literature on written production. In Chapter 9, Emmorey (this volume) discusses signed production and compares it to spoken production, and in Chapter 10, De Ruiter (this volume) focuses on the gestures that typically accompany our speech. Finally, while psycholinguistic and neurolinguistic work has often focused on situations in which a single participant produces language in a non-interactive context, recent work pays more and more attention to the social dimension of language production. In Chapters 11 and 12 of this book, production in social context and joint language production is covered by Yoon and Brown-Schmidt (this volume) and by Gambi and Pickering (this volume), respectively.

Although the book covers a wide number of topics, several other important aspects of language production could not be addressed in this volume. One such topic concerns planning what to say or "Conceptualizing" in Levelt's (1989) terminology. Second, our ability to produce language is obviously learned in childhood, and it is fine-tuned even in adulthood by life-long learning processes (Slevc, this volume). Third, in a different field of science (artificial intelligence and natural language processing [NLP]), remarkable advances have been made in recent years in creating automatic systems that can generate surprisingly coherent texts. Such language models are based on very large neural networks that are trained to predict upcoming words and that are exposed to huge sets of training data. The question can be raised whether the psycholinguistic study of language production and the engineering approach taken in NLP can mutually benefit from each other. Coverage of these and several further topics will have to wait for future books on language production. Nevertheless, we hope that the current volume will give the reader a good introduction to the state of the art of language production. We hope most of all that the reader, like us, will be amazed by this complex, yet fascinating human ability.

Reference

Levelt, W. J. M. (1989). *Speaking: From Intention to Articulation*. Cambridge, MA: MIT Press.

1 Grammatical Encoding

L. Robert Slevc

Introduction

We (as a species) have a lot to say. Exactly how much can be difficult to estimate, but American college students say an average of about 16,000 words each day (Mehl et al., 2007)[1] and I've written nearly 8,000 words in this single chapter. But we do not simply say (or write or sign) thousands of unconnected words, instead we produce sentences where specific words are linked in specific ways to communicate specific meanings. This process of selecting and combining lexical representations into structured sequences is called *grammatical encoding*. This chapter describes a "modal model" of grammatical encoding (i.e., a generally accepted consensus view) which, in broad strokes, has not changed greatly over the last 40 years (Bock & Levelt, 1994; Garrett, 1975, 1988; Levelt et al., 1999). This is not to say that there are not important challenges to this "standard" architecture (and, anyway, the ubiquity of an approach does not necessarily indicate its accuracy), and so the chapter also discusses some longstanding and some relatively new debates challenging and expanding our understanding of grammatical encoding. These include questions about the stages of processing, the nature of grammatical representations, the degree of incrementality and advance planning, and modularity (among others).

Grammatical encoding: The modal model

Grammatical encoding transforms non-linguistic meaning into linguistic representations that can be encoded into relevant phonological or orthographic forms for eventual production. The consensus view of grammatical encoding, illustrated in Figure 1.1, involves two consecutive stages – first a *selection* and then a *retrieval* stage – which occur in two parallel processing streams, one involving *content* and the other involving *structure*. Broadly, this is the process of activating the appropriate lexical representations and word forms (for content) and the appropriate grammatical functions and constituent structures (for structure) to adequately express the intended message, as detailed below. But first, what is this intended message, and what sort of non-linguistic information is involved?

DOI: 10.4324/9781003145790-2

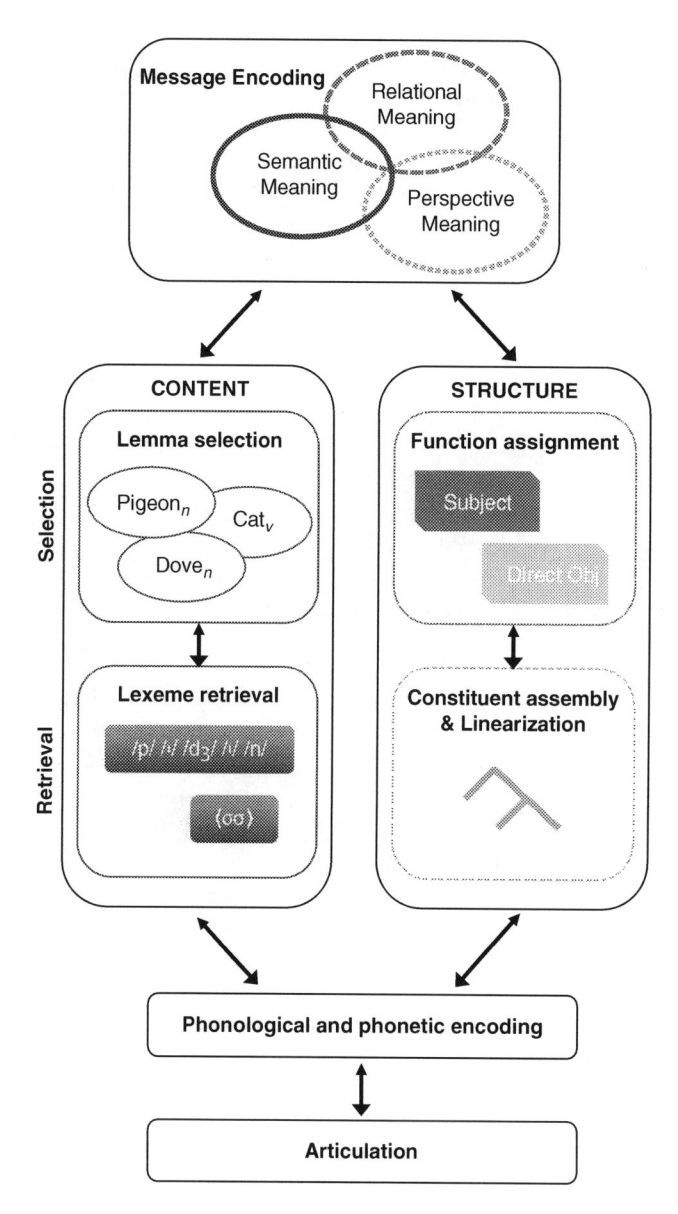

Figure 1.1 Schematic representation of the modal model of grammatical encoding (adapted from Ferreira & Slevc, 2007).

Message encoding

The "job" of grammatical encoding is to convert a non-linguistic *speech act* (an intention to communicate/express some message) into a linguistic expression. But a speech act itself is probably not the input to grammatical encoding;

instead grammatical encoding begins with a *preverbal message* that has already been prepared, to some extent, for linguistic encoding. This preverbal message includes three general types of information that are necessary to linguistically convey the meaning that a speaker wishes to express. One type is information about the to-be-expressed elements – the *semantic meaning* – which includes the entities, actions, events, states, etc. involved in the message. A second type of information in the preverbal message is how these elements relate to each other – the *relational meaning* – for example, who or what is performing or experiencing an action or is in a particular state. Finally, the message must include information about the relative importance or centrality of different elements to the message – the *perspective meaning* – indicating what is topic vs. comment, focused vs. background, etc. For example, if one wanted to communicate a message about a pigeon driving a bus (which probably should be discouraged; Willems, 2003), the semantic meaning would include re-presentations of a particular type of bird, a particular type of vehicle, and an event in which the speed and direction of something is controlled by an operator. The relational meaning would attribute the operator role of the event to the bird entity and the being-controlled role to the vehicle entity. And the perspective meaning might encode that the bird is the topic and the vehicle is the added information (leading to the sentence "The pigeon is driving the bus," as opposed to "The bus is being driven by the pigeon").

The preverbal message typically includes both more and less information than is necessary for grammatical encoding. It contains more than is ne-cessary because some of the information that might be required is a con-sequence of the *language* rather than of the message per se. For example, features like aspect, number, and tense must be linguistically realized in some situations but not in others; thus it is likely that this type of potentially relevant information is part of a preverbal message even when it does not eventually emerge. On the other hand, the preverbal message is often incomplete. Speakers do not necessarily wait for a fully formulated preverbal message before beginning grammatical encoding, and the message can be reformulated "on the fly" mid-production (e.g., Brown-Schmidt & Konopka, 2015; Brown-Schmidt & Tanenhaus, 2006; Lindsley, 1975).

Once a preverbal message (or at least part of one) exists, it becomes the input to grammatical encoding. At this point, the modal model suggests a division of labor where the processing of *content* and of *structure* occurs sepa-rately in parallel. (For more on the processes of message encoding per se, see, e.g., Konopka & Brown-Schmidt, 2014.)

Content stream

The *content stream* of grammatical encoding involves the selection and retrieval of appropriate lexical items to express the elements required by the preverbal message (i.e., the *who, what,* and *whom*). This stream corresponds to lexical access and so in principle (although not always in practice) maps cleanly onto models of lexical access and word production (see Kerr et al., this volume). The selection of appropriate words, according to most models of lexical access, occurs in two stages. First is the selection of *lemmas* (Kempen & Huijbers, 1983), which refer to lexically specific representations (i.e., each word corresponds to an individual lemma). Lemmas are thought to be modality-general such that the same lemmas are involved in speaking/signing and writing (although see the section *Does lexical access involve two stages?* below) and to link to both syntactic (part of speech, grammatical gender, etc.) and formal (phonological, orthographic) properties of the word. The second stage is the retrieval of the corresponding modality-specific word forms, often called *lexemes*. These are whole-word representations that include phonological segments and their order as well as metrical information (e.g., syllable stress).

Note that the *content* stream is not asyntactic; indeed a critical part of a lemma representation is the morpho-syntactic features of a given word. So, to produce the example message above about a pigeon driving a bus, the content stream involves first selecting lemmas for *pigeon*, *drive*, and *bus* (but not *-ing* or *a*, which arise from *constituent assembly* processes described below) and then, for each lemma, retrieving the ordered segments and metrical and syntactic features (e.g., a singular count-noun with one stressed syllable and the segments /b/, /ʌ/, /s/).

Lemma selection, in the modal model, is assumed to be competitive. Activation flows from the message level to the target lemma and to semantically related competitors. So when, for example, naming a picture of a pigeon, activation spreads not only to the lemma for PIGEON but also, to a lesser degree, to related lemmas for DOVE and SPARROW (among others). Lemma selection then requires picking the correct target from a set of candidates, which (by the modal model) is based on exceeding some ratio of target activation (for PIGEON) compared to the activation of activated competitors (e.g., Levelt et al., 1999; Roelofs, 1992). One type of evidence for this comes from the oft-used *picture-word interference* paradigm, where picture naming is slowed when a competitor lemma activation is boosted (that is, people are slower to name a picture of a pigeon when seeing or hearing "dove" compared to some unrelated distractor like "glove").[2]

If lemmas are competing even when producing a single word, one might imagine that the many lemmas involved in expressing a complex preverbal message could lead to quite high levels of competition. One way the production system mitigates this competition is by constraining lexical competition based on syntactic category. Evidence for this is that within-category word exchange errors (like "The bus is driving the pigeon," instead of the intended *The pigeon is driving the bus*) are relatively common, but cases where nouns exchange with verbs (The driving is pigeon the bus?) are vanishingly rare (Fromkin, 1971; Garrett, 1975; Nooteboom, 1969). This pattern is generally taken to show that syntactic category acts as a gatekeeper for lexical competition (cf. Dell et al., 2008) such that nouns only compete with nouns, verbs only compete with verbs, etc. This category-specific competition holds for morphologically complex words as well; for example, saying *running* as a noun (as in *the Olympic athlete's running is very fast*) is unaffected by competition from *walking* as a verb, but not from *walking* as a noun (Momma et al., 2020). One implication of this finding is that at least some types of morphologically complex words are not computed "on the fly" but instead are retrieved as (pre-composed) complex lemmas (i.e., there may be separate lemma representations for the verb *running* and the formally identical nominal gerund *running*).

While the content stream manages the selection and retrieval of content words that represent the semantic meaning of the preverbal message, those items must still be configured into sentences that convey the relational and perspective components of meaning – a process to which we now turn.

Structure stream

In parallel with lexical access, speakers retrieve representations that allow for these lexical items to be configured into grammatical sentences that convey the appropriate relational and perspective meanings. This *structure* stream also consists of two stages: First, *function assignment* (Bock, 1995; Bock & Levelt, 1994) involves selecting the grammatical roles appropriate to the preverbal message. These include functions like *subject* and *direct object* that relate the entities to the actions or states in the message, as well as modifier functions (ranging from single adjectives to full syntactic clauses) that augment other entities in the message. Function assignment can be thought of as the primary way to encode relational meaning.

Following selection of grammatical roles, *constituent assembly* (Ferreira & Slevc, 2007; also called *positional processing*; Bock, 1995; Bock & Levelt, 1994; Garrett, 1975) involves assembling these roles into hierarchical syntactic representations. These representations are not isomorphic to word order, although they are closely linked in languages with relatively fixed word orders like English. (In languages like Japanese with more flexible word orders, this involves the assignment of case markers that indicate relational meaning.) Although not always an explicit part of the modal model, a common assumption is that there is then a separate *linearization* process which creates the specific (grammatical) order in which individual syntactic constituents will be produced (e.g., Ferreira & Rehrig, 2019; Garrett, 1975; Hartsuiker & Westenberg, 2000). This allows ordering flexibility that is necessary for incremental production of earlier-planned information and for implementing order-based aspects of *information structure* (Lambrecht, 1994) arising from the perspective meaning (e.g., producing focused information earlier in a sentence).

On dividing and uniting

Following content and structure encoding, grammatical encoding is faced with a *coordination problem* (Bock, 1987a): The words retrieved via content processes need to somehow be bound to the correct grammatical role. This raises the question of why content and structure would be processed by independent subprocesses to begin with. One answer to this question is that the separation of content (largely covering semantic meaning) from structure (largely covering relational and perspective meaning) allows any semantic information to be combined with any relational/perspective meanings. This allows two bounded systems to be combined in a way that can systematically express boundless meanings (Fodor & Pylyshyn, 1988).

Despite this advantage, it is not yet clear how grammatical encoding solves the coordination problem, and some work has argued that content and structure are not processed independently at all. For example, in lexically based (single-stream) models of grammatical encoding (see especially Levelt, 1989), lexical items include their elementary syntax ("treelets"), which are combined according to various operations (e.g., F. Ferreira, 2000; F. Ferreira et al., 2004). These lexically based approaches not only avoid the coordination problem noted before, but also can easily explain how words of the same grammatical category differ in their "preferences" for different constructions (e.g., verb subcategorization biases; Roland et al., 2006). Another approach assumes content and structure are represented distinctly (as in the modal model), but in a framework where they freely interact (Pickering & Branigan, 1998). Specifically, lemmas combine with lemma-like combinatorial nodes that specify how content lemmas can combine into structures. This approach thus preserves a distinction between the representations involved in content and structure, but without segregated streams of processing.

Nevertheless, most models (even using rather different formalisms, as noted below) maintain a content/structure distinction as in the modal model. In part, this may reflect the difficulty of creating the systematicity and expressive power of language without the advantage of independent combinatorial systems (Chomsky, 1957; Fodor & Pylyshyn, 1988; but see, e.g., Bybee & McClelland, 2005).

Perennial and emerging debates

On stages and representations

Does lexical access involve two stages?

In contrast to the rarely contested content/structure distinction, there is a long-standing (and still unresolved) debate concerning the staged selection-then-retrieval nature of grammatical encoding. Much of this debate has focused on whether the stages of lexical access (the *content* stream) are *discrete* or *interactive*. By discrete theories, lemmas must be selected before lexeme retrieval can begin (Levelt, 1989; Levelt et al., 1999). By interactive theories, lexeme retrieval does start before lemma selection is complete, yielding *cascading* activation and potentially *feedback* such that aspects of lexeme retrieval can influence lemma selection (e.g., Cutting & Ferreira, 1999; Dell, 1986; Rapp & Goldrick, 2000).

Interactive accounts still maintain the fundamental two-stage nature of lexical access (as put by Dell & O'Seaghdha, 1991, they are "globally modular but locally interactive"); however, other work has suggested that lexical access in fact involves only a single stage (Caramazza, 1997). These single-level models are motivated from modality-specific production deficits in neuropsychological patients (Caramazza & Hillis, 1990; Rapp et al., 1997) and thus propose that there are not modality-independent lexical representations (as lemmas are assumed to be). Instead, this model assumes that semantic features activate lexemes directly, as well as their syntactic features. Although a one-stage model seems quite distinct from the modal model described here, this particular debate is really about the existence (or non-existence) of modality-general lexical representations. Aside from this, the one-stage model is roughly equivalent to a two-stage model with discrete (non-interactive) levels. Thus, while this debate is important, it does not necessarily challenge the fundamental hierarchical selection-then-retrieval characteristic of the modal model.

A potentially greater challenge to the selection-than-retrieval nature of the modal model comes from a series of electrophysiological (EEG) and magnetoencephalographic (MEG) studies showing surprisingly early effects of phonological information. In one striking example, differences associated with a phonetic/articulatory manipulation (place of articulation of the word-initial phoneme) and a lexical-semantic manipulation (word frequency) of a to-be-produced word were both detectable with MEG about 200 ms following picture onset (Strijkers et al., 2017; see also Feng et al., 2021; Miozzo et al., 2015; Strijkers et al., 2010). This early distinction among to-be-produced words based only on their phonology is surprising under the modal model: the staged nature of grammatical encoding means that effects based on lexical-semantic information should be evident early in processing, whereas effects based on phonological and phonetic information should arise only relatively later.[3] This evidence for very early activation of phonological information thus poses a significant challenge for the modal model's assumption that word form information is retrieved only after lexical/semantic information is selected.

These findings have motivated a quite different *neural assembly* model of lexical access (and thus of the "left half" of grammatical encoding in Figure 1.1) in which connected neural populations encode all of the various components involved in a lexical item (a *word assembly*) and can be activated in parallel (Strijkers, 2016; Strijkers & Costa, 2016; also see Kerr et al., this volume). In this model, word production begins with an *ignition* phase that activates all information in a word assembly followed by *reverberations* in specific parts of the assembly that allow each component to be available when needed (e.g., phonological/phonetic components to be active when necessary for articulation).

Word assemblies seem, on the surface, quite different from lemma and lexeme representations. Note, however, that lemmas are sometimes criticized for being contentless (and so, as the criticism goes, superfluous), serving only to link together other types of information (Caramazza, 1997). Possible superfluity aside, the contentless but linking nature of lemmas means that word assemblies might be a reasonable way that lemmas could be neurally instantiated. That is, the modal model may, in fact, be compatible with highly distributed lexical representations.

In contrast, the staged selection-then-retrieval tenet of the modal model is not compatible with all information in a word assembly being accessed in parallel. That is, in a neural assembly model, the apparently staged availability of different types of information is not a function of lexical access but is rather due to later reverberations within an already ignited assembly.[4] This aspect of a neural assembly approach thus contrasts significantly with the staged selection-then-retrieval character of the modal model. But before tossing out the modal model completely, note that the EEG and MEG findings that support neural assembly models are still compatible with a strongly cascading version of the modal model. As noted by Feng et al. (2021), these experiments have, so far, assessed only adjacent levels of representation (i.e., lexical and phonological) and it will be important to determine whether information from non-adjacent stages are also available in parallel. As this discussion illustrates, the staged nature of lexical access remains under active investigation.

Does structure building involve two stages?

This debate about stages has, so far, focused mostly on lexical access (i.e., the *content* stream), leaving the staged vs. parallel nature of function assignment and constituent assembly in the *structure* stream relatively unexamined. However, some findings where structural priming (see below) occurs only when both structural *and* linear relationships are shared (not based on structural relationships alone; e.g., Pappert & Pechmann, 2014; Pickering et al., 2002) have motivated theories where a single stage of structure encoding encompasses both function assignment and constituent assembly/linearization (Branigan & Pickering, 2017; Cai et al., 2012; Pickering et al., 2002).

Structure building has also been modeled with *connectionist* approaches (e.g., Chang, 2002), which are similar in some ways to the neural assembly model discussed above (in which representations are not conceptualized as discrete "things" but instead are assumed to reflect highly distributed patterns of activation across the brain; Strijkers, 2016; Strijkers & Costa, 2016). In these connectionist models, activity is distributed not across brain networks, but rather over a computational/cognitive network in which the model maps input states (e.g., states representing preverbal messages) to output states (e.g., strings of words) via a set (or sets) of *hidden units*. Activation patterns in these hidden units replace the discrete representations in the modal model, and cognitive processing is modeled as the spreading of activation across the network combined with changes in the weights of individual connections (e.g., Elman, 2009; see Brehm & Goldrick, 2018, for discussion related to language production).

It may seem odd to think of grammatical functions and hierarchical structures as distributed patterns of activation. However, as noted below, influential theories of structural priming involve incremental learning processes that are well characterized by connectionist models. That is, structural priming can be thought of as a gradual adjustment of connection weights that change how activation flows through the grammatical encoding network in the future (Chang, 2002; Chang et al., 2006). Connectionist approaches to grammatical encoding can also naturally explain how speakers sometimes produce ungrammatical sentences *not* in error, which is somewhat odd if there are discrete structural representations governed by the grammar. (That is, why would a speaker have a stored representation of an ungrammatical structure?) For example, English speakers will sometimes say sentences with resumptive pronouns (e.g., "We're afraid of things that we don't know what they are,") despite judging such sentences unacceptable (e.g., F. Ferreira & Swets, 2017; Morgan et al., 2020). This might occur because it allows speakers to avoid producing an even more problematic structure (i.e., an unlicensed gap like "We're afraid of things that we don't know what __ are"; Morgan & Wagers, 2018) or because it satisfies local constraints (here, "what they are") at the cost of global constraints that might be more cognitively costly to satisfy (Asudeh, 2011).

Another example comes from code switching in bilingualism, where simultaneous activation of representations from both languages can cause incompatible structural constraints from two languages to impact production of a single sentence. These conflicting constraints can lead speakers to produce *doubling constructions*, where a code-switched sentence includes both a word *and* its translation equivalent (e.g., in a code-switch between languages with SVO and SOV word orders, producing the verb in both languages: $S_1V_1O_2V_2$). These doubling constructions can be naturally explained in a gradient approach to syntax where a speaker doubles the verb in order to best satisfy conflicting constraints from the two languages' grammars (Goldrick et al., 2016a, 2016b). Similarly, conflicting constraints within a single language can emerge as *syntactic blend errors* (Bock, 1987a; Coppock, 2010). For example, "Would you turn on the light on," was presumably a blend of two different structural formulations of the same message (Would you turn the light on/ Would you turn on the light; Fay, 1980).

Although connectionist models of grammatical encoding offer a quite different approach from the modal model, some of these differences might be more superficial than deep. The modal model already has features of a connectionist model (in fact, the content stream of the modal model basically *is* a connectionist model that relies on spreading activation through a network; cf. Dell, 1986; Roelofs, 1992). In addition, while the representations in the models differ – discrete units (e.g., lemmas, subjects) in the modal model versus distributed patterns in connectionist models, the encoding of relational and perspective meaning via grammatical roles and linearization need not necessarily involve discrete representations. And some insights from the modal model (the distinction between content and structure) have in fact been instantiated in existing connectionist approaches to grammatical encoding (Chang, 2002; Chang et al., 2006).

However other differences are more profound. Most notably, Chang's (2002; Chang et al., 2006) connectionist models of grammatical production do not progress through a stage of function assignment and then one of constituent assembly. Instead, these models develop sequencing representations based on both lexical and event-semantic knowledge (perhaps analogous to relational meaning). Although there is still relatively little work on such connectionist modeling of grammatical encoding in production, it is possible that these kinds of models will yield a quite different account of sentence production (as has been true in the realm of syntactic parsing; e.g., Christiansen & Chater, 1999).

In sum, the staged nature of the modal model has been questioned for both content and structure processing. Distributed proposals like the neural assembly model (Strijkers & Costa, 2016) and connectionist models of structure building (Chang et al., 2006) offer significant challenges to the selection-then-retrieval character of the modal model, although it remains to be seen how well these approaches can account for the speech error patterns that initially led to the two-stage approach (Garrett, 1975). Other insights from the modal model are, so far, largely preserved even in these quite different neural and connectionist frameworks. For example, connectionist models of grammatical encoding still maintain the distinction between content and structure (and the neural assembly model does too, at least implicitly, by focusing only on lexical access). Perhaps this is unsurprising; as noted above, the separation of content and structure may underlie the infinite expressive potential of language. Alternatively, it may simply be that most research has focused separately on lexical access or structure building, thus potential interactions between streams have received relatively little attention.

What are structural representations (and can structural priming tell us about them)?

Structural priming[5] (also called *syntactic priming, structural persistence, syntactic persistence,* or *structural alignment*) refers to the phenomenon that speakers (and signers and writers) are relatively likely to use the same syntactic structures they have recently produced or perceived (Bock, 1986; Mahowald et al., 2016; Pickering & Ferreira, 2008). This is likely an example of a more general tendency for speakers to reuse aspects of language in the service of communicative efficiency (Pickering & Garrod, 2004), although note that the magnitude of structural priming effects seems insensitive to communicative factors (Ivanova et al., 2020). Structural priming can occur without any lexical or formal overlap (Bock, 1986, 1989; Bock & Loebell, 1990), and in fact can even occur across languages (Hartsuiker et al., 2004; Loebell & Bock, 2003; Schoonbaert et al., 2007; Shin & Christianson, 2009). Priming can also occur among sentences with different thematic roles (Messenger et al., 2012). These kinds of observations suggest that the structural representations that lead to priming do not include semantic information. That is, structural priming seems to reflect persistence of an abstract, content-free, syntactic representation.

However, structural priming *can* be influenced by lexical/semantic overlap even if such overlap is not a prerequisite for priming effects. The most well studied case of this is the *lexical boost,* which refers to the considerably larger priming effects that emerge when lexical items (particularly verbs) are repeated between prime and target (Pickering & Branigan, 1998). In fact, structural priming can occur from even a single isolated verb that has a highly associated structure (Melinger & Dobel, 2005).[6] Other types of lexical overlap such as prepositions (e.g., "by" vs. "for") can impact priming effects as well (Ziegler et al., 2019). And, while structural priming occurs without shared thematic roles, the order of thematic roles can themselves lead to priming (Chang et al., 2003; Song & Lai, 2021). These kinds of observations suggest that structural priming may not be so abstract and content-free after all.

One way to reconcile these observations is to assume that there are two distinct mechanisms underlying structural priming. Indeed, it seems that "abstract" and "lexically based" priming behaves somewhat differently. For example, structural priming can occur without explicit memory of the prime (e.g., in patients with amnesia; Ferreira et al., 2008) and can persist for a very long time (Bock & Griffin, 2000; Kaschak & Borreggine, 2008), supporting theories of priming as a kind of implicit learning process (Chang et al., 2006; Dell & Chang, 2014; Jaeger & Snider, 2013). However, the lexical boost seems to decay quickly relatively (e.g., Hartsuiker et al., 2008), supporting theories where priming reflects residual activation (Pickering & Branigan, 1998) or is a communicative effect (Pickering & Garrod, 2004). Dual process accounts thus assume that long-term abstract priming effects reflect a type of implicit learning process whereas short-term lexical effects are thought to reflect something like transient maintenance in short-term memory (Chang et al., 2006; Ferreira & Bock, 2006; Hartsuiker et al., 2008; Reitter et al., 2011).

Although a dual-process approach seems plausible, evidence that the lexical boost actually reflects persistence in memory is mixed (Yan et al., 2018; Zhang et al., 2020) and it remains possible that these seemingly distinct effects still result from a single process. For example, a model of priming effects based on prediction error (e.g., Jaeger & Snider, 2013) can capture differences between "abstract" and "lexically based" priming by assuming that the informativity of lexical cues decays faster than the informativity of structural cues. (This assumption makes sense if lexical repetition typically occurs over relatively shorter timescales than structural repetition because semantic topics "cluster" in language; Qian & Jaeger, 2012).

At first glance, this all might seem to be a somewhat niche debate about the structural priming paradigm. But, in fact, different theories of structural priming and the lexical boost have important implications for the nature of structural representations. For example, theories of priming as residual activation fit well with symbolic representations of structure, whereas theories of priming based on implicit learning fit well with the idea of syntax as a kind of procedural (rather than declarative) knowledge (cf. Ullman, 2001), and with theories where structural priming indicates a more ubiquitous predictive process that serves production, comprehension, and acquisition (Dell & Chang, 2014; Pickering & Garrod, 2013). Structural priming has even been argued (somewhat controversially) to be an ideal approach to understand the nature of language (see Branigan & Pickering, 2017, and the included commentary).

On incrementality and advance planning

As noted above, one advantage of the linearization process occurring late in grammatical encoding is that it allows for incremental processing. That is, speakers can (and often do) start producing sentences before the structure of the sentence is fully planned. This can sometimes result in disfluencies or can leave a speaker partway through a sentence that cannot be grammatically completed in a way that expresses their intended message (having painted oneself into a syntactic corner; e.g., Shlonsky, 1992). But these disfluencies and errors are a small price to pay given (at least) two significant advantages of incremental production. For one, producing sentences incrementally allows speakers to produce phonological word forms as they become available, thus reducing demand on working memory (WM) (and interference from the contents of WM; e.g., Bock, 1982; Slevc, 2011). Starting to speak before fully planning sentences also allows for the very quick conversational turn taking that is so common in conversational speech (Sacks et al., 1978; Stivers et al., 2009).

These advantages of producing lexical items as they are planned motivates an (often implicit) assumption of many models of production that the order of planning corresponds approximately to the surface order of the sentence (Momma & Ferreira, 2019, call these *sequential* models). That is, sequential models assume that each word is planned in about the same order that it is produced (e.g., Dell et al., 2008; Ferreira & Dell, 2000; Levelt, 1989), although note that the extent to which words are planned in advance can depend on both task and strategic factors (e.g., Ferreira & Swets, 2002; Konopka & Meyer, 2014; Wagner et al., 2010).

Although it seems that speakers *can* start speaking sentence having planned only a single word (Griffin, 2001; Zhao & Yang, 2016), speakers typically plan the initial phrase before starting to speak. Evidence for this is that speakers are slower to start producing sentences starting with coordinate noun phrases compared to sentences starting with simple noun phrases (e.g., it takes longer to start saying *The pigeon and the hat move above the bus*, compared to *The pigeon moves above the hat and the bus*) (Allum & Wheeldon, 2009; Martin et al., 2010; Smith & Wheeldon, 1999; Wheeldon et al., 2013). This phrasal scope of planning may even be obligatory; for example, patients with semantic short-term memory deficits have difficulty producing complex phrases, in which multiple words must presumably be held simultaneously in mind (e.g., *Small angry pigeon*), despite successfully producing the same information in separate simple phrases (e.g., *The pigeon is small and angry*) (Martin & Freedman, 2001; Martin et al., 2004; see also Martin & Schnur, 2019).

At first pass, a sequential model in which words or phrases are produced as they are planned seems reasonable – sentences are, after all, orders of words and phrases. But sentences are not *just* orders of words and phrases, and the syntactic and semantic relationships between these constituents do not necessarily conform to the linear order in which they are produced (e.g., syntactic agreement, coreference, etc.). That is, sentences have both a linear "surface" order and an underlying hierarchical syntactic structure, which together express the preverbal message. And indeed, sentence planning is impacted by syntactic constraints (e.g., Christianson & Ferreira, 2005; Momma & Ferreira, 2019; Momma et al., 2016, 2018).

So how does one usually end up with grammatical sentences under a sequential model? One reason is that the grammar of a language typically includes multiple syntactic structures that can express the same types of syntactic relationships (a feature also critical to the structural priming paradigm discussed above). Thus, it is often possible to construct different meaning-appropriate syntactic structures "on the fly" given different initial starting points. For example, if one wanted to express the message from before about a pigeon driving a bus, and BUS was the most highly accessible item, one could simply produce a passive form ("The bus is being driven by the pigeon"). Speakers do seem to rely on the flexibility of the grammar in this way, possibly motivating why languages so often allow different ways to say the same thing (Ferreira, 1996).

Of course, a passive sentence is not identical in meaning to an active one (as is true for many, perhaps all, structural alternations) and there are differences in the distribution of different structures as a function of the verb. One might imagine that the appropriate structure could still emerge in a sequential model "for free" because the order in which lexical items are selected and retrieved is itself guided by semantic and syntactic relationships in the preverbal message (i.e., the *perspective meaning* mentioned above). For example, aspects of information structure like givenness and focus likely influence the accessibility of relevant lexical items, so if "bus" is especially important in the message, it might also be more likely to be focused in an emergent passive sentence. However, verb/structure biases are hard to explain under a sequential model, as are other ways in which semantic and syntactic relationships constrain sentence form.

Indeed, there is growing evidence that sentence planning is influenced directly by syntactic constraints (not just via higher accessibility for more structurally important items). For example, while speakers may not plan verbs before *external* arguments (like subjects; Schriefers et al., 1998), they do appear to plan verbs before their *internal* arguments (such as direct objects), even when the direct object is produced before the verb (Momma et al., 2016). This also holds for more subtle cases: for example, speakers plan verbs before the subjects of unaccusative verbs (where the subject is, semantically, the object of the action; e.g., *the cat fell*) but not before the subjects of unergative verbs (e.g., *the cat jumped*) (Momma et al., 2018), even when these subject-verb relationships are quite distant in the sentence (Momma & Ferreira, 2019). Similarly, producing long-distance dependencies involves advance planning of the underlying structural relationships (even if not specific lexical items), without necessarily involving planning of intervening material (Do & Kaiser, 2019; Momma, 2021).

The importance of the verb for sentence planning is sensible from a syntactic perspective (see also Antón-Méndez, 2020; Konopka, 2019). Many aspects of verbs' arguments depend on the verb (including syntactic and morphological forms), and this is especially true for *internal* arguments, which are exactly the cases where speakers consistently show advance planning of verbs. This distinction between internal and external arguments also illustrates how linguistic theory can be important for psycholinguistic research: the finding that sentence subjects could be produced prior to verb planning (e.g., Schriefers et al., 1998) would be inconsistent with verb-guided production without considering a more nuanced distinction between internal and external arguments (e.g., Kratzer, 1996; Williams, 2015; see Momma & Ferreira, 2019, for discussion).[7]

In sum, research on the scope of planning reinforces the fundamental insight of the modal model that sentence planning is non-linear. The initial function assignment stage operates over a non-linear relational representation, which (by definition) cannot be planned in a linearly incremental manner. This relational representation then maps to a linear form that is itself planned and executed incrementally. Not only does the order in which relational representations are planned impact form planning, but also the dynamics of form planning modulate exactly which relations get constructed during function assignment. The divisions within grammatical encoding thus do not appear to be independent.

These interactions between stages and streams are internal to grammatical encoding, and so do not challenge the modal model's assumption that grammatical encoding processes are autonomous from other linguistic and non-linguistic processes. However, other work mentioned above (e.g., theories in which domain-general implicit learning processes underlie structural priming effects) suggests grammatical encoding may *not* be strictly independent from other systems.

On modularity

The modal model illustrated in Figure 1.1 is a modular theory (in the sense of Fodor, 1983) in that grammatical encoding is presumed to be distinct from other linguistic and non-linguistic processes, interacting only "at the edges." That is, prior processes of message generation feed into grammatical encoding, which operates largely autonomously of message-level processes and then "outputs" to subsequent processes of phonological encoding and spellout. It is perhaps surprising that the robust debate between modular and domain-general accounts of syntactic *parsing* has been comparatively absent in the literature on grammatical encoding. However, there is evidence that grammatical encoding interacts with both other linguistic and also non-linguistic processes, challenging a strongly modular account.

Of course, influences of message encoding (and earlier conceptual stages) on grammatical encoding are to be expected – the whole point is to encode sentences that express an intended meaning – although it is interesting that different aspects of meaning may exert somewhat independent influences on different stages of grammatical encoding (e.g., Branigan et al., 2008; Ferreira & Rehrig, 2019). Somewhat more surprisingly, grammatical encoding seems to be penetrable by later stages of processing as well. For example, word exchange errors (like the pigeon/bus example above) are more likely for words with shared phonological onsets (Dell & Reich, 1981) and phonological similarity between lexical items can influence choice of grammatical structure (Bock, 1987b; Levelt & Maassen, 1981; Santesteban et al., 2010). Similarly, morphophonological transparency can influence the accuracy of subject-verb agreement production (Hartsuiker et al., 2003; Haskell & MacDonald, 2003) potentially in a modality-specific way (i.e., phonological and orthographic representations influence grammatical encoding in speech and writing, respectively; Franck et al., 2003).

These findings argue against modularity *internal* to grammatical encoding (i.e., they support interactions between levels of grammatical encoding), but research on (non)modularity more often considers the involvement of *external* (non-linguistic/domain-general) processes on grammatical encoding. That is, does grammatical encoding operate largely independently of other cognitive processes (as implied by the modular nature of the modal model), or does it draw on the myriad functions available to other aspects of cognition?

The competitive nature of lemma selection in the modal model (although see endnote 2) naturally motivates work suggesting that domain-general cognitive control underlies the resolution of lexical competition (e.g., Crowther & Martin, 2014; de Zubicaray et al., 2006; Novick et al., 2009; see also Nozari, 2018). And, although structural alternatives do not appear to compete for selection (Ferreira, 1996), production of less preferred structures nonetheless involves brain regions associated with cognitive control (Thothathiri, 2018). Aspects of grammatical encoding also rely on domain-general (short-term/ working) memory processes (e.g., MacDonald, 2013; see Martin & Slevc, 2014, for a review). For example, memory-based accessibility can impact syntactic choice (Ferreira & Firato, 2002; Slevc, 2011) and producing syntactic agreement between subjects and verbs involves domain-general memory processes (Badecker & Kuminiak, 2007; Hartsuiker & Barkhuysen, 2006; Slevc &

Martin, 2016). Memory pressures also can impact the extent of advance planning in production (e.g., Ferreira & Swets, 2002; Martin & Freedman, 2001; Swets et al., 2014; Wagner et al., 2010; but see Klaus et al., 2017, for evidence that this might apply to the scope of phonological rather than grammatical planning). Other evidence for the involvement of domain general processes in grammatical encoding comes from findings that grouping structure in mathematics and in music can prime relative clause attachment in sentence completion (e.g., Scheepers et al., 2011, 2019; Van de Cavey & Hartsuiker, 2016) and that common neural substrates underlie the production of both linguistic and musical structure (Chiang et al., 2018).

However, there are many aspects of grammatical encoding that do *not* seem to involve domain-general processes (e.g., Ivanova & Ferreira, 2019; MacDonald et al., 2016). This may, in part, reflect the non-linear nature of grammatical planning; for example, "long distance dependencies" are far apart in the eventual sequence of words, but are not necessarily planned far apart when encoding the utterance (see section 3.3 above). It may also be the case that many aspects of grammatical encoding are highly automatized (Bock, 1982; Bock & Levelt, 1994), thus fulfilling at least some of the criteria for modularity. Whether such automaticity results from some type of innate cognitive/neural specialization for grammatical encoding (à la Fodor, 1983) or from the emergent modularity of a highly practiced set of processes (e.g., Elman et al., 1996; Johnson, 2011) remains to be seen. Note also that many aspects of grammatical encoding fulfill some, but not *all* criteria for automaticity (e.g., consider the evidence for memory capacity limits noted above), suggesting that automaticity in grammatical encoding is a matter of degree rather than of kind (for discussion, see Hartsuiker & Moors, 2017).

And many more ...

These debates on stages, representations, planning, and modularity are only a few of the many topics where our understanding of grammatical encoding is expanding and being challenged. Another interesting line of work assesses the role of language production (including grammatical encoding) on *comprehension* and *acquisition* of language (e.g., Dell & Chang, 2014; MacDonald, 2013). This complements a broader move away from investigating production independently from other aspects of language and toward models and approaches that apply to production *and* comprehension (e.g., Momma & Phillips, 2018; Pickering & Garrod, 2013; Tooley & Bock, 2014). Broadening the field even more, there is growing evidence that language production processes play important roles in other domains like verbal working memory (MacDonald, 2016), cognitive control (Cragg & Nation, 2010), and even scene/event perception (Sauppe & Flecken, 2021).

A related important topic is whether grammatical encoding can be successfully understood when studied in isolation or if it requires studies of language use in communicative contexts. Increasingly, studies of "monologue" (i.e., participants speaking in some experimental task) are being complemented by controlled laboratory-based studies of multiple speakers in dialogue (Pickering & Garrod, 2004, 2013). Although communicative context is clearly important for many aspects of language use (cf. Clark, 1996), evidence for listener- or dialogue-based effects on grammatical encoding itself has been limited. For example, structural priming effects do not seem to differ between monologue and dialogue situations (Ivanova et al., 2020), which is somewhat unexpected if these effects reflect interactive alignment between communicative partners. Similarly, there is only limited evidence that *audience design* affects syntactic choice; for example, speakers do not seem to avoid producing sentences that would be syntactically ambiguous for a listener (e.g., Ferreira & Dell, 2000; Kraljic & Brennan, 2005; but see Haywood et al., 2005). One challenge is that using confederates in these studies (as is often done to maintain experimental control) may influence results in subtle ways (Kuhlen & Brennan, 2013). However, this may simply mean that the ambiguity of a grammatical structure (for example) is simply not something a speaker is aware of at the point of grammatical encoding. That is, a syntactically ambiguous sentence is only ambiguous if one does not already know the syntax (cf. Ferreira et al., 2005).

Finally, a growing body of work is assessing grammatical encoding in multilingualism and in multiple languages (also see Sánchez et al., this volume). One approach to bi/multilingualism is to assume a straightforward adaptation of the modal model that includes separable grammatical encoding systems for each language (de Bot, 1992). However, more recent work supports highly interactive grammatical encoding processes across languages (e.g., Hartsuiker & Pickering, 2008; Hartsuiker et al., 2004; Shin & Christianson, 2009) or even suggests that there may be no language-specific grammatical encoding processes at all (Lowie & Verspoor, 2011; Tsoukala et al., 2021; cf. Otheguy et al., 2015). Equally critical is work assessing grammatical encoding across different languages (e.g., Christianson & Ferreira, 2005; Norcliffe et al., 2015). Such cross-linguistic work is critical given the diversity across languages (cf. Evans & Levinson, 2009), but there is much to be done: experimental sentence production research has, so far, involved less than 30 of the over 5,000 languages spoken around the world, and most of those languages are typologically similar (Jaeger & Norcliffe, 2009). A greater focus on multilingualism and on cross-linguistic work is likely to not only inform our current theories and understanding of grammatical encoding, but also to help generate new theories and new phenomena to understand.

Conclusion

The modal model of grammatical encoding described here has guided research on sentence production for over 40 years. It has an impressive track record; accounting for a wide variety of findings including speech error patterns, the timing of speech production, and neuroimaging data. It has been used to understand sentence production in monolingual and multilingual speakers, in typical and disordered speech (e.g., aphasia), and in development and aging. Work within this framework has yielded some significant insights on which there is now relatively little debate (contra past debates) within research on grammatical encoding.

One such insight is that linguistic and non-linguistic knowledge are different and involve distinct representational systems.[8] This is not a ubiquitous assumption across psycholinguistics; for example, work on linguistic relativism (Whorf, 1956) argues that the nature of a language impacts the thought patterns of its speakers (e.g., Boroditsky, 2018). Another example is that some connectionist models of reading do not preserve a conceptual/linguistic distinction (e.g., Plaut et al., 1996), which contrasts with connectionist accounts of grammatical encoding (e.g., Chang et al., 2006) that incorporate a relatively rich cognitive architecture including this conceptual/linguistic distinction.

A second insight is that syntax is in there somewhere. This is not uncontroversial in comprehension and acquisition research, where there is a long-standing tension between theories of syntactic knowledge as a cognitive primitive (e.g., Frazier, 1988; Pinker, 1989) and theories of syntactic knowledge as emergent from conceptual and perceptual knowledge (e.g., Tomasello, 2000). However various lines of evidence, especially the syntactic integrity typical of speech errors and the syntactic contributions to structural priming (for discussion, see Bock, 1990; Momma, 2021), have made the role of syntactic structures in sentence production uncontroversial.

Of course, the consensus nature of this model does not mean it is unanimously accepted (nor does it mean that it is an accurate characterization of grammatical encoding). Indeed, there have been significant challenges to the modal model, most especially regarding its staged nature, as described above. However, with some flexibility, it seems likely that some version of the modal model can be maintained to continue informing and structuring future research on grammatical encoding.

Notes

1 Note that the primary point of the Mehl et al. (2007) study was to debunk the persistent claim that women talk more than men.
2 Note, however, that the competitive vs. non-competitive nature of lexical selection is still under active debate and the types of semantic interference often interpreted as support for lexical competition can be explained in other ways (e.g., Mahon et al., 2007; Oppenheim et al., 2010; also see Nozari & Hepner, 2019).
3 More concretely, meta-analytic estimates suggest that lemma-based (i.e., lexical/ semantic) information is typically active about 200–250 ms, and lexeme-based (i.e., phonological) information active around 300–400 ms, from message onset (Indefrey, 2011; Indefrey & Levelt, 2004). Phonological or articulatory effects at 200 ms are clearly inconsistent with these estimates.
4 While the neural assembly model could also be characterized as a two-stage model (*ignition* and *reverberation*), these are rather different from the selection and retrieval stages in the modal model.

5 Which was inconsiderately discussed above despite not being defined until now.
6 Although note that verbs are not critical as structural priming can also occur from sentences that are *missing* a verb (Ivanova et al., 2017).
7 Whether psycholinguistic findings can, in turn, inform linguistic theory (e.g., regarding the underlying syntactic status of the subject of an unaccusative verb) is probably still an open question.
8 A fortunate consequence of this separation was that researchers interested in grammatical encoding could work without having to wrestle with the nature of thought.

References

Allum, P. H., & Wheeldon, L. (2009). Scope of lexical access in spoken sentence production: Implications for the conceptual–syntactic interface. *Journal of Experimental Psychology: Learning, Memory, and Cognition, 35*(5), 1240–1255.

Antón-Méndez, I. (2020). The role of verbs in sentence production. *Frontiers in Psychology, 11*, 189.

Asudeh, A. (2011). Local grammaticality in syntactic production. In E. M. Bender and J. E. Arnold (Eds.), *Language from a cognitive perspective: Grammar, usage, and processing studies in honor of Thomas Wasow* (pp. 51–79). Stanford: CSLI Publications.

Badecker, W., & Kuminiak, F. (2007). Morphology, agreement and working memory retrieval in sentence production: Evidence from gender and case in Slovak. *Journal of Memory and Language, 56*(1), 65–85.

Bock, J. K. (1982). Toward a cognitive psychology of syntax: Information processing contributions to sentence formulation. *Psychological Review, 89*(1), 1–47.

Bock, J. K. (1986). Syntactic persistence in language production. *Cognitive Psychology, 18*(3), 355–387.

Bock, J. K. (1987a). Coordinating words and syntax in speech plans. In A. Ellis (Ed.), *Progress in the psychology of language* (Vol. 3, pp. 337–390). London: Erlbaum.

Bock, J. K. (1995). Sentence production: From mind to mouth. In J. L. Miller, & P. D. Eimas (Eds.), *Handbook of perception and cognition. Vol 11: Speech, language, and communication* (pp. 181–216). Orlando, FL: Academic Press.

Bock, K. (1987b). An effect of the accessibility of word forms on sentence structures. *Journal of Memory and Language, 26*, 119–137.

Bock, K. (1989). Closed-class immanence in sentence production. *Cognition 31*(2), 163–186.

Bock, K. (1990). Structure in language: Creating form in talk. *American Psychologist, 45*(11), 1221.

Bock, K., & Griffin, Z. M. (2000). The persistence of structural priming: Transient activation or implicit learning? *Journal of Experimental Psychology: General, 129*, 177–192.

Bock, K., & Levelt, W. J. (1994). Language production: Grammatical encoding. *Handbook of psycholinguistics* (pp. 945–984). Academic Press.

Bock, K., & Loebell, H. (1990). Framing sentences. *Cognition, 35*(1), 1–39.

Boroditsky, L. (2018). Language and the construction of time through space. *Trends in Neurosciences, 41*(10), 651–653.

Branigan, H. P., & Pickering, M. J. (2017). An experimental approach to linguistic representation. *Behavioral and Brain Sciences, 40*, e282.

Branigan, H. P., Pickering, M. J., & Tanaka, M. (2008). Contributions of animacy to grammatical function assignment and word order during production. *Lingua, 118*(2), 172–189.

Brown-Schmidt, S., & Konopka, A. E. (2015). Processes of incremental message planning during conversation. *Psychonomic Bulletin & Review, 22*(3), 833–843.

Brown-Schmidt, S., & Tanenhaus, M. K. (2006). Watching the eyes when talking about size: An investigation of message formulation and utterance planning. *Journal of Memory and Language, 54*(4), 592–609.

Brehm, L., & Goldrick, M. (2018). Connectionist Principles in Theories of Speech Production. In *The Oxford Handbook of Psycholinguistics* (pp. 372–397). Oxford University Press.

Bybee, J., & McClelland, J. L. (2005). Alternatives to the combinatorial paradigm of linguistic theory based on domain general principles of human cognition. *The Linguistic Review, 22*, 381–410.

Cai, Z. G., Pickering, M. J., & Branigan, H. P. (2012). Mapping concepts to syntax: Evidence from structural priming in Mandarin Chinese. *Journal of Memory and Language, 66*(4), 833–849.

Caramazza, A. (1997). How many levels of processing are there in lexical access?. *Cognitive Neuropsychology, 14*(1), 177–208.

Caramazza, A., & Hillis, A. E. (1990). Where do semantic errors come from? *Cortex, 26*(1), 95–122.

Chang, F. (2002). Symbolically speaking: A connectionist model of sentence production. *Cognitive Science, 26*(5), 609–651.

Chang, F., Bock, K., & Goldberg, A. E. (2003). Can thematic roles leave traces of their places?. *Cognition, 90*(1), 29–49.

Chang, F., Dell, G. S., & Bock, K. (2006). Becoming syntactic. *Psychological Review, 113*(2), 234.

Chiang, J. N., Rosenberg, M. H., Bufford, C. A., Stephens, D., Lysy, A., & Monti, M. M. (2018). The language of music: Common neural codes for structured sequences in music and natural language. *Brain and Language, 185*, 30–37.

Chomsky, N. (1957). *Syntactic structures*. The Hague: Mouton.

Christiansen, M. H., & Chater, N. (1999). Toward a connectionist model of recursion in human linguistic performance. *Cognitive Science, 23*(2), 157–205.

Christianson, K., & Ferreira, F. (2005). Conceptual accessibility and sentence production in a free word order language (Odawa). *Cognition, 98*(2), 105–135.

Clark, H. H. (1996). *Using language*. Cambridge University Press.

Coppock, E. (2010). Parallel grammatical encoding in sentence production: evidence from syntactic blends. *Language and Cognitive Processes, 25*(1), 38–49.

Cragg, L., & Nation, K. (2010). Language and the development of cognitive control. *Topics in Cognitive Science, 2*(4), 631–642.

Crowther, J. E., & Martin, R. C. (2014). Lexical selection in the semantically blocked cyclic naming task: the role of cognitive control and learning. *Frontiers in Human Neuroscience, 8*, 9.

Cutting, J. C., & Ferreira, V. S. (1999). Semantic and phonological information flow in the production lexicon. *Journal of Experimental Psychology: Learning, Memory, and Cognition, 25*(2), 318.

De Bot, K. (1992). A bilingual production model: Levelt's speaking model adapted. *Applied Linguistics, 13*(1), 1–24.

de Zubicaray, G., McMahon, K., Eastburn, M., & Pringle, A. (2006). Top-down influences on lexical selection during spoken word production: A 4T fMRI investigation of refractory effects in picture naming. *Human Brain Mapping, 27*(11), 864–873.

Dell, G. S. (1986). A spreading-activation theory of retrieval in sentence production. *Psychological Review, 93*(3), 283.

Dell, G. S., & Chang, F. (2014). The P-chain: Relating sentence production and its disorders to comprehension and acquisition. *Philosophical Transactions of the Royal Society B: Biological Sciences, 369*(1634), 20120394.

Dell, G. S., & O'Seaghdha, P. G. (1991). Mediated and convergent lexical priming in language production: A comment on Levelt et al. (1991). *Psychological Review, 98*(4), 604–614.

Dell, G. S., & Reich, P. A. (1981). Stages in sentence production: An analysis of speech error data. *Journal of Verbal Learning and Verbal Behavior, 20*(6), 611–629.

Dell, G. S., Oppenheim, G. M., & Kittredge, A. K. (2008). Saying the right word at the right time: Syntagmatic and paradigmatic interference in sentence production. *Language and Cognitive Processes, 23*(4), 583–608.

Do, M. L., & Kaiser, E. (2019). Subjecthood and linear order in linguistic encoding: Evidence from the real-time production of wh-questions in English and Mandarin Chinese. *Journal of Memory and Language, 105*, 60–75.

Elman, J. L. (2009). On the meaning of words and dinosaur bones: Lexical knowledge without a lexicon. *Cognitive Science, 33*(4), 547–582.

Elman, J. L., Bates, E. A., Johnson, M. H., Karmiloff-Smith, A., Parisi, D., & Plunkett, K. (1996) *Rethinking innateness: A connectionist perspective on development*. MIT Press.

Evans, N., & Levinson, S. C. (2009). The myth of language universals: Language diversity and its importance for cognitive science. *Behavioral and Brain Sciences, 32*(5), 429–448.

Fay, D. (1980). Transformational errors. In V. A. Fromkin (Ed.), *Errors in linguistic performance: Slips of the tongue, ear, pen, and hand* (pp. 111–122). New York: Academic Press.

Feng, C., Damian, M. F., & Qu, Q. (2021). Parallel processing of semantics and phonology in spoken production: Evidence from blocked cyclic picture naming and EEG. *Journal of Cognitive Neuroscience, 33*(4), 725–738.

Ferreira, F. (2000). Syntax in language production: An approach using Tree-Adjoining Grammars. In L. Wheeldon (Ed.), *Aspects of language production* (pp. 291–330). Cambridge, MA: MIT Press.

Ferreira, F., & Rehrig, G. (2019). Linearisation during language production: Evidence from scene meaning and saliency maps. *Language, Cognition and Neuroscience, 34*(9), 1129–1139.

Ferreira, F., & Swets, B. (2002). How incremental is language production? Evidence from the production of utterances requiring the computation of arithmetic sums. *Journal of Memory and Language, 46*(1), 57–84.

Ferreira, F., & Swets, B. (2017). The production and comprehension of resumptive pronouns in relative clause "island" contexts. In *Twenty-first century psycholinguistics: Four cornerstones* (pp. 263–278). Routledge.

Ferreira, F., Lau, E. F., & Bailey, K. G. (2004). Disfluencies, language comprehension, and tree adjoining grammars. *Cognitive Science, 28*(5), 721–749.

Ferreira, V. S. (1996). Is it better to give than to donate? Syntactic flexibility in language production. *Journal of Memory and Language, 35*(5), 724–755.

Ferreira, V. S., & Bock, K. (2006). The functions of structural priming. *Language and Cognitive Processes, 21*(7–8), 1011–1029.

Ferreira, V. S., & Dell, G. S. (2000). Effect of ambiguity and lexical availability on syntactic and lexical production. *Cognitive Psychology, 40*(4), 296–340.

Ferreira, V. S., & Firato, C. E. (2002). Proactive interference effects on sentence production. *Psychonomic Bulletin & Review, 9*(4), 795–800.

Ferreira, V. S., & Slevc, L. R. (2007). Grammatical encoding. In Gaskell, M. G. (Ed.), *The Oxford handbook of psycholinguistics* (pp. 453–469). New York: Oxford University Press.

Ferreira, V. S., Bock, K., Wilson, M. P., & Cohen, N. J. (2008). Memory for syntax despite amnesia. *Psychological Science, 19*(9), 940–946.

Ferreira, V. S., Slevc, L. R., & Rogers, E. S. (2005). How do speakers avoid ambiguous linguistic expressions? *Cognition, 96*(3), 263–284.

Fodor, J. A. (1983). *The modularity of mind.* MIT press.

Fodor, J. A., & Pylyshyn, Z. W. (1988). Connectionism and cognitive architecture: A critical analysis. *Cognition, 28*(1–2), 3–71.

Frazier, L. (1988). Grammar and language processing. In F. J. Newmeyer (Ed.), *Linguistics: The Cambridge Survey (iii) Linguistic theory: Extensions and implications* (pp. 15–34). Cambridge: Cambridge University Press.

Franck, J., Bowers, J., Frauenfelder, U., & Vigliocco, G. (2003). Orthographic influences on agreement: A case for modality-specific form effects on grammatical encoding. *Language and Cognitive Processes, 18*, 61–79. 10.1080/01690960143000452.

Fromkin, V. A. (1971). The non-anomalous nature of anomalous utterances. *Language, 47*, 27–52.

Garrett, M. F. (1975). The analysis of sentence production. In Bower, G. H. *Psychology of learning and motivation* (Vol. 9, pp. 133–177). Academic Press.

Garrett, M. F. (1988). Processes in language production. In F. J. Newmeyer (Ed.), *Linguistics: The Cambridge Survey, Vol. 3: Language: Psychological and biological aspects* (pp. 69–96). Cambridge: Cambridge University Press.

Goldrick, M., Putnam, M., & Schwarz, L. (2016a). Coactivation in bilingual grammars: A computational account of code mixing. *Bilingualism: Language and Cognition, 19*(5), 857–876.

Goldrick, M., Putnam, M., & Schwarz, L. (2016b). The future of code mixing research: Integrating psycholinguistic and formal grammatical theories. *Bilingualism: Language and Cognition,* 19(5), 903–906. doi: 10.1017/S1366728916000390

Griffin, Z. M. (2001). Gaze durations during speech reflect word selection and phonological encoding. *Cognition, 82*, 1–14. doi: 10.1016/S0010-0277(01)00138-X

Hartsuiker, R. J., & Barkhuysen, P. N. (2006). Language production and working memory: The case of subject-verb agreement. *Language and Cognitive Processes, 21*(1), 181–204.

Hartsuiker, R. J., Schriefers, H.J., Bock, K., & Kikstra, G. M. (2003). Morphophonological influences on the construction of subject-verb agreement. *Memory & Cognition, 31*, 1316–1326. 10.3758/bf03195814.

Hartsuiker, R. J., & Moors, A. (2017). On the automaticity of language processing. In H.-J. Schmid (Ed.), *Entrenchment and the psychology of language learning: How we reorganize and adapt linguistic knowledge* (pp. 201–225). De Gruyter Mouton: American Psychological Association. 10.1037/15969-010

Hartsuiker, R. J., & Westenberg, C. (2000). Word order priming in written and spoken sentence production. *Cognition, 75*(2), B27–B39.

Hartsuiker, R. J., Bernolet, S., Schoonbaert, S., Speybroeck, S., & Vanderelst, D. (2008). Syntactic priming persists while the lexical boost decays: Evidence from written and spoken dialogue. *Journal of Memory and Language, 58*(2), 214–238.

Hartsuiker, R. J., Pickering, M. J., & Veltkamp, E. (2004). Is syntax separate or shared between languages? Crosslinguistic syntactic priming in Spanish-English bilinguals. *Psychological Science, 15*, 409–414.

Hartsuiker, R. J., & Pickering, M. J. (2008). Language integration in bilingual sentence production. *Acta Psychologica, 128*(3), 479–489.

Haskell, T. R., & MacDonald, M. C. (2003). Conflicting cues and competition in subject–verb agreement. *Journal of Memory and Language*, 48, 760–778. 10.1016/s0749-596x(03)00010-x.

Haywood, S. L., Pickering, M. J., & Branigan, H. P. (2005). Do speakers avoid ambiguities during dialogue? *Psychological Science, 16*(5), 362–366.

Indefrey, P. (2011). The spatial and temporal signatures of word production components: A critical update. *Frontiers in Psychology*, 2, 255.

Indefrey, P., & Levelt, W. J. (2004). The spatial and temporal signatures of word production components. *Cognition, 92*(1–2), 101–144.

Ivanova, I., & Ferreira, V. S. (2019). The role of working memory for syntactic formulation in language production. *Journal of Experimental Psychology: Learning, Memory, and Cognition, 45*(10), 1791–1814.

Ivanova, I., Branigan, H. P., McLean, J. F., Costa, A., & Pickering, M. J. (2017) Do you what I say? People reconstruct the syntax of anomalous utterances. *Language, Cognition and Neuroscience, 32*(2), 175–189.

Ivanova, I., Horton, W. S., Swets, B., Kleinman, D., & Ferreira, V. S. (2020). Structural alignment in dialogue and monologue (and what attention may have to do with it). *Journal of Memory and Language, 110*, 104052.

Jaeger, T. F., & Norcliffe, E. J. (2009). The cross-linguistic study of sentence production. *Language and Linguistics Compass, 3*(4), 866–887.

Jaeger, T. F., & Snider, N. E. (2013). Alignment as a consequence of expectation adaptation: Syntactic priming is affected by the prime's prediction error given both prior and recent experience. *Cognition, 127*(1), 57–83.

Johnson, M. H. (2011). Interactive specialization: A domain-general framework for human functional brain development? *Developmental Cognitive Neuroscience, 1*(1), 7–21.

Kaschak, M. P., & Borreggine, K. L. (2008). Is long-term structural priming affected by patterns of experience with individual verbs? *Journal of Memory and Language, 58*, 862–878.

Kempen, G., & Huijbers, P. (1983). The lexicalization process in sentence production and naming: Indirect election of words. *Cognition, 14*(2), 185–209.

Kerr, E., Ivanova, B., & Strijkers, K. (this volume, 2022). Lexical access in speech production: Psycho- and neurolinguistic perspectives on the spatiotemporal dynamics. In Hartsuiker, R. & Strijkers, K. (Eds.) *Current Issues in the Psychology of Language*. Routledge Press, UK.

Klaus, J., Mädebach, A., Oppermann, F., & Jescheniak, J. D. (2017). Planning sentences while doing other things at the same time: Effects of concurrent verbal and visuospatial working memory load. *Quarterly Journal of Experimental Psychology, 70*(4), 811–883.

Konopka, A. E. (2019). Encoding actions and verbs: Tracking the time-course of relational encoding during message and sentence formulation. *Journal of Experimental Psychology: Learning, Memory, and Cognition, 45*(8), 1486–1510.

Konopka, A. E., & Brown-Schmidt, S. (2014). Message encoding. In M. A. Goldrick, V. S. Ferreira, & M. Miozzo (Eds.), *The Oxford handbook of language production* (pp. 3–20). Oxford University Press.

Konopka, A. E., & Meyer, A. S. (2014). Priming sentence planning. *Cognitive Psychology, 73*, 1–40.

Kraljic, T., & Brennan, S. E. (2005). Prosodic disambiguation of syntactic structure: For the speaker or for the addressee? *Cognitive Psychology, 50*(2), 194–231.

Kratzer, A. (1996). Severing the external argument from its verb. In Rooryck, J. & Zaring, L. *Phrase structure and the lexicon* (pp. 109–137). Dordrecht: Springer.

Kuhlen, A. K., & Brennan, S. E. (2013). Language in dialogue: When confederates might be hazardous to your data. *Psychonomic Bulletin & Review, 20*(1), 54–72.

Lambrecht, K. (1994). *Information structure and sentence form.* Cambridge: Cambridge University Press.

Levelt, W. J. M., & Maassen, B. (1981). Lexical search and order of mention in sentence production. In W. Klein, & W. Levelt (Eds.), *Crossing the boundaries in linguistics* (pp. 221–252). Dordrecht: Reidel.

Levelt, W. J. M. (1989). *Speaking: From intention to articulation.* Cambridge, MA: MIT Press.

Levelt, W. J., Roelofs, A., & Meyer, A. S. (1999). A theory of lexical access in speech production. *Behavioral and Brain Sciences, 22*(1), 1–38.

Lindsley, J. R. (1975). Producing simple utterances: How far ahead do we plan? *Cognitive Psychology, 7,* 1–19.

Loebell, H., & Bock, K. (2003). Structural priming across languages. *Linguistics, 41*(5), 791–824.

Lowie, W., & Verspoor, M. (2011). The dynamics of multilingualism: Levelt's speaking model revisited. *Modeling bilingualism: From structure to chaos* (1st ed., pp. 267–288). Amsterdam and Philadelphia: John Benjamins.

MacDonald, M. C. (2013). How language production shapes language form and comprehension. *Frontiers in Psychology, 4,* 226.

MacDonald, M. C. (2016). Speak, act, remember: The language-production basis of serial order and maintenance in verbal memory. *Current Directions in Psychological Science, 25*(1), 47–53.

MacDonald, M. C., Montag, J. L., & Gennari, S. P. (2016). Are there really syntactic complexity effects in sentence production? A reply to Scontras et al. (2015). *Cognitive Science, 40*(2), 513–518.

Mahon, B. Z., Costa, A., Peterson, R., Vargas, K. A., & Caramazza, A. (2007). Lexical selection is not by competition: A reinterpretation of semantic interference and facilitation effects in the picture-word interference paradigm. *Journal of Experimental Psychology: Learning, Memory, and Cognition, 33*(3), 503–535.

Mahowald, K., James, A., Futrell, R., & Gibson, E. (2016). A meta-analysis of syntactic priming in language production. *Journal of Memory and Language, 91,* 5–27.

Martin, R. C., & Freedman, M. L. (2001). Short-term retention of lexical-semantic representations: Implications for speech production. *Memory, 9*(4–6), 261–280.

Martin, R. C., & Slevc, L. R. (2014). Language production and working memory. In M. Goldrick, V. Ferreira, & M. Miozzo (Eds.), *The Oxford handbook of language production* (pp. 437–450). Oxford University Press.

Martin, R. C., Crowther, J. E., Knight, M., Tamborello, F. P., and Yang, C. L. (2010). Planning in sentence production: Evidence for the phrase as a default planning scope. *Cognition, 116,* 177–192.

Martin, R. C., Miller, M., & Vu, H. (2004). Lexical-semantic retention and speech production: Further evidence from normal and brain-damaged participants for a phrasal scope of planning. *Cognitive Neuropsychology, 21,* 625–644.

Martin, R. C., & Schnur, T. T. (2019). Independent contributions of semantic and phonological working memory to spontaneous speech in acute stroke. *Cortex, 112,* 58–68.

Mehl, M. R., Vazire, S., Ramírez-Esparza, N., Slatcher, R. B., & Pennebaker, J. W. (2007). Are women really more talkative than men? *Science, 317*(5834), 82-82.

Melinger, A., & Dobel, C. (2005). Lexically-driven syntactic priming. *Cognition, 98*(1), B11–B20.

Messenger, K., Branigan, H. P., McLean, J. F., & Sorace, A. (2012). Is young children's passive syntax semantically constrained? Evidence from syntactic priming. *Journal of Memory and Language 66*(4):568–587.

Miozzo, M., Pulvermüller, F., & Hauk, O. (2015). Early parallel activation of semantics and phonology in picture naming: Evidence from a multiple linear regression MEG study. *Cerebral Cortex, 25*, 3343–3355.

Momma, S. (2021). Filling the gap in gap-filling: Long-distance dependency formation in sentence production. *Cognitive Psychology, 129*, 101411.

Momma, S. (2021). Syntax and speaking. In Goodall, G. (Ed.). *The Cambridge handbook of experimental syntax* (Cambridge handbooks in language and linguistics). Cambridge: Cambridge University Press.

Momma, S., & Ferreira, V. S. (2019). Beyond linear order: The role of argument structure in speaking. *Cognitive Psychology, 114*, 101228.

Momma, S., & Phillips, C. (2018). The relationship between parsing and generation. *Annual Review of Linguistics, 4*, 233–254.

Momma, S., Buffinton, J., Slevc, L. R., & Phillips, C. (2020). Syntactic category constrains lexical competition in speaking. *Cognition, 197*, 104183.

Momma, S., Slevc, L. R., & Phillips, C. (2016). The timing of verb selection in Japanese sentence production. *Journal of Experimental Psychology: Learning, Memory, and Cognition, 42*(5), 813.

Momma, S., Slevc, L. R., & Phillips, C. (2018). Unaccusativity in sentence production. *Linguistic Inquiry, 49*(1), 181–194.

Morgan, A. M., & Wagers, M. W. (2018). English resumptive pronouns are more common where gaps are less acceptable. *Linguistic Inquiry, 49*(4), 861–876.

Morgan, A. M., von der Malsburg, T., Ferreira, V. S., & Wittenberg, E. (2020). Shared syntax between comprehension and production: Multi-paradigm evidence that resumptive pronouns hinder comprehension. *Cognition, 205*, 104417.

Nooteboom, S. G. (1969). The tongue slips into patterns. In G. Sciaron, A. van Essen, & A. Van Raad (Eds.), *Leyden studies in linguistics and phonetics* (pp. 114–132). The Hague, Netherlands: Mouton. (reprinted in V. A. Fromkin (Ed.) (1973) *Speech errors as linguistic evidence.* (pp. 144–156). The Hague: Mouton.

Norcliffe, E., Harris, A. C., & Jaeger, T. F. (2015). Cross-linguistic psycholinguistics and its critical role in theory development: Early beginnings and recent advances. *Language, Cognition and Neuroscience, 30*(9), 1009–1032.

Novick, J. M., Kan, I. P., Trueswell, J. C., & Thompson-Schill, S. L. (2009). A case for conflict across multiple domains: Memory and language impairments following damage to ventrolateral prefrontal cortex. *Cognitive Neuropsychology, 26*(6), 527–567.

Nozari, N. (2018). How special is language production? Perspectives from monitoring and control. In Federmeier, K. D. & Watson, D. G. *Psychology of learning and motivation* (Vol. 68, pp. 179–213). Academic Press.

Otheguy, R., García, O., & Reid, W. (2015). Clarifying translanguaging and deconstructing named languages: A perspective from linguistics. *Applied Linguistics Review, 6*(3), 281–307.

Pappert, S., & Pechmann, T. (2014). Priming word order by thematic roles: No evidence for an additional involvement of phrase structure. *Quarterly Journal of Experimental Psychology, 67*(11), 2260–2278.

Pickering, M. J., & Branigan, H. P. (1998). The representation of verbs: Evidence from syntactic priming in language production. *Journal of Memory and Language, 39*(4), 633–651.

Pickering, M. J., & Ferreira, V. S. (2008). Structural priming: A critical review. *Psychological Bulletin, 134*(3), 427.

Pickering, M. J., & Garrod, S. (2004). Toward a mechanistic psychology of dialogue. *Behavioral and Brain Sciences, 27*(2), 169–190.

Pickering, M. J., & Garrod, S. (2013). An integrated theory of language production and comprehension. *Behavioral and Brain Sciences, 36*(4), 329–347.

Pickering, M. J., Branigan, H. P., & McLean, J. F. (2002). Constituent structure is formulated in one stage. *Journal of Memory and Language, 46*(3), 586–605.

Pickering, M. J., & Branigan, H. P. (1998). The representation of verbs: Evidence from syntactic priming in language production. *Journal of Memory and Language, 39*, 633–651.

Pinker, S. (1989). *Learnability and cognition: The acquisition of argument structure*. MIT Press Cambridge, MA.

Plaut, D. C., McClelland, J. L., Seidenberg, M. S., & Patterson, K. (1996). Understanding normal and impaired word reading: Computational principles in quasi-regular domains. *Psychological Review, 103*(1), 56–115.

Qian, T., & Jaeger, T. F. (2012). Cue effectiveness in communicatively efficient discourse production. *Cognitive science, 36*(7), 1312–1336.

Rapp, B., & Goldrick, M. (2000). Discreteness and interactivity in spoken word production. *Psychological Review, 107*(3), 460.

Rapp, B., Benzing, L., & Caramazza, A. (1997). The autonomy of lexical orthography. *Cognitive Neuropsychology, 14*(1), 71–104.

Reitter, D., Keller, F., & Moore, J. D. (2011). A computational cognitive model of syntactic priming. *Cognitive Science, 35*(4), 587–637.

Roelofs, A. (1992). A spreading-activation theory of lemma retrieval in speaking. *Cognition, 42*(1–3), 107–142.

Roland, D., Elman, J. L., & Ferreira, V. S. (2006). Why is that? Structural prediction and ambiguity resolution in a very large corpus of English sentences. *Cognition, 98*(3), 245–272.

Sacks, H., Schegloff, E. A., & Jefferson, G. (1978). A simplest systematics for the organization of turn taking for conversation. In Schenkein, J. *Studies in the organization of conversational interaction* (pp. 7–55). Academic Press.

Sánchez, L. M., Philipp, A. M., Struys, E., & Declerck, M. (this volume, 2022). Bilingual language production: A tale about interference resolution in different linguistic contexts. In Hartsuiker, R. & Strijkers , K. (Eds.) *Current Issues in the Psychology of Language*. Routledge Press, UK.

Santesteban, M., Pickering, M. J., & McLean, J. F. (2010). Lexical and phonological effects on syntactic processing: Evidence from syntactic priming. *Journal of Memory and Language, 63*(3), 347–366.

Sauppe, S., & Flecken, M. (2021). Speaking for seeing: Sentence structure guides visual event apprehension. *Cognition, 206*, 104516.

Scheepers, C., Galkina, A., Shtyrov, Y., & Myachykov, A. (2019). Hierarchical structure priming from mathematics to two-and three-site relative clause attachment. *Cognition, 189*, 155–166.

Scheepers, C., Sturt, P. Martin, C. J., Myachykov, A., Teevan, K., Viskupova, I. (2011). Structural priming across cognitive domains: From simple arithmetic to relative-clause attachment. *Psychological Science, 22*(10), 1319–1326.

Schoonbaert, S., Hartsuiker, R. J., & Pickering, M. J. (2007). The representation of lexical and syntactic information in bilinguals: Evidence from syntactic priming. *Journal of Memory and Language, 56*(2), 153–171.

Schriefers, H., Teruel, E., & Meinshausen, R. M. (1998). Producing simple sentences: Results from picture–word interference experiments. *Journal of Memory and Language, 39*(4), 609–632.

Shin, J. A., & Christianson, K. (2009). Syntactic processing in Korean–English bilingual production: Evidence from cross-linguistic structural priming. *Cognition, 112*(1), 175–180.

Shlonsky, U. (1992). Resumptive pronouns as a last resort. *Linguistic Inquiry, 23*(3), 443–468.

Slevc, L. R. (2011). Saying what's on your mind: Working memory effects on sentence production. *Journal of Experimental Psychology: Learning, Memory, and Cognition, 37*(6), 1503.

Slevc, L. R., & Martin, R. C. (2016). Syntactic agreement attraction reflects working memory processes. *Journal of Cognitive Psychology, 28*(7), 773–790.

Smith, M., & Wheeldon, L. (1999). High level processing scope in spoken sentence production. *Cognition, 73*, 205–246.

Song, Y., & Lai, R. K. (2021). Syntactic representations encode grammatical functions: Evidence from the priming of mapping between grammatical functions and thematic roles in Cantonese. *Language, Cognition and Neuroscience, 36*(10), 1–14.

Stivers, T., Enfield, N. J., Brown, P., Englert, C., Hayashi, M., Heinemann, T., ... & Levinson, S. C. (2009). Universals and cultural variation in turn-taking in conversation. *Proceedings of the National Academy of Sciences, 106*(26), 10587–10592.

Strijkers, K. (2016). A neural assembly–based view on word production: The bilingual test case. *Language Learning, 66*(S2), 92–131.

Strijkers, K., & Costa, A. (2016). The cortical dynamics of speaking: Present shortcomings and future avenues. *Language, Cognition and Neuroscience, 31*(4), 484–503.

Strijkers, K., Costa, A., & Pulvermüller, F. (2017). The cortical dynamics of speaking: Lexical and phonological knowledge simultaneously recruit the frontal and temporal cortex within 200 ms. *NeuroImage, 163*, 206–219.

Strijkers, K., Costa, A., & Thierry, G. (2010). Tracking lexical access in speech production: electrophysiological correlates of word frequency and cognate effects. *Cerebral Cortex, 20*(4), 912–928.

Swets, B., Jacovina, M. E., & Gerrig, R. J. (2014). Individual differences in the scope of speech planning: Evidence from eye-movements. *Language and Cognition, 6*(1), 12–44.

Thothathiri, M. (2018). Statistical experience and individual cognitive differences modulate neural activity during sentence production. *Brain and Language, 183*, 47–53.

Tomasello, M. (2000). Do young children have adult syntactic competence? *Cognition, 74*(3), 209–253.

Tooley, K. M., & Bock, K. (2014). On the parity of structural persistence in language production and comprehension. *Cognition, 132*(2), 101–136.

Tsoukala, C., Broersma, M., van den Bosch, A., & Frank, S. L. (2021). Simulating code-switching using a neural network model of bilingual sentence production. *Computational Brain & Behavior, 4*(1), 87–100.

Ullman, M. T. (2001). The declarative/procedural model of lexicon and grammar. *Journal of Psycholinguistic Research, 30*(1), 37–69.

Van de Cavey, J., & Hartsuiker, R. J. (2016). Is there a domain-general cognitive structuring system? Evidence from structural priming across music, math, action descriptions, and language. *Cognition, 146*, 172–184

Wagner, V., Jescheniak, J. D., & Schriefers, H. (2010). On the flexibility of grammatical advance planning during sentence production: Effects of cognitive load on multiple lexical access. *Journal of Experimental Psychology: Learning, Memory, and Cognition, 36*(2), 423.

Wheeldon, L., Ohlson, N., Ashby, A., & Gator, S. (2013). Lexical availability and grammatical encoding scope during spoken sentence production. *Quarterly Journal of Experimental Psychology, 66*, 1653–1673.

Whorf, B. L. (1956). The relation of habitual thought and behavior to language. In Carroll, J. B. (Ed.), *Language, thought, and reality: Selected writings of Benjamin Lee Whorf* (pp. 134–159). Cambridge, MA: MIT Press.

Willems, M. (2003). *Don't let the pigeon drive the bus*. New York: Hyperion Books for Children.

Williams, A. (2015). *Arguments in syntax and semantics*. Cambridge University Press.

Yan, H., Martin, R. C., & Slevc, L. R. (2018). Lexical overlap increases syntactic priming in aphasia independently of short-term memory abilities: Evidence against the explicit memory account of the lexical boost. *Journal of Neurolinguistics, 48*, 76–89.

Zhao, L.-M., and Yang, Y.-F. (2016). Lexical planning in sentence production is highly incremental: Evidence from ERPs. *PLoS One* 11, e0146359.

Zhang, C., Bernolet, S., & Hartsuiker, R. J. (2020). The role of explicit memory in syntactic persistence: Effects of lexical cueing and load on sentence memory and sentence production. *PLoS one, 15*(11), e0240909.

Ziegler, J., Bencini, G., Goldberg, A., & Snedeker, J. (2019). How abstract is syntax? Evidence from structural priming. *Cognition, 193*, 104045.

2 Lexical Access in Speech Production

Psycho- and Neurolinguistic Perspectives on the Spatiotemporal Dynamics

Emilia Kerr, Bissera Ivanova, and Kristof Strijkers

The speed and ease with which we produce words has puzzled researchers for decades. Uttering a single word comprises a great number of mental operations like conceptual selection ("choosing" the concept we are about to name), lexical retrieval (selecting the correct, and grammatically specified lemma for that concept), phonological encoding (retrieving the phonological form of the word), articulatory preparation, and, lastly, producing the correct sequence of sounds that represent the intended word. All of this is processed by our brain in a few hundreds of milliseconds and is largely error-free. In other words, even though language production is an immensely complex psychomotor skill, we nonetheless manage to achieve it (apparently) quite effortlessly. Hence, our brain must be particularly efficient and successful in organising the re-presentations and dynamics underpinning our ability to speak. Understanding the nature of that organisation has been a key research endeavour in the field of language production. In this chapter we will offer an overview of some of these potential architectures for the retrieval of the mental representation of words, better known as lexical access. To access a word is to retrieve it from the mental lexicon, a vast lexical storage that for an average adult language user comprises, according to different estimates, from 1000 to about 100,000 words (e.g., Levelt, 1989). In essence, for spoken word production, lexical access means coupling conceptual representations and their phonological forms. Below we will give an overview of four different types of word production models, which serve as a guide to highlight the different possible cognitive and neurobiological architectures that can support lexical access. First, we will review traditional serial and interactive theories (Part I and Part II), and then we will move onto some more recent models, namely dual-stream (Part III) and parallel (Part IV) models of lexical access in speech production.

The sequential (serial)[1] model of lexical access in word production

The first model that we will cover is the serial model developed by Willem J.M. Levelt and colleagues (Levelt et al., 1999; see also Levelt, 1989) and later

DOI: 10.4324/9781003145790-3

expanded into a neural model (Indefrey & Levelt, 2004; see also Indefrey, 2011). As the name suggests, one of the main principles is the sequentiality underlying lexical access during word production (see note 1). It advocates progressive step-by-step processing of each linguistic level before advancing to the next level in the hierarchy (Levelt et al., 1999) and considers functional specialisation[2] of brain areas that are involved in the representation of word components (Indefrey & Levelt, 2004). According to this model, the mental lexicon concerns an independent processing layer within the speech production architecture preceded in time by conceptual processing and followed by form encoding, housed in the left mid temporal gyrus (MTG) and functionally active at a specific point in time (roughly between 150 and 250 ms of processing). Below we will outline the main principles and spatiotemporal dynamics behind this model.

While most prior language production models were motivated by aphasic speech and speech error data (e.g., Dell, 1986; Garrett, 1975; Fromkin, 1971), the Levelt et al. model deviates from that tradition by being based on reaction time data of psycholinguistic experiments in healthy speakers (Glaser, 1992; Levelt, 1989; Levelt et al., 1991; Levelt & Kelter, 1982; Meyer, 1992; Schriefers et al., 1990). Figure 2.1 represents a schematic overview of the word production system as proposed by Levelt and colleagues (1999; see also Levelt, 2001). The first step is lexical selection, that is, when a speaker selects an item from their mental lexicon. The way this works is that a speaker activates an intended concept s/he wants to utter (i.e., conceptual focusing), which in turn will activate word candidates in the mental lexicon until an appropriate lemma, i.e., a morpho-syntactic representation of a lexical concept, is being singled out. During lexical selection there is thought to be competition between different lexical candidates due to spreading activation: That is, when activating an intended concept (e.g., CAT) related concepts (e.g., DOG) become (partially) activated as well because of their association with the target concept (spreading activation between strongly interconnected representations). This in turn will activate different lemma representations (e.g., cat and dog) which enter into a competitive process for selection, since after the lemma stage the system is thought to continue processing with a single representation, namely, the target lemma intended for articulation. The empirical input supporting these notions that lexical access is a competitive process where only a single lexical representation will be selected for further phonological processing stems from semantic interference experiments, namely the well-known picture-word interference (PWI) paradigm (Glaser & Düngelhoff, 1984; Levelt et al., 1991; Roelofs, 1992; Schriefers et al., 1990; Damian & Bowers, 2003; for review see: Abdel Rahman & Melinger, 2009; Piai et al., 2012) when a distractor word is either visually superimposed on the picture to be named or auditorily presented during stimulus (picture) presentation. The critical manipulation is that distractor words can either be semantically related to the target word or semantically unrelated. What is consistently shown is that semantically related distractors increase naming

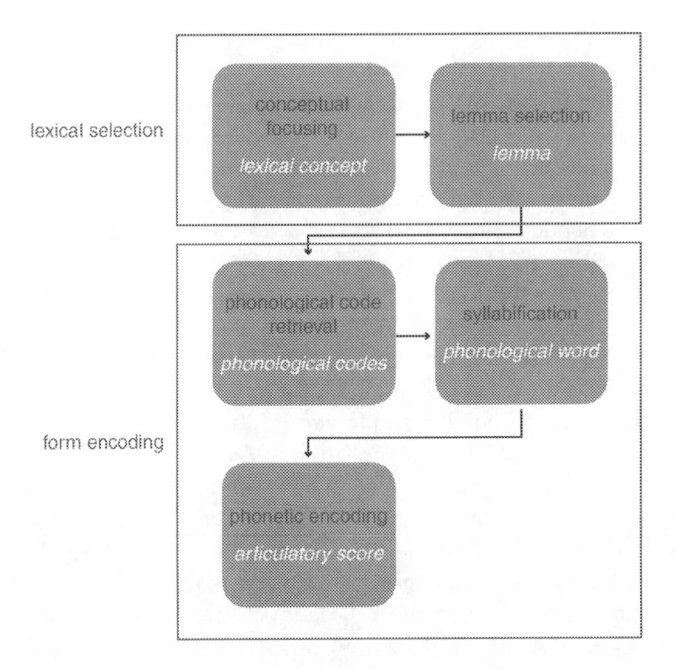

Figure 2.1 Schematic representation of the serial/sequential model language production model, where lexical selection concerns the process of translating a lexical concept into a lemma representation, and form encoding concerns the retrieval of the phonological and phonetic information of the activated lemma (based on Levelt, 2001).

latency. That is, upon presentation of related distractors subjects are normally slower in naming than when an unrelated distractor is presented. This is because the speed of selecting a target item is proportional to the cumulative activation of all the lemmas that are competing for selection. Let us explain this with an example: when selecting the lemma "dog," the lemma "cat" is also activated for selection as a closely related conceptual item. If participants, when asked to name a picture of a dog, are presented with the word *cat* superimposed on that picture, the lemma "cat" receives additional activation resulting in a longer naming latency. If, however, an unrelated word that is not part of the competitive selection process is presented over the picture, e.g., *hat,* it affects the response latency much less. These types of semantic interference effects are amongst the most cited evidence favouring the notion that lexical access is a competitive selection process (but see: e.g., Mahon et al., 2007; Dhooge & Hartsuiker, 2010).

When the target lemma is selected, it triggers the next step, form encoding, which comprises the retrieval of the morpho-phonological form of the selected lemma, structuring those speech sounds in the appropriate order (syllabification) and generating the appropriate articulatory (motor) commands.

In contrast to lexical selection, during form encoding there is no competition since only a single lexical representation is selected for phonological and phonetic processing (e.g., Levelt et al., 1991; the only exception being synonyms when the phonological codes for both synonymous words are activated simultaneously, e.g., Jescheniak & Schriefers, 1998). To show this empirically, PWI experiments also show that when distractor words are phonologically related to the target word (e.g., *cap* for the target *CAT*) the opposite effect is observed, that is, phonological facilitation, which results in shorter naming latencies (e.g., Lupker, 1982; Glaser & Düngelhoff, 1984; Glaser & Glaser, 1989; Meyer & Schriefers, 1991; Cutting & Ferreira, 1999; Ferreira & Pashler, 2002; Jescheniak et al., 2003). The rationale here is thus the following: with semantic distractors we observe naming interference because lexical selection is competitive, but with phonological distractors we observe faster naming latencies as there is no competition anymore (that has been resolved at the lexical level) and what matters is the overlap in sounds between target and distractor (but see: e.g., Starreveld & La Heij, 1996; Cutting & Ferreira, 1999; Damian & Bowers, 2003; Bloem & LaHeij, 2003; Navarrete & Costa, 2005). And even though the exact nature of semantic interference and phonological facilitation in picture naming remains a debated issue (e.g., Mahon et al., 2007; Abdel Rahman & Melinger, 2019; Runnqvist et al., 2019), the context effects on lexical processing as assessed with the PWI paradigm represent one of the most used and important approaches to assess the nature of the mental lexicon (for recent reviews see: e.g., de Zubicaray & Piai, 2019; Nozari & Pinet, 2020), and is the cornerstone paradigm that has informed the serial model of lexical access (e.g., Levelt et al., 1999; Meyer et al., 2019).

Furthermore, PWI experiments were also of importance to obtain initial chronometric evidence on the time course of lemma selection and form encoding. In their classic PWI experiment, Schriefers and colleagues (1990; see also Levelt et al., 1991) explored both semantic interference and phonological facilitation within the same study while manipulating the stimulus-onset asynchrony (SOA). SOA (here) refers to the time between the presentation of the (auditory) distractor and the target picture to name: the distractor could either be presented prior to the target (e.g., −150 ms SOA), at the same time (0 ms SOA), or after target presentation (e.g., +150 ms SOA). The authors showed that the semantic interference effect was maximal when the distractor was presented before the picture target (−150 ms SOA), while the phonological facilitation effect was maximal when distractor and target were presented at the same time (0 ms SOA) or when the distractor was presented after the target (+150 ms SOA). From this result, it was concluded that lexical access and phonological encoding are two dissociable processing stages with a temporal delay between them of around 150 ms. This sequence of events was furthermore successfully simulated by Roelofs in a computational model (e.g., 1992; 1997), adding to the dominant view at that time for a temporal segregation of approximately 100–150 ms between the initiation of lemma selection and the start of form encoding (but see e.g., Alario et al., 2000; Bloem & LaHeij, 2003, Costa et al., 2005; Strijkers & Costa, 2011).

Given the enormous impact of the serial/sequential model developed by Levelt et al. (1999), and its very precise functional and temporal predictions to go from a concept to the utterance of that concept, it offered an ideal blueprint to implement at the neural level and link its different, sequential processing stages to their respective spatial and temporal brain correlates. In order to do so, Indefrey and Levelt (2004) performed a meta-analysis of most available neuroscientific data on picture naming at that point to identify those brain regions and their respective time course of cortical activation involved in the different word production components of the Levelt et al. model (1999). First, to identify the brain regions that are reliably active during word production they looked at 82 production experiments and 26 perception experiments from neuroimaging localisation studies (see Table 2 in Indefrey & Levelt, 2004). By contrasting the patterns of brain activity found in all 108 experiments, Indefrey and Levelt propose that the set of brain areas reliably found for both the picture naming and word generation tasks can be regarded as the core set of brain areas responsible for word production. These include 11 areas in the left hemisphere (posterior inferior frontal gyrus, ventral precentral gyrus, supplementary motor area, mid and posterior superior and middle temporal gyri, posterior temporal fusiform gyrus, anterior insula, thalamus, and medial cerebellum) and four in the right hemisphere (mid superior temporal gyrus, medial and lateral cerebellum, and the supplementary motor area). Next, the authors mapped these regions to the different word production components as proposed in the Levelt et al. (1999) model (see Figure 2.2): mid temporal regions linked to lexical access, superior temporal regions involved in phonological encoding, the inferior frontal gyrus for speech segmentation (syllabification), motor regions associated with phonetics and articulation, and finally the superior temporal cortex for speech monitoring (for more details on the neurobiological basis of speech monitoring see: Runnqvist, 2022 in this handbook). The result of the meta-analysis and its association with the sequential model of word production thus suggest a functional specialisation of brain areas (see note 2): each brain area is responsible for a particular kind of linguistic computation (i.e., conceptual, lexical, phonological, articulatory) during word production. In this view the linguistic computations underpinning speech planning are neurally discrete and the different brain areas "communicate" hierarchically: the output of one becomes the input of another. This hierarchical conceptualisation of word processing therefore copies the key property of the Levelt et al. (1999) model, namely the serial/sequential activation of brain regions linked to a specific word production component (see also later extensions: e.g., Indefrey, 2011; and also: WEAVER++/ARC model (Roelofs, 2014; 2018)).

Importantly, Indefrey and Levelt (2004) provided their model also with temporal estimates, hereby portraying not only the spatial components of word production, but also its temporal dynamics. This is an important addition in

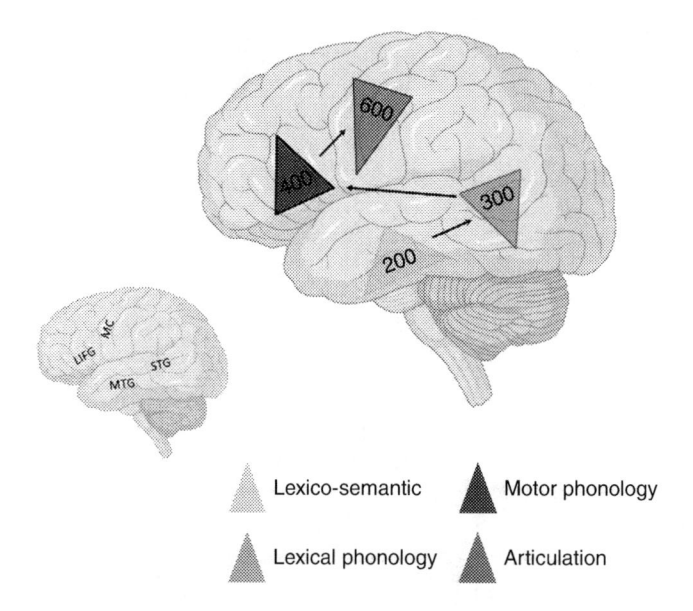

Figure 2.2 Schematic representation in time and space of the sequential brain language model of word production. See text for explanations (based on Indefrey & Levelt, 2004; and adapted from Strijkers & Costa, 2016).

comparison to all previous brain language models of language production which solely focused on where in the brain language production processes may come about, but not when. In order to do so, Indefrey and Levelt adopted the following strategy: First, they estimated time-windows when each word production process would happen in the course of speech planning, and next they compared those temporal estimates with the results of magnetoencephalography (MEG) studies. With regard to the first step, the authors relied on ERP data of object categorisation studies (e.g., Thorpe et al., 1996; Hauk et al., 2007; Johnson & Olshausen; 2005; Schmitt et al., 2000) to estimate that conceptual processing (of an image) takes about 150–200 ms. With that as starting point, they subsequently added the chronometric estimates as assessed with the PWI studies mentioned above and their computational simulations (e.g., Roelofs, 1992; 1997). The following temporal picture emerged for word production (assuming an average naming latency of 600 ms): 0–175 ms = conceptual processing; 175–250 ms = lexical selection; 250–330 ms = phonological encoding; 330–455 ms = syllabification; 455–600 ms = articulatory preparation. Armed with these time-windows associated with different word production components, in the second step, they looked at MEG studies of object naming. The big advantage of MEG is that one obtains both temporal and spatial data. In this manner, Indefrey and Levelt (2004) explored the above-mentioned time-windows in three MEG studies of language production (Levelt et al., 1998; Maess et al., 2002; Salmelin et al., 1994), and checked which brain regions that where maximally activated in that specific functional time-window corresponded to one of the brain regions defined in their meta-analysis. This resulted in the following spatiotemporal map of word production (see Figure 2.2): Lexico-semantic processing taking place around 200 ms after picture presentation in the MTG. Word form (lexical phonology) encoding of the selected lemma manifesting around 300 ms after picture presentation in the posterior STG. Syllabification (motor phonology) emerging after 400 ms in the IFG. And finally, activating the motor commands necessary to move the articulators taking place around 600 ms after stimulus onset in the pre- and post-central gyri.

In summary, the sequential model of lexical access in word production proposes that lexical access is a hierarchically organised process which begins with a concept and moves step-by-step in a feedforward manner through linguistic levels of representation until a motor command is carried out to articulate the utterance. The core of this model postulates that the two parts of the lexical access system, i.e., lexical selection and form encoding, serving two different functions (selecting a target lexical item, and producing an articulatory score for that selected item, respectively), are segregated in time and space. That is, according to the model, information spreads in a feedforward manner, where each step is neurally realised at a well-defined time-window by a distinct brain area, which specialises in one linguistic function only. This model is considered to be a detailed mapping of the neural dynamics supporting word production and to be a valuable tool and theoretical basis for producing precise predictions and hypotheses and testing them (e.g., Aristei et al., 2011; Christoffels et al., 2007; Habets et al., 2008; Koester & Schiller, 2008; Hulten et al., 2009; Hanulová et al., 2011; Dell'Acqua et al., 2010; Laganaro et al., 2009; 2012; Sahin et al., 2009; Piai et al., 2014; Fargier & Laganaro, 2017). Other researchers, however, have questioned the model's strictly sequential and highly localised properties (e.g., Strijkers & Costa, 2016; Munding et al., 2016), and alternative models of lexical access have been proposed; some of which we will discuss below. Nevertheless, and in spite that certain properties of the sequential model have led to much debate, most of the alternatives are directly built on Levelt's model and still have many aspects in common. The latter is remarkable in itself, especially when taken into account that there is no model in language production that has been as extensively tested as the sequential model of lexical access.

Interactive models

The next model we will discuss is the one proposed by Dell in 1986 (see also: Dell & O'Seaghdha, 1992; Dell et al., 1997; Dell et al., 2007; Dell et al., 2013), which introduced the notion of interactivity in lexical access (see also: e.g., Dell & Reich, 1977; Harley, 1984), and inspired many following models and much research in psycho- and neurolinguistics (e.g., Caramazza, 1997; Rapp & Goldrick, 2000; Vigliocco & Hartsuiker, 2002;

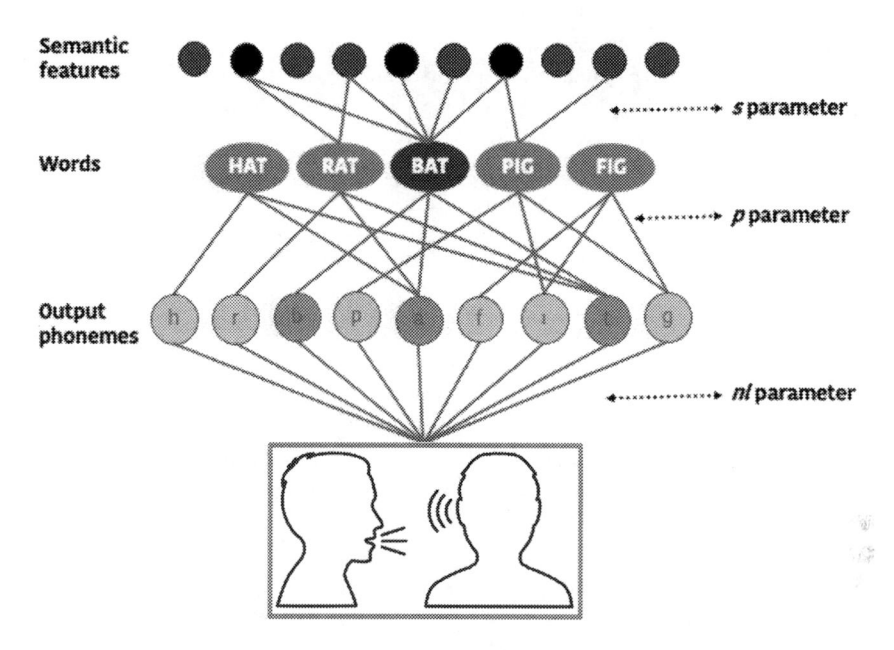

Figure 2.3 Schematic illustration of the two-step interactive activation model of Dell. The two steps of the model during word production are from the semantic (features) to the lexical level (words), and from the lexical to the phonological level (output phonemes). Weights refer to the parameters s, p, and nl in the computational model that represent the connections between the linguistic levels (see main text). Adapted from Dell et al. (2013).

Pickering & Garrod, 2004; 2013; Strijkers & Costa, 2011; Ueno et al., 2011; Strijkers, 2016; Walker & Hickok, 2016; Abdel Rahman & Melinger, 2019; Roelofs & Ferreira, 2019; Nozari & Pinet, 2020). The central characteristic of this model is that while just like sequential models it assumes linguistic representations are organised hierarchically in functionally dissociable processing layers, it allows for interactivity between those levels, meaning that information can flow bidirectionally between processing layers (see Figure 2.3). In this manner, and compared to the serial view on lexical access as discussed before, an interactive account of lexical access is somewhat more flexible in that there is some degree of processing overlap in both time and space. Below we will first detail the computational principles of Dell's interactive lexical model further and subsequently give an overview of its proposed neural implementation.

Interactive lexical access in the Dell-model is, as in the serial model (Levelt et al., 1999; but see Caramazza, 1997), regarded as a two-step process where activation flows through the lexical system in the following manner: The first step is initialised by a jolt of activation at the conceptual level ("Semantic features" in Fig. 3), continues as spreading activation through the network and activates a number of relevant units at the lexico-syntactic level ("Words"). Units at this level are called lemmas and are abstract symbols that unify the semantic-syntactic representation of a word. The first step is finalised when the lemma with the highest level of activation is selected, regulated via an "insertion" rule that checks whether the lemma is semantically and syntactically suitable (e.g., "swim" if a verb is required and "swimming" if a noun), and activation of other lemmas is inhibited. The second step of word production begins with a jolt of activation spreading from the lemma to the phonological level ("Output phonemes"), activating the phonological units corresponding to the selected lemma representation. At this stage, beyond for example differences in compositionality (e.g., Roelofs, 1997b), the previously discussed serial model and Dell's interactive activation model are quite similar in their dynamics of lexical access. Crucially, however, interactive models propose that information travels bi-directionally in the lexical network. That is, while in the serial model (Levelt et al., 1999) lexical access is entirely feedforward, in Dell's model (1986) activation can flow back between the representational layers (see Figure 2.3). This means that even if linguistic levels are globally modular and initially become activated in a sequential manner, they are locally interactive, displaying temporal overlap in the activation of lexical representations: when level x is most active, there will be some activity too in levels $x+1$ and $x-1$ (Dell & O'Seaghdha, 1992). For example, spreading activation from the concept BAT will activate the lemmas "bat" and "pig" because they are categorically related. Then, spreading activation from the lemma "bat" will activate the phonological units "b," "a," and "t," and those phonological units will in their turn send activation back to those lemmas associated with the phonological features, hereby "boosting" the activation of the target lemma "bat" and reducing the activation linked to the semantically related word "pig" (see Figure 2.3). Or put differently, within such interactive framework, the intended lexical entry for speech receives two sources of activation: the bottom-up driven feedforward activation from the concept a speaker wishes to utter and the feedback-driven activation from the phonological level of processing allowing to "check" that the activated sounds indeed correspond to the word we wish to convey.[3]

Importantly, beyond offering a mechanism on how our lexical system can avoid mis-selecting words, the interaction between levels allows for explaining common speech errors that people make. In fact, the original model of Dell (1986) was constructed exactly for that purpose. Indeed, while overall, we make surprisingly few speech errors when speaking, when we do make an error it seldomly is random, but instead follows linguistic constraints (e.g., Fromkin, 1973; Garrett, 1975; Dell, 1986; Rapp & Goldrick, 2000). In this manner, speech errors have been an important source of information to understand the architecture underpinning language production (for more recent overviews: e.g., Goldrick, 2011; Dell et al., 2014; Runnqvist, this volume). At the level of lexical access, three types of errors have been particularly informative: semantic, phonological, and mixed errors. Semantic errors refer to saying for example "pig" instead of the intended "bat" and are explained in the model because of the spreading activation from related concepts (i.e., other animals) (see Figure 2.3). Phonological errors refer to saying for example "hat" instead of "bat" and come about in the second phase of activation in the model, namely when the selected lexical item activates overlapping phonological units. Finally, and most importantly here, the mixed error effect refers to errors which are both semantically and phonologically related, like saying "rat" instead of "bat." Furthermore, these mixed errors occur more frequently than predicted in light of semantic or phonological errors in isolation (e.g., Dell & Reich, 1981; Harley, 1984; Goldrick & Rapp, 2002; Ferreira & Griffin, 2003); an observation which is assumed to be a consequence of interactivity. That is, keeping with the above example, it is more likely that the target "bat" will be substituted by "rat" than by "pig," because "rat" will receive activation from two sources, namely the spreading activation (from the target concept "bat") from the semantic layer and the feedback activation (interactivity) from the phonological layer (because it has two phonological units that overlap with the phonological units of "bat"), while "pig" will only receive activation from one source, namely the spreading activation from the semantic layer (see Figure 2.3). In other words, due to the interactivity, mixed errors are readily explained in Dell's model (1986; Dell et al., 2013). In contrast, in discrete and serial models like that of Levelt et al. (1999), such mixed error effects are particularly difficult to explain, since the holistic word forms do not affect the lexical representations, and thus mixed errors should not happen.

Another important behavioural observation that has typically been cited to support interactivity concerns the lexical bias effect (Baars et al., 1975; Dell & Reich, 1981; Humphreys, 2002; Hartsuiker, et al., 2005; 2006; Nooteboom, 2005; Nozari & Dell, 2009; Runnqvist et al., 2016; 2021). The lexical bias effect is the tendency of phonological errors to also be real words, for example, people are more likely to substitute "bat" with "hat" than with "lat." Interactive models explain this because phonological units follow phonological rules in a language, they will favour the grouping together of legal over illegal phonological activations. Since in an interactive model activated phonological units feedback to the lexical system, it logically follows that a speech error will more likely be a word than a non-word for the simple fact that words are represented in our mental lexicon, while non-words are not. Hence, when making a phonological speech error like a phoneme substitution (e.g., changing the first phoneme of a word), within an interactive system it is predicted that the substitution will more likely result in an actual word ("hat" instead of "lat"), because it receives activation from the lexical layer, while a nonword does not. Similarly as for the mixed error effect, in a serial model (Levelt et al., 1999), this is not necessarily predicted (but see: e.g., Roelofs, 2004).

Finally, behavioural evidence for the interactive nature of the language production system also comes from aphasia studies (e.g., Nozari et al., 2010). For example, in a study by Jefferies et al. (2006) aphasic patients were asked to repeat words while the processing load on the phonological or semantic system was manipulated. The results demonstrated that the semantic manipulation effect was larger in the phonologically straining than the phonologically undemanding task for the phonetically impaired group. The phonetic manipulation effect however was larger in the semantically straining than the semantically undemanding task for the semantically impaired group. This suggests that the phonological system plays a more important role in repetition when the semantic system is impaired and vice versa, providing evidence for interactivity between semantics and phonology in brain-damaged speakers.

In terms of neural implementation, the notion of interactivity can fit different neuroanatomical architectures (e.g., Indefrey, 2011; Strijkers & Costa, 2011; Hickok, 2012). For example, it could be consistent with the previously described Indefrey and Levelt (2004) model if some more temporal and spatial flexibility between the different brain regions (linked to distinct functional word components) is allowed. However, while the Indefrey and Levelt (2004) model suggests a single feedforward processing pathway, going from mid temporal via superior temporal towards frontal brain regions, Dell and colleagues have linked their specific interactive model to a dual-route architecture (Dell et al., 2013; see also Nozari et al., 2010; Ueno et al., 2011), hereby integrating established neuroanatomical ideas from the perception literature (e.g., Hickok & Poeppel, 2000; 2004; 2007; Scott & Johnsrude, 2003; Rauschecker & Scott, 2009). In this manner, Dell et al. (2013) suggest that lexical access in an interactive model is realised by two partially distinct brain networks, a more ventral stream and a more dorsal stream (roughly corresponding to the red and blue patches in Figure 2.4). Previous research

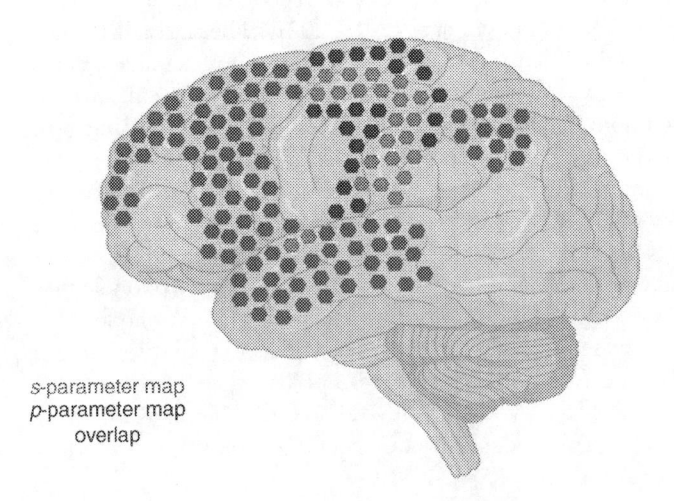

s-parameter map
p-parameter map
overlap

Figure 2.4 The maps of two of the parameters from the interactive computational model suggest that semantic and lexical processing on the one hand and phonological and articulatory processing on the other have only a few brain areas in common (based on Dell et al., 2013).

implicates the dorsal stream in phonological processing as there is evidence that phonological form retrieval takes place in the pSTG (e.g., de Zubicaray et al., 2002; Graves et al., 2008; Edwards et al., 2010), phonological short-term memory is processed by temporo-parietal and inferior parietal regions (e.g., Buchsbaum et al., 2011), and phonologically related errors stem from the dorsal pathway (e.g., Cloutman et al., 2009; Duffau et al., 2008; Schwartz et al., 2012). The ventral stream, on the contrary, has been implicated in more lexical-semantic processing as evidence suggests that lemma processing takes place in the MTG and pITG (e.g., Damasio et al., 1996; Graves et al., 2007; de Zubicaray & McMahon, 2009; de Zubicaray et al., 2015; Riès et al., 2017), objects and events are represented in the ATL and AG (e.g., Binder & Desai, 2011), and damage to the ventral stream, including the MTG, ITG, ATL, AG, and IFG results in semantically based word retrieval difficulties (e.g., Antonucci et al., 2008; DeLeon et al., 2007; Schnur et al., 2009).

Dell and colleagues (2013) further confirmed and extended this two-step neural architecture to brain-damaged aphasic speakers via voxel-based lesion parameter mapping. The study used the interactive activation computational model to simulate the individual error pattern of 103 aphasic patients in three different tasks: word production, word repetition, and non-word repetition. Parameters corresponding to the connections between linguistic levels were adjusted so that the model can account for the variability in errors for all three tasks. The lesion status of a voxel was then used to predict the three critical parameters: s representing the ability to map from the conceptual to the lexical level, p the mapping from the lexical to the phonological level, and nl the mapping from auditory input to the phonological level (see Figures 2.3 and 2.4). While the p and nl parameters shared a significant proportion of their brain maps, for the s and p parameters overlap was much less pronounced (see Figure 2.4), suggesting that the brain areas responsible for realising the lexical and phonological levels of word production are at least in part neurally distinct.

Based on these lesion mapping results (as well as the neuroimaging in healthy speakers) Dell and colleagues (2013) proposed the following neural implementation of the interactive two-step model: The first step, semantic encoding and lemma access, is realised by a rather large left-lateralised network, including the aSTG, aMTG, temporal pole, MFG, IFG, TPJ, and AG (red and purple locations in Figure 2.4). The second step, the access of the phonological form of a word, is implemented more dorsally and more posteriorly (blue and purple locations in Figure 2.4), including regions such as the STG, TPJ, the planum temporale, and the pre- and post-central gyri. In other words, while the neural implementation of the two-step interactive activation model by Dell et al. (2013) shares with the Indefrey and Levelt model (2004) the notion that lexico-semantic and phonological processing are achieved by largely dissociable neural circuits, these circuits themselves are much less localised compared to the Indefrey and Levelt model, recruiting an extensive network of brain regions in frontal, temporal, and parietal cortex both for the lexical and phonological layers of processing.

Regarding the time course of lexical access, as mentioned earlier, interactive models assume that the first pass activation of each representation proceeds sequentially, and thus propose a temporal dynamic which initially can mimic the time course proposed by the Indefrey and Levelt model (2004): lexical processing around 175 ms and phonological form encoding some 100 ms later around 250–300 ms (Dell & O'Seaghdha, 1991; 1992). But in contrast to the serial model, more than one layer can be active at same time, given that when the interactivity (feedback) kicks in, (at the least) adjacent processing layers should display an overlapping time-course. Specifically, for the implementation of interactive lexical access in a dual-route neuroanatomical structure as envisioned by Dell and colleagues (2013), speech planning would thus first trigger ventral brain regions linked to lexico-semantic knowledge (see Figure 2.4), some 100 ms later more dorsal brain regions linked to the phonological knowledge associated with the intended word for speech (see Figure 2.4), and subsequently feed the dorsal activity back to the ventral brain regions, allowing for the interactivity between the lexico-semantic and phonological representations a speaker is about to utter.

To summarise, lexical access in an interactive model (e.g., Dell, 1986; Dell et al., 2013) has some very similar assumptions to lexical access in a serial/sequential model (e.g., Levelt et al., 1999; Indefrey & Levelt, 2004), because it considers lexical access to involve sequential steps of processing which work with different kinds of representations, stored in different brain areas. Specifically, in this view, words in the brain have lexical and phonological representations, which are independent of each other and activation flows from the concept through the lemma and onto the phonological form in functionally distinct time steps. In contrast to the serial/sequential model of lexical access, however, these lexical and phonological layers are "globally modular, but locally interactive" (cf. Dell & O'Seaghdha, 1992), in that they are much more distributed in our brain, and can have a functional and temporal influence upon each other through feedback interactivity.

Dual-stream feedback models

The two previous sections were devoted to the traditional models of lexical access in speech production which have been of enormous impact on the neurocognitive research in language production. Thanks to their pioneering role, the field has advanced much, in particular with regard to the integration of the cognitive mechanisms of word production at the level of the brain, allowing the development of novel brain language models on lexical access. In the final two sections of the present chapter we will describe two such novel brain language models, which lend many insights from the traditional serial and interactive models, but also extend and/or differ from them in important ways.

The first model that we are going to discuss, the hierarchical state feedback control model (HSFC), has been developed by Hickok (2012; see also

Hickok, 2014; Walker & Hickok, 2016) and is part of a larger integrated theory on speech processing, the dual-route model (see Figure 2.5; Hickok & Poeppel, 2000; 2004; 2007). The dual-route architecture, which we already mentioned in the previous section with regard to a specific neural implementation of Gary Dell's (1986) interactive activation model of lexical access, is borrowed from research in the visual domain where this processing mechanism, namely, the division of labour between the ventral and dorsal streams, has been well established and demonstrated empirically (e.g., Milner & Goodale, 1993; Ungerleider & Mishkin, 1982). The dual-route model of speech processing proposes two pathways, or streams, that underlie the neuroanatomy of language processing: the ventral stream, concentrated in the superior and middle parts of the temporal lobe, is responsible for the comprehension of speech, and the dorsal stream, involving structures in the posterior planum temporale and posterior frontal lobe, is engaged in speech production through sensory-motor integration (more on this below) (see Figure 2.5). While originally the dual-route architecture was developed to explain language comprehension (Hickok & Poeppel, 2000; 2004; 2007), here we will focus on the recent extension to language production (Hickok, 2012; 2014). This model serves as a neat bridge with the prior two sections in this chapter, since it borrows many properties of the sequential and interactive models discussed before but embeds it within the neuroanatomical principle of dual-stream processing and adds the concepts of feedback control and predictive processing (see for similar psycholinguistic feedback/predictive models of language production e.g., Pickering & Garrod, 2013; Dell & Chang, 2014).

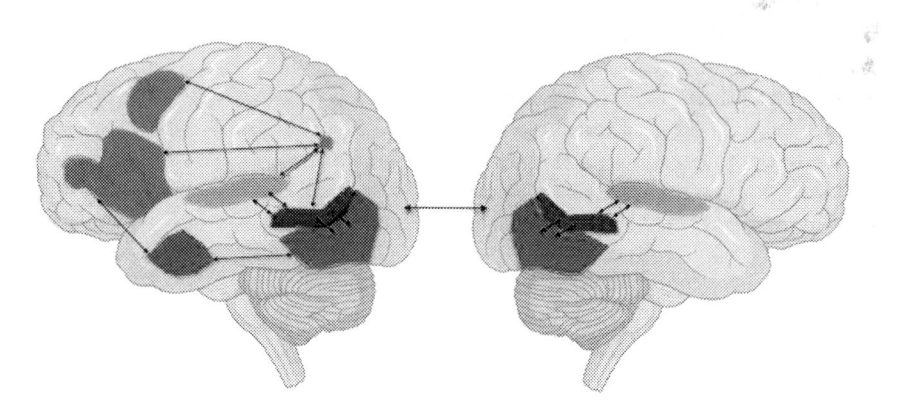

Figure 2.5 The dual-stream model of speech processing. Bilateral auditory regions in the dorsal STG (yellow) and STS (green) are engaged in the early stages of speech processing, which later diverges into two streams: the ventral stream responsible for speech comprehension (blue) and a left dominant dorsal stream involved in speech production (purple) (based on and adapted from Hickok & Poeppel, 2007).

The HSFC model attempts to bridge two traditions of speech processing research – psycholinguistics on the one hand (e.g., Dell, 1986; Levelt et al., 1999), and motor control theories on the other (e.g., Gracco & Lofqvist, 1994; Guenther, 2006; Golfinopoulos et al., 2010; Tourville & Guenther, 2011; Perkell, 2012). Drawing from the previous psycholinguistic theories (e.g., Dell, 1986; Levelt et al., 1999), the model agrees that the main stages of word production comprise conceptual and lexical selection, phonological encoding and articulatory preparation. These stages are considered to be implemented in a hierarchical manner where lexico-semantic processes give rise to phonological processes (Hickok, 2012; 2014; 2019). Neurally, this hierarchy is organised in the following regions: lexical selection occurs in the middle temporal regions and phonological processing takes place in the posterior STG (word forms), inferior parietal and inferior frontal and premotor cortex (motor phonology) (see Figure 2.6).

The main idea adopted from the motor control theory is the notion of feedback control which aids in achieving an action with minimal errors between a planned action and the sensorimotor output (e.g., Fairbanks, 1954; Shadmehr & Krakauer, 2008; Tian & Poeppel, 2010). Within motor control theories, it has been suggested that a smooth implementation of the feedback control system is solved through an internal model of the body. In essence, this means that the system builds a predictive model that controls the motor commands sent to the effector and the most recent state of that effector. This control mechanism is implemented via an efference copy of a given motor command being sent to the internal model. This allows the brain to detect and correct errors almost immediately through predicting the consequences of a motor command before its actual implementation, that is, before feedback occurs (Shadmehr et al., 2010; Shadmehr & Krakauer, 2008; Wolpert et al., 1995). The idea of the internal predictive model attempts to explain why we generally have little trouble and make very few to no errors in our everyday actions including speech. Moreover, the cortical regions that have been shown to be engaged in motor control overlap with those that are proposed to be actively involved in phonological processes in psycholinguistic models of speech production. These regions include IFG, somatosensory-motor cortex, premotor cortex, posterior STG, and temporal-parietal junction (Guenther, 2006; Houde & Nagarajan, 2011) (see Figure 2.6).

According to HSFC, motor control is implemented at the phonological level of processing which comprises two main components – a motor-phonological (output) and an auditory-phonological (input) component. This division is an essential difference compared to prior psycholinguistic models and their neural implementations we discussed above. Since the model ascertains that internal feedback is auditory (Burnett et al., 1998; Houde & Jordan, 1998; Stuart et al., 2002), the split of the phonological level into two is justified via the logic of feedback control: the motor system executes an act (in our case, a speech act), which is evaluated against previously formed predictions about the sensory consequences of that act; in case of an error, the

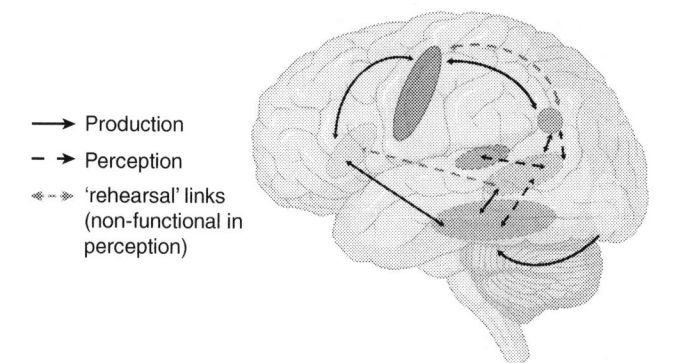

→ Production

- → Perception

◄-→ 'rehearsal' links
(non-functional in
perception)

Figure 2.6 Simplified schematic representation of Hickok's dual-stream HSFC model,
where lexical representations (lemmas) are triggered (for example from a visual
information – yellow area – we wish to utter) in the (posterior) MTG (orange)
and activate two streams of processing: (1) towards inferior frontal regions (blue),
in order to retrieve the motor syllable representations linked to the intended
lexical representation for speech, and thereafter towards the motor cortex (red)
to activate the motor phoneme programs for articulation; at the same time (2) a
more dorsal stream is activated from the lexical level towards superior temporal
regions (green and dark blue) to activate auditory syllable predictions (and
thereafter towards supramarginal gyrus to activate somatosensory phoneme
predictions). Crucially, the auditory syllable/phoneme targets are predictions of
what the sensory outcome (i.e., efference copy) of the articulation of the syl-
lables/phonemes would sound like. These syllable representations in temporal
brain regions are then used to check the syllable representations in frontal brain
regions (via area Spt and the cerebellum): when they overlap, articulation is
triggered, when they don't overlap, reprocessing is required to correct speech
planning towards the intended syllable representations. In this manner, the
HSFC thus integrates prediction (efference copies) and feedback control
(checking mechanism between motor and auditory representations) within its
hierarchical neuroanatomical dual-stream architecture. Finally, note that the
time-course estimates are purely illustrative (the HSFC does not make explicit
temporal predictions) in that the model agrees with a sequential progression of
activation from higher towards lower levels of processing as in interactive or
serial psycholinguistic models (figure roughly based and adopted from Hickok,
2012; 2014).

difference between the prediction and the resulted output is assessed for error
correction. This, according to the HSFC model, dictates the necessity for the
dual organisation of the phonological level – the motor component responsible for execution of a speech act and the auditory component that is
involved in the prediction and monitoring of that act (see Figure 2.6).

An important body of evidence in favour of this view concerns conduction aphasia. This language impairment traditionally manifests in poor
phonemic planning, that is, patients normally produce fluent speech and
have preserved speech comprehension, but they often make phonemic

errors, or paraphasias, which they sometimes are conscious of but find hard to correct. It has been difficult to pinpoint the exact link between these symptoms and prior language production models since none of them seem to find a coherent explanation (for a more detailed review see Baldo et al., 2008; Buchsbaum et al., 2011; Hickok, 2014; 2019), and this is where the dissociation between the motor and auditory phonological systems comes into play. If such a dissociation is assumed, then the symptoms can be explained by a disrupted connection between the auditory (sensory) and motor systems: both the motor and sensory systems are not impaired, hence, speech fluency and comprehension are intact but due to the disconnection between the two systems, the sensory system no longer affects the motor one, which results in frequent paraphasias. Moreover, lesion location for conduction aphasia corresponds to the area Spt, a region in the posterior Sylvian fissure at the parietal-temporal junction (Buchsbaum, et al., 2001; Hickok, et al., 2009), which is hypothesised to be the mediating interface between the auditory and motor phonological systems.

Other data, from healthy speakers, that finds an elegant explanation in the HSFC model concerns neuroimaging data related to (1) auditory suppression and to (2) speech monitoring. Concerning (1), auditory suppression refers to the phenomenon that the auditory cortex's response to one's own speech is reduced compared to the speech of others (e.g., Houde et al., 2002). The fact that this phenomenon seems to occur ultra-rapidly (already within 100 ms of processing; e.g., Heinks-Maldonado et al., 2006) fits well with the notion of forward prediction as implemented in Hickok's HSFC model: That is, because one can predict one's own speech better than that of others, the neural response in the auditory cortex is attenuated since there is a good match between the action (motor) and its consequence (auditory) and no further reprocessing is necessary. Concerning (2), and recent neuroimaging finding that goes well with the predictions of the HSFC, are studies where the speech monitoring system is investigated by using a slip task (e.g., Runnqvist et al., 2016; 2021). In a slip-task (e.g., Motley et al., 1982) researchers attempt to experimentally induce speech errors by priming people to make phoneme substitutions (e.g., barn door → cgqt investigate this phenomenon with TMS and fMRI for correct trials (that is, trials where the participant didn't make the error – the phoneme substitution – but the likelihood of making such error was high; put differently, conditions that tax the speech monitoring system). The authors observed the involvement of the right cerebellum and superior temporal brain regions (amongst a relevant set of other brain regions: e.g., Runnqvist et al., 2016; 2021). Given the cerebellum's role in forward modelling (e.g., Blakemore et al., 2001; Ito, 2008), the link of right cerebellar activity and left superior temporal regions to monitor phoneme substitutions fits neatly with the predictions of the HSFC (Hickok, 2012; 2014).

In summary, lexical access in the HSFC shares some key elements with prior serial and interactive models of speech production, but also adds some additional features that predict different spatial and temporal dynamics underpinning the mental lexicon. With regard to the similarities, one of the key elements of the HSFC model is that it assumes a hierarchical and sequential, interactive relationship between different stages of processing (i.e., lexico-semantic and phonological steps) (see Figure 2.6). Furthermore, the model shares with the Indefrey and Levelt model (2004) the notion of functionally specialised processing regions in the brain, with a clear division of labour between temporal and frontal brain regions (note that this aspect is different from the Dell et al. model (2013; see also Ueno et al., 2011), where there was also functional segregation of brain regions, but not necessarily in function of temporal versus frontal brain structures). It also shares with the sequential and interactive models of lexical access the hierarchical structure and by consequence functionally distinct time-course of activation for different word components (see Figure 2.6). However, by incorporating a dual-stream architecture and predictive feedback control, some key differences with sequential and interactive models become apparent as well: For one, in terms of temporal dynamics, after the activation of words at the lemma level (mid temporal brain regions) a (more or less) parallel activation time-course for frontal motor syllables and temporal auditory syllables is predicted. Second, at the functional spatial level, given the important role predictive feedback control play in the model, inferior frontal and superior temporal brain regions engage in a novel functional dynamic, namely one where their cross-talk serves a checking mechanism for speech production. In this manner, the HSFC model has a more task-dependent structure where a brain region's functional role can dynamically shift in function of task (and become asymmetrical, for example, between production and perception). Another attractive and novel feature of the HSFC model is that it suggests a generalised neuroanatomy across the language modalities, namely that of a dorsal-ventral organisational structure.

The parallel assembly model

The last model we will describe proposes the notion of fast parallel processing where lexico-semantic and phonological-articulatory stages occur in the same temporal windows and simultaneously integrate distributed cortical activations. This model differs from previous models in that it does not assume a hierarchical structure underpinning the different linguistic components making up a word, but rather the full integration of all word components into a single functional whole; the word as the neural Gestalt of language in the brain. Another interesting difference this model has compared to the previous ones is that its basis is inspired by system neuroscience theory rather than psycholinguistics and neuropsychology. That is, while the previous models were mainly guided by reaction time data (Levelt et al., 1999), speech error patterns (Dell, 1986; Dell et al., 2013), or patient data (Hickok, 2012; 2014), the parallel assembly model took the reverse approach and is mainly driven by neurophysiological processing principles. More concretely, the driving principle behind the model is Hebbian-based learning, which in broad terms states that "what fires together wires together" (Hebb, 1949), and which Friedemann Pulvermüller used to develop a model of how our brain would represent words (Pulvermüller, 1999; and later: Pulvermüller, 2002; 2005; 2018; Pulvermüller & Fadiga, 2010). Recently this Hebbian-based assembly model of language was then adopted to the issue of lexical access in speech production (Strijkers, 2016; Strijkers & Costa, 2016).

In short, Hebbian-based learning (or assembly coding) means that those neural representations that are active at the same time will bind together into a single functional unit (e.g., Hebb, 1949; Braitenberg, 1978; Singer & Gray, 1995; Fries, 2005; Buzsáki, 2010; Singer, 2013). Or, put differently, if for a given event X there is temporal correlation (or coherence) between neural population A and neural population B, and this temporal correlation occurs often, then for that specific event X those two neural populations A and B will bind together in a novel, overarching neural assembly C that can reflect event X as a whole. Translating Hebb's postulate to words, the idea is that since the meaning and sounds of a given word always co-occur (e.g., when speaking about a "ball," the semantic features and sound features of "ball" will always be active at the same time), through Hebbian-like learning they form a single functional unit capable to reflect a word in its totality: a word assembly (e.g., Pulvermüller, 1999; 2005; 2018; Pulvermüller & Fadiga, 2010). Note that the starting point is not so different from the previously discussed models, namely a system dedicated to meaning-related processes and to sound-related processes that are (partially) separated and independent from one another. The difference emerges during development where, according to Pulvermüller's Hebbian model, the key to word learning lies in binding together meaning and sounds that form a coherent word. Viewing words in this way results in a substantially different spatiotemporal dynamic of lexical access when adopted to word production compared to the previously discussed serial and interactive theories (see Figure 2.7) (Strijkers, 2016; Strijkers & Costa, 2016): (a) the time course of lexical access would be parallel instead of sequential; (b) the spatial recruitment would involve distributed networks both for lexico-semantic and phonological knowledge, instead of localised brain regions or processing streams for the lexico-semantic (lemmas) representations on the one hand and phonological representations on the other (see Figure 2.7).

First, we will look at the temporal dynamics and the main differences between the parallel assembly and sequential or interactive models. Traditional language production theories suggest that the firing of the lower-level cells (input) spreads to the firing of the higher-level cells (output), thus constructing a hierarchy of activations that occur in a sequential manner, i.e., segregated in time with differences between lexico-semantic and phonological activation often estimated in the range of 100 ms (e.g., Dell & O'Sheagdha, 1992; Indefrey & Levelt, 2004; Indefrey, 2011). Note, as mentioned above for models incorporating interactive (and the same holds for cascading) properties (e.g., Hickok, 2012; 2014;

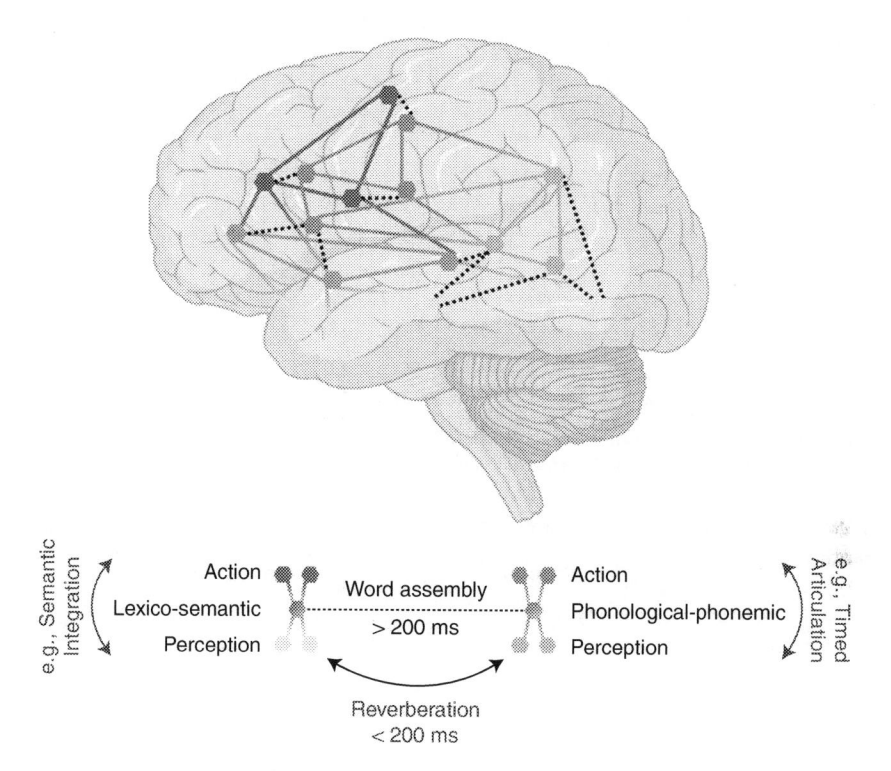

Figure 2.7 A schematic visualisation of the parallel assembly model. A widely distributed lexico-semantic network embedded in action (red) – perception (yellow) circuits and a widely distributed phonological-phonemic network embedded action (blue) – perception (green) circuits form a word assembly which ignites as a whole within the first 200 ms of processing. After ignition activity may remain active in the whole word assembly or reverberate in specific parts of the assembly to generate well-timed (sequential) spatiotemporal dynamics (adapted from Strijkers & Costa, 2016).

Dell et al., 2013), that some overlapping (and in that sense "parallel") activation is predicted in such models. However, and crucially, this overlapping activation occurs at a later point in time after initial sequential activation (for example, in an interactive model, first there is sequential activation of the hierarchical layers before they can start interacting with each other and overlap occurs). This is different from the parallel dynamics envisioned by Hebbian-based assembly models where the parallel activation of the meaning and sounds of a word occurs immediately during the first pass activation. Indeed, given that in a parallel assembly model words are reflected as integrated functional units, neuronal firing triggers the near-synchronous ignition of a word as a whole, because lexico-semantics and phonology are bound together in a single parallel distributed processing network.

While there is quite convincing data (some of which presented in the sections above) that speech production involves a sequential component (for an overview see: e.g., Indefrey & Levelt, 2004; Indefrey, 2011; 2016), whether sequential dynamics is enough has been questioned (e.g., Strijkers & Costa, 2011; 2016), and many of the data used to assess the temporal dynamics did either not rely on immediate and overt speech production (e.g., Strijkers & Costa, 2011) or assessed only a single word production component at a time (e.g., Strijkers & Costa, 2016). Therefore, Strijkers et al. (2017) conducted a MEG study on overt picture naming, and to explore the spatiotemporal dynamics of word production, they manipulated within the same experiment lexico-semantic (words with either lower or higher frequency: e.g., stool vs. table) and articulatory-acoustic properties (minimal pair words with either an initial labial or coronal speech sound: e.g., Monkey vs. Donkey). The crucial finding in this study is that the obtained spatiotemporal patterns of activation correlated with both the words' frequency and initial phonemes during early stages of language production. More precisely, between 160 and 240 ms after stimulus onset activity in the left inferior frontal and middle temporal gyri was modulated by the words' lexical frequency, and in the same time-window initial phoneme-specific dissociations (labial vs. coronal) were observed in the sensorimotor cortex and the superior temporal gyrus. In other words, this study showed that the phonological component is accessed alongside the lexical word properties (for more evidence favouring a parallel processing view in speech production: e.g., Feng et al., 2021; Miozzo et al., 2015; Riès et al., 2017; Strijkers et al., 2010).

Nevertheless, while such results pose serious problems for purely serial processing theories, it remains debated whether they fit word production models with a sequential time-course. That is, the type effects presented above where a lexico-semantic and phonological variable both emerge within (roughly) 250 ms of processing may still reflect a sequential activation over hierarchically distinct processing layers (lexico-semantic → phonological), but simply where activation spreads from one layer onto the other in a faster manner than previously assumed, namely in 10s of ms instead of 100s of ms (e.g., Mahon & Navarrete, 2016; Strijkers et al., 2017). To assess this, Fairs et al. (2021) approached the issue differently and compared the time-course of lexico-semantic (targeted through lexical frequency) and phonological word processing (targeted through phonotactic frequency) during both production and perception. The logic here was the following: Given the hierarchical nature of sequential models, they predict the reverse time-course between production and perception. In production the lexical frequency effect, linked to lexico-semantic word knowledge, should emerge before the phonotactic frequency effect, linked to phonological word knowledge, while in perception the reverse should happen (regardless of whether this happens fast in 10s of ms or slow in 100s of ms). In contrast, according to a parallel assembly model, a word ignites as a whole both in production and perception and thus for both language modalities the lexical and phonotactic frequency effects should manifest simultaneously. The latter is indeed the result found by Fairs et al. (2021), where for both production and perception lexical frequency and phonotactic frequency variables modulated the ERP effects in the early time-windows (74–145 ms and 186–287 ms). Differences between the language modalities occurred only in a later time-window (316–369 ms after stimulus onset).

The results by Fairs et al. (2021) are particularly intriguing because they demonstrate the parallel effects (early on) and the sequential effects (later on) within the same study. Indeed, their data showed that after 300 ms of processing lexical and phonotactic frequency only modulated word production not perception, hereby showing modality and task-specific reverberations at later stages of processing. In this manner, a parallel assembly model explains the temporal dynamics underpinning lexical access in the following manner (see Figure 2.8): After early initial sensorial activation in response to the input, (1) the first linguistic activation emerges roughly between 75 and 150 ms after onset denoting the start of "globally" activating potential words fitting the initial sensory analyses (this ultra-rapid lexical access may be achieved via prediction); (2) next, this initial "global word space" activation is further

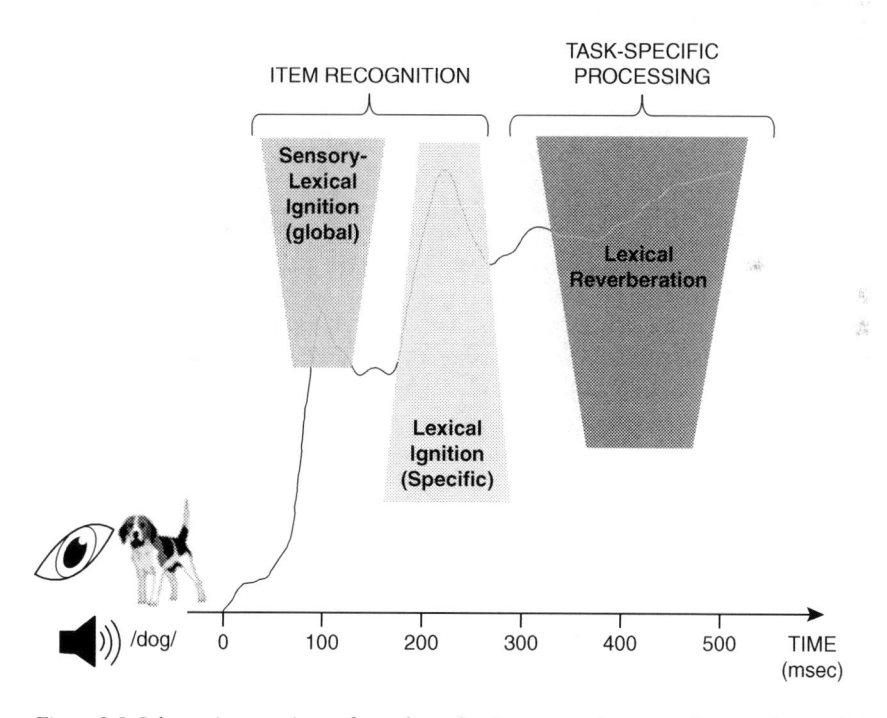

Figure 2.8 Schematic overview of word production processing according to the parallel assembly model. First, up to about 300 ms lexical ignition takes place where the word assembly becomes active simultaneously. Second, task- and stimulus-specific reverberations occur after 300 ms of processing (taken from Fairs et al. (2021).

refined and delineated within roughly 150–250 ms leading to the ignition and recognition of the specific lexical item associated with the input; (3) finally, roughly after 300 ms, slower, sequential-like reverberation upon the activated word assembly takes effect in order to embed the recognised target word into the proper linguistic and task context to be able to perform the intended behaviour, and modality-specific processing effects become visible. Note the last point is key, because it highlights that the parallel assembly model of language production does not invalidate all the studies reporting sequential activation time-courses observed in word production experiments, but rather offers an alternative interpretation to the same data. In particular, rather than reflecting the initial activation of word components in a sequential manner, the observed sequential effects reflect sensitivity to the later task- and language-specific processes upon a parallelly retrieved word representation (see e.g., Strijkers, 2016; Strijkers et al., 2017; Fairs et al., 2021). In a similar vein, dissociations between lexico-semantics and phonology in patients or as observed for speech errors (e.g., Brehm & Goldrick, 2016) would in this model be due to problems during reverberatory processing rather than initial word retrieval (for more details see: e.g., Strijkers, 2016; Strijkers & Costa, 2016b). In sum, this temporal dynamic of lexical access is markedly different from those described for the models in the previous sections in that there is not a single time frame (serial or interactive) where a given linguistic component is active, but (at the least) two functionally distinct time frames: a parallel linked to word activation (i.e., ignition) and a sequential one linked to task-specific operations upon that ignited word assembly (i.e., reverberation) (see Figures 2.7 and 2.8).

Another important difference between prior models and the parallel assembly model lies in the distinct language-to-brain mapping (e.g., Pulvermüller & Fadiga, 2010; Strijkers, 2016; Strijkers & Costa, 2016; Pulvermüller, 1999; 2018). While in the previous models that we discussed the link between brain localisation and linguistic function was mainly driven by a one-to-one (for example, lexical representations in MTG, phonological representations in STG, etc.; e.g., Indefrey & Levelt, 2004), or one-to-many relationship (for example, lexical processing in a ventral stream, phonological processing in a dorsal stream; e.g., Hickok, 2012; 2014; Dell et al., 2013), in the parallel assembly model mapping is many-to-many. This means that the neural organisation of linguistic components during word production (lexico-semantics and phonology) is reflected in distributed frontotemporal and parietal circuits that integrate sensorimotor networks (see Figure 2.7). The reason why different word components will map onto different overlapping and distributed neural networks in parallel assembly models is similar as to why time-course of lexical access manifests rapidly and simultaneously in these models, namely because of the Hebbian neural binding between consistently co-activated input (perception) and output (production) (see Figure 2.7). This is the reason why an assembly model can explain "embodied-like" responses during language perception (for example, the word "kick" activating the leg-region in the motor cortex) (e.g., Watkins et al., 2003;

Hauk et al., 2004; Pulvermuller et al., 2006; Carota et al., 2012; Dreyer et al., 2015), and why during object naming Strijkers and colleagues (2017) observed parallel distributed frontotemporal networks activated in response to both lexical and phonological properties (see also: e.g., Munding et al., 2016; Riès et al., 2017), with (just as in perception) feature-specific topographies in the sensorimotor cortex (e.g., bilabial phonemes linked to lip motor cortex and alveolar phonemes linked to tongue motor cortex; see also Fairs et al., 2021).

In summary, contrary to the previous models we have discussed, lexical access for word production in a parallel assembly model does not assume there is a localisable mental lexicon that is activated at a single, specific point in time. In fact, according to the neural assembly view on language, in general, and word production, specifically, there is no lexical layer of processing. Instead, lexical representations in this model are the binding of meaning-features and sound-features across time and across neural space, resulting in integrated word assemblies. The prediction that there is no specific lexical layer, and thus no dedicated stage of lexical access, is quite a big conceptual difference with the prior models. Nevertheless, it does not mean either that we move away from a representationalism view on cognition and language, but rather that the unit of processing is the "word," the word as the Gestalt of language processing.

Conclusion

In this chapter we have outlined the main theories on lexical access during language production. Lexical access as a process of binding conceptual semantic information with its phonological form has been analysed from different perspectives: as a serial/sequential hierarchical system (e.g., Levelt, 1999; Indefrey & Levelt, 2004; Indefrey, 2011), as an interactive system that allows more communication between its levels (e.g., Dell, 1986; Hickok, 2012; Dell et al., 2013), and as a parallel non-hierarchical system (e.g., Pulvermüller, 1999; 2018; Strijkers, 2016; Strijkers & Costa, 2016). The development of these theories spans a few decades of research, and the topic still remains a vital area of research with many exciting issues to resolve. Traditional serial and interactive accounts on word production have played an essential role in advancing the field by providing the first clear models where the main components of word production were identified. Recently, the advancements of research methods and imaging techniques have allowed to investigate word production in more fine-grained detail and ecologically valid conditions. This, in turn, has triggered some reconsideration of past ideas and postulates that have been considered undeniable, especially the hierarchical and serial nature of speech production processing.

Notes

1 The terms seriality and sequentiality do not denote the same concept: seriality (or discreteness as also often associated historically with these types of models) means that

stage B can only be initiated after stage A has been completed; sequentiality, on the other hand, allows some degree of overlap between stage A and B (i.e., like "cascading" where a representational layer lower in the hierarchy can become activated prior to selection of a representation higher in the processing hierarchy), though stage A would still initiate well before stage B. Historically, the Levelt et al. (1999) model is serial (discrete). However, nowadays, most proponents of this model would agree with some degree of sequentially (cascading) instead strict seriality. For the present chapter, we group the serial and sequential models together (and thus also the historic division between serial and cascaded processing), since their differences are less relevant for present purposes.

2 To avoid confusion, functional specialisation means a given brain region X supports a function Y that other brain regions do not support, which is different from functional specificity where a given brain region X "uniquely" supports a given function Y and nothing else (for discussion related to lexical access see: e.g., Indefrey, 2016; Strijkers & Costa, 2016).

3 While the Dell and colleagues' model does not include inhibitory connections, other interactive models do, suggesting this a biologically plausible mechanism for limiting interaction and cascading within the system. For more detail look at Harley (1993) and Schade and Berg (1992).

References

Abdel Rahman, R., & Melinger, A. (2019). Semantic context effects in language production: A swinging lexical network proposal and a review. *Language and Cognitive Processes*, *24*(5), 713–734.

Alario, F.-X., Segui, J., & Ferrand, L. (2000). Semantic and associative priming in picture naming. *Q. J. Exp. Psychol.*, *A 53A*, 741–764.

Antonucci, S. M., Beeson, P. M., Labiner, D. M., & Rapcsak, S. Z. (2008). Lexical retrieval and semantic knowledge in patients with left inferior temporal lobe lesions. *Aphasiology*, *22*(3), 281–304.

Aristei, S., Melinger, A., & Abdel Rahman, R. (2011). Electrophysiological chronometry of semantic context effects in language production. *Journal of Cognitive Neuroscience*, *23*(7), 1567–1586.

Baars, B. J., Motley, M. T., & MacKay, D. G. (1975). Output editing for lexical status in artificially elicited slips of the tongue. *Journal of Verbal Learning & Verbal Behavior*, *14*(4), 382–391.

Baldo, J. V., Klostermann, E. C., & Dronkers, N. F. (2008). It's either a cook or a baker: Patients with conduction aphasia get the gist but lose the trace. *Brain and Language*, *105*(2), 134–140.

Binder, J. R., & Desai, R. H. (2011). The neurobiology of semantic memory. *Trends in Cognitive Sciences*, *15*(11), 527–536.

Blakemore, S.-J., Frith, C. D., & Wolpert, D. M. (2001) The cerebellum is involved in predicting the sensory consequences of action. *Neuroreport*, *12*(9), 1879–1884.

Bloem, I., & LaHeij, W. (2003). Semantic facilitation and semantic interference in word translation: Implications for models of lexical access in language production. *J. Mem. Lang.*, *48*, 468–488.

Braitenberg, V. (1978). Cell assemblies in the cerebral cortex. In Heim, R. & Palm, G. (eds). *Theoretical approaches to complex systems* (pp. 171–188). Berlin, Heidelberg: Springer.

Brehm, L., & Goldrick, M. (2016). Empirical and conceptual challenges for neurocognitive theories of language production. *Language, Cognition and Neuroscience*, *31*(4), 504–507.

Buchsbaum, B., Hickok, G., & Humphries, C. (2001). Role of left posterior superior temporal gyrus in phonological processing for speech perception and production. *Cognitive Science, 25*, 663–678.

Buchsbaum, B. R., Baldo, J., Okada, K., Berman, K. F., Dronkers, N., D'Esposito, M., & Hickok, G. (2011). Conduction aphasia, sensory-motor integration, and phonological short-term memory–an aggregate analysis of lesion and fMRI data. *Brain and Language, 119*(3), 119–128.

Burnett, T. A., Freedland, M. B., Larson, C. R., & Hain, T. C. (1998). Voice F0 responses to manipulations in pitch feedback. *J. Acoust. Soc. Am., 103*(6), 3153–3161.

Buzsáki, G. (2010). Neural syntax: Cell assemblies, synapsembles, and readers. *Neuron, 68*, 362–385.

Caramazza, A. (1997). How many levels of processing are there in lexical access?. *Cognitive Neuropsychology, 14*(1), 177–208.

Carota, F., Moseley, R., & Pulvermüller, F. (2012). Body-part-specific representations of semantic noun categories. *Journal of Cognitive Neuroscience, 24*(6), 1492–1509.

Christoffels, I. K., Firk, C., & Schiller, N. O. (2007). Bilingual language control: An event-related brain potential study. *Brain Research, 1147*, 192–208.

Cloutman, L., Gottesman, R., Chaudhry, P., Davis, C., Kleinman, J. T., Pawlak, M., Herskovits, E. H., Kannan, V., Lee, A., Newhart, M., & Heidler-Gary, J. (2009). Where (in the brain) do semantic errors come from? *Cortex, 45*(5), 641–649.

Costa, A., Alario, F.-X., & Caramazza, A. (2005). On the categorical nature of the semantic interference effect in the picture–word interference paradigm. *Psychon. Bull. Rev., 12*, 125–131.

Cutting, J. C., & Ferreira, V. S. (1999). Semantic and phonological information flow in the production lexicon. *Journal of Experimental Psychology. Learning, Memory, and Cognition, 25*(2), 318–344.

Damasio, H., Grabowski, T. J., Tranel, D., Hichwa, R. D., & Damasio, A. R. (1996). A neural basis for lexical retrieval. *Nature, 380*(6574), 499–505.

Damian, M., & Bowers, J. (2003). Locus of semantic interference in picture-word interference tasks. *Psychonomic Bulletin & Review, 10*, 111–117.

de Zubicaray, G. I., McMahon, K. L., Eastburn, M. M., & Wilson, S. J. (2002). Orthographic/phonological facilitation of naming responses in the picture-word task: An event-related fMRI study using overt vocal responding. *NeuroImage, 16*(4), 1084–1093.

de Zubicaray, G. I., McMahon K. L., & Howard D. (2015). Perfusion fMRI evidence for priming of shared feature-to-lexical connections during cumulative semantic interference in spoken word production. *Language, Cognition and Neuroscience, 30*(3), 261–272.

de Zubicaray, G. I., & McMahon, K. L. (2009). Auditory context effects in picture naming investigated with event-related fMRI. *Cognitive, Affective, & Behavioral Neuroscience, 9*, 260–269.

DeLeon, J., Gottesman, R. F., Kleinman, J. T., Newhart, M., Davis, C., Heidler-Gary, J., Lee, A., & Hillis, A. E. (2007). Neural regions essential for distinct cognitive processes underlying picture naming. *Brain, 130*(5), 1408–1422.

Dell, G. S. (1986). A spreading-activation theory of retrieval in sentence production. *Psychological Review, 93*(3), 283.

Dell, G. S., & Chang, F. (2014). The P-chain: Relating sentence production and its disorders to comprehension and acquisition. *Philosophical Transactions of the Royal Society of London. Series B, Biological Sciences, 369*(1634), 20120394.

Dell, G. S., & O'Seaghdha, P. G. (1991). Mediated and convergent lexical priming in language production: A comment on Levelt et al. (1991). *Psychological Review, 98*(4), 604–614.

Dell, G. S., & O'Seaghdha, P. G. (1992). Stages of lexical access in language production. *Cognition, 42*(1–3), 287–314.

Dell, G. S., & Reich, P. A. (1977). A model of slips of the tongue. *The Third LACUS Forum, 3*, 448–455.

Dell, G. S., Schwartz, M. F., Nozari, N., Faseyitan, O., & Branch Coslett, H. (2013). Voxel-based lesion-parameter mapping: Identifying the neural correlates of a computational model of word production. *Cognition, 128*(3), 380–396.

Dell, G., Nozari, N., Oppenheim, G. M., Ferreira, V., Goldrick, M., & Miozzo, M. (2014). Word production: Behavioral and computational considerations. In Goldrick, M., Ferreira, V. S., & Miozzo, M. (Eds.), *The Oxford handbook of language production*, Oxford University Press.

Dell, G. S., & Reich, P. A. (1981). Stages in sentence production: An analysis of speech error data. *Journal of Verbal Learning and Verbal Behavior, 20*(6), 611–629.

Dell, G. S., Martin, N., & Schwartz, M. F. (2007). A case-series test of the interactive two-step model of lexical access: Predicting word repetition from picture naming. *Journal of Memory and Language, 56*(4), 490–520.

Dell, G. S., Schwartz, M. F., Martin, N., Saffran, E. M., & Gagnon, D. A. (1997). Lexical access in aphasic and nonaphasic speakers. *Psychological Review, 104*(4), 801.

de Zubicaray, G. I. , & Piai, V. (2019). Investigating the spatial and temporal components of speech production. *The Oxford handbook of neurolinguistics*. Oxford University Press.

Dell'Acqua, R., Sessa, P., Peressotti, F., Mulatti, C., Navarrete, E., & Grainger, J. (2010). ERP evidence for ultra-fast semantic processing in the picture-word interference paradigm. *Frontiers in Psychology, 1*, 177.

Dhooge, E., & Hartsuiker, R. J. (2010). The distractor frequency effect in picture–word interference: Evidence for response exclusion. *Journal of Experimental Psychology: Learning, 36*(4), 878.

Dreyer, F. R., Frey, D., Arana, S., Saldern, S. V., Picht, T., Vajkoczy, P., & Pulvermüller, F. (2015). Is the motor system necessary for processing action and abstract emotion words? Evidence from focal brain lesions. *Frontiers in Psychology, 6*, 1661.

Duffau, H., Gatignol, P., Mandonnet, E., Capelle, L., & Taillandier, L. (2008). Intraoperative subcortical stimulation mapping of language pathways in a consecutive series of 115 patients with Grade II glioma in the left dominant hemisphere. *Journal of Neurosurgery, 109*(3), 461–471.

Edwards, E., Nagarajan, S. S., Dalal, S. S., Canolty, R. T., Kirsch, H., Barbaro, N. M., & Knight, R. T. (2010). Spatiotemporal imaging of cortical activation during verb generation and picture naming. *Neuroimage, 50*, 291–301.

Fairbanks, G. (1954). Systematic research in experimental phonetics: 1. A theory of the speech mechanism as a servosystem. *Journal of Speech and Hearing Disorders, 19*, 133–139.

Fairs, A., Michelas, A., Dufour, S., & Strijkers, K. (2021). The same ultra-rapid parallel brain dynamics underpin the production and perception of speech. *Cerebral Cortex Communications, 2*(3), tgab040.

Fargier, R., & Laganaro, M. (2017). Spatio-temporal dynamics of referential and inferential naming: Different brain and cognitive operations to lexical selection. *Brain Topography, 30*(2), 182–197.

Feng, C., Damian, M. F., & Qu, Q. (2021). Parallel processing of semantics and phonology in spoken production: Evidence from blocked cyclic picture naming and EEG. *Journal of Cognitive Neuroscience*.33(4), 725–738.

Ferreira, V. S., & Pashler, H. (2002). Central bottleneck influences on the processing stages of word production. *Journal of Experimental Psychology. Learning, Memory, and Cognition, 28*(6), 1187–1199.

Ferreira, V. S., & Griffin, Z. M. (2003). Phonological influences on lexical (mis) selection. *Psychological Science, 14*(1), 86–90.

Fries, P. (2005). A mechanism for cognitive dynamics: Neuronal communication through neuronal coherence. *Trends in Cognitive Sciences, 9*(10), 474–480.

Fromkin, V. A. (1971). The non-anomalous nature of anomalous utterances. *Language, 47,* 27–52.

Fromkin, V. A. (1973). Slips of the tongue. *Scientific American, 229*(6), 110–117.

Garrett, M. F. (1975). The analysis of sentence production. In *The psychology of learning and motivation: Vol. 9, ed. G. H. Bower.* Academic Press.

Glaser, W. R. (1992). Picture naming. *Cognition 42,* 61–105.

Glaser, W. R., & Glaser, M. O. (1989). Context effects in Stroop-like word and picture processing. *Journal of Experimental Psychology: General, 118,* 13–42.

Glaser, W. R., & Düngelhoff, F.-J. (1984). The time-course of picture-word interference. *Journal of Experimental Psychology: Human Perception and Performance, 10,* 640–654.

Goldrick, M. (2011). Linking speech errors and generative phonological theory. *Language and Linguistics Compass, 5,* 397–412.

Goldrick, M., & Rapp, B. (2002). A restricted interaction account (RIA) of spoken word production: The best of both worlds. *Aphasiology, 16*(1–2), 20–55.

Golfinopoulos, E., Tourville, J. A., & Guenther, F. H. (2010). The integration of largescale neural network modeling and functional brain imaging in speech motor control. *Neuroimage, 52*(3), 862–874.

Gracco, V. L., & Lofqvist, A. (1994). Speech motor coordination and control: Evidence from lip, jaw, and laryngeal movements. *Journal of Neuroscience., 14*(11 Pt 1), 6585–6597.

Graves, W. W., Grabowski, T. J., Mehta, S., & Gordon, J. K. (2007). A neural signature of phonological access: Distinguishing the effects of word frequency from familiarity and length in overt picture naming. *Journal of Cognitive Neuroscience, 19*(4), 617–631.

Graves, W. W., Grabowski, T. J., Mehta, S., & Gupta, P. (2008). The left posterior superior temporal gyrus participates specifically in accessing lexical phonology. *Journal of Cognitive Neuroscience, 20*(9), 1698–1710.

Guenther, F. H. (2006). Cortical interactions underlying the production of speech sounds. *J Commun Disord, 39*(5), 350–365.

Habets, B., Jansma, B. M., & Münte, T. F. (2008). Neurophysiological correlates of linearization in language production. *BMC Neurosci, 9,* 77.

Hanulová, J., Davidson, D. J., & Indefrey, P. (2011). Where does the delay in L2 picture naming come from? Neurocognitive evidence on second language word production. *Language and Cognitive Processes, 26*(7), 902–934.

Harley, T. A. (1984). A critique of top-down independent levels models of speech production: Evidence from non-plan-internal speech errors. *Cognitive Science, 8,* 191–219.

Harley, T. A. (1993). Phonological activation of semantic competitors during lexical access in speech production. *Language and Cognitive Processes, 8,* 291–309.

Hartsuiker, R. J., Antón-Méndez, I., Roelstraete, B., & Costa, A. (2006). Spoonish spanerisms: A lexical bias effect in spanish. *Journal of Experimental Psychology: Learning, Memory, and Cognition, 32*(4), 949–953.

Hartsuiker, R. J., Corley, M., & Martensen, H. (2005). The lexical bias effect is modulated by context, but the standard monitoring account doesn't fly: Related beply to Baars et al. (1975). *Journal of Memory and Language, 52*(1), 58–70.

Hauk, O., Patterson, K., Woollams, A., Cooper-Pye, E., Pulvermuller, F., & Rogers, T. T. (2007). How the camel lost its hump: The impact of object typicality on event-related potential signals in object decision. *J. Cogn. Neurosci. 19*, 1338–1353.

Hauk, O., Johnsrude, I., & Pulvermüller, F. (2004). Somatotopic representation of action words in human motor and premotor cortex. *Neuron, 41*(2), 301–307.

Hebb, D. O. (1949). *The organization of behavior; a neuropsychological theory.* Psychology Press.

Heinks-Maldonado, T. H., Nagarajan, S. S., & Houde, J. F. (2006). Magnetoencephalographic evidence for a precise forward model in speech production. *Neuroreport, 17*(13), 1375–1379.

Hickok, G. (2012). Computational neuroanatomy of speech production. *Nature Reviews Neuroscience, 13*(2), 135–145.

Hickok, G. (2014). The architecture of speech production and the role of the phoneme in speech processing. *Language and Cognitive Processes, 29*, 2–20.

Hickok, G., & Poeppel, D. (2000). Towards a functional neuroanatomy of speech perception. *Trends in Cognitive Sciences, 4*(4), 131–138.

Hickok, G., & Poeppel, D. (2004). Dorsal and ventral streams: A framework for understanding aspects of the functional anatomy of language. *Cognition, 92*(1–2), 67–99.

Hickok, G., & Poeppel, D. (2007). The cortical organization of speech processing. *Nature Reviews Neuroscience, 8*(5), 393–402.

Hickok, G., Okada, K., & Serences, J. T. (2009). Area Spt in the human planum temporale supports sensory-motor integration for speech processing. *Journal of Neurophysiology, 101*(5), 2725–2732.

Houde, J. F., & Nagarajan, S. S. (2011). Speech production as state feedback control. *Frontiers in Human Neuroscience, 5*, 82.

Houde, J. F., Nagarajan, S. S., Sekihara, K., & Merzenich, M. M. (2002). Modulation of the auditory cortex during speech: an MEG study. *Journal of Cognitive Neuroscience, 14*(8), 1125–1138.

Houde, J. F., & Jordan, M. I. (1998). Sensorimotor adaptation in speech production. *Science, 279*, 1213–1216.

Hultén, A., Vihla, M., Laine, M., & Salmelin, R. (2009), Accessing newly learned names and meanings in the native language. *Human Brain Mapping, 30*(3), 976–989.

Humphreys, K. R. (2002). Lexical bias in speech errors. *University of Illinois at Urbana-Champaign.*

Indefrey, P. (2011). The spatial and temporal signatures of word production components: A critical update. *Front. Psychol. 2*, 255.

Indefrey, P., & Levelt, W. J. M. (2004). The spatial and temporal signatures of word production components. *Cognition, 92*(1–2), 101–144.

Ito, M. (2008). Control of mental activities by internal models in the cerebellum. *Nat Rev Neurosci 9*, 304–313.

Jefferies, E., Crisp, J., & Ralph, M. A. L. (2006). The impact of phonological or semantic impairment on delayed auditory repetition: Evidence from stroke aphasia and semantic dementia. *Aphasiology, 20*(9), 963–992.

Jescheniak, J. D., & Schriefers, H. (1998). Discrete serial versus cascaded processing in lexical access in speech production: Further evidence from the co-activation of near-synonyms. *Journal of Experimental Psychology: Learning, Memory, and Cognition, 24*, 1256–1274.

Jescheniak, J. D., Hahne, A., & Schriefers, H. (2003). Information flow in the mental lexicon during speech planning: Evidence from event-related brain potentials. *Brain Research. Cognitive Brain Research*, *15*(3), 261–276.

Johnson, J. S., & Olshausen, B. A. (2005). The earliest EEG signatures of object recognition in a cued-target task are postsensory. *J. Vis.* *5*, 299–312.

Koester, D., & Schiller, N. O. (2008). Morphological priming in overt language production: Electrophysiological evidence from Dutch. *NeuroImage*, *42*(4), 1622–1630.

Laganaro, M., Morand, S., Schwitter, V., Zimmermann, C., Camen, C., & Schnider, A. (2009). Electrophysiological correlates of different anomic patterns in comparison with normal word production. *Cortex*, *45*(6), 697–707.

Laganaro, M., Valente, A., & Perret, C. (2012). Time course of word production in fast and slow speakers: A high density ERP topographic study. *NeuroImage*, *59*(4), 3881–3888.

Levelt W. J. (2001). Spoken word production: a theory of lexical access. *Proceedings of the National Academy of Sciences of the United States of America*, *98*(23), 13464–13471.

Levelt, W. J. M. (1989). *Speaking: From intention to articulation*. The MIT Press.

Levelt, W. J. M., & Kelter, S. (1982). Surface form and memory in question answering. *Cognitive Psychology*, *14*, 78–106.

Levelt, W. J. M., Praamstra, P., Meyer, A. S., Helenius, P., & Salmelin, R. (1998). An MEG study of picture naming. *Journal of Cognitive Neuroscience*, *10*(5), 553–567.

Levelt, W. J., Roelofs, A., & Meyer, A. S. (1999). A theory of lexical access in speech production. *Behavioral and Brain Sciences*, *22*(1), 1–38.

Levelt, W. J. M., Schriefers, H., Vorberg, D., Meyer, A. S., Pechmann, T., & Havinga, J. (1991). The time course of lexical access in speech production: A study of picture naming. *Psychological Review*, *98*, 122–142.

Lupker, S. J. (1982). The role of phonetic and orthographic similarity in picture-word interference. *Canadian Journal of Psychology*, *36*, 349–367.

Maess, B., Friederici, A. D., Damian, M., Meyer, A. S., & Levelt, W. J. M. (2002). Semantic category interference in overt picture naming: Sharpening current density localization by PCA. *Journal of Cognitive Neuroscience*, *14*(3), 455–462.

Mahon, B. Z., Costa, A., Peterson, R., Vargas, K. A., & Caramazza, A. (2007). Lexical selection is not by competition: A reinterpretation of semantic interference and facilitation effects in the picture-word interference paradigm. *Journal of Experimental Psychology: Learning, Memory, and Cognition*, *33*(3), 503.

Mahon, B. Z., & Navarrete, E. (2016). Modelling lexical access in speech production as a ballistic process. *Language, Cognition and Neuroscience*, *31*(4), 521–523.

Meyer, A. S. (1992). Investigation of phonological encoding through speech error analyses: Achievements, limitations, and alternatives. *Cognition*, *42*, 181–211.

Meyer, A. S., & Schriefers, H. (1991). Phonological facilitation in picture-word interference experiments: Effects of stimulus onset asynchrony and types of interfering stimuli. *Journal of Experimental Psychology: Learning, Memory, and Cognition*, *17*(6), 1146–1160.

Meyer, A. S., Roelofs, A., & Brehm, L. (2019). Thirty years of Speaking: An introduction to the Special Issue, Language. *Cognition and Neuroscience*, *34*(9), 1073–1084.

Milner, A. D., & Goodale, M. A. (1993). Visual pathways to perception and action. In T. P. Hicks, S. Molotchnikoff, & T. Ono (Eds.), *Progress in brain research, Vol. 95* (pp. 317–337). Amsterdam: Elsevier.

Miozzo, M., Pulvermüller, F., & Hauk, O. (2015). Early parallel activation of semantics and phonology in picture naming: Evidence from a multiple linear regression MEG study. *Cereb Cortex*, *25*, 3343–3355.

Motley, M. T., Camden, C. T., & Baars, B. J. (1982). Covert formulation and editing of anomalies in speech production: Evidence from experimentally elicited slips of the tongue. *Journal of Verbal Learning and Verbal Behavior*, *21*(5), 578–594.

Munding, D., Dubarry, A.-S., & Alario, F.-X. (2016). On the cortical dynamics of word production: A review of the MEG evidence. *Language, Cognition and Neuroscience*, *31*(4), 441–462.

Navarrete, E., & Costa, A. (2005). Phonological activation of ignored pictures: Further evidence for a cascade model of lexical access. *Journal of Memory and Language*, *53*(3), 359–377.

Nooteboom, S. G. (2005). Lexical bias revisited: Detecting, rejecting and repairing speech errors in inner speech. *Speech Communication*, *47*(1–2), 43–58.

Nooteboom, S. G. (2005). Listening to oneself: Monitoring speech production. In *Phonological encoding and monitoring in normal and pathological speech* (pp. 179–198). Psychology Press.

Nozari, N., & Dell, G. S. (2009). More on lexical bias: How efficient can a "lexical editor" be?. *Journal of Memory and Language*, *60*(2), 291–307.

Nozari, N., & Pinet, S. (2020). A critical review of the behavioral, neuroimaging, and electrophysiological studies of co-activation of representations during word production. *Journal of Neurolinguistics*, *53*, Article 100875.

Nozari, N., Kittredge, A. K., Dell, G. S., & Schwartz, M. F. (2010). Naming and repetition in aphasia: Steps, routes, and frequency effects. *Journal of Memory and Language*, *63*(4), 541–559.

Perkell, J. S. (2012). Movement goals and feedback and feedforward control mechanisms in speech production. *Journal of Neurolinguistics*, *25*(5), 382–407.

Piai, V., Roelofs, A., Jensen, O., Schoffelen, J. M., & Bonnefond, M. (2014). Distinct patterns of brain activity characterise lexical activation and competition in spoken word production. *PLOS ONE 9*(2): e88674.

Piai, V., Roelofs, A., & van der Meij, R. (2012). Event-related potentials and oscillatory brain responses associated with semantic and Stroop-like interference effects in overt naming. *Brain Research*, *1450*, 87–101.

Pickering, M. J., & Garrod, S. (2013). An integrated theory of language production and comprehension. *The Behavioral and Brain Sciences*, *36*(4), 329–347.

Pickering, M. J., & Garrod, S. (2004). Toward a mechanistic psychology of dialogue. *Behavioral and Brain Sciences*, *27*(2), 169–190.

Pulvermüller F. (1999). Words in the brain's language. *The Behavioral and Brain Sciences*, *22*(2), 253–336.

Pulvermüller, F. (2002). *The neuroscience of language*. Cambridge: Cambridge University Press.

Pulvermüller, F. (2005). Brain mechanisms linking language and action. *Nature Reviews Neuroscience*, *6*(7), 576–582.

Pulvermüller, F. (2018), Neurobiological mechanisms for semantic feature extraction and conceptual flexibility. *Top Cogn Sci*, *10*, 590–620.

Pulvermüller, F., & Fadiga, L. (2010). Active perception: Sensorimotor circuits as a cortical basis for language. *Nature Reviews Neuroscience*, *11*(5), 351–360.

Pulvermüller, F., Huss, M., Kherif, F., Moscoso del Prado Martin, F., Hauk, O., & Shtyrov, Y. (2006). Motor cortex maps articulatory features of speech sounds. *Proceedings of the National Academy of Sciences*, *103*(20), 7865–7870.

Rapp, B., & Goldrick, M. (2000). Discreteness and interactivity in spoken word production. *Psychological Review*, *107*(3), 460.

Rauschecker, J. P., & Scott, S. K. (2009). Maps and streams in the auditory cortex: Nonhuman primates illuminate human speech processing. *Nature Neuroscience*, *12*(6), 718–724.

Riès, S. K., Dhillon, R. K., Clarke, A., King-Stephens, D., Laxer, K. D., Weber, P. B., … Knight, R. T. (2017). Spatiotemporal dynamics of word retrieval in speech production revealed by cortical high-frequency band activity. *Proc Natl Acad Sci.*, *114*, E4530–E4538.

Roelofs, A. (1992). A spreading-activation theory of lemma retrieval in speaking. *Cognition*, *42*, 107–142.

Roelofs, A. (1997b). A case for non-decomposition in conceptually driven word retrieval. *Journal of Psycholinguistic Research 26*, 33–67.

Roelofs, A. (2004). Error biases in spoken word planning and monitoring by aphasic and nonaphasic speakers: comment on Rapp and Goldrick (2000). *Psychological Review*, *111*, 579–580.

Roelofs, A. (2014). A dorsal-pathway account of aphasic language production: The WEAVER++/ARC model. *Cortex*, *59*, 33–48.

Roelofs, A. (2018). A unified computational account of cumulative semantic, semantic blocking, and semantic distractor effects in picture naming. *Cognition*, *172*, 59–72.

Roelofs, A., & Ferreira, V. (2019). The architecture of speaking. In P. Hagoort (Ed.), *Human language: From genes and brains to behavior* (pp. 35–50). Cambridge, MA: MIT Press.

Runnqvist, E., Bonnard, M., Gauvin, H. S., Attarian, S., Trébuchon, A., Hartsuiker, R. J., & Alario, F.-X. (2016). Internal modeling of upcoming speech: A causal role of the right posterior cerebellum in non-motor aspects of language production. *Cortex*, *81*, 203–214.

Runnqvist, E. (2022). Self-Monitoring: The Neurocognitive Basis of Error Monitoring in Language Production. In Hartsuiker , R. & Strijkers, K. *Language Production*. UK: Routledge press (Taylor & Francis).

Runnqvist, E., Strijkers, K., & Costa, A. (2019). Error-based learning and lexical competition in word production: Evidence from multilingual naming. *PloS One*, *14*(3), e0213765.

Runnqvist, E., Chanoine, V., Strijkers, K., Pattamadilok, C., Bonnard, M., Nazarian, B., Sein, J., Anton, J.-L., Dorokhova, L., Belin, P., & Alario, F-X. (2021). Cerebellar and cortical correlates of internal and external speech error monitoring. *Cerebral Cortex Communications*, *2*(2), tgab038.

Sahin, N. T., Pinker, S., Cash, S. S., Schomer, D., & Halgren, E. (2009). Sequential processing of lexical, grammatical, and phonological information within Broca's area. *Science (New York, N.Y.)*, *326*(5951), 445–449.

Salmelin, R., Hari, R., Lounasmaa, O. V., & Sams, M. (1994). Dynamics of brain activation during picture naming. *Nature*, *368*, 463–465.

Schade, U., & Berg, T. (1992). The role of inhibition in a spreading-activation model of language production. II. The simulational perspective. *Journal of Psycholinguistic Research*, *21*, 435–462.

Schmitt, B. M., Münte, T. F., & Kutas, M. (2000). Electrophysiological estimates of the time course of semantic and phonological encoding during implicit picture naming. *Psychophysiology, 37,* 473–484.

Schnur, T. T., Schwartz, M. F., Kimberg, D. Y., Hirshorn, E., Coslett, H. B., & Thompson-Schill, S. L. (2009). Localizing interference during naming: Convergent neuroimaging and neuropsychological evidence for the function of Broca's area. *Proceedings of the National Academy of Sciences, 106*(1), 322–327.

Schriefers, H., Meyer, A. S., & Levelt, W. J. M. (1990). Exploring the time course of lexical access in speech production: Picture-word interference studies. *Journal of Memory and Language, 29,* 86–102.

Schwartz, M. F., Faseyitan, O., Kim, J., & Coslett, H. B. (2012). The dorsal stream contribution to phonological retrieval in object naming. *Brain, 135*(12), 3799–3814.

Scott, S., & Johnsrude, I. (2003). The organisation and functional organisation of speech perception. *Trends in Neurosciences, 26*(2), 100–107.

Shadmehr, R., Krakauer, J. W. (2008). A computational neuroanatomy for motor control. *Exp. Brain. Res., 185*(3), 359–381.

Shadmehr, R., Smith, M. A., & Krakauer, J. W. (2010). Error correction, sensory prediction, and adaptation in motor control. *Annual Review of Neuroscience, 33,* 89–108.

Singer, W. (2013). Cortical dynamics revisited. *Trends Cogn Sci., 17,* 616–626.

Singer, W., & Gray, C. M. (1995). Visual feature integration and the temporal correlation hypothesis. *Annu Rev Neurosci., 18,* 555–586.

Starreveld, P. A., & La Heij, W. (1996). Time-course analysis of semantic and orthographic context effects in picture naming. *Journal of Experimental Psychology: Learning, Memory, and Cognition, 22*(4), 896–918.

Strijkers, K. (2016) A neural assembly–based view on word production: The bilingual test case. *Language Learning, 66,* 92–131.

Strijkers, K., & Costa, A. (2016) The cortical dynamics of speaking: Present shortcomings and future avenues. *Language, Cognition and Neuroscience, 31*(4), 484–503.

Strijkers, K., & Costa, A. (2016b). On words and brains: Linking psycholinguistics with neural dynamics in speech production. *Language, Cognition and Neuroscience, 31*(4), 524–535.

Strijkers, K., & Costa, A. (2011). Riding the lexical speedway: A critical review on the time course of lexical selection in speech production. *Frontiers in Psychology, 2*(December), 1–16.

Strijkers, K., Costa, A., & Pulvermüller, F. (2017). The cortical dynamics of speaking: Lexical and phonological knowledge simultaneously recruit the frontal and temporal cortex within 200 ms. *NeuroImage, 163,* 206–219.

Strijkers, K., Costa, A., & Thierry, G. (2010). Tracking lexical access in speech production: Electrophysiological correlates of word frequency and cognate effects. *Cerebral Cortex, 20*(4), 912–928.

Stuart, A., Kalinowski, J., Rastatter, M. P., & Lynch, K. (2002). Effect of delayed auditory feedback on normal speakers at two speech rates. *J. Acoust. Soc. Am., 111*(5 Pt 1), 2237–2241.

Thorpe, S., Fize, D., & Marlot, C. (1996). Speed of processing in the human visual system. *Nature, 381,* 520–522.

Tian, X., & Poeppel, D. (2010). Mental imagery of speech and movement implicates the dynamics of internal forward models. *Frontiers in Psychology, 1,* 166.

Tourville, J. A., & Guenther, F. H. (2011). The DIVA model: A neural theory of speech acquisition and production. *Language and Cognitive Processes*, *26*(7), 952–981.

Ueno, T., Saito, S., Rogers, T. T., & Ralph, M. A. L. (2011). Lichtheim 2: Synthesizing aphasia and the neural basis of language in a neurocomputational model of the dual dorsal-ventral language pathways. *Neuron*, *72*(2), 385–396.

Ungerleider, L. G., & Mishkin, M. (1982). Two cortical visual systems. In D. J. Ingle, M. A. Goodale, & R. J. W. Mansfield (Eds.), *Analysis of visual behavior* (pp. 549–586). Cambridge, MA: MIT Press.

Vigliocco, G., & Hartsuiker, R. J. (2002). The interplay of meaning, sound, and syntax in sentence production. *Psychological Bulletin*, *128*(3), 442–472.

Walker, G. M., & Hickok, G. (2016). Bridging computational approaches to speech production: The semantic-lexical-auditory-motor model (SLAM). *Psychonomic Bulletin & Review*, *23*(2), 339–352.

Watkins, K. E., Strafella, A. P., & Paus, T. (2003). Seeing and hearing speech excites the motor system involved in speech production. *Neuropsychologia*, *41*(8), 989–994.

Wolpert, D. M., Ghahramani, Z., & Jordan, M. I. (1995). An internal model for sensorimotor integration. *Science*, *269*(5232), 1880–1882.

3 Phonological Processing

Planning the Sound Structure of Words from a Psycholinguistic Perspective

Audrey Bürki

This chapter is concerned with the planning of the sound structure of words and utterances. In dominant psycholinguistic models of language production and in keeping with generative linguistics, the sound structure of words is encoded at two different stages: phonological encoding and phonetic encoding. The present review starts with a summary of the evidence in favour of this distinction. It then summarizes open issues and relevant findings pertaining to each of these processes and their interaction.

Speech consists in sequences of physical events, i.e., articulatory movements. The translation of thoughts into speech requires knowledge about how concepts map onto articulatory gestures and processes by which this mapping occurs. The system that maps thoughts into articulated sounds is not a simple mapping/translation system. Whereas the same configuration of articulatory gestures leads to the same sounds, the inverse is not true, a given sound can be realized with different configurations. Speech produced with a pen in the mouth is nevertheless understood. Moreover, the realization of a given phoneme depends on the preceding and following phonemes; e.g., the articulators are not exactly in the same position to produce the vowel /ae/ in *cat* or in *saddle*. Unsurprisingly, no consensus has been reached regarding the architecture of that system, i.e., the knowledge that speakers have in long-term memory about the sound structure of words (i.e., representations) or the processes by which these representations are accessed and transformed into physical events (e.g., Gafos & van Lieshout, 2020).

The generation of the sound structure of words and utterances has been extensively studied in psycholinguistics but is not the prerogative of this field. A review of this topic will necessary be inter-disciplinary and incomplete. The planning of the sound structure of words is studied in related fields such as (laboratory) phonology (e.g., Pierrehumbert et al., 2000), phonetic sciences, or speech motor control (e.g., Parrell et al., 2019). The integration of the different perspectives is not always straightforward, the different fields seldom talk to one another (see Hickok, 2014; Kearney & Guenther, 2019 for explicit attempts to relate models across fields) and use different terminologies. Similar terms are used to refer to different concepts, likewise, different terms are used

DOI: 10.4324/9781003145790-4

to describe the same reality. In this chapter, we take, as a starting point, the theoretical standpoint, concepts, and terminology of the psycholinguistic perspective. We stop where these models stop, i.e., with the description of the phonetic encoding process and leave it to others to describe the processes occurring during articulation itself. Proposals from other fields are discussed in reference to this specific field and its terminology.

The encoding of sound structure is traditionally thought to involve two sub-steps or components: phonological processing and phonetic processing. In the first section, we review the evidence supporting this distinction. In the second and third sections, we discuss important issues and findings pertaining to the representations and processes involved at each of these processing steps. We then discuss the time course of these processes within and across processing components. The last section is concerned with the role of usage in the generation of sound structure. Note that in this chapter, we only occasionally refer to studies with impaired participants or involving neuroimaging methods. Impairments that involve the sound structure and the implementation of phonological/phonetic processes in the brain are the focus of other chapters in this volume (see Chapters 4 and 5 of this volume: De Zubicaray, 2022; Piai & Borges, 2022).

The phonological/phonetic divide

In keeping with the generativist view, models of language production in psycholinguistics (Dell, 1988; Levelt et al., 1999) assume that the sound structure of words is encoded in two distinct components, the phonological and the phonetic components. During phonological encoding, speakers access and order abstract units (e.g., syllables or segments). During phonetic encoding, these abstract phonological units are mapped onto motor programmes. This distinction is first supported by patterns of speech errors in individuals without language impairments. When two phonemes are substituted, they adapt to their new phonological context (Fromkin, 1971; Garrett, 1980; see also Goldrick, 2011). For instance, in English, voiceless plosives such as /p/, /t/, and /k/ are aspirated at word onset but not at word offset. When a voiceless plosive is erroneously produced at word offset instead of word onset, it is realized without aspiration. This suggests that the error occurs at a level of representation/processing where phonemes are represented in an abstract, context-independent way. Further empirical arguments in favour of the distinction between phonological and phonetic encoding come from patients with language disorders (see also Goldrick, 2014). For instance, Buchwald and Miozzo (2011) performed acoustical analyses of s-deletion errors in two patients. As mentioned already, in English, word initial plosives are produced with aspiration. However, this is not the case when they are preceded by /s/ (as in *sport*). Buchwald and Miozzo (2011) observed that the word-initial plosives (following the deletion of /s/) of one patient were produced without aspiration whereas the word initial plosives of the other patient were produced with aspiration. The authors argued that the errors of the first patient speak in favour of a level of representation where phonemes are represented in a context independent way. More generally and as for instance reviewed in Laganaro (2019), whereas some patients produce mainly errors that involve whole phonemes (phonological errors such as substitutions or meta theses), other patients produce mainly phonetic errors.

The distinction between phonological and phonetic levels of processing and representation has not been unchallenged. Most theoretical frameworks that dispense with this distinction assume that there is no independent level of representation and processing where sounds are represented as abstract (usually phoneme-size) linguistic units. Semantic representations map directly onto physically defined units. In Articulatory Phonology, for instance (Browman & Goldstein, 1992), the words in the lexicon are defined in terms of vocal tract tasks, not phonemes. Given that these representations are already specified in the spatio-temporal dimension, there is no need to assume an additional level of processing in which phonological units are translated into gestures. These vocal tract tasks are phonological (rather than phonetic) in the sense that they are abstract and linguistically defined (see also Gafos & Benus, 2006; Pouplier & Goldstein, 2010 and references therein). Note that in this framework, the terms "phonological processing" or "phonological representations" are used to refer to vocal tract tasks whereas other models locate vocal tract tasks in the phonetic (or speech motor control) component (see below). As will be reviewed below, the evidence from speech errors is difficult to reconcile with the view that the phoneme is not a functional unit in language production.

In Hickok's proposal (2014) syntactico-semantic representations (or lemmas) activate motor programmes and auditory targets directly. Here again, the term "phonological component" is used to refer to motor and auditory targets where models assuming a distinction between phonological and phonetic encoding would locate these "targets" in the phonetic component (see also Rapp et al., 2014). In Hickok's proposal, the default motor and auditory targets used for production are syllable-sized. As discussed for instance in Roelofs (2014), a model with direct links between semantic representations and syllabic motor programmes can hardly be extended to connected speech, at least in languages where words are re-syllabified when produced in the context of other words.

Another class of models with no intermediate level involving abstract sound representations are exemplar-based models (e.g., Bybee, 2007; Goldinger 1998; Kirchner et al., 2010; Port, 2007). In these models, speakers (and listeners) are assumed to store detailed phonetic exemplars for each word or sometimes utterance they use/hear. As a result, each semantic representation has a set of corresponding phonetic representations. "Abstraction" may arise as a result of how exemplars are organized. Exemplars that correspond to a word or word variant may be grouped under the same category label. These models have mostly been discussed in the context of word recognition tasks (e.g., Goldinger, 1998; Hawkins, 2003; Johnson, 1997) and rarely specify the processes by which the speaker chooses an exemplar and maps this exemplar onto motor programmes (see Kirchner et al., 2010, for an attempt) in production tasks. Moreover, whereas the storage of a huge number of representations might be neuro-biologically possible, the question of the efficiency of such a system must be raised (Baayen et al., 2013; Hendrix 2017, see also Fink & Goldrick, 2015 for discussion and further limitations).

Finally, Baayen et al. (2019) discuss a model that dispenses with the very notions of representations and processes. The model has no static representations (at the form or meaning level) and no sub-processes (e.g., grammatical, phonological, or phonetic encoding). It builds on the idea that the relationship between meaning and form is discriminative. The model uses simple linear networks to map the two. Baayen et al. (2019) show that their model can predict response times in written and auditory comprehension tasks. To simulate data for production, semantic vectors map directly onto triphones using linear discriminative learning. Here again, simulations show that the model is accurate in predicting how meaning relates to sequences of triphones. Much remains to be done, however, to determine the extent to which this proposal can explain data on speech errors and response times in language production tasks.

In sum, the evidence from speech errors in individuals with and without speech disorders point to a level of phonological representation that is context-independent. Models without a phonological level of representation still need to provide convincing accounts of these data. In the next section, we describe the phonological component in details.

Phonological encoding

Frames, fillers, and segmental spell-out

In psycholinguistic models of language production, word forms (also called lexemes) are not holistic entities but must be assembled from smaller units. Psycholinguistic models use the concepts of *frame* and *fillers* to describe this process. Words are stored in two parts: a set of segments or phonemes (the fillers) and a word frame or metrical structure, in which the fillers are to be inserted (Dell, 1986; Fromkin, 1971; Shattuck-Hufnagel Cooper 1979). The word (or metrical frame) represents information about how abstract syllables group into feet and how these group into phonological words. In Levelt et al. (1999) for instance, and for languages with lexical stress, the metrical frame is specified for the number of syllables and main stress position should this position not correspond to the default position in the language (but see Cutler, 1984). During the production process, the speaker accesses the frame and fillers and inserts the latter in the first (a process sometimes called segmental spell-out).

The distinction between frame and fillers is supported by several empirical arguments, including speech error patterns. When phonemes are exchanged across words, they tend to keep their position in the syllable (e.g., a phoneme at syllable onset ends up in another syllable onset). In addition, speech errors have been shown to follow phonotactic constraints (e.g., Fromkin, 1971; MacKay, 1972; Vousden et al., 2000), that is, restrictions regarding sound combinations or positions in a given language. For instance (example taken from Goldrick, 2004), English does not allow the sound /ŋ/ at word onset and it is unlikely that a speaker will produce an error that violates this constraint. This again suggests that building the sound structure of words involves using knowledge about phonemes (and their positions). In Psycholinguistic models, phonotactic knowledge is assumed to be used during segmental spell-out, when segments are assigned to the metrical frame.

Another oft-cited argument in favour of the frame and filler view is the fact that in many languages, words re-syllabify in connected speech. For instance, the syllabic structure of the words *car* and *is,* when produced in isolation are CVC and VC, respectively. When these two words are produced one after the other, such as in *the car is mine,* the syllable structure changes and becomes /kae-riz/, i.e., CV-CVC (see also Levelt et al., 1999). If word forms were stored as holistic entities, there would be no opportunity for their syllabic structure to be modified. In the frame and filler view, the word frames of two words can be combined, resulting in a phonological word frame.

Units of phonological encoding

In psycholinguistic models of language production, the minimal unit of phonological encoding is generally assumed to be the phoneme or segment (the two terms being often used interchangeably). In linguistics, units of phonological encoding are a matter of continuous debates. These concern for instance the relevance of phonemes/segments, syllables, or features.

Each phoneme can be described as a set of phonological features. For instance, the phoneme /b/ is +voiced, +plosive, +labial. Features correspond to the phonetic properties of sounds that are distinctive in a given language (e.g., Rialland et al., 2015). Features play a central role in many phonological theories (e.g., Chomsky & Halle, 1968; Goldrick, 2004 and references therein). Some of these theories further assume that features organize in phonemes, whereas others have proposed that phonemes are not needed. Patterns of speech errors do not support the latter view, as most phonological errors concern single segments, not single features. In a study on speech errors, Stemberger (1990) further found that whereas repetition of the same phoneme (as in *blue foot,* where the vowel is the same in the two words) increased the probability of errors, repetition of a feature did not. This does not necessarily mean; however, that features are not important units of processing (see below).

If the general principles governing the phonological encoding process were derived from speech errors, many further details about this process were tested with priming paradigms. In these paradigms, participants in an experiment have to produce a linguistic stimulus (can be a word or syllable) and the context in which the stimulus is presented is manipulated. In one version of the paradigm, the picture-word interference paradigm, the context is another linguistic stimulus, presented in a spoken or written form, and often called distractor (e.g., Lupker, 1979; Posnansky & Rayner, 1977 for early studies with this paradigm). In another version of the paradigm, the implicit priming (or form preparation) paradigm, the context is given by the other stimuli in the experimental block. Participants are first asked to learn pairs of words (e.g., tree-chair). In the test phase, they are presented with the first word and must produce the second out loud. The set of target stimuli in one block are either made of words with similar properties only (homogeneous set or block) or of unrelated stimuli (heterogeneous block). Using the implicit priming paradigm, Roelofs (1999) found that naming latencies were facilitated when participants produced monosyllabic words in homogeneous blocks with words in the block overlapping in their initial segments (i.e., onset facilitation effect), but that there was no such facilitation when the words in the homogeneous blocks shared initial segments with the same voicing feature or place of articulation only. This study suggests that phonemes (not features) are units of phonological encoding but does not inform on whether features have or do not have a psychological reality (or functional role) in speaking. Other studies suggest that they do. Goldrick (2004) examined whether speakers can learn phonotactic constraints at the featural level and showed that this was indeed the case. Mousikou et al. (2015) reported that the time to initiate the overt production of written words was reduced when these words were preceded by a masked nonword prime which shared either the first phoneme or all features but voicing with the to be produced word.

Taken together, the available empirical data from speech errors and chronometric paradigms suggest that the segment plays a crucial role during phonological encoding, but that features also have a psychological reality. The available evidence is more difficult to reconcile with models in which phonemes do not have an independent level of representation, including models in which phonological units are not features but vocal tract tasks (e.g., Browman & Goldstein, 1989; Hickok, 2014).

The role of larger units and, in particular, of the syllable, is also a matter of debate. Speech error patterns highlight the functional role of the syllable (see Meyer, 1992 for a critical review) and dominant psycholinguistic models of language production all assume that the syllable is a functional unit of phonological encoding. Models differ, however, as to how and where in the production system syllables are encoded. In Dell's (1986, 1988) version of the frame and filler view, the frame of a word is specified for the word's syllabic structure (number and types of syllables) as well as for the kind of phonemes (i.e., consonant or vowel) that belong to the slots in the frame. In other words, the stored phonological code is pre-syllabified. The fillers (phonemes) are specified for their type (vowel vs. consonant) and consonants are specified for whether they are to be inserted in the onset of the syllable or its offset. In Levelt et al. (1999) or the Weaver++ model (Roelofs, 1997), by contrast, syllables are computed online during the phonological encoding process but form units of representations at the phonetic encoding level (see next section). The main argument in favour of the latter view is again the need for words to re-syllabify in connected speech. However, as acknowledged, for instance, by Cholin (2006) the degree to which re-syllabification occurs varies across languages and in some languages (e.g., Mandarin where re-syllabification is inexistent), it could make sense to assume a pre-syllabified phonological code.

Chronometric studies on the role of syllables during phonological encoding in European languages have generated mixed results. In a series of experiments on French using a masked priming paradigm (a prime or distractor word is presented for a brief period of time before a picture or written word to be named), Ferrand et al. (1996) reported that their participants were faster to name pictures and read words or nonwords aloud when the prime word shared the first syllable as opposed to one letter less or one letter more with the to be produced word (see Ferrand et al., 1997, for a replication in English, with words that have clear syllables). Several studies failed to replicate these effects in Dutch, German, or French (Perret et al., 2006; Schiller, 2000; Schiller et al., 2008) and found instead that the number of shared phonemes determined the amount of priming, irrespective of syllabic structure.

As noted above, the role of syllables may differ across languages. As reviewed in O'Seaghdha et al. (2010) whereas errors rarely involve syllables in English, they do in Mandarin (Chen, 2000). Likewise, chronometric studies suggest that the syllable is an important unit of phonological encoding in this language. Using the implicit priming paradigm described above, Chen et al. (2002) found that response times were facilitated when disyllabic target words in a block shared the first syllable, but not when they shared the first consonant (with some differences across phonemes and participants). O'Seaghdha et al. (2010) replicated this result as well as the onset facilitation effect in English (we note however that effects in the two languages were never directly compared and that not all statistical analyses confirmed the interaction between type of prime (onset vs. syllable) and block in this study). According to O'Seaghdha et al. (2010), differences in priming effects across languages suggest that for speakers of Mandarin, the first unit of phonological encoding retrieved for production is the syllable whereas the first unit retrieved by speakers of European languages (at least the languages investigated so far) is the phoneme. Additional evidence seems however necessary to confirm these claims.

Time course of phonological encoding

Using an implicit priming paradigm, Meyer (1990) investigated whether the successive syllables of a word are encoded in parallel or sequentially. Participants in her experiments were asked to learn pairs of words. They were then presented with the first of these words and asked to produce the second. In homogeneous sets, all the words to be produced had the same first syllable, in heterogeneous sets, they had variable first syllables. Meyer observed that production latencies were shorter in homogeneous sets. This was not the case when the words in the homogenous sets shared the second syllable unless they also shared the first. These results were taken to suggest that phonological encoding proceeds syllable per syllable. In a subsequent study, Meyer (1991) had participants produce monosyllabic words in homogeneous blocks where words shared the onset, and in heterogeneous blocks where this was not the case. She found shorter naming latencies in the first. No facilitation of this kind was obtained when the words in the homogeneous set shared the rhyme. In addition, there was stronger facilitation when the whole syllable was shared as opposed to only the onset and nucleus of the syllable (but not the coda). These results were taken to reveal that phonological encoding within syllables proceeds sequentially, from left to right.

Further evidence in favour of the hypothesis that the phonological encoding process proceeds sequentially comes from the picture-word interference paradigm. Shared onsets between the word to be produced and a written or spoken distractor facilitate naming when compared to target-distractor pairs that do not share phonological information (phonological facilitation effect, e.g., Posnansky & Rayner, 1977; Rayner & Posnansky, 1978). Using spoken distractors, Meyer and Schriefers (1991) examined the impact of distractors related to the onset and offset of the target word, at different SOAs (or Stimulus Onset Asynchrony, i.e., time between target presentation and onset of distractor presentation). When a spoken distractor sharing phonological information at word onset with the to-be-produced word started playing 150 ms before, or at the same time as the picture, there was a phonological facilitation effect. This effect was not present when the distractor started playing 150 ms before picture onset. For distractors sharing information at word offset, the effect occurred at a later SOA. These findings are expected under the hypothesis that phonological encoding starts with the onset of the word and proceeds sequentially.

Phonetic encoding

In generative linguistics as well as in psycholinguistics, phonetic encoding refers to the representations and processes at the interface between abstract phonological content and execution of articulatory movements. Phonetic encoding takes as input the output of the phonological encoding process and delivers the corresponding motor programmes. The phonetic encoding process is the poor cousin in psycholinguistics, as it did not generate as much enthusiasm and empirical data as lexical access or phonological encoding. By contrast, debates regarding the phonetic encoding process take place in related fields, i.e., cognitive/laboratory phonology[1] or speech motor control. Note that the latter is not only concerned with phonetic encoding but also details the mechanisms by which phonetic representations are used to control the articulators. In other words, theories of speech motor control are theories of phonetic encoding and movement control during articulation. The mechanisms by which articulatory movements are controlled (see, for instance, Parrell et al., 2019) are usually of little interest in psycholinguistics, and will not be reviewed here. We will focus on units of phonetic encoding (or phonetic representations).

Units of phonetic encoding

In his account of the phonetic encoding process, Levelt (1989) assumes that phonetic representations are made of abstract gestural scores. This idea is also at the centre of the task dynamic model of Saltzman and Munhall (1989), which posits that speech targets consist in the locations and degrees of constrictions in the vocal tract. A similar view is found in Articulatory Phonology (Browman & Goldstein, 1992), where discrete constriction actions (also called gestures) are the basic units of phonetic encoding (recall that in Articulatory Phonology, there is no additional phonological representation between these gestures and lexical representations, gestures are both physical events and phonological units).

The DIVA (Directions into Velocities of Articulators) model takes a different perspective. Here speakers use motor, auditory, and sensorimotor targets. The motor target involves a set of motor commands or learned sequences of articulatory movements. Unlike in the task dynamic model, where motor targets are dynamic tasks, in DIVA, motor plans correspond to "time-varying desired articulatory position" (Parrell et al., 2019, p. 1470). The corresponding auditory and somatosensory targets provide information on the state the auditory and somatosensory systems must be in to produce the target sound. Unlike in Articulatory Phonology, the DIVA model assumes that the input of the phonetic process is the output of the phonological encoding process, as described in Levelt's model. The phonological sequence activates the sounds' neural representations (see Kearney & Guenther, 2019). This, in turn, initiates the readout of a motor target and corresponding auditory and somatosensory targets (see Kearney & Guenther, 2019, for details and Guenther, 2016, for a detailed mathematical implementation of the model).

Size of phonetic units

The dominant theory of phonetic encoding in psycholinguistics builds on Crompton's (1982) idea that the phonological syllables resulting from the phonological encoding process are mapped onto syllable-sized abstract motor programmes (Levelt, 1989, 1992). This account further assumes that the phonetic encoding process has two possible routes. For frequent syllables, speakers have a syllable-sized motor programme in long-term memory (stored in a so-called *mental syllabary*, see, for instance, Levelt & Wheeldon, 1994). For less frequent syllables or novel sound sequences, speakers access sub-syllabic motor programmes which they assemble into syllables. When a gestural score is stored in the syllabary, its parameter values for the vocal tract action needed to implement that score can just be read out. The hypothesis that speakers use syllabic (as opposed to phonemic) motor programmes fits well with patterns of coarticulation, i.e., "local articulatory adjustment of all phoneme instantiations to their current neighbours" (Wood, 1996), which mostly take place within the syllable (but see Krause & Kawamoto, 2020). If motor plans are syllabic, the motor commands of a given phoneme in the syllable can depend on the motor commands of other segments in the syllable more than on motor commands of segments outside the syllable.

Many of the experimental studies on phonetic encoding in psycholinguistics have attempted to find evidence in support of the mental syllabary hypothesis. These studies often capitalized on frequency manipulations. The mental syllabary hypothesis predicts that more frequent syllables can be prepared more quickly for production. In a seminal paper, Levelt and Wheeldon (1994) argued that syllable frequency influences production speed, as predicted by the theory. An advantage for more frequent syllables was then reported in several studies performed in different labs with different languages and different tasks (Carreiras & Perea, 2004; Cholin et al., 2006; Croot et al., 2017; Laganaro & Alario, 2006). Notably, however, the effect was not found in other studies (Bürki et al., 2015; Bürki et al., 2020; Croot & Rastle, 2004) and a closer look at studies reporting a difference between low- and high-frequency syllables suggests that this effect is not only very small, it often does not meet the standard criteria in the field to conclude that it is statistically reliable or generalizes over participants and items. A preliminary meta-analysis of the effect, considering data from 22 datasets (experiments or experiment parts) in 11 published papers shows that the meta-analytic estimate is centred at 5.8 ms, with a 95% credible interval ranging between 1.8 and 10.9 (see Figure 3.1 and Appendix 1 for details on the studies included and https://osf.io/4nmbj/ for scripts and data). As is often the case in meta-analyses based on published studies, the meta-analytic estimate is likely over-estimated as a result of a publication bias. The funnel plot in Appendix 2 exhibits a pattern compatible with such bias.

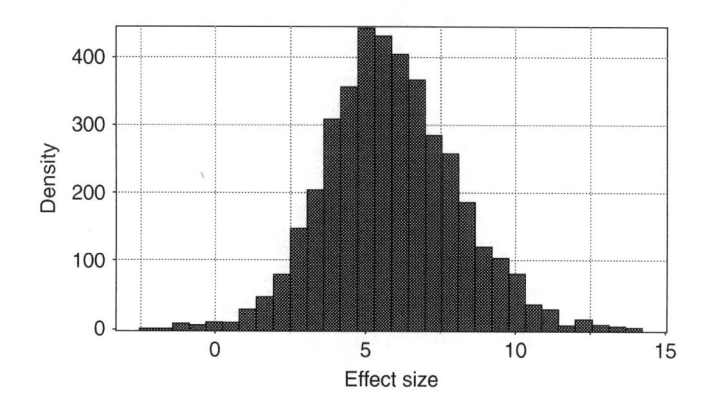

Figure 3.1 Posterior distribution of the meta-analytic estimate of the syllable frequency effect.

This preliminary meta-analysis clearly points to the need to consider additional data and, more importantly, potential datasets with inconclusive findings, to obtain a more precise picture and determine whether more frequent syllables are indeed processed faster. It is important to note, however, that a reliable syllable frequency effect would be compatible with the mental syllabary hypothesis, but would not rule out other accounts. For instance, syllable frequency effects are expected if syllabic (or more generally supra-segmental) motor programmes are not stored as such but computed from segment-size programmes, a computation that benefits from experience (for similar debates about computational vs. storage accounts of frequency effects at the utterance level, see Jeong et al., 2021 or Onnis & Huettig, 2021). Moreover, an advantage for more frequent syllables does not necessarily originate during the phonetic encoding process but could reflect the fact that more frequent syllables can be formed more quickly during segmental spell out. Alternatively, in models where word forms contain information about their syllabic structure (e.g., Dell, 1988), more frequent syllables could have higher activation levels.

Several studies attempted to pinpoint the functional locus of syllable frequency effects, with mixed findings. For instance, Laganaro and Alario (2006) compared effects of syllable frequency in immediate production tasks, delayed production tasks (where participants are assumed to prepare all aspects of their speech in advance) and delayed production tasks with articulatory suppression (where speakers are assumed to prepare everything until phonetic encoding). They observed an advantage for frequent syllables in all but the delayed production task and took this result to suggest that the effect arises during phonetic encoding rather than during phonological encoding or execution. In English Croot et al. (2017, but see Croot et al., 2004) replicated the effect in the immediate production task but not in the delayed task with articulatory suppression. Another attempt to determine the locus of syllable frequency effects is found in Cholin and Levelt (2009). Their participants were presented with a set of four nonwords that they had to read silently, then the four nonwords appeared one by one and the participant had to read them aloud. This was repeated for different sets of four nonwords. The four items in a set could either share the first syllable or have different first syllables. Moreover, syllable frequency was manipulated. The authors observed a syllable frequency effect in heterogeneous sets and concluded that the syllable frequency effect arises during phonetic encoding. This conclusion, however, heavily relies on a series of assumptions regarding priming effects and their absence in the paradigm. Independent evidence is still needed.

The production of low- and high-frequency syllables has also been compared in the neuroimaging literature. Functional magnetic resonance imaging (fMRI) studies comparing the brain response to high- and low-frequency syllables reported higher activation for low-frequency than for high-frequency syllables but no difference in the opposite contrast (Carreiras et al., 2006; Papoutsi et al., 2009, see Riecker et al., 2008 for an effect of syllable complexity but no effect of syllable frequency). This pattern has been taken to suggest that the same brain areas are involved in the preparation of high- and low-frequency syllables but that less frequent units require higher processing costs. This result can be explained within – but does not require – the mental syllabary hypothesis. Bürki et al. (2015) used topographic analyses of the Electroencephalography (EEG) signal and found different topographies for high versus non-existing syllables or low-frequency syllables, a result taken to indicate that different brain networks are involved in the preparation of existing vs. novel syllables, as predicted by the mental syllabary hypothesis. Note, however, that topographies in a follow-up study using similar stimuli and task (Bürki et al., 2020) were quite different from that of the first study and additional data are needed to confirm these observations.

As reviewed in Laganaro (2019), support for the role of syllables during phonetic encoding also comes from the study of patients with apraxia of speech, a disorder associated with the phonetic encoding process. These patients were reported to make more errors on words and pseudowords with low- as opposed to high-frequency syllables (e.g., Aichert & Ziegler, 2004; Laganaro, 2005; Laganaro et al., 2012). Finally, it has been argued that the fine phonetic details of a syllable are influenced by the frequency of that syllable. In Herrmann et al. (2008) high-frequency monosyllabic words were found to have greater coarticulation and a shorter duration than low-frequency monosyllabic words. Schweitzer and Möbius (2004) observed that the relationship between the duration of the syllable and that of the phonemes in the syllable was stronger for low- than for high-frequency syllables. Again such syllable frequency effects could arise because frequent syllables are stored or because they can be assembled faster.

In sum, the available evidence so far does not warrant clear conclusions regarding the existence of a mental syllabary. It suggests that syllables play a role during the preparation of word forms but the exact mechanisms underlying this influence remain unclear. Syllables play a role in models that do not necessarily assume a mental syllabary. The syllable is for instance a relevant processing unit in the DIVA model. In this model, the typical input unit is syllabic but the model also allows for larger units, for instance for frequent multisyllabic words, or smaller units (individual phonemes). Similarly, the model proposed by Ziegler and colleagues also considers that the syllable is a functional unit, but here there is no distinction between units that are stored and units that are not stored. In this model, developed to account for speech errors in apraxia of speech (e.g., Ziegler, 2009; Ziegler, 2014) phonetic plans are hierarchical structures with different tiers and connections between them. On the first tier are gestures, defined as transitions between phonetic features of consecutive phonemes. These gestures are part of a tree-like hierarchical structure, with connections between tiers. There is a tier for syllables as well as for larger units such as the metrical foot and word, but also for sub-syllabic units such as consonant clusters. Connections between units that are frequently produced together are stronger than connections between units that are less often produced together.

Abstraction and details in phonetic units

In the mental syllabary account, motor commands are abstract and independent of contextual information. For instance, the production of the words *carrot*, *cabin*, and *Caroline* require access to the same phonetic unit /kæ/. The exact realization of syllables (and segments) in the model depends on how parameters such as intensity, duration, or strength are set once the abstract motor commands have been retrieved from the mental syllabary or computed (Levelt, 1989). Several empirical observations have been taken to challenge the view that phonetic units are abstract and context-independent. Studies reported for instance that speakers imitate the speech of their interlocutor(s). Phonetic imitation (or convergence) has been reported in several studies in the lab (e.g., Dufour & Nguyen, 2013; Goldinger & Azuma, 2004; Nielsen, 2011; Shockley et al., 2004) and in natural conversations (e.g., Pardo, 2006; Pardo et al., 2010) and taken to support an exemplarist view of the lexicon (e.g., Goldinger, 1998a). Imitation effects are often assessed by independent judges (e.g., Goldinger, 1998, for details on the procedure). Notably, imitation effects tend to be small (when measured in experimental settings) and are not always found. Moreover, several studies examined the phonetic correlates of imitation, but the resulting picture is heterogeneous; the phonetic parameters that are imitated in one study are not necessary the same parameters that are imitated in another study (see Pardo et al., 2017, for review, see also Kraljic et al., 2008).

Another line of evidence taken to challenge the idea that phonetic representations are abstract comes from studies showing an influence of word-specific details on pronunciation (see also Pierrehumbert, 2002). More frequent words are, for instance, produced with shorter durations (see Bell et al., 2009, for review), tend to have vowels produced with more contraction (e.g., Munson & Solomon, 2004) and are produced with more segment deletions (e.g., Hinskens, 2011; Jurafsky et al., 2000; Racine & Grosjean, 2002). Similarly, the number of similar sounding words (phonological neighbourhood) influences the realization of words (e.g., Munson & Solomon, 2004; Scarborough, 2010; Wright, 2004) with hyper or hypo-articulation for words in dense neighbourhoods depending on the study. Gahl (2008) further reported that homophones have distinct acoustic realizations. Finally, support for long-term storage of acoustic details comes from studies on sound change. As, for instance, summarized in Pierrehumbert (2002) changes in the realization of words (reduction, lenition) start with high-frequent words and disseminate across the lexicon with different rates across words (e.g., Bybee, 2001). These effects are hard to explain under the view that phonetic representations are abstract.

Finally, the observation that many variation phenomena seem to be gradient rather than categorical has sometimes been taken as an argument in favour of detailed phonetic representations. Early studies and theories of variation phenomena assumed that many of these phenomena were categorical.

For instance, words with a schwa vowel (e.g., *camera* /kæmərə/) would either be produced with or without (i.e., [kæmrə]) the schwa. Similarly, assimilation (i.e., a phoneme adapts to its context and becomes more similar to a neighbouring phoneme as in fun /fʌn/ realized as /fʌm/ in *fun beach*) would either result in one phoneme or in the other. Fine-grained acoustic and articulatory analyses revealed however that the produced variants could not so easily be distinguished. Traces of the other phoneme (e.g., of the /n/ in /fʌm/), have then been taken to support the idea that words are not represented in abstract phonological ways but in phonetically detailed ways (e.g., of studies suggesting gradient changes between two variants of the same word, see Ernestus et al., 2006; Niebuhr et al., 2011; Nolan, 1992; Snoeren et al., 2006; Wright & Kerswill, 1989).

These different findings have been taken to support the hypothesis that phonetic representations entail phonetic details. In exemplar-based accounts, such details are part of the lexicon (as already discussed, there is no intermediate level of processing with abstract phonological units in these models). Each word is associated with a cloud of exemplars. In her attempt to reconcile the afore-mentioned evidence with evidence from speech errors, Pierrehumbert (2002) describes a hybrid model in which the output of the phonological encoding process maps onto phonetically detailed syllabic or sub-syllabic representations. As we will see next, the evidence discussed here has also been explained within the standard psycholinguistic approach, with either cascading activation or coordination mechanisms.

Interface and interactions between phonological and phonetic encoding

Interaction between phonological and phonetic information

An important issue in modelling language production concerns the extent to which the information activated or selected at one processing level can in-fluence subsequent levels. The influential model of Levelt and colleagues is sequential, modular and discrete. Encoding processes take place in a strictly sequential fashion. Phonological encoding is initiated once a semantic re-presentation or lemma has been selected. Moreover, only the word form corresponding to this lemma is then activated. Other lemmas activated during the lexical-semantic process do not send activation to the next level. Then, once the phonological encoding process is completed to a certain extent (see next section), phonetic encoding may start. Moreover, the model does not allow feedback from the phonetic level to the phonological level. Given the above and the assumption that phonological and phonetic processes are context-independent, the articulation of a given syllable or segment is ex-pected to be the same irrespective of the word in which it occurs. Several lines of empirical evidence have highlighted the limitations of this view. First, and as reviewed earlier, articulation is influenced by word-specific properties.

suggesting that some information activated at the lexical-semantic level is passed on to the articulators. One way to account for these findings in the sequential-modular approach is to assume an external control mechanism that informs the articulators about the strength of activation at each level. The level of activation is then used by the articulators to modulate execution (Bell et al., 2009; Pierrehumbert, 2002; Pluymaekers et al., 2005). We note, however, that this option only saves the modular view on the surface. The mere existence of a mechanism by which information at the lexical level influences articulation is at odds with a fully modular encapsulated view of the language production system.

A second line of evidence that has proven difficult to reconcile with a modular view comes from detailed acoustical analyses of speech errors. Early studies on speech sound errors mostly reported categorical errors (i.e., phoneme deletions, insertions, substitutions, see, e.g., Fromkin, 1971; Stemberger, 1990, see also Meyer, 1992). More fine-grained analyses of these errors have shown however that often, a substituted phoneme contains traces of the intended phoneme (e.g., Alderete et al., 2021; Goldrick & Blumstein, 2006; Goldrick et al., 2011, see also Goldstein et al., 2007; Pouplier & Goldstein, 2010). The sequential-modular view cannot account for these findings, because in this model, only the units selected at the phonological level are used as input for the phonetic process.

Cascading models (e.g., Goldrick, 2006) of language production provide an elegant explanation of error patterns within the psycholinguistic multi-component view of language production. In cascading activation models, a unit activated at a given encoding level can influence subsequent levels, even if it has not been selected. For instance, if the speaker intended to produce a /b/ but ends up producing an /m/ instead, if /b/ has received some activation, this activation may reach the subsequent (phonetic) process. Note that the same mechanism can explain "incomplete" variation phenomena, i.e., the observation that variants (e.g., schwa deleted variant, assimilated variant) bare traces of the other variant (see also Bürki, 2018) or the influence of word-specific properties on articulation (Baese-Berk and Goldrick (2009).

Timing of phonological and phonetic encoding processes

Models with a distinction between phonological and phonetic encoding all assume that the phonological encoding takes as input the output of the lexical-semantic process and that the phonetic encoding process takes as input the output of the phonological process. The assumption that access to motor programmes follows access to abstract phonological code is little debated. If motor programmes can be accessed before or at the same time as abstract phonological representations, then there is little need for the latter. In their description of the time course of encoding processes, considering a mean response time in a picture naming experiment of about 600 ms, Indefrey and Levelt (2004) concluded that the phonological encoding process takes place between about 275 and 450 ms after the onset of picture presentation (i.e., between 325 and 150 ms before articulation onset). According to Indefrey and Levelt (2004, see also Indefrey, 2011), the last 150 ms before speech onset are dedicated to the phonetic encoding process. When speech onsets are defined based on information from spectrograms/oscillograms or using a vocal key, they inform on when the articulatory gestures start making (visible) noise. Take an unvoiced plosive like /p/. The articulation of /p/ starts with the closure of the lips. This closure, which lasts about 30 ms is not visible on the spectrogram or oscillogram and cannot be detected by the vocal key either. More generally, articulation starts as soon as the articulators start moving, not when they have reached their target. Hence the last 150 ms before vocal onset in most studies are likely associated with execution processes rather than with phonetic encoding. As a consequence the phonetic encoding process has started much earlier and the last 150 ms before response onset are dedicated to post-phonetic processes.

Several EEG or MEG studies in the last decade have attempted to determine the timing of encoding processes directly. A few studies showed that effects that can be assumed to originate in the phonological and/or phonetic component are, as expected under Indefrey and Levelt's proposed time course, visible in the response-aligned event-related potentials (or ERPs), starting at about 400 ms before the vocal response (e.g., Bürki et al., 2015; Bürki et al., 2016; Bürki et al., 2020; Laganaro et al., 2013). The exact and relative time course of the two processes requires however additional inquiries. Considering the existing EEG/MEG (Magnetoencephalography) evidence Laganaro (2019) concludes for instance that contrary to Indefrey and Levelt (2004)'s proposal, "far more than 150 ms seem to separate the moment phonetic encoding is engaged from the onset of articulation". Potentially relevant data come from studies examining ERPs for elicited speech errors. Laganaro (2019), Möller et al. (2007) and Monaco et al. (2017) all reported differences between error free and error trials starting at around 370 ms after stimulus onset.

Notably, other studies reported effects of phonological manipulations or variables in ERPs aligned on picture onset, sometimes in very early time windows. Miozzo et al. (2014) in a MEG study using multiple linear regression reported effects of semantic and phonological variables in similar time windows, starting at around 150 ms after picture onset. Strijkers et al. (2010) observed lexical frequency and cognate effects in what they call the P2 range (i.e., around 180 ms after picture onset). As rightly noted by Strijkers et al. (2017) these early effects cannot unambiguously be associated with phonological processing because the variables assumed to reflect phonological processing in these studies have been shown to also influence lexical-semantic processes in other studies. To address this issue further, Strijkers et al. (2017) manipulated whether the first phoneme of the response started with a labial or non-labial phoneme (lip movement vs. tongue) as well as lexical frequency. They reported effects of both manipulations in the same early time window, from 160 to 240 ms after picture onset in left frontal (left inferior frontal gyrus) and temporal (middle temporal gyrus) cortical regions for the frequency manipulation and in the superior temporal gyrus for the phonological/articulatory manipulation. These results are compatible with the hypothesis that phonological or phonetic information is available early. These data have been taken to challenge sequential models of production processes, where the encoding of word form follows the encoding of lexical/semantic information.

To summarize, the empirical evidence available to date does not allow reaching firm conclusions regarding the exact timing of phonological and phonetic encoding processes. The fact that naming latencies greatly vary across participants and studies further complicates the picture. Some recent data seem to suggest that phonological information is available much earlier than assumed by traditional psycholinguistic models, additional studies are now needed to confirm these findings. We note that the parallel vs. sequential nature of word production processes is the focus of intense debates and refer the reader to Munding et al. (2015) for a detailed discussion and review of the MEG evidence.

Scope of advanced planning

Speaking, as any other cognitive task that results in a motor output requires advanced planning. Different actions need to be organized/coordinated ahead. Under the assumption that the preparation of the sound structure of words and utterances involves a phonological and a phonetic component, the question arises of how much is planned at a given component, before the onset of the subsequent component. Studies in psycholinguistics have mostly focused on two (related) issues. The first concerns the minimal planning unit at the phonological encoding level, i.e., how much speakers must minimally plan at this level before they initiate the phonetic encoding process[2] and articulation. The second is whether speakers always plan ahead using minimal units (i.e., incremental planning strategy) or whether they use variable planning units.

Levelt et al. (1999) originally assumed that speakers only begin speaking once the phonetic plans for the whole phonological word have been prepared. Under this assumption, the whole phonological word has been prepared before articulation. A phonological word contains at least a lexical word and may contain clitics (unstressed function words, e.g., *the* in *the car* produced without focus on *the*) as well (e.g., Levelt, 1989; Wheeldon & Lahiri, 1997). It has later been argued that the minimal planning unit could be the syllable rather than the phonological word (Indefrey, 2011; Indefrey & Levelt, 2004; Meyer et al., 2003). Accordingly, speakers can initiate the phonetic encoding process as soon as the first phonological syllable is available (i.e., fillers for that syllable have been inserted in the metrical frame). Finally, others have argued that speakers can plan less than a syllable. In Kawamoto et al. (2014), Kawamoto et al. (2015), or MacKay (1987), the minimal planning unit is the segment.

Studies on the scope of advanced planning show heterogeneous outcomes. For instance, several studies examined the production of simple noun phrases such as determiner-adjective-noun (e.g., *the big dog)*, and concluded that the whole noun phrase is planned before subsequent processes are initiated (Costa & Caramazza, 2002; Damian & Dumay, 2007; Spalek et al., 2010; Wheeldon & Lahiri, 1997, but see Michel Lange & Laganaro, 2014). A few studies even suggested that the scope of phonological encoding can encompass whole sentences (Oppermann et al., 2010; Schnur, 2011). These studies all examined production latencies (time required to prepare the vocal response following the presentation of a stimulus). By contrast, studies using eye-movements as an index of planning (Griffin, 2001; Griffin & Bock, 2000) tended to conclude that the scope of phonological planning does not extend beyond the phonological word. Finally, considering reading aloud latencies and first phoneme duration (for words with regular vs. irregular pronuncia-tions), Kawamoto et al. (1998) concluded that the scope of advanced planning can encompass the whole word or just the first phoneme.

Heterogeneity of results across studies led several authors to suggest that the scope of advanced planning, beyond the minimal planning unit, is variable – or flexible (e.g., Ferreira 2002; Martin et al., 2010; Michel Lange & Laganaro, 2014; Schriefers, 1999). This hypothesis, as well as the factors that generate and constrain this variability were addressed in a few studies. Meyer et al. (2003) examined word length effects on naming latencies. Under the hypothesis that speakers wait until the phonological word is fully implemented before in-itiating phonetic encoding, longer words should take longer to prepare. Meyer et al. (2003) found differences between long and short words (for words at utterance onset or produced in isolation) when the short and long words were presented in separate lists (i.e., made of only monosyllabic words or only of dissyllabic words), but not when they were intermixed. The authors took this finding to suggest that speakers can use different response criteria and either plan the whole word or only the first syllable before the onset of articulation (note however that other studies failed to find any length effect, e.g., Bachoud-Lévi et al., 1998). Martin et al. (2010) argue that variability in the syntactic structures that participants produce during the experiment may in-fluence the scope of advanced planning (see also Oppermann et al., 2010) but did not test this hypothesis directly.

Ferreira and Swets (2002) examined the role of time pressure. They reported that participants seemed to plan less when pressured to respond quickly. Importantly, however, not all participants in their study reduced the scope of advanced planning in this context, suggesting that this scope may vary across participants. Other studies examined the hypothesis that the scope of advanced planning is modulated by cognitive load. Here again, findings are heterogeneous. Klaus et al. (2017) reported a link between the scope of advanced ponological planning and working memory. In a recent study, Ivanova and Ferreira (2019) reported shorter naming latencies under cognitive load, a result in line with the hypothesis that the scope of advanced planning is reduced under cognitive load. By contrast, Martin et al. (2014) failed to find evidence supporting the claim that the scope of advanced planning is modulated by cognitive load.

The scope of advanced planning likely also depends on the language and possibly, in some languages, on the utterances being produced. In some utterances/languages, the minimal units of advanced planning are constrained by linguistic dependencies between words. In many French noun phrases, for instance, the phonological form of the determiner depends on the phonology of the next word (i.e., *phonological constraint*, e.g., *le chat* "the cat" vs. *l'âne* "the donkey"). The same is also true for many pre-nominal adjectives (e.g., *le bel âne* "the nice donkey" vs. *le beau chat* "the nice cat"). To produce these utterances without errors, speakers must encode the utterance up to the noun before the onset of articulation. This is not necessary in other languages, such as English (for a convincing demonstration that advanced planning and phonological variation are related, see Kilbourn-Ceron & Goldrick, 2021).

To summarize, the available evidence tends to support the idea that the scope of advanced planning at the phonological level is variable. We note here that a flexible scope of advanced planning has several advantages over a rigid system. It could allow speakers to avoid dysfluencies while maximizing response speed when necessary. Speaking is mostly used in conversations. In such settings, speakers cannot defer the start of articulation as much as they wish, because if they do, they might miss their turn. On the other hand, a strategy that would consist in initiating the articulation as soon as possible would favour dysfluencies. If the speaker intends to say *the octopus* and starts the articulation as soon as *the* is ready, if *octopus* is not yet encoded, a pause will occur between the two words. Whereas such dysfluencies do exist, they are not frequent within noun phrases. Notably, Ferreira and Swets (2002a) observed that when speakers initiated the articulation quickly, the duration of the produced utterance tended to be longer. In line with this observation, exploratory analyses of published data (Jeong et al., 2021) revealed a negative relationship between utterance duration and naming latency. These observations are expected if speakers adapt the scope of advanced planning on the fly and use the duration of the execution phase to avoid disfluencies when they plan their speech incrementally. Additional studies are clearly needed to determine the conditions and factors that modulate the scope of advanced planning.

Probabilistic knowledge in the generation of sound structure

It has been shown early on that the frequency of a word influences the time needed to retrieve this word for production (Oldfield & Wingfield, 1965, see also, e.g., Alario et al., 2004; Jescheniak & Levelt, 1994). Goldrick (2014) reviews some of the evidence suggesting that this effect originates at least partly in the phonological component and summarizes two accounts of this influence. According to the first, experience is encoded in the phonological structure of words. Less frequent words have weaker connections to phonological units. According to the second account, experience is reflected at the word-form level, with less frequent words having lower resting activation levels or higher selection thresholds. Irrespective of the underlying mechanism, frequency effects, if they indeed arise in phonological encoding, show that representations and processes at this level are influenced by the speaker's use of the language. This conclusion is in line with Bürki et al. (2010)'s finding that picture-naming latencies for French words produced with and without the schwa (e.g., the word fenêtre 'window' can be produced as /fənɛtʀ/ or /fnɛtʀ/) can be predicted by the frequency with which a given speaker produces these variants.

Notably, several studies show that the impact of usage can even be measured over the course of an experiment, suggesting that representations are constantly updated. In some of these studies, participants were asked to repeat sequences of segments, some of which following novel phonotactic regularities (e.g., Dell et al., 2000; Goldrick, 2004; Goldrick & Larson, 2008). Participants started producing errors following the experiment-wide phonotactic regularities after limited exposure (see also Kittredge & Dell, 2016 or Warker et al., 2009). To account for these findings, the model of Warker and Dell (2006) assumes links between segments as well as between segments and syllabic positions. The weight associated with these links can be modified with experience. Bürki et al. (2020) compared the time needed to produce novel and high frequency syllables as well as the neural networks involved in the production of these two types of stimuli using EEG. They also tested their participants after exposure to these sequences/syllables embedded in pseudo-words. They observed a difference in the EEG signal recorded during the production of high frequency vs. novel syllables. Notably, this difference disappeared after exposure. This finding suggests that whichever processes underlie the electrophysiological difference (phonological or phonetic), these are influenced by usage. Finally, we discussed phonetic imitation effects above. Assuming with the dominant accounts of these effects that they reflect the representation of phonetic details in memory, they indicate that the processes and representations underlying the generation of sound structure for production are sensitive to usage.

In sum several lines of evidence suggest that phonological and phonetic knowledge are influenced by the speaker's use of the language. Models of word production and representation in psycholinguistics do not account for this influence beyond lexical frequency effects.

Conclusion

The chapter presented an overview of important issues and findings pertaining to the representations and processes underlying the sound structure of words. The available evidence so far is compatible with models assuming that the generation of sound structure during language production tasks requires two components, a phonological and a phonetic component. The first involves the retrieval of abstract phonological units – most likely of the size of segments – and a process by which these units are inserted in a metrical word frame. The second involves the retrieval of motor programmes. The evidence is further compatible with the hypothesis that these two components are not fully modular and that activation at any level of processing can cascade into subsequent levels, and as a result, influence the articulation. The evidence often taken to support exemplar-based views of word form knowledge can easily be explained in the context of cascading activation models of language production. Finally, representations of sound structure are sensitive to usage and constantly updated. The review further highlights the need for additional evidence in favour of the proposal that speakers store syllable-sized abstract programmes and calls for further inquiries into the time course of the phonological and phonetic encoding processes. As a final note, the study of the generation of sound structure is at the crossroad of different disciplines. This multi-disciplinarity is both a real challenge and a strength. Significant advances in the understanding of sound structure will undeniably require interdisciplinary research programmes spanning over these disciplines.

Acknowledgements

This research was partly funded by the Deutsche Forschungsgemeinschaft (DFG, German Research Foundation, project number BU 3542/2-1, PI. Audrey Bürki).

Notes

1 In cognitive/laboratory phonology, the phonetic encoding process is often discussed under the terms "speech production."
2 The scope of advanced planning at the interface between phonetic encoding and articulation (i.e., how much do speakers plan at the phonetic encoding level before articulation is initiated?) is beyond the scope of psycholinguistic models. For a discussion and review of relevant evidence, see Krause and Kawamoto (2020).

References

Aichert, I., & Ziegler, W. (2004). Syllable frequency and syllable structure in apraxia of speech. *Brain and Language, 88*(1), 148–159. 10.1016/s0093-934x(03)00296-7
Alario, F. X., Ferrand, L., Laganaro, M., New, B., Frauenfelder, U. H., & Segui, J. (2004). Predictors of picture naming speed. *Behavior Research Methods, Instruments, & Computers: A Journal of the Psychonomic Society, Inc, 36*(1), 140–155.
Alderete, J., Baese-Berk, M., Leung, K., & Goldrick, M. (2021). Cascading activation in phonological planning and articulation: Evidence from spontaneous speech errors. *Cognition, 210*, 104577. 10.1016/j.cognition.2020.104577
Baayen, R. H., Chuang, Y.-Y., Shafaei-Bajestan, E., & Blevins, J. P. (2019). *The Discriminative Lexicon: A Unified Computational Model for the Lexicon and Lexical Processing in Comprehension and Production Grounded Not in (De)Composition but in Linear Discriminative Learning* [Research Article]. Complexity; Hindawi. 10.1155/2019/4895891

Baayen, R. H., Hendrix, P., & Ramscar, M. (2013). Sidestepping the Combinatorial Explosion: An Explanation of n-gram Frequency Effects Based on Naive Discriminative Learning. *Language and Speech*, *56*(3), 329–347. 10.1177/0023830913484896

Bachoud-Lévi, A.-C., Dupoux, E., Cohen, L., & Mehler, J. (1998). Where Is the Length Effect? A Cross-Linguistic Study of Speech Production. *Journal of Memory and Language*, *39*(3), 331–346. 10.1006/jmla.1998.2572

Baese-Berk, M., & Goldrick, M. (2009). Mechanisms of interaction in speech production. *Language and Cognitive Processes*, *24*(4), 527–554. 10.1080/01690960802299378

Bell, A., Brenier, J. M., Gregory, M., Girand, C., & Jurafsky, D. (2009). Predictability Effects on Durations of Content and Function Words in Conversational English. *Journal of Memory and Language*, *60*(1), 92–111.

Browman, C. P., & Goldstein, L. (1989). Articulatory gestures as phonological units★. *Phonology*, *6*(2), 201–251. 10.1017/S0952675700001019

Browman, C. P., & Goldstein, L. (1992). Articulatory Phonology: An Overview. *Phonetica*, *49*(3–4), 155–180. 10.1159/000261913

Buchwald, A., & Miozzo, M. (2011). Finding Levels of Abstraction in Speech Production Evidence From Sound-Production Impairment. *Psychological Science*, *22*(9), 1113–1119. 10.1177/0956797611417723

Bürki, A., Ernestus, M., & Frauenfelder, U. H. (2010). Is there only one "fenêtre" in the production lexicon? On-line evidence on the nature of phonological representations of pronunciation variants for French schwa words. *Journal of Memory and Language*, *62*(4), 421–437. 10.1016/j.jml.2010.01.002.

Bürki, A. (2018). Variation in the speech signal as a window into the cognitive architecture of language production. *Psychonomic Bulletin & Review*, *25*(6), 1973–2004. 10.3758/s13423-017-1423-4

Bürki, A., Cheneval, P. P., & Laganaro, M. (2015). Do speakers have access to a mental syllabary? ERP comparison of high frequency and novel syllable production. *Brain and Language*, *150*, 90–102. 10.1016/j.bandl.2015.08.006

Bürki, A., Sadat, J., Dubarry, A.-S., & Alario, F.-X. (2016). Sequential processing during noun phrase production. *Cognition*, *146*, 90–99. 10.1016/j.cognition.2015.09.002

Bürki, A., Viebahn, M., & Gafos, A. (2020). Plasticity and transfer in the sound system: Exposure to syllables in production or perception changes their subsequent production. *Language, Cognition and Neuroscience*, *35*(10), 1371–1393. 10.1080/23273798.2020.1782445

Bybee, J. (2001). Frequency effects on French liaison. *Frequency and the Emergence of Linguistic Structure*, 337–360. DOI: 10.1075/tsl.45.17byb

Bybee, J. (2007). *Frequency of Use and the Organization of Language*. Oxford University Press. http://www.oxfordscholarship.com/view/10.1093/acprof:oso/9780195301571.001.0001/acprof-9780195301571-chapter-10

Carreiras, M., Alvarez, C. J., & Devega, M. (1993). Syllable Frequency and Visual Word Recognition in Spanish. *Journal of Memory and Language*, *32*(6), 766–780. 10.1006/jmla.1993.1038

Carreiras, M., Mechelli, A., & Price, C. J. (2006). Effect of Word and Syllable Frequency on Activation During Lexical Decision and Reading Aloud. *Human Brain Mapping*, *27*(12), 963–972. 10.1002/hbm.20236

Carreiras, M., & Perea, M. (2004). Naming pseudowords in Spanish: Effects of syllable frequency. *Brain and Language*, *90*(1–3), 393–400. 10.1016/j.bandl.2003.12.003

Chen, J.-Y. (2000). Syllable errors from naturalistic slips of the tongue in Mandarin Chinese. *Psychologia: An International Journal of Psychology in the Orient, 43*(1), 15–26.

Chen, J.-Y., Chen, T.-M., & Dell, G. S. (2002). Word-form encoding in Mandarin Chinese as assessed by the implicit priming task. *Journal of Memory and Language, 46*(4), 751–781. 10.1006/jmla.2001.2825

Cholin, J., & Levelt, W. J. M. (2009). Effects of syllable preparation and syllable frequency in speech production: Further evidence for syllabic units at a post-lexical level. *Language and Cognitive Processes, 24*(5), 662–684. 10.1080/01690960802348852

Cholin, J., Levelt, W., & Schiller, N. (2006). Effects of Syllable Frequency in Speech Production. *Cognition, 99*(2), 205–235.

Chomsky, N., & Halle, M. (1968). *The sound pattern of English.* Harper & Row.

Costa, A., & Caramazza, A. (2002). The Production of Noun Phrases in English and Spanish: Implications for the Scope of Phonological Encoding in Speech Production. *Journal of Memory and Language, 46*(1), 178–198. 10.1006/jmla.2001.2804

Crompton, A. (1982). Syllables and segments in speech production. In *Slips of the tongue and language production* (A. Cutler, pp. 109–162). Mouton de Gruyter.

Croot, K., Lalas, G., Biedermann, B., Rastle, K., Jones, K., & Cholin, J. (2017). Syllable frequency effects in immediate but not delayed syllable naming in English. *Language, Cognition and Neuroscience, 32*(9), 1119–1132. 10.1080/23273798.2017. 1284340

Croot, K., & Rastle, K. (2004). Is there a syllabary containing stored articulatory plans for speech production in English. Proceedings of the *10th Australian International Conference on Speech Science and Technology,* 376–381.

Cutler, A. (1984). Stress and Accent in Language Production and Understanding. In D. Gibbon & H. Richter (Eds.), *Intonation, Accent and Rhythm.* DE GRUYTER. 10.1515/9783110863239.77

Damian, M. F., & Dumay, N. (2007). Time pressure and phonological advance planning in spoken production. *Journal of Memory and Language, 57*(2), 195–209. 10.1016/j.jml.2 006.11.001

Dell, G. S. (1986). A spreading-activation theory of retrieval in sentence production. *Psychological Review, 93*(3), 283–321.

Dell, G. S. (1988). The retrieval of phonological forms in production: Tests of predictions from a connectionist model. *Journal of Memory and Language, 27*(2), 124–142. 10.1016/ 0749-596X(88)90070-8

Dell, G. S., Reed, K. D., Adams, D. R., & Meyer, A. S. (2000). Speech errors, phonotactic constraints, and implicit learning: A study of the role of experience in language production. *Journal of Experimental Psychology. Learning, Memory, and Cognition, 26*(6), 1355–1367. 10.1037//0278-7393.26.6.1355

Dufour, S., & Nguyen, N. (2013). How much imitation is there in a shadowing task? *Frontiers in Psychology, 4.* http://www.ncbi.nlm.nih.gov/pmc/articles/PMC3689145/

Ernestus, M., Lahey, M., Verhees, F., & Baayen, R. H. (2006). Lexical frequency and voice assimilation. *The Journal of the Acoustical Society of America, 120*(2), 1040–1051. 10.1121/ 1.2211548

Ferrand, L., Segui, J., & Grainger, J. (1996). Masked Priming of Word and Picture Naming: The Role of Syllabic Units. *Journal of Memory and Language, 35*(5), 708–723. 10.1006/ jmla.1996.0037

Ferrand, L., Segui, J., & Humphreys, G. W. (1997). The syllable's role in word naming. *Memory & Cognition, 25*(4), 458–470. 10.3758/BF03201122

Ferreira, F., & Swets, B. (2002). How Incremental Is Language Production? Evidence from the Production of Utterances Requiring the Computation of Arithmetic Sums. *Journal of Memory and Language*, *46*(1), 57–84. 10.1006/jmla.2001.2797

Fink, A., & Goldrick, M. (2015). The Influence of Word Retrieval and Planning on Phonetic Variation: Implications for Exemplar Models. *Linguistics Vanguard: Multimodal Online Journal*, *1*(1), 215–225. 10.1515/lingvan-2015-1003

Fromkin, V. (1971). The non-anomalous nature of anomalous utterances. *Language*, *47*, 27–52.

Gafos, A. I., & Benus, S. (2006). Dynamics of phonological cognition. *Cognitive Science*, *30*(5), 905–943. 10.1207/s15516709cog0000_80

Gafos, A., & van Lieshout, P. (2020). Editorial: Models and Theories of Speech Production. *Frontiers in Psychology*, *11*. 10.3389/fpsyg.2020.01238

Gahl, S. (2008). Time and Thyme Are not Homophones: The Effect of Lemma Frequency on Word Durations in Spontaneous Speech. *Language*, *84*(3), 474–496. 10.1353/lan.0.0035

Garrett, M. F. (1980). Levels of processing in sentence production. In B. Butterworth, *Language production* (Academic Press., Vol. 1, pp. 177–220).

Goldinger, S. D. (1998). Echoes of echoes? An episodic theory of lexical access. *Psychological Review*, *105*(2), 251–279.

Goldinger, S. D., & Azuma, T. (2004). Episodic memory reflected in printed word naming. *Psychonomic Bulletin & Review*, *11*(4), 716–722. 10.3758/BF03196625

Goldrick, M. (2004). Phonological features and phonotactic constraints in speech production. *Journal of Memory and Language*, *51*(4), 586–603. 10.1016/j.jml.2004.07.004

Goldrick, M. (2006). Limited interaction in speech production: Chronometric, speech error, and neuropsychological evidence. *Language and Cognitive Processes*, *21*(7–8), 817–855. 10.1080/01690960600824112

Goldrick, M. (2011). Linking Speech Errors and Generative Phonological Theory. *Linguistics and Language Compass*, *5*(6), 397–412. 10.1111/j.1749-818X.2011.00282.x

Goldrick, M. (2014). Phonological Processing. In *The Oxford Handbook of Language Production (M. Goldrick, V. Ferreira, M. Miozzo)*. Oxford University Press. http://www.oxfordhandbooks.com/view/10.1093/oxfordhb/9780199735471.001.0001/oxfordhb-9780199735471-e-015

Goldrick, M., & Blumstein, S. E. (2006). Cascading activation from phonological planning to articulatory processes: Evidence from tongue twisters. *Language and Cognitive Processes*, *21*(6), 649–683. 10.1080/01690960500181332

Goldrick, M., & Larson, M. (2008). Phonotactic probability influences speech production. *Cognition*, *107*(3), 1155–1164. 10.1016/j.cognition.2007.11.009

Goldrick, M., Ross Baker, H., Murphy, A., & Baese-Berk, M. (2011). Interaction and representational integration: Evidence from speech errors. *Cognition*, *121*(1), 58–72. 10.1016/j.cognition.2011.05.006

Goldstein, L., Pouplier, M., Chen, L., Saltzman, E., & Byrd, D. (2007). Dynamic action units slip in speech production errors. *Cognition*, *103*(3), 386–412. 10.1016/j.cognition.2006.05.010

Griffin, Z. M. (2001). Gaze durations during speech reflect word selection and phonological encoding. *Cognition*, *82*(1), B1–B14.

Griffin, Z. M., & Bock, K. (2000). What the eyes say about speaking. *Psychological Science*, *11*(4), 274–279.

Guenther, F. H. (2016). *Neural Control of Speech*. MIT Press.

Hawkins, S. (2003). Roles and representations of systematic fine phonetic detail in speech understanding. *Journal of Phonetics, 31*(3–4), 373–405. 10.1016/j.wocn.2003.09.006

Hendrix, P., Bolger, P., & Baayen, H. (2016). Distinct ERP Signatures of Word Frequency, Phrase Frequency, and Prototypicality in Speech Production. *Journal of Experimental Psychology. Learning, Memory, and Cognition.* 10.1037/a0040332

Herrmann, F., Whiteside, S. P., & Cunningham, S. (2008). An acoustic investigation into coarticulation and speech motor control: High vs. low frequency syllables. *Proceedings of Meetings on Acoustics, 4*(1), 060007. 10.1121/1.3085742

Hickok, G. (2014). The architecture of speech production and the role of the phoneme in speech processing. *Language, Cognition and Neuroscience, 29*(1), 2–20. 10.1080/01 690965.2013.834370

Hinskens, F. (2011). "Lexicon, phonology and phonetics. Or: Rule-based and usage-based approaches to phonological variation". In *Linguistic Universals and Language Variation* (P. Siemund, pp. 416–456). Mouton de Gruyter.

Indefrey, P. (2011). The Spatial and Temporal Signatures of Word Production Components: A Critical Update. *Frontiers in Psychology, 2.* 10.3389/fpsyg.2011.00255

Indefrey, P., & Levelt, W. J. M. (2004). The spatial and temporal signatures of word production components. *Cognition, 92*(1–2), 101–144. 10.1016/j.cognition.2002.06.001

Ivanova, I., & Ferreira, V. S. (2019). The role of working memory for syntactic formulation in language production. *Journal of Experimental Psychology: Learning, Memory, and Cognition, 45*(10), 1791–1814. 10.1037/xlm0000672

Jeong, H., van den Hoven, E., Madec, S., & Bürki, A. (2021). Behavioral and Brain Responses Highlight the Role of Usage in the Preparation of Multiword Utterances for Production. *Journal of Cognitive Neuroscience, 33*(11), 2231–2264. 10.1162/jocn_a_01757

Jescheniak, J. D., & Levelt, W. J. M. (1994). Word frequency effects in speech production: Retrieval of syntactic information and of phonological form. *Journal of Experimental Psychology: Learning, Memory, and Cognition, 20*(4), 824–843. 10.1037/0278-7393.20.4.824.

Johnson, K. (1997). Speech perception without speaker normalization: An exemplar model. In *Talker Variability in Speech Processing* (K. Johnson & W. Mullennix, pp. 145–165). Academic Press.

Jurafsky, D., Bell, A., Gregory, M., & Raymond, W. D. (2000). Probabilistic relations between words: Evidence from reduction in lexical production. In J. Bybee, & P. Hopper (Eds.), *Frequency and the emergence of linguistic Structure* (pp. 229–254). John Benjamins.

Kawamoto, A. H., Kello, C. T., Jones, R., & Bame, K. (1998). Initial phoneme versus whole-word criterion to initiate pronunciation: Evidence based on response latency and initial phoneme duration. *Journal of Experimental Psychology: Learning, Memory, and Cognition, 24*(4), 862–885. 10.1037/0278-7393.24.4.862

Kawamoto, A. H., Liu, Q., & Kello, C. T. (2015). The segment as the minimal planning unit in speech production and reading aloud: Evidence and implications. *Frontiers in Psychology, 0.* 10.3389/fpsyg.2015.01457

Kawamoto, A. H., Liu, Q., Lee, R. J., & Grebe, P. R. (2014). The segment as the minimal planning unit in speech production: Evidence based on absolute response latencies. *Quarterly Journal of Experimental Psychology (2006), 67*(12), 2340–2359. 10.1080/1747021 8.2014.927892

Kearney, E., & Guenther, F. H. (2019). Articulating: The neural mechanisms of speech production. *Language, Cognition and Neuroscience, 34*(9), 1214–1229. 10.1080/23273798. 2019.1589541

Kilbourn-Ceron, O., & Goldrick, M. (2021). Variable pronunciations reveal dynamic intra-speaker variation in speech planning. *Psychonomic Bulletin & Review*. 10.3758/s13423-021-01886-0

Kirchner, R., Moore, R. K., & Chen, T.-Y. (2010). Computing phonological generalization over real speech exemplars. *Journal of Phonetics*, *38*(4), 540–547. 10.1016/j.wocn.2010.07.005

Kittredge, A. K., & Dell, G. S. (2016). Learning to speak by listening: Transfer of phonotactics from perception to production. *Journal of Memory and Language*, *89*, 8–22. 10.1016/j.jml.2015.08.001

Klaus, J., Mädebach, A., Oppermann, F., & Jescheniak, J. D. (2017). Planning sentences while doing other things at the same time: Effects of concurrent verbal and visuospatial working memory load. *Quarterly Journal of Experimental Psychology (2006)*, *70*(4), 811–831. 10.1080/17470218.2016.1167926

Kraljic, T., Brennan, S. E., & Samuel, A. G. (2008). Accommodating Variation: Dialects, Idiolects, and Speech Processing. *Cognition*, *107*(1), 54–81. 10.1016/j.cognition.2007.07.013

Krause, P. A., & Kawamoto, A. H. (2020). On the timing and coordination of articulatory movements: Historical perspectives and current theoretical challenges. *Language and Linguistics Compass*, *14*(6), e12373. 10.1111/lnc3.12373

Laganaro, M. (2005). Syllable frequency effect in speech production: Evidence from aphasia. *Journal of Neurolinguistics*, *18*(3), 221–235. 10.1016/j.jneuroling.2004.12.001

Laganaro, M. (2019). Phonetic encoding in utterance production: A review of open issues from 1989 to 2018. *Language, Cognition and Neuroscience*, *34*(9), 1193–1201. 10.1080/23273798.2019.1599128

Laganaro, M., & Alario, F.-X. (2006). On the locus of the syllable frequency effect in speech production. *Journal of Memory and Language*, *55*(2), 178–196. 10.1016/j.jml.2006.05.001

Laganaro, M., Croisier, M., Bagou, O., & Assal, F. (2012). Progressive apraxia of speech as a window into the study of speech planning processes. *Cortex; a Journal Devoted to the Study of the Nervous System and Behavior*, *48*(8), 963–971. 10.1016/j.cortex.2011.03.010

Laganaro, M., Python, G., & Toepel, U. (2013). Dynamics of phonological–phonetic encoding in word production: Evidence from diverging ERPs between stroke patients and controls. *Brain and Language*, *126*(2), 123–132. 10.1016/j.bandl.2013.03.004

Levelt, W. (1989). *Speaking: From intention to Articulation*. MIT Press.

Levelt, W. J. (1992). Accessing words in speech production: Stages, processes and re-presentations. *Cognition*, *42*(1–3), 1–22.

Levelt, W. J., Roelofs, A., & Meyer, A. S. (1999). A theory of lexical access in speech production. *The Behavioral and Brain Sciences*, *22*(1), 1–38; discussion 38-75.

Levelt, W. J., & Wheeldon, L. (1994). Do speakers have access to a mental syllabary? *Cognition*, *50*(1–3), 239–269.

Lupker, S. J. (1979). The semantic nature of response competition in the picture-word interference task. *Memory & Cognition*, *7*(6), 485–495. 10.3758/BF03198265

MacKay, D. G. (1972). The structure of words and syllables: Evidence from errors in speech. *Cognitive Psychology*, *3*(2), 210–227. 10.1016/0010-0285(72)90004-7

MacKay, D. G. (1987). *The organization of perception and action: A theory for language and other cognitive skills*. Springer-Verlag.

Martin, R. C., Crowther, J. E., Knight, M., Tamborello, F. P., & Yang, C.-L. (2010). Planning in sentence production: Evidence for the phrase as a default planning scope. *Cognition*, *116*(2), 177–192. 10.1016/j.cognition.2010.04.010

Martin, R. C., Yan, H., & Schnur, T. T. (2014). Working memory and planning during sentence production. *Acta Psychologica, 152*, 120–132. 10.1016/j.actpsy.2014.08.006

Meyer, A. S. (1990). The time course of phonological encoding in language production: The encoding of successive syllables of a word. *Journal of Memory and Language, 29*(5), 524–545. 10.1016/0749-596X(90)90050-A

Meyer, A. S. (1991). The time course of phonological encoding in language production: Phonological encoding inside a syllable. *Journal of Memory and Language, 30*(1), 69–89. 10.1016/0749-596X(91)90011-8

Meyer, A. S. (1992). Investigation of phonological encoding through speech error analyses: Achievements, limitations, and alternatives. *Cognition, 42*(1–3), 181–211. 10.1016/0010-0277(92)90043-h

Meyer, A. S., Roelofs, A., & Levelt, W. J. M. (2003). Word length effects in object naming: The role of a response criterion. *Journal of Memory and Language, 48*(1), 131–147. 10.1016/S0749-596X(02)00509-0

Michel Lange, V., & Laganaro, M. (2014). Inter-subject variability modulates phonological advance planning in the production of adjective-noun phrases. *Language Sciences, 5*, 43. 10.3389/fpsyg.2014.00043

Miozzo, M., Pulvermüller, F., & Hauk, O. (2014). Early Parallel Activation of Semantics and Phonology in Picture Naming: Evidence from a Multiple Linear Regression MEG Study. *Cerebral Cortex (New York, N.Y.: 1991).* 10.1093/cercor/bhu137

Möller, J., Jansma, B. M., Rodriguez-Fornells, A., & Münte, T. F. (2007). What the Brain Does before the Tongue Slips. *Cerebral Cortex, 17*(5), 1173–1178. 10.1093/cercor/bhl028

Monaco, E., Cheneval, P. P., & Laganaro, M. (2017). Facilitation and interference of phoneme repetition and phoneme similarity in speech production. *Language, Cognition and Neuroscience, 32*(5), 650–660. 10.1080/23273798.2016.1257730

Mousikou, P., Roon, K. D., & Rastle, K. (2015). Masked primes activate feature representations in reading aloud. *Journal of Experimental Psychology: Learning, Memory, and Cognition, 41*(3), 636–649. 10.1037/xlm0000072

Munding, D., Dubarry, A.-S., & Alario, F.-X. (2015). On the cortical dynamics of word production: A review of the MEG evidence. *Language, Cognition and Neuroscience, 0*(0), 1–22. 10.1080/23273798.2015.1071857

Munson, B., & Solomon, N. P. (2004). The effect of phonological neighborhood density on vowel articulation. *Journal of Speech, Language, and Hearing Research: JSLHR, 47*(5), 1048–1058.

Niebuhr, O., Clayards, M., Meunier, C., & Lancia, L. (2011). On place assimilation in sibilant sequences—Comparing French and English. *Journal of Phonetics, 39*(3), 429–451. 10.1016/j.wocn.2011.04.003

Nielsen, K. (2011). Specificity and abstractness of VOT imitation. *Journal of Phonetics, 39*(2), 132–142. 10.1016/j.wocn.2010.12.007

Nolan, F. (1992). The descriptive role of segments: Evidence from assimilation. *Papers in Laboratory Phonology II: Gesture, Segment, Prosody*, 261–280. http://idiom.ucsd.edu/~arvaniti/Nolan1992.pdf

Oldfield, R. C., & Wingfield, A. (1965). Response latencies in naming objects. *Quarterly Journal of Experimental Psychology, 17*(4), 273–281. 10.1080/17470216508416445

Onnis, L., & Huettig, F. (2021). Can prediction and retrodiction explain whether frequent multi-word phrases are accessed "precompiled" from memory or compositionally constructed on the fly? *Brain Research, 1772*, 147674. 10.1016/j.brainres.2021.147674

Oppermann, F., Jescheniak, J. D., & Schriefers, H. (2010). Phonological advance planning in sentence production. *Journal of Memory and Language, 63*(4), 526–540. 10.1016/j.jml. 2010.07.004

O'Seaghdha, P. G., Chen, J.-Y., & Chen, T.-M. (2010). Proximate units in word production: Phonological encoding begins with syllables in Mandarin Chinese but with segments in English. *Cognition, 115*(2), 282–302. 10.1016/j.cognition.2010. 01.001

Papoutsi, M., de Zwart, J. A., Jansma, J. M., Pickering, M. J., Bednar, J. A., & Horwitz, B. (2009). From Phonemes to Articulatory Codes: An fMRI Study of the Role of Broca's Area in Speech Production. *Cerebral Cortex (New York, NY), 19*(9), 2156–2165. 10.1093/ cercor/bhn239

Pardo, J. S. (2006). On phonetic convergence during conversational interaction. *The Journal of the Acoustical Society of America, 119*(4), 2382–2393.

Pardo, J. S., Jay, I. C., & Krauss, R. M. (2010). Conversational role influences speech imitation. *Attention, Perception & Psychophysics, 72,* 2254–2264.

Pardo, J. S., Urmanche, A., Wilman, S., & Wiener, J. (2017). Phonetic convergence across multiple measures and model talkers. *Attention, Perception, & Psychophysics, 79*(2), 637–659. 10.3758/s13414-016-1226-0

Parrell, B., Lammert, A. C., Ciccarelli, G., & Quatieri, T. F. (2019). Current models of speech motor control: A control-theoretic overview of architectures and properties. *The Journal of the Acoustical Society of America, 145*(3), 1456–1481. 10.1121/1.5092807

Perea, M., & Carreiras, M. (1998). Effects of syllable frequency and syllable neighborhood frequency in visual word recognition. *Journal of Experimental Psychology: Human Perception and Performance, 24*(1), 134–144. 10.1037/0096-1523.24.1.134

Perret, C., Bonin, P., & Méot, A. (2006). Syllabic Priming Effects in Picture Naming in French. *Experimental Psychology, 53*(2), 95. 10.1027/1618-3169.53.2.95

Pierrehumbert, J. B. (2002). Word-specific phonetics. *Laboratory Phonology* 7. Berlin: Mouton de Gruyter, 101–139.

Pierrehumbert, J., Beckman, M., & Ladd, D. R. (2000). Conceptual Foundations of Phonology as a Laboratory Science. In *Phonological Knowledge* (Burton-Roberts, P. Carr, and G. Docherty, pp. 273–303). Oxford University Press.

Pluymaekers, M., Ernestus, M., & Baayen, R. H. (2005). Lexical frequency and acoustic reduction in spoken Dutch. *The Journal of the Acoustical Society of America, 118*(4), 2561–2569.

Port, R. (2007). How are words stored in memory? Beyond phones and phonemes. *New Ideas in Psychology, 25*(2), 143–170. 10.1016/j.newideapsych.2007.02.001

Posnansky, C. J., & Rayner, K. (1977). Visual-feature and response components in a picture-word interference task with beginning and skilled readers. *Journal of Experimental Child Psychology, 24*(3), 440–460. 10.1016/0022-0965(77)90090-X

Pouplier, M., & Goldstein, L. (2010). Intention in Articulation: Articulatory Timing in Alternating Consonant Sequences and Its Implications for Models of Speech Production. *Language and Cognitive Processes, 25*(5), 616–649. 10.1080/01690960903395380

Racine, I., & Grosjean, F. (2002). La production du E caduc facultatif est-elle prévisible? Un début de réponse. *Journal of French Language Studies, 12*(03), 307–326. 10.1017/S095 9269502000340

Rapp, B., Buchwald, A., & Goldrick, M. (2014). Integrating accounts of speech production: The devil is in the representational details. *Language, Cognition and Neuroscience, 29*(1), 24–27. 10.1080/01690965.2013.848991

Rayner, K., & Posnansky, C. (1978). Stages of processing in word identification. *Journal of Experimental Psychology: General*, *107*(1), 64–80. 10.1037/0096-3445.107.1.64

Rialland, A., Ridouane, R., & Hulst, H. van der. (2015). Features in Phonology and Phonetics: The contributions of George N. Clements. In *Features in Phonology and Phonetics* (pp. 3–16). De Gruyter Mouton. https://www.degruyter.com/document/doi/10.1515/9783110399981-004/html

Riecker, A., Brendel, B., Ziegler, W., Erb, M., & Ackermann, H. (2008). The influence of syllable onset complexity and syllable frequency on speech motor control. *Brain and Language*, *107*(2), 102–113. 10.1016/j.bandl.2008.01.008

Roelofs, A. (1997). The WEAVER Model of Word-Form Encoding in Speech Production. *Cognition*, *64*(3), 249–284.

Roelofs, A. (1999). Phonological Segments and Features as Planning Units in Speech Production. *Language and Cognitive Processes*, *14*(2), 173–200. 10.1080/016909699386338

Roelofs, A. (2014). Integrating psycholinguistic and motor control approaches to speech production: Where do they meet? *Language, Cognition and Neuroscience*, *29*(1), 35–37. 10.1080/01690965.2013.852687

Saltzman, E. L., & Munhall, K. G. (1989). A dynamical approach to gestural patterning in speech production. *Ecological Psychology*, *1*(4), 333–382. 10.1207/s15326969eco0104_2

Scarborough, R. (2010). Lexical and contextual predictability: Confluent effects on the production of vowels. *Laboratory Phonology*, *10*, 557–586.

Schiller, N. O. (2000). Single word production in English: The role of subsyllabic units during phonological encoding. *Journal of Experimental Psychology. Learning, Memory, and Cognition*, *26*(2), 512–528.

Schiller, N. O., Costa, A., & Colomé, A. (2008). Phonological encoding of single words: In search of the lost syllable. In *Laboratory Phonology 7* (pp. 35–60). De Gruyter Mouton. https://www.degruyter.com/document/doi/10.1515/9783110197105.1.35/html

Schnur, T. T. (2011). Phonological planning during sentence production: Beyond the verb. *Language Sciences*, *2*, 319. 10.3389/fpsyg.2011.00319

Schriefers, H. (1999). Phonological Facilitation in the Production of Two-word Utterances. *European Journal of Cognitive Psychology*, *11*(1), 17–50. 10.1080/713752301

Schweitzer, A., & Möbius, B. (2004). *Exemplar-based production of prosody: Evidence from segment and syllable durations*. Speech Prosody, Nara, Japan.

Shattuck-Hufnagel, S. (1979). Speech errors as evidence for a serial-ordering mechanism in sentence production. In *Sentence processing: Psycholinguistic studies presented to Merrill Garrett* (W. E. Cooper & E. C. T. Walker.). Erlbaum.

Shockley, K., Sabadini, L., & Fowler, C. A. (2004). Imitation in shadowing words. *Perception & Psychophysics*, *66*(3), 422–429. 10.3758/BF03194890

Snoeren, N. D., Hallé, P. A., & Segui, J. (2006). A voice for the voiceless: Production and perception of assimilated stops in French. *Journal of Phonetics*, *34*(2), 241–268. 10.1016/j.wocn.2005.06.001

Spalek, K., Bock, K., & Schriefers, H. (2010). A purple giraffe is faster than a purple elephant: Inconsistent phonology affects determiner selection in English. *Cognition*, *114*(1), 123–128. 10.1016/j.cognition.2009.09.011

Stemberger, J. (1990). Wordshape errors in language production. *Cognition*. 10.1016/0010-0277(90)90012-9

Strijkers, K., Costa, A., & Pulvermüller, F. (2017). The cortical dynamics of speaking: Lexical and phonological knowledge simultaneously recruit the frontal and temporal cortex within 200 ms. *NeuroImage*, *163*, 206–219. 10.1016/j.neuroimage.2017.09.041

Strijkers, K., Costa, A., & Thierry, G. (2010). Tracking Lexical Access in Speech Production: Electrophysiological Correlates of Word Frequency and Cognate Effects. *Cerebral Cortex*, *20*(4), 912–928. 10.1093/cercor/bhp153

Vousden, J. I., Brown, G. D., & Harley, T. A. (2000). Serial control of phonology in speech production: A hierarchical model. *Cognitive Psychology*, *41*(2), 101–175. 10.1006/cogp.2000.0739

Warker, J. A., & Dell, G. S. (2006). Speech errors reflect newly learned phonotactic constraints. *Journal of Experimental Psychology. Learning, Memory, and Cognition*, *32*(2), 387–398. 10.1037/0278-7393.32.2.387

Warker, J. A., Xu, Y., Dell, G. S., & Fisher, C. (2009). Speech errors reflect the phonotactic constraints in recently spoken syllables, but not in recently heard syllables. *Cognition*, *112*(1), 81–96. 10.1016/j.cognition.2009.03.009

Wheeldon, L., & Lahiri, A. (1997). Prosodic Units in Speech Production. *Journal of Memory and Language*, *37*(3), 356–381. 10.1006/jmla.1997.2517

Wood, S. A. J. (1996). Assimilation or coarticulation? Evidence from the temporal coordination of tongue gestures for the palatalization of Bulgarian alveolar stops. *Journal of Phonetics*, *24*(1), 139–164. 10.1006/jpho.1996.0009

Wright, R. A. (2004). Factors of lexical competition in vowel articulation. In J. Local, R. Ogden, & R. Temple (Eds.), *Phonetic interpretation* (pp. 75–87). Cambridge University Press. 10.1017/CBO9780511486425.005

Wright, S., & Kerswill, P. (1989). Electropalatography in the analysis of connected speech processes. *Clinical Linguistics & Phonetics*, *3*(1), 49–57. 10.3109/02699208908985270

Ziegler, P. D. W. (2009). Modelling the architecture of phonetic plans: Evidence from apraxia of speech. *Language and Cognitive Processes*, *24*(5), 631–661. 10.1080/01 690960802327989

Ziegler, W. (2014). The rhythmic organisation of speech gestures and the sense of it. *Language, Cognition and Neuroscience*, *29*(1), 38–40. 10.1080/01690965.2013.849810

Appendix 1. Studies entered in the preliminary meta-analysis of the syllable frequency effect

Paper	Experiment
Bürki et al. (2015)	Experiment 1
Bürki et al. (2020)	Experiment 1
Levelt and Wheeldon (1994)	Experiment 1
	Experiment 2 – 1st syllable
	Experiment 2 – 2nd syllable
	Experiment 3
Laganaro and Alario (2006)	Experiment 1
	Experiment 3
Croot et al. (2017)	Experiment 3
Cholin et al. (2009)	Experiment 3
Cholin et al. (2006)	Experiment 1
Croot and Rastle (2004)	Experiment 3
Carreiras and Perea (2004)	Experiment 1 – 1st syllable
	Experiment 2 – 1st syllable

(*Continued*)

Paper	Experiment
	Experiment 1 – 2nd syllable
	Experiment 2 – 2nd syllable
Perea and Carreiras (1998)	Experiment 2
Carreiras et al. (1993)	Experiment 2
	Experiment 4 – words
	Experiment 4 – nonwords
	Experiment 5 – words
	Experiment 5 – nonwords

Appendix 2. Funnel plot with studies included in a preliminary meta-analysis of the syllable frequency effect

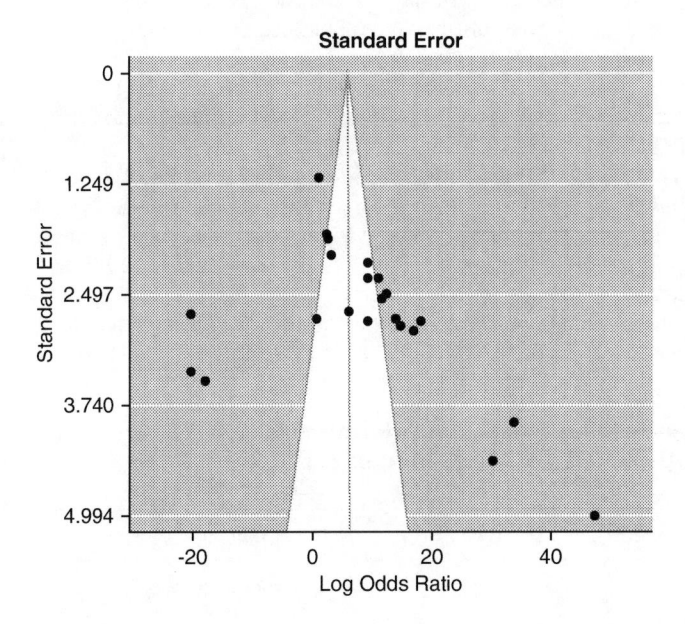

4 The Neural Organization of Language Production

Evidence from Neuroimaging and Neuromodulation

Greig I. de Zubicaray

Our knowledge of the neural mechanisms responsible for language production has improved considerably since 1861, when Paul Broca first proposed that the foot of the third left frontal convolution (i.e., Broca's area) was the centre for "articulated language." In the century following Broca, aphasiologists characterized the neural mechanisms of production primarily in terms of motor and auditory regions connected via a single dorsal white matter pathway (e.g., Geschwind, 1979). Progress from this modest base accelerated in the mid-to-late 1990s when non-invasive neuroimaging and neuromodulation (i.e., brain stimulation) techniques were developed and applied to production research (de Zubicaray & Schiller, 2019; Kemmerer, 2019). The accumulation of new knowledge afforded by these techniques resulted in the obsolescence of the classical Broca-Wernicke-Geschwind model of the neurobiology of language (e.g., Tremblay & Dick, 2016).

Despite the advances, this new knowledgebase does have some limitations. The overwhelming majority of neuroimaging and neuromodulation studies have targeted single word production, so there is currently relatively little evidence available concerning the neurobiology of sentence/narrative production or production in social/conversational contexts. This situation reflects both the constraints of designing psycholinguistic manipulations to target specific production components as well as the limitations of the technologies themselves. The movements that produce continuous overt speech can introduce artefacts that compromise the validity of functional magnetic resonance imaging (fMRI) and near infrared spectroscopy (fNIRS) techniques based on haemodynamic signals, while safety considerations and the temporary nature of neuromodulatory effects limit the scope of those experiments (for an overview, see de Zubicaray & Piai, 2019). Although fMRI has relatively poor temporal resolution compared to electrophysiological recordings, it does provide superior spatial resolution. In addition, neuromodulation with online non-invasive transcranial magnetic stimulation (TMS) protocols can support causal inferences about the involvement of critical cortical regions, as can lesion-symptom mapping (LSM) approaches. Further, TMS can support causal inferences about chronometric or time-course information with respect to

DOI: 10.4324/9781003145790-5

production stages that electrophysiology recordings cannot. Hence, these methods provide complementary "where and when" information. Box 4.1 provides an overview of how each of the neuroimaging and neuromodulation techniques afford inferences about the neurobiology of language production.

This chapter will review the neuroimaging and neuromodulation evidence that demonstrates how our ability to produce spoken, written, and signed words relies upon a predominantly left-hemisphere network of cortical and subcortical brain regions. The first section provides an overview of the neural mechanisms engaged by the intention to communicate up to and including motor output for spoken production, followed by written and signed production. The second section is devoted to neural mechanisms engaged by the interaction of language specific and domain general monitoring and control mechanisms during production. This is followed by an overview of the white matter network architecture underlying production, i.e., its "connectome." I do not refer to studies using language comprehension tasks or findings from reviews and meta-analyses that combined data from both production and comprehension (e.g., Binder, 2015; Binder et al., 2009; cf. Kemmerer, 2019; Nozari, 2020), unless the latter used data/dimensionality reduction techniques such as principal component or factor analysis to identify shared components. This approach serves both to highlight the extent (and limits) of the current production evidence and avoid unsupported assumptions about identical re-presentations and mechanisms. Finally, I also eschew labels such as "Broca's and Wernicke's areas" in favour of anatomical specificity (e.g., Tremblay & Dick, 2016).

Box 4.1   Neuroimaging and neuromodulation techniques

The dependent variable in functional neuroimaging studies is usually a component of the brain's haemodynamic response to neural activity. In positron emission tomography (PET) investigations, a local increase in task-based neuronal activity is associated with an increase in regional cerebral blood flow (rCBF; e.g., Brownsett & Wise, 2010). fMRI studies typically measure the blood oxygen level dependent (BOLD) signal, although a measure of local cerebral perfusion can also be employed (i.e., rCBF). The BOLD signal reflects a change in the ratio of oxygenated (oxy-Hb) to deoxygenated blood (deoxy-Hb) that reaches its peak around four to six seconds following neuronal activation (Heim & Specht, 2019). fNIRS studies measure task-related changes in concentrations of oxy-Hb and/or deoxy-Hb via optical sensors placed on the scalp (Minagawa & Cristia, 2019). Whereas PET and fMRI studies achieve whole brain coverage at relatively high spatial resolution ($\sim$5 and $\sim$3 mm^3, respectively), fNIRS is only able to measure haemodynamic signals at the cortical surface ($\sim$1.5 cm^3).

Structural neuroimaging studies support inferences about functional brain architecture via correlating behaviour with grey and/or white matter tissue characteristics on MRI scans. In voxel- and surface-based morphometry (VBM and SBM) studies, the dependent variable is usually a measure of regional volume, grey matter density, cortical thickness, or surface area (e.g., de Zubicaray et al., 2011). Diffusion weighted imaging (DWI) sequences (Catani & Forkel, 2019) provide more precise measures of white matter tract integrity and connectivity, the latter determined via tractography algorithms. In patients with acute, focal brain injuries, lesion-symptom mapping (LSM) techniques allow determination of critical regions by correlating task performance (e.g., error rates) with lesioned voxels on brain images. However, LSM studies in brain tumour or chronic stroke patients are less helpful for drawing inferences about critical regions in healthy networks due to compensatory functional reorganization occurring over time (Karnath et al., 2020).

Non-invasive neuromodulation techniques include TMS and direct current stimulation (tDCS). Invasive direct electrical stimulation (DES) is only employed during surgical interventions, e.g., for brain tumours and epilepsy. Neuromodulation techniques afford inferences about critical brain regions via manipulating local neuronal excitation or inhibition to disrupt or facilitate task performance. To accomplish this, TMS uses a pulsed magnetic field to induce current flows in the brain via a coil placed over the scalp (Schuhmann, 2019). In tDCS, local electrical currents are induced via electrode placement on the scalp. With TMS and tDCS, stimulation may be applied online or offline (i.e., immediately prior to task performance). TMS is able to deliver relatively focal stimulation to the cortical surface (within ~2 cm) and for discrete (~50 ms) or longer periods. Conversely, tDCS diffuses through a large portion of brain tissue and may take several minutes to influence sustained task performance (Hartwigsen, 2014). As DES is applied in patients who are likely to have experienced reorganization of function due to tumour infiltration or seizure propagation, it is less suitable for drawing inferences about healthy cortical mechanisms, although sub-cortical connectivity is relatively preserved (Duffau, 2019).

Production stages and their neural mechanisms

There are two complementary approaches to researching the neurobiology of speech production. Broadly characterized, the *psycholinguistic* approach (e.g., Dell, 1986; Levelt, 1989; Roelofs & Ferreira, 2019) seeks to integrate knowledge about proposed cognitive architectures (i.e., representations and processing) while the *speech motor control* approach seeks to integrate knowledge about the coordination of auditory, somatosensory and motor systems with neural mechanisms (e.g., Guenther, 1995; Kearney & Guenther, 2019; Tremblay et al., 2019). The psycholinguistic approach is largely concerned with processing stages beginning with the formulation of a meaningful idea to communicate, the retrieval of the appropriate lexical-semantic representation from the mental lexicon and assembly of its sound units for production. The speech motor control approach is often described as commencing with the output from the latter stage and ending with articulation. It is primarily concerned with mapping the relevant speech sounds to a learned set of motor commands that guide articulation, ensuring the appropriate acoustic signal is produced. However, describing the two approaches in this linear manner omits areas where they converge, particularly with respect to self-monitoring and control mechanisms that I will address later in this chapter.

The greater proportion of neuroimaging and neuromodulatory studies of spoken word production have employed picture naming as an exemplar task, and this evidential bias is reflected in the sections below. These studies provide accuracy (speech error) and chronometric (speech latency) data informative for psycholinguistic/neurolinguistic accounts. Speech motor control studies have largely employed repetition and sequencing (e.g., word or syllable) tasks based on written or auditory input. The latter tasks also engage short-term or working memory mechanisms that may involve dedicated storage buffers or an interplay of comprehension and production mechanisms (for a review, see Schwering & MacDonald, 2020).

Conceptual preparation

Speaking commences with the preparation of a preverbal/prelexical conceptual representation or message to be expressed, and the information to be retrieved is typically characterized as being part of semantic memory. For early aphasiologists such as Lichtheim (1885), amodal conceptual representations were distributed throughout the cortex, abstracted away from the modality specific representations underlying perception and action. This perspective was mostly unchallenged until the end of the 20th century when new proposals about the structure of semantic memory began to gain prominence. One is that conceptual representations are instead grounded or *embodied* in the modality specific brain regions responsible for accomplishing perception and action (e.g., Barsalou, 2008, Gallese & Lakoff, 2005; Zwaan, 2004). However, there is comparatively little empirical work addressing conceptual preparation during production from an embodied perspective. Another is that amodal conceptual representations arise from connections with modality-specific regions via cross-modal processing in cortical "hubs" or "convergence zones." Evidence for these "hub-and-spokes" models has been amassed from both comprehension and production paradigms (for a review, see Lambon Ralph et al., 2017).

A large body of evidence from production paradigms supports a role for the left anterior temporal lobe (ATL) as a cortical hub for retrieving information

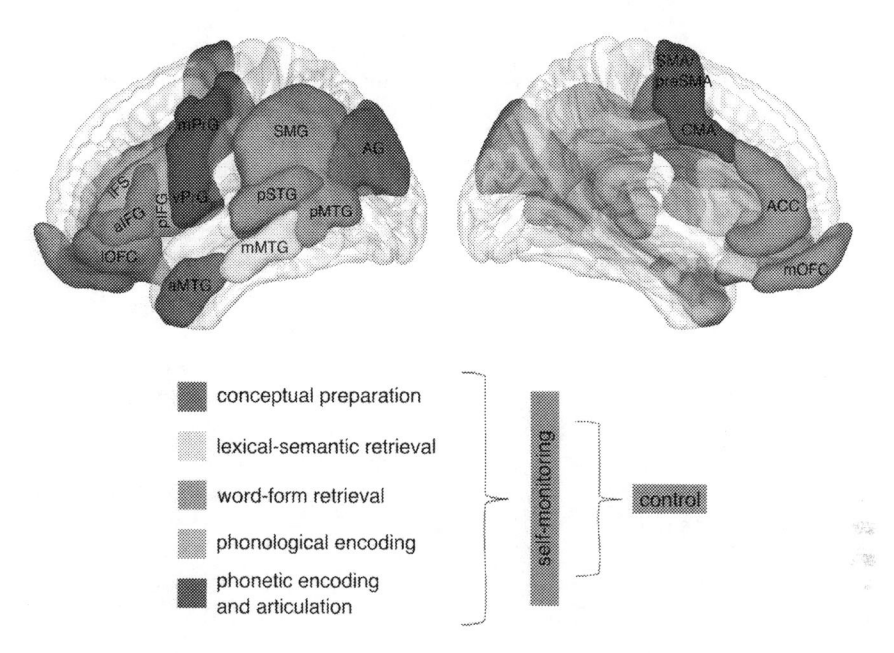

Figure 4.1 Brain regions reliably engaged during spoken word production processes across neuroimaging, neuromodulation and LSM studies, rendered on left lateral and medial cortical surfaces according to the parcellation scheme of Fan et al. (2016). lOFC, lateral orbitofrontal cortex; aIFG, anterior inferior frontal gyrus; IFS, inferior frontal sulcus; pIFG, posterior inferior frontal gyrus; aMTG, anterior middle temporal gyrus; mMTG, mid-middle temporal gyrus; pMTG, posterior middle temporal gyrus; pSTG, posterior superior temporal gyrus; AG, angular gyrus; SMG, supramarginal gyrus; vPrG, ventral precentral gyrus; mPrG, mid-precentral gyrus; SMA, supplementary motor area; CMA, cingulate motor area; ACC, anterior cingulate cortex; mOFC, medial orbitofrontal cortex.

from semantic memory (Figure 4.1). Early functional neuroimaging investigations with PET and fMRI reliably showed ATL activation during naming paradigms compared to high-level baseline tasks controlling for other production processes (Price et al., 2005). Some fMRI studies have targeted conceptual preparation using experimental manipulations. For example, Geranmayeh et al. (2015) employed picture description, a task that requires participants to retrieve facts about the attributes of a depicted object, in conjunction with functional connectivity analyses to demonstrate the ATL is part of the core brain network for production. The *negative priming* effect, whereby naming of a target object is slowed after it has been previously presented as a distractor to be ignored is generally assumed to have its locus in abstract conceptual representations (e.g., Tipper, 1985) and has been shown to elicit activity in the anterior portion of the middle temporal gyrus (MTG; e.g., de Zubicaray et al., 2006a). In addition, structural MRI studies show grey matter density in the left anterior MTG correlates with a common abstract or amodal conceptual component extracted from various production and comprehension paradigms in both healthy adults and neurologically impaired patients (e.g., Butler et al., 2014; de Zubicaray et al., 2011; Han et al., 2013; Mirman et al., 2015; see Kemmerer, 2019 for a review).

Several neuromodulation studies have provided evidence that the ATL is specifically engaged in conceptual preparation during picture naming via manipulations targeting semantic feature processing. Across TMS studies, the region for ATL stimulation was situated approximately 10 mm posterior from the tip of the temporal pole along the MTG. Pobric et al. (2007) reported slower naming of objects at the specific (e.g., *sparrow*) compared to basic level (e.g., *bird*), a task that places greater demand on semantic feature extraction. Woollams (2012) observed slower naming of objects that were low compared to high typicality concepts. Concept typicality is an important component of semantic representations reflecting strength of feature overlap among category exemplars (Rosch, 1975). Less typical exemplars share fewer features with other category coordinate members and overlap more with exemplars of other categories (Rosch & Mervis, 1975; e.g., an *apple* is more typical of the category of fruits, whereas an *olive* is less so). Finally, Chiou et al. (2014) reported that TMS to the ATL eliminated the colour con-gruency advantage in object naming (e.g., a yellow *lemon* is typically named faster than a red one). Using tDCS, Binney et al. (2018) found cathodal stimulation to the ATL increased gaze-fixation durations on key semantic features (e.g., the head of an animal) during picture naming compared to a pre-stimulation baseline.

Together, these results from neuromodulation studies strongly implicate the ATL in feature-driven conceptual preparation during production. They therefore lend support to proposals for decomposed semantic feature re-presentations in production models rather than non-decomposed lexical concepts (e.g., Dell et al., 1997; cf. Kemmerer, 2019). This is because de-compositional models assume accessing a word's semantic representation is a bottom-up process whereby single conceptual features of objects connect directly to lexical representations. Non-decompositional models assume that access to semantic representations is a top-down process, whereby whole lexical concepts are organized according to categorical nodes (e.g., Levelt et al., 1999; Roelofs, 1992). However, there is currently no evidence available from neuromodulation studies to inform us as to *when* the ATL becomes engaged during the production process. If Indefrey's (2011) proposed timecourse of production stages is accurate, then online TMS applied to the ATL for the first 175 ms from picture onset should slow selection of the target concept.

Another conceptual hub or convergence zone that has been proposed to be relevant for production is the left inferior parietal lobule (IPL), comprising the angular gyrus (AG), intraparietal sulcus (IPS), and the supramarginal gyrus (SMG). In his review, Indefrey (2011) considered this region to have an unclear role in production. The SMG is more consistently reported in studies of word form retrieval than conceptual preparation (see section next). For example, left AG and IPS (see Figure 4.1) are engaged by more complex verb argument structures and semantic interference during action naming in neu-roimaging studies (fMRI and LSM; e.g., de Zubicaray et al., 2017; den Ouden et al., 2019). In addition, TMS to the left IPS elicits anomic speech errors during action naming (Ntemou et al., 2021) and slows naming of highly versus non-manipulable objects (Pobric et al., 2010). A role for the left AG in the-matic speech errors during picture naming has been reported in LSM studies (e.g., *worm* for apple; Schwartz et al., 2011). In addition, the facilitated naming observed for thematically related (e.g., *cheese*-MOUSE) versus unrelated (e.g., *pram*-MOUSE) distractor words in the picture-word interference (PWI) paradigm is associated with left IPL/AG activity (e.g., Abel et al., 2012; de Zubicaray et al., 2013). In their PET study, Brownsett and Wise (2010) re-ported the AG was the only parietal region to play a role in mediating amodal representations across both spoken and written narrative production.

Finally, Indefrey (2016) suggested that conceptual preparation could involve motor regions, following from the proposals of grounded or embodied cog-nition accounts that attribute a role for these regions in action semantics (see Barsalou, 2020), in addition to their well-established role in motor pro-gramming for articulation (see the next section). However, TMS studies have consistently failed to observe effects of motor cortex stimulation on naming latencies when applied at 0, 100, or 300 ms after picture onset, placing the beginning of motor cortex engagement well past the conceptual preparation stage (Mottaghy et al., 2006; Töpper et al., 1998).

Lexical-semantic retrieval

Following conceptual preparation, conceptual representations are mapped to words (for a historical overview on theories of lexical access, see Chapter 2 of this volume). Many concepts can be active and so activate multiple entries in the mental lexicon, and this process ultimately culminates in the selection of the appropriate lexical candidate for production. Some theories propose decomposed semantic features or whole lexical concepts spread activation to *lemmas*, a type of mediating representation in declarative memory that codes conceptual and syntactic (e.g., word class and grammatical gender) re-presentations of a word but not its morpho-phonological characteristics (e.g., Levelt et al., 1999; see Roelofs & Ferreira, 2019), while others propose only one level of lexical representation, i.e., *lexemes* (e.g., Caramazza, 1997; Dell et al., 1997). Indefrey and Levelt's (2000, 2004) meta-analyses of neuroima-ging data were predicated on the lemma model (see also Kemmerer, 2019). Evidence from neuroimaging and neuromodulation studies largely supports a distinct stage of processing between conceptual preparation and the retrieval of a word's sound units for production, consistent with lemmas.

Indefrey and Levelt (2004; also Indefrey, 2011) reasoned that comparing picture naming with reading aloud of words and nonwords would assist with the identification of region(s) engaged by lexical-semantic retrieval, particularly because nonword reading engages all production stages excepting it. This process of elimination resulted in them ascribing the role to the left mid-portion of the MTG within a time-window of 200–290 ms. Thus far, only two TMS studies have targeted mid-MTG online during picture naming (Acheson et al., 2011; Schuhmann et al., 2012). Schumann et al. (2012) reported naming was slowed when stimulation was applied at 225 ms post onset, whereas Acheson et al. (2011) reported stimulation applied between 100 ms before and 200 ms after picture onset facilitated naming latencies. The latter result may reflect potentiation of local neural activity due to stimulation applied prior to picture presentation (see Luber & Lisanby, 2014).

Two LSM studies showed mid-MTG lesions are likely to be critical for lexical-semantic errors during naming after controlling for other production processes (Baldo et al., 2013; Walker et al., 2011). Multiple LSM studies have also implicated lesions in left mid-to-posterior MTG by contrasting semantic verbal fluency tasks requiring retrieval of category exemplars (e.g., animals) with letter/phonemic fluency tasks (Baldo et al., 2006; Biesbroek et al., 2021; Chouiter et al., 2016; Schmidt et al., 2019; Thye et al., 2021). Thus, the lesion evidence supports a critical role for the mid-MTG in lexical-semantic retrieval (Figure 4.1).[1]

Additional evidence for mid-to-posterior MTG involvement in lexical-semantic retrieval comes from multiple neuroimaging and neuromodulatory studies employing semantic context manipulations in experimental naming paradigms (for a detailed review, see de Zubicaray & Piai, 2019). These include but are not limited to the PWI (Rosinsky et al., 1975), continuous naming (Howard et al., 2006) and blocked cyclic naming paradigms (Kroll & Stewart, 1994). The principal finding is that naming latencies are slower in contexts comprising category coordinates (e.g., exemplars of *animals*) than in unrelated contexts that comprise exemplars selected from multiple categories (e.g., *animals, tools, vegetables, vehicles*, etc.), an effect termed *semantic interference*. Several of these studies also reported separate clusters in mid-MTG and pMTG, leading de Zubicaray and colleagues (2001, 2006b, 2013) to propose mid-to-pMTG activation during lexical semantic retrieval likely involves word forms of multiple lexical candidates being co-activated prior to selection, consistent with the architecture of cascaded/interactive production models (see the next section; e.g., Cutting & Ferreira, 1999; Dell & O'Seaghdha, 1992; Harley, 1993; Peterson & Savoy, 1998; Schade & Berg, 1992).

Several fMRI studies have also reported mid-posterior STG activation during semantic interference across various naming paradigms (e.g., Abel et al., 2012; de Zubicaray et al., 2006b, 2013; Hocking et al., 2009; Piai et al., 2013). While some suggest a role for the STG in lexical-semantic retrieval (e.g., Abel et al., 2012), alternative explanations for these findings invoke self-monitoring mechanisms (e.g., Hocking et al., 2009; Indefrey, 2011; Maess et al., 2002; see further sections). Piai et al. (2020) recently reported that applying TMS to pSTG did not influence the semantic interference effect in the PWI paradigm.

Other studies have also shown that TMS applied to pSTG at 0, 100, or 200 ms post picture onset does not influence picture naming latencies, indicating the region is unlikely to be engaged during the time-window established for conceptual preparation or lexical-semantic retrieval (Mottaghy et al., 2006; Schuhmann et al., 2012; Töpper et al., 1998).

Word-form retrieval

Indefrey (2011) ascribed a role for the posterior middle (pMTG) and superior temporal gyri (pSTG) in word form retrieval and suggested processing *from the first phoneme segment onwards* occurs between 290 and 370 ms after picture onset. However, he noted the duration of phonological code retrieval may extend well beyond the commencement of phonetic encoding as there is no reason to assume the latter process waits until all phonemes have been retrieved. Not surprisingly then, many neuroimaging studies targeting word-form retrieval also report engagement of regions implicated in phonetic encoding due to their relatively coarse temporal resolution (see the next section). Here, chronometric evidence from TMS is informative.

Some reviews (e.g., Binder, 2015; Nozari, 2020) have drawn on findings from neuroimaging studies of comprehension when discussing brain regions involved in word form encoding during production. However, evidence from people with aphasia shows input and output phonological lexicons are largely separate (e.g., Howard & Nickels, 2005; Jacquemot et al., 2007; see Kemmerer, 2019), and there is ongoing debate about whether phonological working memory required for nonword or syllable repetition involves separate storage buffers or the interplay of comprehension and production mechanisms (see Schwering & MacDonald, 2020 for a review; e.g., Acheson et al., 2011). Consequently, I focus my review below on results from naming paradigms.

Neuroimaging studies have reported activation in the left pSTG and supramarginal gyrus (SMG) for the word frequency (WF) effect in picture naming, in which pictures with high-frequency (HF) names are named faster than pictures with low-frequency (LF) names (e.g., Graves et al., 2007; Wilson et al., 2009). These fMRI studies employed regression analyses to separate the contribution of WF from other linguistic variables such as object familiarity and word length. The WF effect is generally considered to occur at the level of word form retrieval (e.g., Dell, 1990; Jescheniak & Levelt, 1994; but see Caramazza et al., 2004). Other studies of phonological facilitation effects in naming have reported pMTG/pSTG involvement (e.g., Bles & Jansma, 2008; de Zubicaray & McMahon, 2009; Pisoni et al., 2017). Production models typically attribute the facilitation effects observed during performance of these tasks to word form overlap. Additional evidence for the involvement of SMG in word form retrieval comes from LSM studies. Schwartz et al. (2012; see also Dell et al., 2013) reported that phonological errors during naming were associated with SMG lesions while Mirman and Graziano (2013) reported pSTG and SMG lesions were associated with increased error rates for words with denser phonological neighbourhoods. One tDCS study reported faster naming latencies with anodal stimulation over pMTG/STG and SMG (Sparing et al., 2008).

Two of three TMS studies reported faster naming latencies when stimulation was applied to pSTG *prior* to picture onset, which could be due to potentiation of local neural activity (see Luber & Lisanby, 2014; e.g., Mottaghy et al., 2006; Töpper et al., 1998; cf. Acheson et al., 2011). Yet, three chronometric TMS studies failed to observe a significant effect on naming latencies when stimulation was applied to pSTG between 200 and 300 ms after picture onset (Mottaghy et al., 2006; Schuhmann et al., 2012; Töpper et al., 1998). Note that Schuhmann et al. (2012) did observe an effect at 400 ms post picture onset but interpreted this as being consistent with a verbal self-monitoring mechanism (see the next section). According to this explanation, pSTG receives the *output* of word form retrieval as *input* for internal monitoring by the speech comprehension system (e.g., Indefrey & Levelt, 2004).

This leaves pMTG and SMG as more plausible candidate regions for word form retrieval in production (see Figure 4.1). It seems likely that related mechanisms in both regions are necessarily intertwined during word form retrieval. For example, Gow (2012) and Dell et al. (2013) consider left SMG to house articulatorily organized word form representations in contrast to more auditory-based lexical phonological representations in pMTG. In Guenther's (1995, 2016) Directions into Velocities of Articulators (DIVA) model, SMG is considered part of the somatosensory feedback control subsystem that monitors current proprioceptive information from the speech articulators to ensure the intended and current state are matched. Hickok's (2012) hierarchical state feedback control (HSFC) model also ascribes a similar somatosensory feedback role in production to a region in the posterior sylvian fissure at the parietotemporal boundary (area Spt), which can extend laterally to SMG. This implies that whenever the phonological output lexicon is engaged in a naming paradigm, its somatosensory analogue is likely to be engaged in parallel (see Strijkers et al. 2017, for a similar conclusion based on magnetoencephalography data). Although there are currently no TMS studies targeting word form retrieval during picture naming, phonological manipulations during word naming (i.e., reading aloud) have confirmed reliable roles for both left pMTG and SMG (Costanzo et al., 2012; Nakamura et al., 2006; Pattamadilok et al., 2015; see Figure 4.2).

Phonological encoding

Phonological encoding is often represented as the first point of contact between psycholinguistic (see also Chapter 3 of this volume) and speech motor control accounts (see Kearney & Guenther, 2019; Tremblay et al., 2019). According to the former approach, as individual phonemes are retrieved for a given word, they are assembled online segment by segment into sequences (syllabification) and a lexical stress pattern is assigned. Indefrey (2011) ascribed

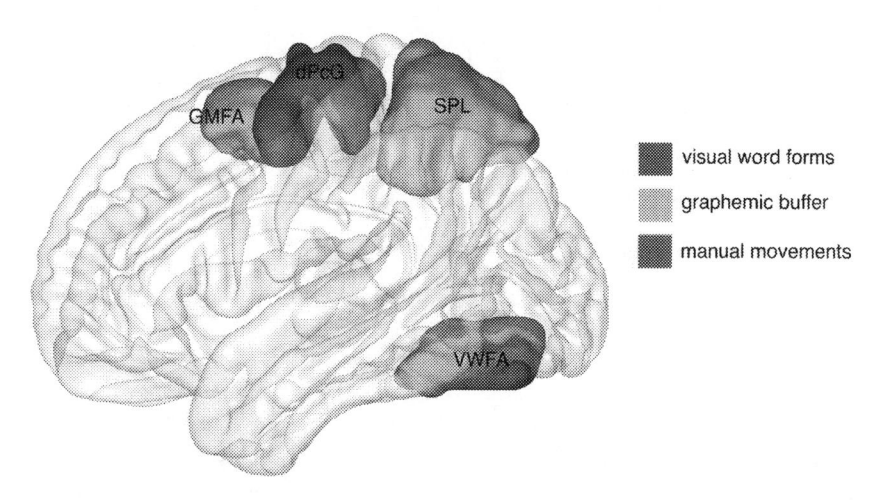

Figure 4.2 Brain regions proposed to be relatively specific to written versus spoken production processes across neuroimaging, neuromodulation and LSM studies,
rendered on a left lateral cortical surface according to the parcellation scheme of
Fan et al. (2016). GMFA, graphemic/motor frontal area; dPcG, dorsal precentral
gyrus; SPL, superior parietal lobule; VWFA, visual word form area.

this post-lexical process to the left posterior inferior frontal gyrus (pIFG) based
upon a comparison of neuroimaging studies employing covert and overt articulation and assigned a time window between 355 and 455 ms. The gradient
order DIVA (GODIVA; Bohland et al., 2010) speech motor control model
originally assigned roles of encoding phonemic sequences and representing
abstract syllable frames (but not phonemic content), respectively, to the inferior frontal sulcus (IFS) and pre-supplementary motor area (preSMA).
Markiewicz and Bohland (2016) later suggested preSMA might instead be
involved in selecting the appropriate response/motor programme (see the next
section). Hickok (2012) proposed a hierarchical mapping between lexical-
semantic representations (lemmas) and syllable motor programmes, with parallel input from the latter to both auditory and motor-phonological systems
(e.g., Hickok, 2012) but has more recently entertained the notion that area Spt
might be involved in coordinating phoneme sequences or prosodic information during production (Rong et al., 2018).

    To distinguish phonological encoding and articulatory mechanisms, neuroi-
maging studies have manipulated the amount of segmental information in
auditory repetition tasks. These studies have shown that dorsal pIFG and adjacent IFS are sensitive to word length but not biphone frequency and respond
differentially when producing multisyllabic versus monosyllabic nonwords,
consistent with a role in phonological encoding (e.g., Ghosh et al., 2008;
Guenther et al., 2006; Papoutsi et al., 2009; Rong et al., 2018; see Figure 4.1).
Converging evidence for pIFG/IFS involvement in phonological encoding

comes from multiple LSM, neuroimaging and neuromodulatory studies of letter/phonemic fluency and rhyme generation tasks. Phonemic fluency tasks require participants to produce a set of words with onset phonemes constrained by a commencing letter and are considered to entail a serial search based on systematic syllabification (e.g., Baldo et al., 2010; Costafreda et al., 2006; Heim et al., 2009; Katzev et al., 2013; Schmidt et al., 2019). Rhyme generation tasks require participants to produce words with word-final phonemes matching a cue word (e.g., Klaus & Hartwigsen, 2019; Lurito et al., 2000). An additional TMS study found stimulation of pIFG reduced the facilitation effect typically observed when pictures are named alongside auditory distractor words that share initial phonemes (Sakreida et al., 2019).

Multiple neuromodulatory studies of picture naming have targeted left pIFG with chronometric TMS across Dutch, English, Japanese, and Chinese languages (e.g., Chouinard et al., 2009; Schuhmann et al., 2009, 2012; Shinshi et al., 2015; Wheat et al., 2013; Zhang et al., 2018; see Figure 4.1). A consistent finding from these studies is that naming latencies are slowed when stimulation is applied 300–400 ms following picture presentation, consistent with Indefrey's (2011) estimate for phonological encoding. These studies also provide little evidence for an earlier role for pIFG in production processes as stimulation applied 100–200 ms following picture onset did not significantly affect naming latencies in all but one study (Schuhmann et al., 2009, 2012; Shinshi et al., 2015; Wheat et al., 2013). Hence, they do not support proposals of parallel activation of lexical-semantic and phonological-articulatory stages (cf. Strijkers & Costa, 2016). The exception was Zhang et al.'s (2018) study in Chinese in which the maximal effect occurred at 225 ms. The authors attributed this discrepant finding to differences in phonological encoding between languages as the fundamental phonological unit in Chinese is the (atonal) syllable rather than the phoneme. Note that the *mora* is considered the fundamental phonological unit in Japanese (it typically consists of a CV or V but never a single consonant). Shinshi et al.'s (2015) result indicates a similar temporal window for phonological encoding in left IFG across Japanese, Dutch, and English.

Phonetic encoding and articulation

Phonetic encoding involves translating the output of phonological encoding to abstract articulatory representations (*speech sound mapping*; Guenther et al., 2006), which may involve retrieving representations for more frequent syllables from a mental repository (a *syllabary*; Levelt et al., 1999) as well as those for individual phonemes necessary for producing novel syllables (see also Chapter 3 of this volume: Bürki, 2022). These representations are then realized by a learned set of motor commands (*articulatory gestures*) that guide the respiratory system and speech musculature to produce the requisite sounds (see Figure 4.1). Speech motor control accounts also integrate predictive feedforward and feedback mechanisms (or monitoring *loops*) to enable motor, auditory and somatosensory targets for speech gestures to be mapped to the intended utterance and any mismatches corrected prior to articulation (e.g., Guenther et al., 2006; Hickok, 2012). I will address monitoring mechanisms in a later section. Indefrey (2011) proposed phonetic encoding encompasses the last 150 ms prior to articulation. However, Laganaro (2019) suggests this is likely an underestimate influenced by disproportionate evidence from tasks employing written rather than pictorial stimuli.

Neuroimaging and neuromodulation studies have consistently implicated the ventral precentral gyrus (vPrG) in phonetic encoding during production, demonstrating its activation is scalable to syllable structure (e.g., Markiewicz & Bohland, 2016; Peeva et al., 2010; Tremblay & Small, 2011) and diminishes as new syllable sequences are learned (e.g., Segawa et al., 2015). These findings support proposals that vPrG houses speech motor programmes for well-practiced sounds in a syllabary or speech sound map (Kearney & Guenther, 2019). Novel (usually non-native language syllables or vowels) and more complex speech sequences are also reported to engage the anterior insula and most of the IFG, often bilaterally (Carey et al., 2017; Moser et al., 2009; Park et al., 2011; Riecker et al., 2008; Treutler & Sörös, 2021), but other studies have failed to observe anterior insula activation (e.g., Bohland & Guenther, 2006; Fedorenko et al., 2015; Rong et al., 2018). The evidence for anterior insula involvement from LSM investigations of apraxia of speech, a disorder of motor speech planning, is likewise equivocal (for a review, see Kemmerer, 2019).

Beyond phonetic encoding, production mechanisms progressively engage cortical and subcortical regions also implicated in more general (i.e., action) motor control (see Tremblay et al., 2019). These include selection, initiation, and timing mechanisms. To identify regions involved in voluntary selection of an appropriate speech motor programme, neuroimaging and neuromodulatory studies have typically varied constraints on spoken word production (e.g., by comparing repetition with generation tasks; Alario et al., 2006; Crosson et al., 2001; Hartwigsen et al., 2013; Tremblay & Gracco, 2009) and orofacial movements (speech versus non-speech; Tremblay & Gracco, 2009, 2010). A consistent finding across studies is that the preSMA is engaged during voluntary selection of both speech and non-speech motor programmes. Initiation mechanisms are responsible for launching the selected speech motor programme at the appropriate moment in time (Kearney & Guenther, 2019). In healthy participants, initiating speech movements involves activation of a broad bilateral network of cortical and subcortical motor regions (Brendel et al., 2010). However, it is worth noting that production is frequently reported to be *unaffected* by focal strokes involving the basal ganglia, with deficits instead attributed to damage to adjacent white matter pathways and/or vascular territories resulting in cortical hypoperfusion (for a review, see Radanovic & Mansur, 2017).

Regarding timing mechanisms, cerebellar lesions have long been associated with *ataxic dysarthria*, a disorder characterized by poorly timed articulation, application of incorrect or indeterminate stress, and pitch and loudness variations (e.g., Schoch et al., 2006; see Kearney & Guenther, 2019). However, it is important to note early LSM studies included patients with lesions extending into other areas and spoken production has also been reported to be *unaffected* after focal cerebellar lesions (e.g., Geva et al., 2021). Neuroimaging studies in healthy participants have typically varied the rate of self-generated speech or instructed participants to simulate dysfluencies to identify regions implicated in speech motor timing (e.g., De Nil et al., 2008; Marchina et al., 2018; Riecker et al., 2006; Theys et al., 2020). Across studies, vPrG, SMA, middle frontal gyrus (MFG), basal ganglia, and cerebellum are relatively consistently reported.

Movements of the articulators (e.g., tongue, lips, jaw) and larynx are executed by somatotopically organized areas of the primary (M1) and secondary motor areas (e.g., cingulate motor area [CMA] and SMA). To investigate cortical and subcortical regions engaged in laryngeal related activity during vocalization, fMRI studies have typically employed comparisons of covert, whispered and overt speech. Overall, these studies have reported inconsistent results (see review by Belyk & Brown, 2017). Some of this inconsistency may be due to the presence of speech-related movement and respiration confounds in standard fMRI acquisition protocols (see de Zubicaray & Piai, 2019). It seems likely there are separate dorsal and ventral larynx representations active in PrG during vocalization (Correia et al., 2020; Eichert et al., 2020). Laryngeal activity in M1 has also been reported to overlap with activity associated with movement of the jaw depressor muscles, indicating a functional coupling of phonation and articulation mechanisms that might have some evolutionary significance (Brown et al., 2020).

Written production

The neural mechanisms engaged by written production, including handwriting and typing, have been relatively under-investigated compared to vocal utterances (see also Chapter 8 of this handbook: Kandel, 2022). While writing and speaking engage some common neural mechanisms (e.g., Longcamp et al., 2019), writing entails additional mechanisms to translate visual representations of words into manual motor programmes. Most research has been conducted from the perspective of alphabetic languages for which writing a word necessitates that its spelling can be retrieved. Cognitive models of writing distinguish between central and peripheral processes. The former entail conceptual, lexical, orthographic (or graphemic) and phonological processes, while the latter involve letter shape (allograph) selection, generation of graphomotor representations and motor execution (for a review, see Rapp & Damian, 2018). Muscular control of the complex finger movements supporting writing is executed by somatotopically organized areas of the primary (M1) and secondary motor areas (e.g., CMA and SMA).

Both speaking and writing commence with the generation of a preverbal message for communication, followed by lexical-semantic retrieval. However, there is debate as to whether the latter might involve common or different abstract lemma representations or conceptual preparation instead being followed by access to modality-specific lexemes (Rapp & Caramazza, 2002). If speaking and writing share the same lexico-semantic retrieval mechanism(s), then comparisons of written word production with low-level motor tasks (e.g., tapping, holding a pen, or drawing geometric figures) would be expected to reveal left mid-MTG activation. Some fMRI studies have reported activation in left mid-MTG for these contrasts (e.g., Planton et al., 2017a; Potgieser et al., 2015) but not others (e.g., Beeson et al., 2003; Rapp & Dufor, 2011). The two earlier fMRI studies that did not report MTG activation used relatively small sample sizes for fMRI studies (12 and 8 participants, respectively), so may have had limited statistical power to detect effects. One PET study reported overlapping left mid-MTG activation when both spoken and written narrative production were contrasted with repetition of spoken syllables and written repeated single graphemes (Brownsett & Wise, 2010).

Neuroimaging studies have typically employed subvocal (i.e., covert) naming or reading as linguistic control tasks to identify central orthographic and graphomotor mechanisms (e.g., Baldo et al., 2018; Palmis et al., 2019; Planton et al., 2013, 2017a; Potgieser et al., 2015; Vinci-Booher et al., 2019). A network of cortical and subcortical regions has been consistently reported across fMRI studies, some of which have been characterized as specific to writing. These include the posterior portion of the left superior frontal sulcus (pSFS), the superior parietal lobule (SPL) and IPS, dorsal IFG/vPrG, ventral occipitotemporal cortex (vOTC; including fusiform gyrus), striatum, thalamus, and right cerebellum (Planton et al., 2013).

Across reading and writing tasks, the vOTC (also referred to as the visual word form area; VWFA) and dorsal IFG/vPrG are considered to play roles in long term storage of visual orthographic/graphemic representations of words and phoneme-grapheme conversion, respectively (Baldo et al., 2018; Purcell et al., 2017; Rapp et al., 2015). Longcamp et al. (2019) noted the left IFG, vPrG and SMA showed overlapping activation during spoken and written production in their fMRI study. The dorsal IFG and vPrG may thus store graphomotor programmes in a syllabary for handwriting analogous to the one proposed for speech (e.g., Kandel et al., 2006). Lending support to this notion, fMRI studies have reported that handwriting activation in IFG/vPrG is sensitive to manipulations of word frequency (Rapp & Dufor, 2011) as well as regularity (Palmis et al., 2019). Given that writing is acquired later than speech and requires formal training, this likely represents co-opting of an existing speech resource.

Of the regions proposed to be relatively specific to writing, the pSFS, also referred to as the graphemic/motor frontal area (GMFA; Roux et al., 2009) and SPL/IPS have been proposed to act in concert to support orthographic working memory (also referred to as the *graphemic buffer*) in which letter-shape representations are temporarily activated and maintained as they are serially selected for production (e.g., Rapp & Dufor, 2011; Figure 4.2). The relative importance of the two regions is debated. Evidence from LSM, fMRI, and TMS studies provides mixed support for a critical role for either region (e.g., Baldo et al., 2018; Planton et al., 2017a, b; Potgieser et al., 2015; Rapp et al., 2015; Segal & Petrides, 2012).

The involvement of subcortical regions such as the bilateral striatum and right cerebellum has been characterized in terms of integrating letter shape representations with motor planning and execution of complex finger movements (e.g., Barton et al., 2020; Planton et al., 2017a; Potgieser et al., 2015). Longcamp et al. (2019) noted that the considerable overlap of activity in these regions for spoken and written production in their fMRI study suggests they could mediate effector-independent representations. The frequently reported right lateralized activity in the cerebellum is consistent with its ipsilateral motor contribution to hand movements in right-handed participants. Proposals for a writing specific role for the cerebellum have been reconsidered recently because comparisons with control tasks requiring more complex manual movements (e.g., drawing) do not result in differential cerebellar activity (e.g., Planton et al., 2017; Potgieser et al., 2015).

Sign production

Sign languages have similar linguistic properties to spoken languages (Corina & Lawyer, 2019; Emmorey et al., 2016; see also Chapter 9 of this volume). They therefore involve equivalent stages of production with retrieval and assembly of "phonological" components accomplished via gestural configurations (hand shape, movement, and position). The articulatory-motor gestures for the intended lexical sign are next specified, producing a "manual utterance." Spoken and sign production engage common neural mechanisms. However, differences arise from the use of visual-manual compared to auditory-vocal modalities that tend to involve greater engagement of bilateral cerebral regions (see Figure 4.3). Neuroimaging investigations have been conducted in congenitally deaf signers and in *bimodal bilinguals*, i.e., people with intact hearing who have acquired a spoken and a signed language.

Neuroimaging evidence has confirmed a similar role for the ATLs in conceptual preparation in both sign and spoken production. For example, Emmorey et al. (2013) observed increased PET activation in the bilateral ATLs of deaf signers that extended into middle temporal areas for comparisons of naming objects with lexical signs versus producing spatial modifiers (e.g., location, motion) and object type classifiers (e.g., long, thin). Lexical signs identify objects at the basic level (e.g., banana), whereas spatial modifiers and object type classifiers require extraction of more specific conceptual features (e.g., yellow, long, curved). In addition, Blanco-Elorieta et al. (2018) reported overlapping activity in the left ATL in deaf signers and monolingual speakers during production of noun-phrases describing objects and their colour features (e.g., *white lamp*) compared to a lexical control task that involved merely describing the background colour and producing the

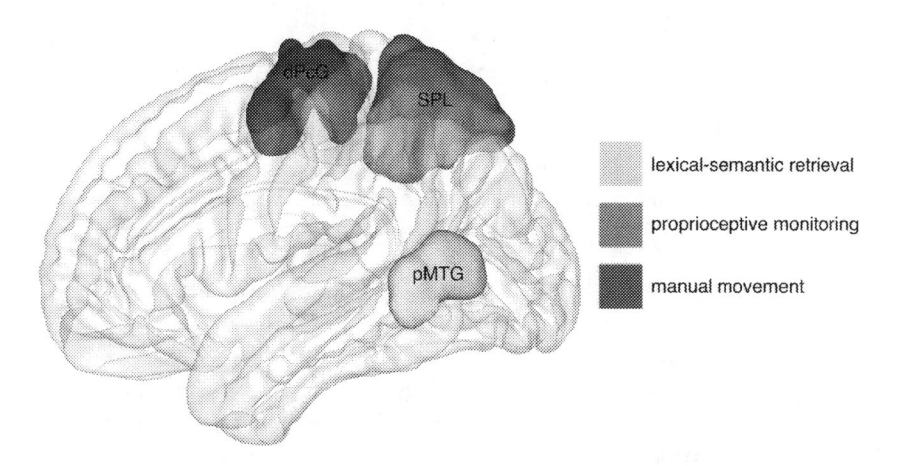

Figure 4.3 Brain regions proposed to have differential roles in signed versus spoken production processes across neuroimaging studies, rendered on a left lateral cortical surface according to the parcellation scheme of Fan et al. (2016). dPcG, dorsal precentral gyrus; SPL, superior parietal lobule; pMTG, posterior middle temporal gyrus.

object name. Okada and colleagues (2016) found no evidence that conceptual preparation during sign production involves motor cortical regions. In their fMRI study, the production of action related signs by deaf signers did not differentially engage the motor system compared to object related signs. In addition, Emmorey et al. (2004) reported cerebral activation elicited during the production of motor-iconic verbs (i.e., signs involving miming of object use) did not significantly differ to that of non-iconic verbs. Consequently, the evidence from sign production does not support proposals of grounding or embodiment of action semantics in motor regions (cf. Barsalou, 2020; Indefrey, 2016).

Early neuroimaging studies (e.g., San Jose-Robertson et al., 2004) assumed equivalent lexical-semantic retrieval mechanisms operated for sign and spoken production (lemma selection). However, Emmorey et al. (2008; see also Emmorey et al., 2016) proposed that the locus of lexical selection in sign production occurs later because bimodal bilinguals show a preference for language mixing (or *code-blending*) rather than switching when communicating. As most code-blends are congruent in meaning, this indicates different lexical-semantic representations may be activated across modalities without interfering with each other. One possibility is that lexical-semantic retrieval during sign production might instead entail conceptual preparation being followed by access to modality-specific lexemes, as has been proposed for writing (e.g., Rapp & Caramazza, 2002). The neuroimaging evidence is broadly consistent with this proposal. For example, both PET and fMRI studies of naming in bimodal bilinguals have reported increased activation in left pMTG for sign compared to spoken production (e.g., Emmorey et al., 2013; Kovelman et al., 2009; Zou et al., 2012a). This pMTG region is also consistently reported as showing increased activation in deaf signers when naming is compared to low level control tasks, rather than mid-MTG as reported for spoken production (e.g., Emmorey et al., 2004; Hu et al., 2011; Okada et al., 2016; San Jose-Robertson et al., 2004).

Several neuroimaging studies have demonstrated that the left IFG is involved similarly in both speech and sign production in bimodal bilinguals (e.g., Emmorey et al., 2007; Emmorey et al., 2013; Zou et al., 2012a). In both bimodal bilinguals and deaf signers, covert sign production also engages left IFG (e.g., Hu et al., 2011; Kassubek et al., 2004), as does covert repetition of pseudosigns in deaf signers (i.e., manual gestures that conform to the phonotactic rules of a sign language but do not convey any meaning; e.g., Buchsbaum et al., 2005; Pa et al., 2008). In sign languages, syllables are composed via combinations of hand locations and movements (see Baus et al., 2014). Although monosyllabic words are much more frequent in sign languages, disyllabic and multisyllabic words do exist, and reduplication is used to denote plurals or inflected forms. Consequently, IFG might serve a cross-modal role in terms of a syllabary.

Studies in bimodal bilinguals typically report increased activation in bilateral STG during spoken compared to sign production attributable to hearing/monitoring speech output (e.g., Emmorey et al., 2013; Kovelman et al., 2009; Li et al., 2015; Zou et al., 2012a). In addition, these studies have consistently reported increased activation in bilateral dorsal parietal cortex, especially the superior parietal lobule (SPL; Figure 4.3), for sign compared to spoken production (e.g., Emmorey et al., 2013; Kovelman et al., 2009; Zou et al., 2012a). In deaf signers, the SPL also shows increased activation for sign production compared to low level manual control tasks (e.g., Hu et al., 2011). Emmorey et al. (2004) noted that as both iconic and non-iconic signs activate SPL similarly, its activation is unlikely to reflect retrieval of object knowledge. Producing location and motion classifiers also engages SPL similarly (Emmorey et al., 2013). One possibility is that the activation occurs due to visuomotor integration processes analogous to the auditory-motor integration processes proposed for speech motor control (e.g., Buchsbaum et al., 2005; Pa et al., 2008). However, visual inputs from self- and other-produced signs differ considerably, unlike the auditory inputs from self- and other-produced speech. Alternatively, as Emmorey et al. (2004, 2007, 2014) proposed, the increased SPL activity might be due to the use of a proprioceptive rather than visual feedback mechanism that monitors for errors during sign production.

Self-monitoring

Both psycholinguistic and speech motor control accounts of spoken production assume that speakers monitor their own inner (i.e., pre-articulatory) and overt speech so they can avoid committing errors and repair them when committed, without the need for prompting by a conversational partner (see also Chapter 6 of this handbook). According to the psycholinguistic tradition, self-produced speech is monitored via two feedback "loops" (Levelt et al., 1999). The internal loop monitors the output of phonological encoding to detect errors prior to articulation, while the external loop monitors auditory targets from overt utterances using the same system for comprehending others' speech. Speech motor control accounts integrate both feedforward models (also referred to as predictive coding, efference copies, or corollary discharges) and feedback mechanisms to enable motor, auditory and somatosensory targets for speech gestures to be mapped to the intended utterance and any mismatches corrected prior to articulation (e.g., Guenther et al., 2006; Hickok, 2012). In the HSFC model (Hickok, 2012), auditory targets are predominantly syllabic, whereas in the DIVA model they are lower-level speech motor programmes (see Kearney & Guenther, 2019). Feedforward models have also been proposed to monitor language production stages prior to phonological encoding but are yet to be linked to neural mechanisms (e.g., Pickering & Garrod, 2013). Other accounts invoke domain general mechanisms such as conflict or competition-based monitoring operating at different stages of production (e.g., de Zubicaray et al., 2001, 2006b; Gauvin & Harstuiker, 2020; Hockey, 2006; Hockey et al., 2005; Nozari et al., 2011).

Indefrey and Levelt (2004) ascribed the monitoring of both pre-articulatory and overt utterances to the entirety of the STG bilaterally, noting they were unable to differentiate the mechanisms for internal and external loops based on their meta-analysis of early studies. Speech motor control accounts (e.g., Hickok, 2012; Kearney & Guenther, 2019) have ascribed a relatively specific role for the pSTG in monitoring auditory targets for external speech (auditory error mapping), based primarily on neuroimaging findings from tasks designed to induce vocal changes by delivering altered auditory feedback (e.g., via distortion, delay, or masking). However, Meekings and Scott's (2021) meta-analysis of these studies instead identified reliable activation that was slightly more anterior to the proposed pSTG area, in addition to activation in the transverse temporal gyrus and precentral gyrus. External monitoring of an incorrect utterance has been reported to engage bilateral pSTG in two recent fMRI studies employing paradigms designed to increase the likelihood of actual speech errors (Hansen et al., 2019; Runnqvist et al., 2021; see Figure 4.1).

Only two neuroimaging studies have explicitly investigated the neural mechanisms of internal monitoring for natural speech errors. Both employed tongue-twisters to increase the likelihood of speech errors and demands for error detection while precluding auditory feedback from externally produced speech. Okada et al. (2018) employed imagined speech (i.e., inner) and silent articulation (i.e., without phonation). They reasoned that a comparison of the two should reveal monitoring of the output of phonetic encoding, as silent articulation is assumed to entail phonetic encoding whereas imagined speech does not. They found increased activation for silent articulation in bilateral anterior-to-posterior STG and MTG, precentral gyrus, ACC, bilateral para-hippocampal gyrus, cerebellum, and basal ganglia. Gauvin et al. (2016) pre-cluded auditory feedback/external monitoring with noise-masking. They reported activation in left preSMA/ACC, anterior insula and bilateral IFG.

In speech motor control accounts, feedforward models assume that speech plans lead to predictions of their sensorimotor consequences before they are enacted, allowing mismatches between predicted and actual outcomes to be monitored. In both DIVA and HSFC accounts, the cerebellum plays a key role in generating these feedforward commands to the articulators in addition to feedback control from auditory and somatosensory targets for speech sounds (e.g., Hickok, 2012; Kearney & Guenther, 2019). While some studies report cerebellar engagement during speech errors (e.g., Peng et al., 2021; Runnqvist et al., 2016, 2021) most do not (e.g., Gauvin et al., 2016; Hansen et al., 2019; see Meekings & Scott, 2021). Of note, in Meekings and Scott's (2021) meta-analysis of 17 studies that used altered auditory feedback to induce vocal changes, only two reported cerebellar engagement. Three studies compared high versus low probabilities of natural speech error occurrence (i.e., word vs. nonword errors), with only one reporting cerebellar activation sensitive to error predictability (e.g., Okada et al., 2018; Runnqvist et al., 2016; cf. Runnqvist et al., 2021). Consequently, the evidence supporting a role for the cerebellum in monitoring is not compelling. The cerebellum's role in the timing/sequencing of articulation (see the previous section) might be an al-ternative explanation for some of the positive results (but see Geva et al., 2021), particularly in fMRI studies employing tongue twisters given the de-mands on coarticulation and syllable sequencing.

Feedforward models have also been proposed to operate during language production beyond speech motor control (e.g., Pickering & Garrod, 2013). According to this account, speakers predict their own utterances and compare these forward production models with forward comprehension models of the predicted output (i.e., the perceptual representation of the utterance). The forward production models are assumed to include re-presentations from conceptual preparation to phonological encoding stages but are relatively impoverished to facilitate faster processing. As Dell (2013) noted, the use of feedforward models and predicted perceptions corresponds well with mechanisms of cascading processing and feedback in interactive models of production.

Pickering and Garrod's (2013) account assumes production and compre-hension are forms of action and action perception, so invokes domain general mechanisms. Although the neural mechanisms supporting these forward models are yet to be specified, there is some evidence from neuroimaging and LSM studies that is consistent with the involvement of a domain general prediction mechanism operating during production. For example, lateral and medial orbitofrontal cortex (OFC; Brodmann areas 10, 11, and 47; Figure 4.1) engagements have been consistently reported during production paradigms requiring a correct utterance to be suppressed *and* replaced with another, such as the Hayling Sentence Completion Test (HSCT; e.g., Allen et al., 2008; Collette et al., 2001; de Zubicaray et al., 2000; Hornberger et al., 2011; Robinson et al., 2015; Volle et al., 2012). These paradigms require a predicted outcome to be avoided (e.g., a word with a high cloze probability in a sentence context) and an alternative utterance that mismatches it to be generated. Early explanations for OFC involvement in these production tasks ascribed it a role in inhibitory control. However, a critical role in representing predicted outcomes and their current value across multiple domains is now supported by both animal and human studies (e.g., Rolls & Deco, 2016; Rudebeck & Murray, 2014; Stalnaker et al., 2015). Orbitofrontal cortex engagement is observed reliably during manipulations of linguistic and syntactic predictability in reading (e.g., Bonhage et al., 2015; Carter et al., 2019; Hofmann et al., 2014). It does not have white matter connections with premotor or primary motor cortices (Rudebeck & Murray, 2014), but does have connections with MTG/STG (see the next section). Hence, this potential predictive role during production can be distinguished from the forward models described in speech motor control accounts (e.g., Hickok, 2012; Kearney & Guenther, 2019).

Initial proposals that a domain general conflict or competition monitoring mechanism might operate during spoken production were based on the relatively reliable observation of medial frontal/anterior cingulate (ACC) activation during the performance of paradigms designed to promote coactivation of multiple candidates (e.g., de Zubicaray et al., 2001, 2002, 2006b; see Gauvin & Harstuiker, 2020; Figure 4.1). As a central conflict monitoring mechanism in the ACC had already been implicated in cognitive control paradigms in domains other than language (e.g., Botvinick et al., 2001), de Zubicaray and colleagues proposed the addition of this mechanism to interactive activation production models as they already incorporated the necessary feedforward and feedback connections and lateral inhibition (e.g., Berg & Schade, 1992; Harley, 1993). Conflict is defined operationally as the simultaneous activation of incompatible, mutually inhibiting representations (Botvinick et al., 2001). Once detected, a control mechanism in the prefrontal cortex (PFC) intervenes to guide activation in the network to meet current task goals (see the next section). A computational implementation appending this conflict monitoring mechanism to Harley's (1993) interactive activation model was able to successfully simulate the semantic interference effect in naming latencies in the PWI paradigm (Hockey, 2006; Hockey et al., 2005). The choice of an interactive activation model incorporating inhibitory links both within and between production stages was deemed important (e.g., Harley, 1993; Schade & Berg, 1992; cf. Dell, 1986), as they provide flexibility for conflict to arise among representations at any level of the production system, not merely the response level (see Berg & Schade, 1992; cf., Roelofs et al., 2006). In addition, these models are biologically plausible given the existence of both excitatory and inhibitory synaptic inputs. Nozari et al. (2011) later implemented a different type of conflict monitoring mechanism for detecting speech errors at the point of response selection, one that does not involve inhibitory links. As the evidence above shows, the ACC is reliably reported across studies of internal and external monitoring of natural speech errors (e.g., Abel et al., 2009; Gauvin et al., 2016; Hansen et al., 2019; Okada et al., 2018; Runnqvist et al., 2021). However, it has not been reliably reported in studies employing altered auditory feedback to induce vocal changes (e.g., Meekings & Scott, 2021). This suggests the ACC likely monitors conflict at stages of production earlier than phonological encoding.

Additional evidence for ACC involvement in monitoring of competing lexical representations comes from neuroimaging studies of bilingual production. Abutalebi and Green (2007) proposed that the ACC monitoring mechanism identified in fMRI studies of monolinguals (e.g., de de Zubicaray et al., 2006b) should also be engaged when bilingual and multilingual speakers switch between languages due to the need to monitor for L1 intrusions during L2 or L3 production. Supporting this proposal, fMRI studies of bilingual language switching in picture naming have reliably reported differential activation in the ACC (e.g., Abutalebi et al., 2013; De Baene et al., 2015; de Bruin et al., 2014; Fu et al., 2017; Garbin et al., 2011; Guo et al., 2011; Reverberi et al., 2018; Yuan et al., 2021). Notably, most of these studies did not report STG activation. Approximately half of these studies also reported activation in the cerebellum, attributing it to a greater demand for articulatory control in the less proficient language, rather than to the operation of a monitoring mechanism. The available evidence from bimodal bilinguals likewise indicates a reliable role for the ACC in language switching during picture naming (Blanco-Elorrieta et al., 2018; Li et al., 2015; Zou et al., 2012a). The latter fMRI studies also reported STG and cerebellar activation attributed to switching between visual-manual and auditory-vocal modalities rather than monitoring per se.

Control mechanisms

Spoken production is remarkably error free in a speaker's native language, with only one or two errors committed every 1,000 words (Levelt et al., 1999). Hence, natural speech affords limited opportunities to observe the operation of control mechanisms unless errors are produced as a consequence of aphasia or elicited by an experimental paradigm. Control mechanisms are assumed to govern interruptions and repairs, i.e., new attempts to produce the correct utterance before an erroneous word has been entirely articulated (see Gauvin & Harstuiker, 2020; Mandal et al., 2020). Proposals for cognitive control mechanisms have also been motivated by observations of refractory effects in production paradigms designed to promote coactivation of multiple candidates (e.g., de Zubicaray et al., 2001; Schnur et al., 2009). In bilingual production, inhibitory control mechanisms are proposed to operate when switching between languages (e.g., Abutalebi & Green, 2007). Most production accounts assume that some form of control is needed to ensure the correct candidate is selected for production, either by reducing (i.e., inhibiting) the activation of non-target candidates or enhancing (i.e., boosting) the activation of the target.

The early production literature focused upon a role for the lateral prefrontal cortex (PFC), particularly left anterior IFG (comprising pars orbitalis and/or pars triangularis; BAs 47 and 45), in implementing top-down control during semantic interference in various naming paradigms (e.g., Belke & Stielow, 2013; Oppenheim et al., 2010; Roelofs, 2018). However, a comprehensive review of the lesion, neuroimaging and neuromodulation literature failed to identify consistent evidence for such a role across paradigms (see de Zubicaray & Piai, 2019).[2] The review did find evidence for a reliable role for aIFG in resolving conflict introduced by competing *linguistic* information (e.g., incongruent versus congruent or neutral stimuli). Note that early proposals for a selective role for aIFG in controlled semantic retrieval in verbal fluency tasks have also not been supported by more recent findings from fMRI meta-analyses (e.g., Wagner et al., 2014) or large-scale LSM studies (e.g., Baldo et al., 2006; Biesbroek et al., 2021; Schmidt et al., 2019; Thye et al., 2021). These studies do support a role for the aIFG in more general control of linguistic information during production (Figure 4.1).

In naturalistic speech error inducing paradigms, aIFG recruitment is a relatively reliable finding and generally interpreted as reflecting greater demands for inhibitory control (e.g., Gauvin et al., 2016; Runnqvist et al., 2021; Severens et al., 2012). Experimental paradigms that explicitly require participants to suppress or inhibit a prepotent *correct* utterance such as the HSCT or Stop Signal Task (SST) are reliably associated with aIFG engagement across numerous LSM, fMRI, and PET studies (e.g., Allen et al., 2008; Collette et al., 2001; de Zubicaray et al., 2000; Hansen et al., 2019; Hornberger et al., 2011; Robinson et al., 2015; Volle et al., 2012; Xue et al., 2008). Across the latter studies, left, right, or bilateral involvement are reported with approximately equal frequency. However, the role of the right aIFG is currently debated, having also been attributed to post-error monitoring processes (see Hansen et al., 2019). A recent LSM study of unsuccessful compared to successful speech error detection by people with aphasia implicated a large portion of the left PFC and underlying white matter (Mandal et al., 2020). This result was due primarily to phonological errors, as semantic errors were not significantly associated with lesions to the same area.

In unimodal bilingual language production, two regions have been implicated in implementing inhibitory control particularly during language switching: aIFG and the head of the caudate nucleus (e.g., Abutalebi & Green, 2007). The evidence for aIFG involvement is relatively mixed, with studies reporting left-sided activation (e.g., De Baene et al., 2015; Yuan et al., 2021), bilateral activation (de Bruin et al., 2014; Fu et al., 2017; Reverberi et al., 2018) or no involvement (Abutalebi et al., 2013; Garbin et al., 2011; Guo et al., 2011). This is also the case for the caudate, with studies reporting right-sided or bilateral activation (de Bruin et al., 2014; Garbin et al., 2011;

Reverberi et al., 2018) or no involvement during language switching (Abutalebi et al., 2013; De Baene et al., 2015; Fu et al., 2017; Guo et al., 2011). In bimodal bilinguals, two studies reported caudate involvement but not aIFG (Li et al., 2015; Zou et al., 2012b). Note that a key moderating factor for reports of significant aIFG or caudate activation during language switching is likely to be proficiency in the non-dominant language (see Abutalebi et al., 2013; de Bruin et al., 2014).

It is worth noting an alternative explanation has attributed (tentatively or otherwise) engagement of the aIFG to top-down regulation of response selection processes (e.g., Oppenheim et al., 2010; Roelofs et al., 2006; Roelofs, 2018). According to this account, aIFG enhances or "boosts" the activation of lexical concepts in mid-MTG until retrieval of the correct candidate (lemma) is achieved. Roelofs and colleagues (2006; see also Roelofs, 2018) also ascribed a similar role to the ACC in selectively enhancing the activation of the correct response until a selection threshold is exceeded. The primary evidence cited to support a regulatory control rather than conflict monitoring role for the ACC in production comes from a Stroop fMRI study showing faster responses and increased ACC activity for congruent compared to neutral stimuli, a comparison that does not involve *response* conflict (e.g., Roelofs et al., 2006). However, this result is consistent with protracted *task* conflict, i.e., the conflict between the relevant colour naming task and the irrelevant word reading task (also referred to as *task set competition*, e.g., Monsell et al., 2001; Steinhauser & Hübner, 2009). Computational simulations implementing monitoring and control for both types of conflict in the Stroop task have been able to successfully model both behavioural and neuroimaging findings (see De Pisapia & Braver, 2006; Kalanthroff et al., 2018). An fMRI study by Aarts et al. (2009) indicates common regions of the ACC are likely to be engaged by both response and task conflict during Stroop performance.

Connectivity

As noted at the beginning of this chapter, our knowledge of the white matter network supporting language (also referred to as its "connectome") has progressed considerably from the classical Broca-Wernicke-Geschwind model. Information from tractography-based diffusion-weighted imaging (DWI; see Catani & Forkel, 2019) and neuromodulation via DES (see Duffau, 2019) supports a more extensive left hemisphere network of multiple white matter pathways. Much of the recent research into the language connectome has focused upon a "dual route" architecture comprising relatively specialized dorsal and ventral pathways (see Dick et al., 2014). Below I offer a production-centric perspective of this connectome in relation to its processing stages.

Relatively consistent evidence indicates conceptual preparation and lexical-semantic retrieval rely on the integrity of the ventrally located inferior

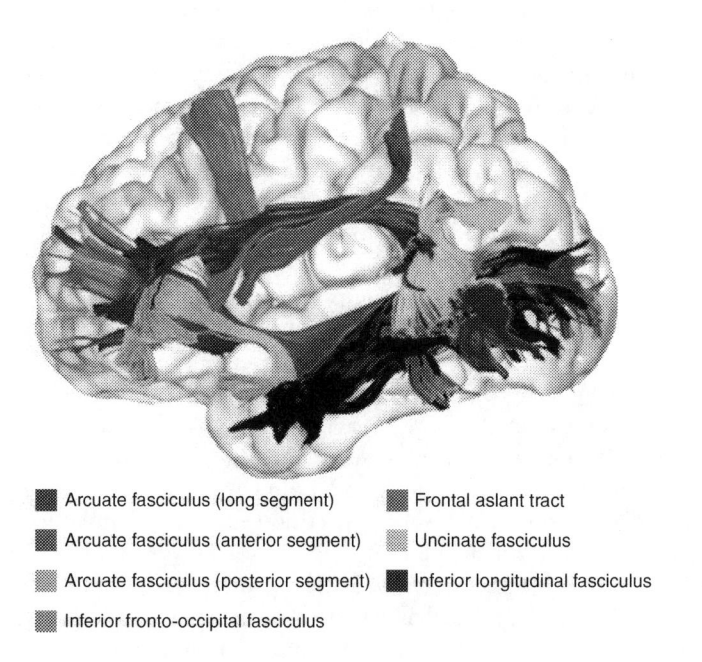

Arcuate fasciculus (long segment) Frontal aslant tract

Arcuate fasciculus (anterior segment) Uncinate fasciculus

Arcuate fasciculus (posterior segment) Inferior longitudinal fasciculus

Inferior fronto-occipital fasciculus

Figure 4.4 Major white matter fibre tracts implicated in production across tractography and electrical stimulation studies. Reprinted from "Imaging white-matter pathways of the auditory system with diffusion imaging tractography" by Maffei et al. (2015), *Handbook of Clinical Neurology* (Vol. 129, pp. 277–288), with permission from Elsevier.

fronto–occipital fasciculus (IFOF; see Figure 4.4), a long associative fibre tract that connects OFC and IFG with lateral temporal (MTG/STG) and occipital regions (e.g., Binney et al., 2012; Martino et al., 2009; Sarubbo et al., 2013). Multiple studies in healthy participants and lesion patients have confirmed the IFOF is implicated in semantic processing during naming tasks (e.g., Butler et al., 2014; de Zubicaray et al., 2011; Han et al., 2013; Hula et al., 2020; Sierpowska et al., 2019). In addition, stimulation of multiple portions of the IFOF disrupts semantic processing during picture naming, resulting in co-ordinate or subordinate speech errors (for reviews, see Cocquyt et al., 2020; Duffau et al., 2014). In Harvey and Schnur's (2015) LSM study of semantic interference in blocked cyclic naming, increases in error rates were associated with lesions disrupting the IFOF, whereas in Janssen et al.'s (2020) LSM study using the PWI paradigm, reduced semantic interference in naming latencies was associated with lower IFOF integrity.

More equivocal evidence implicates three other fibre tracts in conceptual preparation and lexical-semantic retrieval during production. These are the ventrally located uncinate fasciculus (UF), a tract connecting the OFC and IFG with the ATL bidirectionally, the inferior longitudinal fasciculus (ILF) connecting the ATL and occipitotemporal areas, and the dorsally located indirect posterior segment of the arcuate fasciculus (AF) that connects pMTG/STG and IPL. For the UF and ILF, the evidence from tractography investigations is relatively consistent in lesion patients but less so in young healthy participants, yet most stimulation studies have failed to observe an effect on production (for reviews, see Cocquyt et al., 2020; Ivanova et al., 2016). One possibility is that this pattern of evidence reflects an indirect, compensatory role for these tracts in conceptual preparation or lexical semantic retrieval when the ATL and/or IFOF are lesioned (see Herbet et al., 2019). Unfortunately, there are no neuromodulation studies explicitly targeting the posterior indirect segment of the AF and relatively few LSM studies (Cocquyt et al., 2020). Recent tractography investigations have shown an association between the integrity of the posterior indirect AF segment and naming accuracy (e.g., Ivanova et al., 2021) and, more importantly, semantic paraphasias in people with aphasia (e.g., Hula et al., 2020).

Roelofs (2014), influenced by the classical model of Geschwind (1979; see Roelofs & Ferreira, 2019), proposed the AF was critical for lexical-semantic retrieval rather than the IFOF, instead ascribing the latter a role in top down cognitive control (see Harvey & Schnur, 2015, for a similar perspective of the IFOF). Note that Roelofs' proposal is based on a two-segment model of the AF (Glasser & Rilling, 2008) rather than the more commonly accepted three segment model of Catani et al. (2005) that includes the posterior indirect segment of the AF mentioned above (see Figure 4.4). According to the two-segment model, a part of the AF that connects pMTG/STG with pIFG is assumed to be a pathway that maps lexical-semantic representations onto output phonemes. Stimulation and tractography studies of the AF pathway(s) between pMTG and IFG have typically not observed an association with lexical-semantic retrieval during production (see Cocquyt et al., 2020). While more work is needed, it does seem likely that lexical semantic retrieval is accomplished by a combination of ventral (IFOF) and dorsal (i.e., posterior indirect segment of the AF) pathways, not exclusively one or the other (see Hula et al., 2020 for a similar conclusion).

Relatively consistent evidence implicates the long segment of the AF that connects pSTG directly with the pIFG in word form retrieval and phonological encoding, with tractography studies in both people with aphasia (e.g., Hula et al., 2020; McKinnon et al., 2018) and healthy older adults all showing associations with phonological errors during production (Stamatakis et al., 2011; Troutman & Diaz, 2020). These include tip-of-the-tongue (TOT) states as well as phonemic paraphasias. Phonemic paraphasias are also reliably elicited by stimulation of the long segment of the AF during surgery (for a review, see Duffau et al., 2014).

Two fibre tracts have been implicated consistently in phonetic encoding and articulation. Multiple LSM studies have shown damage to the anterior segment of the AF that connects the IPL to the IFG is largely responsible for impairments of fluent speech production (typically defined in terms of words per minute; e.g., Fridriksson et al., 2013; Gajardo-Vidal et al., 2021; Ivanova et al., 2021; Marchina et al., 2011). The second pathway, now referred to as the frontal aslant tract (FAT), was only identified via DWI tractography in recent years and connects the preSMA and ACC with the IFG (for review, see Dick et al., 2019; see Figure 4.2). Stimulation of the FAT during surgery induces speech arrest and multiple neuroimaging studies have implicated this pathway in speech initiation difficulties (see Dick et al., 2019). Finkl et al. (2020) noted the FAT connectivity profiles of non-speaking, congenitally deaf signers were significantly reduced compared to non-hearing-impaired speakers, further supporting a crucial role in speech articulation.

Surprisingly little neuromodulation or tractography research has directly addressed the white matter tracts involved in monitoring during production, although both internal and external speech monitoring is typically assumed to be accomplished via dorsal pathways such as the AF (e.g., Roelofs, 2014). Some reviews of the language connectome do not mention monitoring at all (e.g., Dick et al., 2014). For speech motor control, a more elaborate network of cortico-striatal-cerebellar pathways and corticobulbar and corticospinal tracts is involved for auditory, motor and proprioceptive feedforward and feedback loops in addition to the AF (e.g., Kearney & Guenther, 2019; Hickok, 2012). The corticobulbar and corticospinal tracts of the pyramidal system innervate motor nuclei in the brainstem and spinal cord associated with the cranial nerves relevant for muscle control to achieve respiration, phonation, and articulation (see Tremblay et al., 2019). Neuromodulatory studies of the cortical control of speech muscles with TMS and electromyographic (EMG) recordings have confirmed left-lateralized enhanced excitability of the corticobulbar M1 pathway during word and sentence production (e.g., Sowman et al., 2009).

A relatively recent proposal implicates the right FAT in conflict monitoring and inhibitory control during production following from its connections with the ACC, preSMA, and IFG (Dick et al., 2019). However, a combined neuromodulation and tractography study did not find an effect of stimulation or resection of the right FAT on Stroop test performance (Palmis et al., 2019). This study instead reported a critical role for the fronto-striatal tract (FST; also referred to as the subcallosal fasciculus, e.g., Duffau et al., 2002; Figure 4.5) that connects superior medial frontal regions (ACC, preSMA, SMA) to the caudate nucleus (Draganski et al., 2008; Leh et al., 2007; Lehéricy et al., 2004). Of note, multiple stimulation studies have also implicated the left FST in speech errors, especially *perseverations* (e.g., Corrivetti et al., 2019; Duffau et al., 2002; Kinoshita et al., 2015; Mandonnet et al., 2019). As corticostriatal connections from the caudate include the OFC, IFG, and MTG (Draganski et al., 2008; Leh et al., 2007; Lehéricy et al., 2004), I consider the FST to be a more plausible candidate for a critical role in conflict monitoring and inhibitory control during production, complementing the FAT's more likely role in initiation of articulation (cf. Dick et al., 2019).

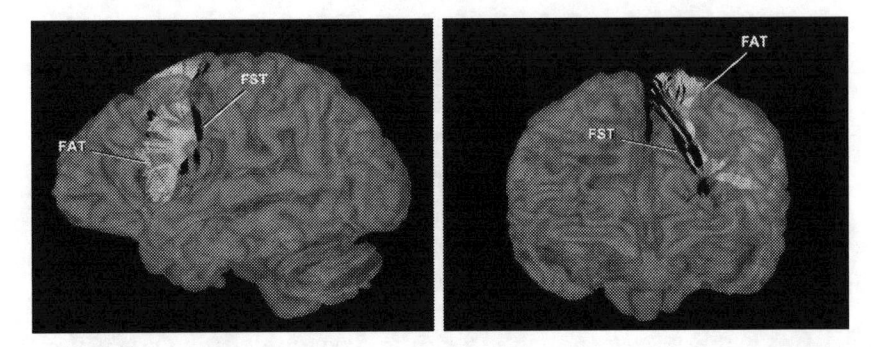

Figure 4.5 The left frontostriatal (FST; blue) and frontal aslant (FAT; green) tracts in relation to each other. Adapted from Bozkurt et al. (2017). Fiber connections of
the supplementary motor area revisited: Methodology of fiber dissection, DTI,
and three-dimensional documentation. *Journal of Visualized Experiments*,
Vol. 123, p. e55681, doi:10.3791/55681.

Conclusion

This chapter reviewed evidence from neuroimaging and neuromodulatory
investigations of spoken, written, and signed production to provide a comprehensive overview of the neural mechanisms engaged from conceptual
preparation to motor output, as well as domain general processes that interact
with the production system. Converging evidence across methods was used to
provide support for the engagement of regions and their connectivity. Further,
neuromodulation studies provided some chronometric evidence concerning
the timecourse of engagement of different regions, which should prove useful
to constrain accounts of spreading activation between stages, but more is
needed. The review also identified other topics in need of further investigation. For example, more work is needed beyond the spoken word, i.e., with
sentence/narrative production or social/conversational contexts to understand
the neural mechanisms supporting the interplay between production and
comprehension systems. Despite a relatively large neuroimaging literature
devoted to sign production, neuromodulation investigations are scarce, and no
studies have compared written and signed production. Little research with
either method has attempted to address the debate about whether working
memory mechanisms active during production involve dedicated storage
buffers or an interplay of comprehension and production mechanisms.

The review also revealed some issues that the field needs to address.
Neuroimaging and neuromodulatory data have contributed significantly to the
obsolescence of the Broca-Wernicke-Geschwind model, yet contemporary
reviews and computational simulations continue to defer to the classical
model, despite its well-recognized limitations. In addition, many studies and
reviews incorporate findings from comprehension tasks without providing
adequate explanation for why identical representations or input/output

mechanisms should be assumed. To the extent that all models are wrong, but some are useful (e.g., Box, 1976), it would be helpful if future accounts of the neurobiology of language production addressed these issues squarely.

Notes

1 The posterior inferior temporal cortex has also been implicated in lexical-semantic retrieval during picture naming based on LSM evidence from surgical resections in patients with chronic temporal lobe epilepsy or low-grade gliomas (e.g., Binder et al., 2020; Herbet et al., 2016). This region is typically not reported in post-stroke LSM studies and there is little evidence from neuroimaging investigations in healthy participants, although the region is difficult (but not impossible) to image with fMRI due to magnetic susceptibility artefacts. Its involvement in glioma and epilepsy patients may be due to functional reorganization in response to tumour infiltration and long-term seizure propagation in the temporal lobe, respectively.

2 The review revealed the left aIFG is not reliably engaged during semantic interference in continuous naming, with mixed evidence for its engagement in PWI and blocked cyclic naming. Unlike PWI or continuous naming, semantic interference in blocked cyclic naming is also reported to engage the hippocampus but not the ACC (e.g., de Zubicaray et al., 2014, 2017; Grappe et al., 2018; Harvey & Schnur, 2015; Llorens et al., 2016; Schnur et al., 2009). This differential engagement of neural mechanisms across paradigms is difficult to reconcile with models proposing "unified" accounts of semantic interference (e.g., Oppenheim et al., 2010; Roelofs, 2018). Alternatively, aIFG might play a relatively small role in resolving semantic interference and so require greater experimental power to be detected, thus accounting for some mixed findings (see Gauvin et al., 2021).

References

Aarts, E., Roelofs, A., & van Turennout, M. (2009). Attentional control of task and response in lateral and medial frontal cortex: Brain activity and reaction time distributions. *Neuropsychologia*, 47, 2089–2099.

Abel, S., Dressel, K., Kümmerer, D., Saur, D., Mader, I., Weiller, C., & Huber, W. (2009). Correct and erroneous picture naming responses in healthy subjects. *Neuroscience Letters*, 463, 167–171.

Abel, S., Dressel, K., Weiller, C., & Huber, W. (2012). Enhancement and suppression in a lexical interference fMRI-paradigm. *Brain and Behavior*, 2, 109–127.

Abutalebi, J., & Green, D. W. (2007). Bilingual language production: The neurocognition of language representation and control. *Journal of Neurolinguistics*, 20, 242–275.

Abutalebi, J., Della Rosa, P. A., Ding, G., Weekes, B., Costa, A., & Green, D. W. (2013). Language proficiency modulates the engagement of cognitive control areas in multilinguals. *Cortex*, 49, 905–911.

Abutalebi, J., Della Rosa, P. A., Green, D. W., Hernandez, M., Scifo, P., Keim, R., Cappa, S. F., & Costa, A. (2011). Bilingualism tunes the anterior cingulate cortex for conflict monitoring. *Cerebral Cortex*, 22(9), 2076–2086. 10.1093/cercor/bhr287.

Acheson, D. J., Hamidi, M., Binder, J. R., & Postle, B. R. (2011). A common neural substrate for language production and verbal working memory. *Journal of Cognitive Neurosciences*, 23, 1358–1367.

Alario, F. X., Chainay, H., Lehéricy, S., & Cohen, L. (2006). The role of the supplementary motor area (SMA) in word production. *Brain Research*, 1076, 129–143.

Allen, P., Mechelli, A., Stephan, K. E., Day, F., Dalton, J., Williams, S., & McGuire, P. K. (2008). Fronto-temporal Interactions during overt verbal initiation and suppression. *Journal of Cognitive Neuroscience, 20*, 1656–1669.

Baldo, J. V., Arévalo, A., Patterson, J. P., & Dronkers, N. F. (2013). Grey and white matter correlates of picture naming: Evidence from a voxel-based lesion analysis of the Boston Naming Test. *Cortex, 49*, 658–667.

Baldo, J. V., Kacinik, N., Ludy, C., Paulraj, S., Moncrief, A., Curran, B., Turkan, A., Herron, T., & Dronkers, N. F. (2018). Voxel-based lesion analysis of brain regions underlying reading and writing. *Neuropsychologia, 115*, 51–59.

Baldo, J. V., Schwartz, S., Wilkins, D. P., & Dronkers, N. F. (2010). Double dissociation of letter and category fluency following left frontal and temporal lobe lesions. *Aphasiology, 24*, 1593–1604.

Baldo, J. V., Schwartz, S., Wilkins, D., & Dronkers, N. F. (2006). Role of frontal versus temporal cortex in verbal fluency as revealed by voxel-based lesion symptom mapping. *Journal of the International Neuropsychological Society, 12*, 896–900.

Barsalou, L. W. (2008). Grounded cognition. *Annual Review of Psychology, 59*, 617–645.

Barsalou, L. W. (2020). Challenges and opportunities for grounding cognition. *Journal of Cognition, 3*, 31.

Bartoň, M., Fňašková, M., Rektorová, I., Mikl, M., Maracek, R., Rapcsak, S. Z., & Rektor, I. (2020). The role of the striatum in visuomotor integration during handwriting: An fMRI study. *Journal of Neural Transmission, 127*, 331–337.

Baus, C., Gutiérrez, E., & Carreiras, M. (2014). The role of syllables in sign language production. *Frontiers in Psychology, 5*, 1254.

Beeson, P., Rapcsak, S., Plante, E., Chargualaf, J., Chung, A., Johnson, S., et al. (2003). The neural substrates of writing: A functional magnetic resonance imaging study. *Aphasiology, 17*, 647–665.

Belke, E., & Stielow, A. (2013). Cumulative and non-cumulative semantic interference in object naming: Evidence from blocked and continuous manipulations of semantic context. *Quarterly Journal of Experimental Psychology, 66*, 2135–2160.

Belyk, M., & Brown, S. (2017). The origins of the vocal brain in humans. *Neuroscience and Biobehavioral Reviews, 77*, 177–193.

Berg, T., & Schade, U. (1992). The role of inhibition in a spreading-activation model of language production. I. The psycholinguistic perspective. *Journal of Psycholinguistic Research, 21*, 405–434.

Biesbroek, J. M., Lim, J-S., Weaver, N. A., Arikan, G., Kang, Y., Kim, B. J., Kuijf, H. J., Postma, A., Lee, B-C., Lee, K-J., You, K-H., Bae, H-J., & Biessels, G. J. (2021). Anatomy of phonemic and semantic fluency: A lesion and disconnectome study in 1231 stroke patients. *Cortex, 143*, 148–163.

Binder, J. R. (2015). The Wernicke area: Modern evidence and a reinterpretation. *Neurology, 85*, 2170–2175.

Binder, J. R., Desai, R. H., Graves, W. W., & Conant, L. L. (2009). Where is the semantic system? A critical review and meta-analysis of 120 functional neuroimaging studies. *Cerebral Cortex, 19*, 2767–2796.

Binder, J. R., Tong, J. Q., Pillay, S. B., Conant, L. L., Humphries, C. J., Raghavan, M., Mueller, W. M., Busch, R. M., Allen, L., Gross, W. L., Anderson, C. T., Carlson, C. E., Lowe, M. J., Langfitt, J. T., Tivarus, M. E., Drane, D. L., Loring, D. W., Jacobs, M., Morgan, V. L., Allendorfer, J. B., Szaflarski, J. P., Bonilha, L., Bookheimer, S., Grabowski, T., Vannest, J., & Swanson, S. J. (2020). fMRI in anterior temporal epilepsy surgery (FATES) study. Temporal lobe regions essential for preserved picture naming after left temporal epilepsy surgery. *Epilepsia, 61*, 1939–1948.

Binney, R. J., Ashaie, S. A., Zuckerman, B. M., Hung, J., & Reilly, J. (2018). Frontotemporal stimulation modulates semantically-guided visual search during confrontation naming: A combined tDCS and eye tracking investigation. *Brain and Language, 18*, 14–23.

Binney, R. J., Parker, G. J., & Lambon Ralph, M. A. (2012). Convergent connectivity and graded specialization in the rostral human temporal lobe as revealed by diffusion-weighted imaging probabilistic tractography. *Journal of Cognitive Neuroscience, 24*, 1998–2014.

Blanco-Elorrieta, E., Emmorey, K., & Pylkkanen, L. (2018). Language switching decomposed through MEG and evidence from bimodal bilinguals. *Proceedings of the National Academy of Science USA, 115*, 9708–9713.

Blanco-Elorrieta, E., Kastner, I., Emmorey, K., & Pylkkänen, L. (2018). Shared neural correlates for building phrases in signed and spoken language. *Scientific Reports, 8*, 5492.

Bles, M., & Jansma, B. M. (2008). Phonological processing of ignored distractor pictures, an fMRI investigation. *BMC Neuroscience, 9*, 20.

Bohland, J. W., Bullock, D., & Guenther, F. H. (2010). Neural representations and mechanisms for the performance of simple speech sequences. *Journal of Cognitive Neurosciences, 22*, 1504–1529.

Bonhage, C. E., Mueller, J. L., Friederici, A. D., & Fiebach, C. J. (2015). Combined eye tracking and fMRI reveals neural basis of linguistic predictions during sentence comprehension. *Cortex, 68*, 33–47.

Botvinick, M. M., Braver, T. S., Barch, D. M., Carter, C. S., & Cohen, J. D. (2001). Conflict monitoring and cognitive control. *Psychological Review, 108*, 624–652.

Box, G. (1976). Science and statistics. *Journal of the American Statistical Association. 71*(356), 791–799.

Bozkurt, B., Yagmurlu, K., Middlebrooks, E. H., Cayci, Z., Cevik, O. M., Karadag, A., Moen, S., Tanriover, N., & Grande, A. W. (2017). Fiber connections of the supplementary motor area revisited: Methodology of fiber dissection, DTI, and three dimensional documentation. *Journal of Visualized Experiments, 123*, e55681, doi:10.3791/55681.

Bohland, J. W., & Guenther, F. H. (2006). An fMRI investigation of syllable sequence production. *NeuroImage, 32*, 821–841. 10.1016/j.neuroimage.2006.04.173.

Brendel, B., Hertrich, I., Erb, M., Lindner, A., Riecker, A., Grodd, W., & Ackermann, H. (2010). The contribution of mesiofrontal cortex to the preparation and execution of repetitive syllable productions: An fMRI study. *NeuroImage, 50*, 1219–1230.

Brown, S., Yuan, Y., & Belyk, M. (2020). Evolution of the speech-ready brain: The voice/jaw connection in the human motor cortex. *Journal of Comparative Neurology, 529*, 1018–1028.

Brownsett, S. L., Wise, R. J. (2010). The contribution of the parietal lobes to speaking and writing. *Cerebral Cortex, 20*, 517–523.

Buchsbaum, B., Pickell, B., Love, T., Hatrak, M., Bellugi, U., & Hickok, G. (2005). Neural substrates for verbal working memory in deaf signers: fMRI study and lesion case report. *Brain and Language, 95*, 265–272.

Butler, R. A., Lambon Ralph, M. A., & Woollams, A. M. (2014). Capturing multi-dimensionality in stroke aphasia: Mapping principal behavioural components to neural structures. *Brain, 137*, 3248–3266.

Caramazza, A. (1997). How many levels of processing are there in lexical access? *Cognitive Psychology, 14*, 177–208.

Caramazza, A., Bi, Y., Costa, A., & Miozzo, M. (2004). What determines the speed of lexical access: Homophone or specific-word frequency? A reply to Jescheniak et al. (2003). *Journal of Experimental Psychology: Learning, Memory, and Cognition, 30*, 278–282.

Carey, D., Miquel, M. E., Evans, B. G., Adank, P., & McGettigan, C. (2017). Functional brain outcomes of L2 speech learning emerge during sensorimotor transformation. *NeuroImage, 159*, 18–31.

Carter, B. T., Foster, B., Muncy, N. M., & Luke, S. G. (2019). Linguistic networks associated with lexical, semantic and syntactic predictability in reading: A fixation-related fMRI study. *NeuroImage, 189*, 224–240.

Catani, C., & Forkel, S. J. (2019). Diffusion imaging methods in language sciences. In G. I. de Zubicaray, & N. O. Schiller (Eds.), *The Oxford handbook of neurolinguistics* (pp. 212–227). New York: Oxford University Press.

Catani, M., Jones, D. K., & Ffytche, D. H., 2005. Perisylvian language networks of the human brain. *Annals of Neurology, 57*, 8–16.

Chiou, R., Sowman, P. F., Etchell, A. C., & Rich, A. N. (2014). A conceptual lemon: Theta burst stimulation to the left anterior temporal lobe untangles object representation and its canonical color. *Journal of Cognitive Neuroscience, 26*, 1066–1074.

Chouinard, P. A., Whitwell, R. L., & Goodale, M. A. (2009). The lateral-occipital and the inferior-frontal cortex play different roles during the naming of visually presented objects. *Human Brain Mapping*, 30, 3851–3864. 10.1002/hbm.20812.

Chouiter, L., Holmberg, J., Manuel, A. L., Colombo, F., Clarke, S., Annoni, J. M., & Spierer, L. (2016). Partly segregated cortico-subcortical pathways support phonologic and semantic verbal fluency: A lesion study. *Neuroscience, 329*, 275–283.

Cocquyt, E. M., Lanckmans, E., van Mierlo, P., Duyck, W., Szmalec, A., Santens, P., De Letter, M. (2020). The white matter architecture underlying semantic processing: A systematic review. *Neuropsychologia, 136*, 107182.

Collette, F., Van der Linden, M., Delfiore, G., Degueldre, C., Luxen, A., & Salmon, E. (2001). The functional anatomy of inhibition processes investigated with the Hayling task. *NeuroImage, 14*, 258–267.

Corina, D. P., Gibson, E. K., Martin, R., Poliakov, A., Brinkley, J., & Ojemann, G. A. (2005). Dissociation of action and object naming: Evidence from cortical stimulation mapping. *Human Brain Mapping, 24*, 1–10.

Corina, D. P., & Lawyer, L. A. (2019). The neural organisation of signed language. In G. I. de Zubicaray, & N. O. Schiller (Eds.), *The Oxford handbook of neurolinguistics* (pp. 402–424). New York: Oxford University Press.

Correia, J. M., Caballero-Gaudes, C., Guediche, S., & Carreiras, M. (2020). Phonatory and articulatory representations of speech production in cortical and subcortical fMRI responses. *Scientific Reports, 10*, 4529.

Corrivetti, F., de Schotten, M. T., Poisson, I., Froelich, S., Descoteaux, M., Rheault, F., & Mandonnet, E. (2019). Dissociating motor-speech from lexico-semantic systems in the left frontal lobe: Insight from a series of 17 awake intraoperative mappings in glioma patients. *Brain Structure and Function, 224*, 1151–1165.

Costafreda, S. G., Fu, C. H., Lee, L., Everitt, B., Brammer, M. J., & David, A. S. (2006). A systematic review and quantitative appraisal of fMRI studies of verbal fluency: Role of the left inferior frontal gyrus. *Human Brain Mapping, 27*, 799–810.

Costanzo, F., Menghini, D., Caltagirone, C., Oliveri, M., & Vicari, S. (2012). High frequency rTMS over the left parietal lobule increases non-word reading accuracy. *Neuropsychologia, 50,* 2645–2651.

Crosson, B., Sadek, J. R., Maron, L., Gökçay, D., Mohr, C. M., Auerbach, E. J., Freeman, A. J., Leonard, C. M., & Briggs, R. W. (2001). Relative shift in activity from medial to lateral frontal cortex during internally versus externally guided word generation. *Journal of Cognitive Neuroscience, 13,* 272–283.

Cutting, J. C., & Ferreira, V. S. (1999). Semantic and phonological information flow in the production lexicon. *Journal of Experimental Psychology. Learning, Memory, and cognition, 25,* 318–344.

De Baene, W., Duyck, W., Brass, M., & Carreiras, M. (2015). Brain circuit for cognitive control is shared by task and language switching. *Journal of Cognitive Neuroscience, 27,* 1752–1765.

de Bruin, A., Roelofs, A., Dijkstra, T., & Fitzpatrick, I. (2014). Domain-general inhibition areas of the brain are involved in language switching: fMRI evidence from trilingual speakers. *NeuroImage, 90,* 348–359.

De Nil, L. F., Beal, D. S., Lafaille, S. J., Kroll, R. M., Crawley, A. P., & Gracco, V. L. (2008). The effects of simulated stuttering and prolonged speech on the neural activation patterns of stuttering and nonstuttering adults. *Brain and Language, 107,* 114–123.

De Pisapia, N., & Braver, T. S. (2006). A model of dual control mechanisms through anterior cingulate and prefrontal cortex interactions. *Neurocomputing, 69,* 1322–1326.

de Zubicaray, G. I., Fraser, D., Ramajoo, K., & McMahon, K. (2017). Interference from related actions in spoken word production: Behavioural and fMRI evidence. *Neuropsychologia, 96,* 78–88.

de Zubicaray, G. I., Hansen, S., & McMahon, K. L. (2013). Differential processing of thematic and categorical conceptual relations in spoken word production. *Journal of Experimental Psychology: General, 142,* 131–142.

de Zubicaray, G., Johnson, K., Howard, D., & McMahon, K. (2014). A perfusion fMRI investigation of thematic and categorical context effects in the spoken production of object names. *Cortex, 54,* 135–149.

de Zubicaray, G. I., & McMahon, K. L. (2009). Auditory context effects in picture naming investigated with event-related fMRI. *Cognitive, Affective and Behavioral Neuroscience, 9,* 260–269.

de Zubicaray, G. I., McMahon, K. L., Eastburn, M. M. (2006a). Classic negative priming involves accessing semantic representations in the left anterior temporal cortex. *NeuroImage, 33,* 383–390.

de Zubicaray, G. I., McMahon, K. L., Eastburn, M. M., & Pringle, A. (2006b). Top-down influences on lexical selection during spoken word production: A 4T fMRI investigation of refractory effects in picture naming. *Human Brain Mapping, 27,* 864–873.

de Zubicaray, G. I., McMahon, K., & Howard, D. (2015). Perfusion fMRI evidence for priming of shared feature-to lexical connections during cumulative semantic interference in spoken word production. *Language and Cognitive Neuroscience, 30,* 261–272.

de Zubicaray, G. I., & Piai, V. (2019). Investigating the spatial and temporal components of speech production. In G. I. de Zubicaray, & N. O. Schiller (Eds.), *The Oxford handbook of neurolinguistics* (pp. 472–497). New York: Oxford University Press.

de Zubicaray, G., Rose, S. E., & McMahon, K. L. (2011). The structure and connectivity of semantic memory in the healthy older adult brain. *NeuroImage, 54,* 1488–1494.

de Zubicaray, G., & Schiller, N. (eds.). (2019). *The Oxford handbook of neurolinguistics.* New York: Oxford University Press.

de Zubicaray, G. I., Wilson, S. J., McMahon, K. L., & Muthiah, S. (2001). The semantic interference effect in the picture-word paradigm: An event-related fMRI study employing overt responses. *Human Brain Mapping, 14*, 218–227.

de Zubicaray, G. I., Zelaya, F. O., Andrew, C., Williams, S. C. R., & Bullmore, E. T. (2000). Cerebral regions associated with verbal response initiation, suppression and strategy use. *Neuropsychologia, 38*, 1292–1304.

de Zubicaray, G. I., McMahon, K., Eastburn, M., & Wilson, S. (2002). Orthographic/ phonological facilitation of naming responses in the picture-word task: an event-related fMRI study using overt vocal responding. *NeuroImage, 16*(4), 1084–1093. 10.1006/ nimg.2002.1135.

Dell, G. S. (1986). A spreading-activation theory of retrieval in sentence production. *Psychological Review, 93*, 283–321.

Dell, G. S. (1990). Effects of frequency and vocabulary type on phonological speech errors. *Language and Cognitive Processes, 5*, 313–349.

Dell, G. S. (2013). Cascading and feedback in interactive models of production: A reflection of forward modeling? *Behavioral and Brain Sciences, 36*, 351–352.

Dell, G. S., & O'Seaghdha, P. G. (1992). Stages of lexical access in language production. *Cognition, 42*, 287–314.

Dell, G. S., Schwartz, M. F., Martin, N., Saffran, E. M., & Gagnon, D. A. (1997). Lexical access in normal and aphasic speakers. *Psychological Review, 104*, 801–838.

Dell, G. S., Schwartz, M. F., Nozari, N., Faseyitan, O., & Coslett, H. B. (2013). Voxel-based lesion-parameter mapping: Identifying the neural correlates of a computational model of word production. *Cognition, 128*, 380–396.

den Ouden, D. B., Malyutina, S., Basilakos, A., Bonilha, L., Gleichgerrcht, E., Yourganov, G., Hillis, A. E., Hickok, G., Rorden, C., & Fridriksson, J. (2019). Cortical and structural connectivity damage correlated with impaired syntactic processing in aphasia. *Human Brain Mapping, 40*, 21532173.

Dick, A. S., Bernal, B., & Tremblay, P. (2014). The language connectome: New pathways, new concepts. *The Neuroscientist, 20*, 453–467.

Dick, A. S., Garic, D., Graziano, P., & Tremblay, P. (2019). The frontal aslant tract (FAT) and its role in speech, language and executive function. *Cortex, 111*, 148–163.

Draganski, B., Kherif, F., Klöppel, S., Cook, P. A., Alexander, D. C., Parker, G. J., Deichmann, R., Ashburner, J., & Frackowiak, R. S. (2008). Evidence for segregated and integrative connectivity patterns in the human basal ganglia. *Journal of Neuroscience, 28*, 7143–7152.

Duffau, H. (2019). What has direct cortical and subcortical electrical stimulation taught us about neurolinguistics? In G. I. de Zubicaray & N. O. Schiller (Eds.), *The Oxford handbook of neurolinguistics* (pp. 186–211). New York: Oxford University Press.

Duffau, H., Capelle, L., Sichez, N., Denvil, D., Lopes, M., Sichez, J. P., & Fohanno, D. (2002). Intraoperative mapping of the subcortical language pathways using direct stimulations. An anatomo-functional study. *Brain, 125*, 199–214.

Duffau, H., Moritz-Gasser, S., & Mandonnet, E. (2014). A re-examination of neural basis of language processing: proposal of a dynamic hodotopical model from data provided by brain stimulation mapping during picture naming. *Brain and Language, 131*, 1–10.

Eichert, N., Papp, D., Mars, R. B., & Watkins K. E. (2020). Mapping human laryngeal motor cortex during vocalization. *Cerebral Cortex, 30*, 6254–6269.

Emmorey, K., Giezen, M., & Gollan, T. (2016). Psycholinguistic, cognitive, and neural implications of bimodal bilingualism. *Bilingualism: Language and Cognition, 19*, 223–242.

Emmorey, K., Grabowski, T., McCullough, S., Damasio, H., Ponto, L., Hichwa, R., & Bellugi, U. (2004). Motor-iconicity of sign language does not alter the neural systems underlying tool and action naming. *Brain and Language, 89*, 27–37.

Emmorey, K., Luk, G., Pyers, J. E., & Bialystok, E. (2008). The source of enhanced cognitive control in bilinguals: Evidence from bimodal bilinguals. *Psychological Science, 19*, 1201–1206.

Emmorey, K., McCullough, S., Mehta, S., & Grabowski, T. J. (2014). How sensory-motor systems impact the neural organization for language: direct contrasts between spoken and signed language. *Frontiers in Psychology*, 5. 10.3389/fpsyg.2014.00484.

Emmorey, K., McCullough, S., Mehta, S., Ponto, L. L. B., & Grabowski, T. J. (2013). The biology of linguistic expression impacts neural correlates for spatial language. *Journal of Cognitive Neuroscience, 25*, 517–533.

Emmorey, K., Mehta, S., & Grabowski, T. J. (2007). The neural correlates of sign versus word production. *NeuroImage, 36*, 202–208.

Federenko, E., Fillmore, P., Smith, K., Bonilha, L., & Fridriksson, J. (2015). The superior precentral gyrus of the insula does not appear to be functionally specialized for articulation. *Journal of Neurophysiology, 113*, 2376–2382.

Finkl, T., Hahne, A., Friederici, A. D., Gerber, J., Mürbe, D., & Anwander, A. (2020). Language without speech: Segregating distinct circuits in the human brain. *Cerebral Cortex, 30*, 812–823.

Fridriksson J., Guo D., Fillmore P., Holland A., Rorden C. (2013). Damage to the anterior arcuate fasciculus predicts non-fluent speech production in aphasia. *Brain, 136*, 3451–3460.

Fan, L., Li, H., Zhuo, J., Zhang, Y., Wang, J., Chen, L., Yang, Z., Chu, C., Xie, S., Laird, A. R., Fox, P. T., Eickhoff, S. B., Yu, C., & Jiang, T. (2016). The human brainnetome atlas: A new brain atlas based on connectional architecture. *Cerebral Cortex, 26*, 3508–3526. 10.1093/cercor/bhw157.

Fu, Y., Lu, D., Kang, C., Wu, J., Ma, F., Ding, G., & Guo, T. (2017). Neural correlates for naming disadvantage of the dominant language in bilingual word production. *Brain and Language, 175*, 123–129.

Gajardo-Vidal, A., Lorca-Puls, D. L., Team, P., Warner, H., Pshdary, B., Crinion, J. T., Leff, A. P., Hope, T. M. H., Geva, S., Seghier, M. L., Green, D. W., Bowman, H., & Price, C. J. (2021). Damage to Broca's area does not contribute to long-term speech production outcome after stroke. *Brain, 144*, 817–832.

Gallese, V., & Lakoff, G. (2005). The brain's concepts: The role of the sensory-motor system in reason and language. *Cognitive Neuropsychology, 22*, 455–479.

Garbin, G., Costa, A., Sanjuan, A., Forn, C., Rodriguez-Pujadas, A., Ventura, N., et al. (2011). Neural bases of language switching in high and early proficient bilinguals. *Brain and Language, 119*, 129–135.

Gauvin, H. S., & Hartsuiker, R. J. (2020). Towards a new model of verbal monitoring, *Journal of Cognition, 3*, 17.

Gauvin, H. S., De Baene, W., Brass, M., & Hartsuiker, R. J. (2016). Conflict monitoring in speech processing: An fMRI study of error detection in speech production and perception. *NeuroImage, 126*, 96–105.

Gauvin, H. S., McMahon, K. L., & de Zubicaray, G. I. (2021). Top-down resolution of lexico-semantic competition in speech production and the role of the left inferior frontal gyrus: An fMRI study. *Language, Cogniton and Neuroscience, 36*, 1–12.

Geranmayeh, F., Leech, R., & Wise, R. J. S. (2015). Semantic retrieval during overt picture description: Left anterior temporal or the parietal lobe? *Neuropsychologia, 76*, 125–135.

Geschwind, N. (1979). Specializations of the human brain. *Scientific American, 241*, 180–199.

Geva, S., Schneider, L. M., Roberts, S., Khan, S., Gajardo-Vidal, A., Lorca-Puls, D. L., Ploras team, Hope T. M. H., Green, D. W., & Price, C. J. (2021). Right cerebral motor areas that support accurate speech production following damage to cerebellar speech areas. *NeuroImage: Clinical, 32*, 102820.

Ghosh, S. S., Tourville, J. A., & Guenther, F. H. (2008). A neuroimaging study of pre-motor lateralization and cerebellar involvement in the production of phonemes and syllables. *Journal of Speech, Language, and Hearing Research, 51*, 1183–1202.

Glasser, M. F., & Rilling, J. K. (2008). DTI tractography of the human brain's language pathways. *Cerebral Cortex, 18*, 2471–2482.

Gow, D. W. (2012). The cortical organization of lexical knowledge: A dual lexicon model of spoken language processing. *Brain and Language, 121*, 273–288.

Grappe, A., Sarma, S. V., Sacré, P., González-Martínez, J., Liégeois-Chauvel, C., & Alario, F.-X. (2018). An intracerebral exploration of functional connectivity during word production. *Journal of Computational Neuroscience, 46*, 125–140. 10.1007/s10827-018-0699-3.

Graves, W. W., Grabowski, T. J., Mehta, S., & Gordon, J. (2007). A neural signature of phonological access: Distinguishing the effects of word frequency from familiarity and length in overt picture naming. *Journal of Cognitive Neuroscience, 19*, 617–631.

Guenther, F. H. (1995). Speech sound acquisition, coarticulation, and rate effects in a neural network model of speech production. *Psychological Review, 102*, 594–621.

Guenther, F. H. (2016). *Neural control of speech.* Cambridge, MA: MIT Press.

Guenther, F. H., Ghosh, S. S., & Tourville, J. A. (2006). Neural modeling and imaging of the cortical interactions underlying syllable production. *Brain & Language, 96*, 280–301.

Guo, T., Liu, H., Misra, M., & Kroll, J. F. (2011). Local and global inhibition in bilingual word production: fMRI evidence from Chinese-English bilinguals. *NeuroImage, 56*, 2300–2309.

Han, Z., Ma, Y., Gong, G., He, Y., Caramazza, A., & Bi, Y. (2013). White matter structural connectivity underlying semantic processing: Evidence from brain damaged patients. *Brain, 136*, 2952–2965.

Hansen, S., McMahon, K., & de Zubicaray, G. (2019). Neural mechanisms for monitoring and halting of spoken word production. *Journal of Cognitive Neuroscience, 31*, 1946–1957.

Harley, T. A. (1993). Phonological activation of semantic competitors during lexical access in speech production. *Language and Cognitive Processes, 8*, 291–309.

Hartwigsen, G. (2014). The neurophysiology of language: Insights from non-invasive brain stimulation in the healthy human brain. *Brain and Language, 148*, 81–94.

Hartwigsen, G., Saur, D., Price, C. J., Ulmer, S., Baumgaertner, A., & Siebner, H. R. (2013). Perturbation of the left inferior frontal gyrus triggers adaptive plasticity in the right homologous area during speech production. *Proceedings of the National Academy of Sciences of the USA, 110*, 16402–16407.

Harvey, D., & Schnur, T. T. (2015). Distinct loci of lexical and semantic access deficits in aphasia: Evidence from voxel-based lesion-symptom mapping and diffusion tensor imaging. *Cortex, 67*, 37–58.

Heim, S., Eickhoff, S. B., & Amunts, K. (2009). Different roles of cytoarchitectonic BA 44 and BA 45 in phonological and semantic verbal fluency as revealed by dynamic causal modelling. *NeuroImage, 48*, 616–624.

Heim, S., & Specht, K. (2019). Studying language with functional magnetic resonance imaging. In G. I. de Zubicaray & N. O. Schiller (Eds.), *The Oxford handbook of neurolinguistics* (pp. 72–93). New York: Oxford University Press.

Herbet, G., Moritz-Gasser, S., Boiseau, M., Duvaux, S., Cochereau, J., & Duffau, H. (2016). Converging evidence for a cortico-subcortical network mediating lexical retrieval. *Brain, 139*, 3007–3021.

Herbet, G., Moritz-Gasser, S., Lemaitre, A. L., Almairac, F., & Duffau, H. (2019). Functional compensation of the left inferior longitudinal fasciculus for picture naming. *Cognitive Neuropsychology, 6*, 1–18.

Hickok, G. (2012). Computational neuroanatomy of speech production. *Nature Reviews Neuroscience, 13*, 135–145.

Hockey, A. (2006). *Computational modelling of the language production system: semantic memory, conflict monitoring, and cognitive control processes.* [Unpublished Masters Thesis, University of Queensland].

Hockey, A., Wiles, J., & de Zubicaray, G. (2005, November). *Interactivity, conflict and cognitive control: Computational modelling of the language production system.* Poster presented at the Dynamical Neuroscience Conference, Washington, DC.

Hocking, J., McMahon, K., & de Zubicaray, G. (2009). Semantic context and visual feature effects in object naming: An fMRI study using arterial spin labelling. *Journal of Cognitive Neuroscience, 21*, 1571–1583.

Hofmann, M. J., Dambacher, M., Jacobs, A. M., Kliegl, R., Radach, R., Kuchinke, L., Plichta, M.-M., Fallgatter, A. J., Herrmann, M. J. (2014). Occipital and orbitofrontal hemodynamics during naturally paced reading: An fNIRS study. *NeuroImage, 94*, 193–202.

Hornberger, M., Geng, J., & Hodges, J. R. (2011). Convergent grey and white matter evidence of orbitofrontal cortex changes related to disinhibition in behavioural variant frontotemporal dementia. *Brain, 134*, 2502–2512.

Howard, D., & Nickels, L. (2005). Separating input and output phonology: Semantic, phonological, and orthographic effects in short-term memory impairment. *Cognitive Neuropsychology, 22*, 42–77.

Howard, D., Nickels, L., Coltheart, M., & Cole-Virtue, J. (2006). Cumulative semantic inhibition in picture naming: experimental and computational studies. *Cognition, 100*(3), 464–482. 10.1016/j.cognition.2005.02.006.

Hu Z., Wang W., Liu H., Peng D., Yang Y., Li K., Zhang, J. X., & Ding, G. (2011). Brain activations associated with sign production using word and picture inputs in deaf signers. *Brain and Language, 116*, 64–70.

Hula, W. D., Panesar, S., Gravier, M. L., Yeh, F. C., Dresang, H. C., Dickey, M. W., & Fernandez-Miranda, J. C. (2020). Structural white matter connectometry of word production in aphasia: An observational study. *Brain, 143*, 2532–2544.

Indefrey, P. (2011). The spatial and temporal signatures of word production components: A critical update. *Frontiers in Psychology, 2*, 255.

Indefrey, P. (2016). On putative shortcomings and dangerous future avenues: Response to Strijkers & Costa. *Language, Cognition & Neuroscience, 31*, 517–520.

Indefrey, P., & Levelt, W. J. M. (2000). The neural correlates of language production. In M. Gazzaniga (Ed.), *The new cognitive neurosciences* (pp. 845–865). Cambridge, MA: MIT Press.

Indefrey, P., & Levelt, W. J. M. (2004). The spatial and temporal signatures of word production components. *Cognition*, *92*, 101–144.

Ivanova, M. V., Zhong, A., Turken, A., Baldo, J. V., & Dronkers, N. F. (2021). Functional contributions of the arcuate fasciculus to language processing. Frontiers in Human Neuroscience, *15*, 672665.

Ivanova, M. V., Isaev, D. Y., Dragoy, O. V., Akinina, Y. S., Petrushevskiy, A. G., Fedina, O. N., Shklovsky, V. M., & Dronkers, N. F. (2016). Diffusion-tensor imaging of major white matter tracts and their role in language processing in aphasia. *Cortex*, *85*, 165–181.

Jacquemot, C., Dupoux, E., & Bachoud-Lévi, A.-C. (2007). Breaking the mirror: Asymmetrical disconnection between the phonological input and output codes. *Cognitive Neuropsychology*, *24*, 3–22.

Janssen, N., Roelofs, A., Mangnus, M., Sierpowska, J., Kessels, R. P. C., & Piai, V. (2020). How the speed of word finding depends on ventral tract integrity in primary progressive aphasia. *NeuroImage: Clinical*, *28*, 102450.

Jescheniak, J. D., & Levelt, W. J. M. (1994). Word frequency effects in speech production: Retrieval of syntactic information and of phonological form. *Journal of Experimental Psychology: Learning, Memory, and Cognition*, *20*, 824–843.

Kalanthroff, E., Davelaar, E. J., Henik, A., Goldfarb, L., & Usher, M. (2018). Task conflict and proactive control: A computational theory of the Stroop task. *Psychological Review*, *125*, 59–82.

Kandel, S., Álvarez, C. J., & Vallée, N. (2006). Syllables as processing units in handwriting production. *Journal of Experimental Psychology: Human Perception and Performance*, *32*, 18–31.

Karnath, H-O., Sperber, C., Wiesen, D., & de Haan, B. (2020). Lesion-behaviour mapping in cognitive neuroscience: A practical guide to univariate and multivariate approaches. In S. Pollmann (Ed.), *Spatial Learning and Attention Guidance. Neuromethods*, vol. 151 9 (pp. 209–238). New York: Humana Press.

Kassubek, J., Hickok, G., & Erhard, P. (2004). Involvement of classical anterior and posterior language areas in sign language production, as investigated by 4 T functional magnetic resonance imaging. *Neuroscience Letters*, *364*, 168–172.

Katzev, M., Tuscher, O., Hennig, J., Weiller, C., & Kaller, C. P. (2013). Revisiting the functional specialization of left inferior frontal gyrus in phonological and semantic fluency: The crucial role of task demands and individual ability. *Journal of Neuroscience*, *33*, 7837–7845.

Klaus, J., & Hartwigsen, G. (2019). Dissociating semantic and phonological contributions of the left inferior frontal gyrus to language production. *Human Brain Mapping*, *40*, 3279–3287. 10.1002/hbm.24597.

Kearney, E., & Guenther, F. (2019). Articulating: The neural mechanisms of speech production. *Language, Cognition and Neuroscience*, *34*, 1214–1229.

Kemmerer, D. (2019). From blueprints to brain maps: The status of the Lemma Model in cognitive neuroscience. *Language, Cognition and Neuroscience*, *34*, 1085–1116.

Kinoshita, M., de Champfleur, N. M., Deverdun, J., Moritz-Gasser, S., Herbet, G., & Duffau, H., (2015). Role of fronto-striatal tract and frontal aslant tract in movement and speech: An axonal mapping study. *Brain Structure and Function*, *220*, 3399–3412.

Kovelman, I., Shalinsky, M. H., White, K. S., Schmitt, S. N., Berens, M. S., Paymer, N., & Petitto, L.-A. (2009). Dual language use in sign-speech bimodal bilinguals: fNIRS brain-imaging evidence. *Brain and Language*, *109*, 112–123.

Kroll, J. F., & Stewart, E. (1994). Category interference in translation and picture naming: Evidence for asymmetric connections between bilingual memory representations. *Journal of Memory and Language, 33*, 149–174.

Laganaro, M. (2019). Phonetic encoding in utterance production: A review of open issues from 1989 to 2018. *Language, Cognition and Neuroscience, 34*, 1193–1201.

Lambon Ralph, M., Jefferies, E., Patterson, K., & Rogers, T. (2017). The neural and computational bases of semantic cognition. *Nature Reviews Neuroscience, 18*, 42–55.

Leh, S. E., Ptito, A., Chakravarty, M. M., & Strafella, A. P. (2007). Fronto-striatal connections in the human brain: A probabilistic diffusion tractography study. *Neuroscience Letters, 419*, 113–118.

Lehéricy, S., Ducros, M., Krainik, A., Francois, C., Van de Moortele, P. F., Ugurbil, K., & Kim, D. S. (2004). 3-D diffusion tensor axonal tracking shows distinct SMA and pre-SMA projections to the human striatum. *Cerebral Cortex, 14*, 1302–1309.

Levelt, W. J. M. (1989). *Speaking: From intention to articulation.* Cambridge, MA: MIT Press.

Levelt, W. J. M., Roelofs, A., & Meyer, A. S. (1999). A theory of lexical access in speech production. *Behavioral and Brain Sciences, 22*, 1–38.

Li, L., Abutalebi, J., Zou, L., Yan, X., Liu, L., Feng, X., Wang, R., Guo, T., & Ding, G. (2015). Bilingualism alters brain functional connectivity between "control" regions and "language" regions: Evidence from bimodal bilinguals. *Neuropsychologia, 71*, 236–247.

Lichtheim, L. (1885). On aphasia. *Brain, 7*, 433–484.

Longcamp, M., Hupe, J. M., Ruiz, M., Vayssiere, N., & Sato, M. (2019). Shared premotor activity in spoken and written communication. *Brain and Language, 199*, 104694.

Llorens, A., Dubarry, A.-S., Trébuchon, A., Chauvel, P., Alario, F.-X., & Liégeois-Chauvel, C. (2016). Contextual modulation of hippocampal activity during picture naming. *Brain and Language, 159*, 92–101. 10.1016/j.bandl.2016.05.011.

Luber, B., & Lisanby, S. H. (2014). Enhancement of human cognitive performance using transcranial magnetic stimulation (TMS). *NeuroImage, 85*, 961–970.

Lurito, J. T., Kareken, D. A., Lowe, M. J., Chen, S. H. A., & Mathews, V. P. (2000). Comparison of rhyming and word generation with FMRI. *Human Brain Mapping, 10*, 99–106.

Maess, B., Friederici, A. D., Damian, M., Meyer, A. S., & Levelt, W. J. (2002). Semantic category interference in overt picture naming: Sharpening current density localization by PCA. *Journal of Cognitive Neuroscience, 14*, 455–462.

Maffei, C., Soria, G., Prats-Galino, A., & Cantani, M. (2015). Imaging white-matter pathways of the auditory system with diffusion imaging tractography. *Handbook of Clinical Neurology, 129C*, 277–288. 10.1016/B978-0-444-62630-1.00016-0.

Mandal, A. S., Fama, M. E., Skipper-Kallal, L. M., DeMarco, A. T., Lacey, E. H., & Turkeltaub, P. E. (2020). Brain structures and cognitive abilities important for the self-monitoring of speech errors. *Neurobiology of Language, 1*, 319–338.

Mandonnet, E., Herbet, G., Moritz-Gasser, S., Poisson, I., Rheault, F., & Duffau H. (2019). Electrically induced verbal perseveration: A striatal deafferentation model. *Neurology, 92*, e613–e621.

Marchina, S., Norton, A., Kumar, S., & Schlaug, G. (2018). The effect of speech repetition rate on neural activation in healthy adults: Implications for treatment of aphasia and other fluency disorders. *Frontiers in Human Neuroscience, 12*, 69.

Marchina, S., Zhu, L. L., Norton, A., Zipse, L., Wan, C. Y., & Schlaug, G. (2011). Impairment of speech production predicted by lesion load of the left arcuate fasciculus. *Stroke, 42*(8), 2251–2256. 10.1161/strokeaha.110.606103.

Markiewicz, C. J., & Bohland, J. W. (2016). Mapping the cortical representation of speech sounds in a syllable repetition task. *NeuroImage*, *141*, 174–190.

Martino, J., Brogna, C., Robles, S. G., Vergani, F., & Duffau, H. (2009). Anatomic dissection of the inferior fronto-occipital fasciculus revisited in the lights of brain stimulation data. *Cortex*, *46*, 691–699.

McKinnon, E. T., Fridriksson, J., Basilakos, A., Hickok, G., Hillis, A. E., Spampinato, M. V., Gleichgerrcht, E., Rorden, C., Jensen, J. H., Helpern, J. A., & Bonilha, L. (2018). Types of naming errors in chronic post-stroke aphasia are dissociated by dual stream axonal loss. *Scientific Reports*, *8*, 14352.

Meekings, S., & Scott, S. K. (2021). Error in the superior temporal gyrus? A systematic review and activation likelihood estimation meta-analysis of speech production studies. *Journal of Cognitive Neuroscience*, *33*, 422–444.

Minagawa, Y., & Cristia, A. (2019). Shedding light on language function and its development with optical brain imaging. In G. I. de Zubicaray, & N. O. Schiller (Eds.), *The Oxford handbook of neurolinguistics* (pp. 154–185). New York: Oxford University Press.

Mirman, D., Chen, Q., Zhang, Y., Wang, Z., Faseyitan, O. K., Coslett, H. B., & Schwartz, M. F. (2015). Neural organization of spoken language revealed by lesion-symptom mapping. *Nature Communications*, *6*, 6762.

Mirman, D., & Graziano, K. M. (2013). The neural basis of inhibitory effects of semantic and phonological neighbors in spoken word production. *Journal of Cognitive Neuroscience*, *25*, 1504–1516. 10.1162/jocn_a_00408.

Monsell, S., Taylor, T. J., & Murphy, K. (2001). Naming the color of a word: Is it responses or task sets that compete? *Memory and Cognition*, *29*, 137–151.

Moser, D., Fridriksson, J., Bonilha, L., Healy, E. W., Baylis, G., Baker, J. M., & Rorden, C. (2009). Neural recruitment for the production of native and novel speech sounds. *NeuroImage*, *46*, 549–557.

Mottaghy, F. M., Sparing, R., & Töpper, R. (2006). Enhancing picture naming with transcranial magnetic stimulation. *Behavioral Neurology*, *17*, 177–186.

Nakamura, K., Hara, N., Kouider, S., Takayama, Y., Hanajima, R., Sakai, K., & Ugawa, Y. (2006). Task-guided selection of the dual neural pathways for reading. *Neuron*, *52*, 557–564.

Nozari, N. (2020). Neural basis of word production. In L. R. Gleitman, A. Papafragou, & J. C. Trueswell (Eds.), *The Oxford handbook of the mental lexicon*. New York: Oxford University Press.

Nozari, N., Dell, G. S., & Schwartz, M. F. (2011). Is comprehension necessary for error detection? A conflict-based account of monitoring in speech production. *Cognitive Psychology*, *63*, 1–33.

Ntemou, E., Ohlerth, A-K., Ille, S., Krieg, S. M., Bastiaanse, R., & Rofes, A. (2021). Mapping verb retrieval with nTMS: The role of transitivity. *Frontiers in Human Neuroscience*, *15*, 719461.

Okada K., Rogalsky C., O'Grady L., Hanaumi L., Bellugi U., Corina D., & Hickok, G. (2016). An fMRI study of perception and action in deaf signers. *Neuropsychologia*, *82*, 179–188.

Okada, K., Matchin, W., & Hickok, G. (2018). Neural evidence for predictive coding in auditory cortex during speech production. *Psychonomic Bulletin and Review*, *25*, 423–430.

Oppenheim, G. M., Dell, G. S., & Schwartz, M. F. (2010). The dark side of incremental learning: A model of cumulative semantic interference during lexical access in speech production. *Cognition*, *114*, 227–252.

Pa, J., Wilson, S. M., Pickell, H., Bellugi, U., & Hickok, G. (2008). Neural organization of linguistic short-term memory is sensory modality-dependent: Evidence from signed and spoken language. *Journal of Cognitive Neuroscience, 20,* 2198–2210.

Palmis, S., Velay, J.-L., Fabiani, E., Nazarian, B., Anton, J.-L., Habib, M., Kandel, S., & Longcamp, M. (2019). The impact of spelling regularity on handwriting production: A coupled fMRI and kinematics study. *Cortex, 113,* 111–127.

Papoutsi, M., de Zwart, J. A., Jansma, J. M., Pickering, M. J., Bednar, J. A., & Horwitz, B. (2009). From phonemes to articulatory codes: An fMRI study of the role of Broca's area in speech production. *Cerebral Cortex, 19,* 2156–2165.

Park, H., Iverson, G. K., & Park, H. J. (2011). Neural correlates in the processing of phoneme-level complexity in vowel production. *Brain and Language, 119,* 158–166.

Pattamadilok, C., Bulnes, L. C., Devlin, J. T., Bourguignon, M., Morais, J., Goldman, S., & Kolinsky, R. (2015). How early does the brain distinguish between regular words, irregular words, and pseudowords during the reading process? Evidence from neuro-chronometric TMS. *Journal of Cognitive Neuroscience, 27,* 1259–1274.

Peeva, M. G., Guenther, F. H., Tourville, J. A., Nieto-Castanon, A., Anton, J. L., Nazarian, B., & Alario, F. X. (2010). Distinct representations of phonemes, syllables, and suprasyllabic sequences in the speech production network. *NeuroImage, 50,* 626–638.

Peng, D., Lin, Q., Chang, Y., Jones, J. A., Jia, G., Chen, X., Liu, P., & Liu, H. (2021). A causal role of the cerebellum in auditory feedback control of vocal production. *The Cerebellum, 20*(4), 584–595. 10.1007/s12311-021-01230-1.

Peterson, R. R., & Savoy, P. (1998). Lexical selection and phonological encoding during language production: Evidence for cascaded processing. *Journal of Experimental Psychology: Learning, Memory & Cognition, 24,* 539–557.

Piai, V., Nieberlein, L., & Hartwigsen, G. (2020). Effects of transcranial magnetic stimulation over the left posterior superior temporal gyrus on picture-word interference. *PLoS ONE, 15,* e0242941.

Piai, V., Roelofs, A., Acheson, D. J., & Takashima, A. (2013). Attention for speaking: Domain-general control from anterior cingulate cortex in spoken word production. *Frontiers in Human Neuroscience, 7,* 832.

Piai, V., Roelofs, A., Jensen, O., Schoffelen, J. M., & Bonnefond, M. (2014). Distinct patterns of brain activity characterise lexical activation and competition in spoken word production. *PLoS One, 9*(2), e88674.

Pickering, M. J., & Garrod, S. (2013). An integrated theory of language production and comprehension. *Behavioral Brain Sciences, 36,* 329–347.

Pisoni, A., Cerciello, M., Cattaneo, Z., & Papagno, C. (2017). Phonological facilitation in picture naming: When and where? A tDCS study. *Neuroscience, 352,* 106–121.

Planton, S., Jucla, M., Démonet, J.-F., & Soum-Favaro, C. (2017b). Effects of orthographic consistency and word length on the dynamics of written production in adults: Psycholinguistic and rTMS experiments. *Reading and Writing, 32,* 115–146.

Planton, S., Jucla, M., Roux, F.-E., & Démonet, J.-F. (2013). The "handwriting brain": A meta-analysis of neuroimaging studies of motor versus orthographic processes. *Cortex, 49,* 2772–2787.

Planton, S., Longcamp, M., Péran, P., Démonet, J.-F., & Jucla, M. (2017a). How specialized are writing specific brain regions? An fMRI study of writing, drawing and oral spelling. *Cortex, 88,* 66–80.

Pobric, G., Jefferies, E., & Ralph, M. A. (2007). Anterior temporal lobes mediate semantic representation: Mimicking semantic dementia by using rTMS in normal participants. *Proceedings of the National Academy of Sciences of the USA, 104*(50), 20137–20141.

Pobric, G., Jeffries, E., & Lambon Ralph, A. (2010). Amodal semantic representations depend on both anterior temporal lobes: Evidence from repetitive transcranial magnetic stimulation. *Neuropsychologia, 48,* 1336–1342.

Potgieser, A. R. E., van der Hoorn, A., & de Jong, B. M. (2015). Cerebral activations related to writing and drawing with each hand. *PLoS ONE, 10,* e0126723.

Price, C. J., Devlin, J. T., Moore, C. J., Morton, C., & Laird, A. R. (2005). Meta-analyses of object naming: Effect of baseline. *Human Brain Mapping, 25,* 70–82.

Purcell, J. J., Jiang, X., & Eden, G. F. (2017). Shared orthographic neuronal representations for spelling and reading. *NeuroImage, 147,* 554–567.

Radanovic, M., & Mansur, L. L. (2017). Aphasia in vascular lesions of the basal ganglia: A comprehensive review. *Brain and Language, 173,* 20–32.

Rapp, B., & Caramazza, A. (2002). Selective difficulties with spoken nouns and written verbs: A single case study. *Journal of Neurolinguistics, 15,* 373–402.

Rapp, B., & Damian, M. (2018). From thought to action: Producing written language. In S-A. Rueschemeyer, & G. Gaskell (Eds.), *The Oxford handbook of psycholinguistics (2 ed.)* (pp. 398–431). Oxford University Press.

Rapp, B., & Dufor, O. (2011). The neurotopography of written word production: An fMRI investigation of the distribution of sensitivity to length and frequency. *Journal of Cognitive Neuroscience, 23,* 4067–4081.

Rapp, B., Purcell, J., Hillis, A. E., Capasso, R., & Miceli, G. (2015). Neural bases of orthographic long-term memory and working memory in dysgraphia. *Brain, 139,* 588–604.

Reverberi, C., Kuhlen, A. K., Seyed-Allaei, S., Greulich, R. S., Costa, A., Abutalebi, J., & Haynes, J. D. (2018). The neural basis of free language choice in bilingual speakers: Disentangling language choice and language execution. *NeuroImage, 177,* 108–116.

Reverberi, C., Kuhlen, A., Abutalebi, J., Greulich, R. S., Costa, A., Seyed-Allaei, S., & Haynes, J.-D. (2015). Language control in bilinguals: Intention to speak vs. execution of speech. *Brain and Language, 144,* 1–9. 10.1016/j.bandl.2015.03.004.

Riecker, A., Brendel, B., Ziegler, W., Erb, M., & Ackermann, H. (2008). The influence of syllable onset complexity and syllable frequency on speech motor control. *Brain and Language, 107,* 102–113.

Riecker, A., Kassubek, J., Gröschel, K., Grodd, W., & Ackermann, H. (2006). The cerebral control of speech tempo: Opposite relationship between speaking rate and BOLD signal changes at striatal and cerebellar structures. *NeuroImage, 29,* 46–53.

Roelofs, A. (1992). A spreading-activation theory of lemma retrieval in speaking. *Cognition, 42,* 107–142.

Roelofs, A. (2014). A dorsal-pathway account of aphasic language production: The WEAVER++/ARC model. *Cortex, 59,* 33–48.

Roelofs, A. (2018). A unified computational account of cumulative semantic, semantic blocking, and semantic distractor effects in picture naming. *Cognition, 172,* 59–72.

Robinson, G. A., Cipolotti, L., Walker, D. G., Biggs, V., Bozzali, M., & Shallice, T. (2015). Verbal suppression and strategy use: a role for the right lateral prefrontal cortex? *Brain, 138*(Pt 4), 1084–1096. 10.1093/brain/awv003.

Roelofs, A., & Ferreira, V. S. (2019). The architecture of speaking. In P. Hagoort (Ed.), *Human language: From genes and brains to behavior* (pp. 35–50). MIT Press.

Roelofs, A., van Turennout, M., & Coles, M. G. (2006). Anterior cingulate cortex activity can be independent of response conflict in Stroop-like tasks. *Proceedings of the National Academy of Sciences USA, 103,* 13884–13889.

Rolls, E. T., & Deco, G. (2016). Non-reward neural mechanisms in the orbitofrontal cortex. *Cortex, 83,* 27–38.

Rong, F., Isenberg, A. L., Sun, E., & Hickok, G. (2018). The neuroanatomy of speech sequencing at the syllable level. *PLoS ONE, 13,* e0196381.

Rosch, E., and Mervis, C. B. (1975). Family resemblances: Studies in the internal structure of categories. *Cognitive Psychology, 7,* 573–605.

Rosinski, R. R., Golinkoff, R. M., & Kukish, K. S. (1975). Automatic semantic processing in a picture-word interference task. *Child Development, 46,* 247–253.

Roux, F.-E., Dufor, O., Giussani, C., Wamain, Y., Draper, L., Longcamp, M., et al. (2009). The graphemic/motor frontal area Exner's area revisited. *Annals of Neurology, 66,* 537–545.

Rudebeck, P. H., & Murray, E. A. (2014). The orbitofrontal oracle: Cortical mechanisms for the prediction and evaluation of specific behavioral outcomes. *Neuron, 84,* 1143–1156.

Runnqvist, E., Bonnard, M., Gauvin, H. S., Attarian, S., Trébuchon, A., Hartsuiker, R. J., & Alario, F. X. (2016). Internal modeling of upcoming speech: A causal role of the right posterior cerebellum in non-motor aspects of language production. *Cortex, 81,* 203–214.

Runnqvist, E., Chanoine, V., Strijkers, K., Pattamadilok, C., Bonnard, M., Nazarian, B., Sein, J., Anton, J. L., Dorokhova, L., Belin, P., & Alario, F. X. (2021). Cerebellar and cortical correlates of internal and external speech error monitoring. *Cerebral Cortex Communications, 2,* tgab038.

Sakreida, K., Blume-Schnitzler, J., Heim, S., Willmes, K., Clusmann, H., & Neuloh, G. (2019). Phonological picture-word interference in language mapping with transcranial magnetic stimulation: An objective approach for functional parcellation of Broca's region. *Brain Structure and Function, 224,* 2027–2044.

San Jose´-Robertson L., Corina D. P., Ackerman D., Guillemin A., & Braun A. R. (2004). Neural systems for sign language production: Mechanisms supporting lexical selection, phonological encoding, and articulation. *Human Brain Mapping, 23,* 156–167.

Sarubbo, S., De Benedictis, A., Maldonado, I. L., Basso, G., & Duffau, H. (2013). Frontal terminations for the inferior fronto-occipital fascicle: Anatomical dissection, DTI study and functional considerations on a multi-component bundle. *Brain Structure and Function, 218,* 21–37.

Schade, U., & Berg, T. (1992). The role of inhibition in a spreading-activation model of language production. II. The simulational perspective. *Journal of Psycholinguistic Research, 21,* 435–462.

Schmidt, C. S. M., Nitschke, K., Bormann, T., Römer, P., Kümmerer, D., Martin, M., et al. (2019). Dissociating frontal and temporal correlates of phonological and semantic fluency in a large sample of left hemisphere stroke patients. *NeuroImage: Clinical, 23,* 101840.

Schnur, T. T., Schwartz, M. F., Kimberg, D. Y., Hirshorn, E., Coslett, H. B., & Thompson-Schill, S. L. (2009). Localizing interference during naming: Convergent neuroimaging and neuropsychological evidence for the function of Broca's area. *Proceedings of the National Academy of Sciences USA, 106,* 322–327.

Schoch, B., Dimitrova, A., Gizewski, E., & Timmann, D. (2006). Functional localization in the human cerebellum based on voxelwise statistical analysis: A study of 90 patients. *NeuroImage*, *30*, 36–51.

Schuhmann, T. (2019). Transcranial magnetic stimulation (TMS) to study the neural network account of language. In G. I. de Zubicaray, & N. O. Schiller (Eds.), *The Oxford handbook of neurolinguistics* (pp. 94–114). New York: Oxford University Press.

Schuhmann, T., Schiller, N. O., Goebel, R., & Sack, A. T. (2009). The temporal characteristics of functional activation in Broca's area during overt picture naming. *Cortex*, *45*, 1111–1116.

Schuhmann, T., Schiller, N. O., Goebel, R., & Sack, A. T. (2012). Speaking of which: Dissecting the neurocognitive network of language production in picture naming. *Cerebral Cortex*, *22*, 701–709.

Sowman, P. F., Flavel, S. C., McShane, C. L., Sakuma, S., Miles, T. S., & Nordstrom, M. A. (2009). Asymmetric activation of motor cortex controlling human anterior digastric muscles during speech and target-directed jaw movements. *Journal of Neurophysiology*, *102*(1), 159–166. 10.1152/jn.90894.2008.

Schwartz, M. F., Faseyitan, O., Kim, J., & Coslett, H. B. (2012). The dorsal stream contribution to phonological retrieval in object naming. *Brain*, *135*, 3799–3814.

Schwartz, M. F., Kimberg, D. Y., Walker, G. M., Brecher, A., Faseyitan, O., Dell, G. S., Mirman, D., & Coslett, H. B. (2011). A neuroanatomical dissociation for taxonomic and thematic knowledge in the human brain. *Proceedings of the National Academy of Sciences*, *108*, 8520–8524.

Schwering, S. C., & MacDonald, M. C. (2020). Verbal working memory as emergent from language comprehension and production. *Frontiers in Human Neuroscience*, *14*, 68.

Segal E., & Petrides M. (2012). The anterior superior parietal lobule and its interactions with language and motor areas during writing. *European Journal of Neuroscience*, *35*, 309–322.

Segawa, J. A., Tourville, J. A., Beal, D. S., & Guenther, F. H. (2015). The neural correlates of speech motor sequence learning. *Journal of Cognitive Neuroscience*, *27*, 819–831.

Severens, E., Kühn, S., Hartsuiker, R. J., & Brass, M. (2012). Functional mechanisms involved in the internal inhibition of taboo words. *Social Cognitive and Affective Neuroscience*, *7*, 431–435.

Sparing, R., Dafotakis, M., Meister, I. G., Thirugnanasambandam, N., & Fink, G. R. (2008). Enhancing language performance with non-invasive brain stimulation—A transcranial direct current stimulation study in healthy humans. *Neuropsychologia*, *46*, 261–268. 10.1016/j.neuropsychologia.2007.07.009.

Shinshi, M., Yanagisawa, T., Hirata, M., Goto, T., Sugata, H., Araki, T., Okamura, Y., Hasegawa, Y., Ihara, A. S., & Yorifuji, S. (2015). Temporospatial identification of language-related cortical function by a combination of transcranial magnetic stimulation and magnetoencephalography. *Brain and Behavior*, *5*, e00317.

Sierpowska, J., Gabarrós, A., Fernández-Coello, A., Camins, À., Castañer, S., Juncadella, M., François, C., & Rodríguez-Fornells, A. (2019). White-matter pathways and semantic processing: Intrasurgical and lesion-symptom mapping evidence. *Neuroimage: Clinical*, *22*, 101704.

Stalnaker, T. A., Cooch, N. K., & Schoenbaum, G. (2015). What the orbitofrontal cortex does not do. *Nature Neuroscience*, *18*, 620–627.

Stamatakis, E. A., Shafto, M. A., Williams, G., Tam, P., & Tyler, L. K. (2011) White matter changes and word finding failures with increasing age. *PLoS ONE*, *6*, e14496.

Steinhauser, M., & Hübner, R. (2009). Distinguishing response conflict and task conflict in the Stroop task: Evidence from ex-Gaussian distribution analysis. *Journal of Experimental Psychology: Human Perception and Performance, 35*, 1398–1412.

Strijkers K., & Costa A. (2016). The cortical dynamics of speaking: Present shortcomings and future avenues. *Language, Cognition and Neuroscience, 31*, 484–503.

Strijkers, K., Costa, A., & Pulvermüller, F. (2017). The cortical dynamics of speaking: Lexical and phonological knowledge simultaneously recruit the frontal and temporal cortex within 200 ms. *NeuroImage, 163*, 206–219.

Theys, C., Kovacs, S., Peeters, R., Melzer, T. R., van Wieringen, A., & De Nil, L. F. (2020). Brain activation during non-habitual speech production: Revisiting the effects of simulated disfluencies in fluent speakers. *PLoS ONE, 15*, e0228452.

Thye, M., Szaflarski, J. P., & Mirman, D. (2021). Shared lesion correlates of semantic and letter fluency in post-stroke aphasia. *Journal of Neuropsychology, 15*, 143–150.

Tipper, S. P. (1985). The negative priming effect: Inhibitory priming by ignored objects. *Quarterly Journal of Experimental Psychology, 37A*, 571–590.

Töpper, R., Mottaghy, F. M., Brugmann, M., Noth, J., & Huber, W. (1998). Facilitation of picture naming by focal transcranial magnetic stimulation of Wernicke's area. *Experimental Brain Research, 121*, 371–378.

Tremblay, P., & Dick, A. (2016). Broca and Wernicke are dead, or moving past the classic model of language neurobiology. *Brain & Language, 162*, 60–71.

Tremblay, P., & Gracco, V. L. (2009). Contribution of the pre-SMA to the production of words and non-speech oral motor gestures, as revealed by repetitive transcranial magnetic stimulation (rTMS). *Brain Research, 1268*, 112–124.

Tremblay, P., & Gracco, V. L. (2010). On the selection of words and oral motor responses: Evidence of a response-independent fronto-parietal network. *Cortex, 46*, 15–28.

Tremblay, P., & Small, S. L. (2011). Motor response selection in overt sentence production: A functional MRI study. *Frontiers in Psychology, 2*, 253.

Tremblay, P., Deschamps, I., & Dick, A. S. (2019). Neuromotor Organization of Speech Production. In G. I. de Zubicaray, & N. O. Schiller (Eds.), *The Oxford handbook of neurolinguistics* (pp. 371–401). New York: Oxford University Press.

Treutler, M., & Sörös, P. (2021). Functional MRI of native and non-native speech sound production in sequential German-English bilinguals. *Frontiers in Human Neuroscience, 15*, 683277.

Troutman, S. B. W., & Diaz, M. T. (2020). White matter disconnection is related to age-related phonological deficits. *Brain Imaging and Behavior, 14*, 1555–1565.

Vinci-Booher, S., Cheng, H., & James, K. H. (2019). An analysis of the brain systems involved with producing letters by hand. *Journal of Cognitive Neuroscience, 31*, 138–154.

Volle, E., Costello, A. L., Coates, L. M., McGuire, C., Towgood, K., Gilbert, S., Kinkingnehun, S., McNeil, J. E., Greenwood, R., Papps, B., van den Broeck, M., & Burgess, P. W. (2012). Dissociation between verbal response initiation and suppression after prefrontal lesions. *Cerebral Cortex, 22*, 2428–2440.

Wagner, S., Sebastian, A., Lieb, K., Tüscher, O., & Tadić, A. (2014). A coordinate-based ALE functional MRI meta-analysis of brain activation during verbal fluency tasks in healthy control subjects. *BMC Neuroscience, 15*, 19.

Walker, G. M., Schwartz, M. F., Kimberg, D. Y., Faseyitan, O., Brecher, A., Dell, G. S., & Coslett, H. B. (2011). Support for anterior temporal involvement in semantic error production in aphasia: New evidence from VLSM. *Brain and Language, 117*, 110–122.

Wheat, K. L., Cornelissen, P. L., Sack, A. T., Schuhmann, T., Goebel, R., & Blomert, L. (2013). Charting the functional relevance of Broca's area for visual word recognition and picture naming in Dutch using fMRI-guided TMS. *Brain and Language*, *125*, 223–230.

Wilson, S. M., Isenberg, A. L., & Hickok, G. (2009). Neural correlates of word production stages delineated by parametric modulation of psycholinguistic variables. *Human Brain Mapping*, *30*, 3596–3608.

Woollams, A. M. (2012). Apples are not the only fruit: the effects of concept typicality on semantic representation in the anterior temporal lobe. *Frontiers in Human Neuroscience*, *6*, 85.

Xue, G., Aron, A. R., & Poldrack, R. A. (2008). Common neural substrates for inhibition of spoken and manual responses. *Cerebral Cortex*, *18*, 1923–1932.

Yuan, Q., Wu, J., Zhang, M., Zhang, Z., Chen, M., Ding, G., Lu, C., & Guo, T. (2021). Patterns and networks of language control in bilingual language production. *Brain Structure and Function*, *226*, 963–977.

Zhang, Q., Yu, B., Zhang, J., Jin, Z., & Li, L. (2018). Probing the timing recruitment of Broca's area in speech production for Mandarin Chinese: A TMS study. *Frontiers in Human Neuroscience*, *12*, 133.

Zou, L., Abutalebi, J., Zinszer, B., Yan, X., Shu, H., Peng, D., & Ding, G. (2012a). Second language experience modulates functional brain network for the native language production in bimodal bilinguals. *NeuroImage*, *62*, 1367–1375.

Zou, L., Ding, G., Abutalebi, J., Shu, H., & Peng, D. (2012b). Structural plasticity of the left caudate in bimodal bilinguals. *Cortex*, *48*, 1197–1206.

Zwaan, R. A. (2004). The immersed experiencer: Toward an embodied theory of language comprehension. In B. H. Ross (Ed.), *The psychology of learning and motivation* (pp. 35–62). New York: Academic Press.

5 The Electrophysiology of Language Production

Vitória Piai and Priscila Borges

In the past decade, the well-established psycholinguistics tradition of using behavioral measures to study language production has been increasingly complemented with electrophysiological investigations. The electrophysiological signal has excellent temporal resolution, which is critical for understanding processes that unfold at the subsecond time scale. Here, we provide a selective review of single-word production studies, focusing mostly on conceptually driven word production tasks performed by healthy adult speakers. We also provide pointers to the literature on speech-motor aspects of production, multi-word production, and word production by speakers with brain damage. The reviewed topics include how the field has evolved over time, what kinds of questions researchers have tried to answer using electrophysiology, and what some of the challenges and future directions might be. The overview provided assumes background knowledge of the psycholinguistics of word production (see Chapter 2 of this volume: Kerr et al., 2022).

Electrophysiology

The electrophysiological signal measured over the scalp is thought to reflect post-synaptic potentials of thousands of synchronously activated neurons (Lopes da Silva, 2013). This activity generates a complex pattern of signals varying in amplitude at different frequencies. Given that electricity travels nearly at the speed of light, what happens at the level of neurons is immediately recorded over the scalp, giving the electrophysiological signal excellent temporal resolution. However, given the effect of volume conduction, spatial resolution is poor and, in particular, underlying sources cannot be inferred from observations of a scalp topography alone. Magnetoencephalography (MEG) measures the magnetic field produced by the same electrical currents that are measured with the electroencephalogram (EEG), so for most psycholinguistic-research purposes, these two techniques (EEG and MEG) can be treated as very similar (for an overview and a discussion on the comparability between the two, see e.g., Lopes da Silva, 2013; Malmivuo, 2012). EEG signals can also be recorded intracranially, i.e., through invasive recordings (iEEG henceforth) in individuals

DOI: 10.4324/9781003145790-6

requiring neurosurgery (for an overview applied to language research, see Flinker et al., 2018; Llorens et al., 2011). Since the signal is recorded from electrodes in direct contact with the brain, iEEG has excellent spatial resolution in addition to exquisite temporal resolution. Henceforth, we will use the term MEEG to refer to the electrophysiological signal in a way that is neutral to the specific recording technique.

Besides the technique for data acquisition (EEG, MEG, iEEG), there are also differences in the way the MEEG signal is processed. In the case of EEG event-related potentials (ERPs) or MEG event-related fields (ERFs), sometimes also termed local field potentials (LFPs) in the case of iEEG, the signal is not decomposed in the frequency domain. For scalp ERP/Fs, the signal is usually averaged over trials, whereas for LFPs, single-trial analyses are common, given the higher signal-to-noise ratio of iEEG data. By averaging the signal over trials, any amplitude modulation that is not consistent over trials is averaged out in the event-related response. Amplitude modulations that are not consistent over trials can originate from noise, in which case the ERP/Fs are the result of keeping brain responses consistently evoked by the stimulus. However, in certain cases, inter-trial inconsistent modulations originate from brain activity not phase-locked to a stimulus, in which case they would not be considered noise (see e.g., Mazaheri & Jensen, 2010; for a specific word-production demonstration, see Piai et al., 2014).

A different way of analyzing the MEEG signal consists of taking spectral information into account, yielding what is often termed "neural oscillations" in the literature. Oscillations are argued to enable a neuronal population to control the timing of neuronal firing, creating optimal windows for neuronal communication (e.g., Buzsaki & Draguhn, 2004). A power spectrum can be computed over a time window, thus disregarding the time course of power changes (e.g., Piai et al., 2015). Alternatively, a time-resolved power spectrum can be computed, providing a representation of how power changes for different frequencies over time (e.g., Piai et al., 2014a). In both cases, both phase-locked and non–phase-locked brain activity is kept in the signal. A different approach, microstate analysis, consists of characterizing the MEEG signal (either event-related responses or spectral information) in terms of changes in topographical configurations over time (e.g., Laganaro, 2014). Finally, for iEEG, it is common to analyze the signal focusing on a frequency range typically above 70 Hz (also called the high gamma range; "broadband" signal henceforth; e.g., Dubarry et al., 2017). This broadband signal is known to correlate with single-neuron spiking (Manning et al., 2009).

Importantly, the most appropriate way of pre-processing the MEEG signal will depend on one's research question, with no particular method being superior to the others in an absolute sense (for examples of word production studies showing distinct effects between two approaches, see Laaksonen et al., 2012; Piai et al., 2012; Piai et al., 2014a). In the overview below, we discuss examples from the production literature using these different approaches.

Event–related responses

Early studies were interested in establishing the brain areas involved in speaking, particularly hemispheric lateralization effects occurring before speech, therefore not focusing on conceptually driven word production. Focusing on the readiness potential, i.e., a slow rising negative-going potential linked to motor response preparation, preceding a speech task (i.e., saying words beginning with /p/ or /k/) and a non-speech task (i.e., spitting or coughing), McAdam and Whitaker (1971) found an enhanced negativity over left scalp locations prior to speech production but symmetrical potentials over left and right scalp locations before the non-speech gestures. These results were presented as the first physiological evidence for left–hemisphere dominance in speech production in non–brain-damaged participants. By contrast, Levy (1977) found larger readiness potential amplitudes over left scalp locations prior to the sequenced production of both speech and non-speech movements but symmetrical readiness potentials over left and right sites when the movements were produced singly rather than in sequence. The results were taken to suggest that the hemispheric dominance effect was a function of task complexity rather than linguistic content. Expanding on these findings, Deecke et al. (1986) analyzed the averaged potentials elicited before the production of words beginning with /p/. To avoid respiration-related effects, participants were instructed to hold their breath prior to producing the words. Deecke et al. found an initial bilateral readiness potential that became stronger over left electrode sites in the final 100 ms preceding word onset. The results were interpreted as evidence that, while speech initiation involves both hemispheres, the left hemisphere dominates the execution of final speech motor operations.

Seeking clearer interpretations for the findings of lateralized motor control, Wohlert and Larson (1991) compared the ERPs preceding a lip protrusion task with those preceding a right-finger extension task performed by the same participants. The results showed that slow negative potentials became larger over left electrode sites before finger movements but remained even over right- and left sites before lip movements. The authors concluded that the control of basic oral movements is unlikely to be dominated by the left hemisphere, but that left-hemispheric dominance could be involved in the motor control of more complex speech movements (see also Wohlert, 1993).

By focusing on motor speech, these earlier studies also highlight how speech preparation per se modulates the MEEG signal and, as such, how this phenomenon needs careful consideration when interpreting effects in terms of cognitive factors, a point to which we return later (see e.g., for a critique, Piai et al., 2015a). In a seminal study, Van Turennout and colleagues (1997) used ERPs to investigate the time course of semantic and phonological processes in word production. In the context of a two-choice reaction go/no-go paradigm, participants performed a categorization task before naming pictures. In the categorization task, participants determined the hand of their response based on semantic information (i.e., animacy of picture referents; e.g., picture: BEAR, "animate" – right-hand button), and the execution of their response based on phonological information (e.g., words ending in /r/ cued a go response, words ending in /n/ cued a no-go response; BEAR is a go response). Given the assumption made by models of language production that semantic information becomes available before phonological information during naming (e.g., Levelt et al., 1999), the authors expected that hand response preparation could start before the phonological information cued participants on whether or not to respond. In turn, this preparation would be reflected on the lateralized readiness potential (LRP), the onset of which would indicate when different types of information are used for response preparation. Specifically, the authors expected an LRP to appear on both go and no-go trials when the response hand was cued by semantic properties (i.e., animacy) and naming execution by phonological information (i.e., end phoneme). By contrast, in the reversed case, when phoneme decisions cued the response hand and semantic information cued naming execution, an LRP was expected only for go trials. Another prediction was that the LRP appearing for no-go trials would be insensitive to the location of the phonological information cueing response execution (i.e., word-initial or word-final). The results of the experiments confirmed all of these predictions. The findings were interpreted as evidence that semantic activation precedes phonological encoding during naming, and that the onset of a word is encoded before its end. Moreover, the study propelled the combination of LRP with a go/no-go paradigm as a way to investigate the timing of semantic activation and phonological encoding in word production (see also van Turennout et al., 1999).

However, it was soon evident that this approach had limitations. Firstly, the LRP might not be a reliable index of the exact moment at which a given type of linguistic information is processed (Laganaro & Perret, 2011). Secondly, the task required participants to carry out cognitive operations other than those involved in the preparation of a verbal response, making it difficult to exclusively link the EEG patterns to production processes (Perret & Laganaro, 2013). Thus, ERP studies on word production later began to use delayed production paradigms as a way to more closely approximate real-world production scenarios while still avoiding motor-preparation effects and artifacts in the signal. In these paradigms, participants prepare their response but produce it only after some delay period, which makes effects/artifacts related to motor execution fall outside the analyzed window. For example, Jescheniak and colleagues (2002) showed how a delayed picture-naming task associated with a priming procedure could be used to study the activation of semantic and phonological information during word planning. Participants named pictures upon seeing a response cue that appeared after a delay period. During this period, words holding different relations to the picture name were presented auditorily. The authors found that the ERPs were less negative-going when participants heard prime words that were phonologically or semantically related to the to-be-named object compared to unrelated controls. Additionally, they found that the phonological effect was absent when participants performed a nonlinguistic task involving judgement of object size. The results were considered evidence that semantic information does not automatically lead to activation of phonological information, thus being incompatible with models that allow for unconstrained cascading of activation from semantic to phonological representations (see for recent discussions e.g., Strijkers et al., 2017). Beyond its theoretical implications at the time, the study extended the LRP approach used in language production studies thus far to allow for investigating the types of code that are automatically activated during naming, leaving behind the need to rely on tasks requiring explicit and conscious extraction of semantic and phonological information. Nonetheless, this approach is also limited, as delaying naming might lead to alterations in the time course of the processes involved in speech production as well as to incomplete implementation of later processes such as phonological encoding and phonetic encoding (Laganaro & Perret, 2011).

Based on demonstrations that ERPs could be analyzed preceding overt naming, Costa and colleagues (2009) investigated the time course of lexical selection. Specifically, by manipulating the position of pictures belonging to the same semantic categories in a series of pictures named overtly (the cumulative semantic interference effect, Howard et al., 2006), Costa and collaborators attempted to identify when lexical selection takes place during production. Their results, depicted in Figure 5.1, showed significant correlations between the ordinal position of pictures, naming latencies, and ERP mean amplitudes starting around 200 ms post-picture onset and lasting 180 ms. The onset of these correlations was taken as evidence that lexical selection happens around 200 ms after picture presentation.

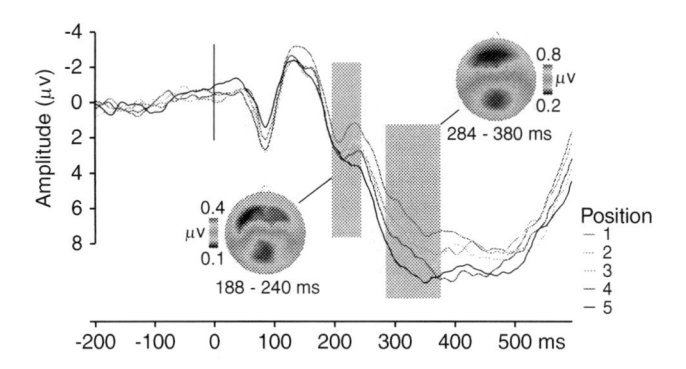

Figure 5.1 Event-related potentials in a continuous picture naming task corresponding to the five ordinal positions within semantic categories, time-locked to picture onset. The waveforms originate from ten posterior scalp electrodes. A cumulative increase in signal amplitude over ordinal positions is observed during the time period indicated by the light-shaded area. Scalp topographies are shown for the averaged difference waves (the ERP for each position subtracted from its subsequent position), averaged over the two time windows indicated (dark-shaded areas). Figure modified from courtesy of Kristof Strijkers.

Also focusing on lexical selection, Aristei and colleagues (2011) investigated the time course of semantic interference and facilitation effects by comparing ERPs in a task that combined picture-word interference and semantic blocking. In this task, participants overtly named pictures presented in either categorically homogeneous, associatively homogeneous or heterogeneous blocks after hearing distractors that were either categorically related, associatively related or unrelated to the pictures. The manipulations of both types of semantic context (distractor word and block) produced temporally overlapping ERP modulations around 200–250 ms post-picture onset, in addition to an overall interaction of distractor and blocking effects on ERPs around the same time. These findings were interpreted as indicating that facilitative and interfering semantic context effects originate from processing stages that are closely connected and that interact relatively early during word planning, being compatible with lexical competition models (e.g., Levelt et al., 1999). For a review of semantic context effects in word production, we refer the reader to Anders et al. (2019) and de Zubicaray and Piai (2019). For a discussion on the theoretical limitations of picture-word interference and semantic context effects studies, see Nozari & Pinet (2020).

In line with Costa et al. (2009), other studies have found that a positive deviation around 200 ms after stimulus onset (termed the P2 component) might be an electrophysiological marker of lexical selection (Aristei et al., 2011; Fargier & Laganaro, 2020; Rabovsky et al., 2021; Rose et al., 2019; Strijkers et al., 2010). Rabovsky and colleagues (2021) compared ERP amplitudes related to naming objects with different levels of semantic richness and intercorrelational semantic feature density. Naming performance was better for semantically richer objects (i.e., objects whose names had many associated semantic features) and worse for objects whose features were more intercorrelated. In the ERPs, concepts with many semantic features and concepts with high feature density induced more positive amplitudes in posterior electrode sites between 200–550 ms post-picture onset. In addition, more positive amplitudes at these posterior regions correlated with slower naming times between 230 and 380 ms. This correlation was taken as evidence that the posterior positivity reflected the difficulty of lexical selection. In sum, several ERP studies on the time course of word-production stages support the idea that the P2 component might be a marker of lexical selection.

Whereas most EEG-ERP studies do not provide information on the neuronal generators of the brain responses, many MEG studies on picture naming do. Salmelin and colleagues (1994) reported the first MEG study on picture naming including source localization of ERFs. The authors showed that, upon seeing a picture, visual areas show increased activity first, followed by temporo-parietal-occipital junctions bilaterally between around 200–400 ms. Around 500 ms post-picture onset, activity in bilateral ventral premotor cortex and inferior frontal gyrus was increased. Other studies from

Salmelin and colleagues have provided further evidence on the neuronal generators of temporally circumscribed responses associated with word production. For example, Sörös and colleagues (2003) analyzed MEG data recorded while healthy participants named drawings using either a verb or a noun. The pattern of activity, which did not differ between the two types of naming tasks, followed bilaterally from occipital cortices in the first 200 ms post-picture onset, to bilateral posterior temporoparietal regions around 200–400 ms, and was left-lateralized in sensorimotor and occipital cortices around 400–800 ms post-picture onset (see also e.g., Liljeström et al., 2009; Vihla et al., 2006). In addition, the study reports behavioral and MEG data of one individual with left-hemisphere damage who presented with anomia that was particularly severe for nouns. In contrast to non-brain-damaged participants, the sources of cortical activity identified in this individual were different for nouns and verbs: Responses in the left middle temporal lobe were found only in object naming, and the latter was also linked to earlier and stronger activity in left inferior frontal gyrus (LIFG) relative to the action naming task. For studies focusing on individuals with aphasia following brain damage, see e.g., Laganaro et al. (2008, 2009).

The extent to which the spatiotemporal patterns of activity during picture naming are replicable is an important issue, as it has a direct bearing on the interpretation of patterns that deviate from this "default." A recent study examined the test–retest reliability of brain activity in a delayed picture naming task relative to a visual task (i.e., participants said 'yes' if a target picture was presented) performed over two different sessions (Ala-Salomäki et al., 2021). The results are shown in Figure 5.2. From 200 ms onwards, activity increased in perisylvian language regions, including the middle temporal cortex and frontal cortex from 400 ms onwards, on both measurement days (rows D1 and D2 in Figure 5.2). Consistent activity across the two sessions (ICC rows in Figure 5.2) was detected in various left-hemisphere regions, namely sensorimotor (200–800 ms), parietal (200–600 ms), temporal (200–800 ms), frontal (400–800 ms), occipital (400–800 ms), and cingulate (600– 800 ms). Additionally, consistent activity was found in the right superior temporal region (600–800 ms). Notably, the consistent pattern of spatiotemporal activity that emerged for delayed picture naming was in line with the proposed set of cortical areas typically associated with language production (e.g., Indefrey & Levelt, 2004). For a demonstration of variability and consistency of EEG microstates in word production, see Laganaro (2017; see also Laganaro et al., 2012, for a comparison between fast and slow speakers using EEG microstates analyses). Importantly, both studies underscore the relevance of evaluating group-level and individual-level consistency in studies of language production. For reviews on ERPs/ERFs in word production, we refer the reader to Ganushchak et al. (2011), Munding et al. (2016), Perret and Laganaro (2013), Salmelin (2007), and Strijkers and Costa (2016).

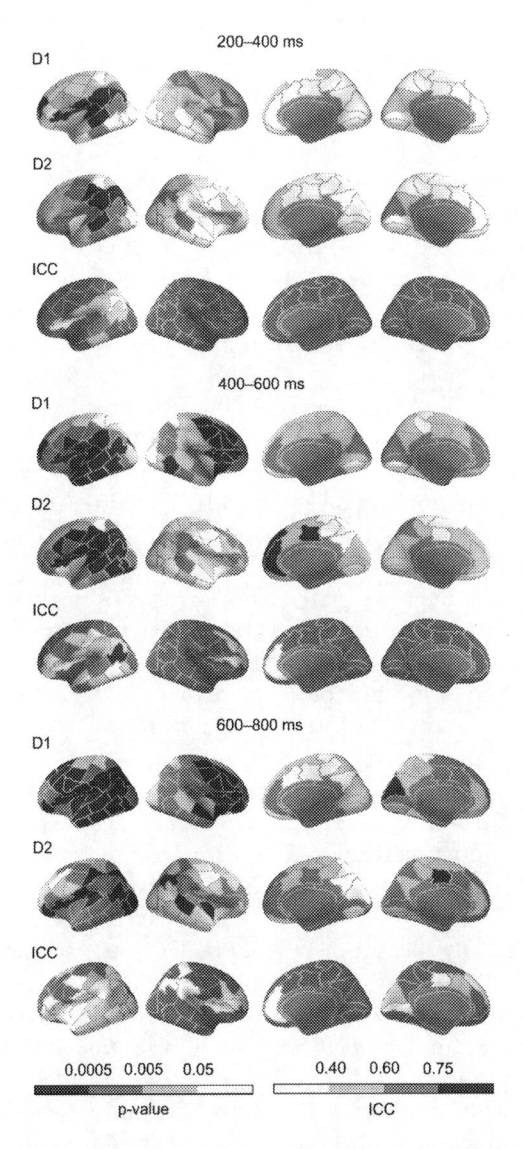

Figure 5.2 Source localization of the activity during delayed picture naming relative to the visual task for three different time windows relative to picture onset, as indicated on top of each panel/triplet. For session 1 (D1) and session 2 (D2), the blue colours indicate p-value thresholds. For the consistency of significant effects across the two sessions (ICC), the green colours indicate the intraclass correlation coefficients. The grey parcels were not used for the across-session consistency analysis. Reprinted from NeuroImage, 227, Ala-Salomäki, H., Kujala, J., Liljeström, M., and Salmelin, R. "Picture naming yields highly consistent cortical activation patterns: Test–retest reliability of magnetoencephalography recordings," 117651, Copyright (2021), with permission from Elsevier. Picture naming yields highly consistent cortical activation patterns: Test–retest reliability of magnetoencephalography recordings. NeuroImage, 227, 117651.

Multi-word production

Following a common criticism to single-word production studies that this is hardly how we speak, researchers have also investigated noun-phrase production (e.g., saying "the brown cat") and multi-word utterances. Bürki and Laganaro (2014) found that the production of "cat" corresponded to a shorter window of stable topography than the production of "the cat" or "the big cat" around 190–300 ms. This time window is in agreement with estimates of the timing of grammatical encoding processes (Indefrey & Levelt, 2004). Additionally, from around 530 ms post-picture onset, a stable topographical pattern was longer for the production of "the big cat" relative to the other two types of utterances. The authors interpreted this difference as corresponding to the longer duration of phonological encoding for utterances with additional syllables and words. For additional multi-word production studies, see Eulitz et al. (2000), Pylkkänen et al. (2014), and Sikora et al. (2016).

Recently, Ries and colleagues (2021) extracted ERP components time-locked to the vocal onset of individual words presented in the context of multi-word utterances. Using a paradigm that required participants to recite four-word tongue twisters from memory at a regular pace, the authors were able to isolate two ERP components related to speech monitoring and word planning mechanisms, namely the error-related negativity and a late left anterior negativity, respectively. Although not tapping into conceptually driven production processes, this paradigm opens the door for future studies to investigate relevant operations involved in sequential word production such as phonological encoding and articulation.

Oscillatory responses

It is well known that during (finger or limb) movement preparation and execution, power between 15–30 Hz decreases (often termed "suppression") over motor-related regions (Pfurtscheller & Lopes da Silva, 1999), subsequently increasing after movement execution (often termed "rebound"). This "suppression" in fact reflects the active involvement of brain regions. Among the first studies to investigate the oscillations underlying speech-motor activity was Salmelin and colleagues (1995). By comparing participants moving their toes, fingers, or mouth, the authors showed that the 20-Hz rhythm is modulated by movement, but in a "motorotopic" manner (i.e., modulation over the hand area when moving the fingers, but over the face area when moving the mouth). In a later study (Salmelin & Sams, 2002), 20-Hz suppression and rebound over the motor face area in motor cortex were examined for both oral non-verbal tasks (e.g., making a kissing movement) and verbal tasks (e.g., silently articulating a vowel). The results showed that, for verbal tasks, the timing of the 20-Hz suppression was correlated between left and right mouth areas, whereas the rebound was left-lateralized. Moreover, the 20-Hz suppression was also present over the hand areas in the non-verbal tasks.

Thus, as the linguistic content of lip and tongue movements increased, modulations of the 20-Hz rhythm became more focal or even left-lateralized.

The MEG study by Salmelin and colleagues (1994) was amongst the first to examine frequency-specific activity during picture naming. Activity in the 9–13 Hz range was suppressed during picture naming, starting from the occipital lobe, followed by bilateral frontal areas, and finally bilateral motor cortex. This suppression was strongest and lasted longer for overt naming versus covert naming and passively viewing pictures. Besides picture naming, oscillations in conceptually-driven production have often been studied with verb generation using MEG. In this task, a verb is produced in response to a noun (e.g., "nightingale," response: *sings*). Power decreases in the 15–30 Hz range are commonly observed, with sources being often found in the language dominant hemisphere, particularly in inferior and middle frontal gyri, and temporal and inferior parietal regions (Findlay et al., 2012; Fisher et al., 2008; Pavlova et al., 2019; see also Youssofzadeh et al., 2020 for a demonstration using visual and auditory naming).

Following up on these findings, Pavlova et al. (2019) used MEG to investigate whether these oscillations are sensitive to semantic retrieval demands. Materials were such that a presented noun was either strongly associated with a single verb (e.g., "nightingale," response: *sings*, less demanding) or weakly associated with multiple verbs (e.g., "paper," many responses, more demanding). Power decreases in the 15–30 Hz range were found to be stronger for more demanding responses, an effect that was visible 700–500 ms before speech onset and that was localized to medial aspects of the frontal lobe bilaterally. The time window of this effect is consistent with the proposed timing of retrieval stages, prior to articulatory planning (Indefrey & Levelt, 2004).

Power decreases in the 10–30 Hz range are also typically found in association with conceptual and lexical retrieval. To study the initial stages of word production in a manner that tries to approximate real-life word production, Piai and collaborators have employed a context-driven word production task in which to-be-named pictures are presented following sentences with differing amounts of constraint (e.g., "the farmer milked a" versus "the child drew a" preceding the picture of a cow), see Figure 5.3A. During the prepicture interval (red box in Figure 5.3A), conceptual and lexical retrieval are initiated following constrained sentences. Thus, the contrast between constrained and unconstrained sentences in this window provides a measure of the speaker's internally driven conceptual and lexical preparation. A series of studies has shown that power is decreased in the 10–25 Hz range in the prepicture interval following constrained relative to unconstrained sentences (Gastaldon et al., 2020; Klaus et al., 2020; Piai et al., 2017, 2018, 2020; Piai et al., 2014b; Piai et al., 2015c). These power decreases have been most consistently localized to the left inferior parietal lobule and left temporal lobe (mostly posterior), as shown in Figure 5.3B. The across-session consistency of this pattern in these left posterior brain regions was further established in an

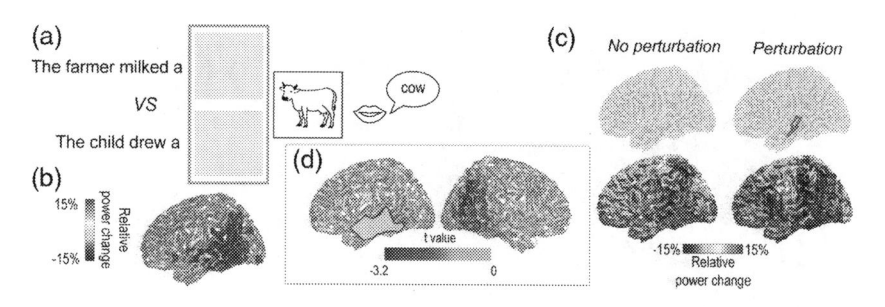

Figure 5.3 A. Context-driven picture naming with a constrained (upper) and unconstrained (lower) context. The pre-picture interval is marked by the red box. B. Source localization of the across-session consistent relative power changes in the 10–20 Hz range for constrained vs unconstrained contexts during the pre-picture interval (Roos & Piai, 2020). C. Source localization of relative power changes as in B following no perturbation (left) and perturbation (right) of the left middle temporal gyrus (through continuous theta burst stimulation, Klaus et al., 2020). D. Source localization of the context effect as in B and C (expressed as t values) for one individual with a stroke lesion in the left temporal lobe (in grey, Piai et al., 2017).

MEG study using the same task with two sessions spaced 2–4 weeks apart (Roos & Piai, 2020, Figure 5.3B). As previously mentioned, the consistency of this pattern is important for interpreting deviations from it following perturbation with non-invasive brain stimulation (Klaus et al., 2020, Figure 5.3C) and in individuals with brain damage (Piai et al., 2017, 2018; Figure 5.3D).

The study on the test–retest reliability of delayed picture-naming mentioned above also examined oscillations (Ala-Salomäki et al., 2021). From 400 ms post-picture onset onwards, power decreases were consistent in bilateral occipital, occipitotemporal, and parietal areas in the ranges of 4–7 Hz, 8–13 Hz, and 14–20 Hz. Power was also consistently decreased in the 14–20 Hz and 21–30 Hz ranges over motor regions in the time window of 800–1200 ms post-picture onset (see also Laaksonen et al., 2012).

A number of studies have examined oscillatory effects associated with picture-word interference, a demanding picture-naming task where participants have to ignore a superimposed distractor word. Using MEG, Piai, Roelofs, Jensen, and colleagues (2014) analyzed oscillatory activity associated with picture-naming with semantically related (most demanding condition), semantically unrelated, and congruent (least demanding condition) distractors. The results are shown in Figure 5.4. Increases in 4–8 Hz activity between 350–650 ms were found for related compared to unrelated distractors and for related compared to congruent distractors. The generators of this effect were found in superior frontal gyrus, possibly including the anterior cingulate cortex. This effect was interpreted to reflect the attentional control required to select the picture name under distracting conditions. Similar results were

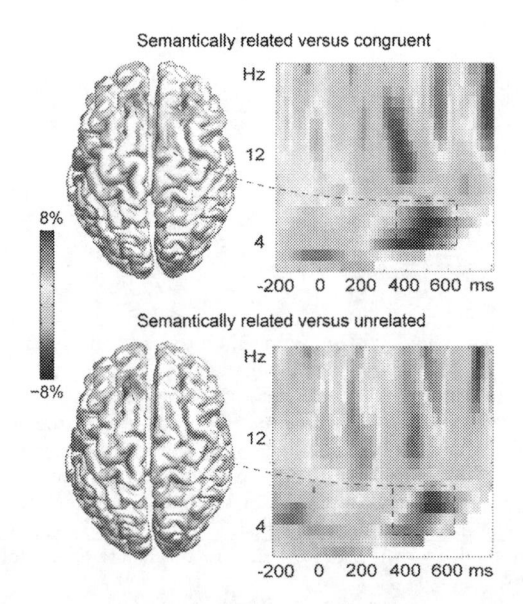

Figure 5.4 Spectro-temporal profile of the relative power differences originating from the superior frontal gyrus for the contrasts semantically related versus congruent distractors (upper) and semantically related versus unrelated distractors (lower) during picture naming. Modified from Piai, V., Roelofs, A., Jensen, O., Schoffelen, J.-M., & Bonnefond, M. (2014). Distinct patterns of brain activity characterise lexical activation and competition in spoken word production. PloS One, 9(2), e88674.

obtained by Shitova et al. (2017) and Krott et al. (2019) using EEG, even though a different pre-processing approach was taken to account for speech-related artifacts in each one of these studies (see also Piai & Zheng, 2019, for similar effects in language switching).

In summary, power decreases in the 10–30 Hz range are commonly found in tasks requiring conceptually driven word production. The generators of this effect are found not only in sensorimotor areas, in line with a motor speech role, but also in temporal and inferior parietal areas, which are commonly implicated in conceptual, lexical, and phonological aspects of word production (Indefrey & Levelt, 2004). There is also tentative evidence that power increases in the 4–8 Hz range, possibly originating from frontal areas commonly associated with cognitive control, underlie the regulatory processes involved in speaking (Roelofs & Piai, 2011), but this phenomenon is less understood than the pattern of power decreases in the 10–30 Hz range. For more studies on response and sentence planning, the reader is referred to Bögels et al. (2015), Jongman et al. (2020), Piai et al. (2015b), and Sauppe et al. (2021). For a more detailed review and discussion of oscillatory activity in word production, see Piai and Zheng (2019).

Intracranial EEG

Crone and collaborators (2001) provided one of the first illustrations of the broadband signal during word production tasks (i.e., picture naming, auditory word repetition, and word reading). Contrasting different input (visual vs. auditory) and output (signed vs. spoken) modalities, the authors found early broadband responses over the superior temporal gyrus (STG) for word repetition and over temporal-occipital cortex for picture naming and word reading. They also found late broadband responses over the tongue area of sensorimotor cortex for spoken responses and over hand areas for signed responses, with latencies varying according to the participant's behavioral response latencies across tasks.

Since this pioneering study, several iEEG studies have used the broadband signal to track language production processes. For example, employing a picture naming task, Edwards et al. (2010) found that activity related to motor-speech production began ~300 ms before verbal responses in peri-Rolandic cortices (pre- and post-central gyri), peaking around 100–200 ms after response onset (Figure 5.5; see Edwards et al. for results on verb generation). Interestingly, one electrode in the posterior middle temporal gyrus (light blue in Figure 5.5) showed increased activity starting around 300 ms post-picture onset, which remained sustained until about 200 ms before response, in line with the proposed time course of planning processes preceding articulation (Indefrey & Levelt, 2004). By contrast, electrodes over posterior STG (the two dark blue dots and lines in Figure 5.5) showed no increased activity during the same period.

An important question about the cognitive architecture of the language-production system relates to whether processes unfold serially or in parallel. Using the iEEG broadband signal, Dubarry et al. (2017) addressed this issue with a picture naming task and the analysis of significant activity concurrent between regions at the single-trial level. Figure 5.6 shows the results of these analyses. The data averaged over trials showed temporal overlap in the activity time courses between various regions, which would be interpreted as parallel processing. Critically, the single-trial analysis revealed a different pattern. The temporal overlap of activity between regions was relatively high for sensory cortices (e.g., striate cortex, transverse temporal gyrus, pink and purple colours in Figure 5.6), but substantially low in other regions (blue colours), including regions previously associated with aspects of conceptually-driven word production. These results were interpreted to indicate that there are limits to the amount of parallel processing involved across word production stages (see also Munding et al., 2016, and subsequent commentaries).

Many iEEG production studies have focused on conceptually-driven production tasks other than picture naming. For example, Williams Roberson and colleagues (2020) investigated verbal fluency and found increases in broadband activity over prefrontal regions in a timeframe attributed to conceptual

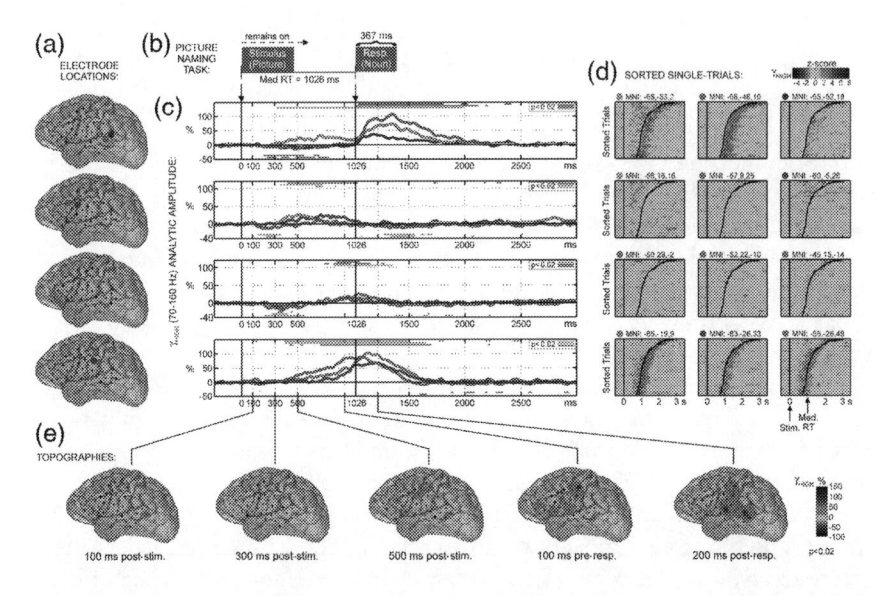

Figure 5.5 Broadband signal for picture naming for Patient 1. a. Locations of the recording sites. The colours correspond to the signal time courses in c. b. Trial events (stimulus and response). c. Broadband signal time courses. Vertical lines indicate stimulus onset and median response onset. Coloured horizontal lines indicate periods of significant amplitude change relative to the pre-stimulus baseline. d. Single-trial broadband amplitude sorted according to response time, which is indicated by the curved black lines in each plot. e. Topographies of the broadband signal over the latencies indicated below each topography. Reprinted from NeuroImage, 50/1, Edwards, E., Nagarajan, S. S., Dalal, S. S., Canolty, R. T., Kirsch, H. E., Barbaro, N. M., & Knight, R. T. "Spatiotemporal imaging of cortical activation during verb generation and picture naming," 291–301, Copyright (2010), with permission from Elsevier.

search mechanisms (earlier than 600 ms prior to speech onset). Using a sentence completion task, Wang and colleagues (2021) found that sentences with more demanding lexical selection (i.e., with low cloze probability) were linked to increased activity in the LIFG as well as to stronger interactions within the LIFG and between the LIFG and the left posterior temporal cortex. For iEEG studies examining semantic context-effects in picture naming, see Anders et al. (2019), Llorens et al. (2016), and Riès et al. (2017).

In a study involving iEEG, functional neuroimaging, and direct cortical stimulation (Forseth et al., 2018), auditory naming to definition and visual object naming were shown to be underlain by three stages of cortical activity, which were identified through consistent patterns of broadband activity preceding speech onset (see also Kojima et al., 2013). The first stage involved modality-dependent sensory processing in early auditory or visual cortex. The second stage was characterized by heteromodal lexical-semantic processing in the middle fusiform gyrus, the intraparietal sulcus, and the IFG. The final stage

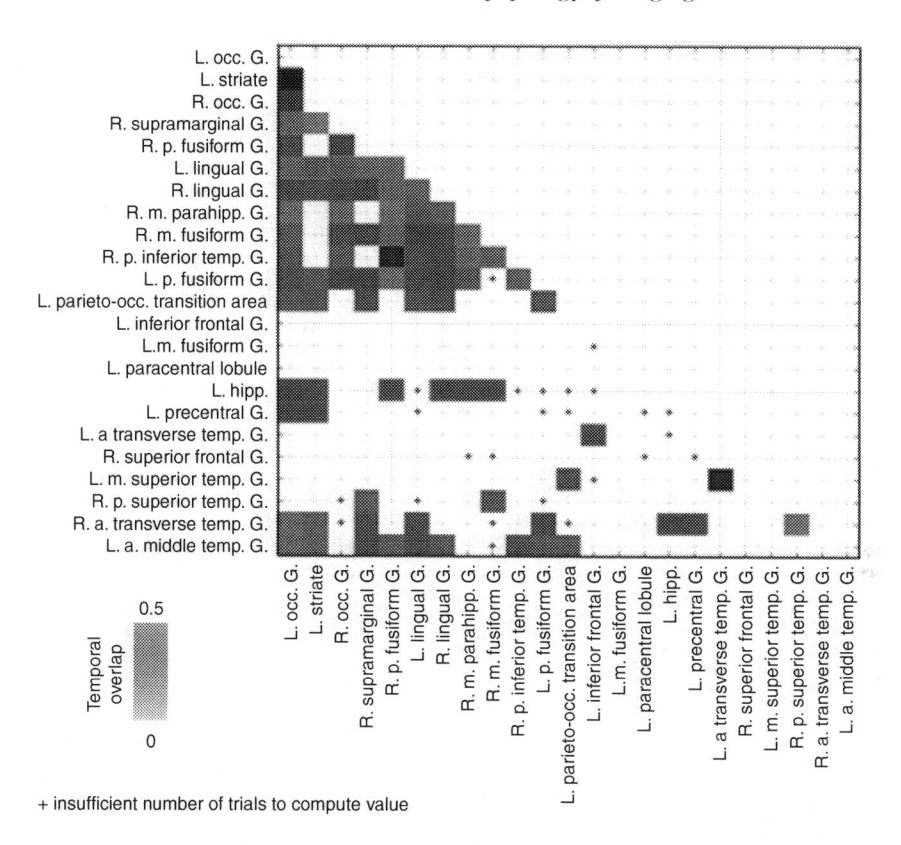

Figure 5.6 Overview of the temporal overlap between regions that were found to be consistently active during picture naming. Overlap was computed for cases when the total number of trials showing significant activity was at least 20 (an insufficient number of trials is indicated by the + sign). The maximum temporal overlap observed in the supra-threshold activity between all pairs of regions post-picture onset is indicated by the colour coding. L. = left; R. = right; G. = gyrus; occ. = occipital; p. = posterior; m. = medial; (para)hipp. = (para)hippocampus; temp. = temporal; a. = anterior. Figure modified from courtesy of Anne Sophie Dubarry.

was linked to heteromodal articulatory planning in the supplementary motor area, mouth sensorimotor cortex, and early auditory cortex. Importantly, the identification of lexical-semantic-specific regions was corroborated by the significant reduction in broadband activity observed in these areas during control tasks involving nonsense stimuli (reversed speech or scrambled images). For a review of word-production studies using iEEG, see Llorens et al. (2011).

Sahin et al. (2009) examined the time course and spatial localization of grammatical encoding using LFPs recorded in and around the LIFG. Silently, participants either read nouns and verbs or produced their inflected forms following a preamble [e.g., overt inflection condition: *Yesterday they___(walked)*; null inflection condition: *Everyday they ___ (walk)*]. Three LFP components linked to distinct processing stages were reported: a first component, elicited ~200 ms after target presentation, was taken to index lexical access because, among other reasons, it was sensitive to the lexical frequency of target words. A second component, which became apparent ~320 ms post-target onset, was linked to grammatical operations, as it was exclusively sensitive to the inflection requirements of the task. The third component, visible around 450 ms post-target onset, was taken to reflect phonological, phonetic, and articulatory programming processes because it varied according to the number of syllables in the words and because it differentiated between the overt inflection condition, which required additional phonological programming, and the other two conditions, which did not.

As one of the approaches used by Lee and colleagues (2018) to investigate the production of functional morphemes (e.g., past tense "-ed" attached to a verb), the authors analyzed LFPs from posterior brain regions during a structured word production task. Sites within the posterior STG and below the temporoparietal junction showed differences in LFPs starting ~1.5 s before speech onset between a condition in which morphological manipulations were required (e.g., overtly producing "walked" after seeing "Yesterday, we [walk]") and a control condition in which only the articulation of the target word was necessary through reading aloud (e.g., producing "walked" after "Yesterday, we [walked]"). Combined with evidence from lesion evaluations and focal cortical disruption through electrical current stimulation, these results were interpreted as being consistent with the idea that the posterior STG implements a discrete step during word production that is specific to functional morphological operations.

Chartier and colleagues (2018) investigated articulatory dynamics during continuous speech production by relating broadband iEEG responses to vocal tract movements. The authors found that specific neural populations in the ventral sensorimotor cortex (vSMC) encode articulatory kinematic trajectories (AKTs), which are coordinated to make specific vocal-tract configurations, and which exhibit out-and-back trajectory profiles with damped oscillatory dynamics. In addition, the AKTs encoded in the vSMC represented the coarticulation of successive AKTs, indicating that the vSMC does not locally encode phonemes, as these would elicit similar neural activity regardless of phonemic or kinematic contexts.

In summary, by capitalizing on the high temporal and spatial resolution afforded by iEEG and on the broadband signal as an index of task-specific cortical activity, studies have provided insights into *when* different brain areas are involved in speaking. More recently, studies have also started to relate these patterns to more specific word production operations, contributing to the refinement of language production models.

Some (methodological) challenges

Empirical results are only as good as the quality of the methods from which they are derived. Over the past decade, it has become clearer that the scalp MEEG signal can be analyzed in combination with overt production, but special considerations during analysis are needed to allow for sound interpretations. Some methodological approaches have been proposed to deal with speech-related artefacts in the signal (Ouyang et al., 2011; Porcaro et al., 2015; Vos et al., 2010), but little validation work and cross-methods comparisons have been conducted. Although critical, this is a challenging task for obvious reasons, and also because it is not immediately clear what such validations should consist of (see also Piai et al., 2015a, for a critical discussion of this and related issues).

Nonetheless, recent studies have tackled methodological issues involved in the analysis of the electrophysiological signal closest to articulation onset. For example, Fargier and colleagues (2018) showed that a phonetic feature such as voicing of a word's initial plosive (i.e., /p/ vs. /b/) influence the EEG signal in a way consistent in timing with the duration of the voicing period preceding the burst (see also Ouyang et al., 2016). Conducting microstate ERP analysis on data related to a delayed pseudoword production task, Jouen and colleagues (2021) confirmed previous observations that articulation starts several hundred milliseconds before vocal onsets and that the duration of the articulatory to acoustic onset interval (AAI) varies according to initial phoneme. As its main contribution, this study also shows that the onset of a specific ERP microstate may index the onset of articulation, as the microstate covered the known articulatory to acoustic gap for specific onset phonemes. Thus, future studies could be better equipped to visualize AAI differences between conditions, making it easier to investigate the final stages of speech production and to distinguish between cognitive and motor processes.

A different type of challenge is faced by the field of cognitive neuroscience more broadly: The extent to which neural data can be used to address cognitive questions remains debatable. This is because cognitive theories in their strict sense are not formulated at the same level as the information provided by neural data (see for discussion Poeppel, 2012). Given that this is not an issue with electrophysiology in particular, we will not address it further, but refer the reader to relevant discussions for example by Page (2006) and Coltheart (2013).

The value of MEEG-based measures

While it may be argued that brain data cannot be (easily) used to address theories about cognition, there are some cases in which MEEG-based measures can be of particular value (although not necessarily to adjudicate between cognitive theories in their strict sense). Besides the future directions already mentioned throughout the chapter, here we highlight other avenues that exemplify the relevance of electrophysiological data.

One special case is offered by the excellent temporal resolution of the MEEG signal. In some cases, one may wish to know when a particular brain area is engaged in a task. Even though there are criticisms to using the MEEG signal to make claims about when precisely things happen (e.g., Piai, 2016), one can be absolutely certain that a particular modulation (in a brain area) occurred during word planning versus after articulation. Haemodynamic-based measures, by contrast, do not allow for this level of temporal scrutiny, so one can never easily disentangle word planning from post-articulation processes using these measures. Therefore, MEEG-based measures may provide special information in the context of language production. One concrete example is illustrated by discussions about the recruitment of the right hemisphere in cases of left-hemisphere brain damage. If one finds right-hemisphere recruitment using MEEG-based measures, one can be certain about whether this recruitment happened during word planning or after articulation (e.g., Chupina et al., 2022; Piai et al., 2017, 2020).

Some scholars have argued that MEEG-based measures such as neural oscillations may provide a way to elucidate how general neuronal computational principles support language (e.g, Friederici & Singer, 2015; Piai & Zheng, 2019). Under this view, the finding of overlapping brain regions between two different domains is not enough evidence in favour of shared mechanisms between these domains. Instead, stronger evidence for shared mechanisms would be provided by finding overlapping features in the multidimensional space that constitute the oscillatory signal, that is, space, time, spectrum, and direction of the modulation (see Piai & Zheng, 2019, for extensive discussion).

Conclusion

In this chapter, we have presented a selective review of studies focusing on spoken language production using electrophysiology. Albeit incompletely, we attempted to outline some of the evolution within the field, highlighting what kinds of questions researchers have focused on. From this exercise, it is clear that methodological rigour has to go hand-in-hand with our theoretical investigations, and that, given the relatively young age of this subfield, there is still much ground to cover. The emerging convergence of findings highlighted here will hopefully solidify as the field matures.

References

Ala-Salomäki, H., Kujala, J., Liljeström, M., & Salmelin, R. (2021). Picture naming yields highly consistent cortical activation patterns: Test–retest reliability of magnetoencephalography recordings. *NeuroImage, 227*. 10.1016/j.neuroimage.2020.117651

Anders, R., Llorens, A., Dubarry, A. S., Trébuchon, A., Liegeois-Chauvel, C., & Alario, F.-X. (2019). Cortical dynamics of semantic priming and interference during word

Production: An intracerebral study. *Journal of Cognitive Neuroscience*, *31*(7), 978–1001. 10.1162/jocn_a_01406

Aristei, S., Melinger, A., & Rahman, R. A. (2011). Electrophysiological chronometry of semantic context effects in language production. *Journal of Cognitive Neuroscience*, *23*(7), 1567–1586. 10.1162/jocn.2010.21474

Bögels, S., Magyari, L., & Levinson, S. C. (2015). Neural signatures of response planning occur midway through an incoming question in conversation. *Scientific Reports*, *5*(1), 12881. 10.1038/srep12881

Bürki, A., & Laganaro, M. (2014). Tracking the time course of multi-word noun phrase production with ERPs or on when (and why) cat is faster than the big cat. *Frontiers in Psychology*, *1*, 586. 10.3389/fpsyg.2014.00586

Buzsaki, G., & Draguhn, A. (2004). Neuronal oscillations in cortical networks. *Science*, *304*(5679), 1926–1929. 10.1126/science.1099745

Chartier, J., Anumanchipalli, G. K., Johnson, K., & Chang, E. F. (2018). Encoding of articulatory kinematic trajectories in human speech sensorimotor cortex. *Neuron*, *98*(5), 1042–1054. 10.1016/j.neuron.2018.04.031

Chupina, I., Sierpowska, J., Zheng, X. Y., Dewenter, A., Piastra, M.-C., & Piai, V. (2022). Time course of right-hemisphere recruitment during word production following left-hemisphere damage: A single case of young stroke. *European Journal of Neuroscience*, *56*, 5235–5259. 10.1111/ejn.15813.

Coltheart, M. (2013). How can functional neuroimaging inform cognitive theories? *Perspectives on Psychological Science*, *8*(1), 98–103. 10.1177/1745691612469208

Costa, A., Strijkers, K., Martin, C., & Thierry, G. (2009). The time course of word retrieval revealed by event-related brain potentials during overt speech. Proceedings of the *National Academy of Sciences of the United States of America*, *106*(50), 21442–21446. 10.1073/pnas. 0908921106

Crone, N. E., Hao, L., Hart, J., Boatman, D., Lesser, R. P., Irizarry, R., & Gordon, B. (2001). Electrocorticographic gamma activity during word production in spoken and sign language. *Neurology*, *57*(11), 2045–2053. 10.1212/WNL.57.11.2045

de Zubicaray, G. I., & Piai, V. (2019). Investigating the spatial and temporal components of speechproduction. In G. I. de Zubicaray, & N. O. Schiller (Eds.), *The Oxford handbook of neurolinguistics*. Oxford University Press.

Deecke, L., Engel, M., Lang, W., & Kornhuber, H. H. (1986). Bereitschaftspotential preceding speech after holding breath. *Experimental Brain Research*, *65*, 219–223. 10.1 007/BF00243845

Dubarry, A. S., Llorens, A., Trébuchon, A., Carron, R., Liégeois-Chauvel, C., Bénar, C. G., & Alario, F. X. (2017). Estimating parallel processing in a language task using single-trial intracerebral electroencephalography. *Psychological Science*, *28*(4), 414–426. 10.1177/ 0956797616681296

Edwards, E., Nagarajan, S. S., Dalal, S. S., Canolty, R. T., Kirsch, H. E., Barbaro, N. M., & Knight, R. T. (2010). Spatiotemporal imaging of cortical activation during verb generation and picture naming. *NeuroImage*, *50*(1), 291–301. 10.1016/j.neuroimage.2009.12.035

Eulitz, C., Hauk, O., & Cohen, R. (2000). Electroencephalographic activity over temporal brain areas during phonological encoding in picture naming. *Clinical Neurophysiology*, *111*(11), 2088–2097. 10.1016/S1388-2457(00)00441-7

Fargier, R., Bürki, A., Pinet, S., Alario, F. X., & Laganaro, M. (2018). Word onset phonetic properties and motor artifacts in speech production EEG recordings. *Psychophysiology*, *55*(2), e12982. 10.1111/psyp.12982

Fargier, R., & Laganaro, M. (2020). Neural dynamics of the production of newly acquired words relative to well-known words. *Brain Research*, *1727*, 146557. 10.1016/j.brainres. 2019.146557

Findlay, A. M., Ambrose, J. B., Cahn-Weiner, D. A., Houde, J. F., Honma, S., Hinkley, L. B. N., Berger, M. S., Nagarajan, S. S., & Kirsch, H. E. (2012). Dynamics of hemispheric dominance for language assessed by magnetoencephalographic imaging. *Annals of Neurology*, *71*(5), 668–686. 10.1002/ana.23530

Fisher, A. E., Furlong, P. L., Seri, S., Adjamian, P., Witton, C., Baldeweg, T., Phillips, S., Walsh, R., Houghton, J. M., & Thai, N. J. (2008). Interhemispheric differences of spectral power in expressive language: A MEG study with clinical applications. *International Journal of Psychophysiology*, *68*(2), 111–122. 10.1016/j.ijpsycho.2007.12.005

Flinker, A., Piai, V., & Knight, R. T. (2018). Intracranial electrophysiology in language research. In S. Rueschemeyer, & M. G. Gaskell (Eds.), *The Oxford handbook of psycholinguistics*. Oxford University Press.

Forseth, K. J., Kadipasaoglu, C. M., Conner, C. R., Hickok, G., Knight, R. T., & Tandon, N. (2018). A lexical semantic hub for heteromodal naming in middle fusiform gyrus. *Brain*, *141*(7), 2112–2126. 10.1093/brain/awy120

Friederici, A. D., & Singer, W. (2015). Grounding language processing on basic neurophysiological principles. *Trends in Cognitive Sciences*, *19*(6), 329–338. 10.1016/j.tics. 2015.03.012

Ganushchak, L. Y., Christoffels, I. K., & Schiller, N. O. (2011). The use of electroencephalography in language production research: A review. *Frontiers in Psychology*, *2*, 208. 10.3389/fpsyg.2011.00208

Gastaldon, S., Arcara, G., Navarrete, E., & Peressotti, F. (2020). Commonalities in alpha and beta neural desynchronizations during prediction in language comprehension and production. *Cortex*, *133*, 328–345. 10.1016/j.cortex.2020.09.026

Howard, D., Nickels, L., Coltheart, M., & Cole-Virtue, J. (2006). Cumulative semantic inhibition in picture naming: Experimental and computational studies. *Cognition*, *100*(3), 464–482. 10.1016/j.cognition.2005.02.006

Indefrey, P., & Levelt, W. J. M. (2004). The spatial and temporal signatures of word production components. *Cognition*, *92*(1–2), 101–144. 10.1016/j.cognition.2002.06.001

Jescheniak, J. D., Schriefers, H., Garrett, M. F., & Friederici, A. D. (2002). Exploring the activation of semantic and phonological codes during speech planning with event-related brain potentials. *Journal of Cognitive Neuroscience*, *14*(6), 951–964. 10.1162/089892902 760191162

Jongman, S. R., Piai, V., & Meyer, A. S. (2020). Planning for language production: The electrophysiological signature of attention to the cue to speak. *Language, Cognition and Neuroscience*, *35*(7), 915–932. 10.1080/23273798.2019.1690153

Jouen, A. L., Lancheros, M., & Laganaro, M. (2021). Microstate ERP analyses to pinpoint the articulatory onset in speech production. *Brain Topography*, *34*, 29–40. 10.1007/s1054 8-020-00803-3

Klaus, J., Schutter, D. J. L. G., & Piai, V. (2020). Transient perturbation of the left temporal cortex evokes plasticity-related reconfiguration of the lexical network. *Human Brain Mapping*, *41*(4), 1061–1071. 10.1002/hbm.24860

Kojima, K., Brown, E. C., Matsuzaki, N., Rothermel, R., Fuerst, D., Shah, A., Mittal, S., Sood, S., & Asano, E. (2013). Gamma activity modulated by picture and auditory naming tasks: Intracranial recording in patients with focal epilepsy. *Clinical Neurophysiology*, *124*(9), 1737–1744. 10.1016/j.clinph.2013.01.030

Krott, A., Medaglia, M. T., & Porcaro, C. (2019). Early and late effects of semantic distractors on electroencephalographic responses during overt picture naming. *Frontiers in Psychology*, *10*, 696. 10.3389/fpsyg.2019.00696

Laaksonen, H., Kujala, J., Hultén, A., Liljeström, M., & Salmelin, R. (2012). MEG evoked responses and rhythmic activity provide spatiotemporally complementary measures of neural activity in language production. *NeuroImage*, *60*(1), 29–36. 10.1016/j.neuroimage.2011.11.087

Laganaro, M. (2014). ERP topographic analyses from concept to articulation in word production studies. *Frontiers in Psychology*, *5*, 493. 10.3389/fpsyg.2014.00493

Laganaro, M. (2017). Inter-study and inter-individual consistency and variability of EEG/ERP microstate sequences in referential word production. *Brain Topography*, *30*(6), 785–796. 10.1007/s10548-017-0580-0

Laganaro, M., Morand, S., & Schnider, A. (2009). Time course of evoked-potential changes in different forms of anomia in aphasia. *Journal of Cognitive Neuroscience*, *21*(8), 1499–1510. 10.1162/jocn.2009.21117

Laganaro, M., Morand, S., Schwitter, V., Zimmermann, C., & Schnider, A. (2008). Normalisation and increase of abnormal ERP patterns accompany recovery from aphasia in the post-acute stage. *Neuropsychologia*, *46*(8), 2265–2273. 10.1016/j.neuropsychologia.2008.02.013

Laganaro, M., & Perret, C. (2011). Comparing electrophysiological correlates of word production in immediate and delayed naming through the analysis of word age of acquisition effects. *Brain Topography*, *24*(1), 19–29. 10.1007/s10548-010-0162-x

Laganaro, M., Valente, A., & Perret, C. (2012). Time course of word production in fast and slow speakers: A high density ERP topographic study. *NeuroImage*, *59*(4), 3881–3888. 10.1016/j.neuroimage.2011.10.082

Lee, D. K., Fedorenko, E., Simon, M. V., Curry, W. T., Nahed, B. V., Cahill, D. P., & Williams, Z. M. (2018). Neural encoding and production of functional morphemes in the posterior temporal lobe. *Nature Communications*, *9*, 12. 10.1038/s41467-018-04235-3

Levelt, W. J. M., Roelofs, A., & Meyer, A. S. (1999). A theory of lexical access in speech production. *Behavioral and Brain Sciences*, *22*(1), 1–38. 10.1017/S0140525X99001776

Levy, R. S. (1977). The question of electrophysiological asymmetries preceding speech. In *Studies in neurolinguistics* (Vol. 3, pp. 287–318). Elsevier. 10.1016/b978-0-12-746303-2.50013-0

Liljeström, M., Hultén, A., Parkkonen, L., & Salmelin, R. (2009). Comparing MEG and fMRI views to naming actions and objects. *Human Brain Mapping*, *30*(6), 1845–1856. 10.1002/hbm.20785

Llorens, A., Dubarry, A.-S., Trébuchon, A., Chauvel, P., Alario, F.-X., & Liégeois-Chauvel, C. (2016). Contextual modulation of hippocampal activity during picture naming. *Brain and Language*, *159*, 92–101. 10.1016/j.bandl.2016.05.011

Llorens, A., Trébuchon, A., Liégeois-Chauvel, C., & Alario, F. X. (2011). Intra-cranial recordings of brain activity during language production. *Frontiers in Psychology*, *2*, 375. 10.3389/fpsyg.2011.00375

Lopes da Silva, F. (2013). EEG and MEG: Relevance to neuroscience. *Neuron*, *80*(5), 1112–1128. 10.1016/j.neuron.2013.10.017

Malmivuo, J. (2012). Comparison of the properties of EEG and MEG in detecting the electric activity of the brain. *Brain Topography*, *25*, 1–19. 10.1007/s10548-011-0202-1

Manning, J. R., Jacobs, J., Fried, I., & Kahana, M. J. (2009). Broadband shifts in local field potential power spectra are correlated with single-neuron spiking in humans. *Journal of Neuroscience, 29*(43), 13613–13620. 10.1523/JNEUROSCI.2041-09.2009

Mazaheri, A., & Jensen, O. (2010). Rhythmic pulsing: Linking ongoing brain activity with evoked responses. *Frontiers in Human Neuroscience, 4*, 177. 10.3389/fnhum.2010.00177

McAdam, D. W., & Whitaker, H. A. (1971). Language production: Electroencephalographic localization in the normal human brain. *Science, 172*(3982), 499–502. 10.1126/science.172.3982.499

Munding, D., Dubarry, A.-S., & Alario, F.-X. (2016). On the cortical dynamics of word production: A review of the MEG evidence. *Language, Cognition and Neuroscience, 31*(4), 441–462. 10.1080/23273798.2015.1071857

Nozari, N., & Pinet, S. (2020). A critical review of the behavioral, neuroimaging, and electrophysiological studies of co-activation of representations during word production. *Journal of Neurolinguistics, 53*, 100875. 10.1016/j.jneuroling.2019.100875

Ouyang, G., Herzmann, G., Zhou, C., & Sommer, W. (2011). Residue iteration decomposition (RIDE): A new method to separate ERP components on the basis of latency variability in single trials. *Psychophysiology, 48*(12), 1631–1647. 10.1111/j.1469-8986.2011.01269.x

Ouyang, G., Sommer, W., Zhou, C., Aristei, S., Pinkpank, T., & Abdel Rahman, R. (2016). Articulation artifacts during overt language production in event-related brain potentials: Description and correction. *Brain Topography, 29*(6), 791–813. 10.1007/s1054 8-016-0515-1

Page, M. P. A. (2006). What can't functional neuroimaging tell the cognitive psychologist? *Cortex, 42*(3), 428–443. 10.1016/S0010-9452(08)70375-7

Pavlova, A. A., Butorina, A. V., Nikolaeva, A. Y., Prokofyev, A. O., Ulanov, M. A., Bondarev, D. P., & Stroganova, T. A. (2019). Effortful verb retrieval from semantic memory drives beta suppression in mesial frontal regions involved in action initiation. *Human Brain Mapping, 40*(12), 3669–3681. 10.1002/hbm.24624

Perret, C., & Laganaro, M. (2013). Dynamic of verbal response preparation and Electroencephalography: A review. *L'Année Psychologique, 113*(04), 667–698. 10.4074/S0003503313014073

Pfurtscheller, G., & Lopes da Silva, F. H. (1999). Event-related EEG/MEG synchronization and desynchronization: Basic principles. *Clinical Neurophysiology, 110*(11), 1842–1857. 10.1016/S1388-2457(99)00141-8

Piai, V. (2016). The role of electrophysiology in informing theories of word production: A critical standpoint. *Language, Cognition and Neuroscience, 31*(4), 471–473. 10.1080/23273 798.2015.1100749

Piai, V., Klaus, J., & Rossetto, E. (2020). The lexical nature of alpha-beta oscillations in context-driven word production. *Journal of Neurolinguistics, 55*, 100905. 10.1016/j.jneuroling.2020.100905

Piai, V., Meyer, L., Dronkers, N. F., & Knight, R. T. (2017). Neuroplasticity of language in left-hemisphere stroke: Evidence linking subsecond electrophysiology and structural connections. *Human Brain Mapping, 38*(6), 3151–3162. 10.1002/hbm.23581

Piai, V., Riès, S. K., & Knight, R. T. (2015a). The electrophysiology of language production: What could be improved. *Frontiers in Psychology, 5*, 1560. 10.3389/fpsyg.2014.01560

Piai, V., Roelofs, A., Jensen, O., Schoffelen, J.-M., & Bonnefond, M. (2014a). Distinct patterns of brain activity characterise lexical activation and competition in spoken word production. *PLoS ONE, 9*(2), e88674. 10.1371/journal.pone.0088674

Piai, V., Roelofs, A., & Maris, E. (2014b). Oscillatory brain responses in spoken word production reflect lexical frequency and sentential constraint. *Neuropsychologia*, *53*, 146–156. 10.1016/j.neuropsychologia.2013.11.014

Piai, V., Roelofs, A., Rommers, J., Dahlslätt, K., & Maris, E. (2015b). Withholding planned speech is reflected in synchronized beta-band oscillations. *Frontiers in Human Neuroscience*, *9*, 549. 10.3389/fnhum.2015.00549

Piai, V., Roelofs, A., Rommers, J., & Maris, E. (2015c). Beta oscillations reflect memory and motor aspects of spoken word production. *Human Brain Mapping*, *36*(7), 2767–2780. 10.1002/hbm.22806

Piai, V., Roelofs, A., & van der Meij, R. (2012). Event-related potentials and oscillatory brain responses associated with semantic and Stroop-like interference effects in overt naming. *Brain Research*, *1450*, 87–101. 10.1016/j.brainres.2012.02.050

Piai, V., Rommers, J., & Knight, R. T. (2018). Lesion evidence for a critical role of left posterior but not frontal areas in alpha-beta power decreases during context-driven word production. *European Journal of Neuroscience*, *48*(7), 2622–2629. 10.1111/ejn.13695

Piai, V., & Zheng, X. (2019). Speaking waves: Neuronal oscillations in language production. In *Psychology of learning and motivation* (Vol. 71, pp. 265–302). Elsevier. 10.1016/bs.plm.2019.07.002

Poeppel, D. (2012). The maps problem and the mapping problem: Two challenges for a cognitive neuroscience of speech and language. *Cognitive Neuropsychology*, *29*(1–2), 34–55. 10.1080/02643294.2012.710600

Porcaro, C., Medaglia, M. T., & Krott, A. (2015). Removing speech artifacts from electroencephalographic recordings during overt picture naming. *NeuroImage*, *105*, 171–180. 10.1016/j.neuroimage.2014.10.049

Pylkkänen, L., Bemis, D. K., & Blanco Elorrieta, E. (2014). Building phrases in language production: An MEG study of simple composition. *Cognition*, *133*(2), 371–384. 10.1016/j.cognition.2014.07.001

Rabovsky, M., Schad, D. J., & Abdel Rahman, R. (2021). Semantic richness and density effects on language production: Electrophysiological and behavioral evidence. *Journal of Experimental Psychology: Learning, Memory, and Cognition*, *47*(3), 508–517. 10.1037/xlm0000940

Riès, S. K., Dhillon, R. K., Clarke, A., King-Stephens, D., Laxer, K. D., Weber, P. B., Kuperman, R. A., Auguste, K. I., Brunner, P., Schalk, G., Lin, J. J., Parvizi, J., Crone, N. E., Dronkers, N. F., & Knight, R. T. (2017). Spatiotemporal dynamics of word retrieval in speech production revealed by cortical high-frequency band activity. Proceedings of the *National Academy of Sciences*, *114*(23), E4530–E4538. 10.1073/pnas.1620669114

Riès, S. K., Pinet, S., Nozari, N. B., & Knight, R. T. (2021). Characterizing multi-word speech production using event-related potentials. *Psychophysiology*, *58*(5), 1–16. 10.1111/psyp.13788

Roelofs, A., & Piai, V. (2011). Attention demands of spoken word planning: A review. *Frontiers in Psychology*, *2*, 307. 10.3389/fpsyg.2011.00307

Roos, N. M., & Piai, V. (2020). Across-session consistency of context-driven language processing: A magnetoencephalography study. *European Journal of Neuroscience*, *52*(5), 3457–3469. 10.1111/ejn.14785

Rose, S. B., Aristei, S., Melinger, A., & Abdel Rahman, R. (2019). The closer they are, the more they interfere: Semantic similarity of word distractors increases competition in language production. *Journal of Experimental Psychology: Learning, Memory, and Cognition*, *45*(4), 753–763. 10.1037/xlm0000592

Sahin, N. T., Pinker, S., Cash, S. S., Schomer, D., & Halgren, E. (2009). Sequential processing of lexical, grammatical, and phonological information within Broca's area. *Science, 326*(5951), 445–449. 10.1126/science.1174481

Salmelin, R. (2007). Clinical neurophysiology of language: The MEG approach. *Clinical Neurophysiology, 118*(2), 237–254. 10.1016/j.clinph.2006.07.316

Salmelin, R., Hámáaláinen, M., Kajola, M., & Hari, R. (1995). Functional segregation of movement-related rhythmic activity in the human brain. *NeuroImage, 2*(4), 237–243. 10.1006/nimg.1995.1031

Salmelin, R., Hari, R., Lounasmaa, O. V., & Sams, M. (1994). Dynamics of brain activation during picture naming. *Nature, 368*(6470), 463–465. 10.1038/368463a0

Salmelin, R., & Sams, M. (2002). Motor cortex involvement during verbal versus nonverbal lip and tongue movements. *Human Brain Mapping, 16*(2), 81–91. 10.1002/hbm.10031

Sauppe, S., Choudhary, K. K., Giroud, N., Blasi, D. E., Norcliffe, E., Bhattamishra, S., Gulati, M., Egurtzegi, A., Bornkessel-Schlesewsky, I., Meyer, M., & Bickel, B. (2021). Neural signatures of syntactic variation in speech planning. *PLoS Biology, 19*(1), 1–20. 10.1371/journal.pbio.3001038

Shitova, N., Roelofs, A., Schriefers, H., Bastiaansen, M., & Schoffelen, J.-M. (2017). Control adjustments in speaking: Electrophysiology of the Gratton effect in picture naming. *Cortex, 92*, 289–303. 10.1016/j.cortex.2017.04.017

Sikora, K., Roelofs, A., & Hermans, D. (2016). Electrophysiology of executive control in spoken noun-phrase production: Dynamics of updating, inhibiting, and shifting. *Neuropsychologia, 84*, 44–53. 10.1016/j.neuropsychologia.2016.01.037

Sörös, P., Cornelissen, K., Laine, M., & Salmelin, R. (2003). Naming actions and objects: Cortical dynamics in healthy adults and in an anomic patient with a dissociation in action/object naming. *NeuroImage, 19*(4), 1787–1801. 10.1016/S1053-8119(03)00217-9

Strijkers, K., Costa, A., & Pulvermüller, F. (2017). The cortical dynamics of speaking: Lexical and phonological knowledge simultaneously recruit the frontal and temporal cortex within 200 ms. *NeuroImage, 163*, 206–219. 10.1016/j.neuroimage.2017.09.041

Strijkers, K., & Costa, A. (2016). The cortical dynamics of speaking: Present shortcomings and future avenues. *Language, Cognition and Neuroscience, 31*(4), 484–503. 10.1080/23273798.2015.1120878

Strijkers, K., Costa, A., & Thierry, G. (2010). Tracking lexical access in speech production: Electrophysiological correlates of word frequency and cognate effects. *Cerebral Cortex, 20*(4), 912–928. 10.1093/cercor/bhp153

van Turennout, M., Hagoort, P., & Brown, C. (1999). The time course of grammatical and phonological processing during speaking: Evidence from event-related brain potentials. *Journal of Psycholinguistic Research, 28*, 649–676. 10.1023/A:1023221028150

Van Turennout, M., Hagoort, P., & Brown, C. M. (1997). Electrophysiological evidence on the time course of semantic and phonological processes in speech production. *Journal of Experimental Psychology: Learning Memory and Cognition, 23*(4), 787–806. 10.1037/0278-7393.23.4.787

Vihla, M., Laine, M., & Salmelin, R. (2006). Cortical dynamics of visual/semantic vs phonological analysis in picture confrontation. *NeuroImage, 33*(2), 732–738. 10.1016/j.neuroimage.2006.06.040

Vos, D. M., Riès, S., Vanderperren, K., Vanrumste, B., Alario, F.-X., Huffel, V. S., & Burle, B. (2010). Removal of muscle artifacts from EEG recordings of spoken language production. *Neuroinformatics, 8*(2), 135–150. 10.1007/s12021-010-9071-0

Wang, Y., Korzeniewska, A., Usami, K., Valenzuela, A., & Crone, N. E. (2021). The dynamics of language networks interactions in lexical selection: An intracranial EEG study. *Cerebral Cortex*, *31*(4), 2058–2070. 10.1093/cercor/bhaa344

Williams Roberson, S., Shah, P., Piai, V., Gatens, H., Krieger, A. M., Lucas, T. H., & Litt, B. (2020). Electrocorticography reveals spatiotemporal neuronal activation patterns of verbal fluency in patients with epilepsy. *Neuropsychologia*, *141*, 107386. 10.1016/j.neuropsychologia.2020.107386

Wohlert, A. B. (1993). Event-related brain potentials preceding speech and nonspeech oral movements of varying complexity. *Journal of Speech, Language, and Hearing Research*, *36*(5), 897–905. 10.1044/jshr.3605.897

Wohlert, A. B., & Larson, C. R. (1991). Cerebral averaged potentials preceding oral movement. *Journal of Speech, Language, and Hearing Research*, *34*(6), 1387–1396. 10.1044/jshr.3406.1387

Youssofzadeh, V., Stout, J., Ustine, C., Gross, W. L., Conant, L. L., Humphries, C. J., Binder, J. R., & Raghavan, M. (2020). Mapping language from MEG beta power modulations during auditory and visual naming. *NeuroImage*, *220*, 117090. 10.1016/j.neuroimage.2020.117090

6 Self-Monitoring

The Neurocognitive Basis of Error Monitoring in Language Production

Elin Runnqvist

Speakers' tongues sometimes slip such as in Ronald Reagan's famous misquotation of John Adams: "Facts are stupid things ... stubborn things, I should say" (Reagan, 1988). Similar error patterns to those of spoken language production have also been reported for other modalities such as typing or signing (e.g., Hohenberger et al., 2002; Pinet & Nozari, 2018; see also Emmorey, 2022, this volume). However, when considering the great complexity of language production, both from an anatomical and cognitive point of view, involving the use and orchestration of several organs, body parts, and mental representations, an intriguing question is why speech errors only occur about once every thousand words (e.g., Levelt, 1992; Meyer, 1992)? Several phenomena indicate that part of the answer to this question is that speakers inspect their utterances for errors. In this chapter, we will provide a succinct overview of core phenomena leading researchers to assume the existence of such self-monitoring (Part 1). We will then focus on how some of the more influential models of language production have incorporated this self-monitoring component either in the periphery or as part of the core mechanisms sustaining language processing, leading to a classification of comprehension-based, production-based, and integration-based monitoring (Part 2). Afterwards, we will dedicate a part to the brain bases of monitoring (Part 3), focusing on the links that have been made between three broad brain regions (temporal cortex, cerebellum, and medial frontal cortex) and the cognitive theories reviewed previously. Lastly, we will consider how both behavioral and neurophysiological techniques have provided evidence suggesting that monitoring may rely on several mechanisms, contrary to what is currently assumed by most models of language production (Part 4).

Part 1. What is the evidence that speakers inspect their utterances for errors?

The most obvious evidence that speakers monitor their own speech for errors is that they can interrupt and correct themselves (self-repairs, Levelt, 1983), or accurately report having committed an error (Postma & Noordanus, 1996).

DOI: 10.4324/9781003145790-7

An intuitive and parsimonious explanation for how speakers detect errors in cases such as the Reagan example above is that they hear themselves producing an utterance that did not match what was intended. That is, an external channel relying on sensorial information would allow speakers to detect their own errors just as they might detect those of another speaker. Compelling evidence that speakers make use of this type of sensorial feedback for monitoring purposes comes from studies in which altering the feedback can result in speakers admitting to errors that they did not produce. Both in spoken and typed language production, there are studies showing that replacing participants' responses (such as modifying the auditory or visual feedback of the produced word "green" to "gray") goes undetected in a majority of cases, indicating a strong reliance of the external channel to monitor language production (e.g., Lind et al., 2014; Logan & Crump, 2010). Further evidence that speakers actually detect their own errors and thus monitor their speech production is that speakers are generally slower in subsequent production upon committing an error (e.g., post-error slowing, Freund & Nozari, 2018; Ganushchak & Schiller, 2006). Moreover, when asked to press a button if they think their utterance contained an error, speakers are quite accurate in estimating the accuracy of their self-produced speech (e.g., Gauvin et al., 2016). Interestingly, several empirical findings indicate that speakers also count on mechanisms allowing them to detect errors during speech planning, before articulation.

A first example of this is that errors are sometimes interrupted or repaired almost immediately after they start to be pronounced. Producing a repair for an error requires the speaker to perceive the error, decide that it is an error, interrupt the erroneous utterance, and prepare and initiate articulation of a new one, processes that all necessitate a certain amount of time. Hence, a near-zero interval between the error and the repair indicates that error detection and repair had already been prepared internally, before the error was even audible (Hartsuiker & Kolk, 2001; Levelt, 1983). Certain authors have argued that such near-zero intervals might not require assuming an inner monitoring channel after all (e.g., Lind 2014, 2015). However, not only the latency indicates the existence of an inner and an external channel, but also the fact that there is a bimodal distribution in error to cut-off latencies. That is, a first group of errors is interrupted almost immediately after articulation is initiated, while a second group of errors is on average interrupted some 500 ms later (e.g., Nooteboom & Quené, 2017). While this bimodal distribution is predicted by an error detection system relying on an inner and an external channel, it is hard to account for when assuming all errors are detected externally.

A second finding supporting the existence of inner monitoring is that certain types of errors such as taboo words or non-words, occur below chance in contexts where they would be considered as inappropriate utterances (Baars et al., 1975; Hartsuiker et al., 2005; Nooteboom & Quené, 2008), indicating that the monitor can filter out impending errors before articulation. This holds true both in corpora and in laboratory settings in which participants are primed to produce errors (e.g., Hartsuiker et al., 2006). For example, a classical psycholinguistic error-inducing task is the SLIP task (e.g., Baars et al., 1975). Speakers are presented with a series of word pairs that they are instructed to read silently, and upon an unpredictable cue, they are instructed to produce the last word pair they saw as quickly as possible. On the critical trials, a target (e.g., "barn door") is preceded by several primes in which the word onsets are in the opposite order compared to the target (i.e., "duck ball", "dish bell"). This manipulation makes speakers substantially more prone to producing a spoonerism error such as "darn bore" instead of the targeted "barn door". However, this tendency is very much reduced if the spoonerism leads the speaker to produce something embarrassing or nonsensical. Moreover, certain physiological responses that are linked to emotional arousal (e.g., the galvanic response) show sensitivity to an increased risk of producing this kind of error even though the correct utterance is ultimately produced (e.g., Motley et al., 1981, 1982; Severens et al., 2012).

A third finding supporting the existence of internal monitoring processes is that speakers can report having committed an error just as accurately in a noisy environment when relying on an audition is not possible, as in a regular setting (e.g., Postma & Kolk, 1992; Nooteboom & Quené, 2017). Finally, adaptation phenomena such as slowing on subsequent trials is not only observed after overt error commission as discussed above but also after correct trials in conditions that are error-prone (e.g., Freund & Nozari, 2018), indicating the presence of internal monitoring processes (e.g., Verguts et al., 2011). Interestingly, there is certain evidence that the use of internal or external monitoring can vary flexibly depending on different variables. The first variable would be the availability of external feedback: reliance on external monitoring decreases as feedback is less available (e.g., Pinet & Nozari, 2020). Another variable that might condition the degree of reliance on internal or external monitoring is the modality of the language production behavior involved. For example, typing might rely more heavily on external monitoring than oral language production because keeping track of the precise external feedback is useful for correcting a single keystroke as typewriters do frequently, while in oral language production corrections often involve starting from scratch and so detection and correcting errors before they become overt is more efficient for fluent communication (e.g., Pinet & Nozari, 2020). By contrast, and as reviewed by Emmorey, this volume, signers rarely look at their hands when signing and do not seem to rely on visual feedback of their self-produced signs while obviously relying on a vision for comprehension of signed language produced by others (Emmorey et al., 2009). Thus, signers seem to rely almost exclusively on internal monitoring involving somatosensory rather than visual representations (see also Riès et al., 2020). Alternatively, proprioceptive feedback might be at the basis of signers' external language production monitoring. In summary, evidence relying on the timing of error cut-offs and repairs, certain error patterns, physiological responses to correct utterances in error-prone situations and the noise insensitivity of self-reported errors support the existence of an inner monitoring channel in addition to the external monitoring channel that may rely on the auditory, visual, or proprioceptive detection of overtly committed errors. Despite the quite general consensus regarding the existence of both inner and external error monitoring processes, their cognitive basis remains contentious.

Part 2. Monitoring in models of language production

The contention regarding the cognitive basis of self-monitoring is intrinsic to the broader dynamics of language production models. The amount of cross-talk (i.e., the extent to which information may be processed simultaneously at different levels and information may be exchanged across levels) and integration between different levels (from semantics to articulation) and modalities (production and comprehension) of language processing, as well as between language and other cognitive domains (motor control, cognitive control) varies substantially in different theoretical frameworks. Consequently, the implementation of monitoring also differs in whether it is located at a unique stage or rather distributed, whether it relies on mechanisms exclusively related to producing or comprehending speech or rather on mechanisms integrating both sensory and motor aspects, and whether it is conceived as something specific to language processing, or rather shared with monitoring processes of other human actions. This can be illustrated through two of the most influential psycholinguistic models of language production, namely that of Levelt and colleagues (Levelt, 1983; 1992; Levelt et al., 1999) and that of Dell (1986, 1995).

The model of Levelt and colleagues is strictly serial so there is no cross-talk or integration across levels. It also conceives language production as a separate architecture from language comprehension, though the two are connected via an external loop (relying on audition) and an inner loop (relying on phonologically encoded inner speech). The motivation of the external loop connecting comprehension and production is clear as comprehending language leads to activating the same conceptual information as the one that is used to produce speech. The motivation of the inner loop seems to be primarily to account for the relative frequencies of naturally occurring errors. As discussed before, errors do not occur randomly but in patterns, seemingly obeying rules such as well-formedness, appropriateness, etc. One way of accounting for these patterns in speech errors is to integrate them as filtering biases on which a monitoring system is based. This is exactly what was done in Levelt and colleagues' speech production model (Levelt et al., 1999; see also Hartsuiker & Kolk, 2001; Roelofs, 2020). In this model, errors occurring at any level of speech planning or during overt speech production can be detected because the inner and external loops, respectively, both feed into the speech comprehension system leading to a central monitor. This monitor is then thought to take into account the appropriateness of a to-be-produced word, explaining why inappropriate errors such as taboo or non-words occur less frequently. That is, in a normal conversation, a non-word would never be appropriate and hence it would be easier for the monitor to intercept an impending non-word error compared to a word error. This mechanism can account for a large spectrum of error patterns, though the constraints in what might be considered as a filtering bias by the central monitor could be more specified (i.e., any error pattern could be a filter).

Now let's turn to the model of Dell. This model shares with Levelt et al.'s model the properties of considering production as separate from comprehension, but it differs in that distinct levels of processing are thought to be carried out in a cascaded and interactive fashion, allowing for some cross-talk. Thanks to the latter, certain error patterns can be explained as a natural by-product of the inner workings of language production (e.g., Dell, 1995). In this way, this model has a ready explanation for certain error distributions that are difficult to explain on the sole basis of filtering biases. A typical example of this is the fact that mixed errors (such as saying "stop" instead of "start" that are both semantically and phonologically related) occur more frequently than errors with only a single source (semantic or phonological). If the language production system is interactive and both semantics and phonology can be active at the same time, there is a double source of potential errors when "start" has to be produced, leading to the disproportional occurrence of these errors relative to errors with a single source. Note that while this is an elegant account of the source of certain error patterns that does not require any additional monitoring mechanism, it does not preclude the existence of monitoring either and it does not provide an account for the other phenomena discussed above (Part 1) supporting the existence of internal monitoring. Furthermore, action monitoring to optimize performance is thought to exist in many other domains than language under different forms (e.g., Gehring & Knight, 2000; Hoffmann & Falkenstein, 2012; Imamizu et al., 2000). Capitalizing on this, several proposals of more recent years have integrated monitoring mechanisms borrowed from other domains of cognition such as cognitive control and motor control. The basic idea here is that dealing with response conflict and performance optimization is equally necessary when driving a car or descending the stairs as when speaking, so perhaps the monitoring mechanisms regulating all human actions might share processes. For example, Nozari et al. (2011) proposed a model integrating an interactive speech production model with a conflict monitoring mechanism borrowed from the domain of cognitive control (e.g., Botvinick et al., 2001; see also Gauvin & Hartsuiker, 2020, for another model adapted to speech monitoring). Conflict is quantified as the amount of competition either at the lexical or at the phonological level, predicting respectively the occurrence of semantic and phonological errors. Moreover, in healthy speakers, the conflict can be used as an error signal for the purpose of error monitoring (a high amount of conflict would signal that something is going wrong at that level). If, on the contrary, the language production architecture is deteriorated due to a lesion, conflict will be increased in general at the level affected by the lesion, rendering it less useful to detect errors resulting in these occurring more frequently. The latter property of this model has the advantage of accurately predicting the performance of people with aphasia.

However, in a framework that completely prescinds of the notion of feedback correction, there is no obvious account for phenomena such as online speech adaptation to altered auditory feedback. That is, it is well known that if speakers have to produce a target such as "bet" but hear themselves saying "bit" because of an alteration in the auditory feedback they are given, they will adjust their production based on the auditory feedback (e.g., Savariaux et al., 1995; Niziolek & Guenther, 2013). Such phenomena are arguably related to speech monitoring because speakers sometimes experience the need to adjust their speech in response to external events coming from an interlocutor, noise, unexpected changes in the environment, etc. One possibility put forward by Gauvin and Hartsuiker (2020) is to implement the conflict-based monitoring both in the stream of language production and in that of language comprehension. That is, a conflict between highly active nodes, whether during response selection or comprehension, triggers error detection and leads to repair through a domain-general mechanism.

A different class of models is similarly inspired by mechanisms at work beyond the processing of language, concretely capitalizing on language production as a motor activity. It is widely held that the control of somatic movement involves internal models, which predict and correct the motor command before its effective output as a physical action (e.g., Jeannerod, 1988; Wolpert et al., 1995). More concretely, it has been proposed that this is done by having motor actions produce expectations of their sensory consequences (i.e., efference copies, Jeannerod, 1988). Thanks to processes of sensory-motor integration, these predicted percepts can then be compared to the output of the motor preparation process at different stages, potentially providing an error signal in case of a mismatch. Because of the predictive nature of the percepts, sensory feedback control of motor actions can be carried out internally, before the action becomes overt. The continuous communication between action and perception hence requires a highly integrated architecture across motor and sensory domains. This general architecture of sensory-motor integration has naturally been a key notion also for models focusing on post-lexical processes and speech-motor control (e.g., Guenther et al., 2006; Hickok, 2012, 2014). For example, the Hierarchical State Feedback Control model (HSFC) (Hickok, 2012, 2014) focuses on the processes that take place after lexical encoding to the moment of articulation. In this theoretical proposal, the activation of auditory targets (stored sound patterns) triggers a motor attempt to "hit" that target. Error-signal computation – speech monitoring – takes place as follows: if an auditory target is activated and there is no activity in the motor units, then the excitatory inputs from auditory-to-motor will correct this non-activation "error" by activating the corresponding motor units. If an auditory target is activated and the corresponding motor units are also activated, then

inhibitory motor-to-auditory inputs will cancel the auditory-to-motor excitation, thus squashing the error signal (i.e., the motor network is on the
right track and does not need any "correction" from the auditory network).
If an auditory target is activated and the wrong (non-corresponding) motor
units are activated, the motor-to-sensory feedback will inhibit non-target
auditory units and therefore "allow" the actual auditory target to continue
sending excitatory inputs to the corresponding motor units thus correcting
the error. Finally, if the wrong auditory target is activated, an error will be
produced.

However, the scope of such models being limited to processes occurring after
lexical selection, they remain silent about whether the mechanisms they integrate might apply also to higher levels of language processing and can hence
not account for certain speech error phenomena and their detection. Pickering
and Garrod (2013) proposed an integrated model of the complete process of
language production and comprehension with a monitoring mechanism borrowed from the domain of motor control. In a nutshell, they hypothesize that, in
parallel to speech formulation, speakers construct efference copies of their
predicted utterances. These predictions, constructed rapidly at the cost of being
impoverished representations, are then compared with the more slowly constructed output of the production process proper at different internal stages
(corresponding to the different levels of linguistic performance), and this
comparison between the predicted and actual utterance percept constitutes
speech monitoring. Adding support to this proposal, the use of internal modeling beyond motor actions have already received empirical and theoretical
support in other domains (e.g., Ito, 2008). Nevertheless, as integrating sensory
and motor aspects of speech is less straightforward at higher levels of processing
than for aspects of production that are directly speech-motor related (e.g.,
Hartsuiker, 2013; Strijkers et al., 2013), a more detailed mechanistic account
would be desirable. One possibility is that sensory-motor integration at higher
levels is possible because in language use sound and meaning always cooccur.
Over time, this arguably leads the two dimensions to form an interconnected
distributed representation (Fairs et al., 2021; Strijkers, 2016). This holistic format
of linguistic representations would entail that sound and meaning dimensions
would become active in parallel both when producing and understanding
speech, hence over time also sharing processing dynamics. In this way, motor
control processes could be directly applied to any level of language processing.

In summary, from a cognitive point of view, three types of monitoring have
been proposed so far in the literature: (1) purely comprehension-based monitoring through internal and external loops connecting the speech production
system with the speech comprehension system; (2) purely production-based
monitoring operating through conflict, a quantified measure of competition
at different linguistic levels; and (3) monitoring arising as a consequence of
the integration between speech production and perception, allowing for
inner comparisons between predicted percepts and motor outcomes (see
Figure 6.1). As has been highlighted throughout this part, all three models have

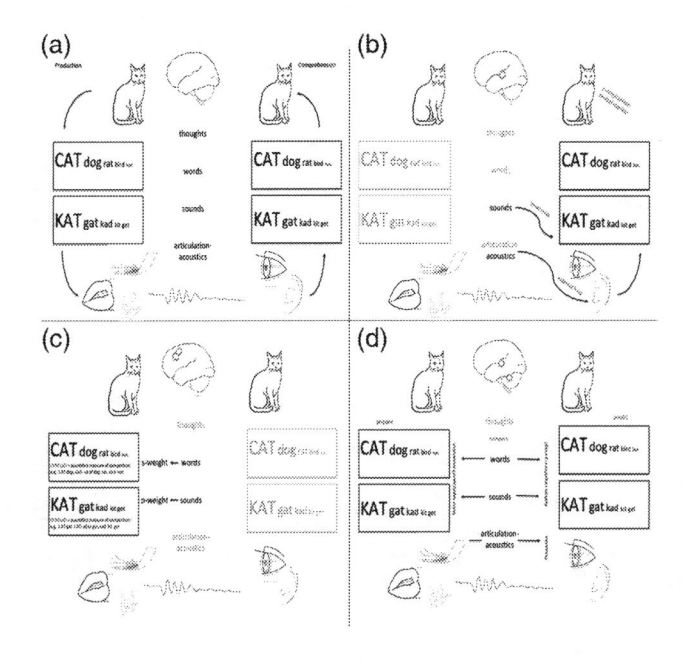

Figure 6.1 Schematic illustration of three types of monitoring models. (Panel A) The basic processes involved in producing and comprehending speech. In the case of production, a concept (cat) triggers activation of lexical (cat, dog, rat bird, lion) and phonological (cat, gat, kad, kit, get) representations (the target is represented in a capital case, the competitors in a small case, font size represents the level of activation). Ultimately, the candidate with the highest level of activation is articulated, usually corresponding to the target. The acoustic signal is the input of speech comprehension that ends with the activation of the corresponding concept. (Panel B) A comprehension-based model of monitoring (e.g., Hartsuiker & Kolk, 2001; Levelt et al., 1999; Roelofs, 2020): phonologically encoded inner speech (inner loop) or articulated speech (external loop) feed into speech comprehension and a central monitor at the conceptual level is in charge of assessing appropriateness. The proposed neural correlates of this process are the pSTG. (Panel C) A production-based monitoring model in which a domain-general monitoring mechanism operates based on conflict (e.g., Nozari et al., 2011): conflict is a quantified measure of competition (word or sound) and serves as an error signal in speakers with intact language processing (default s and p weights). Damage to the s and p weights renders conflict less useful as an error signal and leads to level-specific error patterns. Neural correlates of conflict-based monitoring have been observed in the medial frontal cortex and insula. (Panel D) An integration-based monitoring model (e.g., Hickok, 2012; Pickering & Garrod, 2013): the production system prepares speech guided by predictions or targets that are comprehension-based, and the continuous comparison between both streams provides an error signal upon a mismatch, concretely through a decreased reafference cancellation. The comparison process of such monitoring is thought to have at least part of its basis in the cerebellum, while reafference cancellation in response to speech has been attributed to posterior regions in the temporal cortex (pSTG, SPT).

advantages and limitations as currently conceived, but no model alone seems to satisfactorily account for all phenomena related to speech errors and their detection. As pointed out in the beginning of this chapter, producing language is a complex cognitive-motor skill, involving several organs, processes, and representations. One possibility that is receiving increasing empirical support and that will be further discussed at the end of the chapter (Part 4) is that monitoring is equally complex and multi-componential.

Part 3. Brain basis of monitoring

Another approach to the cognitive architecture of monitoring can be made through its brain bases. This is because all three broad mechanisms accounting for monitoring that were specified in Part 2 (sensory feedback, conflict, and internal modeling) can be linked to different brain regions either directly (proposed in the models) or indirectly through knowledge about the neuro-biological substrates of the components on which they are based (see Figure 6.1). In combination with experimental designs isolating monitoring processes, the differential involvement of such regions can thus be used as evidence supporting one mechanism or another. However, using neuroimaging techniques can also be useful to redefine our hypotheses and theoretical assumptions about monitoring. In what follows we will first focus on how the cognitive accounts can be linked to brain hypotheses, and then we will briefly illustrate with some examples how the knowledge about the brain bases in turn can be linked back to cognitive components.

Temporal cortex and comprehension-based monitoring

One of the first attempts to provide the full process of language production (from semantics to articulation) with a brain basis was carried out by Indefrey and Levelt (2004). These authors used the model of Levelt and colleagues as a framework for the general cognitive architecture of language production. They then conducted a large meta-analysis on neuroimaging data in search for neural correlates of the cognitive functions that were proposed by Levelt and colleagues. In this way, for conditions requiring increased speech monitoring (e.g., manipulated auditory feedback, Hirano et al., 1997; auditory halluci-nations, Shergill et al., 2000), enhanced bilateral activation of posterior su-perior temporal gyrus (pSTG) was observed, fitting well with the idea that monitoring processes are comprehension based. Also models of speech-motor control typically implement error detection as a feedback circuit comparing auditory perception to an internal auditory target, and the proposed locus of this comparison is also pSTG (e.g., Golfinopoulos et al., 2010) or the neighboring region SPT (Sylvian fissure at the parieto-temporal boundary, e.g., Hickok, 2012). However, another meta-analysis including several studies argued to support the implication of the pSTG in monitoring concluded that existing neuroimaging evidence is insufficient to make such an argument (e.g., Meekings & Scott, 2021). In particular, there was a mismatch between the pSTG regions proposed as responsible for error detection in the previous literature and the regions identified in an activation likelihood estimate (ALE) analysis. Also, the studies themselves were found to be methodologically and theoretically inconsistent with one another. In addition, none of the studies on which the models were built was actually based on natural speech errors, but rather on feedback alterations. On the other hand, it was recently shown that the pSTG also becomes differentially activated for overt speech errors compared to correct utterances (e.g., Runnqvist et al., 2021) as well as for trials in which speakers were unsuccessful in halting their production upon a stop signal compared to successful halting (Hansen et al., 2019). The contrast between errors and correct trials has often been used to isolate monitoring processes based on the observation that speakers detect their own errors in a majority of cases (e.g., Gauvin et al, 2016). A similar rationale can be applied to unsuccessful halting. Thus, this evidence clearly indicates a role of the pSTG in the monitoring of speech errors. The exact nature of this role merits further attention (e.g., is it reflecting speech comprehension or sensory feedback that could be internally generated through predictive internal modeling?), as does its role in connection to the other brain regions (e.g., cerebellum and areas of the medial frontal cortex) that consistently have been documented in monitoring demanding tasks and that do not follow from a purely comprehension-based account of monitoring.

Cerebellum and forward modeling

The involvement of the cerebellum has been reported in studies involving manipulations of participants' auditory feedback to their own speech (e.g., distorted or noisy feedback, Christoffels et al., 2007; Tourville et al., 2008), and verbal fluency (e.g., produce as many words as possible beginning with "s", Leggio et al., 2000). To understand this cerebellar involvement for speech production, one can turn to what is known about the monitoring of non-verbal actions. The cerebellum has been ascribed a crucial role in the monitoring of motor actions through the theoretical construct of forward modeling (also labeled "internal modeling" or "predictive coding"). As discussed in Part 2, in a forward modeling framework, the correction of motor commands is ensured by producing expectations of the commands' sensory consequences before their output is effective as physical actions (i.e., through corollary discharges or efference copies; Jeannerod, 1988; McCloskey, 1981; Wolpert et al., 1995). Cerebellar activity, particularly in the posterior lobules, is modulated by the predictability of the consequences of self-generated movements (Blakemore et al., 2001; Imamizu et al., 2000). Hence, the cerebellum has been proposed as an important center of this forward modeling of motor actions (Blakemore et al., 2001; Imamizu et al., 2000; Miall & King, 2008).

The hypothesis of cerebellar forward modeling has also been incorporated into theories and empirical investigations of mental activities, including language processing (Argyropoulos, 2016; Hickok, 2012; Ito, 2008; Lesage et al., 2017; Pickering & Garrod, 2013; Strick et al., 2009). For example, Ito (2008) proposed to extend the domain of forward models from sensorimotor actions to mental activities based on a review of anatomical (i.e., appropriate neural wiring between the cerebellum and the cerebral cortex), functional (appropriate mental activity in the cerebellum) and neuropsychological data (the association of some mental disorders with cerebellar dysfunction). In line with this proposal, it has been shown that a gradient within the posterolateral cerebellum supports cognitive control of both concrete, proximal actions (motor-adjacent sub-regions) and abstract future processing (motor-distal sub-regions, e.g., D'Mello et al., 2020). Thus, one possibility is that all self-generated actions, whether motor or mental, may be supervised through forward modeling enabled by connections from the cerebellum, an important neural center of forward modeling, to different areas of the cortex (Ito, 2008; Strick et al., 2009). The cerebellum would generate the prediction of the sensory or mental consequences of the action (efference copying), while the cortical region in question would be in charge of inhibiting the neural response that the action is expected to generate (reafference cancellation). In the case of language, the modeling of different levels of linguistic representation might result in reafference cancellation in different areas of cortex. Several theoretical models of the motor control of speech incorporate some form of forward modeling (i.e., Guenther et al., 2006; Hickok, 2012; 2014; Tian & Poeppel, 2010; Tourville & Guenther, 2011) involving, among other brain regions, the cerebellum (for a detailed account of the neural bases of such models we refer to Golfinopoulos (2010), or, for a review, see Nozari (2020), here we will focus on the role of the cerebellum which might be generalizable to monitoring of the full language production process). For example, Golfinopoulos et al. (2010) propose that auditory feedback control would be complemented by a cerebellar module (superior lateral cerebellum) and a feedforward control subsystem mediated by a trans-cerebellar pathway (anterior paravermal parts of the cerebellum). Hickok (2012) proposes that the cerebellum is in charge of the comparison (coordinate transform) between auditory and motor targets at the phonetic encoding stages of speech production. The integration of the cerebellum in these models is based on evidence from feedback manipulations as discussed previously (e.g., Ghosh et al., 2008), and on the role of the cerebellum in ataxic dysarthria studies (e.g., Ackermann et al., 1992). A less explored hypothesis states that linguistic levels of processing that are beyond speech-motor control are also monitored through forward models (Pickering & Garrod, 2013). Furthermore, this psycholinguistic proposal has not been neurobiologically specified. However, given the increasing evidence of a role of the cerebellum in cognitive processing, an extension of the mechanisms operating on speech-motor aspects to language processing proper is conceivable. In line with this hypothesis, two recent studies have reported a role of the cerebellum in the production and detection of speech errors beyond articulatory levels of processing (Runnqvist et al., 2016, 2021).

Medial frontal cortex and conflict-based monitoring or vocal feedback control

The involvement of several areas in the medial frontal cortex such as the pre-supplementary motor area (pre-SMA) and the anterior cingulate cortex (ACC) has been reported in studies investigating error-related processing in language production (De Zubicaray et al., 2001; Gauvin et al., 2016; Möller et al., 2007; Riès et al., 2011). These areas are the same ones that have been linked to error detection and conflict monitoring in domains other than language, such as in cognitive control (Botvinick et al., 2001; Nachev et al., 2005). The conflict monitoring theory holds that medial frontal structures constantly evaluate current levels of conflict and that, when a conflict threshold is passed, they relay this information on to other regions in the frontal cortex responsible for control, triggering them to adjust the strength of their influence on processing. A need for greater control is thus indicated by the occurrence of conflict itself. Such theory can account both for inner and external monitoring through a single mechanism operating on a continuum of conflict on which overt errors would be the most extreme case.

As discussed above (Part 2), the idea of conflict monitoring as a means of preventing and detecting errors has been incorporated into a model of language production (Nozari et al., 2011) that successfully simulated error-detection performance in people with aphasia. Moreover, a few studies have obtained evidence for an involvement of the ACC and pre-SMA also on correctly named trials in tasks involving the presence of explicit conflict in the stimulus to be processed for language production (e.g., semantic interference inflicted by the categorical relationship between a picture to be named and a (near-)simultaneously presented distractor; Abel et al., 2012; De Zubicaray et al., 2001). However, the available evidence only bears on the involvement of medial frontal cortex in the presence of inner conflict susceptible of generating sensory feedback (errors or articulatory conflict are susceptible of resulting in auditory and proprioceptive feedback; e.g., Alario et al., 2006; Gauvin et al., 2016) or in the presence of feedback generated through external stimulation (externally provided performance feedback or explicitly presented interfering information De Zubicaray et al., 2001; Loh et al., 2020). Hence, in the context of a task in which the conflict does not result in sensory feedback, it remains an open question whether the medial frontal cortex has a role for monitoring in the absence of overt errors. An alternative account for activations of regions in the medial frontal cortex observed for speech errors might consist in linking speech monitoring in humans with vocal feedback monitoring across human and non-human primates (Loh et al., 2017; 2020; Procyk et al., 2016) rather than with conflict. Several authors have argued that, across primates, pars opercularis of the inferior frontal gyrus (IFG), also known as area 44, is in charge of cognitive control of orofacial and non-speech vocal responses, and the midcingulate cortex is in charge of analyzing vocal non-speech feedback driving response adaptation. Furthermore, the cognitive control of human–specific speech vocal information would require the additional recruitment of pars triangularis of the IFG, also known as area 45, and pre-SMA. The most direct evidence supporting this vocal feedback control network comes from studies that actually provided external vocal feedback. However, recent evidence suggests that such external feedback might also be provided through the acoustic signal of self-produced speech (Runnqvist et al., 2021).

Part 4. Behavioral and neuroimaging studies suggesting multiple mechanisms of monitoring

As discussed in the beginning of this chapter, there is a general consensus regarding the existence of monitoring processes both during speech planning and upon articulation. An inherent assumption of the models discussed previously is that both types of monitoring would rely on the same mechanisms applied at different stages of processing (before and after articulation). While this is a parsimonious assumption, there could be good reasons to assume differently. First, from a purely theoretical point of view, most models of language production agree that different levels of language differ in how directly they are linked to sensory-motor aspects (e.g., Dell, 1986; Levelt et al., 1999; but see Strijkers, 2016 and Fairs et al., 2021 for an account of parallel and distributed processing in language production). Hence, it would be easy to imagine that levels directly connected to sensory-motor aspects of speech capitalize on monitoring mechanisms based on feedback from these properties while higher levels might have to rely on properties of information processing such as activation and conflict. Instead, the models that were reviewed in Part 2 assume either an inner perceptual level (inner speech, auditory target, inner percept) or that the same properties of information processing are used throughout the language production process for the purpose of monitoring, rendering perceptual variables irrelevant even for the monitoring of overt errors. Second, some studies have shown that inner speech and articulated speech display different error patterns. For example, Oppenheim and Dell (2008) showed that in imagined speech, lexical errors occurred more frequently than non-lexical errors just as in overt speech. However, only overt speech was sensitive to phonetic variables (i.e., increase in exchanges of consonant onsets when onsets share phonetic features). This result suggests that monitoring of different levels of processing may be carried out at different time points and that monitoring of inner speech and overt speech potentially rely on different mechanisms. Consistent with this, it has also been shown that while error detection during speech planning entails a very quick initiation of repairs, this is not the case when an error is externally detected (e.g., Nooteboom & Quené, 2017). One interpretation of this is that inner repairs are based on the available activation of the correct candidate that was mistakenly not initially selected, while repairs to externally detected errors would not be able to rely on such remaining activation and thus need to be prepared from scratch. Third, several studies using neuroimaging techniques have found evidence of distinct neural correlates of internal and external monitoring. Hansen et al. (2019) conducted a picture naming task in which participants were asked to halt their speech upon hearing an auditorily presented word (stop signal). The stop signal word could either share onset with the picture to be named or not. The authors reasoned that if internal monitoring relies on phonologically encoded inner speech and given that it is well known in speech comprehension that onsets have a privileged position in the temporal stream of processing, stop signals sharing onsets with the picture to be named should result in an impaired ability of halting caused by a delay of the inner monitor to detect the stop signal as such. Moreover, the authors reasoned that contrasting trials of successful halting of speech with unsuccessful halting of speech should reveal the brain regions involved in speech error commission and monitoring in relation to an external cue interrupting speech production.

The authors did not find any evidence for an inner speech monitoring mechanism operating at the level of phonologically encoded phonemic plans in either the behavioral or fMRI data. For external monitoring contrast, however, they found increased pSTG, anterior STG, and IFG activation which they interpreted as, respectively, based on participants' hearing their own erroneous spoken responses, speech-based properties of the response being produced and domain-general post-error monitoring. Another study (Okada et al., 2018) included a manipulation targeting speech production involving either only lexical processing (imagined speech) or engaging motor-phonological processing (speech articulation without phonation). Crucially, none of the conditions involved participants receiving auditory speech feedback. The authors observed an increased activation of pSTG in the condition requiring motor phonological processing compared to imagined speech, something they took to indicate forward modeling and hence that overt articulation (i.e., the actual execution of motor speech plans) results in stronger forward predictions than imagined speech. That is, external monitoring would rely on internal modeling to a greater extent than internal monitoring. Finally, yet another study recently aimed at dissociating internal and external monitoring processes (Runnqvist et al., 2021). For internal monitoring, the higher or lower probability of committing an error was manipulated across conditions that were contrasted on correct trials. For external monitoring, correct trials were contrasted with incorrect trials. While both internal and external monitoring revealed differential activations in the cerebellum indicating the presence of internal modeling, only external monitoring engaged additional pSTG and regions in the medial frontal cortex. This was taken as evidence that monitoring relies on forward modeling across the board, but also recruits additional mechanisms more dependent on the sensorial feedback to detect errors once these become overt.

In sum (see Figure 6.2), several studies have found converging evidence for an involvement of pSTG in the monitoring of overt speech errors, but so far, no manipulation targeting inner monitoring has revealed the

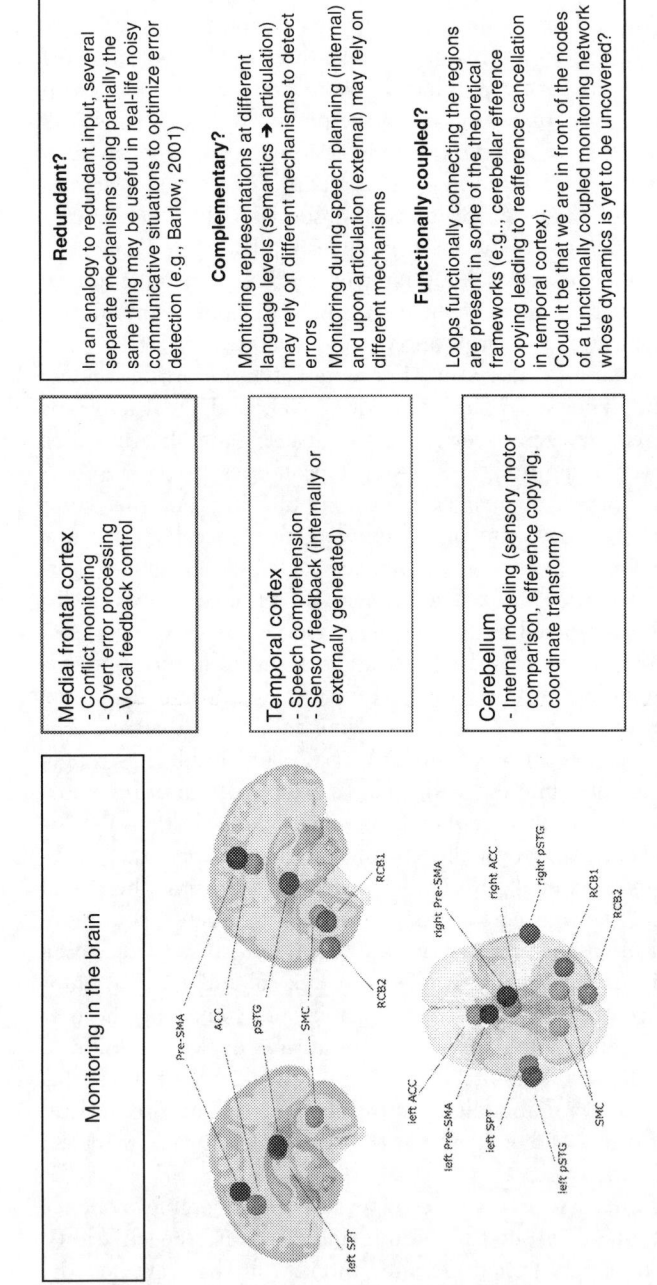

Monitoring in the brain

Medial frontal cortex
- Conflict monitoring
- Overt error processing
- Vocal feedback control

Temporal cortex
- Speech comprehension
- Sensory feedback (internally or externally generated)

Cerebellum
- Internal modeling (sensory motor comparison, efference copying, coordinate transform)

Redundant?

In an analogy to redundant input, several separate mechanisms doing partially the same thing may be useful in real-life noisy communicative situations to optimize error detection (e.g., Barlow, 2001)

Complementary?

Monitoring representations at different language levels (semantics ➔ articulation) may rely on different mechanisms to detect errors

Monitoring during speech planning (internal) and upon articulation (external) may rely on different mechanisms

Functionally coupled?

Loops functionally connecting the regions are present in some of the theoretical frameworks (e.g.., cerebellar efference copying leading to reafference cancellation in temporal cortex).

Could it be that we are in front of the nodes of a functionally coupled monitoring network whose dynamics is yet to be uncovered?

Figure 6.2 Illustration of brain regions (left) that have been linked to different monitoring proposals (middle panels). As discussed in the text, these may be redundant or complementary mechanisms, or nodes of a functionally coupled network (see right panel). Pre-SMA, presupplementary motor area; ACC, anterior cingulate cortex; pSTG, posterior superior temporal gyrus; SPT, Sylvian fissure at the temporoparietal boundary; SMC, superior medial cerebellum; RCB, right posterior cerebellum.

involvement of this brain region. Furthermore, several studies have observed an involvement of the medial frontal cortex in the processing of overt errors, in the presence of conflict or feedback generated through external stimulation (e.g., De Zubicaray et al., 2001; Loh et al., 2020), or for articulatory conflict susceptible of providing proprioceptive feedback (e.g., Alario et al., 2006). However, the implication of this region in the inner monitoring of levels beyond those susceptible of providing sensory feedback (semantic and lexical levels as opposed to post-lexical, articulation-related levels) seems to be more circumscribed and elusive. Finally, studies have reported an involvement of the cerebellum both in situations taxing inner monitoring and upon commission of overt errors. This complex picture indicates that one mechanism accounting for the totality of monitoring in the production of language is unlikely. Why would there be several mechanisms devoted to monitoring language production? Note that, though at first glance it would seem inefficient, the different systems could to some extent redundant, justified by the need to optimize communication situations often involving noise (e.g., Barlow, 2001). Assuming some functional segregation, at least three, not mutually exclusive, hypotheses can be made.

A first hypothesis is that the different mechanisms are complementary and are in charge of monitoring different representations. As reviewed above, so far mostly the boundary around articulation has been examined, splitting up monitoring in internal and external. However, one could also imagine other variables such as the levels of language being monitored as key in accounting for the prevalence of one mechanism or another. For instance, as discussed briefly above, though post-lexical processes (syllabification, articulatory planning, and execution) form part of speech planning as they take place at least partly prior to phonation, they differ from lexical or grammatical processes in that they generate proprioceptive feedback.

A second possibility similarly related to the different levels of linguistic (and non-linguistic) representations is that monitoring follows a functional hierarchy, ranging from primary to transmodal processing. This hypothesis could provide an elegant account for the differences in location elicited by monitoring related tasks reported *within* the temporal cortex, medial frontal cortex, and cerebellum. The heterogeneity within regions reported across (e.g., for a review of regions in the temporal cortex see Meekings & Scott, 2021) and sometimes even within studies (e.g., for different regions within the cerebellum see Runnqvist et al., 2021) would follow a functional gradient ranging from more sensory-motor-related representations to more abstract and associative representations. Such gradients were already proposed for the temporal lobe by Mesulam (1998), accounting for the relationship between the macrostructure of the brain and hierarchical cognitive function. Accordingly, a gradient in the temporal cortex would range from basic auditory functions (primary auditory area) to speech comprehension (Wernicke's area) and lexical and semantic processing (mid-temporal gyrus). Similarly, a gradient along the rostro-caudal axis of the frontal lobe would range from more basic motor function (primary motor area) to more complex motor behaviors such as cognitive control and speech production (Broca's region; e.g., Badre & D'Esposito, 2009). Finally, two gradients have recently been described for the cerebellum, similarly going from more basic motor processing to trans-modal processing (e.g., D'Mello et al., 2020; Guell et al., 2018). In sum, two roles can be hypothesized for the level of language representation in self-monitoring for errors: (a) different mechanisms monitoring different levels of representation reflected through the recruitment of distinct brain regions, and (b) monitoring different levels of representation might result in differential activations *within* a broad region corresponding to a functional, hierarchical gradient.

A third hypothesis is that some or all of the regions that regularly are re-ported in studies isolating monitoring are in fact the nodes of a functionally coupled network. It has been shown that cognitive functions can emerge as a result of different, possibly distant brain regions working together, rather than of the isolated activation of an area (Bressler & Menon, 2010), and that be-havioral task performance can be predicted from the integration of the area specialized for a task-specific function into large scale brain networks (Park & Friston, 2013). Arguably, the forward modeling explanation of monitoring already contains a network encompassing the cerebellum and somatosensory parts of cortex. For instance, the forward modeling taking place in the cere-bellum is thought to be functionally coupled with the auditory suppression taking place in the temporal cortex for speech production (e.g., Knolle et al., 2012, 2013). Interestingly, other evidence suggests that there is no direct functional connectivity between the cerebellum and auditory regions (e.g., Buckner et al., 2011), meaning that this functional network must be mediated by another structure. In contrast, the cerebellum and the medial frontal cortex are functionally connected (e.g., Bostan & Strick, 2018), as are temporal and medial frontal cortex (e.g., LaCruz et al., 2007). Could it be that the medial frontal cortex, temporal cortex, and the cerebellum are coordinated compe-titively or collaboratively? This intriguing possibility would have profound consequences for the interpretation of the cognitive processes that these re-gions are thought to sustain (Figure 6.2).

Conclusion

In conclusion, language production is a complex cognitive-motor skill, not surprisingly the way in which people monitor their production is as well. The behavioral and neurobiological data reviewed in this chapter point to a multi-mechanism, gradient-based, or network model of monitoring, and possibly to an important role of the level of representation in triggering distinct me-chanisms, different hierarchical positions along a functional gradient, or dif-ferent parts of the network. These are all exciting directions that future research will have to address to gain a better understanding of the complex cognitive skill of self-monitoring for errors during language production.

References

Abel, S., Dressel, K., Weiller, C., & Huber, W. (2012). Enhancement and suppression in a lexical interference fMRI-paradigm. *Brain and Behavior, 2*(2), 109–127.

Ackermann, H., Vogel, M., Petersen, D., & Poremba, M. (1992). Speech deficits in ischaemic cerebellar lesions. *Journal of Neurology, 239*(4), 223–227.

Alario, F. X., Chainay, H., Lehericy, S., & Cohen, L. (2006). The role of the supplementary motor area (SMA) in word production. *Brain Research, 1076*(1), 129–143.

Argyropoulos G. P. (2016). The cerebellum, internal models and prediction in 'non-motor'aspects of language: A critical review. *Brain and Language, 161*, 4–17.

Baars B. J., Motley M. T., & MacKay D. G. (1975). Output editing for lexical status in artificially elicited slips of the tongue. *Journal of Verbal Learning and Verbal Behavior, 14*(4), 382–391.

Badre, D., & D'esposito, M. (2009). Is the rostro-caudal axis of the frontal lobe hierarchical?. *Nature Reviews Neuroscience, 10*(9), 659–669.

Barlow H. (2001). Redundancy reduction revisited. *Network: Computation in Neural Systems, 12*(3), 241–253.

Blakemore S. J., Frith C. D., Wolpert D. M. (2001). The cerebellum is involved in predicting the sensory consequences of action. *Neuroreport, 12*(9), 1879–1884.

Bostan & Strick, (2018).The basal ganglia and the cerebellum: nodes in an integrated network. *Nature Reviews Neuroscience, 19*(6), 338–350

Botvinick M. M., Braver T. S., Barch D. M., Carter C. S., & Cohen J. D. (2001). Conflict monitoring and cognitive control. *Psychological Review, 108*(3), 624.

Bressler, S. L., & Menon, V. (2010). Large-scale brain networks in cognition: Emerging methods and principles. *Trends in Cognitive Sciences, 14*(6), 277–290.

Buckner, R. L., Krienen, F. M., Castellanos, A., Diaz, J. C., & Yeo, B. T. (2011). The organization of the human cerebellum estimated by intrinsic functional connectivity. *Journal of Nneurophysiology, 106*(5), 2322–2345.

Christoffels I. K., Formisano E., & Schiller N. O. (2007). Neural correlates of verbal feedback processing: An fMRI study employing overt speech. *Human Brain Mapping, 28*(9), 868–879.

Dell G. S. (1986). A spreading-activation theory of retrieval in sentence production. *Psychological Review, 93*(3), 283–321.

Dell, G. S. (1995). Speaking and misspeaking. *An Invitation to Cognitive Science, 1*, 183–208.

De Zubicaray G. I., Wilson S. J., McMahon K. L., & Muthiah M. (2001). The semantic interference effect in the picture-word paradigm: An event-related fMRI study employing overt responses. *Human Brain Mapping, 14*(4), 218–227.

D'Mello A. M., Gabrieli J. D., & Nee D. E. (2020). Evidence for hierarchical cognitive control in the human cerebellum. *Current Biology, 30*(10), 1881–1892.

Emmorey K. (this volume, 2022). Signing vs. speaking: How does the biology of linguistic expression affect production?

Emmorey, K., Bosworth, R., & Kraljic, T. (2009). Visual feedback and self-monitoring of sign language. *Journal of Memory and Language, 61*, 398–411. 10.1016/j.jml.2009.06.001.

Fairs, A., Michelas, A., Dufour, S., & Strijkers, K. (2021). The same ultra-rapid parallel brain dynamics underpin the production and perception of speech. *Cerebral Cortex Communications, 2*(3), 1–17. 10.1093/texcom/tgab040.

Freund, M., & Nozari, N. (2018). Is adaptive control in language production mediated by learning?. *Cognition, 176*, 107–130.

Ganushchak, L. Y., & Schiller, N. O. (2006). Effects of time pressure on verbal self-monitoring: An ERP study. *Brain Research, 1125*(1), 104–115.

Gauvin H. S., De Baene W., Brass M., & Hartsuiker R. J. (2016). Conflict monitoring in speech processing: An fMRI study of error detection in speech production and perception. *NeuroImage, 126*, 96–105.

Gauvin, H. S., & Hartsuiker, R. J. (2020). Towards a new model of verbal monitoring. *Journal of Cognition, 3*(1), 1-37. 10.5334/joc.81.

Gehring, W. J., & Knight, R. T. (2000). Prefrontal–cingulate interactions in action monitoring. *Nature Neuroscience, 3*(5), 516–520.

Ghosh S. S., Tourville J. A., & Guenther F. H. (2008). A neuroimaging study of premotor lateralization and cerebellar involvement in the production of phonemes and syllables. *Journal of Speech, Language, and Hearing Research, 51*(5), 1183–1202. 10.1044/1092-43 88(2008/07-0119).

Golfinopoulos E., Tourville, J. A., & Guenther F. H. (2010). The integration of large-scale neural network modeling and functional brain imaging in speech motor control. *Neuroimage, 52*(3), 862–874.

Guell, X., Schmahmann, J. D., Gabrieli, J. D., & Ghosh, S. S. (2018). Functional gradients of the cerebellum. *Elife*, 7, e36652.

Guenther F. H., Ghosh S. S., & Tourville J. A. (2006). Neural modeling and imaging of the cortical interactions underlying syllable production. *Brain and Language, 96*(3), 280–301.

Hansen, S. J., McMahon, K. L., & de Zubicaray, G. I. (2019). Neural mechanisms for monitoring and halting of spoken word production. *Journal of Cognitive Neuroscience, 31*(12), 1946–1957.

Hartsuiker, R. J. (2013). Are forward models enough to explain self-monitoring? Insights from patients and eye movements. *Behavioral and Brain Sciences, 36*(4), 357.

Hartsuiker, R. J., Antón-Méndez, I., Roelstraete, B., & Costa, A. (2006). Spoonish spanerisms: A lexical bias effect in spanish. *Journal of Experimental Psychology: Learning, Memory, and Cognition, 32*(4), 949.

Hartsuiker R. J., Corley M., & Martensen H. (2005). The lexical bias effect is modulated by context, but the standard monitoring account doesn't fly: Related reply to Baars, Motley, and MacKay (1975) *Journal of Memory and Language, 52*, 58–70.

Hartsuiker R. J., & Kolk, H. H. (2001). Error monitoring in speech production: A computational test of the perceptual loop theory. *Cognitive Psychology, 42*(2), 113–157.

Hickok G. (2012). Computational neuroanatomy of speech production. *Nature Reviews Neuroscience, 13*(2), 135–145.

Hickok G. (2014). The architecture of speech production and the role of the phoneme in speech processing. *Language, Cognition and Neuroscience, 29*(1), 2–20.

Hirano S., Kojima H., Naito Y., Honjo I., Kamoto Y., Okazawa H., Ishizu K., Yonekura Y., Nagahama Y., Fukuyama H., Konishi J. (1997). Cortical processing mechanism for vocalization with auditory verbal feedback. *NeuroReport, 8*, 2379–2382.

Hoffmann, S., & Falkenstein, M. (2012). Predictive information processing in the brain: Errors and response monitoring. *International Journal of Psychophysiology, 83*(2), 208–212.

Hohenberger, A., Happ, D., & Leuninger, H. (2002). Modality-dependent aspects of sign language production: Evidence from slips of the hands and their repairs in German Sign Language. In Cheek, C., Cheek, A., Knapp, H., & Rathmann, C. (Eds.), *Modality and structure in signed and spoken languages*, Cambridge University Press. 112–142.

Imamizu H., Miyauchi S., Tamada T., Sasaki Y., Takino R., Puetz B., ... Kawato M. (2000). Human cerebellar activity reflecting an acquired internal model of a new tool. *Nature, 403*(6766), 192–195.

Indefrey P., & Levelt W. J. (2004). The spatial and temporal signatures of word production components. *Cognition, 92*(1), 101–144.

Ito M. (2008). Control of mental activities by internal models in the cerebellum. *Nature Reviews Neuroscience, 9*(4), 304–313.

Jeannerod M. (1988). *The neural and behavioural organization of goal-directed movements.* Clarendon Press/Oxford University Press.

Knolle, F., Schröger, E., Baess, P., & Kotz, S. A. (2012). The cerebellum generates motor-to-auditory predictions: ERP lesion evidence. *Journal of Cognitive Neuroscience, 24*(3), 698–706.

Knolle, F., Schröger, E., & Kotz, S. A. (2013). Cerebellar contribution to the prediction of self-initiated sounds. *Cortex, 49*(9), 2449–2461.

Lacruz, M. E., Garcia Seoane, J. J., Valentin, A., Selway, R., & Alarcon, G. (2007). Frontal and temporal functional connections of the living human brain. *European Journal of Neuroscience, 26*(5), 1357–1370.

Leggio M. G., Silveri M. C., Petrosini L., & Molinari M. (2000). Phonological grouping is specifically affected in cerebellar patients: A verbal fluency study. *Journal of Neurology, Neurosurgery & Psychiatry, 69*(1), 102–106.

Lesage E., Hansen P. C., & Miall R. C. (2017). Right lateral cerebellum represents linguistic predictability. *Journal of Neuroscience, 37*(26), 6231–6241.

Levelt, W. J. (1992). Accessing words in speech production: Stages, processes and representations. *Cognition, 42*(1–3), 1–22.

Levelt W. J. (1983). Monitoring and self-repair in speech. *Cognition, 14*(1), 41–104.

Levelt W. J., Roelofs A., & Meyer A. S. (1999). A theory of lexical access in speech production. *Behavioral and Brain Sciences, 22*(1), 1–38.

Lind, A., Hall, L., Breidegard, B., Balkenius, C., & Johansson, P. (2014). Speakers' acceptance of real-time speech exchange indicates that we use auditory feedback to specify the meaning of what we say. *Psychological Science, 25*(6), 1198–1205.

Lind, A., Hall, L., Breidegard, B., Balkenius, C., & Johansson, P. (2015). Auditory Feedback Is Used for Self-Comprehension. *Psychological Science, 26*, 1978–1980. 10.1177/0956797615599341.

Logan, G. D., & Crump, M. J. (2010). Cognitive illusions of authorship reveal hierarchical error detection in skilled typists. *Science, 330*(6004), 683–686.

Loh, K. K., Petrides, M., Hopkins, W. D., Procyk, E., & Amiez, C. (2017). Cognitive control of vocalizations in the primate ventrolateral-dorsomedial frontal (VLF-DMF) brain network. *Neuroscience & Biobehavioral Reviews, 82*, 32–44.

Loh K. K., Procyk E., Neveu R., Lamberton F., Hopkins W. D., Petrides M., & Amiez C. (2020). Cognitive control of orofacial motor and vocal responses in the ventrolateral and dorsomedial human frontal cortex. *Proceedings of the* National Academy of Sciences, *117*(9), 4994–5005.

McCloskey D. I. (1981). Corollary discharges: Motor commands and perception. *Comprehensive Physiology, 2,* 1415–1447.

Meekings S., & Scott S. K. (2021). Error in the superior temporal gyrus? A systematic review and activation likelihood estimation meta-analysis of speech production studies. *Journal of Cognitive Neuroscience, 33*(3), 422–444.

Mesulam, M. M. (1998). From sensation to cognition. *Brain: A Journal of Neurology, 121*(6), 1013–1052.

Meyer, A. S. (1992). Investigation of phonological encoding through speech error analyses: Achievements, limitations, and alternatives. *Cognition, 42*(1–3), 181–211.

Miall R. C., King D. (2008). State estimation in the cerebellum. *The Cerebellum, 7*(4), 572–576.

Möller J., Jansma B. M., Rodriguez-Fornells A., Münte T. F. (2007). What the brain does before the tongue slips. *Cerebral Cortex, 17*(5), 1173–1178.

Motley, M. T., Camden, C. T., & Baars, B. J. (1982). Covert formulation and editing of anomalies in speech production: Evidence from experimentally elicited slips of the tongue. *Journal of Verbal Learning and Verbal Behavior, 21*, 578–594.

Motley, M. T., Camden, C. T., & Baars, B. J. (1981). Towards verifying the assumptions of laboratory- induced slips of the tongue: The output-error and editing issues. *Human Communication Research, 8*, 3–15.

Nachev, P., Rees G., Parton A., Kennard C., & Husain M. (2005). Volition and conflict in human medial frontal cortex. *Current Biology, 15*(2), 122–128.

Niziolek, C. A., & Guenther, F. H. (2013). Vowel category boundaries enhance cortical and behavioral responses to speech feedback alterations. *Journal of Neuroscience, 33*(29), 12090–12098.

Nooteboom S. G., & Quené H. (2008). Self-monitoring and feedback: A new attempt to find the main cause of lexical bias in phonological speech errors. *Journal of Memory and Language, 58*(3), 837–861.

Nooteboom, S. G., & Quené, H. (2017). Self-monitoring for speech errors: Two-stage detection and repair with and without auditory feedback. *Journal of Memory and Language, 95*, 19–35.

Nozari, N. (2020). Neural basis of word production. In A. Papafragou, J. C. Trueswell, & L. R. Gleitman (Eds.), *The Oxford handbook of the mental Lexicon,* Oxford Academic. (pp. 552–574).

Nozari N., Dell G. S., & Schwartz M. F. (2011). Is comprehension necessary for error detection? A conflict-based account of monitoring in speech production. *Cognitive Psychology, 63*(1), 1–33.

Okada K., & Hickok G. (2006). Left posterior auditory-related cortices participate both in speech perception and speech production: Neural overlap revealed by fMRI. *Brain and Language, 98*(1), 112–117.

Okada, K., Matchin, W., & Hickok, G. (2018). Neural evidence for predictive coding in auditory cortex during speech production. *Psychonomic Bulletin & Review, 25*(1), 423–430.

Oppenheim, G. M., & Dell, G. S. (2008). Inner speech slips exhibit lexical bias, but not the phonemic similarity effect. *Cognition, 106*(1), 528–537.

Park, H. J., & Friston, K. (2013). Structural and functional brain networks: from connections to cognition. *Science, 342*(6158), 579.

Pickering M. J., & Garrod S. (2013). An integrated theory of language production and comprehension. *Behavioral and Brain Sciences, 36*(04), 329–347.

Pinet, S., & Nozari, N. (2020). Electrophysiological correlates of monitoring in typing with and without visual feedback. *Journal of Cognitive Neuroscience, 32*(4), 603–620.

Pinet, S., & Nozari, N. (2018). "Twisting fingers": The case for interactivity in typed language production. *Psychonomic Bulletin & Review, 25*(4), 1449–1457.

Postma, A., & Noordanus, C. (1996). Production and detection of speech errors in silent, mouthed, noise-masked, and normal auditory feedback speech. *Language and Speech, 39*(4), 375–392.

Postma, A., & Kolk, H. (1992). The effects of noise masking and required accuracy on speech errors, disfluencies, and self-repairs. *Journal of Speech, Language, and Hearing Research*, *35*, 537–544. 10.1044/jshr.3503.537.

Procyk, E., Wilson, C. R., Stoll, F. M., Faraut, M. C., Petrides, M., & Amiez, C. (2016). Midcingulate motor map and feedback detection: Converging data from humans and monkeys. *Cerebral Cortex*, *26*(2), 467–476.

Riès, S., Janssen, N., Dufau, S., Alario, F. X., & Burle, B. (2011). General-purpose monitoring during speech production. *Journal of Cognitive Neuroscience*, *23*(6), 1419–1436.

Riès, S. K., Nadalet, L., Mickelsen, S., Mott, M., Midgley, K. J., Holcomb, P. J., & Emmorey, K. (2020). Pre-output language monitoring in sign production. *Journal of Cognitive Neuroscience*, *32*(6), 1079–1091.

Roelofs, A. (2020). Self-monitoring in speaking: In defense of a comprehension-based account. *Journal of Cognition*, *3*(1), 1-13. 10.5334/joc.61.

Runnqvist E., Bonnard M., Gauvin H. S., Attarian S., Trébuchon A., Hartsuiker R. J., Alario F. X. (2016). Internal modeling of upcoming speech: A causal role of the right posterior cerebellum in non-motor aspects of language production. *Cortex*, *81*, 203–214.

Runnqvist, E., Chanoine, V., Strijkers, K., Patamadilok, C., Bonnard, M., Nazarian, B., ... & Alario, F. (2021). Cerebellar and cortical correlates of internal and external speech error monitoring. *Cerebral Cortex Communications*, *31*(2), tgab038.

Savariaux, C., Perrier, P., Orliaguet, J. P., & Schwartz, J. L. (1999). Compensation strategies for the perturbation of French [u] using a lip tube. II. Perceptual analysis. *The Journal of the Acoustical Society of America*, *106*(1), 381–393.

Savariaux, C., Perrier, P., & Orliaguet, J. P. (1995). Compensation strategies for the perturbation of the rounded vowel [u] using a lip tube: A study of the control space in speech production. *The Journal of the Acoustical Society of America*, *98*, 2428–2442. 10.1121/1.413277.

Severens, E., Kühn, S., Hartsuiker, R. J., & Brass M., (2012). Functional mechanisms involved in the internal inhibition of taboo words. *Social Cognitive and Affective Neuroscience*, *7*(4), 431–435.

Shergill, S. S., Brammer, M. J., Williams, S. C. R., Murray R. W., & McGuire, P. K. (2000). Mapping auditory hallucinations in schizophrenia using functional magnetic resonance imaging. *Archives of General Psychiatry*, *57*, 1033–1038.

Strick, P. L., Dum, R. P., & Fiez, J. A. (2009). Cerebellum and nonmotor function. *Annual Review of Neuroscience*, *32*, 413–434.

Strijkers, K., Runnqvist, E., Costa, A., & Holcomb, P. (2013). The poor helping the rich: How can incomplete representations monitor complete ones?. *Behavioral and Brain Sciences*, *36*(4), 374.

Strijkers, K. (2016). A neural assembly-based view on word oroduction: The bilingual test case. *Language Learning*, 66, 92–131. 10.1111/lang.12191.

Strijkers, K., & Costa, A. (2016). On words and brains: linking psycholinguistics with neural dynamics in speech production. *Language, Cognition and Neuroscience*, *31*, 524–535. 10.1080/23273798.2016.1158845.

Strijkers, K., Costa, A., & Pulvermüller, F. (2017). The cortical dynamics of speaking: Lexical and phonological knowledge simultaneously recruit the frontal and temporal cortex within 200 ms. *NeuroImage*, *163*, 206–219. 10.1016/j.neuroimage. 2017.09.041.

Tian X., & Poeppel D. (2010). Mental imagery of speech and movement implicates the dynamics of internal forward models. *Frontiers in Psychology*, *1*, 166.

Tourville J. A., & Guenther F. H. (2011). The DIVA model: A neural theory of speech acquisition and production. *Language and Cognitive Processes*, *26*(7), 952–981.

Tourville J. A., Reilly K. J., & Guenther F. H. (2008). Neural mechanisms underlying auditory feedback control of speech. *Neuroimage*, *39*(3), 1429–1443.

Verguts, T., Notebaert, W., Kunde, W., & Wühr, P. (2011). Post-conflict slowing: Cognitive adaptation after conflict processing. *Psychonomic Bulletin & Review*, *18*(1), 76–82.

Wolpert, D. M., Ghahramani, Z., & Jordan M. I. (1995). An internal model for sensorimotor integration. *Science*, *269*(5232), 1880.

7 Bilingual Language Production

A Tale About Interference Resolution in Different Linguistic Contexts

Luz María Sánchez, Andrea M. Philipp, Esli Struys, and Mathieu Declerck

Over the past few decades, research has shown that language processing in monolinguals and bilinguals, here understood as individuals who speak more than one language even when one of their languages is not characterized by native-like proficiency, is clearly distinct. As argued by Gollan and Ferreira (2009), the lexicon of a bilingual is larger than that of a monolingual due to the simple fact that the lexicon of a bilingual contains items from two languages. Since both languages have to share production time instead of a single language being used constantly, the frequency with which lexical items in one or the other language are accessed is lower for bilinguals than monolinguals. Consequently, a bilingual might take slightly longer to select the right word than a monolingual will (e.g., Runnqvist et al., 2011). Next to lower frequency, there is also ample evidence that the nontarget language is activated when producing in the target language (e.g., Costa et al., 2000; Giezen & Emmorey, 2016; Hoshino & Kroll, 2008), which results in pervasive interference from the nontarget language during target language processing. Some studies have even shown that this cross-language activation can lead to selection of nontarget language words (e.g., Declerck et al., 2017, 2021; Gollan et al., 2011; Poulisse & Bongaerts, 1994). One might question how bilinguals manage to employ the target language in the right context without too much cross-language interference. The process responsible for resolving this issue and increasing the chances of selecting words in the target language is called bilingual language control (henceforth referred to as "language control"; e.g., Declerck & Philipp, 2015; Green, 1998) and it is the focus of the present chapter.

Two types of language control processes have been discussed in the literature. Reactive language control is the most investigated of these two and it entails the control process that is implemented when selection of the target language word is disrupted by the nontarget language. As an example, picture a scenario where an English–German bilingual finds themselves in a supermarket in Germany. The bilingual has been speaking and listening to German all day, but shortly before reaching the cashier they call their English-speaking partner to ask (in English) whether there is a last-minute request and so their English becomes activated.

DOI: 10.4324/9781003145790-8

When the cashier then asks a question in German, there is a conflict between the customer's recently activated English and their knowledge that they are expected to reply in German. Here, the customer must rely on reactive language control to overcome the cross-language interference from English in order to respond in German. Reactive language control is hence implemented to resolve interference from the nontarget language (English in our example) so that the target language (German in our example) can be produced fluently. Proactive language control, on the other hand, is the language control process that is implemented in anticipation of any nontarget language disruption. Referring back to the previous example, imagine the customer had never made the phone call in English. Before being addressed by the cashier, the English–German bilingual would have suppressed their English in anticipation to using German, and thus would have optimized their German language production before any cross-language interference from English arose. This should result in fluent German language production, as German words will be more available for selection, relative to English words.

Inhibition stands out as the most prominent mechanism thought to underlie reactive and proactive language control throughout the literature (e.g., Declerck et al., 2015; Grainger et al., 2010; Green, 1998). Green's Inhibitory Control Model (ICM; Green, 1998; see also Green, 1986), the most influential bilingual language production model that relies on inhibition, postulates that bilingual language production starts with the activation of the corresponding task schema, which is a "mental program" applied to reach a goal (e.g., speaking in the first [L1] or second [L2] language, or performing a specific task such as multiplying two numbers). The first language control process occurs between the different active task schemas related to speaking specific languages (e.g., L1 and L2). In turn, the task schemas affect their corresponding language tags, which are mental language representations connected to all word representations of that language. The language tag of the target language will inhibit all lemmas that are not a part of the target language, once these representations have been activated by the concept. Finally, inhibition is also assumed to occur from the target lemma to its translation-equivalent lemma. The amount of inhibition applied in this model is assumed to be proportional to the initial level of activation of a given language or lemma. That is, a language that has a higher initial activation level, for instance, due to a higher proficiency compared to the other language or due to recent use of that language, is also inhibited more strongly. It is important to note that Green's ICM also has a proactive component, as the appropriate task schema can be activated in anticipation (i.e., preparation for speaking in a specific language is possible).

Even though models relying on inhibitory control prevail in the field, there are also several models that do not rely on inhibition but advocate for a different underlying mechanism. Some even view the issue of language control as irrelevant, as they presume that only the vocabulary of the target language is up for selection (e.g., Costa et al., 1999). Other models do not deny the possibility that nontarget lemmas/words are available for selection but propose that word selection is channeled by additional activation of the target language, rather than inhibition of the nontarget language (e.g., La Heij, 2005; see also Blanco-Elorrieta & Caramazza, 2021). La Heij (2005), for example, argues for a model where lexical selection is guided by a preverbal message and a "language cue" that provides additional activation to words from the target language. This implies that even though the translation-equivalent word in the nontarget language will be activated, the word corresponding to the target language will be more highly activated due to the language cue included in the message. Therefore, words of the target language are more likely to be selected, while cross-language interference is also accounted for.

In the sections to follow, we aimed to cover how language control operates in different linguistic contexts, since bilingual language production is not static, the performance of a bilingual speaker in a given language can depend on a series of external factors such as linguistic context. The main focus of this chapter will be on three prominent behavioral measures of language control (for a discussion on neuronal aspects of language control, see Calabria et al., 2018; Strijkers, 2016; Sulpizio et al., 2020; see also Chapter 6 of this volume: Runnqvist, 2022), namely asymmetrical switch costs, reversed language dominance, and language mixing costs. Before delving into these measures, we will first briefly discuss how language control might differ depending on the linguistic context from a more theoretical viewpoint, as well as the corresponding methodology that has been employed to investigate language control in different linguistic contexts.

Language control in different linguistic contexts

Rather than assuming that language control processes are rigidly applied in the same way in every situation, the Adaptive Control Hypothesis (Green & Abutalebi, 2013) argues that control processes are dynamic and can be adjusted to the needs of a given linguistic context. Reportedly, language control results from a combination of various cognitive processes including conflict monitoring, task disengagement, suppression of interference, and goal maintenance. The way in which these processes work together depends on the situation at hand, be it a context where the bilingual speaker uses their languages in complementary situations (e.g., Spanish at home, French at work; *single language context*), a context where the use of two languages can occur in the same situation but with different people (*dual-language context*), or one where the bilingual can switch at will between their two languages in a conversation (*dense code-switching context*). Quite some cross-language interference might have to be resolved in the first two situations, especially in the dual-language context. In turn, a higher degree of language control will be necessary in these contexts. However, this is not necessarily the case in the dense code-switching context, since both interlocutors can use whichever language might be easier or more appropriate, as long as they are both sufficiently proficient in their two languages.

The three linguistic contexts described in the Adaptive Control Hypothesis (Green & Abutalebi, 2013) also correspond to different variants of the most prominent paradigm in the language control literature, that is, the language-switching paradigm. In the rest of this section, we will present an overview of the two most prominent variants of the language-switching paradigm that have been employed to test theoretical models of language control empirically: cued language switching and voluntary language switching.[1]

Cued language switching is the most commonly used paradigm in the language control literature. Usually, it involves naming a series of digits or images in one language or the other, based on a visual or an auditory cue. An example can be found in the seminal paper by Costa and Santesteban (2004), who employed this paradigm to test the performance of a group of Spanish–Catalan and Korean–Spanish bilinguals. The participants completed a picture naming task, where the language they had to employ was indicated by the color background of the image. Mixed language blocks demanded responses in both languages and thus included both switch trials, in which the participants used a different language in the previous trial relative to the current trial, and repetition trials, where the participants used the same language in two consecutive trials. The authors observed significantly worse performance during switch trials than during repetition trials. A comparable pattern has been reported by a multitude of other cued language-switching studies (e.g., Bonfieni et al., 2019; Campbell, 2005; Christoffels et al., 2007; de Bruin et al., 2020; Declerck et al., 2012; Filippi et al., 2014; Ivanova & Hernandez, 2021; Jylkkä et al., 2021; Kirk et al., 2021; Li & Gollan, 2021; Linck et al., 2012; Meuter & Allport, 1999; Peeters, 2020; Philipp et al., 2007; Timmer et al., 2019; Verhoef et al., 2009; Wang et al., 2009). The costs that come with language switching from one trial to another, relative to repeating the same language across trials, have been termed "language switch costs", and are assumed to be an index of language control (Declerck & Philipp, 2015; Green, 1998).

Some scholars have argued that in real-life conversations bilinguals tend to switch languages when they decide to, rather than solely switch languages based on external cues, such as the arrival of a person who speaks a different language. Following this line of thought, several studies have tested the robustness of switch costs when bilinguals were allowed to switch whenever they wanted to (i.e., voluntary language switching; e.g., Blanco-Elorrieta & Pylkkänen, 2018; de Bruin et al., 2018, 2020; Gollan & Ferreira, 2009; Grunden et al., 2020). De Bruin et al. (2018), for instance, designed a picture naming task with both single language blocks (where participants only used one language) and mixed language blocks (where they could use both Spanish and Basque whenever they wanted to). Once again, bilinguals showed significant switch costs during mixed language blocks. However, voluntary switching studies by Blanco-Elorrieta and Pylkkänen (2017) and Experiment 2 in Gollan and Ferreira (2009) reported no significant switch costs. So, while most voluntary language-switching studies do still find switch costs, the effect might not be as robust as with cued language-switching studies (for a review on this topic, see Blanco-Elorrieta & Pylkkänen, 2018).

When comparing the different language-switching paradigms, one could argue that they have similarities with the different language contexts introduced in the Adaptive Control Hypothesis (Green & Abutalebi, 2013). Cued language switching most closely resembles a dual-language context where the speaker knows they must employ their two languages in a specific context, but the implementation of one or the other depends on a language cue, which in real life could be parallel to the arrival of a speaker with whom normally a different language is used. The Adaptive Control Hypothesis predicts that even if bilinguals are highly trained in switching between their languages, such a context would still require a high degree of language control processes. In contrast, a language-switching experiment where the language of production can be chosen voluntarily corresponds to the dense code-switching context, where a speaker has the freedom to use whichever language they please without fearing their interlocutor will not understand them. The Adaptive Control Hypothesis predicts that in such a setting little to no control processes must be engaged. Lastly, the single language context of the Adaptive Control Hypothesis resembles single language blocks in language-switching studies, which are blocks that require production in solely one language as opposed to the mixed language blocks discussed so far. The prediction of the Adaptive Control Hypothesis is that mainly activation of the relevant language is engaged to maintain the speech goal, while some conflict monitoring and interference suppression make sure no lemmas from another language will be selected.

It seems that control is not implemented in the same manner in every task and in each situation, which could explain the different models that attempt to account for the results as well as the different empirical findings. In the upcoming section, we will turn to three prominent measures of language control that can be investigated with the language-switching paradigm, next to switch costs, and discuss them in light of how they might be affected by different linguistic contexts.

Measures of language control

Asymmetrical switch costs

The first measure of control to be discussed is the asymmetry of switch costs across languages, which entails larger switch costs when switching to L1 than when switching to L2. Meuter and Allport (1999) were the first to report the presence of asymmetrical switch costs using a cued language-switching experiment. The authors tested the performance of bilinguals who spoke English as a first or second language in combination with one of five other Romance or Germanic languages. The participants were asked to name digits 1–9 in their L1 or L2 depending on the colored background of the image. Meuter and Allport (1999) reported switch costs being greater when switching back to the speakers' L1 relative to switching to their L2. This asymmetry has since been replicated in several studies testing non-balanced bilinguals (e.g., Gollan et al., 2014; Martin et al., 2013; Schwieter & Sunderman, 2008; for a review, see Bobb & Wodniecka, 2013).

Such a pattern might seem counterintuitive at a first glance, as one would assume that switching to a more proficient language would be easier than going back to a less proficient language. However, the phenomenon can be interpreted as a consequence of persisting, reactive inhibition (cf. Green,1998; Meuter & Allport, 1999).[2] As previously stated, the central claim of the ICM is that language control is attained through the inhibition of the nontarget language. Meaning that in order to produce in Language A on Trial 1, Language B has to be inhibited. The inhibition of Language B will carry over into the next trial. If the next trial (Trial 2) requires the usage of Language B (i.e., switch trial), the inhibition from Trial 1 will persist and make it more difficult to speak in Language B, simply because it takes time to overcome the inhibition that was put on that language in Trial 1. This explains why switch costs are present: There is no persisting inhibition to overcome in a repetition trial because target and nontarget language are the same as in the previous trial. But when a switch occurs, the persisting inhibition from the previous trial will affect the performance on the current trial to some degree as the recently inhibited language now needs to be used. Furthermore, inhibition is assumed to be proportional, in that languages with a larger activation will require more inhibition. So, when producing in L2, more inhibition is required to reduce the activation of L1, because L1 is used more and thus has a higher base activation, than the inhibition on L2 when producing in L1. As a consequence, more inhibition will persist when switching from L2 to L1 than vice versa, resulting in asymmetrical switch costs.

While Green's ICM is the most widely used model to explain asymmetrical switch costs, there are other alternative ways to explain this phenomenon that are not solely based on inhibition. Philipp et al. (2007) suggested that persistent relative activation of the previous target language could also explain asymmetrical switch costs. The authors proposed that when using Language A on Trial 1, additional activation will go to Language A during this trial to make sure that words from that language will be selected. When Language B is required in Trial 2, the activation of Language A from the previous trial will still be relatively high and thus result in high competition of Language A words with the target word in Language B. This will make a switch trial more cognitively demanding than a trial where no switch occurs, explaining switch costs. The asymmetry reported by Meuter and Allport (1999) and others is then due to L2 requiring a higher increase of activation than L1, because of the larger L1 base activation. As such, more L2 activation will interfere with L1 production when switching to L1 as opposed to switching to L2.

Another account was brought forward by Finkbeiner and colleagues (2006), namely the response selection account. When naming a stimulus in a mixed language block, corresponding words from both languages will be activated and one of the two languages has to be selected. In a repetition trial, the same selection criteria from the previous trial will be reused, thereby resulting in relatively fast responses. During such trials, responses in the L1 will be faster, as L1 responses are usually more rapidly available due to it being the dominant language. In a switch trial, performance is less efficient because the same selection criteria cannot be reutilized anymore, so a reconfiguration of the response selection criteria is in order. Asymmetrical switch costs are assumed to occur because fast responses will be rejected in the more difficult context of a switch trial in order to prevent errors. Since L1 tends to be faster overall than L2, more initial L1 responses would be rejected (and would have to be selected again) when switching to L1 than L2 responses would be rejected when switching to the L2, generating a switch cost asymmetry.

While these three accounts could all explain the typical pattern of asymmetrical switch costs, they are not always in line with more recent findings (e.g., Costa & Santesteban, 2004; Gambi & Hartsuiker, 2016; Peeters et al., 2014; Schwieter & Sunderman, 2008). For example, all three accounts have problems with explaining the reversed language dominance effect (i.e., worse L1 than L2 performance in mixed language blocks; see next section for more details) in combination with asymmetrical switch costs (e.g., Costa & Santesteban, 2004). If L1 performance is worse than L2 performance, and thus L1 activation is most probably lower than L2 activation, all of the accounts above would predict larger L2 than L1 switch costs. However, this is not what some studies have shown (e.g., Costa & Santesteban, 2004; Schwieter & Sunderman, 2008). So, more research is necessary to further delve into how asymmetrical switch costs can be explained.

Moreover, while asymmetrical costs have been widely reported in the literature (Costa & Santesteban, 2004; Ma et al., 2016; Macizo et al., 2012; Meuter & Allport, 1999; Reynolds et al., 2016; Schwieter & Sunderman, 2008), their presence is not ubiquitous (for a recent meta-analysis, see Gade et al., 2021). Some experiments in which such a pattern would have been expected did not find an asymmetry (e.g., Christoffels et al., 2007; Declerck et al., 2012; Kang et al., 2017), or rather found the opposite effect by showing larger L2 than L1 switch costs (i.e., *reversed* asymmetrical switch costs, e.g., Bonfieni et al., 2019; Declerck et al., 2015; Zheng et al., 2020). Many studies have tried to find evidence for specific characteristics, either methodological or related to specific bilinguals, that invariably allow for the occurrence of asymmetrical switch costs, or lack thereof. One such characteristic that has consistently been observed to have an impact is voluntary language switching. Studies that rely on this language-switching variant usually do not find asymmetrical switch costs (de Bruin et al., 2018, 2020; Gollan & Ferreira, 2009; Gollan et al., 2014; Gross & Kaushanskaya, 2015; Grunden et al., 2020; Jevtović et al., 2020). Jevtović et al. (2020) even showed significantly smaller asymmetrical switch costs relative to the pattern observed in cued language switching. Gollan and Ferreira (2009) attributed the lack of asymmetrical switch costs to a combination of two factors. First, in a voluntary setting, bilinguals tend to produce difficult (e.g., low frequency) words in their L1 so that the relative activation for the used words might be more similar across languages. Second, bilinguals probably implement proactive inhibitory control upon their L1. Both these factors should lead to more similar L1 and L2 activation levels and thus might result in symmetrical switch costs.

Since asymmetrical switch costs, and switch costs in general, have been found relatively often in cued language-switching studies (e.g., Meuter & Allport, 1999; Philipp et al., 2007), but not in voluntary language-switching studies (see above), we can deduce that language control processes are influenced by the linguistic context. In line with the Adaptive Control Hypothesis (Green & Abutalebi, 2013), asymmetrical switch costs decrease, or are entirely absent, in voluntary language switching relative to cued language switching. Put differently, less reactive control processes are implemented on L1 relative to L2 in a dense code-switching context (cf. voluntary language switching) than in a dual-language context (cf. cued language switching). So, reactive language control is different in distinct linguistic contexts. In the following sections, we will turn to measures of proactive language control.

Reversed language dominance

A language control measure that might, on the surface at least, be connected to asymmetrical switch costs is the reversed language dominance effect (e.g., Christoffels et al., 2016; Declerck et al., 2013; Declerck et al., 2020; Li & Gollan, 2018; Stasenko et al., 2021; Tarlowski et al., 2012; Verhoef et al., 2009). This phenomenon entails worse overall L1 performance during a mixed block (i.e., more errors and/or slower reaction times) than L2 performance, whereas typically a reversed pattern is observed in single language blocks (e.g., Strijkers et al., 2013; for a review, see Runnqvist et al., 2011).

A reversed language dominance effect might occur in mixed language blocks because of worse performance in L1 switch trials than in L2 switch trials (while L1 repetition trials still might show a better performance than L2 repetition trials, e.g., Meuter & Allport, 1999). However, this explanation has been challenged by reported instances where switch costs were symmetrical, and yet a reversed language dominance was observed, making it unlikely that the reversed language dominance effect is solely caused by asymmetrical switch costs. Experiments 2 and 3 of Costa and Santesteban (2004) showed that while switch costs were symmetrical across the two languages, overall L2 performance was better, thus pointing towards a reversed language dominance effect in the absence of asymmetrical switch costs. Peeters and Dijkstra (2018) found a similar pattern when testing both color-cued language switching and language switching cued through virtual interlocutors. Their results support those of Costa and Santesteban (2004) and also show that such a pattern can result from a more ecologically valid experimental setup.

A second explanation for the reversed language dominance effect relies on proactive inhibition. Based on this account (e.g., Christoffels et al., 2007; Gollan & Ferreira, 2009), the reversed dominance effect results from an attempt to have a more similar L1 and L2 activation in mixed language blocks, which is assumed to increase overall performance in mixed language blocks. To get a more similar L1 and L2 activation in mixed language blocks, and thus a similar overall L1 and L2 performance, L1 will be inhibited. It could be argued that an inhibition process that lowers the activation of L1 to that of L2 activation should not result in overall worse L1 than L2 activation. So, to account for the reversed language dominance effect with inhibition, it has been suggested that there is an inability to decide the exact amount of inhibition. Accordingly, the reversed language dominance effect is believed to result from an unintentional over-shooting of L1 inhibition (e.g., Gollan & Ferreira, 2009).

Declerck et al. (2015) proposed a third explanation for the reversed lan-guage dominance pattern based on relative activation. Instead of being a consequence of proactive inhibition, the better L2 than L1 performance could be occasioned by an increase of L2 activation throughout mixed language blocks, applied proactively in an attempt to equalize the activation of the two languages. Along the same vein as the proactive inhibition account (e.g., Christoffels et al., 2007; Gollan & Ferreira, 2009), the reversal of language dominance could then be due to an overshooting of increased L2 activation.

A fourth hypothesis was brought forward by Costa and Santesteban (2004). These authors argue that different selection thresholds can be established for each language. In order to make L1 and L2 activation levels more similar, the threshold is set higher for L1, which might generate a reversed dominance effect. According to their account, only highly proficient bilinguals should be able to modulate the selection thresholds for their languages, but this as-sumption is not congruent with the fact that reversed dominance effects have also been encountered in studies with less proficient bilinguals (e.g., Declerck et al., 2020; Peeters & Dijkstra, 2018).

Unfortunately, the reversed language dominance effect is not a robust finding across studies (for a meta-analysis, see Gade et al., 2021). Language-switching studies are seemingly divided between finding a better L1 perfor-mance in mixed language blocks (e.g., Reynolds et al., 2016; Wang et al., 2009), a similar performance in both languages (e.g., Calabria et al., 2015; Filippi et al., 2014), or a reversed dominance effect (i.e., better L2 perfor-mance e.g., Christoffels et al., 2016; Tarlowski et al., 2012).

Importantly, previous studies identified key variables affecting the reversed language dominance effect. For example, the total number of trials has been shown to influence the results, as evidenced by Kleinman and Gollan (2018). They re-analyzed data from a picture naming task performed by 416 Spanish–English bilinguals using a cued language-switching paradigm and found that the reversed language dominance effect increased progressively as bilinguals got further in the mixed language block. These results can be in-terpreted as a reflection of an adaptive response to a given linguistic setting (see Green & Abutalebi, 2013). More specifically, experience in a specific linguistic context tends to alter the control processes that are implemented in said linguistic context.

Despite this influence of the linguistic context on reversed dominance, the effect is still sometimes observed in voluntary language switching (e.g., de Bruin et al., 2018; Gollan & Ferreira, 2009; Gollan et al., 2014) – similar to cued language switching. Moreover, whether the implemented language-switching paradigm is cued or voluntary does not seem to have a robust effect on the reversed language dominance effect (de Bruin et al., 2018; Experiment 2 of Gollan et al., 2014; Jevtović et al., 2020; however, see Experiment 1 of Gollan et al., 2014).

Taken together, there is some evidence that the reversed language dominance effect can adapt to the linguistic context. However, the observed adaptation mainly refers to a short-term adaptation within a given situation (e.g., over the course of an experiment). In contrast, there is no conclusive evidence that proactive language control is different between cued and voluntary language switching. Yet, based on the fact that very little research is available, one should be careful to draw conclusions of a non-existent difference in proactive language control between the dual-language context and the dense code-switching context.

Language mixing costs

The final effect to be discussed here are language mixing costs, another marker of proactive language control. Language mixing costs refer to worse performance in language repetition trials (i.e., the current trial is in the same language as the previous trial) in a mixed block relative to trials in a single language block (e.g., Christoffels et al., 2007; Declerck et al., 2013; Ma et al., 2016; Mosca & de Bot, 2017; Peeters & Dijkstra, 2018; Prior & Gollan, 2011). As an example, Peeters and Dijkstra (2018) had Dutch–English bilinguals perform a picture naming task where their two languages were used based on a color cue in the mixed language block, while only one of the two languages was used in each of the two single language blocks. The authors observed worse performance in repetition trials in mixed language blocks than trials in single language blocks (i.e., language mixing costs) for both languages.

Ma and colleagues (2016) explain language mixing costs by arguing that proactive inhibition on the nontarget language is employed during single language blocks, whereas the target language is proactively activated. In contrast, both languages will be proactively activated in preparation to use either language in mixed language blocks, since bilinguals cannot know in advance which language will be required in the next trial, only that one of the languages will have to be used. As a result, cross-language interference is higher in mixed language blocks, leading to worse performance in repetition trials of a mixed language block relative to trials in a single language block.

Parting from the account of Ma and colleagues (2016), language mixing costs have also been explained without proactive language control. Some authors contend that language mixing costs probably do not solely result from proactive language control, and could also be caused by the increased cognitive cost of maintaining and monitoring the two languages in mixed language blocks relative to single language blocks (e.g., de Bruin et al., 2018; Declerck, 2020).

Regardless of the specific interpretation of language mixing costs, they provide evidence for a qualitative or quantitative difference in control processes implemented during mixed and single language blocks. In line with the Adaptive Control Hypothesis (Green & Abutalebi, 2013), language mixing costs indicate that in general, less language control is required and fewer of its underlying processes are implemented in a single language context (cf. single language block) than in a dual-language context (cf. cued language switching; Christoffels et al., 2007; Ma et al., 2016; Peeters & Dijkstra, 2018).

Though, this is not necessarily the case when comparing performance in single language blocks to that of repetition trials obtained with the voluntary language-switching paradigm (de Bruin et al., 2018; Gambi & Hartsuiker, 2016; Gollan & Ferreira, 2009; Gross & Kaushanskaya, 2015). de Bruin and colleagues observed a language mixing benefit (i.e., worse performance in single language block trials than in repetition trials of mixed language blocks) across both languages when Spanish-Basque bilinguals could voluntarily choose their language on each trial in the mixed language blocks. Gollan and Ferreira (2009) found a language mixing benefit for L2 trials, but not for L1 trials, with Spanish–English bilinguals. The observation of a language mixing benefit with the voluntary language-switching paradigm corresponds with the assumption that fewer control processes would be required in a dense code-switching context than in a single language context as put forward by the Adaptive Control Hypothesis (Green & Abutalebi, 2013).

Gollan and Ferreira (2009) partly attributed the L2 mixing benefit to bilinguals naming only 'easier' words in their less dominant language and avoiding the more difficult words in their L2 by relying on L1, a strategy impossible to implement when the languages are cued. This assumption, however, does not hold in evidence of a similar language mixing benefit found by studies implementing a cued language-switching paradigm (e.g., Mosca & Clahsen, 2016). In order to explain the mixing benefit with cued language switching, Mosca & Clahsen, 2016) put forward that speakers focus additional resources on their less proficient language to try and balance out the difference between the two, an explanation reminiscent of the reversed language dominance effect.

Based on the current state of affairs, the language mixing cost results observed in the literature are mostly in line with the assumptions of the Adaptive Control Hypothesis (Green & Abutalebi, 2013). The results seem to generally correspond with less control being required in a single language context (i.e., single language blocks) than in a dual-language context (i.e., cued language switching), but not in a dense code-switching language context (i.e., voluntary language switching). In turn, we can deduce that the different linguistic contexts recruit different control processes or the same control processes but to different degrees. Still, more research focusing on this measure is required as not all studies found evidence along these lines (e.g., Mosca & Clahsen, 2016).

Open issues

How and when language control is implemented has received quite some attention in the past. Nonetheless, as this overview indicates, these issues are not entirely resolved yet, as are a series of other crucial issues. Here we want to outline some of these other important issues where additional research would greatly benefit our understanding of language control. To start with, it is still unclear how language control is initiated. Green and Abutalebi's (2013) Adaptive Control Hypothesis postulate that language control is triggered by high levels of cross-language interference (see also Declerck et al., 2019), as language control occurs to reduce the costs of such interference. They assume that the the anterior cingulate cortex (ACC) in the brain is responsible for constantly monitoring our actions. The moment the system detects a conflict (e.g., cross-language interference), control processes come into play. Yet this contradicts other models that assume that language control is engaged through the activation of the target language (e.g., Grainger et al., 2010). The handful of studies examining this issue have come up with contradictory results: while some brought forward evidence that conflict monitoring is involved in the initiation of language control (e.g., Branzi et al., 2015), others did not (e.g., Eben & Declerck, 2019). Hence, it is presently unclear how language control is initiated.

The second unresolved issue is the processing stage(s) at which language control is engaged in bilingual language production. It is commonly assumed that control intervenes both at the goal (i.e., task schema) and at the lemma levels (e.g., Green, 1998). So far, there is not much evidence to confirm this hypothesis. Furthermore, it could very well be that the different language control processes stipulated in the Adaptive Control Hypothesis are implemented at different processing stages. However, little to no research has gone into this so far.

Third, there is a need for much more research that provides insight into how control processes contribute to the everyday life of a bilingual outside an experimental setting. Blanco-Elorrieta and Pylkkänen (2018) and Johns and Steuck (2021), for instance, have focused more on ecologically valid experimental setups to test the performance of bilinguals when they switch between languages. These studies show that in settings closer to real-life situations, bilinguals appear to employ overall less language control, since little to no switch costs were observed, but this pattern is not consistently found in the literature (see, for instance, Peeters & Dijkstra, 2018). Further research in this direction with various populations is thus strongly needed before these results can be considered conclusive.

The final question is whether reactive and proactive language control influence one another, and if this is different in distinct linguistic contexts. The literature proposes that different mechanisms are implemented on the basis of indexes of proactive and reactive language control (Declerck, 2020). Both processes aim to resolve cross-language interference, which begs the question whether the two are connected. For instance, it might be that whenever there is an increase in proactive language control, less reactive language control would be necessary, because the cross-language interference would be resolved for the most part by proactive language control. Unfortunately, most of the research that would show whether proactive and reactive language control are interconnected relies on language mixing costs and switch costs, respectively (cf. Declerck, 2020). These two effects are inherently connected since they both rely on repetition trials in mixed language blocks. More specifically, if performance in repetition trials was, for instance, fast in a certain setting, then the reaction time mixing costs would be small and the reaction time switch costs would be large. Moreover, language mixing costs are not a straightforward measure of proactive language control (for more details see the section on language mixing costs above). Consequently, studies that investigate both switch and mixing costs do not allow for a straightforward investigation into whether proactive and reactive language control are interdependent.

Conclusion

In the present chapter, we discussed language control during bilingual language production and how this process might differ across several linguistic contexts. To this end, we focused on three major measures of language control: asymmetrical switch costs, reversed language dominance, and language mixing costs. The evidence gathered from these three measures is mostly in line with the Adaptive Control Hypothesis of Green and Abutalebi (2013), as less control seems to be necessary in a dense code-switching context than in single and dual-language contexts. The evidence seems to suggest that the latter requires even more control than a single language context. While most of the studies discussed here are in line with these assumptions, this is not the case for all studies. Therefore, more research is necessary to further substantiate how language control works, with a specific focus on different linguistic contexts.

Notes

1 Please note that the alternating language-switching variant (e.g., Declerck et al., 2015; Jackson et al., 2001) is also used relatively often in language-switching studies. However, since this language-switching variant does not correspond to one of the linguistic contexts put forward by Green and Abutalebi (2013) in a straightforward fashion, we decided not to include it in this chapter.
2 While other measures of reactive language control have been used in the literature, such as n-2 language repetition costs (e.g., Branzi et al., 2016; Declerck, Thoma et al., 2015; Declerck & Philipp, 2017; Guo et al., 2013; Philipp et al., 2007), none have extensively investigated the impact of linguistic contexts and thus fall outside the scope of the current chapter.

References

Blanco-Elorrieta, E., & Caramazza, A. (2021). A common selection mechanism at each linguistic level in bilingual and monolingual language production. *Cognition*, *213*, 104625. doi: 10.1016/j.cognition.2021.104625

Blanco-Elorrieta, E., & Pylkkänen, L. (2017). Bilingual language-switching in the laboratory versus in the wild: The spatiotemporal dynamics of adaptive language control. *Journal of Neuroscience*, *37*, 9022–9036.

Blanco-Elorrieta, E., & Pylkkänen, L. (2018). Ecological validity in bilingualism research and the bilingual advantage. *Trends in Cognitive Sciences*, *22*, 1117–1126.

Bobb, S. C., & Wodniecka, Z. (2013). Language switching in picture naming: What asymmetric switch costs (do not) tell us about inhibition in bilingual speech planning. *Journal of Cognitive Psychology*, *25*, 568–585. doi:10.1080/20445911.2013.792822

Bonfieni, M., Branigan, H. P., Pickering, M. J., & Sorace, A. (2019). Language experience modulates bilingual language control: The effect of proficiency, age of acquisition, and exposure on language-switching. *Acta Psychologica*, *193*, 160–170.

Branzi, F. M., Calabria, M., Boscarino, M. L., & Costa, A. (2016). On the overlap between bilingual language control and domain-general executive control. *Acta Psychologica*, *166*, 21–30.

Branzi, F. M., Della Rosa, P. A., Canini, M., Costa, A., & Abutalebi, J. (2015). Language control in bilinguals: Monitoring and response selection. *Cerebral Cortex*, *26*, 2367–2380. doi: 10.1093/cercor/bhv052

Calabria, M., Branzi, F. M., Marne, P., Hernández, M., & Costa, A. (2015). Age-related effects over bilingual language control and executive control. *Bilingualism: Language and Cognition*, *18*, 65–78

Calabria, M., Costa, A., Green, D. W., & Abutalebi, J. (2018). Neural basis of bilingual language control. *Annals of the New York Academy of Sciences*, *1426*, 221–235. doi: 10.1111/nyas.13879

Campbell, J. I. D. (2005). Asymmetrical language switching costs in Chinese-English bilinguals' number naming and simple arithmetic. *Bilingualism: Language and Cognition*, *8*, 85–91. doi:10.1017/s136672890400207x

Christoffels, I. K., Firk, C., & Schiller, N. O. (2007). Bilingual language control: An event-related brain potential study. *Brain Research*, *1147*, 192–208.

Christoffels, I., Ganushchak, L., & La Heij, W. (2016). When L1 suffers: Sustained, global slowing and the reversed language effect in mixed language context. In J. W. Schwieter (Ed.), *Cognitive control and consequences of multilingualism* (pp. 171–192). Amsterdam: John Benjamins Publishing Company.

Costa, A., Caramazza, A., & Sebastian-Galles, N. (2000). The cognate facilitation effect: implications for models of lexical access. *Journal of Experimental Psychology: Learning, Memory, and Cognition*, *26*, 1283–1296.

Costa, A., Miozzo, M., & Caramazza, A. (1999). Lexical selection in bilinguals: Do words in the bilingual's two lexicons compete for selection? *Journal of Memory and Language*, *41*, 365–397. doi: 10.1006/jmla.1999.2651

Costa, A., & Santesteban, M. (2004). Lexical access in bilingual speech production: Evidence from language-switching in highly proficient bilinguals and L2 learners. *Journal of Memory, and Language*, *50*, 491–511.

de Bruin, A., Samuel, A. G., & Duñabeitia, J. A. (2020). Examining bilingual language switching across the lifespan in cued and voluntary switching contexts. *Journal of Experimental Psychology: Human Perception and Performance*, *46*, 759–788. doi: 10.1037/xhp0000746 de Bruin, A., Samuel, A. G., & Duñabeitia, J. A. (2018). Voluntary language-switching: When and why do bilinguals switch between their languages? *Journal of Memory and Language, 103*, 28–43.

Declerck, M. (2020). What about proactive language control? *Psychonomic Bulletin & Review, 27*, 24–35. doi: 10.3758/s13423-019-01654-1

Declerck, M., Grainger, J., & Hartsuiker, R. J. (2021). Proactive language control during sentence production. *International Journal of Bilingualism, 25*(6), 1813–1824. doi: 10.11 77/13670069211047803

Declerck, M., Kleinman, D., & Gollan, T. (2020) Which bilinguals reverse language dominance and why? *Cognition, 204*, 104384 doi: 10.1016/j.cognition.2020.104384

Declerck, M., Koch, I., Duñabeitia, J. A., Grainger, J., & Stephan, D. N. (2019). What absent switch costs and mixing costs during bilingual language comprehension can tell us about language control. *Journal of Experimental Psychology: Human Perception and Performance, 45*, 771–789. doi: 10.1037/xhp0000627

Declerck, M., Koch, I., & Philipp, A. M. (2012). Digits vs. pictures: The influence of stimulus type on language switching. *Bilingualism: Language and Cognition, 15*, 896–904. doi: 10.1017/S1366728912000193

Declerck, M., Koch, I., & Philipp, A. M. (2015). The minimum requirements of language control: Evidence from sequential predictability effects in language switching. *Journal of Experimental Psychology: Learning, Memory and Cognition, 41*, 377–394. doi: 10.1037/xlm0000021

Declerck, M., Lemhöfer, K., & Grainger, J. (2017). Bilingual language interference initiates error detection: Evidence from language intrusions. *Bilingualism: Language and Cognition, 20*, 1010–1016.

Declerck, M., & Philipp, A. M. (2015). A review of control processes and their locus in language-switching. *Psychonomic Bulletin & Review, 22*, 1630–1645. doi: 10.3758/s13423-015-0836-1

Declerck, M., & Philipp, A. M. (2017). Is there lemma-based language control? The influence of language practice and language-specific item practice on asymmetrical switch costs. *Language, Cognition and Neuroscience, 32*, 488–493.

Declerck, M., Philipp, A. M., & Koch, I. (2013). Bilingual control: Sequential memory in language-switching. *Journal of Experimental Psychology: Learning, Memory, and Cognition, 39*(6), 1793–1806.

Declerck, M., Stephan, D. N., Koch, I., & Philipp, A. M. (2015). The other modality: Auditory stimuli in language-switching. *Journal of Cognitive Psychology, 27*, 685–691. doi: 10.1080/20445911.2015.1026265

Declerck, M., Thoma, A. M., Koch, I., & Philipp, A. M. (2015). Highly proficient bilinguals implement inhibition: Evidence from n-2 language repetition costs. *Journal of Experimental Psychology: Learning, Memory, and Cognition, 41*, 1911–1916. doi: 10.1037/xlm0000138

Eben, C., & Declerck, M. (2019). Conflict monitoring in bilingual language comprehension? Evidence from a bilingual flanker task. *Language, Cognition and Neuroscience, 34*, 320–325. doi: 10.1080/23273798.2018.1537499

Filippi, R., Karaminis, T., & Thomas, M. S. (2014). Language switching in bilingual production: Empirical data and computational modelling. *Bilingualism: Language and Cognition, 17*, 294–315.

Finkbeiner, M., Almeida, J., Janssen, N., & Caramazza, A. (2006). Lexical selection in bilingual speech production does not involve language suppression. *Journal of Experimental Psychology. Learning, Memory, and Cognition, 32*, 1075–1089. doi: 10.1037/0278-7393.32.5.1075

Gade, M., Declerck, M., Philipp, A. M., Rey-Mermet, A., & Koch, I. (2021). On the existence of asymmetrical switch costs and reversed language dominance effects – a meta-analysis. *Journal of Cognition*, *4*, 55.

Gambi, C., & Hartsuiker, R. J. (2016). If you stay, it might be easier: Switch costs from comprehension to production in a joint switching task. *Journal of Experimental Psychology: Learning, Memory, and Cognition*, 42, 608–626. doi: 10.1037/xlm0000190

Giezen, M. R., & Emmorey, K. (2016). Language co-activation and lexical selection in bimodal bilinguals: Evidence from picture–word interference. *Bilingualism: Language and Cognition*, *19*, 264–276.

Gollan, T. H., & Ferreira, V. S. (2009). Should I stay or should I switch? A cost-benefit analysis of voluntary language-switching in young and aging bilinguals. *Journal of Experimental Psychology: Learning, Memory, and Cognition*, *35*, 640–665. doi: 10.1037/a0014981

Gollan, T. H., Kleinman, D., & Wierenga, C. E. (2014). What's easier: Doing what you want, or being told what to do? Cued versus voluntary language and task switching. *Journal of Experimental Psychology: General*, *143*, 2167–2195.

Gollan, T. H., Sandoval, T., & Salmon, D. P. (2011). Cross-language intrusion errors in aging bilinguals reveal the link between executive control and language selection. *Psychological Science*, *22*, 1155–1164.

Grainger, J. Midgley, K. J., & Holcomb, P. J. (2010). Re-thinking the bilingual interactive-activation model from a developmental perspective (BIA-d). In M. Kail, & M. Hickman (Eds.), *Language acquisition across linguistic and cognitive systems* (pp. 267–284). Philadelphia: John Benjamins.

Green, D. W. (1986). Control, activation, and resource: A framework and a model for the control of speech in bilinguals. *Brain and Language*, *27*, 210–223. doi:10.1016/0093-934 X(86)90016-7

Green, D. W. (1998). Mental control of the bilingual lexico-semantic system. *Bilingualism: Language and Cognition*, *1*, 67–81. doi:10.1017/S1366728998000133

Green, D. W., & Abutalebi, J. (2013). Language control in bilinguals: The adaptive control hypothesis. *Journal of Cognitive Psychology*, *25*, 515–530. doi: 10.1080/20445911.2013. 796377

Gross, M., & Kaushanskaya, M. (2015). Voluntary language-switching in English–Spanish bilingual children. *Journal of Cognitive Psychology*, *27*, 992–1013.

Grunden, N., Piazza, G., García-Sánchez, C., & Calabria, M. (2020). Voluntary Language Switching in the Context of Bilingual Aphasia. *Behavioral Sciences*, *10*, 141. doi:10.3390/bs10090141

Guo, T., Liu, F., Chen, B., & Li, S. (2013). Inhibition of non-target languages in multi-lingual word production: Evidence from Uighur–Chinese–English trilinguals. *Acta Psychologica*, *143*, 277–283.

Hoshino, N., & Kroll, J. F. (2008). Cognate effects in picture naming: Does cross-language activation survive a change of script?. *Cognition*, *106*, 501–511.

Ivanova, I., & Hernandez, D. C. (2021). Within-language lexical interference can be re-solved in a similar way to between-language interference. *Cognition*, *214*, 104760.

Jackson, G. M., Swainson, R., Cunnington, R., & Jackson, S. R. (2001). ERP correlates of executive control during repeated language switching. *Bilingualism*, *4*, 169–178.

Jevtović, M., Duñabeitia, J. A., & de Bruin, A. (2020). How do bilinguals switch between languages in different interactional contexts? A comparison between voluntary and mandatory language-switching. *Bilingualism: Language and Cognition*, *23*, 401–413.

Johns, M. A., & Steuck, J. (2021). Is codeswitching easy or difficult? Testing processing cost through the prosodic structure of bilingual speech. *Cognition*, *211*, 104634. doi: 10.1016/j.cognition.2021.104634

Jylkkä, J., Laine, M., & Lehtonen, M. (2021). Does language switching behavior rely on general executive functions?. *Bilingualism: Language and Cognition*, *24*, 583–595.

Kang, C., Ma, F., & Guo, T. (2017). The plasticity of lexical selection mechanism in word production: ERP evidence from short-term language switching training in unbalanced Chinese-English bilinguals. *Bilingualism, Language and Cognition*, *21*, 296–313. doi: 10.1017/S1366728917000037

Kirk, N., Declerck, M., Kemp, R., & Kempe, V. (2021). Language control in regional dialect speakers – monolingual by name, bilingual by nature? *Bilingualism: Language and Cognition*, *25*(3), 511–520. doi: 10.1017/S1366728921000973

Kleinman, D., & Gollan, T. H. (2018). Inhibition accumulates over time at multiple processing levels in bilingual language control. *Cognition*, 173, 115–132. doi: 10.1016/j.cognition.2018.01.009

La Heij T. (2005) Selection processes in monolingual and bilingual lexical access. In J.F. Kroll, & A.M.B. de Groot (Eds.), *Handbook of bilingualism: Psycholinguistic Approaches* (pp. 289–307). Oxford University Press.

Li, C., & Gollan, T. H. (2018). Cognates interfere with language selection but enhance monitoring in connected speech. *Memory & Cognition*, *46*, 923–939. doi: 10.3758/s13421-018-0812-x

Li, C., & Gollan, T. (2021). What cognates reveal about default language selection in bilingual sentence production. *Journal of Memory and Language*, *118*, 104214. doi: 10.1016/j.jml.2020.104214

Linck, J. A., Schwieter, J. W., & Sunderman, G. (2012). Inhibitory control predicts language switching per- formance in trilingual speech production. *Bilingualism: Language and Cognition*, *15*, 651–662. doi: 10.1017/s136672891100054x

Ma, F., Li, S., & Guo, T. (2016). Reactive and proactive control in bilingual word production: An investigation of influential factors. *Journal of Memory and Language*, *86*, 35–59.

Macizo, P., Bajo, T., & Paolieri, D. (2012). Language switching and language competition. *Second Language Research*, *28*, 131–149. doi: 10.1177/0267658311434893

Martin, C. D., Strijkers, K., Santesteban, M., Escera, C., Hartsuiker, R. J., & Costa, A. (2013). The impact of early bilingualism on controlling a language learned late: an ERP study. *Frontiers in Psychology*, *4*, 815.

Meuter, R. F. I., & Allport, A. (1999). Bilingual language-switching in naming: Asymmetrical costs of language selection. *Journal of Memory and Language*, *40*, 25–40.

Mosca, M., & Clahsen, H. (2016). Examining language switching in bilinguals: The role of preparation time. *Bilingualism: Language and Cognition*, *19*, 415–424. doi: 10.1017/S1366728915000693

Mosca, M., & de Bot, K. (2017). Bilingual language switching: Production vs. Recognition. *Frontiers in Psychology*, *8*, 934. doi: 10.3389/fpsyg.2017.00934

Peeters, D. (2020). Bilingual switching between languages and listeners: Insights from immersive virtual reality. *Cognition*, *195*, 104107. doi: 10.1016/j.cognition.2019.104107

Peeters, D., & Dijkstra, T. (2018). Sustained inhibition of the native language in bilingual language production: A virtual reality approach. *Bilingualism: Language and Cognition*, *21*, 1035–1061. doi: 10.1017/S1366728917000396

Peeters, D., Runnqvist, E., Bertrand, D., & Grainger, J. (2014). Asymmetrical switch costs in bilingual language production induced by reading words. *Journal of Experimental Psychology: Learning, Memory, and Cognition*, *40*, 284–292.

Philipp, A. M., Gade, M., & Koch, I. (2007). Inhibitory processes in language-switching: Evidence from switching language-defined response sets. *European Journal of Cognitive Psychology, 19*, 395–416. doi: 10.1080/09541440600758812.

Poulisse, N., and Bongaerts, T. (1994). 1st Language use in 2nd-language production. *Applied Linguistics, 15*, 36–57.

Prior, A. & Gollan, T. H. (2011). Good language-switchers are good task-switchers: evidence from spanish–english and mandarin–english bilinguals. *Journal of the International Neuropsychological Society, 17*, 682–691. doi:10.1017/S1355617711000580.

Reynolds, M. G., Schlöffel, S., & Peressotti, F. (2016). Asymmetric switch costs in numeral naming and number word reading: Implications for models of bilingual language production. *Frontiers in Psychology, 6*, 2011. doi: 10.3389/fpsyg.2015.02011.

Runnqvist, E. (2022). Self-Monitoring: The neurocognitive basis of error monitoring in language production. In Hartsuiker, R., & Strijkers, K. (Eds.), *Current Issues in the Psychology of Language* (pp. xx–xx). Abingdon: Routledge.

Runnqvist, E., Strijkers, K., Sadat, J., & Costa, A. (2011). On the temporal and functional origin of L2 disadvantagesin speech production: Critical review. *Frontiers in Psychology, 2*, 379. doi: 10.3389/fpsyg.2011.00379

Schwieter, J. W., & Sunderman, G. (2008). Language switching in bilingual speech production: In search of the language-specific selection mechanism. *The Mental Lexicon, 3*(2), 214–238. doi:10.1075/ml.3.2.06sch

Stasenko, A. Kleinman, D., & Gollan T. H. (2021). Older bilinguals reverse language dominance less than younger bilinguals: Evidence for the inhibitory déficit hypothesis. *Psychology and Aging*. doi:10.1037/pag0000618

Strijkers, K. (2016). An assembly based view on word production: The bilingual test case. *Language Learning, 66*, 92–131. doi:10.1111/lang.12191

Strijkers, K., Baus, C., Runnqvist, E., Fritzpatrick, I., & Costa, A. (2013). The temporal dynamics of first versus second language speech production. *Brain & Language, 127*, 6–11. doi: 10.1016/j.bandl.2013.07.008

Sulpizio, S., Del Maschio, N., Fedeli, D., & Abutalebi, J. (2020). Bilingual language processing: A meta-analysis of functional neuroimaging studies. *Neuroscience and Biobehavioral Reviews, 108*, 834–853. doi:10.1016/j.neubiorev.2019.12.014

Tarlowski, A., Wodniecka, Z., & Marzecová, A. (2012). Language-switching in the production of phrases. *Journal of Psycholinguistic Research, 42*, 103–118.

Timmer, K., Christoffels, I. K., & Costa, A. (2019). On the flexibility of bilingual language control: The effect of language context. *Bilingualism: Language and Cognition, 22*, 555–568.

Verhoef, K., Roelofs, A., & Chwilla, D. J. (2009). Role of inhibition in language switching: evidence from event-related brain potentials in overt picture naming. *Cognition, 110*, 84–99. doi: 10.1016/j.cognition.2008.10.013

Wang, Y., Kuhl, P. K., Chen, C., & Dong, Q. (2009). Sustained and transient language control in the bilingual brain. *NeuroImage, 47*, 414–422. doi: 10.1016/j.neuroimage.2008.12.055

Zheng, X., Roelofs, A., Erkan, H., & Lemhöfer, K. (2020). Dynamics of inhibitory control during bilingual speech production: An electrophysiological study. *Neuropsychologia, 140*, 107387. doi: 10.1016/j.neuropsychologia.2020.10738

8 Written Production

The APOMI Model of Word Writing: Anticipatory Processing of Orthographic and Motor Information

Sonia Kandel

This chapter concerns questions that we often ask ourselves in everyday life: How do we write words? How do we recall a word's spelling from memory? How do we execute the movements to produce letters? Although writing is one of the most important communicational tools in humans, it has received considerably less attention than reading. This lack of interest for writing is astonishing, as every word we read has to be written *before* it is ready to be read! From the intention to write a text, to actually seeing the words written down, there are a series of processes of varying cognitive complexity: content processing, semantic and syntax construction, spelling retrieval, letter activation, spatial and muscular adjustments and motor execution. I will focus on word production, which is one of the core processes involved in writing. We generally write words by hand or type them on a keyboard of a computer or smartphone. This chapter focuses on handwriting (and for other non-verbal production skills, see Chapter 9: Emmorey, 2022, and Chapter 10: Ruiter, 2022 of this volume).

Writing a word requires the retrieval of its letter components and producing hand movements with an instrument (e.g., pencil, pen) to transform abstract letter representations into spatial configurations that unfold progressively on a page. The first part of this chapter presents an overview of experimental, neuropsychological, and neuroimaging studies that were designed with the idea that spelling and motor processes are independent and sequential (e.g., Bonin et al., 2001; Bonin et al., 2012; Damian & Stadthagen-Gonzalez, 2009; Ellis, 1982; Margolin, 1984; Miceli & Capasso, 2006; Planton et al., 2013; Purcell et al., 2011; Qu et al., 2011; Rapp et al., 2016; Rapp et al., 2002; Shallice, 1988). In this view, word writing begins with the activation of central orthographic processes that retrieve its letter components before movement production. The letter string is stored in working memory as input for motor production (Costa et al., 2011). Then, the peripheral motor processes execute the movements to trace the letter sequence.

A series of experimental studies revealed that although we need spelling information to trace the letters one after the other, this does not necessarily mean that word writing is a strictly sequential process (Afonso et al., 2015;

DOI: 10.4324/9781003145790-9

2015; Álvarez et al., 2009; Delattre et al., 2006; Buchwald & Falconer, 2014; Kandel et al., 2012; Quémart & Lambert, 2019; Lambert et al., 2011; Roux et al., 2013; Sausset et al., 2012). In this chapter, I present a new approach of the dynamics of word writing. Within the framework of this new model, the orthographic processes involved in spelling retrieval remain active during the processing of the motor aspects of letter production. I review movement production data collected with digitizers indicating that some orthographic processes occur before starting to write while others continue to be active when we are writing the initial letters of the word. Orthographic and motor processes are active at the same time because they anticipate spelling information about the end of the word. Orthographic processing anticipates information on the letters that are further ahead in the word. Motor processing is also anticipatory because some movement parameters like global letter size (e.g., word love, global letter height = 1 cm) are calculated before the more local ones as relative letter size (e.g., if letter height l = 1 cm then o, v, e = 0.5 cm). This kind of processing in turn, takes place before muscular contractions make the hand move. Thus, word writing involves spelling and motor anticipatory processes that are active simultaneously in a hierarchical architecture. This renders word writing movements fast, smooth and readable because the orthographic and motor processes are continuously anticipating forthcoming information at different processing levels. The final part of this chapter presents an outline of this complex architecture.

Traditional orthographic and motor approaches of word writing

Most experimental, neuropsychological, and neuroimaging studies conceived word writing as a linguistic motor task involving two distinct functional processes that operate sequentially: spelling retrieval and motor production. To write a word, we have to know its spelling; that is, which letters compose it. Thus, before we start to write there are a series of processes involved in orthographic retrieval (Bonin et al., 2012; Damian et al., 2011). This kind of "central" processing has also been widely examined in neuropsychology with dysgraphic patients (Fischer-Baum et al., 2010; Rapp et al., 2002; Rapp et al., 2016) and experimental approaches (e.g., Bonin et al., 2001). It led to a dual conception of spelling retrieval resulting from lexical and sub-lexical procedures (Figure 8.1; Caramazza & Miceli, 1989; Shallice, 1988). Suppose we have to write a word in a writing-to-dictation task or picture naming. If we know the word, we privilege the lexical route. This activates previously stored phonological, semantic, and orthographic information of the word (see Miceli & Capasso, 2006 for a review). We recall the information on the letter components from a long-term memory system known as the orthographic lexicon (Bonin et al., 2001; Costa et al., 2011).

The sub-lexical procedure converts each phoneme of the sequence in a specific letter or group of letters called graphemes (e.g., English phoneme /f/ will be

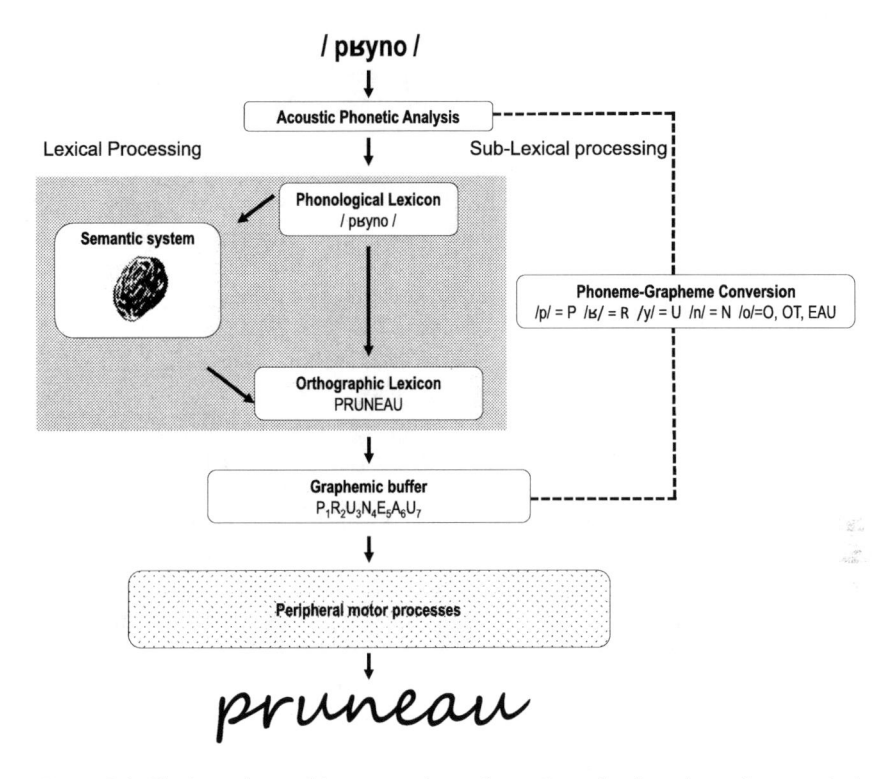

Figure 8.1 Classic orthographic conception of word production (central processing). Example for the French word PRUNEAU (prune, /pʁyno/).

converted into graphemes F (*fate*) or PH (*photo*); English phonemes /ð/ (*this*) and /θ/ (*thing*) will be converted into grapheme TH). The phoneme–grapheme conversion mechanism relies on the application of pre-established language-specific sound-letter transcription rules. In general, the lexical and sub-lexical procedures are active at the same time. The sub-lexical procedure is particularly useful when we do not know the word we have to write. The outcome of both routes is temporarily stored in a sort of working memory that most researchers referred to as the "graphemic buffer" (Costa et al., 2011; Rapp & Kong, 2002; Sage & Ellis, 2004; Tainturier & Rapp, 2003). It stores the letter string as information on letter identity and order. This last stage of the "central" orthographic processing is the interface between orthographic and motor processes. The end of spelling retrieval marks the beginning of the motor production phase, which is considered as "peripheral" processing.

This conception of word writing was influenced by dual-route models of reading. In fact, writing and reading were considered as symmetrically inverse processes (Tainturier & Rapp, 2001, 2003). Thus, the lexical and sub-lexical procedures function the same way but they will be involved in visual letter decoding processes when reading and auditory phonological encoding processes when writing. Although several dysgraphic case studies support this view, it leads, in our opinion, to some misunderstandings of the writing process. Writing is more difficult than reading, not only because it takes more time. Retrieving the correct letter string to write a word involves a stronger cognitive load than recognizing the same letter string in reading. Word recognition can be done correctly with partial information and does not require accessing the complete orthographic detail of the word as in spelling retrieval (Tainturier & Rapp, 2001). I will not discuss all the differences between reading and writing processes here. The point I would like to make is that word writing requires the retrieval of detailed orthographic representations as well as cognitively demanding movement production processes that cannot be assimilated to the ones involved in reading. More specifically, I refer to the anticipatory nature of orthographic and motor processes that take place during writing. I will discuss this in the following paragraphs when presenting my alternative approach to word writing.

This sequential "spelling then movement" conception of word writing is in line with neuropsychological research on the motor components of letter production (Ellis, 1988; Margolin & Goodman-Schulman, 1992). Moreover, the experimental studies on handwriting production followed this view and focused on the aspects of writing that exclusively concerned peripheral processing (e.g., André et al., 2014; Maarse, 1987; Teulings, 1996). In this perspective, the input to the peripheral motor production modules is the letter string that is stored in the graphemic buffer (Figure 8.2). These studies examined movement programming, control, and production of the letters in the graphemic buffer, without considering any top-down activation from the preceding spelling processes.

Therefore, to write a word we execute graphomotor sequences that produce one letter after the other "mechanically". In this perspective, each letter in a word is represented as a specific spatial configuration called "allograph" (Thomassen & Van Galen, 1992). For instance, letter A can be represented as the following shapes: A, a, A, a, A, a. Each shape is an allograph. Allographs are schematic representations of the shape that must be produced. Each allograph has a corresponding motor program or graphic motor pattern that stores a learned movement sequence in long-term memory (Schmidt 2013). When we write a letter, we select an allograph and activate its motor program. The activation of the motor program provides information on the allograph's shape, stroke order, and direction (Thomassen et al., 1991). The writing system then adapts this information to the *global* parameters of the situation, like the adjustment of letter size and mean movement speed (Pick & Teulings, 1983). This processing stage is *effector independent*, which means that it does not consider the part of the body that will execute the writing movement. Finally, the writing system calculates a series of *local* parameters according to the situational constraints of stroke production. This determines the muscular contractions of the hand – or other parts of the body – which holds the pen

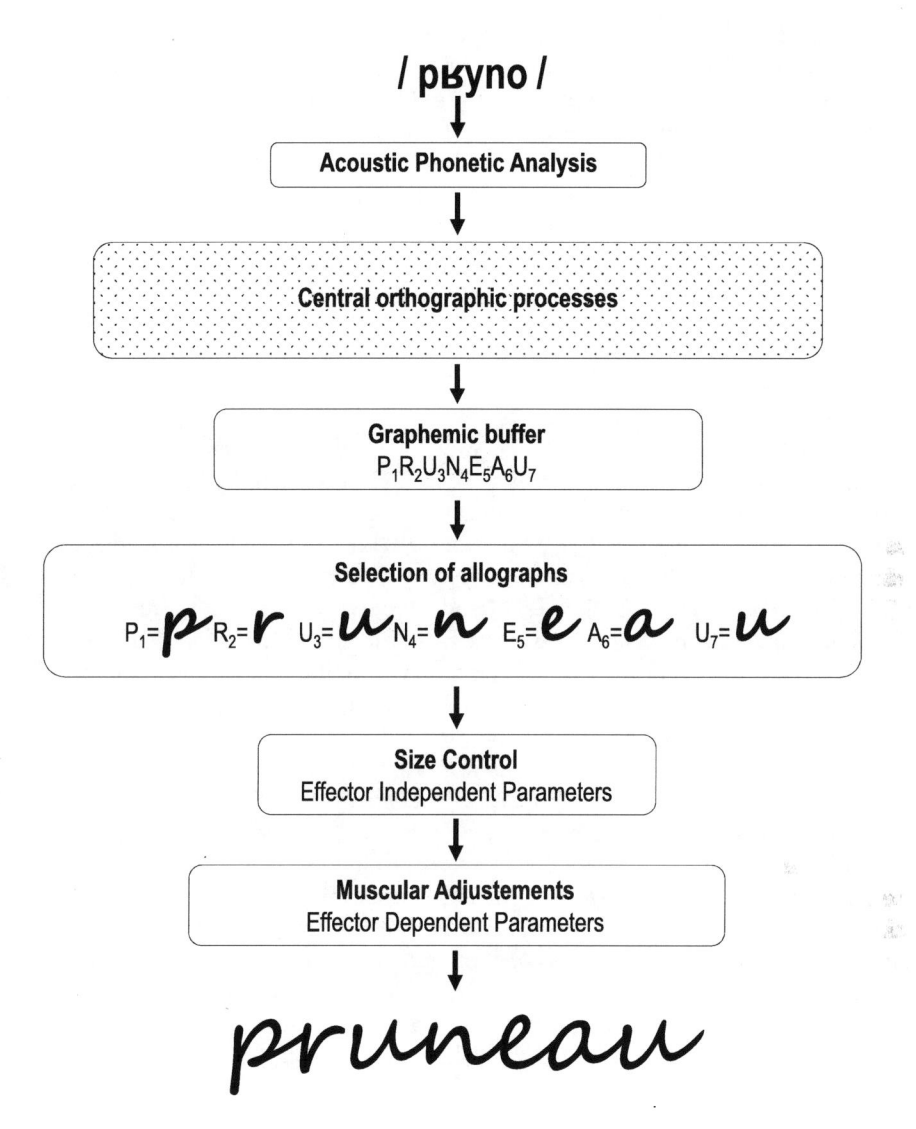

Figure 8.2 Classic motor conception of word production (peripheral processing). Example for the French word PRUNEAU (prune, /pʀyno/).

that produces the trace on the paper. This phase is obviously *effector dependent*, since the calculations apply to the specific muscular groups that execute the writing movement.

An important point of this conception of graphomotor production is that the writing movements result from a series of hierarchical processes that concern different aspects of letter production. The processes are active simultaneously, but the higher–level processing modules (e.g., allographs) are always ahead of the lower-level processing modules (e.g., strokes; Van der Plaats & van Galen, 1990). This is crucial for the articulation of continuous, fast, and smooth handwriting because it implies the anticipatory processing of information on how to produce the forthcoming motor sequences (Keele et al., 1990). Experimental data revealed that while writing a letter we simultaneously process information on the local graphomotor parameters that constrain the movements to produce the following letter (see Boë et al., 1991; Orliaguet & Boë, 1990; Orliaguet et al., 1997 for data on adults; and Kandel & Perret, 2015b for a developmental study).

Although it is common sense that all the processing levels are necessary to write a word, most researchers examined the processes either from *central* or *peripheral* points of view as if they were independent from one another. The former investigated orthographic processing, with experimental methods and concepts from psycholinguistics. They were also strongly influenced by neuropsychological case studies on central dysgraphia. The latter focused exclusively on motor processing, with experimental data and theoretical frameworks of the motor control field (Schmidt & Lee, 2013). Neuropsychological studies on peripheral dysgraphia cases also played a major role in the elaboration of handwriting modeling. As Figures 8.1 and 8.2 show, the graphemic buffer stores the information on identity and order of the letter components of the word resulting from spelling retrieval. This is the input to the motor processing stage. Both conceptions of writing consider the graphemic buffer as the connection point between central and peripheral processing, with orthographic processes concluding before movement initiation. They do not specify how orthographic and motor processes communicate or whether they interact.

Most neuroimaging studies of writing are in agreement with the sequential "spelling then movement" view of word production (Beeson et al., 2003). There are two meta-analyses on writing that clearly distinguish the brain regions that are involved in central and peripheral processing (Planton et al., 2013; Purcell et al., 2011). Orthographic processing involves the left fusiform gyrus, which plays a determinant role in the storage of word forms in an orthographic long-term memory. It is also involved in the access to orthographic representations (Nakamura et al., 2000; Rapp et al., 2016; Ueki et al., 2006). Spelling retrieval processes have also been associated to the left inferior frontal gyrus, in the pars opercularis, but the reasons for its activation still need to be examined in more detail (Baxter & Warrington, 1986; Henry et al., 2007; Roeltgen, 2003). Neuroimaging research on the motor aspects of writing focused on Exner's area which is located in the left superior frontal gyrus (Exner, 1881; Roux et al. (2009). Lesions in this area produce apraxic agraphia (Anderson et al., 1990; De Smet et al., 2011; Hodges, 1991; Magrassi et al., 2010; Sakurai et al., 2007). This led to the idea that this region, which extends to the precentral gyrus, is responsible of the instantiation of motor commands for producing letters (Longcamp et al., 2003; Longcamp et al., 2014; Rapp & Dufor, 2011; Roux et al., 2009; Sugihara et al., 2006). The representation of the letter trajectories seems to be linked to the left superior parietal lobule (Menon & Desmond, 2001; Seitz et al., 1997). These regions, as well as the right cerebellum, specifically respond to writing movements and not to other kinds of movements (Planton et al., 2017).

An attempt to integrate the central and peripheral components of writing was presented by van Galen (1991). He presented a model in which word writing results from a hierarchical architecture of processing modules that function in parallel (Van Galen et al., 1986; Van Galen et al., 1989). Each module receives input from a higher-level temporary working memory system or buffer and uses this information to process a specific processing unit. The latter vary in nature and size: ideas, concepts, phrases, words, graphemes, allographs, and strokes. Van Galen's model includes central aspects that consider linguistic processing, such as the implication of semantic, syntax and spelling processing. These higher-level processing modules were taken from Levelt's (1989) speech production model because they are thought to be common to all linguistic movements. Handwriting differs from speech at the spelling level, so Van Galen proposed an independent spelling module for orthographic processing. The model proposes a one-route orthographic module but does not specify the processes that lead to spelling retrieval and refers to previous neuropsychological studies for descriptions on this issue (e.g., Ellis, 1982; Humphreys & Evett, 1985; Margolin, 1984). Its output feeds the peripheral, motor components of letter writing, via abstract letter information that is stored in what he called the "orthographic buffer".

The orthographic buffer is the equivalent of the graphemic buffer presented in Figures 8.1 and 8.2. It functions as a temporary storage device that keeps the information on the letter order and identity of the word. This is the input to the selection of allographs module. Please note that there are some terminology differences between the "spelling" and "motor" studies. In the figures, I used the terms that I considered as most appropriate. The most salient terminology discrepancy is the concept of *graphemes*. The spelling studies use the term *grapheme* to indicate the graphic representation of a phoneme. According to Tainturier and Rapp (2004) for instance, phoneme /f/ can be represented by grapheme PH. For the motor control studies (e.g., Van Galen, 1991), a *grapheme* refers to the representation of a letter: P and H are two different graphemes, which can be represented by allographs P, p, P, p and H, h, H, h, respectively.

Van Galen (1991) described in detail the different peripheral motor processing stages that follow the spelling module: selection of allographs, size control and muscular adjustment. They are presented in Figure 8.2 with a slightly different terminology but they refer to the same kind of processes. It is also noteworthy that Van Galen's model makes a clear distinction between the central and peripheral components of handwriting. The outcome of the spelling module is an abstract letter string that is stored in the orthographic buffer and is the input to the allograph module. At this level, the system determines which allograph will represent each letter in the word. Then, the corresponding motor programs will be activated. The letters unfold sequentially in the form of allographs, with information on their identity and order. The following step determines the global parameters for the control of movement force, letter size, and slant, as well as information about execution speed (Pick & Teulings, 1983; Van Galen & Teulings, 1983). This information will feed the motor commands that regulate muscle contraction. The outcome specifies the synergies of the agonist and antagonist muscular forces that produce the tracing movements. This processing level involves the control of local parameters.

In summary, the sequential mechanism underlying central and peripheral perspectives, as well as Van Galen's (1991) model, establishes that spelling retrieval is over before we start to write. The spelling of the whole word is the input to the graphemic buffer, which keeps the word to be written as a string of letter components with specifications on letter identity and order (Caramazza et al., 1987; Teulings et al., 1983; Van Galen et al., 1989; Van Galen, 1991). This leads to specific predictions that were tested experimentally with digitizer data. For instance, to write the words THOUGH (/ðoʊ/) and THOUGHT (/θɔːt/), the graphemic buffer temporarily stores the linear sequences $T_1H_2O_3U_4G_5H_6$ and $T_1H_2O_3U_4G_5H_6T_7$, respectively. Since the words share the representation of the first six letters $T_1H_2O_3U_4G_5H_6$, the movements to trace the corresponding six allographs should be identical, despite the phonemic discrepancies between the two words. In addition, the dual-route approaches predict that lexical processing generates $T_1H_2O_3U_4G_5H_6$ and sub-lexical processing $T_1H_2O_3W_4$ (as in THROW /ðroʊ/). The incongruency of these outcomes results in a supplementary cognitive load. The system solves the conflict before feeding the correct spelling information into the graphemic buffer. In this view, the resolution of the conflict is done before starting to write. This generates a latency increase before starting to write the first letter. Several studies analyzing kinematic data of letter production revealed however that these predictions can be challenged by a more interactive dynamics of orthographic and motor processing (e.g., Bloemsaat et al., 2003; Delattre et al., 2006; Lambert et al, 2011; Orliaguet & Boë 1993; Zesiger et al., 1993, for typing). They suggest that the orthographic specificities of the words are still being processed during the graphomotor production of the allographs. Therefore, the independence of central and peripheral processing is not as clear at the functional level as the traditional studies claimed.

Spelling processes modulate motor processes during word production

A series of experimental studies conducted by Kandel and colleagues combined a fine-grained psycholinguistic methodology with precise digitizer data on stroke production. The kinematic data were collected with different kinds of tasks: written picture naming, copying, and writing-to-dictation. This research provides empirical evidence indicating that orthographic and motor processing are not sequential and independent as the traditional spelling and motor research stated. Roux et al. (2013) compared the timing of movement production to trace the same letters that differed in the phonological information they convey in words. For example, MON in the French words MONTAGNE (mountain, /mɔ̃taɲ/) and MONSIEUR (sir, /møsjø/) diverge in the phonemes they represent (I underline the letters that are subject to conflict). The most frequent sound-letter mappings to spell the word /mɔ̃taɲ/ lead to /m/ = M, /ɔ̃/ = ON, /t/ = T, /a/ = A, /ɲ/ = GN. In /møsjø/ the application of these phono-graphemic transcription rules results in an incorrect letter string like MEUSSIEUX or other letter combinations but never a MON onset; the most plausible one should be MEU, like in the word MEUBLÉ (furnished, /møble/). For this reason, MONTAGNE is considered an orthographically *regular* word whereas MONSIEUR is an orthographically *irregular* word (also called *inconsistent* or *exception* words by some researchers; see Bonin et al., 2008; Planton, 2014; Soum, 1997 for quantitative accounts of French phoneme-to-grapheme correspondence frequencies).

When measuring with a digitizer the duration of each stroke in each of the initial letters, the data revealed that movement time in words like MONSIEUR was longer than in MONTAGNE. The longer stroke duration in MONSIEUR arises from the processing of the orthographic discrepancy between the outcomes of the lexical MONSIEUR) and sub-lexical routes (MEUSSIEUX). These results provide evidence that the spelling mismatch is still being processed after movement initiation and while tracing the initial letters. Thus, letter production does not merely depend on the tracing of a specific allograph shape but also on the way the orthographic system encodes the phonology of the letters it represents.

The position of the sound–letter conflict within the word affects the way in which phonology regulates the timing of letter production (Palmis et al., 2019; Roux et al., 2013). In the word /kʁonik/ (chronical, CHRONIQUE) there is an orthographic irregularity at the onset of the word because /k/ = CH instead of C; the most frequent transcription of CH is /ʃ/. This discrepancy will only affect the movement time of the first allographs, when compared to an orthographically regular word (e.g., CHAPITRE, chapter, /ʃapitʁ/). When the mismatch concerns the final letters of the word as in /ʁespe/ (respect, RESPECT) the stroke durations are longer than in regular words from the onset and throughout all the letters preceding the location of the sound–letter incongruency (i.e., when producing the allographs of letters RESPE).

The sub-lexical phonological component of spelling processing while writing letters seems to be stronger than the lexical level. The movement time to produce MON in words (MONTAGNE) is longer than in pseudo-words (e.g., MONFOCHE, /mɔ̃foʃ/). In addition, word frequency affects motor production only during the first years of writing acquisition (Afonso et al., 2018; Kandel & Perret, 2015a). This kind of lexical processing tends to decrease at the end of elementary school and apparently disappears in adulthood. Also, the locus of lexical processing is limited to the initial letters of a word whereas sub-lexical processing may spread throughout the production of the whole word.

In sum, spelling processes continue to be active *while* we write and can last throughout the production of the whole word. The extent of the orthographic impact on the kinematics of movement production depends on the type of activation that is done at the central level. Palmis et al. (2019) confirm these experimental findings at the brain level by using an fMRI-compatible digitizer during the fMRI recordings. They observe that orthographic regularity as well as the effect of its position within the word, modulate the activation of the brain regions that are involved in both motor *and* orthographic processing: left superior parietal lobule, left superior frontal gyrus, right cerebellum for the areas responsible of motor production; and left inferior frontal gyrus, left fusiform gyrus for the regions known to be involved in orthographic processes. Therefore, the neural processing of the central and peripheral components of writing are active simultaneously. Orthographic processes modulate the timing of movement production during word writing.

A multi-level approach of orthographic processing in word production

The experimental and neuroimaging results presented in the previous paragraphs are at odds with the predictions of the classic spelling and motor studies for several reasons. First, they clearly show that central and peripheral processes are active simultaneously. Spelling processing occurs while the motor system is active tracing letters, so orthographic and motor processing cannot be independent. This way of functioning indicates that although there is a hierarchical processing order – from higher to lower levels – the spelling and motor production processes do not function sequentially. It seems as though central processing spreads into peripheral processing. Another important point about these experimental outcomes is that they suggest a different way of functioning for the working memory system. Finally, the data indicate that the production of a given letter does not merely depend on the shape of its allograph – and its specifications for stroke order and direction – but also on the way we encoded it orthographically.

I propose an approach of word writing in which central and peripheral processes are active simultaneously. I called it the APOMI model of word writing: Anticipatory Processing of Orthographic and Motor Information. This perspective attempts to describe *how* and *when* the top-down spelling processes interact with motor production processes. It is an incomplete model that intends to account for the movement production data collected up-to-date with digitizers. I integrate the traditional spelling and motor studies into a more dynamic view of word writing. I am aware that further research complemented by computational approaches is needed to clearly specify the predictions on the timing of spelling and motor processes. The idea underlying this conception is that the tracing of each letter in a word results from top-down multiple orthographic and motor activations.

Orthographic processing involves lexical and sub-lexical routes. However, they do not function exactly as the traditional spelling studies postulated. To understand the rationale underlying my conception of lexical processing, I refer the reader to a series of neuropsychological case studies suggesting a multi-level conception of orthographic representations (Caramazza, 1997; McCloskey et al., 1994). The data on the spelling errors of Italian- and English-speaking dysgraphic patients indicate that orthographic representations are complex structures that code the morphological components of the word (Baddecker et al., 1990), syllable structure (Caramazza & Miceli, 1990) and even graphemic information on how letters represent phonology (Tainturier & Rapp, 2004).

According to this multi-dimensional conception of orthographic representations, the French word PRUNEAU (prune, /pʁyno/) for example, is represented as $PRUN_1EAU_2$ at the morphological level where $1 = root$ and $2 = suffix$; PRU_1NEAU_2 at the syllable level where $1 = syllable 1$ and $2 = syllable 2$; and $P_1R_2U_3N_4EAU_5$ at the graphemic level where 1, 2, 3, and 4 = are one-letter simple graphemes and 5 = complex grapheme EAU (i.e., more than one letter represents the phoneme). The classic spelling and motor perspectives stipulated that once orthographic processing is concluded, the retrieved letter string is stored temporarily in a working memory buffer so that the motor system can start the processes involved in movement execution. The information in the graphemic buffer is an abstract linear sequence of letters that codes letter identity and order. Hence, the graphemic buffer stores $P_1R_2U_3N_4E_5A_6U_7$ and this linear letter string is then "unpacked" in a sequential manner –letter by letter – for motor production (cf. Tainturier & Rapp, 2004, p. 124).

As mentioned in previous paragraphs, digitizer data on word production revealed that orthographic processes spread onto motor production. Furthermore, morphological structure (Kandel et al., 2008, 2012; Quemart & Lambert, 2019), syllable segmentation (Álvarez et al., 2009; Kandel et al., 2006, 2011) and graphemic processing (Afonso et al., 2015; Kandel & Spinelli, 2010; Spinelli et al., 2012) modulate movement duration and fluency during letter production. In other words, motor processing is non-linear and is also constrained by linguistic structure. The impact of morpheme and syllable structures in written word production was also examined in experimental studies in German (Weingarten et al., 2004). The approach I propose therefore points to a more complex architecture that integrates the multi-dimensional aspects of orthographic representations in the lexical route (Figure 8.3).

This multi-level conception of word production should facilitate working memory storage. It is well established that the human cognitive system decreases processing loads by grouping small units of information into bigger chunks that convey meaning (Jenkins & Russel, 1952). Therefore, it should be easier to store and retrieve a long letter string such as PRUNEAU if we have two morpheme units in working memory, namely the root PRUN and suffix EAU, than a mere letter string of seven letters. On the basis of this idea, the APOMI model of word writing proposes a different way of functioning for

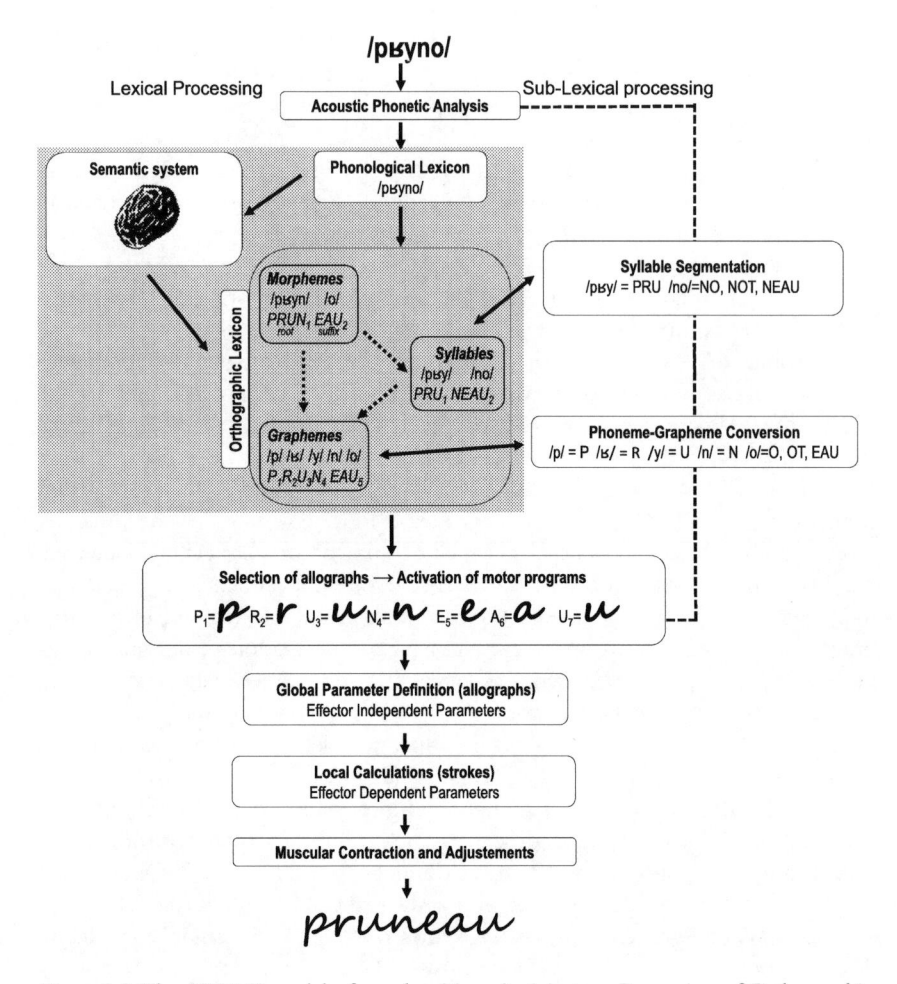

Figure 8.3 The APOMI model of word writing: Anticipatory Processing of Orthographic and Motor Information. Example for the French word PRUNEAU (prune, /pʁyno/).

the working memory system. The spelling of the whole word is not stored in a "graphemic buffer" before peripheral processes are ready to begin (Houghton & Zorzi, 2003; Houghton et al., 1994; Rapp & Kong, 2002). There is a continuous top-down information flow. Once a letter chunk like PRUN is active, it constitutes the input to the selection of allographs processing level directly. The allographs for letters PRUN will be selected and the corresponding motor programs activated. This may take place before allographs for the suffix EAU are selected. This mechanism should be particularly useful to write long words because it optimizes the coding of the spelling in a coherent semantic fashion, facilitates working memory storage and mediates the motor programming of the letter chunks PRUN and EAU. In the same perspective, the letters of a word should be grouped together as processing units according to a phonologically coherent fashion, resulting in syllable letter clusters (PRU and NEAU) and grapheme letter clusters (P, R, U, N, and EAU).

The functioning of the sub-lexical route on the right of Figure 8.3 also processes letter clusters and feeds them as inputs to the motor processing levels. Lexical and sub-lexical routes are active in parallel, as the traditional approaches described. Since this route relies on phonological processing, there is an initial segmentation of the phoneme string into syllable chunks. For example, the pseudo-word /pʁylo/ is segmented /pʁy/$_1$ /lo/$_2$, which leads to syllable chunks PRU$_1$ and LEAU$_2$. This accounts for digitizer data on pseudo-word writing (Kandel et al., 2006). At a lower level, and as in the traditional spelling studies, the processing consists of the application of phoneme–grapheme transcription rules. The letter chunks resulting from this process are a series of simple and complex graphemes, as the ones of the grapheme level of the orthographic lexicon described above. Thus, the pseudo-word PRULEAU should most likely generate a P$_1$R$_2$U$_3$L$_4$EAU$_5$ graphemic representation. Indeed, phoneme /o/ in word-final position is most frequently transcribed as EAU.

The APOMI multi-dimensional framework also includes an aspect of Van Galen's (1991) model, that is very useful to understand how the orthographic components of words impact motor processing. Parallel processing implies that all the levels can be active simultaneously. The higher-order processing levels are always ahead during the execution of a movement than the lower lower-order processing levels. This characteristic allows for anticipatory processing, which is a core concept of the APOMI model. Anticipation has been investigated in the framework of the motor aspects of letter production (e.g., Kandel & Perret, 2015b; Orliaguet & Boë, 1993; Orliaguet et al., 1997; Teulings et al., 1983; Van Galen et al., 1989) but to our knowledge, was not considered in the context of orthographic processing theories in neuropsychology or psycholinguistics.

An anticipatory conception of orthographic processing in word production

Kinematic data collected with digitizers revealed that morphological, syllabic, and graphemic processing in the orthographic lexicon are active simultaneously and function according to a hierarchical and parallel fashion. There is a continuous top-down information flow from orthographic to motor processing levels. This way of functioning generates a multiple anticipation of information on the lower processing levels. Information on the forthcoming letters of the word affect in turn, the programming of the movements that trace each letter in the letter string.

The experimental studies measuring movement duration indicated that the morphological, syllabic, and graphemic structures of the word affect motor programming. They activate information on the forthcoming letters and thus modulate the timing of motor programming. A part of this processing takes place before starting to execute the movements to trace the letters but another important part is done online, during the actual tracing of the letters. There is a continuous top-down information flow that allows for the anticipation of information on other aspects of the writing process. This impacts the timing of letter production. Note that the APOMI model does not consider bottom-up processing and feedback. This does not mean it considers that the system functions in a strict top-down fashion. There is of course some kind of feedback and bottom-up information flow from the peripheral to the central levels (e.g., Van Galen et al., 1989). The reason why APOMI does not mention them is because there is not enough information to describe them and make predictions in the context of the present model. Figure 8.4 provides a schematic view of the timing of morphological, syllabic, and graphemic processing for the French word PRUNEAU.

Before starting to write, morphological processing at the lexical level results in a segmentation of the root $PRUN_1$ and suffix EAU_2 (Kandel et al., 2008, 2012; Quémart & Lambert, 2019). Phonological processes are active simultaneously so that the information on the letters in the root co-exists with the information on the letters in syllable PRU_1 (Kandel et al., 2006, 2009, 2011; Sausset et al., 2012). In addition, throughout the execution of these initial letters, the system also anticipates the programming of the letters that occur later on in the word. The programming of the suffix is done in parallel to the production of the letters of the first syllable and the morpheme boundary. In other words, while executing the movements to produce UN, the system is also processing information on the upcoming letters EAU. This timing pattern applies to suffixed words in derivational morphology. Prefixed words seem to be processed differently because the prefix is activated before

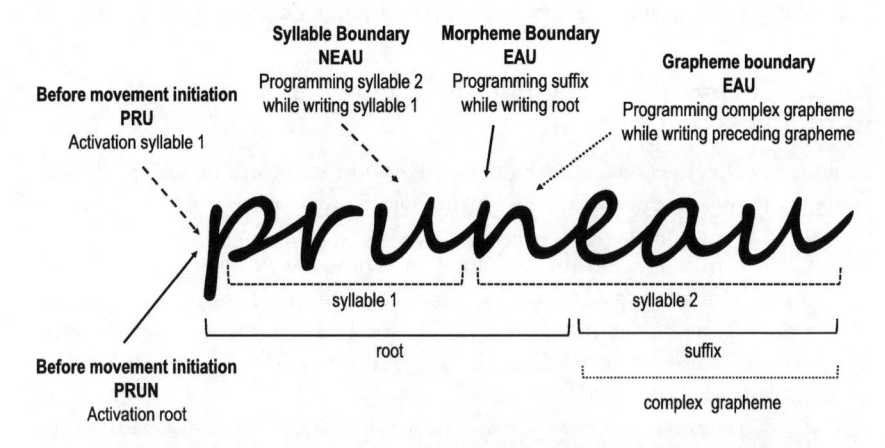

Figure 8.4 Schematic illustration of the timing of morphological, syllabic, and complex graphemic processing for the word PRUNEAU.

starting to write, but the experimental data is not sufficient to describe a specific way of functioning (Kandel et al., 2012).

The syllabic level appears to regulate letter production in a similar anticipatory manner (Kandel et al., 2009, 2006; Lambert et al., 2008). The empirical evidence indicates that most of the orthographic and motor programming of the initial syllable is done before starting to write. While writing the letters around the syllable boundary, the system anticipates the production of the second syllable. Thus, to write PRUNEAU, we activate chunk PRU before starting to write. While writing RU, the system activates NEAU so that the letters at the end of the word can be programmed beforehand. In other words, the allographs for NEAU are selected, their corresponding motor programs are activated. This in turn generates the activation of the motor peripheral processes (effector-independent and effector-dependent) that will lead to the muscular contractions to produce the hand movements that trace the letters. We are permanently programming information of what comes next. This dynamics of letter production was observed in adults and also regulates the acquisition of word writing skills (Kandel & Perret, 2015a). Although most of the empirical data were collected in French, there is evidence that this syllable-oriented programming mechanism operates in other languages, especially if they are syllable-timed like Spanish (Álvarez et al., 2009; Kandel et al., 2006). The phonological information of orthographic representations regulates word production according to syllable structure but also by the way letters represent speech sounds.

In sum, when producing the initial letters of PRUNEAU, the activated information will be the input to lower-level processing. During the execution of the allograph for letter P, it is likely that the system is selecting the allograph for N (anticipation of the end of the root). Since it is the end of the root, morphological processing will signal the anticipation of the production of the suffix EAU_2. Simultaneously, the system also anticipates the effector-independent processes to produce the allograph for U, as well as the effector-dependent parameters to produce the allograph for letter R. Probably, when producing the allograph for R, the system will also select the allograph for N because it is the beginning of the second syllable $NEAU_2$. The timing of the production of the allographs that occur at morpheme and syllable boundaries will also be affected by the motor lower-level processing of the word-final letters. The exact dynamics cannot be described in detail because we do not have enough information on the timing of every processing level. A computational model could be very useful but it does not exist yet.

It is well established that phoneme–grapheme transcription rules are less consistent than the grapheme-phoneme rules involved in reading processes (see Ziegler et al., 1996 for French). These rules are also more complex in languages with deep orthographies than shallow ones (Seymour et al., 2003). In French, for example, there are at least 34 complex graphemes; that is, more than one letter represents a phoneme (Catach, 1995). In addition, complex graphemes are letter chunks that differ in complexity. For instance, phoneme /o/ in word-final position PRUNEAU is most frequently transcribed as EAU but could be written O (like in MOTO, motorcycle), OT (like in ESCA-RGOT, snail), or AUD (like in CRAPAUD, toad). A way to decrease this complexity is to map phonemes to graphemes rather than to letters directly. This renders sound-letter associations more straightforward. Kandel and Spinelli (2010) and Spinelli et al. (2012) conducted word writing experiments with digitizers indicating that grapheme-like chunks modulate the timing of the movements to trace the letters of a word. They found, as with morphemes and syllables, that we tend to anticipate the programming of complex graphemes as a letter chunk rather than a group of single letters (Weingarten, 2005 in for data in German).

The complexity of the grapheme mainly affects the timing of the letter that precedes it, so that the duration of the movement for tracing letter L in the French word PLAINTE (complaint, /plɛ̃t/ where AIN = /ɛ̃/) is longer than in CLAVIER (keyboard, /klavje/ where A = /a/). When writing PLAINTE, keeping in working memory the chunk AIN – instead of A only – while tracing the L facilitates the production of the letters of the end of the word. It is noteworthy that this grapheme-by-grapheme programming strategy is also observed in languages with shallow orthographies like Spanish, indicating that it can render the letter-writing processes more efficient even in languages that are not orthographically complex (Afonso & Álvarez, 2011; Afonso et al., 2015).

Digitizer data also point to other orthographic specificities that affect movement programming in word production. One of them is letter doubling, which is common in many languages. There is neuropsychological evidence on dysgraphic patients revealing that double letters are specifically coded in the orthographic representation of words (Tainturier & Caramazza, 1996). Kandel et al. (2013) observed that letter doubling affects the timing for producing letters. For example, movement duration differs when tracing letters DIS in the words DISSIPATE and DISGRACE. The writing system codes the presence of the double letters before movement initiation. It anticipates letter doubling and remains active while producing the movements that trace the two letters that precede the doublet. The same kind of timing pattern occurs in Italian – e.g., DISSIPARE vs. DISGRAZIA – which are Italian–English cognates (Kandel et al., 2017). Although DIS is pronounced the same way /dis/ in both words, it should be pointed out that in Italian the specific coding of letter quantity could be accounted for by the fact that certain phonemes are represented by complex graphemes that are double letters (e.g., /kaza/, house, CASA vs /kasa/, box, CASSA; Esposito & Di Benedetto, 1999). Letter doubling also affects the dynamics of word writing in French: the production of letters LIS is longer in LISSER (to smooth, /lise/) than LISTER (to list, /liste/; Kandel et al., 2014). The dynamics of letter production in word writing can also be affected by purely orthographic information such as the frequency of letter co-occurrence (Kandel et al., 2011). There is no doubt that tracing letters in frequent bi-grams should be easier – that is, faster and smoother – than letters that we are not used to produce together. In this sense, complex graphemes and doublets should also be considered as frequent bigrams.

The sub-lexical route also operates in an anticipatory fashion. Kinematic data on pseudo-word writing revealed that we program the initial syllable of the pseudo-word before movement initiation. Then, while tracing the last letters of the first syllable, the writing system prepares the information required to produce the second syllable (Kandel et al., 2006). This syllabic segmentation is prior to a processing level where the phonemes are converted into letters by following pre-determined phono-graphological conversion rules. Again, the resulting grapheme letter chunks feed into the motor production processing levels. Since the information flow is continuous and tends to anticipate forthcoming information, it is likely that when having to write the pseudo-word /pʁylo/, we prepare the initial syllable before starting to write, so we activate /pʁy$_1$/ = PRU$_1$. The second syllable /lo$_2$/ is activated while writing RU. At this point, French sound-letter conversion rules stipulate that /lo$_2$/ is L plus transcriptions of phoneme /o/ in final word position (EAU as in PRUNEAU, prune; O as in MOTO, motorcycle; OT as in ESCARGOT, snail). Most of the programming of the grapheme representing phoneme /o/ is done during the tracing of letter L. Since the lexical and sub-lexical routes operate simultaneously, the outcomes of syllable and grapheme processing should be similar for orthographically regular words and discrepant for irregular words.

It is noteworthy that this view of word production questions the widespread idea of the existence of the graphemic buffer as a sort of interface between orthographic and motor processing. Word production results from a *continuous flow of top-down anticipatory information on letter chunks*. Writers program the first chunk of the word before starting to write and activate the second chunk *n* while tracing the letters of chunk *n-1*. If the word is mono-morphemic, then the letter string is only decomposed into syllable-like chunks. Before starting to write, the system activates the information on the letter chunk that composes the initial syllable. While tracing the last letters of this syllable and close to the syllable boundary, there is an activation of the second syllable so that the system gets information on which letters have to be produced. If the word is bi-morphemic and contains a suffix, the system activates the root and first syllable before movement initiation. This processing continues while producing the letters of the root and initial syllable. Simultaneously to the production of the last letters of the initial syllable and the beginning of the syllable boundary, the syllable level programs information on the letters of the second syllable. When tracing the letters of the root that are close to the morpheme boundary, the system activates the suffix so the system knows which letter chunk constitutes the end of the word. The letters that represent complex graphemes and are doubled are also chunked together and processed beforehand, before starting to write and during the production of the letters that precede them. This interactive and anticipatory way of conceiving word writing accounts for experimental movement production data collected with digitizers. It is an attempt to outline how spelling and motor processes communicate and interact during word writing.

Conclusion

AMOPI is a model of word writing that integrates spelling and motor processes in a single architecture. It consists of a hierarchical series of central and peripheral processing levels. Orthographic and motor processes are active simultaneously and generate a continuous flow of top-down information. High-level processes are always ahead of low-level processes because they anticipate information about the letters to be produced later in the word. Orthographic processes involve lexical and sub-lexical routes. The lexical system activates orthographic representations that code information on morphological, syllabic, and graphemic letter chunks. These letter clusters are the input to the motor processing levels. Sub-lexical processing also feeds syllable and grapheme letter chunks as input to the allograph level. This will activate the corresponding motor programs and initiate effector-independent and effector-dependent processes. The letter clusters are activated while producing the movements that trace the initial letters of the word. This model is an attempt to integrate digitizer data into the understanding of adult word writing. Word writing is conceived as a *global* spelling *and* motor production skill. It involves the extremely complex processing of orthography and movement control, so more specific information is definitely needed and should be a matter of future research.

References

Afonso, O., Alvarez C., & Kandel, S. (2015). Effects of Grapheme-to-Phoneme probability on writing durations. *Memory & Cognition, 43,* 579–592.

Afonso, O., & Álvarez, C. J., (2011). Phonological effects in handwriting production: Evidence from the implicit priming paradigm. *Journal of Experimental Psychology: Learning, Memory, and Cognition, 37*(6), 1474–1483.

Afonso, O., Suárez-Coalla, P. & Cuetos, F. (2015). Spelling impairments in Spanish dyslexic adults. *Frontiers in Psychology, 6,* 466.

Afonso, O., Suárez-Coalla, P., González-Martín, N., & Cuetos, F. (2018). The impact of word frequency on peripheral processes during handwriting: A matter of age. *The Quarterly Journal of Experimental Psychology, 71*(3), 695–703.

Álvarez, C. J., Cottrell, D., & Afonso, O. (2009). Writing dictated words and picture names: Syllabic boundaries affect execution in Spanish. *Applied Psycholinguistics, 30*(2), 205–223.

Anderson, S. W., Damasio, A. R., & Damasio, H. (1990). Troubled letters but not numbers: domain specific cognitive impairments following focal damage in frontal cortex. *Brain, 113,*749–766.

André, G., Kostrubiec, V., Buisson, J. C., Albaret, J. M. & Zanone, P. G. (2014). A parsimonious oscillatory model of handwriting. *Biological Cybernetics (Modeling), 108*(3), 321–336.

Baddecker, W., Hillis, A., & Caramazza, A. (1990). Lexical morphology and its role in the writing process: Evidence from a case of acquired dysgraphia. *Cognition, 35*, 205–224.

Baxter, D. M., & Warrington, E. K. (1986). Ideational agraphia: A single case study. *Journal of Neurology, Neurosurgery, and Psychiatry, 49*, 369–374.

Beeson, P. M., Rapcsak, S. Z., Plante, E., Chargualaf, J., Chung, A., Johnson, S. C., & Trouard, T. (2003). The neural substrates of writing: A functional magnetic resonance imaging study. *Aphasiology, 17*, 647–665.

Bloemsaat, J. G., Van Galen, G. P., & Meulenbroek, R. G. J. (2003). Lateralized effects of orthographical irregularity and auditory memory load on the kinematics of tran- scription typewriting. *Psychological Research, 67*(2), 123–133.

Boë, L. J., Orliaguet, J. P., & Belhaj, R. (1991). Effet de contexte inter-lettre sur le déroulement temporel des mouvements d'écriture: Similarités avec la parole. [Inter-letter context effect on the time course of written movements: Similarities with speech]. Proceedings of the *XIIth International Congress of Phonetic Sciences*. Aix-en-Provence, France, August 19–24, vol. 5, pp. 22–25.

Bonin, P., Collay, S., & Fayol, M. (2008). La consistance orthographique en production verbale écrite: une brève synthèse. *L'année Psychologique, 108*(3), 517–546.

Bonin, P., Peereman, R., & Fayol, M. (2001). Do phonological codes constrain the selection of orthographic codes in written picture naming? *Journal of Memory and Language, 45*, 688–720. https://doi.org/10.1006/jmla.2000.2786.

Bonin, P., Roux, J.-S., Barry, C., & Canell, L. (2012). Evidence for a limited-cascading account of written word naming. *Journal of Experimental Psychology: Learning, Memory, & Cognition, 38*(6), 1741–1758.

Buchwald, A., & Falconer, C. (2014). Cascading activation from lexical processing to letter-level processing in written word production. *Cognitive Neuropsychology, 31*, 606–621.

Caramazza, A. (1997). How many levels of processing are there in lexical access? *Cognitive Neuropsychology, 14*, 177–208.

Caramazza, A., & Miceli, G. (1989). Orthographic structure, the graphemic buffer and the spelling process. In C. von Euler (Ed.), *Brain and reading*. Macmillan/Wenner-Gren International Symposium Series (pp. 257–268). Basingstoke, UK: Macmillan.

Caramazza, A., & Miceli, G. (1990). The structure of graphemic representations. *Cognition, 37*, 243–297.

Caramazza, A., Miceli, G., Villa, G., & Romani, C. (1987). The role of the graphemic buffer in spelling: Evidence from a case of acquired dysgraphia. *Cognition, 26*, 59–85.

Catach, N. (1995). *L'orthographe française*. Paris: Nathan.

Costa, V., Fischer-Baum, S., Capasso, R., Miceli, G., & Rapp, B. (2011). Temporal stability and representational distinctiveness: Key functions of ortho- graphic working memory. *Cognitive Neuropsychology, 28*, 338–362.

Damian, M. F., Dorjee, D., & Stadthagen-Gonzalez, H. (2011). Long-term repetition priming in spoken and written word production: Evidence for a contribution of phonology to handwriting. *Journal of Experimental Psychology: Learning, Memory & Cognition, 37*, 813–826.

Damian, M. F., & Stadthagen-Gonzalez, H. (2009). Advance planning of form properties in the written production of single and multiple words. *Language and Cognitive Processes, 24*, 555–579.

Delattre, M., Bonin, P., & Barry, C. (2006). Written spelling to dictation: Sound-to-spelling regularity affects both writing latencies and durations. *Journal of Experimental Psychology: Learning, Memory and Cognition, 32*(6), 1330–1340.

De Smet, H. J., Engelborghs, S., Paquier, P. F., De Deyn, P. P., & Mariën, P. (2011) Cerebellar induced apraxic agraphia: A review and three new cases. *Brain and Cognition*, 76(3), 424–434.

Ellis, A. W. (1982). Spelling and writing (and reading and speaking). In A. W. Ellis (Ed.), *Normality and pathology in cognitive functions* (pp. 113–146). London: Academic Press.

Ellis, A. W. (1988). Spelling and writing. Dans A.W. Ellis & A.W. Young (dir.), *Human cognitive neuropsychology*. Hove, UK: Lawrence Erlbaum Associates Ltd.

Esposito, A., & Di Benedetto, M. G. (1999). Acoustical and perceptual study of gemination in Italian stops. *Journal of the Acoustical Society of America*, 106(4), 2051–2062.

Exner S. (1881). *Untersuchungen über die Localisation der Functionen in der Grosshirnrinde des Menschen* (Wilhelm Braumüller, Wien).

Fischer-Baum, S., McCloskey, M. & Rapp, B. (2010). The representation of grapheme position: Evidence from acquired dysgraphia. *Cognition*, 115, 466–490.

Glasspool, D. W. & Houghton, G. (2005). Serial order and consonant-vowel structure in a graphemic output buffer model. *Brain and Language*, 94, 304–330.

Henry, M. L., Beeson,P. M., Stark, A. J., & Rapcsak, S. Z. (2007). The role of left perisylvian cortical regions in spelling. *Brain and Language*, 100(1), 44–52.

Hodges, J. R. (1991). Pure apraxic agraphia with recovery after drainage of a left frontal cyst. *Cortex*, 27, 469–473.

Houghton, G., Glasspool, W., & Shallice, T. (1994). Spelling and serial recall: Insights from a competitive queuing model. In G. D. A. Brown, & N. C. Ellis (Eds.), *Handbook of spelling: Theory, process and intervention*. New York: John Wiley and Sons Ltd.

Houghton, G. & Zorzi, M. (2003). Normal and impaired spelling in a connectionist dual-route architecture. *Cognitive Neuropsychology*, 20, 115–162.

Humphreys, G. W., & Evett, L. J. (1985). Are there independent lexical and nonlexical routes in word processing? An evaluation of the dual-route theory of reading. *Behavioral and Brain Sciences*, 8(4), 689–740.

Jenkins, J. J., & Russel, W. A. (1952). Associative clustering during recall. *Journal of Abnormal and Social Psychology*, 47, 818–821

Kandel, S., Alvarez C., & Vallée, N. (2008). Morphemes also serve as processing units in handwriting production. In M. Baciu (Ed.), *Neuropsychology and Cognition of Language Behavioural, Neuropsychological and Neuroimaging Studies of Spoken and Written Language* (pp. 87–100). Kerala, India: Research Signpost.

Kandel, S., Álvarez C., & Vallée, N. (2006). Syllables as processing units in handwriting production. *Journal of Experimental Psychology: Human Perception and Performance*, 32(1), 18–31.

Kandel, S., Herault, L., Grosjacques, G., Lambert, E., & Fayol, M. (2009). Orthographic vs. phonologic syllables in handwriting production. *Cognition*, 110(3), 440–444.

Kandel, S., Peereman, R., & Ghimenton, A. (2014). How do we code the letters of a word when we have to write it? Investigating double letter representation in French. *Acta Psychologica*, 148, 56–62.

Kandel, S., Peereman, R., & Ghimenton, A. (2013). Further evidence for the interaction between central and peripheral processes: the impact of double in writing English words. *Frontiers in Psychology (Research Topic "Writing words: From brain to hand(s)" – Section Cognitive Science)*, 4, 729.

Kandel, S., Peereman, R., Ghimenton, A., & Perret, C. (2017). Letter coding affects movement production in word writing: An English-Italian cross-linguistic study. *Reading & Writing: An Interdisciplinary Journal*, 34(3-4), 219–251. 10.1007/s11145-017-9756-y.

Kandel, S., Peereman, R., Grosjacques, G., & Fayol, M. (2011). For a psycholinguistic model of handwriting production: Testing the syllable-bigram controversy. *Journal of Experimental Psychology: Human Perception and Performance, 37*(4), 1310–1322.

Kandel, S., & Perret, C. (2015a). How does the interaction between spelling and motor processes build up during writing acquisition? *Cognition, 136,* 325–336.

Kandel, S., & Perret, C. (2015b). How do movements to produce letters become automatic during writing acquisition? Investigating the development of motor anticipation. *International Journal of Behavioral Development, 32*(9), 113–120.

Kandel, S., & Spinelli, E. (2010). Processing complex graphemes in handwriting production. *Memory & Cognition, 38*(6), 762–770.

Kandel, S., Spinelli, E., Tremblay, A., Guerassimovitch, H., & Alvarez, C. (2012). Processing prefixes and suffixes in handwriting production. *Acta Psychologica, 140,* 187–195.

Keele S. W., Cohen, A. & Ivry, R. (1990). Motor programs: Concepts and issues. In M. Jeannerod (Ed.), *Attention and performance XIII: Motor representation and control* (pp.77–111). Hillsdale, NJ: Lawrence Erlbaum Associates

Lambert, E., Alamargot, D., Larocque, D., & Caporossi, G. (2011). Dynamics of the spelling process during a copy task: Effects of regularity and frequency. *Canadian Journal of Experimental Psychology, 65,* 141–150.

Lambert, E., Kandel, S., Fayol, M., & Espéret, E. (2008). The effect of the number of syllables on handwriting production. *Reading and Writing, 21*(9), 859–883.

Levelt, W. J. M. (1989). *Speaking: From intention to articulation.* Cambridge, MA: The MIT Press.

Longcamp, M., Anton, J.-L., Roth, M., & Velay, J.-L. (2003). Visual presentation of single letters activates a premotor area involved in writing. *NeuroImage, 19*(4), 1492–1500.

Longcamp, M., Lagarrigue, A., Nazarian, B., Roth, M., Anton, J.-L., Alario, F.-X., & Velay, J.-L. (2014). Functional specificity in the motor system: Evidence from coupled fMRI and kinematic recordings during letter and digit writing. *Human Brain Mapping, 35*(12), 6077–6087.

Maarse., F. J. (1987). *The study of handwriting movement: Peripheral models and signal processing techniques.* Lisse: Swets & Zeitlinger.

Magrassi, L., Bongetta, D., Bianchini, S., Berardesca, M., & Arienta, C. (2010). Central and peripheral components of writing critically depend on a defined area of the dominant superior parietal gyrus. *Brain Reseach, 1346,* 145–154.

Margolin, D. I. (1984). The neuropsychology of writing and spelling: semantic, phonological, motor, and perceptual processes. *The Quarterly Journal of Experimental Psychology A, Human Experimental Psychology, 36*(3), 459–489.

Margolin, D. I., & Goodman-Schulman, R. (1992). Oral and written spelling impairments. In D. I. Margolin (Ed.), *Cognitive neuropsychology in clinical practice* (pp. 263–297). Oxford: Oxford University Press.

McCloskey, M., Badecker, W., Goodman-Schulman, R. A., & Aliminosa, D. (1994). The structure of graphemic representations in spelling: Evidence from a case of acquired dysgraphia. *Cognitive Neuropsychology, 11,* 341–392.

Menon, V., & Desmond, J. E. (2001). Left superior parietal cortex involvement in writing: integrating fMRI with lesion evidence. Brain Research. *Cognitive Brain Research, 12*(2), 337–340.

Miceli, G., & Capasso, R. (2006). Spelling and dysgraphia. *Cognitive Neuropsychology, 23* (1), 110–134.

Nakamura, K., Honda, M., Okada, T., Hanakawa T., Toma, K., Fukuyama, H., Konishi, J., & Shibasaki, H. (2000). Participation of the left posterior inferior temporal cortex in writing and mental recall of kanji orthography: A functional MRI study. *Brain*, *123*(5), 954–967.

Orliaguet, J.-P., & Boë, L.-J. (1993). The role of linguistics in the speed of handwriting movements: Effects of spelling uncertainty. *Acta Psychologica*, *82*(1), 103–113

Orliaguet J.-P., & Boë L.-J. (1990). Régulation temporelle des mouvements d'écriture en fonction des contraintes spatiales. [Temporal regulation of handwriting movements as a function of spatial constraints]. In V. Nougier, & J. P. Blanchi (Eds.), *Pratiques sportives et modélisation du geste* [Sport practice and gestural modelling] (pp. 163–177). Grenoble: Collection Grenoble Sciences.

Orliaguet, J.-P., Kandel, S., & Boe, L. J. (1997). Visual perception of motor anticipation in cursive handwriting: Influence of spatial and movement information on the prediction of forthcoming letters. *Perception*, *26*, 905–912.

Palmis, S., Velay, J.-L., Fabiani, E., Nazarian, B., Anton, J.-L., Habib, M., Kandel, S. & Longcamp, M. (2019). The impact of spelling regularity on handwriting production: A coupled fMRI and kinematics study. *Cortex*, *113*, 111–127.

Pick, H. L., & Teulings, H.-L. (1983). Geometric transformations of handwriting as a function of instruction and feedback. *Acta Psychologica*, *54*(1–3), 327–340

Planton, S. (2014). Processus centraux et périphériques en production écrite de mots: études comportementales, en neuroimagerie fonctionnelle et par stimulation magnétique transcrânienne. Unpublished Doctoral Dissertation, Université Toulouse 3 Paul Sabatier.

Planton S., Jucla M., Roux F. E., & Démonet J. F. (2013). The "handwriting brain". A meta-analysis of neuroimaging studies of motor versus orthographic processes. *Cortex*, *49*(10), 2772–2787.

Planton, S., Longcamp, M., Péran, P., Démonet, J.-F., & Jucla, M. (2017). How specialized are writing-specific brain regions? An fMRI study of writing, drawing and oral spelling. *Cortex*, *88*, 66–80.

Purcell, J. J., Turkeltaub, P. E., Eden, G. F., & Rapp, B. (2011). Examining the central and peripheral processes of written word production through a meta-analysis. *Frontiers in Psychology*, *2*, 239.

Qu, Q., Damian, M. F., Zhang, Q., &, Zhu, X. (2011). Phonology contributes to writing: Evidence from written production in nonalphabetic language. *Psychological Science*, *22*(9), 1107–1112.

Quémart, P., & Lambert, E. (2019). The influence of the morphological structure of words on the dynamics of handwriting in adults and fourth and sixth grade children. *Reading and Writing*, *32*(1), 175–195.

Rapp B., & Dufor O. (2011) The neurotopography of written word production: an fMRI investigation of the distribution of sensitivity to length and frequency. *Journal of Cognitive Neuroscience*, *23*(12), 4067–4081.

Rapp, B., Epstein, C., & Tainturier, M.-J. (2002). The integration of information across lexical and sublexical processes in spelling. *Cognitive Neuropsychology*, *19*, 1–29.

Rapp, B., & Kong, D. (2002). Revealing the component functions of the graphemic buffer. *Brain and Language*, *83*, 112–114.

Rapp, B., Purcell, J., Hillis, A. E., Capasso, R., & Miceli, G. (2016) Neural bases of orthographic longterm memory and working memory in dysgraphia. *Brain*, *139*(2), 588–604.

Roeltgen, D. P. (2003) Agraphia. *Clinical Neuropsychology* (pp 126–145). Oxford: Oxford University Press.

Roux, F.-E., Dufor, O., Giussani, C., Wamain, Y., Draper, L., Longcamp, M., & Démonet, J.-F. (2009). The graphemic/motor frontal area Exner's area revisited. *Annals of Neurology, 66*(4), 537–545.

Roux, J.-S., McKeeff, T. J., Grosjacques, G., Afonso, O., & Kandel, S. (2013). The interaction between central and peripheral processes in handwriting production. *Cognition, 127*(2), 235–241.

Sage, K., & Ellis, A. (2004). Lexical influences in graphemic buffer disorder. *Cognitive Neuropsychology, 21*, 381–400.

Sakurai, Y., Onuma, Y., Nakazawa, G., Ugawa, Y., Momose, T., Tsuji, S., & Mannen, T. (2007). Parietal dysgraphia: characterization of abnormal writing stroke sequences, character formation and character recall. *Behavioural Neurology, 18*(2), 99–114.

Sausset, S., Lambert, E., Olive, T., & Larocque, D. (2012). Processing of syllables during handwriting: Effects of graphomotor constraints. *Quarterly Journal of Experimental Psychology, 65*(10), 1872–1879.

Schmidt, R. A., & Lee, T. D. (2013). *Motor learning and performance: From principles to applications* (5th ed.). Champaign, IL: Human Kinetics.

Schmidt, R. A., & Wrisberg, C. A. (2004). *Motor learning and performance: A problem-based learning approach* (pp. 12–13). Campaign, IL: Human Kinetics.

Seitz, R. J., Canavan, A. G., Yáguez, L., Herzog, H., Tellmann, L., Knorr, U., … Hömberg, V. (1997). Representations of graphomotor trajectories in the human parietal cortex: evidence for controlled processing and automatic performance. *The European Journal of Neuroscience, 9*(2), 378–389.

Seymour, P., Aro, M., & Erskine, J. M. (2003) Foundation literacy acquisition in European orthographies. *British Journal of Psychology, 94*(2), 143–174.

Shallice, T. (1988). *From neuropsychology to mental structure.* Cambridge: Cambridge University Press.

Soum, C. (1997). L'apprentissage de l'ecriture contraintes orthographiques & contraintes phonologiques . (Doctoral dissertation, Toulouse 2). *Université de Toulouse* (Vol. 2).

Spinelli, E., Kandel, S., Guerassimovitch, H., & Ferrand, L. (2012). Graphemic cohesion effect in reading and writing complex graphemes. *Language and Cognitive Processes, 27*(5), 770–791.

Sugihara, G., Kaminaga, T., & Sugishita, M. (2006) Interindividual uniformity and variety of the "Writing center": a functional MRI study. *NeuroImage, 32*(4), 1837–1849.

Tainturier, M. J., & Caramazza, A. (1996). The status of double letters in graphemic representations. *Journal of Memory and Language, 36*(1), 53–73.

Tainturier, M. J., & Rapp, B. (2004). Complex graphemes as functional spelling units: Evidence from acquired dysgraphia. *Neurocase, 10*, 122–131.

Tainturier, M.-J., & Rapp, B. (2003). Is a single graphemic buffer used in reading and spelling? *Aphasiology, 17*, 537–562.

Tainturier, M. J., & Rapp, B. (2001). The spelling process. In B. Rapp (Ed.), *The handbook of cognitive neuropsychology.* Philadelphia: Psychology Press.

Teulings, H. L. (1996). Handwriting movement control. In S. W. Keele, & H. Heuer (Eds.), *Handbook of perception and action. Vol.2: Motor Skills* (pp. 561–613). London: Academic Press.

Teulings, H.-L., Thomassen, A. J. W. M., & Van Galen, G. P. (1983). Preparation of partly precued handwriting movements: The size of movements units in handwriting. *Acta Psychologica, 54*, 165–177.

Thomassen, A. J. W. M., Meulenbroek, R. G. J., & Tibosch, H. J. C. M. (1991). Latencies and kinematics reflect graphic production rules. *Human Movement Science, 10*, 271–289.

Thomassen, A. J. W. M., & van Galen, G. (1992). Handwriting as A Motor Task: Experimentation, Modelling, and Simulation. In J. J. Summers (Ed.), *Advances in psychology* (pp. 113–144, 84). Amsterdam: North-Holland.

Ueki,Y., Mima T., Nakamura, K., Oga, T., Shibasaki, H., Nagamine, T., & Fukuyama, H. (2006). Transient functional suppression and facilitation of Japanese ideogram writing induced by repetitive transcranial magnetic stimulation of posterior inferior temporal cortex. *Journal of Neuroscience, 26*(33), 8523–8530.

Van der Plaats, R. E., & van Galen, G. P. (1990). Effects of spatial and motor demands in handwriting. *Journal of Motor Behavior, 22*(3), 361–385

Van Galen, G. P. (1991). Handwriting: Issues for a psychomotor theory. *Human Movement Science, 10*, 165–191.

van Galen, G. P., Meulenbroek, R. G. J., & Hylkema, H. (1986). On the simultaneaous processing of words, letters and strokes in handwriting: evidence for a mixed linear and parallel model. In H. S. R. Kao, G. P. van Galen, & R. Hoosain (Eds.), *Graphonomics: Contemporary research in handwriting (Advances in Psychology)* (Vol. 37, pp. 5–20). Amsterdam: North-Holland.

Van Galen, G. P., Smyth, M. M., Meulenbroek, R. G. J., & Hylkema, H. (1989). The role of short-term memory and the motor buffer in handwriting under visual and non-visual guidance. In R. Plamondon, C. Y. Suen & M. L. Simner (Eds.), *Computer recognition and human production of handwriting* (pp. 253–271). Singapore: World Scientific.

Van Galen, G. P., & Teulings, H. L. (1983). The independent monitoring of form and scale factors in handwriting. *Acta Psychologica, 54*(1–3), 9–22.

Weingarten, R. (2005). Subsyllabic units in written word production. Subsyllabic units in written word production. *Written Language and Literacy, 8*(1), 43–61.

Weingarten, R., Nottbusch, G., & Will, U. (2004). Morphemes, syllables, and graphemes in written word production. In T. Pechmann, & C. Habel (Eds.), *Multidisciplinary approaches to language production* (pp. 529–572). Berlin: Mouton de Gruyter.

Zesiger, P., Mounoud, P., & Hauert, C. A. (1993). Effects of lexicality and trigram frequency on handwriting production in children and adults. *Acta Psychologica, 82*(1–3), 353–365.

Zhang, Q., & Damian, M. F. (2010). Impact of phonology on the generation of handwritten responses: Evidence from picture-word interference tasks. *Memory & Cognition, 38*, 519–528.

Ziegler, J., Jacobs, A., & Stone, G. (1996). Statistical analysis of the bi-directional inconsistency of spelling and sound in French. *Behavior, Research Methods, Instruments, & Computers, 28*, 504–515.

9 Sign Production

Signing vs. Speaking: How Does the Biology of Linguistic Expression Affect Production?

Karen Emmorey

Introduction

Current theories in linguistics, psychology, and cognitive neuroscience have all been developed primarily from investigations of spoken languages. By widening our scientific lens to include sign languages, we gain a deeper understanding of the language production system because we can ask questions that cannot be addressed with spoken languages. This chapter reviews neurobiological principles that are universal to human language production and those that are modulated by the specific sensory-motor systems within which language is instantiated.

The linguistic articulators for sign and speech are dramatically different. The vocal articulators for speech are largely hidden from view, relatively small, arranged along the midline of the body, and coupled with breathing. The manual articulators for sign are larger, symmetrical, directly visible, and move independently within a large space. However, one fundamental discovery from decades of linguistic and psycholinguistic research is that sign languages exhibit structure at the level of form that is parallel, but not identical to spoken language phonology (see Brentari, 2019, for a recent review).

Sublexical structure for sign languages includes contrasts that involve handshapes (including hand orientation), locations on the body (place of articulation), and movements. Lexical contrasts for these phonological parameters constitute minimal pairs. Signs can be one-handed or two-handed, and there are constraints on the form of two-handed signs (e.g., the non-dominant hand is limited in its movement and configuration; Battison, 1978). Handedness is not distinctive in any sign language, and thus linguistic constraints are specified with respect to the dominant hand (e.g., the hand used to produce one-handed signs) and the non-dominant hand. Signs also exhibit a level of syllable structure, and movement is typically analyzed as the syllabic peak, akin to vowels in spoken syllables. Thus, signs without movement (like words without vowels) are generally ill-formed. In addition, similar phonological phenomena such as co-articulation, assimilation, sonority, allophonic variation, and stress patterns exist in sign languages.

Although the hands are the primary articulators for signing, movements of the face, head, and body also convey linguistic information. For example, in

DOI: 10.4324/9781003145790-10

American Sign Language (ASL), raised eyebrows signal a yes/no question, while furrowed brows indicate a content (or WH) question, and these facial expressions are obligatory and often the only interrogative marker in the sentence. Body leans are used for discourse functions, such as expressing contrast (Wilbur & Patschke, 1998) and quotation (Herrmann & Steinbach, 2012). Headshakes in many sign languages are used to indicate negation, but languages vary in whether and how headshakes are deployed within a clause or sentence (Zeshan, 2006). Eyeblinks tend to mark phrase boundaries (e.g., Herrmann, 2010), and eye gaze has a number of referential linguistic functions (e.g., Thompson et al., 2006). Mouth patterns are also important aspects of sign production and have two primary forms: mouth gestures and mouthing (Boyes-Braem & Sutton-Spence, 2001). Mouth gestures are mouth patterns that obligatorily co-occur with a manual sign and have no relation to the surrounding spoken language. In contrast, mouthing refers to the partial articulation of a spoken word that accompanies a sign (typically, but not always, the translation-equivalent word).

The discovery that sign languages exhibit phonological structure, despite dramatic differences in the nature of the linguistic articulators, provides a foundation for comparing speaking and signing. In what follows, we explore a) how differences in the manual and vocal articulators affect the rate of language production, b) modality-dependent and modality-independent properties of lexical access and organization, c) evidence for the assembly of phonological units during sign production, d) how self-monitoring differs for signers and speakers, e) implications of the unique ability of bimodal bilinguals to code-blend (i.e., simultaneously produce signs and words), and f) the neural substrate that supports sign language production.

The impact of multiple independent articulators on language production

Models of language production assume that two unrelated propositions cannot be assembled simultaneously, primarily due to the serial nature of speech production – it's not possible to vocally articulate two different messages simultaneously. For signers, the arms and hands are independent articulators and could in principle produce two unrelated messages at the same time. However, signers do not do this. One hand may be held in space to express a backgrounded element (e.g., a classifier handshape representing a ground object in a spatial description), but the linguistic information expressed by the two hands is related to a single proposition. This pattern may result in part from constraints on bimanual coordination, but it also provides evidence for central limitations on human language processing, i.e., two different messages cannot be easily attended to simultaneously (Levelt, 1980). We will return to this central cognitive bottleneck in the section on code-blending in bimodal bilinguals.

The hands are much larger and slower articulators than the tongue and move through a much larger space (from just below the waist to above the head).

Bellugi and Fischer (1972) first documented that signs take longer than words to articulate, using a within-subject narrative elicitation task with hearing ASL–English bilinguals. The rate of articulation for words was nearly double the rate for signs (see also Grosjean, 1979). However, Bellugi and Fischer (1972) also showed that the proposition rate across the two languages was the same. The use of multiple articulators is one reason that the same amount of information could be conveyed with fewer manual signs. That is, ASL non-manual morphemes are expressed simultaneously with manual signs to convey information such as negation (headshake), adverbial modifications (mouth gestures), and syntactic structure (e.g., raised eyebrows and head tilt indicate conditional clauses). Other linguistic properties that are very common across sign languages also reduce the need for sequentially produced manual signs: pro-drop (i.e., pronouns can be omitted), various types of incorporation (e.g., incorporating numbers into manual signs), and simultaneous verb morphology (e.g., changes in movement, rather than sequential affixes, express temporal aspect). Based on these findings, we can conclude that there are temporal constraints on human language production, perhaps related to our limited working memory capacity (e.g., Cowan, 2010), that shape the linguistic structure of both signed and spoken languages.

For speakers, language output is inextricably linked to respiration, such that inhalation can only take place during a pause in speaking. In contrast, a signer's breathing is almost totally independent of their language production (Grosjean, 1979). Signers' respiratory cycle is regular throughout signing and is not affected much by changes in signing rate. In contrast, speakers typically inhale at the beginning of a sentence or clause and adjust their expiration based on linguistic structure (e.g., syntactic boundaries). Grosjean (1979) found that only 19% of inhalations for signers took place during pauses (vs. 100% for speakers), with the remaining inhalations occurring randomly during signs or transitions between signs. These factors impact how speakers versus signers change their rate of language production. Speakers largely alter the timing and duration of their pauses, while signers primarily change the amount of time they spend articulating (Grosjean, 1979).

In sum, results from studies of sign language production suggest that a) there is a central cognitive bottleneck that limits the simultaneous production of unrelated messages, b) temporal demands for rapid production impact the form of linguistic structure (more simultaneous for sign languages), and c) the impact of linguistic structure on respiration is unique to speech.

Modality-independent and modality-dependent factors that influence lexical access

The speed of lexical access during speech production is known to be influenced by a number of lexical variables. Some of these variables are likely to be modality-independent (e.g., frequency), while others could be specific to speech (e.g., phonological density) or sign (e.g., iconicity). Next, we explore what is known about how these lexical properties impact sign production.

Frequency

An important difference in how frequency effects are studied for spoken compared to sign languages is how lexical frequency is measured. For spoken languages, frequency is typically determined using word counts from corpora that contain millions of words. However, no such large corpora exist for any sign language to date. To determine lexical frequency, experimenters typically use subjective frequency or familiarity ratings from signers (e.g., Carreiras et al., 2008; Sehyr et al., 2022; Vinson et al., 2008). Based on data from a small corpus for British Sign Language (24,823 tokens), Fenlon et al. (2014) found that objective frequency counts were positively correlated ($r = .391$) with subjective frequency ratings for BSL signs ($N = 149$). This result is encouraging and suggests that subjective frequency ratings are a reasonable proxy for objective corpus counts. However, given the small number of signs included in this study, the difference in how lexical frequency is assessed for signed versus spoken languages should be kept in mind when interpreting its effects.

Several studies have now investigated frequency effects for sign production using picture naming tasks (e.g., Baus & Costa, 2015; Emmorey et al., 2012; 2013; Sehyr & Emmorey, in press). All studies found that more frequent signs were retrieved more quickly than less frequent signs. Emmorey et al. (2013) also found that the frequency effect was larger for hearing than deaf ASL signers, likely because ASL was the non-dominant language for hearing signers. Frequency effects are larger for the less dominant language due to less frequent use (Gollan et al., 2008). That is, hearing bilinguals use ASL less often than deaf bilinguals, making low-frequency signs more difficult to access which increases the difference between low- and high-frequency signs. Parallel effects of frequency on lexical retrieval suggest that a similar mechanism is at play for both language modalities, such as variation in resting activation levels for lexical representations or selection thresholds for lexical retrieval (i.e., high-frequency lexical items are assumed to have high activation levels or a low threshold for selection).

Baus and Costa (2015) presented electrophysiological data from a picture-naming task indicating frequency effects for signs that were parallel to words. Low-frequency signs elicited a larger positivity than high-frequency signs 200 ms after picture presentation. This early effect of frequency for signs and words is argued to reflect initial activation and retrieval processes within the lexicon, with more difficult low frequency items generating a larger positivity (Strijkers et al., 2010). Unpublished data from a positron emission tomography study indicated that a region in the left posterior superior parietal lobule (SPL) was more active when naming pictures with low than high-frequency signs (data from Emmorey et al., 2014). Sensitivity to lexical frequency in SPL is not typically observed for spoken language (e.g., Graves et al., 2007). This pattern could reflect differences in where phonological representations are represented in the brain for signs (parietal cortex) and words (superior temporal cortex) since some frequency effects are associated with phonological form (e.g., Jescheniak & Levelt, 1994).

| BIRD | HAMMER | APPLE |

Figure 9.1 Illustration of ASL signs from the ASL-LEX database (http://asl-lex.org).

For speech, it has long been known that shorter words tend to be more frequent than longer words (Zipf, 1949), which reflects articulatory reduction and the need to maximize communication efficiency (Gibson et al., 2019). A corpus analysis of Swedish Sign Language (44,876 tokens) was the first to document that more frequent signs also tend to be shorter (Börstell et al., 2016). Similar results were found for a single signer's productions in the ASL-LEX database of 2,723 signs (Sehyr et al., 2022) and for 20 deaf signers naming ~500 pictures (Sehyr & Emmorey, 2021). Thus, the relationship between frequency of use and word length is not modality-specific, but a universal property of language.

However, it is not known whether *phonological* length, measured in number of segments or syllables, is correlated with frequency in sign languages. All studies thus far have examined phonetic length, that is, the physical duration of signs. It is possible that phonological length is not correlated or is only weakly correlated with frequency because much of the phonological structure of signs is expressed simultaneously. For example, in the signs BIRD, HAMMER, and APPLE illustrated in Figure 9.1, handshape, location, and movement are all produced simultaneously. Compared to spoken words, the number of sequential segments (e.g., sequences of locations) is extremely limited, and the majority of signs are monosyllabic (Brentari, 2019). It is possible, therefore, that the *articulatory* reduction associated with high frequency of use is modality-independent, but the degree of *phonological* reduction is modulated by language modality (potentially larger effects for speech than for sign).

Phonological neighborhood density

For spoken languages, phonological neighborhood density is defined as the number of words that share all but one phoneme with a target word (Luce & Pisoni, 1998). Words from phonologically dense neighborhoods tend to be easier to produce (Vitevitch, 2002), but more difficult to recognize (Vitevitch & Luce, 1998). For comprehension, neighbors activated by a target word compete for recognition which slows identification of the target word. In contrast, for production, activation is top-down rather than bottom-up, and activation from neighboring words boosts activation of the target word's phonological segments, which facilitates production. The data necessary to study possible phonological neighborhood density effects in a sign language has only recently become available through the ASL-LEX database (Caselli et al., 2017; Sehyr et al., 2021).

Phonological neighborhood density for signs is defined as the number of signs that share all but one phonological feature with a target sign, and neighborhoods can vary somewhat depending upon how phonological features are defined, for example, as parameters (handshape, location, movement) or using more specific phonological features (e.g., selected fingers, contact) (Sehyr et al., 2021). Paralleling results from spoken language, Caselli et al. (2021) found that lexical decisions were slower to ASL signs from dense than sparse neighborhoods, particularly for low-frequency signs (see Carreiras et al., 2008, for a similar result with a narrower, sublexical definition of neighborhoods, based on shared location only). For production, in contrast to results from spoken languages, Sehyr and Emmorey (2022) found that phonological neighborhood density had no effect on picture-naming times, in contrast to other lexical variables, such as frequency and name agreement. A lack of facilitation from phonological neighbors during sign production could be due to a more simultaneous assembly of phonological segments, which might allow less time for the bidirectional spread of activation between lexical and segmental representations (Dell, 1986), compared to the more serial production of segments for spoken language. The finding that phonological neighborhood density impacts sign comprehension but not production is intriguing but requires further investigation to identify the underlying mechanism(s).

Iconicity

Iconicity is typically defined as a resemblance between a form and its meaning.[1] Although the potential role of iconicity in language acquisition and processing has long been of interest to sign language researchers, its role in language learning and processing for spoken languages has only recently been investigated since the relation between word forms and meaning was historically considered arbitrary (for recent reviews see Lockwood & Dingemanse, 2015; Nielsen & Dingemanse, 2021). Here we focus specifically on studies investigating whether iconicity impacts language production, rather than those investigating language development or comprehension.

Many studies have now shown that iconic signs are retrieved more quickly than non-iconic signs in picture-naming tasks (Baus & Costa, 2015; McGarry et al., 2021; Navarrete et al., 2017; Pretato et al., 2018; Sehyr and Emmorey, 2022; Vinson et al., 2015). For these studies, iconicity is typically assessed using a rating scale with deaf signers or hearing non-signers rating the degree to which a sign form resembles its meaning (iconicity ratings from these two groups are highly correlated; Sehyr & Emmorey, 2019). Iconicity effects in language production are not easily accounted for within existing psycholinguistic frameworks, since most models assume that semantic and phonological representations are completely independent of each other.

One possible mechanism for the facilitatory effect of iconicity on production is that iconic signs become activated more quickly and robustly because these signs receive additional activation from the perceptual and action-related semantic features that they encode (Navarrete et al., 2017; McGarry et al., 2021). For example, the ASL sign BIRD depicts a bird's beak (a perceptual feature), and the sign HAMMER depicts how a hammer is held and used (action-based features) (see Figure 9.1 for sign illustrations). Under this account, iconic effects are somewhat parallel to semantic concreteness effects. For example, concrete single-character Chinese words are produced (read aloud) more quickly than abstract words (Liu et al., 2007), and concrete words are generally recognized more quickly than abstract words in comprehension (Holcomb et al., 1999). The picture-naming ERP study by McGarry et al. (2021) provides some support for this hypothesis. Pictures named with iconic signs elicited a larger N400 (greater negativity) than non-iconic signs; similarly, concrete words elicit a larger N400 amplitude than abstract words (Barber et al., 2013; Holcomb et al., 1999). The concreteness effect is generally attributed to increased activation of perceptual and action-related semantic features associated with concrete words. The concreteness-like N400 response for iconic sign production observed by McGarry et al. (2021) could reflect more robust encoding of sensory-motor semantic features that are depicted by these signs and that are emphasized by the picture naming task.

In addition, the picture-naming task itself may give rise to facilitatory effects of iconicity. One account of iconicity is that it represents a structured alignment between features of a conceptual representation (which are depicted in the picture) and features of a phonological form (Emmorey, 2014; Taub, 2001). McGarry et al. (2021) found that pictures that aligned with the phonological form of the sign (e.g., a picture of a bird with a prominent beak aligns with the ASL sign BIRD which depicts a bird's beak) were named faster than non-aligned pictures (e.g., a picture of a bird in flight). Thus, pictures that correspond with iconic target signs may be more likely to visually prime the phonological form of the sign, leading to faster and more accurate picture naming (and a reduced N400 response). Support for this account was recently found in an ERP study by Gimeno-Martinéz and Baus (2021) in which picture naming was compared to a word-to-sign translation task with deaf bimodal bilinguals. Faster naming times and ERP effects were found for the production of iconic compared to non-iconic signs but only for the picture-naming task – no effects of iconicity were found for the translation task. Thus, iconicity effects in the picture-naming task could be due to the mapping between the visual features of the picture and features of the phonological form of the sign.

No picture-naming study (to my knowledge) has manipulated iconicity in spoken language, most likely because a) iconic forms are less pervasive in spoken languages, b) iconic features involve cross-modal mappings from sound to other senses, and c) concepts expressed by iconic words may not be easily picturable (e.g., onomatopoeia, manner of motion verbs). Although speakers use prosodic changes to express semantic information such as speed (e.g., "he's so slooooooow") or height (e.g., "it went *up* and *down*" with raising and falling pitch), such expressions have been analyzed as vocal gesture rather than as lexical properties of word forms (Okrent, 2002). Based on data from the English Lexicon Project (Balota et al., 2007), Meteyard et al. (2015) reported that iconic words (e.g., *clang, roar, zing*) were not read aloud more quickly than matched control words (e.g., *swore, doze, slow*), although some people with aphasia were better able to read aloud the iconic words than the control words, suggesting that they may draw on sensory cues in the words to aid production (perhaps engaging the right hemisphere).

A number of studies have documented cross-linguistic patterns of sound-meaning relationships (e.g., Blasi et al., 2016; Dautriche et al., 2017), but it is unclear whether these iconic mappings play any role in lexical access and language production for spoken language. For sign language, the prevalence of iconic forms has afforded more investigation, and the evidence clearly indicates a facilitatory effect on language production, at least as measured by picture naming. However, the precise mechanisms that give rise to this effect require further study (e.g., robust representation of sensory-motor semantic features, task-specific visual form priming, etc.).

Evidence for phonological assembly during sign production

Evidence from linguistic analyses (minimal pairs; constraints on form, etc.) indicate that signs are not wholistic gestures and have an internal structure, composed of sublexical units. But are these units "psychologically real"? Is there evidence that phonological units are assembled online during language production? The answer is emphatically *yes*, with evidence from tip-of-the-fingers experiences (parallel to tip-of-the-tongue states), slips of the hand (parallel to slips of the tongue), and picture–sign interference paradigms.

Tip-of-the-tongue (TOT) states provide evidence for a two-stage model of lexical access in which semantic information can be retrieved (one knows the meaning of the word), but phonological information cannot be retrieved or can only be partially recalled (e.g., the first sound or letter). To examine whether signers experience a similar phenomenon, Thompson et al. (2005) conducted a laboratory study of elicited tip-of-the-fingers states (TOFs) using a translation task (e.g., provide the ASL translation for the English word "Moscow"). TOFs were similar to TOTs in that the majority occurred with proper names and participants sometimes had partial access to the phonological form of the target sign. Remarkably, when in a TOF state, signers often recalled three out of four phonological parameters (hand configuration, palm orientation, location, movement). Movement (the most temporally dynamic aspect of sign structure) was the parameter that was least likely to be recalled in a TOF. Similar results were recently reported by Löffler (2019) and Löffler et al. (2020) for German Sign Language (DGS). Thus, TOFs appear to be qualitatively different from TOTs with respect to the amount of phonological information that is retrieved. Overall, the TOF data argue for a two-stage model of lexical access for sign language and for a separation between semantic and phonological representations (despite the higher prevalence of iconic forms in sign language). Importantly, these data also suggest that much of the phonological structure of a sign may be accessed simultaneously.

Speech errors have long been used as evidence for linguistic structure and for theories of speech production. Sign errors have been less well studied, but the data clearly show that phonological units (handshapes, locations, movements) can be mis-selected during production, providing further evidence that signs are not stored as wholistic gestures (Hohenberger et al., 2002; Newkirk et al., 1980). Like speech errors, sign errors can involve anticipation, perseveration, or exchanges of segmental units. Interestingly, word exchanges were extremely rare in both the ASL corpus (Newkirk et al., 1980) and the DGS corpus (Hohenberger et al., 2002). This rarity could be due to differences in the speed of speech and sign production; that is, whole sign exchanges might be repaired before they are fully articulated.

Vinson et al. (2010) used error data to investigate whether the production of mouthings and manual signs arise from two separate representational systems (speech and sign) or whether mouthings are part of the non-manual phonological representation of signs. Signers were asked to name sets of semantically related and unrelated pictures as quickly as possible. The results revealed that semantic errors occurred either for the manual sign alone or for mouthing alone, but rarely did a semantic error occur simultaneously for both the mouthing and manual components. Vinson et al. (2010) reasoned that if mouthings and manual signs shared the same lexico-semantic representation then the proportion of such errors should have been higher. These results suggest that mouthings may constitute a form of code-blending by bimodal bilinguals (see below) and are not represented as a non-manual phonological feature of signs (see Giustolisi et al., 2017, for supporting evidence from Italian Sign Language).

Finally, further evidence for a stage of phonological encoding during sign language production comes from studies using the picture–word interference (PWI) paradigm. In this paradigm, a video of a sign is superimposed on a to-be-named picture. Parallel to results from spoken language, semantically related signs inhibit picture naming, while phonologically related signs generally facilitate naming (Baus et al., 2008, 2014; Corina & Knapp, 2006). This finding further supports a two-stage model of lexical access for sign production. Importantly, the nature of the phonological overlap differentially impacts sign production. When the distractor sign and the target sign overlap in a single parameter, production facilitation was observed for handshape and for movement, but inhibition (slower naming) was observed for location overlap (Baus et al., 2008). A similar pattern has been observed for sign comprehension using phonological priming or lexical decision paradigms (Carreiras et al., 2008;

Corina & Emmorey, 1993; Meade et al., 2021). One possible explanation for this pattern is that location is a critical organizational factor for representations within the sign lexicon, such that lexical-level competition occurs for signs sharing location (see Gutiérrez et al., 2012; Meade et al., 2021).

When two phonological parameters overlap for the prime and target signs, facilitation is generally observed for comprehension studies (e.g., Mayberry & Witcher, 2005; Meade et al., 2018). Similarly, using a cross-modal, cross-linguistic version of the PWI paradigm, Giezen and Emmorey (2016) found that hearing bimodal bilinguals were faster to name pictures in ASL when they heard an English word whose translation was phonologically related to the target ASL sign (two-parameter overlap). Using a within-language, picture–sign interference paradigm, Baus et al. (2014) investigated whether the type of two-parameter overlap was important. This study found that sign production was facilitated when the distractor and target signs overlapped in movement and location, but no facilitation was observed if the sign pairs overlapped in movement and handshape or in handshape and location (see also Corina & Knapp, 2006). The authors suggested that this pattern of results could be due to a) the greater perceptual salience of movement and location overlap (Hildebrandt & Corina, 2002), b) the greater frequency of movement and location combinations (cf. biphone frequencies) and/or c) the structural unit of movement and location form a syllable, as proposed by some models of sign phonology (Brentari, 2019; Sandler, 1989). Together the results from these PWI studies indicate that the role of each parameter and parameter combination should be considered in an account of phonological re-presentation and encoding for sign production.

Visual feedback and sign language monitoring: Implications for models of output control

In his influential *perceptual loop* theory of language output monitoring, Levelt (1989) proposed that speakers monitor their own speech (via auditory feedback or internally generated speech) the same way they monitor other people's speech, using their comprehension system. This theory runs into problems when applied to sign language because signers do not look at their hands while signing, and they cannot visually perceive their own facial expressions, which contain critical linguistic information. Thus, the visual input to the comprehension system from another person's signing and from one's own signing are quite different. In contrast, auditory input from another person's speech and from one's own speech are very similar, and both are quite comprehensible. Emmorey et al. (2009a) showed that comprehension of self-produced signs (presented in the periphery of vision and from the back, as observed when signing) was significantly poorer than comprehension of other-produced signs (presented in the center of vision, from the front, as when viewing another person's signing). These data argue against the use of a comprehension-based monitor for sign language and indicate that such a mechanism is not a universal property of language production.[2]

Moreover, work by Nozari and colleagues suggests that comprehension-based monitoring cannot be the sole (or even primary) mechanism for controlling speech output (Nozari et al., 2011; Nozari & Novick, 2017). Rather, these authors propose a production-based, conflict-monitoring model in which simultaneous activation of more than one representation during production (e.g., words, phonemes) generates a conflict signal which is relayed to a central monitoring system (see Runqvist, this volume, for a discussion of comprehension-based vs. conflict-monitoring models of self-monitoring). The central monitoring system is hypothesized to operate for both internally generated speech (prior to articulation) and overt speech. Evidence that this conflict-monitoring system is domain-general stems from electrophysiological research involving the error negativity (Ne) or Error Related Negativity (ERN) component which is observed in the EEG signal for both linguistic and non-linguistic tasks (Riès et al., 2011). For speech production, the error negativity (Ne wave) is present for both correct and incorrect naming trials (but larger for errors) and precedes overt articulation, suggesting that this component is involved in internal monitoring of language production.

Recently, Riès et al. (2020) investigated whether the same monitoring system might be involved in sign language production. In this study, deaf and hearing ASL–English bilinguals performed a picture–word interference task in which English words (semantically related or unrelated) preceded a picture to-be-named in ASL. ASL response times were measured from keyboard release, and ERPs were time-locked with this point. For deaf signers, the results revealed a medial frontal negativity (Ne-like wave) that peaked 15 ms after keyboard release, and this negativity was larger in errors than correct trials. The slope of the Ne wave was correlated with an objective measure of ASL proficiency across participants (steeper slope for more proficient signers), suggesting that more skilled signers may have a more efficient monitoring system. Overall, the results indicate that the monitoring mechanism reflected by the Ne/Ne-like wave is universal and engaged in both spoken and signed language monitoring. Further, this mechanism appears to monitor pre-articulatory representations of language. For sign language, these internal representations are likely to be somatosensory in nature, rather than visual. In contrast, for spoken language, these internally generated representations are likely to be both auditory and somatosensory (Hickok, 2012).

What the unique properties of bimodal bilingualism reveal about language production

Bimodal bilinguals know a signed and a spoken language, while unimodal bilinguals know either two spoken languages or two sign languages (see Emmorey et al., 2016, for a review). Because a bimodal bilingual's languages involve distinct primary articulators (the hands vs. the vocal tract), it is physically possible for them to produce words from their two languages at the same time, and this type of language mixing has been called *code-blending*. When hearing bimodal bilinguals interact with each other, they prefer to code-blend rather than to code-switch between speaking and signing (Emmorey et al., 2008). In addition, the majority of code-blends involve translation equivalents (e.g., saying "bird" while producing the sign BIRD), and code-blends refer to the same proposition, even if the signs and words are not translation equivalents (e.g., saying "Tweety" while signing BIRD). These findings further support the hypothesis that there is a central cognitive bottleneck with respect to producing multiple propositions simultaneously. In addition, bimodal bilinguals generally time-lock their vocal and manual productions so that word and sign onsets are temporally aligned, which typically means that speech is delayed given the rate difference between speaking and signing (Bellugi & Fischer, 1972; Emmorey et al., 2012).

The fact that bimodal bilinguals prefer code-blending over code-switching provides evidence that the locus of lexical selection for bilinguals is relatively late since a single lexical representation need not be selected at either the conceptual or lexical level. In addition, studies have shown that code-blending is not costly; for example, naming a picture in ASL alone does not engage more neural resources and does not take any longer than naming a picture simultaneously in both English and ASL, despite the dual-task nature of the latter (Emmorey et al., 2012; Blanco-Elorrieta et al., 2018a). This finding indicates that the bilingual language production system must be capable of shutting off inhibition between languages to allow lexical items from two languages to be produced. However, this finding is also consistent with a model that proposes lexical selection occurs via levels of activation rather than via inhibitory processes (Blanco-Elorrieta & Caramazza, 2021).

Code-blending also provides unique insight into bilingual language control. For unimodal bilinguals, switching between two languages involves two processes that occur at the same time: "turning off" one language and "turning on" the other language. Code-blending allows us to tease apart these two processes because switching into a code-blend (switching from speaking alone to code-blending) only involves turning on a language, while switching out of a code-blend (switching from code-blending to speaking alone) only involves turning off a language. Behavioral data from cued picture-naming tasks indicate a cost to turn off a language, but no cost to turn on a language (Emmorey et al., 2020a; Kaufmann & Philipp, 2017). Further, neuroimaging data indicate that turning off a language engages cognitive control regions, but turning on a language does not (Blanco-Elorrieta 2018a). Although these results are consistent with inhibitory accounts of bilingual lexical selection (e.g., Green & Abutalebi, 2013), they are also consistent with a response exclusion account of task effects (e.g., Finkbeiner et al., 2006; Mahon et al., 2007). Blanco-Elorrieta and Caramazza (2021) argued that when turning on a language (switching into a code-blend), there is no need to reject a response since both languages are allowed to be produced; in contrast, when turning off a language (switching out of a code-blend), a new rejection criterion needs to be applied to ensure that only a single language is produced. Application of a response rejection criterion carries a general cognitive cost (for both linguistic and non-linguistic tasks).

Similarly, recent data from the picture–word interference (PWI) paradigm with bimodal bilinguals supports a response exclusion account, over a lexical selection by competition account of cross-language semantic interference (Emmorey et al., 2020b). In this paradigm, cross-language semantic interference refers to slower naming times when a semantically related word (e.g., "truck" in English) precedes a picture to be named in the other language (e.g., CAR in ASL); see Costa and Caramazza (1999) for evidence of semantic interference using the PWI paradigm for unimodal bilinguals. The response exclusion hypothesis predicts that semantic interference should *not* occur for bimodal bilinguals because sign and word responses do not compete for production within an output buffer, in contrast to the two spoken responses for unimodal bilinguals. The results from Emmorey et al. (2020) supported this prediction. Bimodal bilinguals named pictures in ASL faster (not slower) when preceded by semantically related English words compared to unrelated words, and they showed a reduced N400 amplitude in the semantically related compared to unrelated naming trials. This pattern of results suggests that the semantically related English word facilitated, rather than inhibited, access to the ASL sign and further supports models of bilingual (and monolingual) language production that assume lexical selection occurs without inhibition-based competition.

In sum, the characteristics of language production for bimodal bilinguals provide a unique opportunity to investigate the mechanisms involved in lexical selection and control. Because the phonological and articulatory systems for sign and speech do not overlap, bimodal bilinguals offer a novel way of investigating the role of phonological and/or output competition in language production.

The neural underpinnings of sign language production

Although much is known about the neural underpinnings of speech production (Tourville & Guenther, 2011), we know comparatively little about the neural circuits recruited during sign production. In this section, evidence for shared functional neural substrates for speaking and signing are briefly reviewed, as well as evidence for neural regions that are differentially engaged for sign vs. speech production (see Emmorey, 2021, for a more comprehensive review).

Biology-independent neural substrates for language production

A clear universal property of language production is that it is strongly lateralized to the left hemisphere. Like speakers, signers with left but not right hemisphere damage produce phonological, morphological, and/or semantic errors when signing (e.g., Hickok, Bellugi, & Klima, 1996). Gutiérrez-Sigut and colleagues have also used functional transcranial Doppler sonography (fTCD) to investigate hemispheric lateralization during speech and sign production in neurotypical adults (Gutierrez-Sigut et al., 2015, Gutierrez-Sigut et al., 2016). fTCD measures event-related changes in blood flow velocity within the middle cerebral arteries in the two hemispheres. Hearing bimodal bilinguals exhibited stronger left lateralization for sign than speech production when performing verbal fluency tasks, and a control experiment with sign-naïve participants indicated that the difference in degree of laterality was not driven by greater motoric demands for manual articulation. These authors speculated that greater left lateralization for signing might be due to increased use of somatosensory self-monitoring mechanisms and/or to the nature of phonological encoding for signs.

Within the left hemisphere, the inferior frontal gyrus (IFG) has been implicated as a key region involved in both sign and speech production (Braun et al., 2001; Emmorey et al., 2007; Petitto et al., 2000). In addition, Corina et al. (2003) reported nearly identical left IFG activation for both left- and right-handed signing (using verb generation and repetition tasks), indicating that activation in this region is not driven by motoric demands of right-handed signing. In addition, Horwitz et al. (2003) used probabilistic cytoarchitectonic maps of Brodmann's Area (BA) 45 and 44 within the IFG, along with the functional imaging data from Braun et al. (2001), to show that BA 45 was involved in higher-level linguistic processes (e.g., lexical-semantic processing), while BA 44 (and not BA 45) was engaged in the generation of complex oral and manual movements. Consistent with this finding, cortical stimulation of BA 44 during sign production by a deaf signer resulted in motor execution errors (e.g., lax or imprecise articulation), rather than phonological errors (e.g., handshape substitution) (Corina et al., 1999).

Although the linguistic articulators are different for sign and speech, a recent electrocorticography (ECoG) study with a deaf signer undergoing awake craniotomy revealed surprising parallels in the neural organization and representation of sublexical components for sign and speech (Leonard et al., 2020). For speakers, ECoG data has identified speech-articulator representations (such as the tongue and lips) that are laid out somatotopically along the sensorimotor cortex, and spatiotemporal patterns of neural activity that are hierarchically organized by articulatory-defined phonetic features, such as lip-rounding or tongue position (Bouchard et al., 2013). The Leonard et al. (2020) results for signing were surprisingly parallel. The study revealed neural selectivity for the production of very similar, but linguistically contrastive handshapes and places of articulation for electrodes over pre-central, post-central, and supramarginal cortices. Some of these electrodes showed neural activity that began before the signer moved his hand, which likely reflected planning activity prior to the actual motor movement. Other electrodes exhibited activity that was locked to the onset of movement, which may reflect motor and proprioceptive feedback used to guide the formation and maintenance of a target handshape. Further, Leonard and colleagues provided evidence that these cortical responses were specific to linguistic production, rather than simply reflecting general motor actions of the hand and arm. For example, the spatial distribution of the neural activity across location- and handshape-selective electrodes was clustered along a linguistically relevant hierarchy (e.g., distinguishing fingerspelled words and lexical signs). This rare and novel type of data provides some of the first evidence that sublexical phonological representations are supported by the same neural principles and architecture, regardless of language modality.

With respect to higher-level processes involved in language production, a recent magnetoencephalographic (MEG) study by Blanco-Elorrieta et al. (2018b) investigated whether the same neural circuits support the online construction of linguistic phrases in sign and speech. Two-word compositional phrases and two-word non-compositional "lists" were elicited from signers and speakers using identical pictures. In one condition, participants combined an adjective and a noun to describe the color of the object in the picture (e.g., *white lamp*) and in the control condition, participants named the color of the picture background and then the object (e.g., *white, lamp*). For both signers and speakers, phrase building engaged left anterior temporal and ventromedial cortices, with similar timing. The left anterior temporal lobe may be involved in computing the intersection of semantic features (Poortman & Pylkkänen, 2016), while the ventromedial prefrontal cortex may be more specifically involved in constructing combinatorial plans (Pylkkänen et al., 2014). Overall, this work indicates that the same frontotemporal network achieves the planning of structured linguistic expressions for both signed and spoken languages.

Biology-dependent neural substrates for language production

Several studies have now shown that parietal cortex is more engaged during sign than speech production. For example, the supramarginal gyrus (SMG) is significantly more active during sign than word production when deaf signers are compared to hearing speakers (Emmorey et al., 2007) and when sign and speech production are directly compared within hearing bimodal bilinguals (Braun et al., 2001; Emmorey et al., 2014). The sign production study by Emmorey et al. (2016) also implicated the SMG as a key region for sign production. This study elicited the production of several different sign types using a translation task: one-handed signs (articulated in "neutral" space in front of the signer), two-handed (neutral space) signs, and one-handed body-anchored signs (produced with contact on or near the body). A conjunction analysis comparing the production of each sign type with a baseline task revealed common activation in SMG bilaterally (greater involvement on the left) for all sign types. Importantly, Corina et al. (1999) found that stimulation to left SMG resulted in phonological substitutions, rather than motor execution errors. Further, bilateral SMG activation (larger on the left) has been found during covert rehearsal of pseudosigns, but not during covert rehearsal of pseudowords (Buchsbaum et al., 2005). Together, these results suggest that SMG may be critically involved in phonological encoding for sign language production.

In addition, a recent study of a deaf native signer who underwent direct cortical stimulation (as part of a clinical procedure to remove an insular tumor) suggests that the superior part of the SMG is connected both functionally and anatomically to a posterior, superior region of IFG (Metellus et al., 2017).

Stimulation of this posterosuperior IFG region elicited sign production errors (mistakes in handshape or location or sign blockage) in both object-naming and word-translation tasks. Similar errors were observed when the arcuate fasciculus (the fiber tract connecting IFG and SMG) was stimulated. Further, stimulation of the IFG region induced a later afterdischarge in superior SMG. Together, these data provide novel evidence for a dorsal frontoparietal network that supports sign language production.

Like the SMG, the superior parietal lobule (SPL) is also more active during sign than word production (Emmorey et al., 2007; 2014). One possible explanation for this finding is that SPL is involved in self-monitoring of overt sign output via somatosensory feedback. Results from Emmorey et al. (2016) provide some support for this hypothesis. The production of body-anchored signs resulted in greater activation in SPL compared to signs produced in neutral space. Greater engagement of SPL may reflect the motor control and somatosensory monitoring required to direct the hand toward a specific location on the face or body. When hand and arm movements are not visually guided (as for sign production), SPL plays a role in updating postural representations during movement (Parkinson et al., 2010), and SPL is also known to be a key region for processing proprioceptive hand feedback during reaching movements (Reichenbach et al., 2014).

Data from two ECoG studies with hearing bimodal bilinguals have also provided evidence that sign production activates parietal regions which are not activated during speech (Crone et al., 2001; Shum et al., 2020). Shum et al. (2020) found that activity in SPL immediately preceded sign production (~120 ms prior to initiating hand movement), suggesting that SPL plays an important role in planning sign articulation. Furthermore, this temporal pattern of SPL activity was not observed for non-linguistic reaching movements or for speech production. In addition, Crone et al. (2001) reported that electrical cortical stimulation of regions in SPL interfered with sign (but not speech) production, although the nature of this interference was not specified. Overall, the data indicate that SPL is uniquely involved in the planning and execution of signs, but not spoken words.

Conclusion

This review has identified several ways in which the biology of linguistic expression impacts language production. The larger size and articulatory space of the manual vs. vocal articulators impact the rate of production and may lead to more simultaneous linguistic structure for signs than words. The link between breathing and production is unique to speech. The prevalence of iconicity in sign languages may have a unique impact on production and/or lexical representation (but more work is needed!). Phonological density may not exert the same facilitatory effect on sign production as it does for speech (but again, more research is needed). With respect to language output monitoring, auditory feedback likely plays a larger role in speech production than visual feedback plays in sign production. In addition, the lack of phonological and articulatory competition for a bimodal bilingual's two languages has provided new insights into the nature of language control. Finally, evidence from a variety of different neuroimaging techniques indicates that signing relies on parietal cortex to a greater extent than speaking.

Despite these differences, the production systems for signed and spoken language also exhibit remarkable parallels. Both signs and words are composed of sublexical units that must be assembled during production, and these units can be mis-selected during production. Lexical frequency facilitates both sign and word production, and both follow Zipf's law such that more frequent productions are shorter (at least in articulatory length). A production-based, conflict-monitoring model can be applied to both sign and speech output monitoring. Both sign and speech production are strongly left-lateralized, and similar frontotemporal regions are engaged during both speaking and signing.

To conclude, sign languages provide an important tool for investigating the psycholinguistic and neural mechanisms that underlie language production. Their study can reveal both universal and modality-specific production mechanisms, as well as clarify the nature of biological constraints on language production.

Acknowledgments

This chapter was written with support from the National Institutes of Health (R01 DC010997) and the National Science Foundation (BCS-1918556).

Notes

1 A recent formal definition of iconicity is that "aspects of form have a contextually in-stantiated sense of resemblance to aspects of meaning" (Winter, 2021), which captures both the selective mapping between features of a form and features of its meaning and the subjective nature of this perceived iconic mapping.
2 Although signers are unlikely to use visual feedback to monitor for production errors, they appear to use visual feedback to adjust the size of their signing space (Emmorey et al., 2009b, 2009c).

References

Balota, D. A., Yap, M. J., Hutchison, K. A., Cortese, M. J., Kessler, B., Loftis, B., Neely, J. H., Nelson, D. L., Simpson, G. B., & Treiman, R. (2007). The English Lexicon Project. *Behavior Research Methods*, *39*(3), 445–459. 10.3758/BF03193014

Barber, H. A., Otten, L. J., Kousta, S.-T., & Vigliocco, G. (2013). Concreteness in word processing: ERP and behavioral effects in a lexical decision task. *Brain and Language*, *125*(1), 47–53. 10.1016/j.bandl.2013.01.00

Battison, R. (1978). *Lexical borrowing in American Sign Language*. Linstok Press.

Baus, C., & Costa, A. (2015). On the temporal dynamics of sign production: An ERP study in Catalan Sign Language (LSC). *Brain Research*, *1609*, 40–53. 10.1016/j.brainres.2015.03.013

Baus, C., Gutiérrez, E., & Carreiras, M. (2014). The role of syllables in sign language production. *Frontiers in Psychology*, *5*. 10.3389/fpsyg.2014.01254

Baus, C., Gutiérrez-Sigut, E., Quer, J., & Carreiras, M. (2008). Lexical access in Catalan Sign Language (LSC) production. *Cognition*, *108*(3), 856–865. 10.1016/j.cognition.2008.05.012

Bellugi, U., & Fischer, S. (1972). A comparison of sign language and spoken language. *Cognition*, *1*(2), 173–200. 10.1016/0010-0277(72)90018-2

Blanco-Elorrieta, E., & Caramazza, A. (2021). A common selection mechanism at each linguistic level in bilingual and monolingual language production. *Cognition*, 104625. 10.1016/j.cognition.2021.104625

Blanco-Elorrieta, E., Emmorey, K., & Pylkkänen, L. (2018a). Language switching decomposed through MEG and evidence from bimodal bilinguals. Proceedings of the *National Academy of Sciences*, *115*(39), 9708–9713. 10.1073/pnas.1809779115

Blanco-Elorrieta, E., Kastner, I., Emmorey, K., & Pylkkänen, L. (2018b). Shared neural correlates for building phrases in signed and spoken language. *Scientific Reports*, *8*, 5492. DOI: 10.1038/s41598-018-23915-0

Blasi, D. E., Wichmann, S., Hammarström, H., Stadler, P. F., & Christiansen, M. H. (2016). Sound–meaning association biases evidenced across thousands of languages. Proceedings of the *National Academy of Sciences*, *113*(39), 10818–10823. 10.1073/pnas. 1605782113

Börstell, C., Hörberg, T., & Östling, R. (2016). Distribution and duration of signs and parts of speech in Swedish Sign Language. *Sign Language & Linguistics*, *19*(2), 143–196. 10.1075/ sll.19.2.01bor

Bouchard, K. E., Mesgarani, N., Johnson, K., & Chang, E. F. (2013). Functional organization of human sensorimotor cortex for speech articulation. *Nature*, *495*(7441), 327–332. 10.1038/ nature11911

Boyes-Braem, P., & Sutton-Spence, R. (2001). *The hands are the head of the mouth: The mouth as articulator in sign languages*. Gallaudet University Press.

Braun, A. R., Guillemin, A., Hosey, L., & Varga, M. (2001). The neural organization of discourse: An H215O-PET study of narrative production in English and American Sign Language. *Brain*, *124*(10), 2028–2044. 10.1093/brain/124.10.2028

Brentari, D. (2019). *Sign language phonology*. Cambridge University Press.

Buchsbaum, B., Pickell, B., Love, T., Hatrak, M., Bellugi, U., & Hickok, G. (2005). Neural substrates for verbal working memory in deaf signers: FMRI study and lesion case report. *Brain and Language*, *95*(2), 265–272. 10.1016/j.bandl.2005.01.009

Carreiras, M., Gutiérrez-Sigut, E., Baquero, S., & Corina, D. (2008). Lexical processing in Spanish Sign Language (LSE). *Journal of Memory and Language*, *58*(1), 100–122. 10.1016/ j.jml.2007.05.004

Caselli, N., Emmorey, K., & Cohen-Goldberg, A. (2021). The signed mental lexicon: Effects of phonological neighborhood density, iconicity, and childhood language experience. *Journal of Memory and Language*, *121*. 10.1016/j.jml.2021.104282.

Caselli, N., Sehyr, Z. S., Cohen-Goldberg, A., & Emmorey, K. (2017). ASL-LEX: A lexical database of American Sign Language. *Behavioral Research Methods*, *49*, 784–801. doi: 10.3758/s13428-016-0742-0

Corina, D., & Emmorey, K. (1993). Lexical priming in American Sign Language. Postere presented at the *Psychonomic Society Meeting*, November, Washington, D.C.

Corina, D. P., Jose-Robertson, L. S., Guillemin, A., High, J., & Braun, A. R. (2003). Language lateralization in a bimanual language. *Journal of Cognitive Neuroscience*, *15*(5), 718–730. 10.1162/jocn.2003.15.5.718

Corina, D. P., & Knapp, H. P. (2006). Lexical retrieval in American Sign Language Production. In L. M. Goldstein, D. H. Whalen, & C. T. Best (Eds.), *Varieties of phonological competence* (pp. 213–240). Berlin: Mouton de Gruyter.

Corina, D. P., McBurney, S. L., Dodrill, C., Hinshaw, K., Brinkley, J., & Ojemann, G. (1999). Functional roles of Broca's area and SMG: Evidence from cortical stimulation mapping in a deaf signer. *NeuroImage, 10*(5), 570–581. 10.1006/nimg.1999.0499

Costa, A., & Caramazza, A. (1999). Is lexical selection in bilingual speech production language-specific? Further evidence from Spanish–English and English–Spanish bilinguals. *Bilingualism: Language and Cognition, 2*(3), 231–244. 10.1017/S1366728999000334

Cowan, N. (2010). The magical mystery four: How is working memory capacity limited, and why? *Current Directions in Psychological Science, 19*(1), 51–57. 10.1177/0963721409359277

Crone, N. E., Hao, L., Hart, J., Boatman, D., Lesser, R. P., Irizarry, R., & Gordon, B. (2001). Electrocorticographic gamma activity during word production in spoken and sign language. *Neurology, 57*(11), 2045–2053. 10.1212/WNL.57.11.2045

Dautriche, I., Mahowald, K., Gibson, E., & Piantadosi, S. T. (2017). Wordform similarity increases with semantic similarity: An analysis of 100 languages. *Cognitive Science, 41*(8), 2149–2169. 10.1111/cogs.12453

Dell, G. S. (1986). A spreading-activation theory of retrieval in sentence production. *Psychological Review, 93*(3), 283–321. 10.1037/0033-295X.93.3.283

Emmorey, K. (2021). New perspectives on the neurobiology of sign languages. *Frontiers in Communication: Language Sciences.* 10.3389/fcomm.2021.748430

Emmorey, K. (2014). Iconicity as structure mapping. *Philosophical Transactions of the Royal Society B: Biological Sciences, 369*(1651), 20130301. 10.1098/rstb.2013.0301

Emmorey, K., Borinstein, H. B., Thompson, R., & Gollan, T. H. (2008). Bimodal bilingualism. *Bilingualism: Language and Cognition, 11*(1), 43–61. 10.1017/S1366728907003203

Emmorey, K., Bosworth, R., & Kraljic, T. (2009a). Visual feedback and self-monitoring of sign language. *Journal of Memory and Language, 61*(3), 398–411. 10.1016/j.jml.2009.06.001

Emmorey, K., Gertsberg, N., Korpics, F., & Wright, C. E. (2009b). The influence of visual feedback and register changes on sign language production: A kinematic study with deaf signers. *Applied Psycholinguistics, 30*(1), 187–203. 10.1017/S0142716408090085

Emmorey, K., Giezen, M. R., & Gollan, T. H. (2016). Psycholinguistic, cognitive, and neural implications of bimodal bilingualism. *Bilingualism: Language and Cognition, 19*(2), 223–242. 10.1017/S1366728915000085

Emmorey, K., Korpics, F., & Petronio, K. (2009c). The use of visual feedback during signing: Evidence from signers with impaired vision. *Journal of Deaf Studies and Deaf Education, 14*(1), 99–104. 10.1093/deafed/enn020

Emmorey, K., Li, C., Petrich, J., & Gollan, T. H. (2020a). Turning languages on and off: Switching into and out of code-blends reveals the nature of bilingual language control. *Journal of Experimental Psychology: Learning, Memory, and Cognition, 46*(3), 443–454. 10.1037/xlm0000734

Emmorey, K., McCullough, S., Mehta, S., & Grabowski, T. J. (2014). How sensory-motor systems impact the neural organization for language: Direct contrasts between spoken and signed language. *Frontiers in Psychology, 5.* 10.3389/fpsyg.2014.00484

Emmorey, K., Mehta, S., & Grabowski, T. J. (2007). The neural correlates of sign versus word production. *NeuroImage, 36*(1), 202–208. 10.1016/j.neuroimage.2007.02.040

Emmorey, K., Mehta, S., McCullough, S., & Grabowski, T. J. (2016). The neural circuits recruited for the production of signs and fingerspelled words. *Brain and Language, 160*, 30–41. 10.1016/j.bandl.2016.07.003

Emmorey, K., Mott, M., Meade, G., Holcomb, P. J., & Midgley, K. J. (2020b). Lexical selection in bimodal bilinguals: ERP evidence from picture-word interference. *Language, Cognition and Neuroscience, 0*(0), 1–15. 10.1080/23273798.2020.1821905

Emmorey, K., Petrich, J. A. F., & Gollan, T. H. (2012). Bilingual processing of ASL–English code-blends: The consequences of accessing two lexical representations simultaneously. *Journal of Memory and Language, 67*(1), 199–210. 10.1016/j.jml.2012.04.005

Emmorey, K., Petrich, J. A. F., & Gollan, T. H. (2013). Bimodal bilingualism and the frequency-lag hypothesis. *Journal of Deaf Studies and Deaf Education, 18*(1), 1–11. 10.1093/deafed/ens034

Fenlon, J., Schembri, A., Rentelis, R., Vinson, D., & Cormier, K. (2014). Using conversational data to determine lexical frequency in British Sign Language: The influence of text type. *Lingua, 143*, 187–202. 10.1016/j.lingua.2014.02.003

Finkbeiner, M., Almeida, J., Janssen, N., & Caramazza, A. (2006). Lexical selection in bilingual speech production does not involve language suppression. *Journal of Experimental Psychology: Learning, Memory, and Cognition, 32*(5), 1075–1089. 10.1037/0278-7393.32.5.1075

Gibson, E., Futrell, R., Piantadosi, S. P., Dautriche, I., Mahowald, K., Bergen, L., & Levy, R. (2019). How efficiency shapes human language. *Trends in Cognitive Sciences, 23*(5), 389–407. 10.1016/j.tics.2019.02.003

Giezen, M. R., & Emmorey, K. (2016). Language co-activation and lexical selection in bimodal bilinguals: Evidence from picture–word interference. *Bilingualism: Language and Cognition, 19*(2), 264–276. 10.1017/S1366728915000097

Gimeno-Martínez, M., & Baus, C. (2021). Iconicity in sign production: Task matters. Preprint. https://psyarxiv.com/kf68y/

Giustolisi, B., Mereghetti, E., & Cecchetto, C. (2017). Phonological blending or code mixing? Why mouthing is not a core component of sign language grammar. *Natural Language & Linguistic Theory, 35*(2), 347–365. 10.1007/s11049-016-9353-9

Gollan, T. H., Montoya, R. I., Cera, C., & Sandoval, T. C. (2008). More use almost always means a smaller frequency effect: Aging, bilingualism, and the weaker links hypothesis☆. *Journal of Memory and Language, 58*(3), 787–814. 10.1016/j.jml.2007.07.001

Graves, W. W., Grabowski, T. J., Mehta, S., & Gordon, J. K. (2007). A neural signature of phonological access: Distinguishing the effects of word frequency from familiarity and length in overt picture naming. *Journal of Cognitive Neuroscience, 19*(4), 617–631. 10.1162/jocn.2007.19.4.617

Green, D. W., & Abutalebi, J. (2013). Language control in bilinguals: The adaptive control hypothesis. *Journal of Cognitive Psychology, 25*(5), 515–530. 10.1080/20445911.2013.796377

Grosjean, F. (1979). A study of timing in a manual and a spoken language: American Sign Language and English. *Journal of Psycholinguistic Research, 8*(4), 379–405. 10.1007/BF01067141

Gutiérrez, E., Müller, O., Baus, C., & Carreiras, M. (2012). Electrophysiological evidence for phonological priming in Spanish Sign Language lexical access. *Neuropsychologia, 50*(7), 1335–1346. 10.1016/j.neuropsychologia.2012.02.018

Gutierrez-Sigut, E., Daws, R., Payne, H., Blott, J., Marshall, C., & MacSweeney, M. (2015). Language lateralization of hearing native signers: A functional transcranial Doppler sonography (fTCD) study of speech and sign production. *Brain and Language, 151*, 23–34. 10.1016/j.bandl.2015.10.006

Gutierrez-Sigut, E., Payne, H., & MacSweeney, M. (2016). Examining the contribution of motor movement and language dominance to increased left lateralization during sign generation in native signers. *Brain and Language, 159*, 109–117. 10.1016/j.bandl.2016.06.004

Herrmann, A. (2010). The interaction of eye blinks and other prosodic cues in German Sign Language. *Sign Language & Linguistics*, *13*(1), 3–39. 10.1075/sll.13.1.02her

Herrmann, A., & Steinbach, M. (2012). Quotation in sign languages. In I. Buchstaller, & I. Van Alphen (Eds.), *Quotatives: Cross-linguistic and cross-disciplinary perspectives* (pp. 203–228). Amsterdam: John Benjamins Publishing.

Hickok, G. (2012). Computational neuroanatomy of speech production. *Nature Reviews Neuroscience*, *13*(2), 135–145. 10.1038/nrn3158

Hickok, G., Bellugi, U., & Klima, E. S. (1996). The neurobiology of sign language and its implications for the neural basis of language. *Nature*, *381*(6584), 699–702. 10.1038/381699a0

Hildebrandt, U., & Corina, D. (2002). Phonological similarity in American Sign Language. *Language and Cognitive Processes*, *17*(6), 593–612. 10.1080/01690960143000371

Hohenberger, A., Happ, D., & Leuninger, H. (2002). Modality-dependent aspects of sign language production: Evidence from slips of the hands and their repairs in German Sign Language. In R. P. Meier, K. Cormier, & D. Quinto-Pozos (Eds.), *Modality and structure in signed and spoken languages* (1st ed., pp. 112–142). Cambridge University Press. 10.1017/CBO9780511486777.006

Holcomb, P. J., Kounios, J., Anderson, J. E., & West, W. C. (1999). Dual-coding, context-availability, and concreteness effects in sentence comprehension: An electrophysiological investigation. *Journal of Experimental Psychology: Learning, Memory, and Cognition*, *25*(3), 721–742. 10.1037/0278-7393.25.3.721

Horwitz, B., Amunts, K., Bhattacharyya, R., Patkin, D., Jeffries, K., Zilles, K., & Braun, A. R. (2003). Activation of Broca's area during the production of spoken and signed language: A combined cytoarchitectonic mapping and PET analysis. *Neuropsychologia*, *41*(14), 1868–1876. 10.1016/S0028-3932(03)00125-8

Jescheniak, J. D., & Levelt, W. J. M. (1994). Word frequency effects in speech production: Retrieval of syntactic information and of phonological form. *Journal of Experimental Psychology: Learning, Memory, and Cognition*, *20*(4), 824–843. 10.1037/0278-7393.20.4.824

Kaufmann, E., & Philipp, A. M. (2017). Language-switch costs and dual-response costs in bimodal bilingual language production. *Bilingualism: Language and Cognition*, *20*(2), 418–434. 10.1017/S1366728915000759

Leonard, M. K., Lucas, B., Blau, S., Corina, D. P., & Chang, E. F. (2020). Cortical encoding of manual articulatory and linguistic features in American Sign Language. *Current Biology 30*(22), 4342–4351. 10.1016/j.cub.2020.08.048

Levelt, W. J. M. (1980). On-line processing constraints on the properties of signed and spoken language. In *Signed and spoken language: Biological constraints on linguistic form* (pp. 141–160). Verlag Chemie. https://pure.mpg.de/pubman/faces/ViewItemOverviewPage.jsp?itemId=item_66987

Levelt, W. J. M. (1989). *Speaking: From intention to articulation*. MIT Press.

Liu, Y., Shu, H., & Li, P. (2007). Word naming and psycholinguistic norms: Chinese. *Behavior Research Methods*, *39*(2), 192–198. 10.3758/BF03193147

Lockwood, G., & Dingemanse, M. (2015). Iconicity in the lab: A review of behavioral, developmental, and neuroimaging research into sound-symbolism. *Frontiers in Psychology*, *6*. 10.3389/fpsyg.2015.01246

Löffler, J. (2019). The tip-of-the-fingers phenomenon in German Sign Language – A corpus-based analysis. Poster presented at the Theoretical Issues in Sign Language Research meeting, September, Hamburg, Germany.

Löffler, J., Herrmann, A., & Villwock, A. (2020). Wie ist noch mal die Gebärde … ? Das Tip-of-the-finger Phänomen in Deutsche Gebårdensprache (DGS) [What is the sign again ...? The tip-of-the-finger phenomenon in German Sign Language (DGS)]. *Das Zeichen 114*, 80–94.

Luce, P. A., & Pisoni, D. B. (1998). Recognizing spoken words: The neighborhood activation model. *Ear and Hearing, 19*(1), 1–36. 10.1097/00003446-199802000-00001

Mahon, B. Z., Costa, A., Peterson, R., Vargas, K. A., & Caramazza, A. (2007). Lexical selection is not by competition: A reinterpretation of semantic interference and facilitation effects in the picture-word interference paradigm. *Journal of Experimental Psychology: Learning, Memory, and Cognition, 33*(3), 503–535. 10.1037/0278-7393.33.3.503

Mayberry, R. I., & Witcher, P. (2005). What age of acquisition effects reveal about the nature of phonological processing. *CRL Technical Reports, 17*(3), 1–9.

McGarry, M. E., Mott, M., Midgley, K. J., Holcomb, P. J., & Emmorey, K. (2021). Picture-naming in American Sign Language: An electrophysiological study of the effects of iconicity and structured alignment. *Language, Cognition and Neuroscience, 36*(2), 199–210. 10.1080/23273798.2020.1804601

Meade, G., Lee, B., Massa, N., Holcomb, P. J., Midgley, K. J., & Emmorey, K. (2021). The organization of the American Sign Language lexicon: Comparing one- and two-parameter ERP phonological priming effects across tasks. *Brain and Language, 218*, 104960. 10.1016/j.bandl.2021.104960

Meade, G., Lee, B., Midgley, K. J., Holcomb, P. J., & Emmorey, K. (2018). Phonological and semantic priming in American Sign Language: N300 and N400 effects. *Language, Cognition and Neuroscience, 33*(9), 1092–1106. 10.1080/23273798.2018.1446543

Metellus, P., Boussen, S., Guye, M., & Trebuchon, A. (2017). Successful insular glioma removal in a deaf signer patient during an awake craniotomy procedure. *World Neurosurgery, 98*, 883.e1–883.e5. 10.1016/j.wneu.2016.08.098

Meteyard, L., Stoppard, E., Snudden, D., Cappa, S. F., & Vigliocco, G. (2015). When semantics aids phonology: A processing advantage for iconic word forms in aphasia. *Neuropsychologia, 76*, 264–275. 10.1016/j.neuropsychologia.2015.01.042

Navarrete, E., Peressotti, F., Lerose, L., & Miozzo, M. (2017). Activation cascading in sign production. *Journal of Experimental Psychology: Learning, Memory, and Cognition, 43*(2), 302–318. 10.1037/xlm0000312

Newkirk, D., Klima, E. S., Pedersen, C. C., & Bellugi, U. (1980). Linguistic evidence from slips of the hand. In V. Fromkin (Ed.), *Errors in linguistic performance: Slips of the tongue, ear, pen, and hand* (pp. 165–197). New York: Academic Press.

Nielsen, A. K., & Dingemanse, M. (2021). Iconicity in word learning and beyond: A critical review. *Language and Speech, 64*(1), 52–72. 10.1177/0023830920914339

Nozari, N., Dell, G. S., & Schwartz, M. F. (2011). Is comprehension necessary for error detection? A conflict-based account of monitoring in speech production. *Cognitive Psychology, 63*(1), 1–33.

Nozari, N., & Novick, J. (2017). Monitoring and control in language production. *Current Directions in Psychological Science, 26*(5), 403–410. 10.1177/0963721417702419

Okrent, A. (2002). A modality-free notion of gesture and how it can help us with the morpheme vs. gesture question in sign language linguistics (or at least give us some criteria to work with). In R. Meier, K. Cormier, & D. Quinto-Pozos (Eds.), *Modality and structure in signed and spoken languages* (pp. 175–198). Cambridge University Press.

Parkinson, A., Condon, L., & Jackson, S. R. (2010). Parietal cortex coding of limb posture: In search of the body-schema. *Neuropsychologia, 48*(11), 3228–3234. 10.1016/j.neuropsychologia.2010.06.039

Petitto, L. A., Zatorre, R. J., Gauna, K., Nikelski, E. J., Dostie, D., & Evans, A. C. (2000). Speech-like cerebral activity in profoundly deaf people processing signed languages:

Implications for the neural basis of human language. Proceedings of the *National Academy of Sciences, 97*(25), 13961–13966. 10.1073/pnas.97.25.13961

Poortman, E. B., & Pylkkänen, L. (2016). Adjective conjunction as a window into the LATL's contribution to conceptual combination. *Brain and Language, 160,* 50–60. 10.1016/j.bandl.2016.07.006

Pretato, E., Peressotti, F., Bertone, C., & Navarrete, E. (2018). The iconicity advantage in sign production: The case of bimodal bilinguals. *Second Language Research, 34*(4), 449–462. 10.1177/0267658317744009

Pylkkänen, L., Bemis, D. K., & Blanco Elorrieta, E. (2014). Building phrases in language production: An MEG study of simple composition. *Cognition, 133*(2), 371–384. 10.1016/j.cognition.2014.07.001

Reichenbach, A., Thielscher, A., Peer, A., Bülthoff, H. H., & Bresciani, J.-P. (2014). A key region in the human parietal cortex for processing proprioceptive hand feedback during reaching movements. *NeuroImage, 84,* 615–625. 10.1016/j.neuroimage.2013.09.024

Riès, S. K., Janssen, N., Dufau, S., Alario, F.-X., & Burle, B. (2011). General-purpose monitoring during speech production. *Journal of Cognitive Neuroscience, 23*(6), 1419–1436. 10.1162/jocn.2010.21467

Riès, S. K., Nadalet, L., Mickelsen, S., Mott, M., Midgley, K. J., Holcomb, P. J., & Emmorey, K. (2020). Pre-output language monitoring in sign production. *Journal of Cognitive Neuroscience, 32*(6), 1079–1091. 10.1162/jocn_a_01542

Runqvist, E. (this volume). The neurocognitive basis of error monitoring in language production.

Sandler, W. (1989). *Phonological representation of the sign: Linearity and nonlinearity in American Sign Language.* Dordrecht: Foris. doi: 10.1515/9783110250473

Sehyr, Z. S., Caselli, N., Cohen-Goldberg, A. M., & Emmorey, K. (2021). The ASL-LEX 2.0 project: A database of lexical and phonological properties for 2,723 signs in American Sign Language. *The Journal of Deaf Studies and Deaf Education, 26*(2), 263–277. 10.1093/deafed/enaa038

Sehyr, Z. S., & Emmorey, K. (2022). The effects of multiple linguistic variables on picture naming in American Sign Language. *Behavioral Research Methods, 54,* 2502–2521.

Sehyr, Z. S., & Emmorey, K. (2019). The perceived mapping between form and meaning in American Sign Language depends on linguistic knowledge and task: Evidence from iconicity and transparency judgments. *Language and Cognition, 11*(2), 208–234. doi:10.1017/langcog.2019.18

Shum, J., Fanda, L., Dugan, P., Doyle, W. K., Devinsky, O., & Flinker, A. (2020). Neural correlates of sign language production revealed by electrocorticography. *Neurology, 95*(21), e2880–e2889. 10.1212/WNL.0000000000010639

Strijkers, K., Costa, A., & Thierry, G. (2010). Tracking lexical access in speech production: Electrophysiological correlates of word frequency and cognate effects. *Cerebral Cortex, 20*(4), 912–928. 10.1093/cercor/bhp153

Taub, S. F. (2001). *Language from the body: Iconicity and metaphor in American Sign Language.* Cambridge University Press.

Thompson, R., Emmorey, K., & Gollan, T. H. (2005). "Tip of the Fingers" experiences by deaf signers: Insights into the organization of a sign-based lexicon. *Psychological Science, 16*(11), 856–860. 10.1111/j.1467-9280.2005.01626.x

Thompson, R., Emmorey, K., & Kluender, R. (2006). The relationship between eye gaze and verb agreement in American Sign Language: An eye-tracking study. *Natural Language & Linguistic Theory, 24*(2), 571–604. 10.1007/s11049-005-1829-y

Tourville, J. A., & Guenther, F. H. (2011). The DIVA model: A neural theory of speech acquisition and production. *Language and Cognitive Processes, 26*(7), 952–981. 10.1080/01 690960903498424

Vinson, D. P., Cormier, K., Denmark, T., Schembri, A., & Vigliocco, G. (2008). The British Sign Language (BSL) norms for age of acquisition, familiarity, and iconicity. *Behavior Research Methods, 40*(4), 1079–1087. 10.3758/BRM.40.4.1079

Vinson, D. P., Thompson, R. L., Skinner, R., Fox, N., & Vigliocco, G. (2010). The hands and mouth do not always slip together in British Sign Language: Dissociating articulatory channels in the lexicon. *Psychological Science, 21*(8), 1158–1167. 10.1177/09567976103 77340

Vinson, D., Thompson, R. L., Skinner, R., & Vigliocco, G. (2015). A faster path between meaning and form? Iconicity facilitates sign recognition and production in British Sign Language. *Journal of Memory and Language, 82*, 56–85. 10.1016/j.jml.2015.03.002

Vitevitch, M. S. (2002). The influence of phonological similarity neighborhoods on speech production. *Journal of Experimental Psychology: Learning, Memory, and Cognition, 28*(4), 735–747. 10.1037/0278-7393.28.4.735

Vitevitch, M. S., & Luce, P. A. (1998). When words compete: Levels of processing in perception of spoken words. *Psychological Science, 9*(4), 325–329. 10.1111/1467-9280.00064

Wilbur, R. B., & Patschke, C. G. (1998). Body leans and the marking of contrast in American sign language. *Journal of Pragmatics, 30*(3), 275–303. 10.1016/S0378-2166(98)00003-4

Winter, B. (2021). Iconicity, not arbitrariness, is a design feature of language. Talk presented for the Abralin talk series, May 5: https://aovivo.abralin.org/en/lives/bodo-winter/

Zeshan, U. (2006). *Interrogative and negative constructions in sign language.* Ishara Press. 10.26530/ OAPEN_453832

Zipf, G. K. (1949). *Human behavior and the principle of least effort.* Cambridge, MA: Addison-Wesley Press.

10 Co-Speech Gesture

J.P. de Ruiter

The phenomenon

What is co-speech gesture?

Every observer of human–human communication will have noticed the intri-guing hand movements[1] that speakers make during their production of verbal utterances. The famous gesture researcher Adam Kendon has called these hand motions "visible action as utterance" (Kendon, 2004). This definition alludes to the fact that not every hand motion performed during speech is a co-speech gesture. If someone scratches their nose or adjusts their glasses during an ut-terance, this is usually not related to the content of their speech, so it is not considered to be a co-speech gesture.[2]

A defining aspect of co-speech gestures, implied by their name, is that they are produced by speakers, and not by listeners. Listeners also can and do make gestures, but they then are trivially not "co-speech gestures," and they are very different from co-speech gestures.

Another defining feature of co-speech gestures is that they are tightly *synchronized* with the concurrent speech, both temporally and semantically. Their *temporal* synchronization means that the meaning-carrying part of the hand motion is produced in temporal overlap with the concurrent speech. *Semantic* synchronization means that the gesture expresses a meaning that is intricately related to the meaning of the concurrent speech. It is for these reasons that co-speech gesture is seen as distinctly different from so-called "nonverbal behavior" like body posture, body orientation, or facial expression.

A final defining and often underestimated property of co-speech gestures is that they only occur during *spontaneous* speech, that is speech that is con-ceptualized on the spot by the speaker, as opposed to rehearsed or ritualized speech. This property has important consequences for the study of gesture as well as for their diagnostic value in studying speech and thought processes, both of which are discussed in other sections below.

DOI: 10.4324/9781003145790-11

What co-speech gesture is not

It is tempting to assume that co-speech gesture (henceforth "gesture" for reasons of brevity) is very similar to Sign Language, the native language of deaf people (see Emmorey, this volume, for an in-depth discussion of Sign Language). It is very important to realize that and how this is not the case. Obviously, what Sign Language and gesture have in common is that they express communicative intentions by using hand motions. This common use of articulators leads to some articulatory similarities. Both Sign Language and gestures exploit both hand shape and trajectory for expressing meanings and will for instance often use the index finger to point. But the similarities are deceptive. Sign Languages are full-fledged languages, each with a unique phonology, syntax, and semantics, involving arbitrary form-meaning mappings at all three levels. For phonology, this means that speakers of Sign Languages have recognizable "accents," just like speakers of spoken languages. For syntax, this means that different Sign Languages can have different word orders. And for semantics, it not only means that it is generally not possible for people who do not speak a Sign Language to recognize the meaning of the lexical elements, but also that people speaking different Sign Languages will not automatically understand each other. Just like speakers of spoken languages, they will need to learn the other language. The reason I elaborate on these properties of Sign Language is that none of them holds for gesture (with one specific exception that is discussed below). This means that it is generally not possible to produce an ungrammatical or ill-pronounced gesture. This is not to say that gestures cannot be marked, strange, or otherwise unusual.[3] But in contrast to when someone says "Me banana want" in English, and we can correct the utterance on the basis of the inferred meaning to "I want a banana," in gesture there is no agreed-upon "correct" way to express things.

Typology of gestures

There are different types of gestures, each with unique properties that require different cognitive processes and representations in speakers who produce them. For the purposes of this chapter, I will follow the influential typology by McNeill (1992), which is used by most gesture researchers, albeit often with modifications. McNeill's classification is largely based on semiotic principles, and distinguishes the following categories:

> **Deictic** gestures are what we informally call pointing gestures. There are two subtypes. *Concrete* deictic gestures refer to a concrete direction or object, whereas *abstract* deictic gestures point to a location in the space in front of the speaker that represents a referent from the dialogue discourse.

> **Beats** are repetitive, rhythmic hand movements that do not appear to be related to specific elements from the accompanying speech.

Iconic gestures express meaning through their shape and manner of their execution. In contrast to metaphoric gestures, their referents are concrete entities. The most important property of iconic gestures is that their form-to-meaning relationship is not conventional and shared in the language community (as is the signed or spoken words) but created "on the fly" by the speaker. It is this spontaneous and idiosyncratic form–meaning mapping that makes iconic gestures very interesting for language and communication researchers, and subject to a number of long-standing controversies, which are discussed below. An important sub-type of iconic gesture is the "pantomime." This is a gesture that is produced by performing an action "in the air" to convey the action. For instance, one can make a sawing, hammering, or throwing motion in the air, as if one had an actual saw, hammer, or ball in one's hand. The difference with the "standard" iconic gesture is that the gesture doesn't "draw" something (e.g., when tracing the shape of a coke bottle), but "enacts" an activity. Even though McNeill (1992) classifies both of these as iconic gestures, it is to be expected that they require different cognitive processing.

Metaphoric gestures are iconic gestures that refer to *abstract* concepts instead of concrete ones.

Emblematic gestures (or "emblems") are conventionalized stand-alone gestures that are often produced *instead* of speech and are in that case of course not accompanied by speech. Examples are the thumbs-up for "OK," or the index finger on the lips for "be quiet." Emblems are the types of gestures that are the most similar to words in Sign Language, as they *do* have arbitrary form-meaning mappings that are different for different language communities. This can lead to cross-linguistic confusion. For instance the gesture where the index finger and the thumb together make a ring and the other three fingers are stretched means "excellent" in many Germanic language communities but means "asshole" (as an insult) in some Romance languages.

The scientific study of gesture

Studying gesture using controlled experimental methods is surprisingly difficult. The main reason for this is that gesture is a phenomenon that only occurs during spontaneous speech, and experimental control of spontaneous behavior is an oxymoron.

To compare, in studying speech production, we can show a participant a picture of a duck, and require them to say "duck," and record and time their vocal response. This classical paradigm, called "picture naming" (see Glaser, 1992) has many variants (one can for instance create semantic distractors by printing the word "goose" under the picture of the duck) and has been used very effectively to study the different stages and time course of word production. This would not work with iconic gestures, which is the most frequent and arguably most interesting category of gesture. If we were to present a picture of a duck to someone and ask them to "gesture it," this experiment would not be very informative for a number of reasons. First, there is no conventionalized form-meaning mapping that tells the participant how to gesture "duck." Note that this would work perfectly well with Sign Language because then there *is* a conventional mapping from the concept "duck" to a sign, namely the Sign Language word for "duck." Second, and relatedly, the participant, faced with the request to gesture in response to the picture of a duck, has a wide range of behavioral options, which makes their response behavior unpredictable. This means the dependent variable is very difficult to analyze. Third, even if this did work, it would not tell us anything about gesture as it occurs naturally. The participant could, for instance, move their arms as if flapping wings and accompany this with a quacking sound. This would perhaps do a good job of conveying the concept of "duck," but it would probably not be the same type of gesture as someone who produces a co-speech gesture while producing a sentence featuring a duck.

This methodological limitation makes it hard to study gesture using the "single unit" production experiments and requires the researcher to either study natural or semi-natural data from people telling stories or limit their experimental design to situations where people still produce spontaneous speech. For example, in the gesture experiments by Bangerter (2004) and De Ruiter et al. (2012), a variant of the director-matcher paradigm was used to have people speak and gesture spontaneously while still being in an experimental design, with control over the stimuli. However, because of the difficulty to control independent variables, many gesture studies are based on studying recordings of participants either speaking and gesturing "in the wild" or, more commonly, participants retelling stories that have been presented to them on video (see e.g., Hostetter & Skirving, 2011; Kita & Özyürek, 2003; McNeill, 1992).

Brief history of cognitive-scientific gesture theory

In this section, I will give a brief overview of the development of cognitive-psychological theory regarding the coordinated production of gesture and speech. This overview will necessarily be incomplete, covering only some of the central theories, experiments, and controversies. Readers interested in more information are referred to the provided references and the references therein.

Before the cognitive revolution

Before the cognitive revolution, there has been some observational work on gesture. For a very thorough discussion of the history of pre-20th-century gesture research, I strongly recommend the comprehensive monograph by Kendon (2004). As for the study of both language and gesture during the earlier half of the 20th century, research into gesture was hindered by the predominance of Behaviorism. This then-mainstream approach attempted to explain human behavior in terms of observable responses to observable stimuli, and explicitly avoids invoking internal representations (a notable exception is the work of Edward Tolman). This makes it nearly impossible to establish a relationship between spoken utterances and hand movements, let alone develop theories about their internal processing. But there was some important observational work on gesture. David Efron, a student of Franz Boas, was the first to use visual recordings of gesture, using 16 mm film, to study the differences between East European Jewish and Italian immigrants in Manhattan. He concluded that these differences disappeared in subsequent generations, indicating that the observed differences did not have a racial origin (Efron, 1941). Another observer of gesture was Ray Birdwhistell (1952), whose project on "kinesics," in the words of Kendon (2004, p. 68) "constituted the most ambitious and explicit attempt to extend the methods of structural linguistics beyond the boundaries of spoken utterance." According to Kendon (ibid.), the potential of the work of Birdwhistell and his contemporaries, e.g., Trager's (1958) work on "paralanguage," did not develop into a kind of "linguistics of gesture" because of the rising influence of the work of Noam Chomsky in the late 1950s and early 1960s. Chomsky's work switched the attention of language researchers from observable behavior to the study of linguistic "competence" (Chomsky, 1964). As Kendon (2004, p. 68) astutely observed, gesture, "was consigned, along with much else, to the waste-basket of 'performance' – at the height of Chomsky's influence this meant that it was definitely not worthy of attention."

During the cognitive revolution

Efron pioneered the use of 16-mm film to study gesture and speech in great detail.[4] Subsequent work by Condon and Ogston (1966; 1967) used this medium at different frame rates to perform a micro analysis of body motion and speech of psychiatric patients and neurotypical controls at a high temporal resolution. A similar study was conducted by Kendon (1972). These studies uncovered that speech and body motion are generally synchronized. Larger body movements tend to co-occur with speech units at the level of larger discourse units, and smaller movements (e.g., hand and finger movement) with prosodic phrases. Note that these studies did not look specifically at gesture as an explicit communicative device, but rather provided an 'etic' analysis of speech and general body motion. A modern variant of this approach, taking advantage of modern video technology, can be found in Bente et al. (2001).

During that same period, Ekman and Friesen (1969) also studied hand motion with concurrent speech and created the important distinction between "illustrators" and "emblems," hand movements that carried meaning, and "self-adaptors," where the speaker touches themselves or adjust their clothing.

One of the earliest papers that analyzed gestures as a carrier of meaning together with the concurrent speech was Kendon (1980). This landmark study

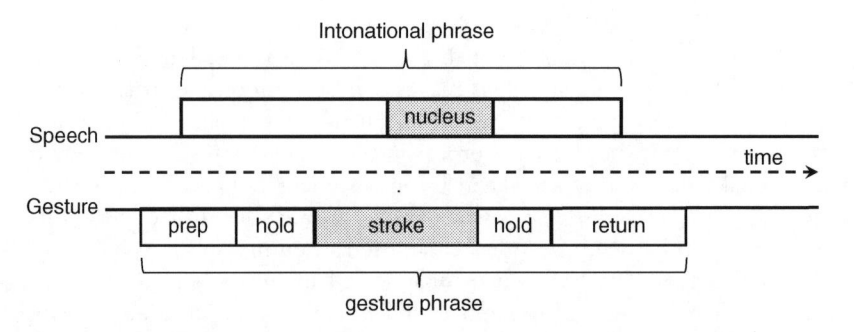

Figure 10.1 Temporal anatomy of gesture and speech.

contributed a few central concepts regarding gesture (which Kendon usually calls "gesticulation") that have had a deep impact on the field. Like Condon and Ogston, Kendon was primarily focused on the temporal synchrony of the gesture and the speech, but it is worth noting here that this *presumes* semantic synchrony, as otherwise it would be impossible to tell which gesture is supposedly aligned with which verbal utterance. Kendon described the temporal anatomy of a gesture and its relation to speech in great detail. The central part, the meaning-carrying phase of the gesture, he called the *stroke*. The stroke is optionally preceded by a *preparation phase*, which is the part where the hand is moved from the resting position (e.g., in the lap or pocket) to the beginning of the stroke. After the stroke, there is an optional *return phase*, in which the hand moves from the end of the stroke back to a resting position. The temporal synchronization of the gesture is such that the stroke either precedes or is concurrent with the *tone nucleus* (usually the last syllable with primary stress) of the intonational phrase in the speech. Because both gesture and speech units vary in duration, the gesture/speech system often needs to maintain this temporal synchronization by inserting pre-stroke and post-stroke *holds*, periods during which the hands remain motionless either right before or right after the stroke. See Figure 10.1 for an overview of the temporal anatomy of a synchronized gesture/speech utterance.

The growth point

In 1985, the developmental psychologist and psycholinguist David McNeill published a landmark article with the provocative and very apt title "So you think gesture is nonverbal?"(McNeill, 1985). It was this article that permanently separated co-speech gesture conceptually from the then highly popular field of "nonverbal behavior" and put gesture on the map as a purely psycholinguistic phenomenon. It features a detailed semiotic analysis of five students retelling a Tweetybird & Sylvester cartoon movie, and was one of the first to point to the defining properties of gesture mentioned in the first page of this article: (a) gesture is a speaker phenomenon, (b) gestures mirror the pragmatic and semantic aspects of the accompanying speech, and (c) gestures are temporally synchronized with speech. McNeill also argued that gesture is affected just as much as speech in people with aphasia and that it develops in children together with speech. These two claims have been disputed in later research (M. Alibali & Goldin-Meadow, 1993; Feyereisen, 1983).

In his subsequent landmark publication "Hand and Mind" (McNeill, 1992), McNeill elaborated on these ideas and provided both a systematic research methodology, a typology (both described above), and a new theory of speech production centered around the notion of the *Growth Point*. The Growth Point (GP) is, roughly speaking, a pre-linguistic thought (McNeill calls it an *idea unit*) from which both linguistic-categorical information (speech) as well as imagistic information (gesture) are developed as overt utterances. The interested reader is referred to McNeill's (1992) book "Hand and Mind" and also McNeill et al. (2008).

GP theory is not formulated in the information processing framework commonly used in the Cognitive Sciences (see De Ruiter, 2000, pp. 285–289 for a more detailed discussion of this particular issue), but it expresses, in a rather poetic way, a number of key insights. The most central one is that a gesture and its accompanying speech originate from a new idea that is about to be introduced in the discourse. This also provides a tentative explanation why gestures occur only during spontaneous speech, and not during rehearsed speech.

Because GP theory was not formulated within the classical information processing framework of the cognitive sciences, it is very hard to derive concrete predictions from it, making it essentially unfalsifiable. As I hope to show in the following sections, the Growth Point theory nevertheless left its mark on the subsequent cognitive and psycholinguistic work on co-speech gesture.

The sketch model

The synchronous production of gesture and speech, descriptively reported mostly in work by Adam Kendon and David McNeill and their colleagues and students, has been captured in a cognitive architecture by De Ruiter (2000). The architecture (see Figure 10.2) was built on the foundation of Levelt's (1989) influential "blueprint for the speaker." It is still the only cognitive model for gesture and speech production that incorporates the production of all but one of the major gesture types from McNeill's (1992) typology (the exception being beat gestures).

The model incorporates four core assumptions about the relation between gesture and speech. (a) A single communicative intention underlies the planning of both gesture and speech, (b) Speech and gesture are planned together in the conceptualizer, but executed separately ("ballistically," in the words of Levelt et al., 1985) by the Formulator and the Gesture Planner, and the temporal

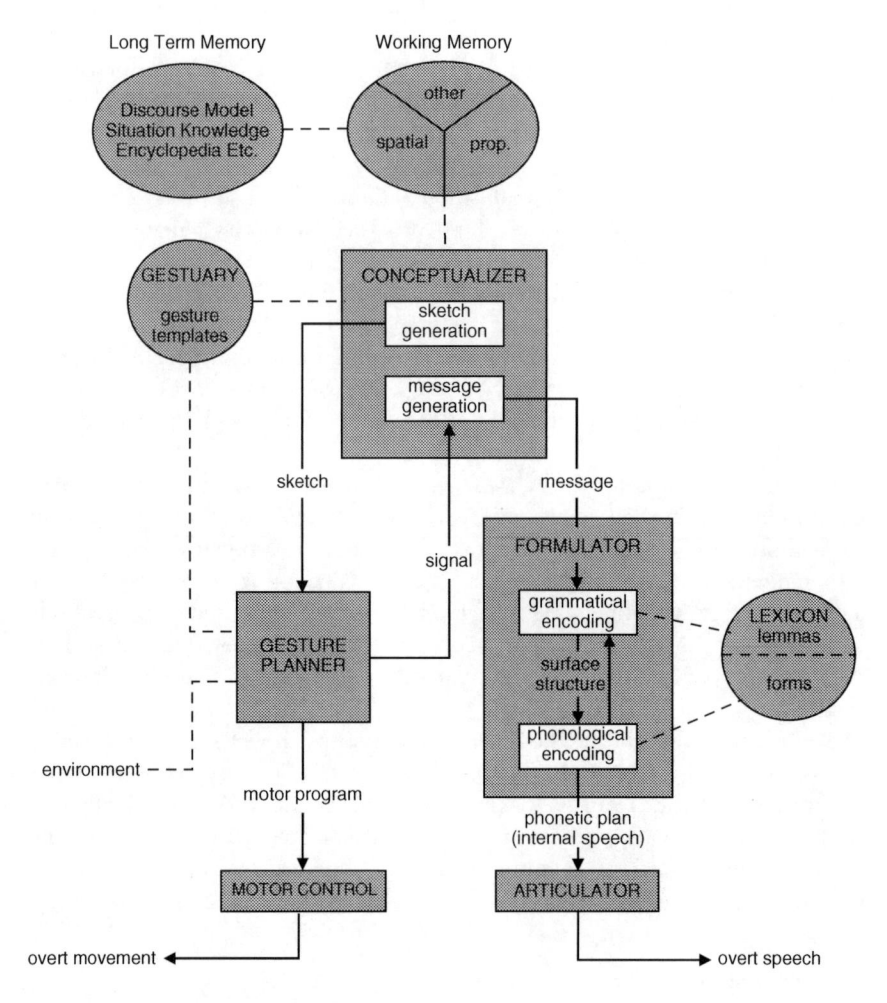

Figure 10.2 The Sketch Model.

synchronization is achieved by a simple signaling mechanism, (c) Gesture and speech are both planned and produced together to express information for the benefit of the interlocutor's understanding, and finally, (d) Gesture and speech are assumed to be mutually adaptive: one channel compensates for expressive limitations of the other.

The planning of a multimodal utterance starts with a representation of a speaker's communicative intention. Based on this communicative intention, the Conceptualizer retrieves the relevant information from working memory. These representations are either propositional or imagistic in nature and are processed independently of one another by the conceptualizer, but are timed to be produced at roughly the same time.

As most of the theoretical debates regarding gesture and speech processing are about iconic gestures, I will only describe in more detail here how an utterance containing an iconic or metaphoric[5] gesture is processed in the model. For the production processes in the Sketch model for pointing gestures and emblems, please see De Ruiter (2000).

In the case of an utterance consisting of both speech and an iconic gesture, the propositional representations from the communicative intention are encoded into a Preverbal Message to be used to plan and produce the spoken part of the utterance (in line with Levelt's 1989 model). The imagistic information from the communicative intention forms the basis for the encoding of a so-called "sketch," which is the functional equivalent of the preverbal message in the gesture modality. The sketch of an iconic gesture contains spatio-temporal and imagistic representations retrieved from working memory. This sketch is further processed and transformed in the gesture planner into a motor program for the hand(s). This motor program is sent to the motor control system of the hand to be converted into the overt movement, i.e., the gesture. This all happens largely in parallel with the Formulator expanding the preverbal message into an articulatory plan. A simple signal mechanism ensures that the gesture and speech are initiated at roughly the same time. This synchronization mechanism has been empirically tested and confirmed using speech hesitation data by Seyfeddinipur (2006).

Controversy 1: The function of gesture

The studies discussed so far have all implicitly or explicitly assumed that the primary function of gesture is to transmit information from the communicative intention to the listener. This is uncontroversial when it comes to deictic (pointing) gestures and emblems. For iconic gestures (which are sometimes called "lexical gestures" or "representational gestures"), however, this has been disputed. Several gesture researchers have claimed that the function of gesture is not to inform the listener, but rather to facilitate internal cognitive processes of the speaker. One of the oldest facilitatory theories was the idea that making gestures facilitates the retrieval of word-form information from the lexicon by cross-modally activating the conceptual representations involved in the verbal message (Hadar & Butterworth, 1997; Krauss et al., 1995, 2000; Rauscher et al., 1996; Rimé et al., 1984).

The view that gesture facilitates lexical retrieval

The assumption that the primary function of gesture is to facilitate word retrieval was also the basis for the model by Krauss et al. (2000). This model was formulated to illustrate how retrieving wordforms from the mental lexicon can be facilitated by speakers producing what the authors call "lexical gestures," which are essentially the same as McNeill's iconic (and perhaps also metaphoric) gestures. The diagram of their model is shown in Figure 10.3 below. Like the Sketch model, it is based on and an extension of Levelt's (1989) blueprint for the

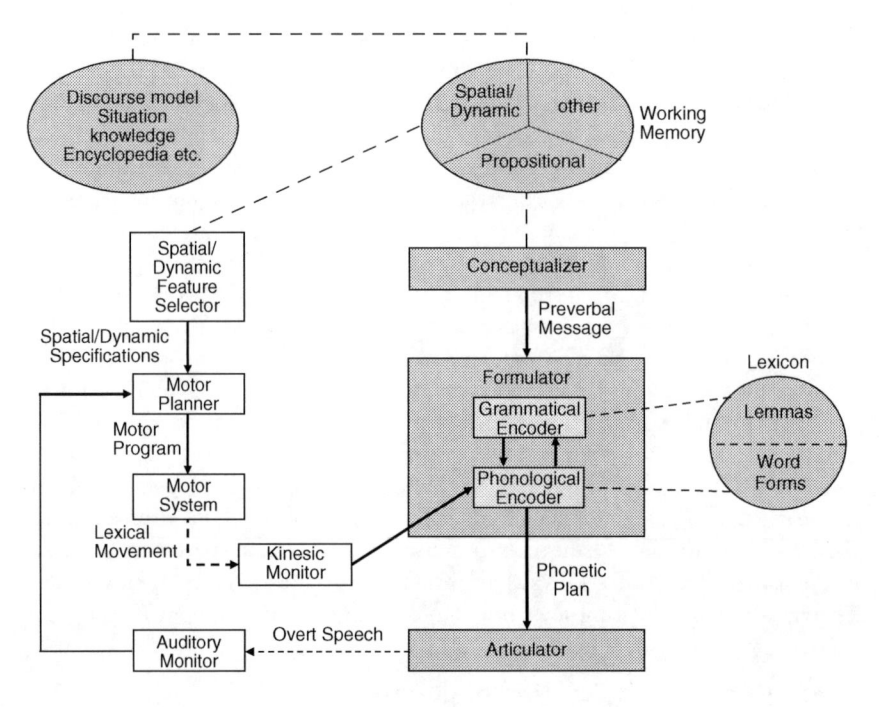

Figure 10.3 The model by Krauss et al. (2000).

speaker.[6] But in contrast to the Sketch model, it assumes that gestures are not generated to communicate information to the listener, but rather to provide speaker-internal cross-modal cues that facilitate word-form retrieval during speech formulation. The spatial/dynamic information in working memory that is related to the verbal message is translated into a motor program for a lexical gesture, which is monitored kinesthetically by the Kinesic Monitor. The features detected by the Kinesic Monitor feed into the Phonological Encoder, providing cross-model cues that facilitate word-form encoding.

According to this "lexical retrieval facilitation" view, the fact that some information might be gleaned from the resulting overt movement is at best a lucky side-effect. There has been a long debate between the proponents of the "communicative" and "lexical retrieval facilitation" (henceforth LRF) views. The discussion between these two camps is complicated because the experimental evidence for either view is often amenable to interpretations that support either view.

Evidence for and against the view that gesture facilitates lexical retrieval

One of the more intriguing phenomena regarding iconic gestures is that they are also produced when there is no visual contact between interlocutors.

People on the telephone tend to gesture quite a lot, and it seems to make little sense to produce these gestures if they cannot be observed by the interlocutor. This suggests that people might produce iconic gestures in order to facilitate their own internal speech processing, rather than to communicate information. But proponents of the Communicative view point out that people also produce facial expressions and other communicative movements (e.g., bowing, by Japanese speakers) while speaking on the phone, and it is highly implausible that these gestures are explicitly intended by the speaker to transmit information because the speaker will be aware that they are not observed by their interlocutor. This suggests that these physical behaviors that tend to occur during speech might just be insuppressible habits. As long as the information expressed in these behaviors is not essential for understanding the speech, it does not matter that they are not being observed. People don't usually use deictic expression combined with pointing on the telephone (although there is anecdotal evidence of young children doing this), or produce emblems without also redundantly expressing the same information in speech, e.g., a "thumbs-up" gesture while saying "OK." It is also a well-established finding that people gesture significantly more when there is visual contact than when there is not (Bavelas et al., 1992; Cohen, 1977; Cohen & Harrison, 1973; De Ruiter et al., 2012).

Another source of support cited by proponents of the LRF view is that the stroke of a gesture tends to start earlier than the affiliated speech (see Figure 10.1 above). Morrel-Samuels & Krauss (1992) argued that this might be because the gesture is performed in order to facilitate word-form retrieval processes. Proponents of the Communicative view would argue that there are other potential reasons why gestures tend to start earlier, for instance, that gesture processing involves fewer computations than speech, giving gesture a head start.

A testable prediction from the LRF view is that it should be harder for people to speak when they are unable to gesture. Rimé et al. (1984) had participants engage in free conversation about some suggested topics. During the second half of the conversation, the head, hand, and arm movements of the participant were immobilized by devices attached to the armchair of the participant. It was found that the vividness of the imagery in the speech decreased when the hands were immobilized. At first sight these results seem to contradict the earlier findings by Graham and Argyle (1975) and Graham and Heywood (1975). They had participants talk about line drawings without gesturing, and found an *increase* in spatial speech, while Rimé et al. found a *decrease* in spatial speech. But these seemingly contradictory results actually make sense from the Communicative view. In the studies by Graham and Argyle (1975), and Graham and Heywood (1975), the participants were requested to speak about a given topic (the line drawings), while in the study by Rimé et al. participants were free to talk about anything. If gesture is a communicative device that is normally used to express spatial information, in the studies by Graham and Argyle (1975), and Graham and Heywood (1975) participants were forced to compensate for the lack of gesture by producing

more spatial descriptions in speech, while in the study by Rimé et al. participants, knowing they could not gesture, could simply have avoided talking
about topics requiring the expression of spatial information. Rauscher et al.
(1996) also prevented their participants from gesturing. The participants in
their study had to describe cartoon animations to listeners. Half of the time
they were not allowed to move their hands. Their findings were: (1) that
speech with spatial content was less fluent when gesturing was not permitted,
(2) speech without spatial content was not affected, and (3) that the frequency
of filled pauses in the speech increased in the no-gesture condition, but only
when the participants were producing speech with spatial content. The authors conclude from these findings that gesture facilitates access to the mental
lexicon, for the effects of preventing gesture are similar to those of word-
finding difficulties. But again, these results can more parsimoniously be interpreted as evidence that gesture functions as a compensatory communicative
device. Given that the gesture modality is much more efficient in expressing
spatial information, the loss of fluency in the no-gesture condition is predictable: the generation of speech with spatial content needs to be more
elaborate when the gesture modality is not available. If the content of the
speech is not spatial, this problem does not occur, which is exactly what the
authors found (see De Ruiter, 2006 for a more extensive discussion).

Beattie and Coughlan (1999) performed the most direct test of the LRF
hypothesis. They elicited Tip Of the Tongue (TOT) states in experimental
participants. TOT states are states in which we "are sure that the information
[about the word we are looking for] is in memory but are temporarily unable to
access it" (Brown, 1991, p. 204). Beattie and Coughlan allowed half of their
participants to gesture but asked the other half to keep their arms folded during
the experiments, preventing them from gesturing. Then the participants were
presented with definitions and were then asked which word is described by the
provided definition. This induced TOT states in their participants. The
Facilitatory view would predict that the people who are allowed to gesture
would resolve a higher proportion of TOT states than those who had their arms
folded. This turned out not to be the case. The main finding of this study was
that "significantly more TOT states were resolved when gestures were absent
than when they were present" (p. 49). In other words, the presence of gesture
lowered the probability of resolving the TOT state. This finding is a straightforward falsification of the LRF hypothesis. In contrast, the Communicative
hypothesis can plausibly explain this finding that the occurrence of gesture goes
together with a lower probability of resolving the word-finding difficulty: the
more difficult it is to find the word, the more likely it is for the gesture channel
to be used to compensate for the processing difficulties in the speech channel, to
get the concept that is in the communicative intention across to the listener. In
other words, the presence of gesture indicated that the word-finding difficulties
are more serious and therefore less likely to be resolved.

Summarizing, most of the studies supporting the LRF view can also, and
often more parsimoniously, be explained by the Communicative view, and

the most direct experimental test of the LRF hypothesis clearly favored the Communicative view.

The view that gesture facilitates conceptualizing

Other facilitatory theories have proposed that gesture facilitates speech production not at the (lexical) level of Levelt's Formulator but rather at the level of the *Conceptualizer*. One of these approaches assumes that performing gestures is a way to (re-)activate spatial representations in short-term memory, making it easier for the Conceptualizer to generate a message (De Ruiter, 1998; Morsella & Krauss, 2004; Wesp et al., 2001). Experimental evidence for this theory came from data suggesting that people produce more gestures when they have to describe images from memory.

Another proposal is Kita's (2000) *Information Packaging Hypothesis* which maintains that gesturing facilitates the process of *packaging* information into units that are suitable for verbal encoding. This view assumes that while speech is based on analytic processing, gesture is based on spatio-motoric processing. Similar to Gibson's (1986) *affordances*, "spatio-motoric thinking organizes information with action schemas and their modulation according to features of the environment." (Kita, 2000, p. 164). During the part of the speech production process that corresponds to Levelt's (1989) *micro-planning*, spatio-motoric and analytic thinking "continuously interact, with a common goal of organizing rich and complicated information into a series of packages that can be verbalized within on planning unit of speaking" (Kita, 2000, p. 169).

Evidence for this hypothesis comes from Mol and Kita (2012) who exploited the fact that in Dutch (as in English) it is possible and common, but not obligatory, to express path and manner in a single clause, as for instance in the sentence "de hond sprong omhoog" (ENG: "the dog jumped upwards"). Participants were shown short animations with figures moving around, with different paths and manners. In one condition, they were requested to describe the event while gesturing manner and path separately, and in the other they were asked to produce gesture combining manner and path during their description. The results showed that in the condition where the participants had to produce separate gestures for manner and path, they would also produce a higher proportion of separated verbal utterances for manner and path, and in the condition where they had to produce a conflated gesture, they produce a higher proportion of conflated verbal utterances. The authors interpreted this result as supporting the idea that the gesturing helped the participants package the visual information from the stimulus into verbal clauses.

It should be noted that, as with some of the evidence for the lexical retrieval facilitation hypothesis discussed above, there is also a plausible communicative interpretation of these results. Participants could have adapted their speech to the gesture they were asked to make, in order to make sure they expressed consistent information in both channels.

The view that gesture facilitates general cognitive processing

More recently, a number of gesture theorists have proposed and explored an additional possible function of gesture, namely facilitating cognitive processes beyond those needed for speech production. The physical nature of gesture and similarities between manual actions and gestures, most visible in panto-mimic gestures, naturally suggests that gesture could play a role in *embodied cognition*, which is an umbrella term for a number of different assumptions about cognition. In a seminal review article, Wilson (2002) identifies six of these views: (1) cognition is situated; (2) cognition is time-pressured; (3) we off-load cognitive work onto the environment; (4) the environment is part of the cognitive system; (5) cognition is for action, and finally (6) off-line cognition is body based. Interestingly, while the author is, for varying well-motivated reasons, highly critical of the first five claims, she writes about the sixth claim that "[it] has received the least attention in the literature on embodied cognition, but it may in fact be the best documented and most powerful of the six claims." It is this view of embodied cognition that has been the focus of attention in recent theoretical work on gesture. These new theories posit a wide range of facilitatory effects of gesturing on cognition, including cognitive development (M. Alibali & Goldin-Meadow, 1993; Goldin-Meadow et al., 1993), mental rotation (Chu & Kita, 2011), bringing out implicit knowledge (Broaders et al., 2007), and reducing learners' cognitive load (Goldin-Meadow & Wagner, 2005). A detailed discussion of the recent theoretical proposals that address the role of gesture in (embodied) cognition would be beyond the scope of this handbook chapter, but the interested reader is referred to Hostetter and Alibali (2008), Goldin-Meadow and Beilock (2010), and Kita et al. (2017).

Concluding remark

The debate between the communicative and facilitatory views on the function of gesture has mostly died down in recent decades. Some authors (e.g., Alibali et al., 2001) have pointed out that the communicative and the facilitatory view are not mutually exclusive: gesture could have both a communicative and a facilitatory function. While this is certainly correct, it is still an interesting question what the *primary* function of gesture is, and which one(s) is a beneficial spin-off. This is especially relevant in the context of the evolution of gesture.

Controversy 2: The semantic relation between gesture and speech

If gestures and speech originate from the same pre-linguistic thought, one would expect some level of redundancy in their content. Otherwise, how could we even tell that the gesture and the thought are related? However, gesture and speech do have very different communicative affordances. Speech is very good at transmitting propositional information. Gesture is not. Gesturing conditionals and tense, for instance ("If it hadn't rained yesterday, I would have taken my bicycle") is very difficult. Gesture, on the other hand (pun not intended), is very good at transmitting analog information. To appreciate this, try describing the shape of a coke bottle without using gesture. So that would suggest that gesture and speech could well be complementary, compensating for each other's expressive limitations.

The Sketch model assumes that while gesture and speech originate from the same pre-linguistic thought, the relation between what the gesture and speech end up expressing is complementary and compensatory. When the information to be expressed is hard to verbalize, gesture takes over the communicative load, and when the information is hard to gesture about, it is expressed in speech. Prima facie this sounds plausible, and this assumption has been adopted by a number of researchers (e.g., Van der Sluis & Krahmer, 2007) and there is some quantitative evidence for it presented by Melinger and Levelt (2004).

There are three relatively recent studies, however, the results of which seem incompatible with the assumption of gesture and speech being complementary and compensatory. Rather, they seem to suggest that they are far more redundant than those who hold the Communicative view (including the author of this chapter) had previously believed. I will discuss these in historical order.

Kita and Özyürek (2003) had speakers of English, Turkish, and Japanese retell episodes from the classic Warner Brothers cartoon "Tweety" and one of the scenes in the cartoon features Sylvester the cat using a rope to swing across the street from one building to another in a failure-doomed attempt to catch Tweetybird. Neither Japanese nor Turkish has a verb that has the same meaning as the verb "to swing" in English. They found that in describing this particular scene, nearly all of the English speakers produced only arc-like gestures, but the Japanese and Turkish speakers either used only a straight gesture, or both a straight and an arc-shaped gesture. English speakers rarely produced any straight gestures, suggesting that the availability of the "swing" verb in English appeared to have forced the shape of the gesture to be arc-like, and the lack of such a verb had prevented the Japanese and Turkish speakers from gesturing an arc-gesture. This would suggest that the effect of language on gesture is actually a lexical effect, and that speakers of Turkish or Japanese, not experiencing the "constraints" on the gesture provided by the verb "swing," are free to either include or exclude the arc-trajectory from their gesture.

Kita and Özyürek have also formulated a model to explain this result, illustrating the process by which both imagistic information and the available concepts in the speaker's language influence the final shape of a gesture. The model diagram is depicted in Figure 10.4 below. The three modules in gray together roughly correspond with the Conceptualizer in the Sketch model, but with very different processing. The Communication Planner generates a communicative intention and determines which modalities are going to be used to express this intention. The shape of the final gesture is then the result of a negotiation process (my term, for details see Kita and Özyürek (2003), pp. 28–29) between the

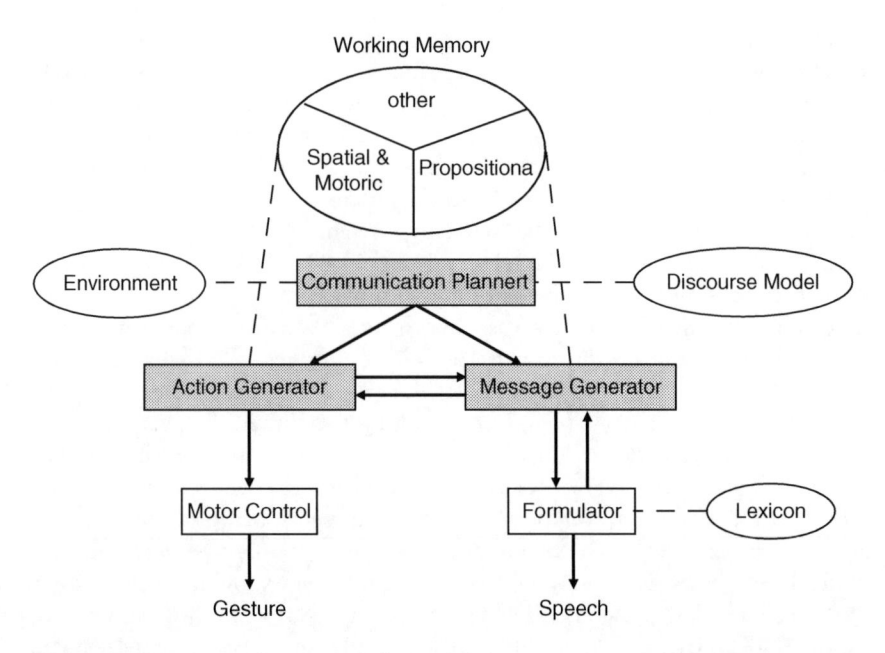

Figure 10.4 The model by Kita and Özyürek (2003).

Action Generator, which has access to action schemata and spatial information from working memory, and the (verbal) Message Generator, which can bi-directionally exchange information with the Formulator (and via the Formulator, also the Lexicon). This allows the model to shape the gesture while simultaneously taking into account (a) the expressive possibilities of the language, (b) the available motoric gesture- and action schemata, and (c) the communicative intention. For a more in-depth discussion of the strengths and weaknesses of this model, the reader is referred to De Ruiter (2017).

Arguably even more intriguing is Kita and Özyürek's (2003) second cross-linguistic finding, also regarding a difference between English on the one hand, and Turkish and Japanese on the other. In describing Sylvester, who has swallowed a bowling ball and moves down the hill in a rolling-like fashion, English allows for coding *manner* in the verb itself, and *path* in a prepositional phrase, in the description "he rolls down the hill," needing only one clause to express both manner and path (See Figure 10.5).

Japanese and Turkish, on the other hand, need separate verb clauses for expressing manner and path. In this study, the majority of English speakers *only* produced a manner-path conflating gesture, describing manner and path together by performing a spiraling motion with the finger while diagonally moving downwards. This mirrors the semantic structure of the unmarked way of describing the rolling event in their language ("rolls down the street"). However, the majority of Turkish and Japanese speakers produced separate

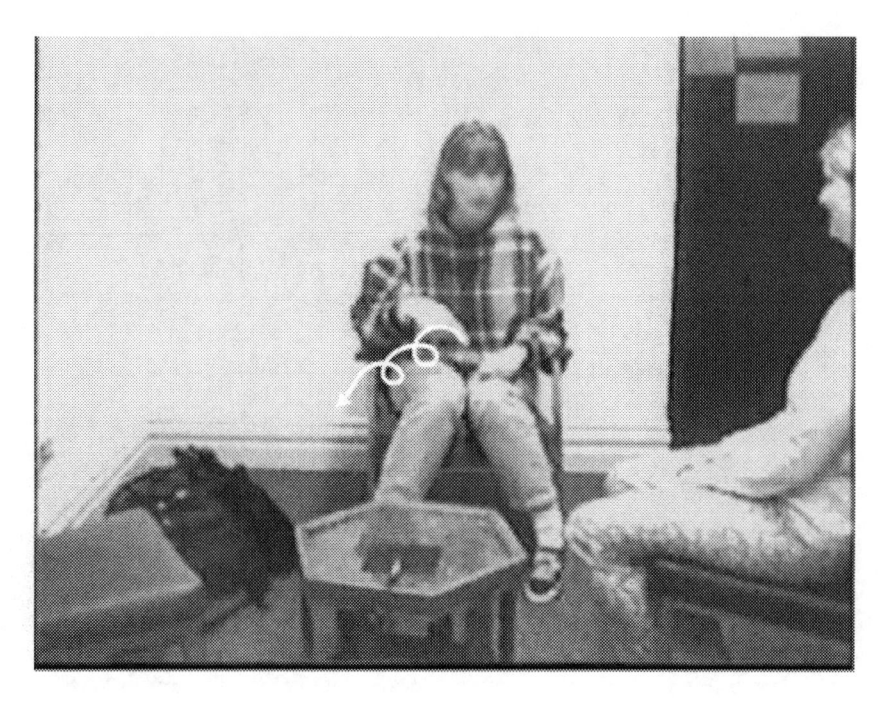

Figure 10.5 English "rolling down the hill" gesture.

gestures that displayed *either* the manner ("rolling") by rotating their finger in a stationary position *or* the path ("down the street") by making a straight diagonal–downward gesture. This matches the two–clause expression that is common in those languages.

These findings strongly suggest that the grammar of the language that is spoken has a dominant influence on the nature of the accompanying iconic gestures. As Kita and Özyürek (2003) point out, this would contradict the assumption that information in iconic gesture is independent of the linguistic information from the pre-linguistic thought, an assumption that is adopted in the Sketch Model.

Interestingly, there seems to be an influence of language structure on iconic gesture, but not the other way around. This is also a priori unlikely because iconic gestures are not lexicalized: contrary to the syntax and semantics of spoken languages, their form-meaning mapping is not conventionalized within a language community. If the structure or shape of gestures is not conventionalized, it is implausible that they could systematically influence the nature of the speech.

The second study is by So et al. (2009) who tested the assumption that gesture compensates for information that is not in the speech, the assumption that is made in the Sketch model (De Ruiter, 2000) but also by for instance Bangerter (2004) and Van der Sluis and Krahmer (2007). So et al. (2009) asked their participants to tell stories based on a "vignette," featuring either two male protagonists or a male and a female protagonist. They then recorded how often the participants referred to these protagonists, either by using noun phrases or pronouns, and whether they performed "abstract deictic" gestures to refer to them. Abstract deictic gestures are pointing gestures to locations in the speaker's space that are used to refer to and keep track of previously introduced discourse entities. They found that instead of gestures occurring to compensate for missing referents in the speech, they tended to co-occur with the speech. They concluded that gesture and speech go "hand in hand" (pun presumably intended). This finding directly contradicts the assumption that gesture compensates for difficulties in speech in the Sketch Model. Again, it seems as if the content of the speech is playing a dominant role in shaping the gesture, and that the gesture is redundant to the speech.

Finally, there is a study that directly tested the assumption in the Sketch model that gesture and speech are compensatory. While there is evidence from Bangerter (2004) and Van der Sluis and Krahmer (2007) that speech can compensate for difficulties in gesture, the opposite had never been studied. De Ruiter et al. (2012) directly tested the assumption that gesture compensates for difficulties in speech. They used a director/matcher experiment with tangram figures on a poster as target and systematically manipulated repetition (how often had the target been referred to before by the director-participant) and codability (how easy it is to come up with a simple and adequate verbal description for that target). Neither factor had any influence on the gesture-per-word rate in directors, but they did have a strong effect on speech preparation times, showing that the manipulation did work as intended. More importantly for the purpose of this discussion, additional correlational analyses revealed that the type of gesture covaried reliably with the type of information that was simultaneously expressed in speech. Feature descriptions were reliably accompanied by iconic gestures, and locative expressions by pointing gestures. The authors concluded that this is additional evidence for the "gesture and speech go hand in hand" hypothesis by So et al. (2009) and incompatible with the idea that gesture and speech compensate for each other. Again, this is evidence not only for redundancy between the two channels but also for the "dominance" of speech over gesture.

So, it appears that while the idea of gesture and speech being compensatory and complementary is plausible and elegant, it is also wrong. In De Ruiter (2017) a successor model to the Sketch model was formulated that incorporates these new findings. In the new model, called the Asymmetric Redundancy Sketch Model (or AR-Sketch model for short) the idea that the Conceptualizer distributes information between the two modalities on the basis of expressibility is replaced by another mechanism: the speech is generated on the basis of the *entire* set of features from the pre-linguistic thought, whereas the gesture is generated only on the basis of the *imagistic subset* of these features. See Figure 10.6 below for an illustration of the difference between the working of the Conceptualizer in the original Sketch model and the new AR-Sketch model.

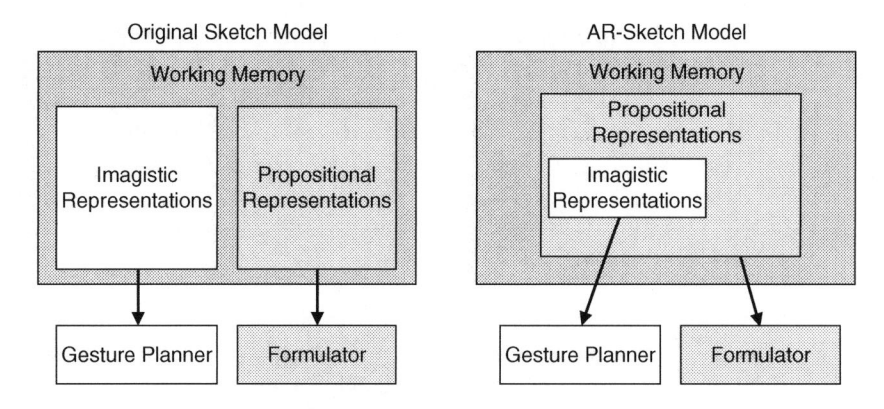

Figure 10.6 Sketch model vs. AR-Sketch model.

This implies, first, that speech always contains more information than gesture, and second, that the gesture is largely redundant with the speech. Not only does this newly defined conceptualizer incorporate the three findings discussed above, it also explains another mystery that several gesture researchers have pointed out (e.g., Kendon, 1994; Krauss et al., 1995): while it is usually perfectly possible to understand speech without seeing the gesture, it is nearly impossible to understand gesture without having access to the accompanying speech. Anyone can experience this by watching a video fragment of a gesture-rich speech fragment with the sound off and trying to discern what is being said purely on the basis of the gesture.

An obvious counter-argument to the notion that gestures are redundant with speech is that there is almost always some information in gestures that is not in the speech. For instance, talking about a cake while gesturing a round shape with the hands gives information about the size of the cake. However, the author argues that this kind of information is not explicitly planned by the conceptualizer as part of the communicative intention, but rather an unavoidable side-effect of expressing another communicative intention in gesture: it is not possible to gesture the shape of a cake without also giving away information about the size. For a more detailed discussion see De Ruiter (2017).

Summary

To summarize, although many researchers believed that gesture and speech represent complementary information, more recent findings indicate that gesture is actually surprisingly redundant with the concurrent speech. To return to the first controversy, one might wonder if this does not in fact support the Facilitatory view rather than the Communicative view on the function of (iconic) gesture. After all, if gesture is mostly redundant with speech, what does it actually contribute to communication? One possibility, suggested by

De Ruiter et al. (2012) is that gesture serves as a *signal enhancer*. Redundancy is an effective way to increase the signal-to-noise ratio of a communicative utterance. Another possibility is that gesture behavior is a residual leftover from our evolutionary past. Some authors, most notably Corballis (2002), have suggested that gesture has evolutionary preceded speech, to be gradually replaced by speech, which has developed because it also works in the dark and over larger distances.

Gesture and aphasia

Because people with aphasia face significant limitations in their production of spoken language, communicative modalities other than speech can gain relevance (Anglade et al., 2021; Damico et al., 2008; Sekine et al., 2013; Sekine & Rose, 2013). In some studies, it was suggested that aphasia leads to a parallel breakdown of gesture and speech as well as other communicative modalities (Cicone et al., 1979; Duffy & Duffy, 1981; Duffy & Liles, 1979). The core assumption of this Asymbolia Hypothesis was that a central underlying deficit, named asymbolia, resulted in processing difficulties of symbols in both modalities (Duffy & Liles, 1979). It was further assumed that a shared underlying deficit resulting in parallel disturbances of gesture and speech prevents people with aphasia from using gestures to effectively compensate for their verbal limitations (Cicone et al., 1979).

However, using gestures to express meaning by complementing or replacing spoken production is of high relevance for people with aphasia, especially for those with severe expressive limitations. Therefore, many scholars have investigated the potential of co-speech gestures to be used by people with aphasia to compensate for problems in speech (Feyereisen, 1983; Herrmann et al., 1988). More recent studies have looked at the role gestures play in the expression of content by people with aphasia (De Beer et al., 2017; Hogrefe et al., 2013, 2017; Wilkinson et al., 2010). A rating study conducted by Hogrefe et al. (2013) revealed that some people with aphasia, and especially people with severe types of aphasia, conveyed more information using gestures than they did using spoken utterances in a narration task. The authors concluded that people with aphasia compensate for their verbal limitations by employing gestures. De Beer et al. (2017) investigated the communicative role of three different gesture types, namely pantomimes, emblems, and referential gestures (a category containing both iconic and deictic gestures) in extracts from spontaneous conversations. The results revealed that the naive raters understood the messages expressed by the people with aphasia of varying severities more accurately when they were expressed using gesture and speech instead of speech alone. This was true for all gesture types under investigation, including iconic gestures. The spontaneous use of iconic gestures by people with aphasias of varying severities has also been described by other researchers (Kong et al., 2015; Sekine et al., 2013) and people with aphasia use iconic gestures to express different aspects of semantic content (De Beer et al., 2018; Dipper et al., 2015).

Taken together, the results of the aforementioned studies suggest that people with aphasia use gesture to add relevant content to their communication and thereby compensate for their limitations in speech processing. They employ various gesture types to express speech–complementing information, including iconic gestures. The assumption of a parallel impairment of gesture and speech in people with aphasia (McNeill, 1985) is not supported by these findings. In fact, these results support the assumption that gestures are employed by people with aphasia to compensate for limitations in the verbal channel.

To summarize, it is debated whether persons with aphasia are able to employ gestures for effective compensation for their verbal difficulties. Furthermore, some authors found that persons with aphasia make less use of gestures in tasks with stronger linguistic constraints. On the other hand, there is evidence suggesting that they use gestures, including iconic gestures, to express important content, and this was found to be particularly evident with increasing verbal limitations, i.e., more severe types of aphasia.

In a recent study by De Beer et al. (2020), it was found that the assumption from the original Sketch model (De Ruiter, 2000) that gesture is complementary and compensatory, even though it does not adequately describe the gesture behavior of neurotypical speakers, *did* in fact apply to the gesture and speech of people with Aphasia. However, the tight temporal synchrony between gesture and its affiliated speech, typical for iconic (and deictic) gestures in neurotypical speakers, was lost. This suggests that the persons with aphasia could have been using a different processing mechanism for producing speech and gesture than neurotypical gesturers. More specifically, it is possible that when the self-monitoring process (see Levelt, 1989) in speakers with aphasia detects problems in the speech production process, the speaker deliberately switches to producing gesture as an alternative strategy. In contrast, the speech and gesture from neurotypical speakers are produced as an integrated process. This is an interesting and urgent issue for further research.

What we don't know about gesture

While gesture researchers in recent decades have been successful in putting gesture on the cognitive-psychological and psycholinguistic map, and have made great progress in understanding, studying, and modeling the phenomenon, there are still a number of mysteries. Here I will discuss what I consider to be one of the greatest of these mysteries.

An aspect of gesture processing that is taken for granted or just assumed in most, if not all, gesture models and theories so far is the process of generating a gesture from an imagistic representation. It seems natural to us while describing a cat rolling down the hill with a bowling ball in its belly to gesture by making a spiraling motion with the tip of our index finger diagonally downwards, as most English-speaking participants did in McNeill's original study (see Figure 10.5). But it actually represents a major feat of information *selection* and *reduction* (De Ruiter, 2007). The original stimulus shows an abundance of detail, involving the street, storefronts, lampposts moving by, the cat frantically moving its paws, and at some point looking directly into the "camera" with a very worried facial expression. Even this fairy rich verbal description conveys only a small subset of information presented in the entire scene, which of course in the original cartoon is dynamic and for that reason alone contains far more information.

So how does a speaker come up with a very stylized, minimalistic gesture of this scene, seemingly effortlessly and even faster than the process of selecting the verbal expression "rolls down the hill" like the one in Figure 10.5? We frankly have no idea how speakers do this. All we can do is analyze and admire the end result. It appears that the gesturer's solution is to take an arbitrary point on the lateral planar projection of the invisible and inferred bowling ball inside the cat and use her fingertip to trace out the movement she imagines that this imaginary point makes inside the cat during its fateful descent, projected on the perpendicular plane in front of her. The rotating index finger, combined with the rightward and downward motion of the hand, are communicating the "rolling down" concept expressed in the speech.

There are some artificial agents that produce iconic gestures (Cassell et al., 1999; Kopp & Wachsmuth, 2004; Lundeberg & Beskow, 1999; Pelachaud, 2005; Stone et al., 2004), but these use predetermined, hard-coded hand movements. More recent approaches rely on data-driven and machine-learning approaches (Bergmann & Kopp, 2009; Tepper, 2014), which avoid the use of pre-stored gestures. So while there is progress in the development of embodied artificial agents, that could perhaps soon pass the iconic gesture equivalent of the Turing Test, we still do not have a theory of how humans represent a given imagistic representation using their hand(s), although some interesting observational work can be found in Enfield (2004).

One might suspect that "pantomime" gestures, a subclass of iconic gestures that depict recognizable actions, are not as mysterious when it comes to the generation of the gesture, because we can simply use our internal knowledge of the action to perform the action "in the air." This is in fact how the Sketch model (De Ruiter, 2000) and by implication the AR-Sketch model (De Ruiter, 2017) assume pantomime gestures are processed. The idea is that one can just use one's motor schema for the action and use it as a gesture. But it turns out that that is another assumption of the Sketch model and its successor that is likely to be wrong. In a fascinating study, Goldenberg (2017) reports a double dissociation between the ability to perform an action and the ability to produce a pantomime gesture about that action. That is, some patients could perform the action (e.g., turning a key in a lock) but not produce the pantomime gesture for it, and other patients could perform the pantomime but not the action. So in generating pantomime gestures people may retrieve certain features from the stored motor action schema, but as Goldenberg showed, the pantomimes are different from the original motor pattern because they are specifically designed to be communicative, which creates different constraints for the gesture motor program than for the functional one. Importantly, this intriguing finding is also at odds with theories of gesture in neurotypical speakers that assume that iconic gestures are constructed from action schemata (Chu & Kita, 2016; Ping et al., 2014).

Conclusion

Arguably the most fascinating aspect of co-speech gesture, especially iconic gesture, is that it is a communication system that is tightly integrated with speech, but that, contrary to speech, has no form-to-meaning mappings that are conventionalized, that is shared in a language community. This feature is also the underlying reason for the controversies and the mystery discussed in the previous sections. Because iconic gesture is not conventionalized, gesture has also been seen as a "privileged window into the mind" (M. Alibali & Goldin-Meadow, 1993; Beattie, 2003; Goldin-Meadow et al., 1993; McNeill, 1992, 2000), allowing the researcher access to pristine pre-linguistic imagistic representations that are untainted by the constraining conventions governing our language system; a kind of "Freudian" view of iconic gesture. However, there is abundant evidence that speakers design their gestures like their speech, that is, they design their gestures to express selected information to their interlocutors (see De Ruiter, 2007 for a more elaborate discussion).

To wrap up, my hope is that this chapter has conveyed to the reader that gesture is a very different phenomenon from "nonverbal behavior," and that gestures have an intimate relation to the speech they accompany. The exact nature of this relationship is still largely a mystery, but there is one thing we can say with certainty: it's complicated.

Notes

1 I will limit the discussion to co-speech gesturing with the hands, omitting head gestures, eye-gaze, and other speech-related physical signals, which is not to suggest that these are less interesting.
2 The main protagonist of the TV series "CSI Miami" always takes off his sunglasses before he says something profound. But even that is not a co-speech gesture.
3 A great source of unusual iconic gestures is video recordings of speeches of world leaders. See for instance this video about Donald Trump's mysterious iconic gestures: https://www.youtube.com/watch?v=1p7sOsDHLiw&ab_channel=BBCNews
4 Unfortunately, I have been informed by Adam Kendon that the film Efron made is lost.
5 Note that iconic and metaphoric gestures are processed identically in the Sketch model, as it doesn't matter for the production of gesture whether the referent of the gesture is abstract or concrete.
6 The dark-shaded parts in the model diagram are the parts that correspond to Levelt's blueprint, and the white parts represent the extensions by the authors.

References

Alibali, M., & Goldin-Meadow, S. (1993). Gesture-speech mismatch and mechanisms of learning: What the hands reveal about a child's state of mind. *Cognitive Psychology, 25,* 468–523.

Alibali, M. W., Heath, D. C., & Myers, H. J. (2001). Effects of visibility between speaker and listener on gesture production: Some gestures are meant to be seen. *Journal of Memory and Language, 44,* 169–188.

Anglade, C., Le Dorze, G., & Croteau, C. (2021). How clerks understand the requests of people living with aphasia in service encounters. *Clinical Linguistics & Phonetics, 35*(1), 84–99.

Bangerter, A. (2004). Using pointing and describing to achieve joint focus of attention in dialogue. *Psychological Science, 15*(6), 415–419.

Bavelas, J., Chovil, N., Lawrie, D. A., & Wade, A. (1992). Interactive gestures. *Discourse Processes, 15,* 469–489.

Beattie, G. (2003). *Visible thought: The new psychology of body language.* London: Routledge.

Beattie, G., & Coughlan, J. (1999). An experimental investigation of the role of iconic gestures in lexical access using the tip-of-the-tongue phenomenon. *British Journal of Psychology, 90,* 35–56.

Bente, G., Krämer, N., Petersen, A., & De Ruiter, J. P. (2001). Computer animated movement and person perception: Methodological advances in nonverbal behavior research. *Journal of Nonverbal Behavior, 25*(3), 151–166.

Bergmann, K., & Kopp, S. (2009). *GNetic—Using Bayesian decision networks for iconic gesture generation* (pp. 76–89). Heidelberg.

Birdwhistell, R. L. (1952). *Introduction to kinesics: An annotation system for analysis of body motion and gesture.* Department of State, Foreign Service Institute.

Broaders, S. C., Cook, S. W., Mitchell, Z., & Goldin-Meadow, S. (2007). Making children gesture brings out implicit knowledge and leads to learning. *Journal of Experimental Psychology: General, 136*(4), 539.

Brown, A. S. (1991). A review of the tip-of-the-tongue experience. *Psychological Bulletin, 109*(2), 204–223. https://doi.org/10.1037/0033-2909.109.2.204

Cassell, J., Bickmore, T., Billinghurst, L., Campbell, K., Chang, H., Vilhjalmsson, H., & Yan, H. (1999). Embodiment in conversational interfaces: Rea. In *Proceedings of the SIGCHI conference on Human Factors in Computing Systems* (pp. 520–527).

Chomsky, N. (1964). *Aspects of the theory of syntax.* Cambridge, Massachusetts: MIT Press.

Chu, M., & Kita, S. (2011). The nature of gestures' beneficial role in spatial problem solving. *Journal of Experimental Psychology: General, 140*(1), 102.

Chu, M., & Kita, S. (2016). Co-thought and co-speech gestures are generated by the same action generation process. *Journal of Experimental Psychology: Learning, Memory, and Cognition, 42*(2), 257.

Cicone, M., Wapner, W., Foldi, N., Zurif, E., & Gardner, H. (1979). The relation between gesture and language in aphasic communication. *Brain and Language, 8*(3), 324–349.

Cohen, A. A. (1977). The communicative functions of hand illustrators. *Journal of Communication, 27,* 54–63.

Cohen, A. A., & Harrison, R. P. (1973). Intentionality in the use of hand illustrators in face-to-face communication situations. *Journal of Personality and Social Psychology, 28*(2), 276.

Condon, W. S., & Ogston, W. D. (1966). Sound film analysis of normal and pathological behavior patterns. *Journal of Nervous and Mental Disease.* p. 233.

Condon, W. S., & Ogston, W. D. (1967). A segmentation of behavior. *Journal of Psychiatric Research, 5*(3), 221–235.

Corballis, M. C. (2002). *From hand to mouth: The origins of language.* Princeton University Press.

Damico, J. S., Wilson, B. T., Simmons-Mackie, N. N., & Tetnowski, J. A. (2008). Overcoming unintelligibility in aphasia: The impact of non-verbal interactive strategies. *Clinical Linguistics & Phonetics, 22*(10–11), 775–782.

De Beer, C., Carragher, M., van Nispen, K., Hogrefe, K., de Ruiter, J. P., & Rose, M. L. (2017). How much information do people with aphasia convey via gesture? *American Journal of Speech-Language Pathology*, 26(2), 483–497.

De Beer, C., Hogrefe, K., & De Ruiter, J. P. (2018). Features of semantic content expressed via gesture by people with aphasia. *Aphasiology*, 32(1), 18–20.

De Beer, C., Hogrefe, K., Hielscher-Fastabend, M., & De Ruiter, J. P. (2020). Evaluating models of gesture and speech production for people with aphasia. *Cognitive Science*, 44(9), e12890.

De Ruiter, J. P. (1998). *Gesture and speech production* [Doctoral Dissertation].

De Ruiter, J. P. (2000). The production of gesture and speech. In D. McNeill (Ed.), *Language and gesture* (pp. 284–311). Cambridge, Massachusetts: Cambridge University Press.

De Ruiter, J. P. (2006). Can gesticulation help aphasic people speak, or rather, communicate? *Advances in Speech-Language Pathology*, 8(2), 124–127.

De Ruiter, J. P. (2007). Postcards from the mind: The relationship between thought, imagistic gesture, and speech. *Gesture*, 7(1), 21–38.

De Ruiter, J. P. (2017). The asymmetric redundancy of gesture and speech. In R. B. Church, M. W. Alibali, & S. D. Kelly (Eds.), *Why gesture? How the hands function in speaking, thinking and communicating* (pp. 59–75). John Benjamins Publishing Company.

De Ruiter, J. P., Bangerter, A., & Dings, P. (2012). The interplay between gesture and speech in the production of referring expression: Investigating the tradeoff hypothesis. *Topics in Cognitive Science*, 4, 232–248.

Dipper, L., Pritchard, M., Morgan, G., & Cocks, N. (2015). The language-gesture connection: Evidence from aphasia. *Clinical Linguistics & Phonetics*, 29(8–10), 748–763.

Duffy, R. J., & Duffy, J. R. (1981). Three studies of deficits in pantomimic expression and pantomimic recognition in aphasia. *Journal of Speech, Language, and Hearing Research*, 24(1), 70–84.

Duffy, R. J., & Liles, B. Z. (1979). A translation of Finkelnburg's (1870) lecture on aphasia as "asymbolia" with commentary. *Journal of Speech and Hearing Disorders*, 44(2), 156–168.

Efron, D. (1941). *Gesture and environment*. New York: King's Crown Press.

Ekman, P. (1969). The repertoire of Nonverbal Behavior: Categories, Origins, Usage, and Coding. *Semiotica*, 1(49–98), 50–98.

Emmorey, K. (2022, this volume). Signing vs. speaking: How does the biology of linguistic expression affect production?

Enfield, N. J. (2004). On linear segementation and combinatorics in co-speech gesture: A symmetry-dominance construction in Lao fish trap descriptions. *Semiotica*, 149(1–4), 57–123.

Feyereisen, P. (1983). Manual activity during speaking in aphasic subjects. *International Journal of Psychology*, 18(1–4), 545–556.

Gibson, J. (1986). *The theory of affordances: The ecological approach to visual perception*. London: L. Erlbaum.

Glaser, W. R. (1992). Picture naming. *Cognition*, 42(1–3), 61–105.

Goldenberg, G. (2017). Facets of pantomime. *Journal of the International Neuropsychological Society*, 23(2), 121–127.

Goldin-Meadow, S., Alibali, M. W., & Church, R. B. (1993). Transitions in concept acquisition: Using the hand to read the mind. *Psychological Review*, 100(2), 279.

Goldin-Meadow, S., & Beilock, S. L. (2010). Action's influence on thought: The case of gesture. *Perspectives on Psychological Science*, 5(6), 664–674.

Goldin-Meadow, S., & Wagner, S. M. (2005). How our hands help us learn. *Trends in Cognitive Sciences*, 9(5), 234–241.

Graham, J. A., & Argyle, M. (1975). A cross-cultural study of the communication of extra-verbal meaning by gestures. *International Journal of Psychology, 10*(1), 57–67.

Graham, J. A., & Heywood, S. (1975). The effects of elimination of hand gestures and of verbal codability on speech performance. *European Journal of Social Psychology, 5*(2), 189–195.

Hadar, U., & Butterworth, B. (1997). Iconic gesture, imagery and word retrieval in speech. *Semiotica, 115*, 147–172.

Herrmann, M., Reichle, T., Lucius-Hoene, G., Wallesch, C.-W., & Johannsen-Horbach, H. (1988). Nonverbal communication as a compensative strategy for severely nonfluent aphasics? - A quantitative approach. *Brain and Language, 33*(1), 41–54.

Hogrefe, K., Ziegler, W., Weidinger, N., & Goldenberg, G. (2017). Comprehensibility and neural substrate of communicative gestures in severe aphasia. *Brain and Language, 171*, 62–71.

Hogrefe, K., Ziegler, W., Wiesmayer, S., Weidinger, N., & Goldenberg, G. (2013). The actual and potential use of gestures for communication in aphasia. *Aphasiology, 27*(9), 1070–1089.

Hostetter, A. B., & Alibali, M. W. (2008). Visible embodiment: Gestures as simulated action. *Psychonomic Bulletin and Review, 15*, 495–514.

Hostetter, A. B., & Skirving, C. J. (2011). The effect of visual vs. Verbal stimuli on gesture production. *Journal of Nonverbal Behavior, 35*(3), 205–223.

Kendon, A. (1994). Do gestures communicate?: A review. *Research in Language and Social Interaction, 27*(3), 175–200.

Kendon, A. (1980). Gesticulation and speech: Two aspects of the process of an utterance. In M. R. Key (Ed.), *The relatinship of verbal and nonverbal communication* (pp. 207–227). Berlin: Mouton.

Kendon, A. (2004). *Gesture: Visible action as utterance.* Cambridge University Press, 175–200.

Kendon, A. (2004). *Gesture: Visible action as utterance.* Cambridge University Press.

Kita, S. (2000). How representational gestures help speaking. In (Ed.), *Language and Gesture: Window into thought and action* (pp. 162–185). Cambridge University Press. D. McNeill.

Kita, S., Alibali, M. W., & Chu, M. (2017). How do gestures influence thinking and speaking? The gesture-for-conceptualization hypothesis. *Psychological Review, 124*(3), 245.

Kita, S., & Özyürek, A. (2003). What does cross-linguistic variation in semantic co-ordination of speech and gesture reveal?: Evidence for an interface representation of spatial thinking and speaking. *Journal of Memory and Language, 48*, 16–32.

Kong, A. P.-H., Law, S.-P., Wat, W. K.-C., & Lai, C. (2015). Co-verbal gestures among speakers with aphasia: Influence of aphasia severity, linguistic and semantic skills, and hemiplegia on gesture employment in oral discourse. *Journal of Communication Disorders, 56*, 88–102.

Kopp, S., & Wachsmuth, I. (2004). Synthesizing multimodal utterances for conversational agents. *Computer Animation and Virtual Worlds, 15*, 39–52.

Krauss, R. M., Chen, Y., & Chawla, P. (1995). Nonverbal behavior and nonverbal communication: What do conversational hand gestures tell us? In M. Zanna (Ed.), *Advances in experimental social psychology* (Vol. 28). Academic Press.

Krauss, R. M., Chen, Y., & Gottesmann, R. F. (2000). Lexical gestures and lexical access: A process model. In D. McNeill (Ed.), *Language and Gesture.* Cambridge University Press.

Levelt, W. J. M. (1989). *Speaking: From intention to articulation.* The MIT Press.

Levelt, W. J. M., Richardson, G., & La Heij, W. (1985). Pointing and voicing in deictic expressions. *Journal of Memory and Language, 24*, 133–164.

Lundeberg, M., & Beskow, J. (1999). Developing a 3D-agent for the August dialogue system. *AVSP'99-International Conference on Auditory-Visual Speech Processing.*

McNeill, D. (1992). *Hand and mind*. The Chicago University Press.

McNeill, D. (2000). *Language and gesture: Window into thought and action*. Cambridge University Press.

McNeill, D. (1985). So you think gestures are nonverbal? *Psychological Review, 92*, 350–371.

McNeill, D., Duncan, S. D., Cole, J., Gallagher, S., & Bertenthal, B. (2008). Growth points from the very beginning. *Interaction Studies, 9*(1), 117–132.

Melinger, A., & Levelt, W. J. M. (2004). Gesture and the communicative intention of the speaker. *Gesture, 4*(2), 119–141.

Mol, L., & Kita, S. (2012). Gesture structure affects syntactic structure in speech. *Proceedings of the Annual Meeting of the Cognitive Science Society, 34*, Article 34.

Morrel-Samuels, P., & Krauss, R. M. (1992). Word familiarity predicts temporal asynchrony of hand gestures and speech. *Journal of Experimental Psychology: Learning, Memory, and Cognition, 18*(3), 615–622.

Morsella, E., & Krauss, R. M. (2004). The role of gestures in spatial working memory and speech. *American Journal of Psychology, 117*(3), 411–424.

Pelachaud, C. (2005). Multimodal expressive embodied conversational agents. *Proceedings of the 13th Annual ACM International Conference on Multimedia*, 683–689.

Ping, R. M., Goldin-Meadow, S., & Beilock, S. L. (2014). Understanding gesture: Is the listener's motor system involved? *Journal of Experimental Psychology: General, 143*(1), 195.

Rauscher, F. B., Krauss, R. M., & Chen, Y. (1996). Gesture, speech, and lexical access: The role of lexical movements in speech production. *Psychological Science, 7*, 226–231.

Rimé, B., Schiaratura, L., & Ghysselinckx, A. (1984). Effects of relative immobilization on the speaker's nonverbal behavior and on the dialogue imagery level. *Motivation and Emotion, 8*(4), 311–325.

Sekine, K., & Rose, M. L. (2013). The relationship of aphasia type and gesture production in people with aphasia. *American Journal of Speech-Language Pathology*, pp. 662–672.

Sekine, K., Rose, M. L., Foster, A. M., Attard, M. C., & Lanyon, L. E. (2013). Gesture production patterns in aphasic discourse: In-depth description and preliminary predictions. *Aphasiology, 27*(9), 1031–1049.

Seyfeddinipur, M. (2006). *Disfluency: Interrupting speech and gesture*. Radboud University Nijmegen.

So, W. C., Kita, S., & Goldin-Meadow, S. (2009). Using the hands to identify who does what to whom: Gesture and speech go hand-in-hand. *Cognitive Science, 33*, 115–125.

Stone, M., DeCarlo, D., Oh, I., Rodriguez, C., Stere, A., Lees, A., & Bregler, C. (2004). Speaking with hands: Creating animated conversational characters from recordings of human performance. *ACM Transactions on Graphics (TOG), 23*(3), 506–513.

Tepper, P. A. (2014). *Unraveling iconicity: Data-driven modeling of iconic gestures in humans and virtual humans* [PhD Thesis]. Northwestern University.

Trager, G. L. (1958). Paralanguage: A first approximation. *Studies in Linguistics, 13*, 1–11.

Van der Sluis, I., & Krahmer, E. (2007). Generating multimodal references. *Discourse Processes, 44*(3), 145–174.

Wesp, R. K., Hesse, J., Keutmann, D., & Wheaton, K. (2001). Gestures maintain spatial imagery. *American Journal of Psychology, 114*, 591–600.

Wilkinson, R., Beeke, S., & Maxim, J. (2010). Formulating actions and events with limited linguistic resources: Enactment and iconicity in agrammatic aphasic talk. *Research on Language & Social Interaction, 43*(1), 57–84.

Wilson, M. (2002). Six views of embodied cognition. *Psychonomic Bulletin & Review, 9*(4), 625–636.

11 Understanding Language Use in Social Contexts

The Role of Past and Present Discourse Contexts

Si On Yoon and Sarah Brown-Schmidt

In this chapter, we discuss classic findings and new insights in the domain of conversational language use, with a focus on the types of contexts that shape language use in conversation. Language in conversation is inherently a social enterprise, involving an interactive exchange between two or more individuals, where the conversational partners may have repeated communicative interactions over time. As a result, conversational partners influence each other in terms of what they say and how they understand what was said to them. Conversation is also influenced by the context in which it occurs, where that context is broadly defined and can include the location (e.g., at a coffee shop), the time-period (e.g., right before a big exam), events and objects in the immediate environment (e.g., a loud espresso machine; a delicious assortment of pastries on the counter), as well as the conversational partners' shared history (e.g., a prior conversation about where to find the best croissants in town).

The mechanisms of conversational language use in social contexts where speech is unscripted have been largely unexplored due to the difficulties in examining this form of language use with classic psycholinguistic approaches. That said there is increasing interest in developing methods to examine unscripted language in more natural contexts where speakers can freely formulate utterances with fewer constraints (Bögels, 2020; Brown-Schmidt & Tanenhaus, 2008, Corps et al., 2022). In unscripted conversation, the presence of a conversational partner shapes the dynamics of language production, and as a result, the form of language is often quite different from traditional laboratory speech. Unlike a typical experimental setting where the speech is controlled by the experimental design, in unscripted conversation, the discussion is driven by the social and discourse contexts, including the conversational partners and their recent experiences and knowledge. As we shall see, empirical investigations of conversational processes often engage participants in task-based conversation (e.g., interactive games with cards or building blocks), and use implicit measures of cognitive processes (e.g., number of words produced; eye-gaze in the game) in order to elicit conversational language in the conditions of

DOI: 10.4324/9781003145790-12

interest, without explicitly instructing participants on what to say or how to respond.

In what follows, we describe both classic and new findings in the domain of language use in interactive settings, with a focus on the way the contexts of conversational language use shape what is said, including how these contextual influences are modulated by cognitive factors such as memory. We then discuss how one's *role* in the conversation, for example as speaker or listener, shapes how the conversation is remembered over time.

Relevant domains of reference: What is said, and not said by whom

In the domain of reference, it has long been known that what is said is shaped by information in the immediate context (Olson, 1970, Osgood, 1971). Theories of referential form posit that a well-formulated definite referring expression, such as "that shoe" or "my son," is designed in a way such that the addressee can uniquely identify the intended referent given the context (Gundel et al., 1993). The referential context against which expressions such as these are interpreted can come from the linguistic discourse itself, but also from the physical context of the conversation (Altmann & Steedman, 1998; Tanenhaus, et al. 2000). For example, in a task-based conversation where a speaker produces a definite re-ferring expression to refer to an entity in the co-present visual world, speakers typically use a detailed enough description to uniquely identify the referent with respect to other entities in the immediate visual context. Often this is accom-plished with modifiers (e.g., *blue, narrow, leather*), or specific rather than generic nouns (e.g., *stiletto* vs. *shoe*) that distinguish the intended referent from others in the context (Brennan & Clark, 1996; Engelhardt et al., 2006; Heller & Chambers, 2014; Heller et al., 2016; Sedivy, 2003). The tendency for speakers to use a modifier in the absence of contextual support varies across adjective classes (Belke, 2006; Konopka & Brown-Schmidt, 2014; Pechmann, 1989; Sedivy, 2005). This likely reflects differences in encodability or salience of the different dimensions (e.g., color vs. size; Tarenskeen et al., 2015). Attributive uses of modifiers are of interest as they reflect, in part, the speaker's character-ization of the thing which they refer to, apart from the interpersonal mechanics of guiding the addressee to uniquely identify what is being referred to (Donnellan, 1966; Heller, 2020).

While the aforementioned empirical work largely explored referential form in task-based conversation where the language is about visible things in the immediate environment, in non-task-based conversation, where the language is about things not in the here and now, we similarly observe sensitivity to discourse context. In language production, the number of entities that have been introduced into the discourse context affects referential form, with speakers less likely to use a pronoun when two animate characters had pre-viously been introduced into the context (Arnold & Griffin, 2007; Fukumura et al., 2010; Fukumura & van Gompel. 2011). Similar findings are observed in paradigms that employ language comprehension and reading as well as paradigms that are about entities that were *previously* seen in a co-present visual world (Arnold et al. 2000; Van Berkum et al., 2003; Van Berkum et al., 1999). For example, when listening to a discourse where multiple "girls" are mentioned, if the story continues to refer to one of them, "the girl … ", this creates temporary confusion, compared to a case where only a single referent in the story matches the expression (Van Berkum et al., 2003). These findings suggest that language users flexibly adapt the processing of language production and comprehension with respect to the prior context they encountered. As a result, then, the relevant discourse context that guides referential form includes both prior and immediate contexts.

Critically, consider the fact that we may talk to more than one person in a single day. Thus, the previous conversations (and past discourse contexts) that are relevant to the current conversation should only be those past contexts that one experienced with the *current* discourse partner. For example, if Si On had a conversation with Rachel and said "I bought a new car," that car might be part of the relevant discourse context in future conversations with Rachel, but not in a future conversation with Sarah (who does not know about the car). Indeed, the effects of discourse context on referential form are modulated by who a person is talking to and what they know (Brown-Schmidt et al., 2015; Horton & Gerrig, 2005). This suggests that one's communicative partner can be thought of as a type of contextual cue that shapes language use in interactive conversation. Indeed, conversational partners design what they say in part based on what they have discussed with that particular partner in the past (Brennan & Clark, 1996; Horton & Gerrig, 2005). Speakers also use different referring expressions depending on the identity of the partner and their relationships (e.g., friend vs. stranger; Fussell & Krauss, 1989b; Yoon et al., 2021b). In sum, the context of conversation shapes what speakers say, where the context must be broadly defined to include both immediate and prior contexts, as well as the conversational partner and their shared knowledge.

Historical models of the discourse

Conversational partners build representations of the discourse context and the discourse history as conversation unfolds, with language use in the moment reflecting, in part, past contexts and past language use (Brennan & Clark, 1996). For example, in referential communication tasks where hard-to-name game-pieces are repeatedly referred to, over time partners develop brief labels with simpler syntactic structures to refer to these entities (Clark & Wilkes-Gibbs, 1986; Hawkins et al., 2020; Krauss & Weinheimer, 1966). This learning is context-sensitive in that these brief labels are expanded with more detail if one partner begins the game anew with a naive partner unfamiliar with the previously developed labels (Wilkes-Gibbs & Clark, 1992; also see Isaacs & Clark, 1987). This sensitivity to the partner is not simply a generic reaction to the presence of a new partner or driven by their feedback, as this sensitivity to the partner's lack of knowledge emerges even before the partner has given any feedback (Horton & Gerrig, 2005; Yoon & Brown-Schmidt, 2018b; 2019a; 2019b).

At the same time, an inherent feature of conversation is that it is interactive, and through the interaction, conversational partners respond to each other (e.g., "*What was that?*"), and shape what each other say, providing follow-up comments and questions, as well as back-channel responses like "uh-huh," and requests for clarification (Brennan et al., 2010; Clark & Schaefer, 1989; Fussell & Krauss, 1989a; Krauss & Weinheimer, 1966). Manipulations of whether the addressee can provide feedback reveal that speakers may produce longer descriptions of abstract images when feedback is absent, compared to when they received appropriate feedback from their partner (Krauss & Weinheimer, 1966). These findings indicate that the way language is produced in conversation is guided both by speaker-driven processes, as well as interactive processes that involve feedback from the partner.

While several of the findings discussed thus far show that speakers adjust what they say based on the knowledge and perspective of their partner, this *audience design* (Clark & Murphy, 1982) process becomes more complicated in larger groups where the knowledge of individuals within the group may vary. In studies of multiparty conversation where the speaker alternates between talking to one partner who does know the labels for particular abstract images, and another partner who does not, we find that the speaker systematically uses expressions with more or less descriptive detail depending on the knowledge of the current addressee (Yoon & Brown-Schmidt, 2018b, 2019a). On the other hand, if the speaker in this task is simultaneously describing the images to a group of 2–4 addressees who *vary* in their knowledge of the image labels, speakers produce expressions with an amount of detail that tracks, more or less, the average knowledge of the group (Yoon & Brown-Schmidt, 2019a). These findings indicate that not only do speakers encode information about what their partner does and does not know, but they maintain this information in memory for more than one conversational partner.

Moreover, speakers combine information from the historical context, including what was discussed in the past, with information in the local immediate context. For example, Yoon and Brown-Schmidt (2019b) examined referential form in multiparty conversation where the speaker and one partner first worked together to establish labels for abstract images. Then in the second phase, the speaker simultaneously addressed the knowledgeable partner and a new partner who was unfamiliar with the image labels. We found that speakers were sensitive to both the immediate context and the discourse history with the knowledgeable partner in the way they designed their expressions. When the immediate context made identification of the intended referent simple for the naïve partner despite their lack of experience with the abstract images, speakers used short expressions. By contrast, when the knowledgeable partner's immediate context was made complex with multiple confusable images, speakers used longer expressions despite their shared knowledge from the prior discourse. This shows that utterance design in multiparty conversation is sensitive to partner-specific communicative needs based on both the discourse history as well as the local context.

Given this sensitivity to the local immediate context, including the discourse history and one's partner, an emerging question is how speakers track the discourse history over time and if and how past referents and contexts influence referring *in the moment*. Consider the following exchange which occurred between a pair of participants playing a game where they each saw different parts of a cubbyhole display. The task was to re-arrange animal game-pieces that were placed in the cubbyholes (see Brown-Schmidt et al., 2008 for details):

1   A: ok … the- the b- the box that I just put that you can't see that's a pig with a hat?
2   B: mmhmm
3   A: NEXT to it is aa
4   B: a cow with
5   A: with shoes
6   B: and then next to it is a cow with shoes
7   A: yeah so then we gotta switch that cow with shoes the one that we both can see
8   A: **WHAT is under the cow with shoes that we both can see?**
9   B: that we both CAN see?
10   A: yeeah … what's under it?
11   A: I can't see the box you can
12   B: you said that we both can see
13   A: no n–no … you see? the pig?
14   B: the *cow that we both can see? ok ok*
15   A: *the cow that we both yeah*
16   A: under it what is it?
17   B: a horse with shoes
18   A: a horse with shoes?
19   B: mmhmm

The associated visual scene for this exchange is shown in Figure 11.1a from participant B's perspective; participant A sat on the opposite side of the display and therefore had a different perspective on the same scene. In the cubbyhole display, there were a total of 36 images with three types of animals (e.g., pig, horse, and cow), each of which featured an accessory (e.g., shoes, hat, glasses). Participant A could see some of the same animals (such as the cow with shoes indicated by the black box), but not others (such as the horse with shoes indicated by the green box). The goal of this task was to rearrange the animals so that matching animals were not adjacent to each other. Participants freely discussed the display with their partners. The use of wh-questions and gaze during interpreting the wh-questions was analyzed.

(a)

(b)

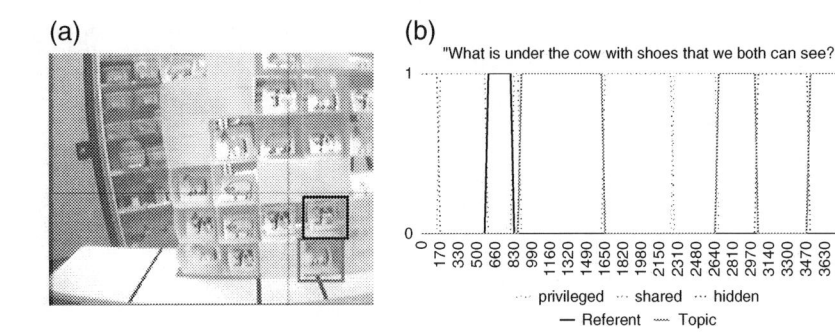

Figure 11.1 **(a) (left):** Screenshot from head-mounted Eyelink eye-tracker with gaze position indicated by the cursor and discourse-relevant entities marked in black (**cow with shoes,** the referent in question) and green (**horse with shoes,** what the question is asking about). **(b) (right):** Plot of B's fixations to different types of objects in the scene as they interpreted A's question "What is under the cow with shoes that we can both see" [8]. The eye-tracking data are plotted in binary form (1 = fixation; 0 = no fixation), over time as Participant B interpreted this question (see Cho et al., 2020 for analysis of eye-tracking data in binary form). The x-axis plots time (in milliseconds, ms), where 0 ms corresponds to the onset of the word "What" in A's question. Black line = referent mentioned in the question (**cow with shoes**); Green line = topic of the question (**horse with shoes**); Gray dotted line = looks to animals only B can see; Blue dotted line = looks to animals both A&B can see; Red dotted line = looks to squares hidden from B's view.

The example exchange in [1–19] is typical of unscripted conversation in that participants use incomplete sentences, finish each other's utterances, and use prosody to mark meaning, as in the use of the declarative questions "that we both CAN see?" [9] (Gunlogson, 2003). Analysis of the production data from this dataset showed that 93% of wh-questions asked about something only the addressee could see (e.g., wh-question in [8]). While the data in Figure 11.1b illustrate the structure of the eye-tracking data for a single question, analysis of all wh-questions in this dataset provides insight into how naturally produced, unscripted questions are interpreted. These data showed that when interpreting these very same wh-questions, addressees looked at things only they could see (i.e., their *privileged ground*) significantly more than things they both could see (i.e., their *common ground*). In contrast, in related tasks, when interpreting imperatives or statements, addressees tend to look at information in the common ground (Hanna et al., 2003; Heller et al., 2008). In sum, information questions (unlike statements) tend to inquire about information that is not known to the speaker but that might be known to the addressee, and this is reflected in the way in which questions are interpreted online.

Figure 11.1b plots participant B's eye movements during [8] in polytomous form (see Brown-Schmidt et al., 2020; Cho et al, 2020 for quantitative methods for polytomous eye-tracking data), where at each time point the participant is looking at a given type of object (=1 on the y-axis) or is not looking at that object type (=0 on the y-axis). The wh-question in [8], "*What is under the cow with shoes that we both can see?*" begins at the zero mark in Figure 11.1a, and lasts approximately 2200 ms, thus the following time points reflect the continued exchange in [9]. While single trial eye-tracking data are a noisy measure of cognitive processes, Figure 1B shows that as participant B interprets the question, they look at the referent mentioned in the question (the cow with shoes that both A and B can see), and then direct attention to the thing the question is asking about (the horse with shoes below it among the four same horses with shoes in the display). This pattern is consistent with the aggregate data pattern in this study and several other investigations of the on-line interpretation of information questions (Brown-Schmidt & Fraundorf, 2015).

While partners A and B negotiate a misunderstanding in this exchange, what is clear from the example is that the production and interpretation of each line in the exchange can only be understood with respect to a combination of the discourse history and the immediate context. The problem discussed in lines [3—7], that there were two cows next to each other, sets the stage for the subsequent attempt to resolve this problem (the rules of the game were such that two animals of the same type were not allowed to be next to each other in the display). It is only by tracking the discourse history, that B understands A's question [16] "*under it what is it?*", and provides the answer, [17] "*a horse with shoes*". Critically, studies of the moment-by-moment understanding in this and related tasks show that partners develop detailed knowledge of the game board and rules that support the use of expressions such as "*the horse with shoes*," that a person not familiar with either the game board or the discourse history would likely find confusing (Brown-Schmidt, et al., 2008; Garrod & Anderson, 1987; Schober & Clark, 1989; also see Fox Tree, 1999).

Findings that speakers successfully adjust what they say depending on experiences they have shared with the addressee(s) clearly reflect sensitivity to the discourse history (Brennan & Clark, 1996; Wilkes-Gibbs & Clark, 1992; Yoon & Brown-Schmidt, 2018a; 2019a). Further, speakers are able to integrate information from the discourse history and the immediate context to design expressions sensitive to both (Brennan & Clark, 1996; Knutsen & Le Bigot, 2014; Yoon & Brown-Schmidt, 2019b). Less well understood, however, is the way in which the immediate context and the historical context together shape speaking *in the moment*.

Consider a noteworthy study by Van Der Wege (2009) which explored the way in which items referred to in past contexts persist and shape referring in future contexts. A key finding from that study was that speakers sometimes produce referring expressions with modifiers to distinguish the intended referent (which is present in the immediate visual context) from a different referent that was previously encountered (but <u>not</u> present in the immediate context). Consider the scene in the top right corner of Figure 11.2, where task is for the speaker to describe the object in the box so that the listener can

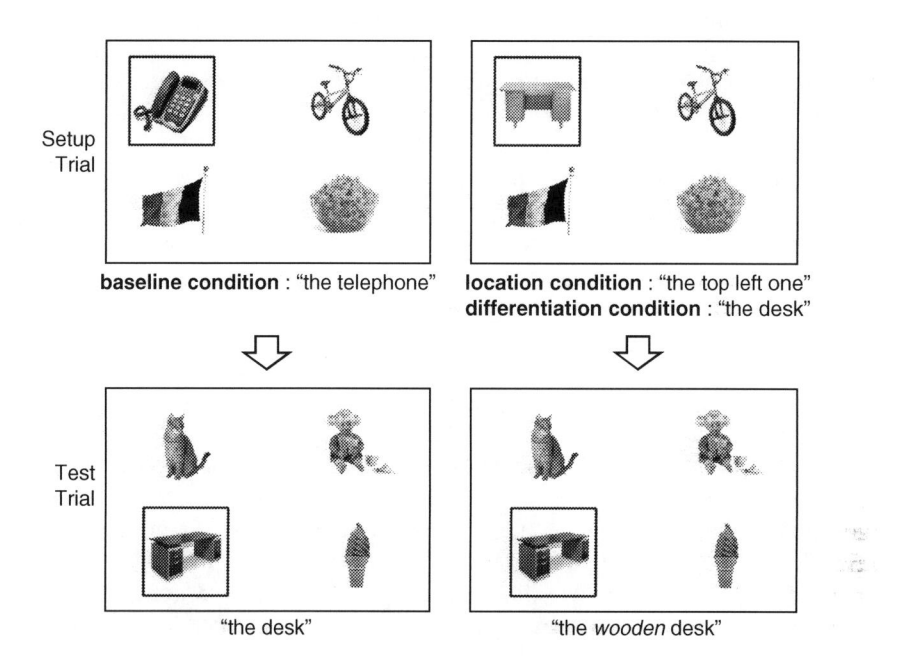

baseline condition : "the telephone"   location condition : "the top left one"
differentiation condition : "the desk"

"the desk"   "the *wooden* desk"

Figure 11.2 Example differentiation procedure for a single pair of critical trials (Yoon et al., 2016). On the setup trial (top), participants labeled a control object (baseline condition, e.g., "the telephone"), located a critical object (location condition, e.g., "the top left one"), or labeled a critical object (e.g., differentiation condition, e.g., "the desk"). On the test trial (bottom), we measured the rate at which participants differentiate the critical object from the previously-mentioned object using modifiers, as in "the wooden desk." Participants used modifiers approximately 20% of the time in the location and differentiation conditions, vs. 14% in the baseline condition, suggesting that the past referents in different visual scenes influenced referential design.

identify it on their own screen. Given there is only a single desk, most speakers would say "the desk" or "the top left one" if they use a locative expression. What Van Der Wege (2009) showed was that if speakers later see a different desk in a scene like the one on the bottom right of Figure 11.2, they frequently say "the wooden desk" despite the fact that the local context only contains one desk, and therefore a bare noun phrase "the desk" would suffice to uniquely identify the intended referent. In a control condition (left side of Figure 11.2), the speaker never sees the first desk (instead they name something unrelated like "the telephone"), and thus, modifiers like "wooden" are uncommon when describing the wooden desk at test (bottom left of Figure 11.2). This phenomenon, termed *lexical differentiation*, occurs when the speaker uses modification to distinguish one object from a different object from the same basic object category that they had *previously* mentioned. While the magnitude of this differentiation effect is somewhat small (4–8% increase in the modification rate in the differentiation condition compared to the baseline condition), it is a consistent effect replicated across different settings (Yoon & Brown-Schmidt, 2013; Yoon et al., 2016). Of note is that the differentiation effect occurs regardless of whether the speaker located the first object within the scene (e.g., "*Click on the top left one*"), or described it (e.g., "*Click on the desk*"). This finding shows that speakers are differentiating *referents* (e.g., two desks), rather than referential labels (e.g., "the desk"), as in the locative condition the label "desk" had not already been produced, yet when referring to the second desk speakers nonetheless differentiated and modified their expression (e.g., "the wooden desk").

A potential mechanism that could drive the lexical differentiation effect could be priming. One study examined how speakers represent past referents and contexts and how this representation of the discourse history affects language production in the moment – whether it is affected solely by priming or not (Yoon et al., 2021a). For example, if a speaker had previously described a closed, unstriped umbrella (e.g., *the closed umbrella*) in the presence of an open, unstriped umbrella, and then they later encounter a third exemplar of an umbrella (e.g., an open, striped umbrella in a scene with a single umbrella), how would they describe it? The "*open* umbrella" or "*striped* umbrella"? If priming shapes referential form, leading conversational partners to converge on similar forms over time (Pickering & Garrod, 2004; 2013), primed expressions should be produced (e.g., the *closed* umbrella → the *open* umbrella; Colombo & Williams, 1990; Perea & Rosa, 2002). While the expression "the open umbrella" would differentiate the current referent from the past referent (the closed unstriped umbrella), it would not differentiate the current referent from the unmentioned item from the past context (the unmentioned open unstriped umbrella). Alternatively, perhaps interlocutors store in memory a representation of past unmentioned contexts as well as past referents. If so, viewing the open striped umbrella would cue the retrieval of this past visual context from memory (which included both the open and closed unstriped umbrellas), prompting the speaker to produce an expression that distinguishes the current referent from both the past referent and its context (e.g., the *closed* umbrella → the *striped* umbrella). The results of this study showed that speakers were less likely to produce the primed form (e.g., the *open* umbrella) when it did not distinguish the current target from the earlier, unmentioned item. Thus, these findings suggest that the lexical differentiation effect is not driven by linguistic representations nor by priming alone. Speakers encode both past referents and non-referents from the visual context to memory and use these representations when planning referring expressions.

How memory constraints shape the role of historical contexts

Previous findings using the lexical differentiation paradigm (Van Der Wege, 2009; Yoon & Brown-Schmidt, 2013; Yoon et al., 2016; 2021) show that memory processes are relevant to understanding how past contexts affect language use in the moment. When the participant had referred to a different object from the same basic level object category in the past, they were more likely to use a modified expression in the moment, even though a modifier was not necessary given the local context. One question, then, is what memory mechanisms allowed the past to influence the present in this way. Retrieval of information from memory is shaped in part by the nature of the retrieval cues used to access that past memory representation. Contextual cues, such as one's location, background images, and even the identity of the partner can all influence retrieval success, with recall tending to be better when the context of encoding and retrieval match (Godden & Baddeley, 1975; Smith & Vela, 2001; also see Tulving & Thomson, 1973). These environmental context (or *contextual reinstatement*) effects are particularly strong when the items are integrated with the context (Eich, 1985; Shin et al., 2021). Moreover, memory retrieval cues can affect the interpretation of ambiguity in language in the moment. For example, Tullis et al. (2014) asked participants to generate interpretations of a series of words that were presented upon distinct background images (such as a cafe scene or an industrial scene). In a critical condition, homographs such as "bank," were preceded by a prior cue word such as "river" that biased the meaning of the homograph. Tullis et al. (2014) found that speakers were significantly more likely to generate the biased meaning of the homograph (e.g., the bank of a river) when the cue and homograph appeared with the same vs. different background image, illustrating the way in which retrieval cues can shape access to past events. In other words, when the ambiguous homograph appeared on the same background image as the cue word, that background acted as a reminder of the cue word and influenced the activated meaning of the homograph. Using a variant of this paradigm, Yoon et al. (2021) asked if contextual cues such as a background image would similarly remind participants of past discourse contexts, increasing the likelihood they would differentiate the current referent from the past referent if they consistently appeared in the same location on the same background image (Figure 11.3). Consistent with this hypothesis, Yoon et al. (2021) reported significantly larger differentiation effects when the past and current contexts were contextually linked (an 18% difference in modification rate over baseline), compared to when those contexts were distinct (an 8% difference over baseline). This finding suggests that when accessing a representation of the discourse history from memory, contextual cues (such as one's physical context) support the retrieval of the discourse history from memory.

Under the people-as-contexts view of partners in conversation (introduced above), one's communicative partner acts as a context cue to facilitate retrieval of associated information much like environmental contexts can cue retrieval of studied items from memory (Brown-Schmidt et al., 2015). Indeed, a variety of findings indicate that language use is tailored to what individual conversational partners do and do not know (Isaacs & Clark, 1987; Wilkes-Gibbs & Clark, 1992). Further, when retrieval of partner information is made

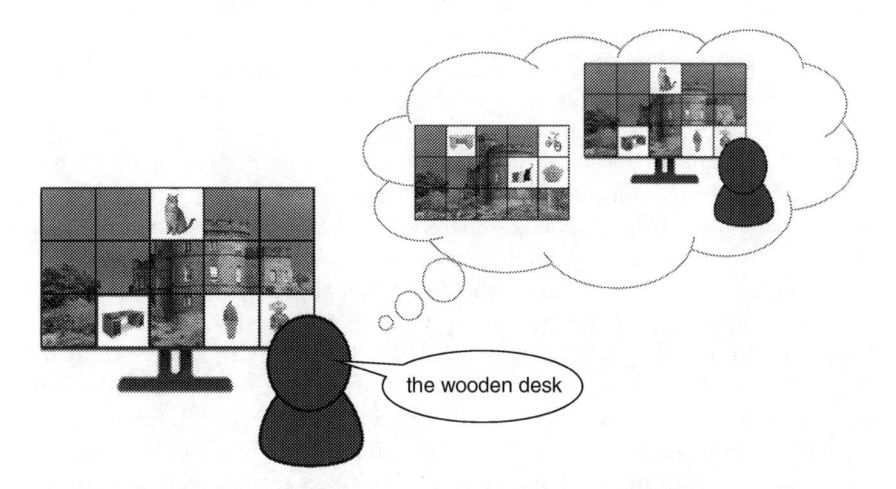

Figure 11.3 Illustration of merging of past and current context representations. The current referent, the wooden desk, serves as a retrieval cue to access related information from memory such as the metal desk. These retrieved items, as well as information in the immediate context together, shape referring in the moment.

easier with clear cues to shared knowledge, partner-specific audience design is more likely (Horton & Gerrig, 2005). Findings that overlapping contextual cues from encoding to retrieval shape homograph interpretation and referential form (Tullis et al 2014; Yoon et al., 2021; see also O'Shea et al., 2021) therefore suggest that contextual cues during language production shape retrieval of relevant information from memory, acting as a memory-based context cue that influences language use in the moment much like the immediate context shapes language use. These findings illustrate the broader observation that ordinary memory processes (Horton & Gerrig, 2005) are likely to be relevant to understanding the contextual factors – historical and immediate – that guide language use in the moment. As we shall see, one such memory process involves the *generation* of information (Slamecka & Graf, 1978), with important implications for how the conversation is remembered as a function of role as speaker (the *generator* of information) vs. listener.

Perception of and memory for discourse contexts

Thus far, we have established that the way in which a speaker communicates their intended meaning is shaped by the contexts of language use. That context can include the immediate physical context (Olson, 1970; Osgood, 1971), or more precisely, what the speaker perceives or notices in the immediate physical context (Brown-Schmidt & Tanenhaus, 2006; Pechmann, 1989). The context also includes what speakers know or believe about their conversational partner's knowledge and physical context (Heller et al., 2012;

Isaacs & Clark, 1987; Horton & Brennan, 2016), or more precisely, what the speaker perceives or remembers about that partner's knowledge or context (Branigan et al., 2011; Horton & Gerrig, 2002; 2005; Horton & Spieler, 2007). Lastly, the context also includes past language use, including past referents and contexts (Galati & Brennan, 2021; Heller & Chambers, 2014; Van Der Wege, 2009; Yoon, et al., 2016; 2021; Yoon & Stine-Morrow, 2019), or more precisely what the speaker recalls about those past contexts (Schmader & Horton, 2019). Critically, then, understanding the influence of context on language use requires considerations of the cognitive processes that shape *perception* of and *memory* for those contexts.

When the current referent is from the same basic level object category as a prior referent, the current referent may offer a strong retrieval cue to access a representation of the prior referent from memory. By contrast past referents that do not share the same features as the current referent may not be cued and not accessed from memory and therefore may not be accessed even if relevant. In dialog, past referents are more likely to be retrieved from memory and influence speaking in the moment when interlocutors perceive the past discourse as relevant to the current discourse and retrieval cues in the moment support memory retrieval (Yoon et al., 2021; see also Hockley, 2008; cf. O'Shea et al., 2021). This suggests that the mechanism by which speakers establish discourse contexts is continuing evaluation of perceived relevance rather than memory for the discourse per se. An open question is how historical and present contexts are represented, specifically whether speakers represent these contexts in one domain with one weighted higher than the other, or if they are represented as being in separate domains that interact with each other (as illustrated in the thought bubble in Figure 11.3).

As discussed above, contextual reinstatement effects – a boost to memory when contextual cues at encoding and retrieval match (Godden & Baddeley, 1975, inter alia), are strongest when the encoded information is integrated with the context (Eich, 1985; Shin et al. 2021). Extended to the conversation, this suggests that one's partner may act as a contextual cue most strongly when that person is perceived to be relevant to the talk at hand. One reason, then, that the differentiation effects are somewhat weak may be due to the fact that the referenced items are not particularly relevant to the conversational partner or to each other. Context effects in language may be stronger when they are seen as relevant to the conversational goals. Stronger effects of one's partner on what a speaker says may be observed when the partner is of special significance (e.g., talking to a friend vs. stranger; Yoon et al., 2021b), or particularly relevant to the task at hand.

Subsequent memory representations after communication

An extensive amount of work has investigated the role of historical contexts and the memory representations that shape language production processes in the moment. A related question is what information guides memories for what one said over longer time scales. Speakers exhibit persistence in both syntactic choices (Bock et al., 2007; Jacobs et al., 2019) and referential choices (Brennan & Clark, 1996; Knutsen & Le Bigot, 2014), consistent with the idea that the process of speaking results in learning (Dell & Chang, 2014; MacDonald, 2013). Persistence may arise at the level of the communicative intention, the linguistic utterance that was planned, or information gleaned from internal monitoring mechanisms (Nozari & Novick, 2017), or some combination of these. For example, after reading a temporarily ambiguous sentence, readers may retain in memory an incorrect interpretation of the literal meaning of the sentence that was generally plausible in the scenario set up by the sentence itself (Christianson et al., 2001; Patson et al., 2009).

Over longer time scales, we can ask what is likely to be retained in memory about what was communicated, including factors that shape what is likely to be recalled after a conversation is over. Studies investigating recall of conversation have typically employed an experimental paradigm in which participants come together for a conversation, followed by a delay of minutes to days, and are then asked to recall, in detail, everything that was said in that original conversation. The researcher can then compare a high-quality audio recording of the original conversation with the participant's recall, and quantify the proportion of *idea units* from the original conversation that were recalled after a delay (an idea unit is typically defined as a unit of meaning with informational or affective value, and often corresponds to a phrase). After delays of several minutes to several weeks (Ross & Sicoly, 1979; Samp & Humphreys, 2007; Stafford et al., 1987; Stafford & Daly, 1984), these studies estimate that on average participants can recall anywhere from 0% to 40% of the total idea units expressed in the original conversation, where perfect recall would be 100%.

Further, analyses of conversational role reveal that conversational partners are more likely to recall and more likely to correctly recognize information that they said themselves in conversation, as compared to what was said to them (Fischer et al., 2015; Knutsen & Le Bigot, 2017; McKinley et al., 2017; Ross & Sicoly, 1979). For example, analyses of memory for the images in lexical differentiation tasks, discussed above, consistently show that speakers had significantly better memory for past referents than listeners (Yoon et al., 2016; 2021). Further, McKinley et al. (2017) find that the generation benefit for referents in conversation persists even when conversational partners have established common ground for the way to refer to the to-be-remembered objects. These findings reflect a widely known set of phenomena in the memory literature that producing and otherwise generating information (e.g., reading words aloud, word stem completion), compared to receiving in-formation (e.g., reading or hearing words), promotes memory for that which is produced or generated (Fawcett et al., 2012; MacLeod, et al., 2010; Slamecka & Graf, 1978; Zormpa et al., 2019). Interestingly, the speaker benefit for past referents in conversation does not appear to extend to unmentioned items in the visual context (Yoon et al., 2016; 2021), suggesting that the asymmetry may be limited to what is explicitly discussed.

This asymmetry in memory is also reflected in what people mention and re-mention in dialog, with speakers more likely to re-mention things that they first introduced into the discourse, than they are to re-mention something their partner first introduced (Knutsen & Le Bigot, 2014). Further, in a study of source monitoring errors following collaborative interaction, Jalbert et al. (2021) reports that participants are more likely to incorrectly attribute their partner's idea to themselves than they are to attribute their idea to their partner. Jalbert et al. (2021) also find that participants were more likely to falsely believe that their own idea was shared with their partner (a false consensus effect) than to believe that their partner's idea was shared with them, again reflecting a type of egocentrism in memories of the shared past. Taken together, these findings show that despite conversation being an inherently interactive enterprise, conversational partners retain different information about the shared past, and these distinct memories shape what is subsequently said. This phenomenon demonstrates that while language use is constructed with respect to both immediate and historical contexts, conversational partners draw on distinct *memories* of what that historical context is, possibly due to differences in the way resources are allocated to carry out successful communication (Hawkins et al., 2021; also see Gopie & MacLeod, 2009). The findings of distinct memories for the discourse context between speakers and listeners have wide-ranging implications, including offering a critique of the common assumption that conversational partners form and share common ground for the discourse history (Heller & Brown-Schmidt, 2021). In addition to potential theoretical implications, these findings have important potential implications for policy and law (Brown-Schmidt & Benjamin, 2018; Spellman & Weaver, 2020). In legal settings, testimony based on memory for prior conversations may be a common occurrence, and if so, limits on memory for conversation deserve closer scrutiny in such settings (see Duke et al., 2007).

Conclusion

Language use in conversation is driven by the speaker's communicative goals and intentions which may be to inform, inquire, motivate, persuade, or more. The way that the speaker communicates their message is shaped by not only linguistic aspects of language production, such as which messages the speaker wishes them to receive, but also social–cognitive factors, such as who the intended addressee or addressees are, and what discourse contexts they encounter. The form of language that a speaker uses is shaped by the different types of contexts. Here we argue that the context of language use is a combination of past and present with the elements of the past and present that shape language use in the moment determined by cognitive processes such as interlocutors' perception and memory. Remembering past referents is necessary but not sufficient to drive referential forms to be reflective of the discourse history. Instead, how interlocutors perceive the relevant discourse context and take that into consideration while planning determines utterance form. Lastly, one reason that conversational partners form distinct memories for conversation may be to divide their responsibilities, each remembering different aspects of the discourse context in order to facilitate successful communication.

Acknowledgments

This material is based on work supported by National Science Foundation Grant BCS 19-21492 to Sarah Brown-Schmidt, and National Institutes of Health Grant R03AG072236 to Si On Yoon. We thank Kaitlin Lord for comments on a draft of this manuscript.

References

Altmann, G., & Steedman, M. (1998). Interaction with context during human sentence processing. *Cognition, 30*(3), 191–238.

Arnold, J. E., Eisenband, J. G., Brown-Schmidt, S., & Trueswell, J. C. (2000). The rapid use of gender information: Evidence of the time course of pronoun resolution from eyetracking. *Cognition, 76*(1), B13–B26.

Arnold, J. E., & Griffin, Z. M. (2007). The effect of additional characters on choice of referring expression: Everyone counts. *Journal of Memory and Language, 56*(4), 521–536.

Belke, E. (2006). Visual determinants of preferred adjective order. *Visual Cognition, 14*(3), 261–294.

Bock, K., Dell, G. S., Chang, F., & Onishi, K. H. (2007). Persistent structural priming from language comprehension to language production. *Cognition, 104*(3), 437–458.

Bögels, S. (2020). Neural correlates of turn-taking in the wild: Response planning starts early in free interviews. *Cognition, 203*, 104347.

Branigan, H. P., Pickering, M. J., Pearson, J., McLean, J. F., & Brown, A. (2011). The role of beliefs in lexical alignment: Evidence from dialogs with humans and computers. *Cognition, 121*, 41–57.

Brennan, S. E., & Clark, H. H. (1996). Conceptual pacts and lexical choice in conversation. *Journal of Experimental Psychology: Learning, Memory & Cognition, 22*, 482–493.

Brennan, S. E., Galati, A., & Kuhlen, A. K. (2010). Two minds, one dialog: Coordinating speaking and understanding. In B. H. Ross (Ed.), *The psychology of learning and motivation: Advances in research and theory* (pp. 301–344). Elsevier Academic Press.

Brown-Schmidt, S., & Benjamin, A. S. (2018). How we remember conversation: Implications in legal settings. *Policy Insights from the Behavioral and Brain Sciences, 5*(2), 187–194.

Brown-Schmidt, S., & Fraundorf, S. (2015). Interpretation of informational questions modulated by joint knowledge and intonational contours. *Journal of Memory and Language, 84*, 49–74.

Brown-Schmidt, S., Gunlogson, C., & Tanenhaus, M. K. (2008). Addressees distinguish shared from private information when interpreting questions during interactive conversation. *Cognition, 107*(3), 1122–1134.

Brown-Schmidt, S., Naveiras, M., De Boeck, P., & Cho, S.-J. (2020). Statistical modeling of intensive categorical time-series eye-tracking data using dynamic generalized linear mixed effect models with crossed random effects. In: K. Federmeier & Schotter, L. (Eds.), *The psychology of learning and motivation, 73*, 1–31.

Brown-Schmidt, S., & Tanenhaus, M. K. (2006). Watching the eyes when talking about size: an investigation of message formulation and utterance planning. *Journal of Memory and Language, 54*, 592–609.

Brown-Schmidt, S., & Tanenhaus, M. K. (2008). Real-time investigation of referential domains in unscripted conversation: A targeted language game approach. *Cognitive Science, 32*, 643–684.

Brown-Schmidt, S., Yoon, S. O., & Ryskin, R. A. (2015). People as Contexts in Conversation. *Psychology of Learning and Motivation, 62*, 59–99.

Cho, S.-J., Brown-Schmidt, S., De Boeck, P., & Shen, J. (2020). Modeling Intensive Polytomous Time Series Eye Tracking Data: A Dynamic Tree-Based Item Response Model. *Psychometrika, 85*, 154–184.

Christianson, K., Hollingworth, A., Halliwell, J. F., & Ferreira, F. (2001). Thematic roles assigned along the garden path linger. *Cognitive Psychology, 42*, 368–407.

Clark, H. H., & Murphy, G. L. (1982). Audience design inmeaning and reference. In Le Ny, J.-F., & Kintsch, W. (Eds.), *Language and comprehension* (pp. 287–299). Amsterdam: North-Holland.

Clark, H. H., & Schaefer, E. F. (1989). Contributing to discourse. *Cognitive Science, 13*, 259–294.

Clark, H. H., & Wilkes-Gibbs, D. (1986). Referring as a collaborative process. *Cognition, 22*, 1–39.

Colombo, L., & Williams, J. (1990). Effects of word- and sentence-level contexts upon word recognition. *Memory & Cognition, 18*, 153–163.

Corps, R. E., Knudsen, B., Meyer, A. S., & Corps, R. E. (2022). Overrated gaps: Inter-speaker gaps provide limited information about the timing of turns in conversation. *Cognition, 223*, 105037.

Dell, G. S., & Chang, F. (2014). The P-chain: Relating sentence production and its disorders to comprehension and acquisition. *Philosophical Transactions of the Royal Society B: Biological Sciences, 369*(1634), 20120394.

Donnellan, K. S. (1966). Reference and definite descriptions. *The Philosophical Review, 75*(3), 281–304.

Duke, S. B., Lee, A. S. E., & Pager, C. K. (2007). A picture's worth a thousand words: Conversational versus eyewitness testimony in criminal convictions. *American Criminal Law Review, 44*, 1.

Eich, E. (1985). Context, memory, and integrated item/context imagery. *Journal of Experimental Psychology: Learning, Memory, and Cognition, 11*(4), 764.

Engelhardt, P. E., Bailey, K. G., & Ferreira, F. (2006). Do speakers and listeners observe the Gricean Maxim of Quantity? *Journal of Memory and Language, 54*(4), 554–573.

Fawcett, J. M., Quinlan, C. K., & Taylor, T. L. (2012). Interplay of the production and picture superiority effects: A signal detection analysis. *Memory, 20*(7), 655–666.

Fischer, N. M., Schult, J. C., & Steffens, M. C. (2015). Source and des-tination memory in face-to-face interaction: A multinomial model-ing approach. *Journal of Experimental Psychology: Applied, 21*(2), 195.

Fox Tree, J. E. (1999). Listening in on monologues and dialogues. *Discourse Processes, 27*(1), 35–53.

Fukumura, K., & Van Gompel, R. P. (2011). The effect of animacy on the choice of referring expression. *Language and Cognitive Processes, 26*(10), 1472–1504.

Fukumura, K., Van Gompel, R. P., & Pickering, M. J. (2010). The use of visual context during the production of referring expressions. *Quarterly Journal of Experimental Psychology, 63*(9), 1700–1715.

Fussell, S. R., & Krauss, R. M. (1989a). The effects of intended audience on message production and comprehension: Reference in a common ground framework. *Journal of Experimental Social Psychology, 25*, 203–219.

Fussell, S. R., & Krauss, R. M. (1989b). Understanding friends and strangers: The effect of audience design on message comprehension. *European Journal of Social Psychology, 19*, 509–525.

Galati, A., & Brennan, S. E. (2021). What is retained about common ground? Distinct effects of linguistic and visual co-presence. *Cognition, 215*, 104809.

Garrod, S., & Anderson, A. (1987). Saying what you mean in dialogue: A study in conceptual and semantic co-ordination. *Cognition, 27*(2), 181–218.

Godden, D. R., & Baddeley, A. D. (1975). Context-dependent memory in two natural environments: On land and underwater. *British Journal of psychology, 66*(3), 325–331.

Gopie, N., & MacLeod, C. M. (2009). Destination memory: Stop me if I've told you this before. *Psychological Science, 20*(12), 1492–1499.

Gundel, J., Hedberg, N., & Zacharski, R. (1993). Cognitive Status and the Form of Referring Expressions in Discourse. *Language, 69*(2), 274–307. doi:10.2307/416535

Gunlogson, C. (2003). *True to form: Rising and falling declaratives as questions in English.* New York, New York: Routledge.

Hanna, J. E., Tanenhaus, M. K., & Trueswell, J. C. (2003). The effects of common ground and perspective on domains of referential interpretation. *Journal of Memory and Language, 49*, 43–61.

Hawkins, R. D., Frank, M. C., & Goodman, N. D. (2020). Characterizing the dynamics of learning in repeated reference games. *Cognitive Science, 44*, e12845.

Hawkins, R. D., Gweon, H., & Goodman, N. D. (2021). The division of labor in communication: Speakers help listeners account for asymmetries in visual perspective. *Cognitive Science, 34*, e12926.

Heller, D. (2020). The production and comprehension of referring expressions: Definite description. *Language and Linguistics Compass, 14*(5), e12370.

Heller, D. & Brown-Schmidt, S. (2021). Common ground is dead. *Spoken presentation at the Cycle Linguists Podcast.*

Heller, D., & Chambers, C. G. (2014). Would a blue kite by any other name be just as blue? Effects of descriptive choices on subsequent referential behavior. *Journal of Memory and Language, 70*, 53–67.

Heller, D., Gorman, K. S., & Tanenhaus, M. K. (2012). To name or to describe: Shared knowledge affects referential form. *Topics in Cognitive Science, 4*(2), 290–305.

Heller, D., Grodner, D., & Tanenhaus, M. K. (2008). The role of perspective in identifying domains of reference. *Cognition, 108*, 831–836.

Heller, D., Parisien, C., & Stevenson, S. (2016). Perspective-taking behavior as the probabilistic weighing of multiple domains. *Cognition, 149*, 104–120.

Hockley, W. E. (2008). The effects of environmental context on recognition memory and claims of remembering. *Journal of Experimental Psychology, 34*, 1412–1429.

Horton, W. S., & Brennan, S. E. (2016). The role of metarepresentation in the production and resolution of referring expressions. *Frontiers in Psychology, 7*, 1111.

Horton, W. S., & Gerrig, R. J. (2002). Speakers' experiences and audience design: Knowing when and knowing how to adjust utterances to addressees. *Journal of Memory and Language, 47*, 589–606.

Horton, W. S., & Gerrig, R. J. (2005). The impact of memory demands on audience design during language production. *Cognition*, *96*(2), 127–142.

Horton, W. S., & Spieler, D. H. (2007). Age-related differences in communication and audience design. *Psychology and Aging*, *22*, 281–290.

Isaacs, E. A., & Clark, H. H. (1987). References in conversation between experts and novices. *Journal of Experimental Psychology: General*, *116*(1), 26.

Jacobs, C. L., Cho, S. J., & Watson, D. G. (2019). Self-Priming in Production: Evidence for a Hybrid Model of Syntactic Priming. *Cognitive Science*, *43*(7), e12749.

Jalbert, M. C., Wulff, A. N., & Hyman Jr, I. E. (2021). Stealing and sharing memories: Source monitoring biases following collaborative remembering. *Cognition*, *211*, 104656.

Knutsen, D., & Le Bigot, L. (2014). Capturing egocentric biases in reference reuse during collaborative dialogue. *Psychonomic Bulletin & Review*, *21*(6), 1590–1599.

Knutsen, D., & Le Bigot, L. (2017). Conceptual match as a determinant of reference reuse in dialogue. *Journal of Experimental Psychology: Learning, Memory, and Cognition*, *43*(3), 350.

Konopka, A. E., & Brown-Schmidt, S. (2014). Message encoding. In V. Ferreira, M. Goldrick, & M. Miozzo (Eds.), *The Oxford handbook of language production* (pp. 1–20). New York, NY: Oxford University Press.

Krauss, R. M., & Weinheimer, S. (1966). Concurrent feedback, confirmation, and the encoding of referents in verbal communication. *Journal of Personality and Social Psychology*, *4*(3), 343.

MacDonald, M. C. (2013). How language production shapes language form and comprehension. *Frontiers in Psychology*, *4*, 226.

MacLeod, C. M., Gopie, N., Hourihan, K. L., Neary, K. R., & Ozubko, J. D. (2010). The production effect: Delineation of a phenomenon. *Journal of Experimental Psychology: Learning, Memory, and Cognition*, *36*, 671–685.

McKinley, G. L., Brown-Schmidt, S., & Benjamin, A. S. (2017). Memory for conversation and the development of common ground. *Memory & cognition*, *45*(8), 1281–1294.

Nozari, N., & Novick, J. (2017). Monitoring and control in language production. *Current Directions in Psychological Science*, *26*(5), 403–410.

Olson, D. R. (1970). Language and thought: aspects of a cognitive theory of semantics. *Psychological review*, *77*, 257–273.

Osgood, C. E. (1971). Exploration in semantic Space: a personal diary. *Journal of Social Issues*, *27*, 5–64.

O'Shea, K. J., Martin, C. R., & Barr, D. J. (2021). Ordinary memory processes in the design of referring expressions. *Journal of Memory and Language*, *117*, 104186.

Patson, N. D., & Darowski, E. S., Moon, N., & Ferreira, F. (2009). Lingering misinterpretations in garden-path sentences: evidence from a paraphrasing task. *Journal of Experimental Psychology: Learning, memory, and Cognition*, *35*, 280–285.

Pechmann, T. (1989). Incremental speech production and referential overspecification. *Linguistics*, *27*(1), 89–110.

Perea, M., & Rosa, E. (2002). The effects of associative and semantic priming in the lexical decision task. *Psychological Research*, *66*, 180–194.

Pickering, M. J., & Garrod, S. (2013). An integrated theory of production and comprehension. *Behavioral and Brain Sciences*, *36*, 329–392.

Pickering, M. J., & Garrod, S. (2004). Toward a mechanistic psychology of dialogue. *Behavioral and Brain Sciences*, *27*, 167–226.

Ross, M., & Sicoly, F. (1979). Egocentric biases in availability and attribution. *Journal of Personality and Social Psychology, 37*(3), 322.

Samp, J. A., & Humphreys, L. R. (2007). "I said what?" Partner familiarity, resistance, and the accuracy of conversational recall. *Communication Monographs, 74,* 561–581.

Schmader, C., & Horton, W. S. (2019). Conceptual effects of audience design in human-computer and human-human dialogue. *Discourse Processes, 56,* 170–190.

Schober, M. F., & Clark, H. H. (1989). Understanding by addressees and overhearers. *Cognitive Psychology, 21*(2), 211–232.

Sedivy, J. C. (2003). Pragmatic versus form-based accounts of referential contrast: Evidence for effects of informativity expectations. *Journal of Psycholinguistic Research, 32*(1), 3–23.

Sedivy, J. C. (2005). Evaluating explanations for referential context effects: evidence for Gricean mechanisms in online language interpretation. In J. C. Trueswell, & M. K. Tanenhaus (Eds.), *Approaches to studying world-situated language use: Bridging the language as product and language as action traditions* (pp. 153–171). Cambridge, MA: MIT press.

Shin, Y. S., Masís-Obando, R., Keshavarzian, N., Dáve, R., & Norman, K. A. (2021). Context-dependent memory effects in two immersive virtual reality environments: On Mars and underwater. *Psychonomic Bulletin & Review, 28*(2), 574–582.

Slamecka, N. J., & Graf, P. (1978). The generation effect: Delineation of a phenomenon. *Journal of Experimental Psychology: Human Learning and Memory, 4,* 592–604.

Smith, S. M., & Vela, E. (2001). Environmental context-dependent memory: A review and meta-analysis. *Psychonomic Bulletin & Review, 8*(2), 203–220.

Spellman, B. A., & Weaver, C. A. (2020). Memory and the Law. Kahane, M., & Wagner, A. (Eds.), *Handbook of Human Memory – Vol. II: Applications. Oxford (Forthcoming),* Virginia Public Law and Legal Theory Research Paper No. 2020-56, Available at SSRN: https://ssrn.com/abstract=3644394

Stafford, L., Burggraf, C. S., & Sharkey, W. F. (1987). Conversational memory: The effects of time, recall, mode, and memory expectancies on remembrances of natural conversations. *Human Communication Research, 14,* 203–229.

Stafford, L., & Daly, J. A. (1984). Conversational memory: The effects of recall mode and memory expectancies on remembrance of natural conversations. *Human Communication Research, 10,* 379–402.

Tanenhaus, M. K., Magnuson, J. S., Dahan, D., & Chambers, C. (2000). Eye movements and lexical access in spoken-language comprehension: Evaluating a linking hypothesis between fixations and linguistic processing. *Journal of Psycholinguistic Research, 29*(6), 557–580. 10.1023/a:1026464108329

Tarenskeen, S., Broersma, M., & Geurts, B. (2015). Overspecification of color, pattern, and size: Salience, absoluteness, and consistency. *Frontiers in Psychology, 6,* 1703.

Tullis, J. G., Braverman, M., Ross, B. H., & Benjamin, A. S. (2014). Remindings influence the interpretation of ambiguous stimuli. *Psychonomic bulletin & review, 21*(1), 107–113.

Tulving, E., & Thomson, D. M. (1973). Encoding specificity and retrieval processes in episodic memory. *Psychological Review, 80,* 352–373.

Van Berkum, J. J., Brown, C. M., & Hagoort, P. (1999). Early referential context effects in sentence processing: Evidence from event-related brain potentials. *Journal of Memory and Language, 41*(2), 147–182.

Van Berkum, J. J., Brown, C. M., Hagoort, P., & Zwitserlood, P. (2003). Event-related brain potentials reflect discourse-referential ambiguity in spoken language comprehension. *Psychophysiology, 40*(2), 235–248.

Van der Wege, M. M. (2009). Lexical entrainment and lexical differentiation in reference phrase choice. *Journal of Memory and Language, 60*(4), 448–463.

Wilkes-Gibbs, D., & Clark, H. H. (1992). Coordinating beliefs in conversation. *Journal of Memory and Language, 31*(2), 183–194.

Yoon, S. O., Benjamin, A. S., & Brown-Schmidt, S. (2016). The historical context in conversation: Lexical differentiation and memory for the discourse history. *Cognition, 154*, 102–117.

Yoon, S. O., Benjamin, A. S., & Brown-Schmidt, S. (2021). Referential form and memory for the discourse history. *Cognitive Science, 45*(4), e12964.

Yoon, S. O., & Brown-Schmidt, S. (2013). Lexical differentiation effects in language production and comprehension. *Journal of Memory and Language, 69*, 397–416.

Yoon, S. O., & Brown-Schmidt, S. (2019a). Audience design in multiparty conversation. *Cognitive Science, 43*(8), e12774.

Yoon, S. O., & Brown-Schmidt, S. (2019b). Contextual integration in multiparty audience design. *Cognitive Science, 43*(12), e12807

Yoon, S. O., & Brown-Schmidt, S. (2018a). The influence of the historical discourse record on language processing in dialogue. *Discourse Processes*, 55, 31–46.

Yoon, S. O., & Brown-Schmidt, S. (2018b). Aim low: Mechanisms of audience design in multiparty conversation. *Discourse Processes, 55*(7), 566–592.

Yoon, S. O., Pratley, B., & Heller, D. (2021a). Invisible, unmentioned entities affect referential forms. Short talk presented at 34th Annual CUNY Conference on Human Sentence Processing, Philadelphia, PA.

Yoon, S. O., Pratley, B., & Heller, D. (2021b). The identity of the partner matters even when naming everyday objects. Proceedings of the 43nd Annual Virtual Meeting of the Cognitive Science Society.

Yoon, S. O., & Stine-Morrow, E. A. L. (2019). Evidence of preserved audience design with aging in interactive conversation. *Psychology and Aging, 34*, 613–623.

Zormpa, E., Brehm, L. E., Hoedemaker, R. S., & Meyer, A. S. (2019). The production effect and the generation effect improve memory in picture naming. *Memory, 27*(3), 340–352.

12 Joint Language Production and the Representation of Other Speakers' Utterances

Chiara Gambi and Martin J. Pickering

Joint language production is the study of the mechanisms involved in producing language jointly with another real or assumed speaker. Using relevant tasks, researchers have asked how (if at all) speakers represent one another's utterances (which we term *co-representation*) and specifically examined how such representations affect language production. They have compared the process of producing language jointly to the process of producing language individually, and have done so to address a question that is important for the study of both comprehension and production: How do language production processes relate to the representation of others' utterances? If production processes contribute to co-representation, then we would expect to find that co-representation affects actual language production.

We use the term *joint language production* to refer both to cases where two people speak at the same time and to cases where people take turns speaking (e.g., *A* names a picture, then *B* names a picture). Furthermore, we include both situations where speakers are simply aware of each other's tasks (e.g., Gambi et al., 2015a; Kuhlen & Abdel Rahman, 2017) and situations where speakers intend to coordinate with each other, such as in choric production (Cummins, 2003, 2009; Jasmin et al., 2016), or when they are instructed to jointly construct a meaningful sentence (e.g., Lelonkiewicz & Gambi, 2020) or to minimize the silent pause between their utterances (e.g., Hoedemaker & Meyer, 2018). Importantly, we use it to refer not only to situations where two people are actually producing, but also to instances when one participant produces while believing that another person is also producing (whether the participant receives any feedback about their partner's production or not, or even whether there is a real partner or not). Finally, speaking individually (the other side of the comparison) can refer either to one speaker performing just half of the joint production task (e.g., *A* names a picture, but then nobody speaks) or to one speaker performing the whole of the task (e.g., *A* names a picture, and then names another picture). Throughout the chapter, we specify exactly what is meant by "jointly" and "individually" with reference to particular studies, but we first explain the theoretical importance of this comparison and thus the unique contribution made by this literature.

Comparing joint to individual production is important because it helps answer the following question: To what extent do a speaker's language

DOI: 10.4324/9781003145790-13

production processes contribute to the representation of another speaker's utterances? Such representation is typically considered to be part of comprehension, but traditional studies of comprehension do not consider the extent to which others' utterances are represented similarly to people's own utterances (as an example, see the chapters in Crocker et al., 2000). The assumption of considerable overlap between representations and processes used in production and comprehension (Gambi & Pickering, 2017) is at the heart of some theories of dialogue (Pickering & Garrod, 2013; Pickering & Garrod, 2021), monitoring (see Gauvin & Hartsuiker, 2020 for a recent review), and prediction (Pickering & Gambi, 2018). However, until recently, very little was known about how the processes that underlie language production in an individual are adapted to incorporate representations of others' utterances in a joint setting. Furthermore, the hypothesis that speakers use the production system to represent the utterances of other speakers as if they were their own (i.e., via simulation; Dell & Chang, 2014; Pickering & Garrod, 2013) has remained controversial (Hickok, 2013).

Note that our question is more specific than the broad question of how others' utterances affect one's own language production. The latter is of course central to the study of dialogue: In referential games (e.g., Brennan & Clark, 1996; Garrod & Anderson, 1987), in work about the effect of feedback and backchannels (e.g., Bavelas et al., 2000; Tolins et al., 2018), in studies of syntactic priming (e.g., Branigan et al., 2000) and priming of language switching across interlocutors (Kootstra et al., 2010), and more recently in studies of turn-taking (e.g., Bögels et al., 2015; Corps et al., 2018), researchers are interested in how an interlocutor's production (lexical and structural choices, language choices, the time course of sentence preparation) is affected by another speaker's utterances.

Most studies of dialogue are not designed to determine whether production processes are involved in the representation of others' utterances, and thus do not include direct comparisons between the effects of others' utterances and one's own previously produced utterances on language production. A few studies of syntactic priming (i.e., the tendency of speakers to re-use recently comprehended or produced structural representations; see Pickering & Ferreira, 2008; Slevc, this volume) have included a comparison between production-to-production priming (i.e., priming within an individual speaker) and comprehension-to-production priming (i.e., priming between speakers) (Bock et al., 2007; Jacobs et al., 2019; Segaert et al., 2013). But they tested isolated speakers (i.e., the other speaker on comprehension-to-production trials was just implied) and it is not clear to what extent the production task used on prime trials reflected only production (and not comprehension) processes (Jacobs et al., 2019).

We are not aware of any experimental study of priming in dialogue that has directly compared within-speaker and between-speaker priming. In contrast, some corpus studies have included this comparison (e.g., Gries, 2005; Reitter et al., 2006). While they found stronger within- than between-speaker priming, it is difficult to be certain about the relationship between comprehension and production mechanisms because the findings could be confounded by other factors such as discourse structure (see Jacobs et al., 2019 for discussion). Finally, Schoot et al. (2019) found larger priming in the presence versus absence of an interlocutor (though see Ivanova et al., 2020, for contrasting findings), but the source of this effect is unclear: The presence of an interlocutor may have encouraged production-based simulation of the primes during comprehension, but the study did not include a comparison to production-to-production priming.

In this chapter we review studies that include direct comparisons between individual and joint production (sometimes, we make brief reference to studies that included only a joint production condition). Taken together, the studies show that language production mechanisms are affected by representations of others' utterances: Speakers represent whether their co-speakers are engaging in language production (i.e., speaking or preparing to speak) and these representations influence the way they produce their own utterances, often in a way that parallels within-speaker effects. However, the extent to which this co-representation alters the dynamics of language production compared to speaking individually appears limited, such that speakers are typically affected by others' utterances in a less specific way or to a lesser extent than by their own utterances. These findings show that representation of others' utterances and production of one's own utterances are based on partly overlapping mechanisms, but also that representations of others' utterances tend to be less detailed.

Below, we organize our review broadly by paradigm. We identify three individual production paradigms for which researchers have developed joint versions: (1) picture naming (including the word-replacement task used by Gambi et al., 2015a – see below); (2) picture-word interference (PWI) and Stroop tasks; (3) language switching tasks. We then briefly review two special cases (4): choric production and joint sentence building. In our conclusion, we consider open questions and the relevance of this research for the study of dialogue.

Joint picture naming

Most of the studies that have investigated joint language production have used variations of the picture naming paradigm, in which speakers are asked to name pictures displayed on a screen. Some details, for instance the number of pictures displayed simultaneously or whether participants sat next to each other or in separate rooms, varied between studies. But in all of them speakers either named pictures on their own or shared the task with another speaker, who might be a (naïve) participant or a confederate.

In one of the earliest studies, Gambi et al. (2015a) had two participants sit next to each other in front of the same screen and take turns naming pictures. On critical trials, a picture changed into a different picture, and participants were instructed to stop speaking as quickly as possible. One group was told that the person who stopped would name the new picture (individual task group), another group was told that the other person would name the new picture (joint task group), and a third group had to ignore the new picture (control group). Participants in the individual task group were less likely to stop mid-word than participants in the control group (replicating Hartsuiker et al. (2008) and Tydgat et al. (2011) in the presence of a partner), thus suggesting that planning the new picture name interfered with the process of stopping speech. Importantly, participants in the joint task group were also less likely to stop mid-word than participants in the individual task group, but not to the same extent as participants in the control group. Thus representing that another person will speak delays the process of stopping speech similarly to representing that one will speak, albeit to a lesser extent.

Two studies manipulated speakers' beliefs about the task their partner was performing in a different room while they prepared to speak (Gambi et al., 2015b; 2022). In Gambi et al. (2015b), speakers named either single pictures or superimposed pairs of pictures and, across four experiments, they were told their partner would produce an utterance that was the same or different from their own utterance, stay silent, or respond yes or no to a semantic categorization question (i.e., did the pictures belong to the same semantic category?). Naming latencies were faster when participants believed their partner was not speaking, or was speaking but not engaging in lexical retrieval (categorization condition), than when they believed their partner was naming pictures. Moreover, Gambi et al. (2022) replicated this finding in a task where speakers produced full active or passive descriptions of transitive events: Across three experiments, description latencies were longer when speakers believed their partner was producing or about to produce a sentence, compared to when they believed their partner remained silent.

Thus, speakers represented whether their partner was engaging in language production – even though doing so brought no obvious benefit to their performance, and in fact slowed down concurrent production. The fact that such representations affected concurrent language production suggests that co-representation of others' utterances makes use of production mechanisms. However, both studies also suggest that co-representation is only partial. Onset latencies were unaffected by whether speakers believed their partner was naming the same or a different picture (or indeed whether they were naming the pictures in the same or different order; Gambi et al., 2015b) and they were similarly unaffected by whether they believed the partner was describing the same event with a syntactic construction of the same or opposite voice (Gambi et al., 2022). There was some evidence that believing the partner was producing a different utterance than one's own increased interference (sometimes leading to increased error rates; Gambi et al., 2015b; or longer descriptions; Gambi et al., 2022), but it was not consistent across experiments, suggesting that co-representation generally lacked detail.

One important question is whether speakers may co-represent others' utterances in greater detail under different conditions than the one tested by Gambi and colleagues (2015b; 2022). First, in those studies, speakers performed a joint task only in a minimal sense: They sat in different rooms and had no requirement to coordinate their utterances with those of their partner. Speakers might be more likely to represent the content of their partner's utterances when their partner's presence is made more salient, or when they are given explicit instructions to coordinate. Second, speakers were co-representing others' utterances while preparing to speak themselves; but since language production is cognitively demanding (Roelofs & Piai, 2011), the resources available for concurrent co-representation may have been limited. It is thus possible that speakers may represent their partners' utterances in greater detail when they do not need to speak at the same time as their partner, but take turns with them. Below, we review studies that help address these questions.

Brehm et al. (2019) manipulated speakers' beliefs about their partner's task (naming the same picture, a different picture, or categorizing it as living/non-living), similar to Gambi et al. (2015b). However, they had participants sit side-by-side. Thus, although speakers wore noise-cancelling headphones, the co-present partner was arguably more salient. Despite this, there were again only inconsistent effects of the content of the partner's utterance. Across two experiments, participants took *longer* to name the pictures when they knew their partner was performing a different task (categorization) than the same task (naming), and this effect was present in the joint task (partner present) but not in an individual control task (when speakers had the same task instructions and stimuli, but were told their partner could not attend the session). Although one experiment found longer latencies when the partner was naming a different than the same picture, this effect was present even in the individual condition, suggesting it was not related to co-representation, and furthermore it was not replicated in the second experiment.

In sum, Brehm et al. (2019) found evidence for co-representation of the partner's task (though the effect was in the opposite direction to Gambi et al., 2015b), but not that they formed detailed representations of the partner's utterances, even when the partner's presence was salient. However, partners' pictures were displayed on the opposite side of the screen (cf. Gambi et al., 2015b, who superimposed the pictures), making it harder for speakers to inspect them (as confirmed by eye-tracking data). Thus, although speakers knew where the partner's pictures would be displayed and although they were told whether the partner's pictures were the same or different from theirs, they may have disregarded this information as task-irrelevant.

More compelling evidence against detailed co-representation, even when it is task-relevant, comes from Hoedemaker and Meyer (2018). In two experiments, they had two speakers sit side-by-side, while one of the speakers was eye-tracked. Three pictures were displayed on each trial, and instructions either required only one participant to name one or more pictures (individual naming) or both participants to take turns (joint naming). When more than one picture was named, speakers were instructed to minimize the silent pause between words. In joint naming, this meant coordinating the production of the utterances with their partner. Speakers could do this well, achieving gaps of comparable lengths to those found in natural conversations (below 300ms on average; Stivers et al., 2009). But although speakers were more likely to look at pictures their partner would later name (in the joint condition) than pictures nobody would name (in the individual condition), those looks were much shorter and closer to speech onset than looks to the same pictures when the speakers themselves would later name them, implying that co-representation stopped well short of planning the partner's utterances. Crucially, this was the case even when the task required speakers to coordinate their utterances, suggesting co-representation lacks detail even when representing the content of others' utterances could facilitate smooth turn-taking.

However, all the studies mentioned so far investigated whether speakers co-represent others' utterances while speaking or preparing to speak themselves. As mentioned above, concurrent production may limit the cognitive resources that speakers have available for co-representation. Thus, we should also consider studies that have tested whether speakers co-represent others' utterances in detail when they remain silent. In order to assess whether co-representation makes use of language production processes, these studies adopted two different approaches. One approach was to look for neural signatures of production processes on trials where the participant did not speak, but their partner did (Baus et al., 2014). The other was to examine onset latencies on subsequent trials on which the participant spoke to look for evidence of co-representation on previous silent trials (Hoedemaker et al., 2017; Kuhlen & Abdel Rahman, 2017, 2021).

Baus et al. (2014) had participants take turns producing high- and low-frequency picture names with a confederate, while their EEG was recorded (there was also an individual condition, tested in a separate block, with no confederate present). In line with previous literature (e.g., Strijkers et al., 2010), the amplitude of the P200 component was larger when participants prepared to produce low- than high-frequency words – a standard frequency effect. Crucially, there was also a frequency effect when the participant remained silent and the confederate prepared to speak, but not when the confederate stayed silent as well (or indeed in the individual condition, when there was no confederate), suggesting speakers performed lexical access for pictures that their partner was about to name. Interestingly, the frequency effect on silent trials was delayed compared to speaking trials (frequency affected the P300, rather than the P200 component), which suggests that the processes underlying co-representation are similar to those underlying production, but slower.

Kuhlen and Abdel Rahman (2017) used a joint version of the cumulative semantic inhibition paradigm. In the (standard) individual version of this paradigm, participants name pictures that belong to a limited number of semantic categories, and naming latencies become slower with each naming instance within a category (Brown, 1981). This effect is thought to result from changes in the strength of connections between conceptual and lexical representations (or between features and concepts), which are caused by previous retrieval episodes (Belke, 2013; Howard et al., 2006; Oppenheim et al., 2010). In the joint version, a coloured frame around pictures indicated whether they should be named by the speaker, named by the partner, or named by neither; the speaker named half of the pictures in each semantic category, but crucially for some categories the partner named the other half of the pictures (joint naming categories), while for other categories half of the pictures were presented but not named by either the speaker or the partner (individual naming categories).

Latencies increased more steeply with successive naming instances for joint than individual naming categories. Crucially, this was the case not only when speakers could hear their partners (as also shown by Hoedemaker et al., 2017), but also when speakers could not hear their co-present partner (because they wore noise-cancelling headphones) or when the partner was seated in a different room (though see Kuhlen & Abdel Rahman, 2021, who did not replicate this last finding). In sum, there was evidence for between-speaker cumulative semantic inhibition, suggesting that speakers co-represented their partner's words using their production system and that these co-representations led to changes in the strength of connections in the mental lexicon that are qualitatively similar to those that occur when speakers produce the words themselves. We do not know how this between-speaker effect compares to the within-speaker effect quantitatively (as the study did not include a condition where the speaker named all pictures from a given category), but the effect is certainly not just due to comprehending the words produced by the partner.

Interestingly, Wudarczyk et al. (2021) suggested that co-representation of a partners' words is specific to interacting with a human partner: They had participants complete the naming task with a humanoid robot that named pictures while standing next to them (both the participant and the robot wore noise-cancelling headphones). When sharing the task with the robot, there was no evidence for co-representation of words (i.e., no increased semantic inhibition). However, participants were facilitated in naming semantic categories that were shared with the robot (compared to categories they named on their own). These findings suggest that the robot's task affected how quickly participants accessed meaning but not the downstream process of lexicalization.

In conclusion, there is good evidence that speakers co-represent whether others are speaking or about to speak, and that such co-representation affects concurrent language production, thus suggesting an involvement of production processes in the representation of others' utterances. It is less clear whether speakers co-represent the content of others' utterances in detail, but if they do, it is more likely when they are not preparing to speak at the same time. When speakers are preparing to speak, increasing the saliency of the production partner or making coordination with the partner a task requirement does not seem to make speakers more likely to engage in detailed co-representation. However, there is some indication that partner presence may increase the strength of co-representation for participants who are not preparing to speak at the same time (compare Kuhlen & Abdel Rahman, 2017, with Kuhlen & Abdel-Rahman, 2021).

Joint stroop and joint picture–word interference tasks

We now review studies in which a picture-word interference (PWI) task or a Stroop task was split across two participants. In both tasks, participants produce a verbal response (picture name or ink colour) while ignoring an irrelevant written word (distractor or colour word); ignoring this information is hard and interferes with participants' responses. In the Stroop task, incongruent trials (where ink colour and colour word mismatch) lead to more errors and longer response times than congruent trials (MacLeod, 1991); in PWI, semantically related distractor words typically lead to more errors and longer naming times than semantically unrelated words (Glaser & Düngelhoff, 1984). In the joint version of these tasks, irrelevant information is associated with a partner's response and the question is how this association affects the level of interference.

The evidence from joint spatial action tasks (e.g., Simon task, SNARC task; Knoblich et al., 2011) is that participants represent their partner's response as well as their own, so when a task-irrelevant feature of the stimulus evokes the partner's response, they respond more slowly because of interference between their own and their partner's response. For example, Sebanz et al. (2003) had participants perform a spatial compatibility ("Simon") task. Participants saw a finger wearing a red or green ring that pointed left or right. When a single participant responded to red stimuli by pressing a button on the left and to green stimuli by pressing a button on the right, they produced faster responses when the finger pointed toward the button that they had to press than when it pointed toward the other button. When participants responded in pairs, if one participant responded to (say) red stimuli and the other participant did not respond, there was no spatial compatibility effect (individual task). But when one participant responded to red stimuli and the other responded to green stimuli, the compatibility effect returned (joint task).

In contrast to this evidence for a "joint" spatial compatibility effect, Saunders and colleagues found no evidence for utterance co-representation in a joint version of the Stroop task (Saunders et al., 2019). In this button-press study, one participant responded to (say) yellow and blue words and the other responded to red and green words. They reasoned that, if the partner's response is represented, then there should be similar interference on incongruent trials where the written word corresponds to the alternative colour assigned to the same participant (own-colour trials; e.g., the word *yellow* written in blue) or one of the two colours assigned to the partner (other-colour trials; e.g., the word *red* written in blue), and there should be greater interference on both own-colour and other-colour trials than when the written word does not correspond to any response alternative (neutral trials; e.g., the word *purple* written in blue). Both of these predictions were supported, but critically a similar pattern was also found in the individual version of the task, when a single participant responded to two colours only, suggesting the results were not due to co-representation of the partner's utterances.

In a joint version of the verbal Stroop task, Pickering et al. (2022) also found no evidence that interference increased in the joint compared to the individual version. In the joint experiment, participants responded to words appearing in one ink colour, while their partners responded to words appearing in the other ink colour; in the individual experiment, participants had the same task but their partners did not respond to the other ink colour. Crucially, however, interference was greater in the joint than in the individual version when participants were additionally asked to monitor their partner's utterances for correctness (i.e., when they had to provide feedback). These findings suggest that the need to monitor another speaker's utterances may encourage a deeper representation of those utterances using the production system, thus leading to increased interference with the production of one's own utterances. Accordingly, when participants' EEG was recorded while performing the joint and individual tasks with feedback (Demiral et al., 2016), the centro-parietal P3 (P3b) component was larger in the joint than the individual task on trials when it was the partner's turn to respond (i.e., silent trials for the participant), which suggests that participants represented their partner's upcoming response on these trials.

Interestingly, Demiral et al. (2016) also found a *reduced* congruency effect on the N2 component, which indexes perceptual conflict (Donkers & Van Boxtel, 2004), when participants responded in the joint compared to the individual task. This finding suggests that representing a co-actor's utterance may not only cause additional interference between competing response alternatives but also attenuate perceptual conflict. Consistent with this hypothesis, a study that compared a joint and an individual version of the picture-word interference task (Sellaro et al., 2020) found a *reduced* semantic interference effect in a condition in which participants named pictures and were (falsely) told they had a partner in another room who read the superimposed distractor words. However, this reduction in the magnitude of the semantic interference effect only occurred when the distractor words were presented in case-alternating font, suggesting that representation of the partner's utterances can sometimes help participants ignore distracting information that is task-relevant for the partner, but only when the processing of that information is made less automatic (in contrast, when the words were presented in regular font, or when participants believed their partner was naming the colour of the pictures, comparable levels of interference were found in joint and individual versions). Finally, Kuhlen and Abdel Rahman (2022) found that when the PWI task is embedded in a communicative game, with one participant naming the distractor words and the other, co-present, participant naming the pictures, semantic interference is also greatly reduced (compared to a non-communicative, standard version of the PWI task). They suggested that naming pictures in a communicative setting may enhance semantic facilitation at the conceptual level (due to distractor and target belonging to the same semantic category).

In sum, there is some suggestive evidence that in joint Stroop and PWI tasks participants co-represent a partner's response, even though this response is associated with stimulus features that are irrelevant for the participants' own task. Specifically, evidence from these tasks suggests that co-representation can alter the way in which task-irrelevant but partner-related information is processed (perhaps reducing perceptual conflict, or facilitating conceptual processing) and the associated response is selected (perhaps increasing response conflict). There is also some evidence that co-representation effects emerge when there is an explicit requirement to monitor the others' utterances or there is a clear communicative goal to the task. However, it is unclear precisely to what extent these effects can be attributed to the co-representation of a partner's response as opposed to the default processing of the irrelevant information. Moreover, these findings do not demonstrate that the production system is involved in co-representation, though they are consistent with others' utterances being represented similarly to one's own utterances.

Joint switching tasks

When unbalanced bilinguals are cued to switch languages while naming pictures, they sometimes (but not consistently; see Gade et al., 2021, for a recent meta-analysis) experience an asymmetrical cost – greater when switching from their second language (L2) into their first language (L1) than vice versa. This cost is thought to index the extent to which bilingual speakers need to inhibit the L1 in order to select an L2 word (e.g., Meuter & Allport, 1999). A few studies have asked whether switch costs are present when switching between speakers (i.e., from comprehension to production) and if so, whether they are also asymmetrical. Such findings would suggest that the language chosen by another speaker needs to be inhibited similarly to the language chosen by the speaker.

Two studies that directly compared switch costs from comprehension to production to switch costs within production found greater costs within production (Liu et al., 2020; Liu et al., 2021b), but they used recordings for the comprehension trials, so no partner was present (or assumed). In contrast, another series of studies used a joint language-switching task with two co-present participants whose EEG was recorded (Liu et al., 2021a; Liu et al., 2018; Liu et al., 2019; Xie et al., 2019; Zhang et al., 2019). Overall, behavioural measures revealed comparable switch costs within and between speakers. But analyses of the EEG data mostly revealed the asymmetric pattern – suggestive of increased inhibition when switching into L1 than into L2 – within but not between speakers. In fact, EEG markers of inhibition suggested that increased inhibition was applied to all between-person trials (relative to within-person trials), regardless of whether they included a language switch or not.

In comparison to cued switching, when unbalanced bilinguals switch language voluntarily in production, switch costs can be reduced, but typically they are not eliminated (e.g., de Bruin et al., 2018). In one study, unbalanced bilinguals switched between their languages voluntarily, while they took turns naming pictures themselves and listening to recordings of another speaker naming pictures (Liu et al., 2021b). While there were within-speaker switch costs, there were no switch costs from comprehension (of the recording) to production, and speakers were more likely to repeat the language they had previously used themselves than the language they had previously heard. But again, both these findings could be due to the absence of a partner. In Gambi and Hartsuiker (2016), two bilinguals took turns naming pictures in a joint task; one of them could voluntarily switch to the L2, while the other named pictures exclusively in the L1. The non-switching bilingual experienced switch costs from comprehending L2 words produced by their partner. Furthermore, individual pictures were named more slowly in L1 by the non-switching bilingual when their partner had previously named them in the L2 compared to when the partner had named them in the L1, showing that one speaker's language choices affected lexical retrieval within the other speaker's production system. However, this study did not include a comparison to within-speaker switching, so it does not address the question of whether production processes are involved in representing the switching partner's utterances.

In sum, there is some evidence for between-speakers switch costs both from cued and voluntary joint language switching paradigms. But more research is needed to clarify the extent to which others' utterances affect language selection mechanisms in production similarly to one's own previously produced utterances: A single study (Gambi & Hartsuiker, 2016) examined between-speaker costs in voluntary language switching in a truly joint task, and the evidence for cued joint language switching is hard to interpret because the behavioural and EEG findings diverge.

Choric speech and joint sentence production

Choric speech – speech produced synchronously with one or more other speakers – is relatively common, for example when people chant, pray, or protest. A few studies have examined the effect of asking speakers to speak synchronously with another speaker versus on their own. Cummins found that speakers are able to synchronize their speech with that of another speaker who is reading the same paragraph of text (Cummins, 2002, 2003, 2009). This synchronization is remarkably precise (discrepancies of only 40 ms), even without much practice; good synchronization is possible both with a "live" speaker and with a recording, but better with a live speaker (who can adapt as well) and with previous knowledge of the text.

Interestingly, choric speech tends to be slower than individual speech, and it tends to be less variable in terms of fundamental frequency, amplitude, and vowel duration (Poore & Ferguson, 2008), which may also facilitate synchronization. Moreover, in an fMRI study, Jasmin et al. (2016) asked participants to speak (1) individually (i.e., as baseline), (2) in sync with a recording, (3) at the same time as another live speaker but not in sync (i.e., with the live speaker producing a different utterance), or (4) in synch with a live speaker (who was producing the same utterance). Typically, speakers' responses to concurrent speech-like sounds in auditory areas are suppressed (so-called speech-induced suppression; e.g., Chang et al., 2013). Jasmin et al. (2016) observed speech-induced suppression for (2) and (3) but not for (4), suggesting that choric speech may be processed like other-produced speech.

In joint sentence production studies, participants produce short sentences with a confederate or another participant, with the constraint that the two speakers alternate and produce one word per turn. To our knowledge, three studies have used this paradigm (Fjaellingsdal et al., 2020; Himberg et al., 2015; Lelonkiewicz & Gambi, 2020). Himberg et al. (2015) showed that speakers entrained to each other's speech rhythm, and Fjaellingsdal et al. (2020) showed that turns were delayed after unexpected words. Taken together, these two studies demonstrate that speakers are able to perform this rather constrained joint production task by carefully monitoring and adapting to their partner's utterances. However, they did not include an individual condition, so it is hard to draw conclusions about the extent to which joint production resembles individual production on the basis of these two studies.

In contrast, Lelonkiewicz and Gambi (2020) asked two participants to type definitions for common English words, either on their own (individual task) or interacting with a naïve partner (joint task), and measured the timing and predictability of the resulting definitions. Consistent with findings from choric speech, interacting participants produced words with less variable delays than individuals; however, the duration of turns was not less variable in the joint than the individual condition, and jointly produced definitions were less predictable than definitions produced by individuals. In sum, there was some evidence for a reduction in variability during joint sentence production, which might help coordination, but it was not consistent across all measures. Overall, choric speech and joint sentence production studies highlight the fact that joint production may involve processes of adaptation to the other speaker or to the joint nature of the task that are absent from individual production.

Discussion

The study of joint production differs both from traditional monologic psycholinguistics and from the study of dialogue. It differs from traditional psycholinguistics because in joint language production tasks speakers do not believe they are producing language in isolation, but instead with a real or assumed partner who is also producing language either concurrently or in turn with the participant. It differs from the study of dialogue because the communicative and interactive aspects of language use in dialogue are typically stripped away or reduced to a bare minimum, in order to achieve greater experimental control and yield measures of performance that can be compared across joint and individual versions of the same task. In this way, researchers have been able to ask to what extent and how the mechanisms of language production – as reflected in traditional psycholinguistic tasks such as picture naming – are affected by representing others' utterances. Overall, the evidence suggests that such co-representation does take place, even when it is not task-relevant. Moreover, it appears to use language production mechanisms, but typically in a manner that lacks detail: Speakers may represent whether their partner is preparing to speak, but not what they are about to say.

Our review highlighted three open issues. First, there is a question about the degree to which co-representation via the production system depends on the situation being a joint task or being perceived as a joint task by the speakers. Some findings suggest that co-representation may be stronger when speakers are co-present (Kuhlen & Abdel Rahman, 2021) and when they are explicitly asked to monitor each other's utterances (Pickering et al., 2022), but other studies have found limited evidence for co-representation even though they explicitly asked speakers to coordinate their utterances (Hoedemaker & Meyer, 2018). A second open question is the extent to which co-representation is cognitively demanding and, relatedly, whether speaking and co-representing simultaneously reduce the resources available for co-representation (compared to co-representing without a simultaneous language production task) and therefore make such representations fairly undetailed. While our review generally supports this claim, no study has yet provided a direct comparison between co-representation when the participant is simultaneously speaking/preparing to speak and when they are not. Finally, choric speech and joint sentence production studies suggest there may be processes that are unique to joint production (adaptation, variability reduction), but these have not been extensively investigated and it is unclear how they may affect the comparison between joint and individual versions of the same task.

In sum, the evidence from joint language production tasks lends some support to simulation-based theories (Dell & Chang, 2014; Pickering & Garrod, 2013; Pickering & Gambi, 2018) – that is, to the hypothesis that speakers can use their own language production system to represent the utterances of other speakers. However, this body of evidence also makes clear that simulation of others' speakers typically stops well short of full lexical access, and that the effects of co-representation on language production do not always parallel the effects of previous production – suggesting that others' utterances are often represented differently from our own previous utterances. This has important implications for theory development, and future research should systematically investigate which factors influence the flexible use of simulation-based mechanisms (e.g., nature of the communicative context, partner's identity, cognitive load).

One possibility, based on the evidence reviewed above, is that comprehenders engage their production system by simulating what they encounter (in part to support prediction; Pickering & Gambi, 2018). The extent to which they simulate may depend on the situation. For example, when their task is to produce one utterance, they may inhibit their simulation of another utterance – accounting for the undetailed nature of co-representation when participants are concurrently engaged in a language production task. Such inhibition of detailed co-representation may be beneficial in communicative contexts, where it may help facilitate conceptual processing (see Kuhlen & Abdel Rahman, 2022). Additionally, comprehenders may be more likely to engage in the simulation of partners that are more human-like (as is the case for simulation of non-verbal actions; e.g., Tsai & Brass, 2007).

Given that the communicative/interactive aspects of joint language use in conversation are intentionally stripped away in these tasks, one might ask whether the findings we have reviewed in this chapter bear relevance to understanding the processes that support successful between-speaker coordination in naturalistic conversations. We argue that they do, for two reasons. First, these tasks allow us to isolate the effect of others' utterances on production above and beyond the known effects of comprehension on production (e.g., priming). In addition, they make it possible to test the involvement of production processes in the representation of others' utterances, because they allow a direct comparison between the effect of comprehension on production and the effect of production on subsequent production. In sum, this body of work contributes to the theoretical understanding of the mechanisms of other-representation in language production, which is relevant to dialogue as well as monologue.

Conclusion

We have reviewed the growing body of work on joint language production. Experimental work comparing how speakers produce language in joint versus individual tasks has begun to uncover when and how speakers engage in co-representation of others' utterances. Taken together these studies show that the process of producing language is susceptible to influence from representations of others' utterances (whether real or assumed). There is also good evidence that co-representation makes use of language production mechanisms, but typically stops short of engaging in detailed simulation of what another person is saying. Future work should systematically investigate which factors influence the flexible use of simulation-based mechanisms (e.g., nature of the communicative context, partner's identity, cognitive load) to further our understanding of how speaking jointly differs from speaking in isolation.

References

Baus, C., Sebanz, N., de la Fuente, V., Branzi, F. M., Martin, C., & Costa, A. (2014). On predicting others' words: Electrophysiological evidence of prediction in speech production. *Cognition, 133*(2), 395–407.

Bavelas, J. B., Coates, L., & Johnson, T. (2000). Listeners as co-narrators. *Journal of Personality and Social Psychology, 79*(6), 941–952.

Belke, E. (2013). Long-lasting inhibitory semantic context effects on object naming are necessarily conceptually mediated: Implications for models of lexical-semantic encoding. *Journal of Memory and Language, 69*(3), 228–256.

Bock, K., Dell, G. S., Chang, F., & Onishi, K. H. (2007). Persistent structural priming from language comprehension to language production. *Cognition, 104*(3), 437–458.

Bögels, S., Magyari, L., & Levinson, S. C. (2015). Neural signatures of response planning occur midway through an incoming question in conversation. *Scientific Reports, 5*, 12881.

Branigan, H. P., Pickering, M. J., & Cleland, A. A. (2000). Syntactic co-ordination in dialogue. *Cognition, 75*(2), B13–B25.

Brehm, L., Taschenberger, L., & Meyer, A. (2019). Mental representations of partner task cause interference in picture naming. *Acta Psychologica, 199*, 102888.

Brennan, S. E., & Clark, H. H. (1996). Conceptual pacts and lexical choice in conversation. *Journal of Experimental Psychology: Learning, Memory, and Cognition, 22*(6), 1482–1493.

Brown, A. S. (1981). Inhibition in cued retrieval. *Journal of Experimental Psychology: Human Learning and Memory, 7*(3), 204–215.

Chang, E. F., Niziolek, C. A., Knight, R. T., Nagarajan, S. S., & Houde, J. F. (2013). Human cortical sensorimotor network underlying feedback control of vocal pitch. *Proceedings of the National Academy of Sciences, 110*(7), 2653–2658.

Corps, R., Crossley, A., Gambi, C., & Pickering, M. J. (2018). Early preparation during turn-taking: listeners use content predictions to determine what to say but not when to say it. *Cognition, 175*, 77–95.

Crocker, M. W., Pickering, M., & Clifton, C. (Eds.) (2000). *Architectures and mechanisms for language processing.* Cambridge: Cambridge University Press.

Cummins, F. (2002). On synchronous speech. *Acoustics Research Letters Online, 3*(1), 7–11.

Cummins, F. (2003). Practice and performance in speech produced synchronously. *Journal of Phonetics, 31*(2), 139–148.

Cummins, F. (2009). Rhythm as entrainment: The case of synchronous speech. *Journal of Phonetics, 37*(1), 16–28.

de Bruin, A., Samuel, A. G., & Duñabeitia, J. A. (2018). Voluntary language switching: When and why do bilinguals switch between their languages? *Journal of Memory and Language, 103*, 28–43.

Dell, G. S., & Chang, F. (2014). The P-chain: Relating sentence production and its disorders to comprehension and acquisition. *Philosophical Transactions of the Royal Society B: Biological Sciences, 369*(1634), 20120394.

Demiral, Ş. B., Gambi, C., Nieuwland, M. S., & Pickering, M. J. (2016). Neural correlates of verbal joint action: ERPs reveal common perception and action systems in a shared-Stroop task. *Brain Research, 1649*, 79–89.

Donkers, F. C., & Van Boxtel, G. J. (2004). The N2 in go/no-go tasks reflects conflict monitoring not response inhibition. *Brain and Cognition, 56*(2), 165–176.

Fjaellingsdal, T. G., Schwenke, D., Scherbaum, S., Kuhlen, A. K., Bögels, S., Meekes, J., & Bleichner, M. G. (2020). Expectancy effects in the EEG during joint and spontaneous word-by-word sentence production in German. *Scientific Reports, 10*, 5460.

Gade, M., Declerck, M., Philipp, A. M., Rey-Mermet, A., & Koch, I. (2021). Assessing the evidence for asymmetrical switch costs and reversed language dominance effects – A meta-analysis. *Journal of Cognition, 4*(1), 55, 1–32. DOI: 10.5334/joc.186

Gambi, C., Cop, U., & Pickering, M. J. (2015a). How do speakers coordinate? Evidence for prediction in a joint word-replacement task. *Cortex, 68*, 111–128.

Gambi, C., & Hartsuiker, R. J. (2016). If you stay, it might be easier: Switch costs from comprehension to production in a joint switching task. *Journal of Experimental Psychology: Learning, Memory, and Cognition, 42*(4), 608–626.

Gambi, C., & Pickering, M. J. (2017). Models linking production and comprehension. In E. M. Fernández & H. Smith Cairns (Eds.), *Handbook of psycholinguistics* (pp. 157–181). Hoboken, NJ: John Wiley & Sons Inc.

Gambi, C., Van de Cavey, J., & Pickering, M. J. (2015b). Interference in joint picture naming. *Journal of Experimental Psychology: Learning, Memory, and Cognition, 41*(1), 1–21.

Gambi, C., Van de Cavey, J., & Pickering, M. J. (2022). Representation of others' synchronous and asynchronous sentences interferes with sentence production. *Quartelrly Journal of Experimental Psychology*, 10.1177/17470218221080766.

Garrod, S., & Anderson, A. (1987). Saying what you mean in dialogue: A study in conceptual and semantic co-ordination. *Cognition, 27*(2), 181–218.

Gauvin, H. S., & Hartsuiker, R. J. (2020). Towards a new model of verbal monitoring. *Journal of Cognition, 3*(1), 17. doi:10.5334/joc.81

Glaser, W. R., & Düngelhoff, F.-J. (1984). The time course of picture-word interference. *Journal of Experimental Psychology: Human Perception and Performance, 10*(5), 640–654.

Gries, S. T. (2005). Syntactic priming: A corpus-based approach. *Journal of Psycholinguistic Research, 34*(4), 365–399.

Hartsuiker, R. J., Catchpole, C. M., De Jong, N. H., & Pickering, M. J. (2008). Concurrent processing of words and their replacements during speech. *Cognition, 108*(3), 601–607.

Hickok, G. (2013). Predictive coding? Yes, but from what source?. *Behavioral and Brain Sciences, 36*(4), 358. doi:10.1017/S0140525X12002750

Himberg, T., Hirvenkari, L., Mandel, A., & Hari, R. (2015). Word-by-word entrainment of speech rhythm during joint story building. *Frontiers in Psychology, 6*, 797.

Hoedemaker, R. S., Ernst, J., Meyer, A. S., & Belke, E. (2017). Language production in a shared task: Cumulative semantic interference from self-and other-produced context words. *Acta Psychologica, 172*, 55–63.

Hoedemaker, R. S., & Meyer, A. S. (2018). Planning and coordination of utterances in a joint naming task. *Journal of Experimental Psychology: Learning, Memory, and Cognition, 45*(4), 732–752. doi:10.1037/xlm0000603.

Howard, D., Nickels, L., Coltheart, M., & Cole-Virtue, J. (2006). Cumulative semantic inhibition in picture naming: Experimental and computational studies. *Cognition, 100*(3), 464–482.

Ivanova, I., Horton, W. S., Swets, B., Kleinman, D., & Ferreira, V. S. (2020). Structural alignment in dialogue and monologue (and what attention may have to do with it). *Journal of Memory and Language, 110*, 104052.

Jacobs, C. L., Cho, S. J., & Watson, D. G. (2019). Self-priming in production: Evidence for a hybrid model of syntactic priming. *Cognitive Science, 43*(7), e12749.

Jasmin, K. M., McGettigan, C., Agnew, Z. K., Lavan, N., Josephs, O., Cummins, F., & Scott, S. K. (2016). Cohesion and joint speech: right hemisphere contributions to synchronized vocal production. *Journal of Neuroscience, 36*(17), 4669–4680.

Knoblich, G., Butterfill, S., & Sebanz, N. (2011). Psychological research on joint action: Theory and data. In B. Ross (Ed.), *The psychology of learning and motivation* (Vol. 54, pp. 59–101). Burlington: Academic Press.

Kootstra, G. J., Van Hell, J. G., & Dijkstra, T. (2010). Syntactic alignment and shared word order in code-switched sentence production: Evidence from bilingual monologue and dialogue. *Journal of Memory and Language, 63*(2), 210–231.

Kuhlen, A., & Abdel Rahman, R. (2017). Having a task partner affects lexical retrieval: Spoken word production in shared task settings. *Cognition, 166*, 94–106.

Kuhlen, A., & Abdel Rahman, R. (2021). Joint language production: An electrophysiological investigation of simulated lexical access on behalf of task partner. *Journal of - Experimental Psychology: Learning, Memory, and Cognition, 47*(8), 1317–1337. doi:10.1037/xlm0001025

Kuhlen, A., & Abdel Rahman, R. (2022). Mental chronometry of speaking in dialogue: Semantic interference turns into facilitation. *Cognition, 219*, 104962.

Lelonkiewicz, J. R., & Gambi, C. (2020). Making oneself predictable in linguistic interactions. *Acta Psychologica, 209*, 103125.

Liu, H., Kong, C., de Bruin, A., Wu, J., & He, Y. (2020). Interactive influence of self and other language behaviors: Evidence from switching between bilingual production and comprehension. *Human Brain Mapping*, *41*(13), 3720–3736.

Liu, H., Li, B., Wang, X., & He, Y. (2021a). Role of joint language control during cross-language communication: evidence from cross-frequency coupling. *Cognitive Neurodynamics*, *15*, 191–205.

Liu, H., Li, W., de Bruin, A., & He, Y. (2021b). Should I focus on self-language actions or should I follow others? Cross-language interference effects in voluntary and cued language switching. *Acta Psychologica*, *216*, 103308.

Liu, H., Xie, N., Zhang, M., Gao, X., Dunlap, S., & Chen, B. (2018). The electrophysiological mechanism of joint language switching: evidence from simultaneous production and comprehension. *Journal of Neurolinguistics*, *45*, 45–59.

Liu, H., Zhang, M., Pérez, A., Xie, N., Li, B., & Liu, Q. (2019). Role of language control during interbrain phase synchronization of cross-language communication. *Neuropsychologia*, *131*, 316–324.

MacLeod, C. M. (1991). Half a century of research on the Stroop effect: an integrative review. *Psychological Bulletin*, *109*(2), 163–203.

Meuter, R. F., & Allport, A. (1999). Bilingual language switching in naming: Asymmetrical costs of language selection. *Journal of Memory and Language*, *40*(1), 25–40.

Oppenheim, G. M., Dell, G. S., & Schwartz, M. F. (2010). The dark side of incremental learning: A model of cumulative semantic interference during lexical access in speech production. *Cognition*, *114*(2), 227–252.

Pickering, M. J., & Ferreira, V. S. (2008). Structural priming: a critical review. *Psychological Bulletin*, *134*(3), 427–459, 10.1037/0033-2909.134.3.427.

Pickering, M. J., & Gambi, C. (2018). Predicting while comprehending language: A theory and review. *Psychological Bulletin*, *144*(10), 1002–1044.

Pickering, M. J., & Garrod, S. (2013). An integrated theory of language production and comprehension. *Behavioral and Brain Sciences*, *36*(4), 329–392. doi:10.1017/S0140525X12001495

Pickering, M. J., & Garrod, S. (2021). *Understanding dialogue: Language use and social interaction*. Cambridge, UK: Cambridge University Press.

Pickering, M. J., McLean, J. F., & Gambi, C. (2022). *Royal Society Open Science*, Interference in the shared-Stroop task: a comparison of self- and other-monitoring. https://royalsocietypublishing.org/doi/full/10.1098/rsos.220107

Poore, M. A., & Ferguson, S. H. (2008). Methodological variables in choral reading. *Clinical Linguistics & Phonetics*, *22*(1), 13–24.

Reitter, D., Moore, J. D., & Keller, F. (2006). *Priming of syntactic rules in task-oriented dialogue and spontaneous conversation*. Paper presented at the 28th Annual Conference of the Cognitive Science Society, Vancouver, BC, Canada.

Roelofs, A., & Piai, V. (2011). Attention demands of spoken word planning: A review. *Frontiers in Psychology*, *2*. doi:10.3389/fpsyg.2011.00307

Saunders, D. R., Melcher, D., & van Zoest, W. (2019). No evidence of task co-representation in a joint Stroop task. *Psychological Research*, *83*(5), 852–862.

Schoot, L., Hagoort, P., & Segaert, K. (2019). Stronger syntactic alignment in the presence of an interlocutor. *Frontiers in Psychology*, *10*, 685.

Sebanz, N., Knoblich, G., & Prinz, W. (2003). Representing others' actions: Just like one's own? *Cognition*, *88*(3), B11–B21.

Segaert, K., Kempen, G., Petersson, K. M., & Hagoort, P. (2013). Syntactic priming and the lexical boost effect during sentence production and sentence comprehension: An fMRI study. *Brain and Language*, *124*(2), 174–183.

Sellaro, R., Treccani, B., & Cubelli, R. (2020). When task sharing reduces interference: Evidence for division-of-labour in Stroop-like tasks. *Psychological Research*, *84*(2), 327–342.

Slevc, L. R. (this volume, 2022). Grammatical encoding.

Stivers, T., Enfield, N. J., Brown, P., Englert, C., Hayashi, M., Heinemann, T., Hoymann, G., Rossano, F., de Ruiter, J. P., Yoon, K-E, & Levinson, S. C. (2009). Universals and cultural variation in turn-taking in conversation. *Proceedings of the National Academy of Sciences*, *106*(26), 10587–10592.

Strijkers, K., Costa, A., & Thierry, G. (2010). Tracking lexical access in speech production: electrophysiological correlates of word frequency and cognate effects. *Cerebral Cortex*, *20*(4), 912–928.

Tolins, J., Zeamer, C., & Fox Tree, J. E. (2018). Overhearing dialogues and monologues: How does entrainment lead to more comprehensible referring expressions? *Discourse Processes*, *55*(7), 545–565.

Tsai, C. C., & Brass, M. (2007). Does the human motor system simulate Pinocchio's actions? Coacting with a human hand versus a wooden hand in a dyadic interaction. *Psychological Science*, *18*(12), 1058–1062.

Tydgat, I., Stevens, M., Hartsuiker, R. J., & Pickering, M. J. (2011). Deciding where to stop speaking. *Journal of Memory and Language*, *64*(4), 359–380.

Wudarczyk, O. A., Kirtay, M., Pischedda, D., Hafner, V. V., Haynes, J. D., Kuhlen, A. K., & Abdel Rahman, R. (2021). Robots facilitate human language production. *Scientific Reports*, *11*, 16737, 10.1038/s41598-021-95645-9

Xie, N., Li, B., Zhang, M., & Liu, H. (2019). Role of top-down language control in bilingual production and comprehension: Evidence from induced oscillations. *International Journal of Bilingualism*, *23*(5), 1041–1063.

Zhang, M., Wang, X., Wang, F., & Liu, H. (2019). Effect of cognitive style on language control during joint language switching: An ERP study. *Journal of Psycholinguistic Research*, *49*(3), 383–400.

Index

Printed in the United States
by Baker & Taylor Publisher Services